with DVD

The Practice of
English
Language
Teaching

Jeremy Harmer

FOURTH EDITION

PEARSON
Longman

Contents

PART 2: THEORIES, METHODS AND TECHNIQUES

PART 3: LEARNERS AND TEACHERS

CHAPTER 20: SPEAKING

PART 8: PLANNING AND SYLLABUSES

CHAPTER 21: PLANNING LESSONS

PART 9: EVALUATION

CHAPTER 22: TESTING AND EVALUATION

Introduction

In a few days (as I write this) I will be going to a large English teachers' conference in the USA which has the title 'Tides of change'. A couple of weeks after that it's Poland and a weekend called 'New challenges for language teaching and learning in the changing world'; and then there's a 'changes' conference somewhere else, and then it's off to another country for a conference on ... changes and how to deal with them! And as the year goes on – and who knows, through into the next year and the years after that – there will continue to be meetings, seminars and articles about how to deal with the pace of newness and innovation in a world where increasingly sophisticated technology is only one manifestation of the way things just keep on moving and developing.

We can only be grateful for this fitful march forwards (and, of course, sometimes sideways and occasionally even backwards). It keeps us on our toes, insists on our engagement with new ideas, technologies and techniques and, whilst occasionally bewildering and unsettling us, makes the world a brighter and more invigorating place. And it demands new editions of a book like *The Practice of English Language Teaching*.

Since the last edition of this book, different new ideas (or shifts in emphasis) have come to prominence and so they are reflected in this fourth edition. There is much more on educational technology, of course, both in Chapter 11 and throughout the rest of book. There is a re-examination of the place and role of English in the world (and about the competing claims of Global English and the newly-observed phenomenon that is sometimes called ELF). The fourth edition of this book is far more concerned about context-sensitive teaching than its predecessors, describing different learning contexts in Chapter 7, and teasing out native-speaker and non-native-speaker teacher issues in Chapter 6 (though, as it happens, I dislike that terminology). The place of the students' mother tongue is examined in more (and more sympathetic) detail than in previous editions, and the discussions on learner autonomy and teacher development in the last two chapters of the book have been extensively re-thought.

But what makes this new edition significantly different from its three predecessors is the inclusion of a DVD of lesson 'stories' (edited-down versions of filmed lessons), together with teacher interviews in which the teachers discuss issues ranging from pronunciation teaching to role-play, from coursebook use to the importance of instructions, from grammar teaching to repetition and correction. These lessons and interviews illuminate much of the content of the book better than my own prose can ever do.

The fourth edition of *The Practice of English Language Teaching* is offered as a record of where English language teaching is right now. But underneath the surface, changes are bubbling away as we speak. Watch this space!

Acknowledgements

Since this book started its (now) long life, it has been informed by the help and counsel of many people through its four editions. From the very beginning I would have been incapable of writing and re-writing it without the encouragement, engagement and critical responses of the many people whom I now wish to acknowledge with very real appreciation and gratitude.

The **first edition** of *The Practice of English Language Teaching* was informed by the input and reactions of teacher colleagues and students at the Instituto Anglo-Mexicano de Cultura, both in Mexico City and Guadalajara. I was given help and advice (and more) by Walter Plumb, Jean Pender and Richard Rossner, and had excellent reporting from Donn Byrne and Jane Willis. Tim Hunt commissioned the book and guided me through it, and Judith King edited it.

For the **second edition**, I was inspired by comments from Richard Rossner, Julian Edge and Nick Dawson, and spurred on by publisher Damien Tunnacliffe, who, together with Helena Gomm and Alyson Lee, saw the work through to its completion.

The **third edition** kicked off (and continued) with advice, encouragement and robustly helpful criticism from Martin Parrott. It benefited enormously from reporting by Sally Blackmore, Hann Kijowska, Katie Head, Kip Tellez and David Bowker. Many people answered questions or helped me out in other ways, including Paul Cane, Chris George, Roger Gower, Kenny Graham, Peter Grundy, Michael Rundell, Michael Swan and Douglas Workman. As with the previous two editions, Anita Harmer provided counsel, support and a sharp and challenging assessment of many ideas I was working with as the book progressed and I was lucky enough to have Brigit Viney as my editor.

When this **fourth edition** of *The Practice of English Language Teaching* was first discussed, Jacqui Hiddleston commissioned some really terrific reports by Guy Cook, Leslie Anne Hendra, David Valente, Lindsay Clandfield and Michael Manser. I think it is safe to say that I could not have got going without reading what they had to say about the things they thought needed to be done. Of course, as with all reporting, I have not always done what they suggested or expected (though I often have), but a real engagement with their various points of view was an absolutely essential part of the thinking that has gone into this book

Later on, Guy Cook, in the most helpful and invigorating way, again provided really useful comments on a part of the manuscript as it emerged, and Jeff Stanford gave some absolutely crucial feedback on one particular chapter.

In my visits to schools, courses and conferences around the world, learning and teaching are always, of course, the main subjects of discussion. I would love to be able to list the literally hundreds of names of the participants in those discussions. But I can thank the following people for various specific kinds of help and comment: Martine Allard, Stephen Bax, Kosta Dimeropoulus, John Evans, Kenny Graham, Clare Griffiths, Philip Harmer, Ian Jasper, Mary O'Leary, Michael Swan and Penny Ur.

It has been extremely exciting (and comforting!) for me to have Helena Gomm working on this edition (as she did on the second edition some years ago). Her firm and experienced hand is evident in every page. However much of a cliché this is, it is important to say that the book would never have made it without her. But without publisher Katy Wright's driving encouragement and her significant engagement with this fourth edition, it wouldn't even have got started – and it almost certainly wouldn't have got finished on time either. All writers deserve to be blessed with a publisher like Katy.

When Katy Wright and I approached Vic Richardson at Embassy CES to see about the possibility of filming teachers who work for that organisation, his immediate openness and support for our ideas was both crucial and inspiring. Thanks to him, we were able to film a number of lessons and conduct in-depth interviews with a range of exceptional professionals. I do not think I can say thank you forcefully enough to express my gratitude to the teachers (Allan Bramall, Barbara Gardner, Bill Harris, Eleanor Spicer-Lundholm, Kit Claxton, Laura Hayward, Ross Wainwright, Rolf Tynan, Tony Rapa, Silvana Richardson and Vanessa Harrison) for allowing us to film them, edit them, cut large chunks from their lessons, interview them and generally disrupt their lives. I hope they will realise how important their contribution has been to the way in which the project has finally turned out. I also want to thank David Rowland, Steve Barratt, Andy Quin and Reg Veale for making it all possible. Luis España's kind counsel was invaluable in the film editing process, and heartfelt thanks are due to Amy Weaver for responding so constructively to being 'thrown in at the deep end'. And finally, as always, once the book got into the hands of production controller Jane Reeve, it really started to move! How would we ever manage without her?

I have wanted to describe the practice of English language teaching as it exists right now. All of the people listed above have helped me enormously in that endeavour. And I pray that they will think I have got it right. If I haven't, it's my fault. If I have, well it's thanks to them.

Jeremy Harmer
Cambridge, UK

The changing world of English

A A language story

By the end of the twentieth century English was already well on its way to becoming a genuine *lingua franca*, that is a language used widely for communication between people who do not share the same first (or even second) language. Just as in the Middle Ages Latin became for a time a language of international communication (at least in the Roman Empire), so English is now commonly used in exchanges between, say, Japanese and Argentinian business people, or between Singaporeans and their Vietnamese counterparts. English is also, of course, a mother tongue for many people in the world, though, as we shall see, such 'native speakers' are increasingly out-numbered by people who have English as a second or third language and use it for international communication.

There is something awe-inspiring about the way English use has grown in the last few decades. In 1985, Braj Kachru estimated that there were between 320 and 380 million people speaking English as a first language and anywhere between 250 and 380 million speakers of English as a second language, but he had already predicted that the balance might change. 'One might hazard a linguistic guess here,' he had written two years earlier. 'If the spread of English continues at the current rate, by the year 2000 its non-native speakers will outnumber its native speakers' (1983: 3).

Kachru's guess was absolutely right, but on a much greater scale than he might have supposed. Estimates vary, but the ratio of native speakers to non-native speakers is anywhere between 1:2 (Rajagopalan 2004) and 1:3 (Crystal 2003a), and this gap is widening all the time. In terms of numbers, Crystal suggests that there are currently around 1.5 billion speakers of English worldwide, of whom only some 329 million are native speakers. 'Moreover,' he writes, 'the population growth in areas where English is a second language is about 2.5 times that in areas where it is a first language' (2003a: 69). A quarter of the world's population speaks English, in other words, and native speakers are in a proportionately ever-decreasing minority. However, it is worth acknowledging, as Crystal does, that these totals are to some extent only guesstimates, and avoid certain difficult questions, such as how good at the language someone has to be before we can say they are a real 'speaker of English'. Is a beginner an English speaker? Does being an English 'speaker' mean only having the ability to speak English, or do we wait until people are functionally literate before we count them?

Despite these uncertainties, it is clear that English is special, and for many people its inexorable rise has been something to celebrate, though for others it causes real unease (see A2 below). The future of English language 'superiority' is also called into question by some (see A4 below), and its growth may one day be halted. The status of English as one language is challenged by the many different 'Englishes' being used around the world (see A3 below), and the ownership of

English has shifted dramatically, as the numbers quoted above will have demonstrated. All of these issues have a bearing on how and why English is taught – and indeed what type of English is taught – and it is these issues which we will be exploring in this chapter.

A1 The triumph of English?

In his book *English Next*, the British applied linguist David Graddol discusses how English – originally the language of a small island people – triumphed, despite being infiltrated by other languages, especially Norman French in the eleventh and twelfth centuries (Graddol 2006: 58). His use of the term *triumph* is deliberately ironic, of course, especially when we consider that the language itself grew from a number of roots and incorporated words and grammar from various languages and language groups (Crystal 2003b: Chapters 2–5). Nevertheless, some people have been tempted to see the history of English as it has spread through the world in terms of an onward march to victory (a view we will challenge below). How, then, did English get where it is today? How do languages become truly global? There are a number of factors which have ensured the widespread use of English.

- **A colonial history:** when the Pilgrim Fathers landed on the Massachusetts coast in 1620 after their eventful journey from Plymouth, England, they brought with them not just a set of religious beliefs, nor only a pioneering spirit and a desire for colonisation, but also their language, and though many years later the Americans broke away from their one-time colonial masters, the language of English remained and it is still the main language of the world's predominant economic and political power.

  It was the same in Australia, too. When Commander Philip planted the British flag in Sydney Cove on January 26th, 1788, it wasn't just a bunch of British convicts and their guardians who disembarked (to be rapidly followed by many 'free' settlers of that land), but also a language.

  In other parts of the British Empire, English rapidly became a unifying/dominating means of control. For example, it became something a little like a lingua franca in India, where a plethora of indigenous languages made the use of any one of them as a whole-country system problematic. The imposition of English as the one language of administration helped maintain the coloniser's power.

  English was not the only language to become widespread in this way, of course. Spanish was imposed on much of the 'new world' by the conquistadores from Castile. Brazil and parts of Africa took on the language of their Portuguese conquerors. The (short-lived) dominance of Russia in the Soviet Union meant that Russian was spoken – or at least learnt – throughout the Warsaw Pact countries (and we have not even mentioned the way Chinese or French, for example, became widespread as a result of political and colonial realities). English, therefore, is not unique in the way it travelled around many parts of the globe (though its predominance is partly the result of the extended reach of British colonial ambitions).

- **Economics:** military prowess may account for the initial establishment of a language, as we have seen, but it is economic power that ensures its survival and growth. A major factor in the growth of English has been the spread of global commerce, pushed on by the dominance of the United States as a world economic power. The English language travelled in the wake of this success, so that now, whatever countries are involved, it is one of the main mediating languages of international businesses. This is the phenomenon of 'globalisation', described by the journalist John Pilger (at the end of the twentieth century) as '... a term which journalists and politicians have made fashionable and which is often used in a positive sense to denote a "global village" of "free trade", hi-tech marvels and all kinds of possibilities that transcend class, historical experience and ideology' (Pilger 1998: 61). Pilger, like many of his contemporaries, sees this globalisation as a threat to the identities of individual countries as a new colonialism stalks the world. But the situation may be somewhat more complex than this. As Suresh Canagarajah points out, 'postmodern globalisation' (his phrase) 'sees many companies outsourcing their economic activity so that now English – in varieties such as Indian or Sri-Lankan English – is a language being beamed back towards its originators from call centres offering technical assistance, marketing and customer service' (Canagarajah 2005: 17). In other words, as this one example shows, commercial activity has helped fan the flames of English, but it is no longer possible to see this only in terms of one-way traffic.

- **Information exchange:** a great deal of academic discourse around the world takes place in English. It is often a lingua franca of conferences, for example, and many journal articles in fields as diverse as astrophysics and zoology have English as a default language.

    The first years of the Internet as a major channel for information exchange also saw a marked predominance of English (though as we shall see in A4, such a situation may change). This probably has something to do with the Internet's roots in the USA and the predominance of its use there in the early days of the World Wide Web (see Chapter 11 for more on the Internet).

- **Travel:** much travel and tourism is carried on, around the world, in English. Of course this is not always the case, as the multilingualism of many tourism workers in different countries demonstrates, but a visit to most airports around the globe will reveal signs not only in the language of that country, but also in English, just as many airline announcements are glossed in English, too, whatever the language of the country the airport is situated in.

    So far, English is also the preferred language of air traffic control in many countries and is used widely in sea travel communication.

- **Popular culture:** in the 'western world', at least, English is a dominating language in popular culture. Pop music in English saturates the planet's airwaves. Thus many people who are not English speakers can sing words from their favourite English-medium songs. Many people who are regular cinemagoers (or TV viewers) frequently hear English on subtitled films coming out of the USA. There is a worldwide audience for the annual Oscars ceremony – though nowhere near the regularly quoted figure of a billion, Daniel Radosh suggests (Radosh 2005). However, we need to remind ourselves that Bollywood (in India) produces more films than Hollywood (in the USA) and that many countries, such as France and South Korea, for example, do their best to fight against the cultural domination of the American movie. Nevertheless, the advent of film and recording technology greatly enhanced the worldwide penetration of English. In addition, countries such as the USA, Britain, Canada and Australia do their best to promote their culture overseas and to attract people to choose them as a study destination.

A2 The effect of English

Not everyone sees the growth of English as a benign or even desirable phenomenon. Many people worry about what it means for the cultures and languages it comes into contact with, seeing its teaching as a form of cultural or linguistic 'imperialism' (e.g. Phillipson 1992, Pennycook 1994, 1998). They argue that, as we have seen, English has been regarded by some as a way of promoting military, cultural or economic hegemony. Nor is it necessarily welcome to those who have been obliged to study it, some of whom see learning English as an unpleasant but sadly necessary occupation (Pennycook 1998: 206–212).

The view that learners and non-native speakers of English are victims of linguistic and cultural imperialism is not shared by everyone. Joseph Bisong points out that Nigerians, for example, may want to operate with two or more languages in a multilingual setting, choosing which one to use depending upon the situation they are in and the people they wish to communicate with. He suggests that great writers like Achebe, Soyinka and Ngugi do not write in English as victims, but out of choice – whatever the reasons for this choice might be (Bisong 1995). But this isn't a free choice, Phillipson (1996) argues. It is determined by their audience, not them. Kanavillil Rajagopalan, on the other hand, suggests that the teaching of English should not be seen as a form of cultural imperialism, '... in a world marked by cultural intermixing and growing multilingualism at a hitherto unprecedented level' (Rajagopalan 1999: 200).

An issue that concerns everyone who follows the rise of English is the impact it has on the other languages it comes into contact with. This concern is articulated in the knowledge that of the approximately 6,000 extant languages in the world, at least half may be lost within the next hundred years – although some commentators are far more apocalyptic and suggest that the figure may be more like 90 per cent. Language death is a frightening and ongoing problem in much the same way that species loss is a threat to the biodiversity on our planet; for once lost, a language cannot be resurrected and its loss takes with it culture and customs and ways of seeing the world through its use of metaphor, idiom and grammatical structuring. In this context, a powerful argument is that as more and more people speak English, languages will gradually be lost. As David Crystal warns (in a widely-quoted phrase), if, in 500 years, English is the only language left to be learnt, 'it will have been the greatest intellectual disaster that the planet has ever known' (Crystal 2003a: 191).

Although there can be no doubt that the spread of English has some impact on other languages, creating a causal link between this and language death seems somewhat simplistic. In the first place, languages are under threat from a wide variety of sources, not just English. Spanish threatens some Andean languages, French battles it out with Euskara and Flemish, and the number of Mandarin and Arabic speakers is growing all the time – not to mention the growing influence that speakers of these languages exert in the international community.

But in a sense, the presence of a new multi-use language such as English is only one side of the picture. A much more important predictor of language survival will be whether there is still a viable community with its own social and cultural identity to keep a language alive. In other words, survival is as much social as linguistic. And here, too, the world is changing. Instead of only seeing language as a one-way street where English is exported, we need to remember that there is massive movement of people and languages around the globe. In London alone, according to a recent survey, more than 300 languages are spoken by schoolchildren, making London one of the most linguistically diverse cities in the world. This means that for at least a third of all London schoolchildren, English is not the language spoken at home.

It is possible, of course, that many of these languages may be lost from one generation to the next (or the one after that). But language is bound up with identity, and there are many examples of successful identity-grounded fightbacks. Since the Balkan wars of the 1990s, for example, Serbians, Bosnians and Croatians have all taken the original 'Yugoslavian' Serbo-Croatian and started to mould it into three new varieties (Serbian, Bosnian and Croatian), emphasising as many differences between these varieties as possible. Catalan and Euskara have mounted a fierce and successful renaissance in Spain. The Welsh language went through something of a resurrection in the second half of the twentieth century, the Singaporean government embeds the preservation of home languages into its national curriculum, and there are many more examples of this kind. Members of the European Parliament who are competent speakers of English nevertheless use their own languages (e.g. Finnish) in plenary sessions as a highly charged statement of political and cultural identity.

We should not be starry-eyed about all this, of course. But rather than fearing English as a destroyer, we should, perhaps, concentrate on how to maintain communities with a strong enough identity to preserve the language they represent. It is even possible that the presence of English as a lingua franca actually provokes speakers of minority languages to protect and promote their own languages (House 2001).

The other charge against English – that of cultural and linguistic imperialism – is also proving more and more difficult to sustain. As we shall see below, neither colonial Britain nor the American giant actually own the language any more, in any real sense. Linguistic imperialism may have once been a function of geopolitical conquest (and it is certainly the case that economic globalisation has had some extremely baleful – as well as benign – consequences), but the world of English has morphed into something very different from what it was in the days of colonisation.

A3 English as a global language

We have already seen how the proportion of native and non-native speakers has altered in the last few decades, but the way this has happened, and its implications, need to be explored further.

In 1985 Kachru described the world of English in terms of three circles. In the inner circle he put countries such as Britain, the USA, Australia, etc. where English is the primary language.

The outer circle contained countries where English had become an official or widely-used second language. These included India, Nigeria, Singapore, etc. Finally, the expanding circle represented those countries where English was learnt as a foreign language

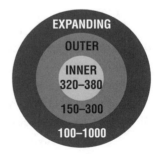

FIGURE 1: Kachru's 1985 circles

(though we will be debating the use of that term in Section B below) – countries such as Poland, Japan, Mexico, Hungary, etc.

We have already seen how Kachru's numbers have been dramatically surpassed. But something else has happened, too. It was once assumed that there was some kind of inbuilt superiority for inner circle speakers. They spoke 'better' English, and there were more of them. Among other things, this situation 'bred an extremely enervating inferiority complex among many a non-native speaker learner/teacher' (Rajagopalan 2004: 114). But since English is now used more often as a lingua franca than as a native language – and since the majority of competent English speakers are not native speakers, but second-language users – the inner circle has lost much of its linguistic power, real or imagined (though there are still many people who advocate using a native-speaker model to teach international English as we shall see in B2 below). As a result, a consensus has emerged that instead of talking about inner, outer and expanding circle Englishes, we need to recognise 'World Englishes' (Jenkins 2006a: 159) or 'Global English' (Graddol 2006: 106). World English (in Rajagopalan's words) '... belongs to everyone who speaks it, but it is nobody's mother tongue' (2004: 111). Nobody owns English any more, in other words – or perhaps we could say that we all, 'native' and 'non-native' speakers alike, own it together in a kind of international shareholders' democracy since whatever English we speak – Indian English, British English or Malaysian English – we have, or should have, equal rights as English users. This does not mean, of course, that there are not 'haves' and 'have-nots' in World Englishes (as there are in any language where 'conflicting interests and ideologies are constantly at play' (Rajagopalan 2004: 113)). But it does mean, suddenly, that native speakers may actually be at a disadvantage, especially if we compare less educated native speakers with highly competent and literate second-language English users. The speaker of World English is, perhaps, capable of dealing with a wider range of English varieties than someone stuck with native-speaker attitudes and competence; indeed, as Rajagopalan suggests, anyone who can't deal with a Punjabi or Greek accent (or, as Canagarajah suggests, with an outsourced call centre operative in Delhi or Kuala Lumpur speaking their own special English variety) is 'communicatively deficient' (Rajagopalan 2004: 115).

The emergence of global English has caused Kachru to propose a new circle diagram where language affiliation (and ethnicity) is less important than a speaker's proficiency (Kachru 2004). He still wishes to make a distinction between the inner core and everyone else, but outside that inner core, the main difference is between high and low proficiency users.

FIGURE 2: World English and English proficiency

A4 The future of English

We have noted that English is spoken by at least a quarter of the world's population. It is important, too, to realise that this means it is *not* spoken by three quarters of that same population. However, it is clear from the way its use has grown in the last decade that this situation is about to change. But by how much?

In 1997 David Graddol considered a number of future possibilities, all of which questioned the certainty of English as the number one world language. He pointed out, for example, that the fastest-growing language community in the USA was (and is) Hispanic. Taken together with the trade agreements which are springing up in both the North and South American continents, it is highly possible that in the foreseeable future the entire American continent will be an English-Spanish bilingual zone. He also suggested that other languages such as Mandarin, Hindu and Arabic would gain in status and importance as their geopolitical and economic power increased – something that is increasingly visible, especially in the case of China. It is still too early to say whether those predictions were right, but he now suggests that there will be about 3 billion English speakers by the year 2040. He thinks it doubtful 'that more than 40% of the global population would ever become functional users of English' (Graddol 2006: 107).

And what of the Internet, the means of e-commerce transmission? In 1999 the company Computer Economics (www.computereconomics.com) said that the proportion of first-language English-speaker users to speakers of other languages was 54%:46%, but that by 2005 that balance would change to 43%:57% – in other words, the number of other-language users would rise sharply. At the time of writing, Global Reach (http://global-reach.biz/globstats/index.php3) estimates that this figure has shifted to 35.8%:64.2%. This does not mean that there is a corresponding breakdown of languages actually used on the Internet – and indeed one of the biggest search engines, Google, only currently lists 35 different language options. However, things are changing and whereas it used to be the case that almost all websites seemed to be in English, nowadays there is an increasing amount of information offered in other languages, too.

What we think we know, then, is that English will grow, but is unlikely to have the catastrophic effect Crystal worried about (see page 16). It faces challengers from other big language groups, and the exponential growth of the IT community may not necessarily favour English in the same way that English dominated the virtual world in its early days.

However, what we do know is that because native speakers are becoming less and less 'powerful' in the daily use of the language, we will have to adjust the way in which both native and non-native speaker experts have traditionally thought about learning and teaching English around the world.

B EFL, ESL, ESOL & ELF

English teaching, like many other professions and disciplines, is almost overwhelmed by acronyms and initials. For example, we talk about *ESP* (English for Specific Purposes – English for specialities such as nursing or paper technology or banking) to differentiate it from general English (English taught in most schools and private language institutes). We use *EAP* (English for Academic Purposes) to describe courses and materials designed specifically to help people who want to use their English in academic contexts.

For many years, scholars and teachers have made a distinction between *EFL* (English as a Foreign Language) and *ESL* (English as a Second Language). EFL described situations where students were learning English in order to use it with any other English speakers in the world – when the students might be tourists or business people. Students often studied EFL in their own country, or sometimes on short courses in Britain, the USA, Australia, Canada, Ireland, New Zealand, etc. ESL students, on the other hand, were described as usually living in a target-language community (e.g. Britain, the USA, etc.) and needed the target language (English) in order to survive and prosper in that community, doing such things as renting apartments, accessing the local health service, etc. It follows from this separation that the language studied in EFL lessons will be different from the language which ESL students concentrate on.

The distinction has become difficult to sustain, however, for two reasons. Firstly, many communities – whether in English- or non-English-speaking countries – are now multilingual, and English is a language of communication. Does that make it a foreign or a second language? Secondly, however, many students of EFL use English in a global context, as we have seen. Using English for international communication, especially on the Internet, means that our students are in fact part of a global target-language community (the target language being not British or American English, but, as we have seen, some form of World English). With the picture shifting like this, it makes sense to blur the distinction and say, instead, that whatever situation we are in, we are teaching *ESOL* (English to Speakers of Other Languages). This does not mean we should ignore the context in which language-learning takes place, but it does reflect a more multilingual global reality.

Recently a new term, *ELF* (English as a Lingua Franca), has become a focus for much discussion and it is to ELF that we will now turn.

B1 English as a Lingua Franca (ELF)

The reality of Global or World English(es) has caused some people to become very interested in what actually happens when it is used as a lingua franca – that is between two people who do not share the same language and for whom English is not their mother tongue. A number of researchers have studied such conversations. In particular, Barbara Seidlhofer at the University of Vienna has noted a number of somewhat surprising characteristics, including:

- Non-use of third person present simple tense -s (*She look very sad*)

- Interchangeable use of the relative pronouns *who* and *which* (*a book who, a person which*)

- Omission of definite and indefinite articles where they are obligatory in native-speaker English, and insertion where they do not occur in native English

- Use of an all-purpose tag question such as *isn't it?* Or *no?* instead of *shouldn't they?* (*They should arrive soon, isn't it?*)

- Increasing of redundancy by adding prepositions (*We have to study about ...* and *Can we discuss about ...?*), or by increasing explicitness (*black colour* versus *black* and *How long time?* versus *How long?*)

- Heavy reliance on certain verbs of high semantic generality, such as *do, have, make, put, take*

- Pluralisation of nouns which are considered uncountable in native-speaker English (*informations, staffs, advices*)

- Use of *that* clauses instead of infinitive constructions (*I want that we discuss about my dissertation*)

Seidlhofer (2004: 220)

Something interesting is happening here. Whereas, as Jennifer Jenkins points out, '... the belief in native-speaker ownership persists among both native and non-native speakers' (Jenkins 2006a: 171), the evidence suggests that non-native speakers are not conforming to a native English standard. Indeed they seem to get along perfectly well despite the fact that they miss things out and put things in which they 'should not do'. Not only this, but they are actually better at 'accommodating' – that is negotiating shared meaning through helping each other in a more cooperative way – than, it is suggested, native speakers are when talking to second language speakers (Jenkins 2004). In other words – and as if to back up Rajagopalan's comments – non-native speakers seem to be better at ELF communication than native speakers are.

We said above that ELF speakers were doing things which they 'should not do'. But, argues Jennifer Jenkins, the evidence suggests that on the contrary, these 'expert' speakers (because they are successful communicators) have just as much right to say what is correct as native speakers do. Jenkins discusses 'the need to abandon the native speaker as the yardstick and to establish empirically some other means of defining an expert (and less expert) speaker of English, regardless of whether they happen to be a native or non-native speaker' (2006a: 175). The traditional 'gatekeepers' of English (inner circle teachers, publishers and testing organisations) may have to think again, in other words, and it is only a short step from this realisation to the suggestion that – knowing what we now know about ELF – we should start to think again about what kind of English to teach.

B2 Teaching English in the age of ELF

For Jennifer Jenkins, the evidence of ELF suggests that we should change what we teach. Instead of conforming to a native standard such as British English, learners 'need to learn not (a variety of) English, but about Englishes, their similarities and differences, issues involved in intelligibility, the strong links between language and identity, and so on' (2006a: 173). Elsewhere (Jenkins 2004: 40) she has wondered whether or not we should cease to correct developing language in the classroom and concentrate instead on helping students to accommodate more. Because in her research she has noticed that some allophonic variation is not evident in ELF conversations (e.g. ELF speakers do not differentiate between strong and weak forms; they substitute voiced and voiceless 'th' with /t/, /s/ and /d/ – *think* becomes *sink* or *tink*), she suggests only concentrating on core phonology. And finally, she suggests that in lexis teaching we should 'avoid idiomatic usage' – because ELF speakers don't use idioms.

Not everyone would be happy with these suggestions. In particular, Ivor Timmis worries that students, for whatever reason, often want to conform to native-speaker norms while teachers, on the contrary, seem to be moving away from such a position. He is clear that we should not foist native-speaker norms on students who neither want nor need them, but 'it is scarcely more appropriate to offer students a target which manifestly does not meet their aspirations' (Timmis 2002: 249).

Vicky Kuo (2006) argues strongly against the view that native speakers are irrelevant or that native-speaker varieties have little prestige. She thinks that ELF applied linguists are erroneously suggesting that 'what is needed for comprehension is all that is needed to be produced.' (2006: 216). She points out that there is more to language use than 'mere international intelligibility'. She says that the phenomenon that people are making use of their imperfect L2 repertoire to communicate more or less effectively 'is interesting and revealing', but doesn't necessarily have any implications for teaching. Based on responses from students in her doctoral research, she suggests that while a degree of inaccuracy may be tolerated in communication, it does not constitute an appropriate model for learning purposes, especially in a highly competitive world where accuracy and linguistic creativity not only in speech, but also in reading and writing (especially in the domain of e-commerce) may contribute towards success. All this leads her to defend a native-speaker variety as an 'appropriate pedagogical model' (2006: 219).

B3 Native speaker varieties and other Englishes

When Vicky Kuo defends the appropriacy of a native-speaker variety, we might want to ask her if she has any preference for which one – or indeed if it matters which variety she or her students would choose. This is not an idle question, since different varieties exhibit different grammar, lexis and pronunciation. This is borne out if we look at the two most analysed varieties of inner circle English: British and American English. In Oscar Wilde's 1887 play *The Canterville Ghost,* one of the British characters says, 'We have really everything in common with America nowadays except, of course, language.'

The differences between British and American English are well documented. For example, British English speakers regularly use the phrase *have got* in utterances such as *I've got a book about it* or *Have you got the time?* when American English speakers are more likely to say *I have a book* and *Do you have the time?* While British speakers in conversation make use of the present perfect in questions such as *Have you read her latest article yet?* an American English speaker might well say *Did you read her latest article yet?* and there are many differences in vocabulary use (*lift/elevator, flat/apartment, trousers/pants*), pronunciation (/lɔː/ – *law* (British English) versus /lɔ/ (American English), ad*ver*tisement (British English) versus *advertisement* (American English)) and even spelling (*analyse/analyze, colour/color*).

But there is a danger in calling a variety by the name of a country, since in so doing we fail to take account of regional variety. If we consider 'British English', for example, it only takes a moment's thought to realise that there are many varieties of English within the British Isles, each with its own vocabulary, pronunciation and grammar. While a Londoner might get a *take-away* meal to eat at home, a Scottish person will order a *carry-out*. While an East-end Londoner might talk about having a '*barf*' (/bɑːf/), a Yorkshireman talks about a *bath* (/bæθ/).

In addition to geography, factors such as social class, ethnic grouping and sex affect the language being used and influence the way in which listeners judge speakers. Until comparatively recently in Britain, it was customary for people to talk about 'BBC English' to describe an accent which derived from the 'received pronunciation' (RP) recorded by the phonetician Daniel Jones in the first half of the twentieth century, and which was considered a sign of status. In Britain, while some accents are admired (such as 'BBC English' and some Scottish varieties), others (such as the 'Birmingham' accent) are still seen by many as less attractive. Though it is true that such attitudes diminished towards the end of the twentieth century – and some accents, such as 'Cockney' and 'Geordie' became widely admired, particularly in broadcast media – it is still the case that many British people ascribe status, educational background and social position to a person largely on the basis of accent.

However, concentrating on British and American varieties of English ignores the many other inner circle varieties on offer, such as Canadian, Australian or Irish, all of which have their own special lexical, grammatical and phonological identities, and all of which have variations of their own. And, as we have made clear in this chapter, even these might seem irrelevant in a world where a number of World Englishes (such as Singaporean English, for example) are on offer as equal status varieties, and where ELF might be considered as a variety in its own right, too. We seem, therefore, to be in something of a fix. What is English for, after all, and what model should we choose to teach it with? Does the fact that something is observable (e.g. ELF behaviour) make it desirable? How important is correctness, and who is going to decide when something is or is not acceptable? Perhaps the answers to these questions will depend on where English is being taught, who the students are, and what they want it for.

B4 World English education

Around the world English is taught in a bewildering variety of situations. In many countries it first appears in the primary curriculum, but many universities in those and other countries continue to find that their entrants are insufficiently competent in English use, even if, as David Graddol points out, good English is an entry requirement for much tertiary education in a global market where English gives the user a 'competitive advantage' (2006: 122). English is taught in private language schools and institutes all over the world, and even in specialised 'English villages' in countries such as Korea and Japan, where pupils live in English-only environments in specially constructed theme-park-like environments. A growing trend has been for Content and Language Integrated Learning (CLIL), where, in secondary schools, a subject is taught through the medium of English. In other words, the students learn the language for mathematics at the same time as they learn the mathematics they are talking about in English. Rather than just teaching maths *in* English (a situation which is common in some bilingual schools), the language and the subject are taught side-by-side. In such situations students might well study another foreign language, too, since there will be no lessons which deal with English only as a foreign language.

We have already seen other situations where English is studied not just for some unspecified general purpose, but, for example, for academic purposes (EAP) or as English for business. Business English learning and teaching has grown enormously over the last 20 years, whether it takes place before students enter commercial life or during their life in the business world.

It is clear from this short summary that the old world of English language teaching is in transition, especially in terms of the language schools which have traditionally taught general English, and for whom many of the teacher exams, such as the CELTA and DELTA schemes run by the local examinations syndicate of Cambridge University, were developed. If CLIL becomes a standard model in secondary schools, for example, the demand for private 'top-up' learning may diminish. If students emerge from primary education with a good working command of English, they may be competent English speakers by the time they get to university level. In such situations language schools and institutes whether in inner circle countries or in other parts of the world (e.g. the Culturas and bi-national centres of Latin America or the worldwide federation of International House schools) may have to think more carefully about what they teach and what 'added value' (in Graddol's words) they can offer. But these are big 'ifs'; we will have to wait to see how things develop. In the meantime we will offer our students the kind of English (general, business, CLIL, etc.) which is most appropriate for their needs at the time.

But whatever kind of English it is, we cannot escape the need to decide on the variety or varieties which students are exposed to and learn. As we have seen, the choice seems to be between adopting one (perhaps native-speaker) variety, or, on the other hand, raising students' awareness or 'pluricentricity' so that they can adjust their speech 'in order to be intelligible to interlocutors from a wide range of L1 backgrounds, most of whom are not inner circle native speakers' (Jenkins 2006a: 174).

Inner circle varieties become noticeably inappropriate when, for example, students in the Far East or South America are taught particularly British idioms such as *I may as well be hanged for a sheep as a lamb* or learn the language for renting a flat in the south of England. But they are more convincing when students learn how they are constructed grammatically and lexically while, at the same time, avoiding their more obviously culture-specific manifestations. Australian, British and American English are still prestige varieties of the language, in other words. What this chapter has shown, however, is that they are not the only prestige varieties which all must aspire to. On the contrary, other World Englishes have equal prestige and can serve as equally appropriate models for teaching. Indeed there may be good psychological reasons why a student actually wants to speak Singaporean English, with its distinctive pronunciation aspects and special lexical and grammatical patterning. Language, as we have said, is bound up with identity. Speaking English with a Singaporean, Argentinian or Turkish accent, for example, may make a clear statement about who the speaker is. On the other hand, as we have seen, some students want to gravitate towards a native-speaker model.

What seems to be the case, therefore, is that, especially for beginner students, a prestige variety of the language (whether from the inner circle or from anywhere else) will be an appropriate pedagogical model. The actual variety may depend on the wishes of the student, the variety the teacher herself uses, the learning materials that are on offer, or the school or education authority policy. Within that variety, it seems entirely appropriate to say what is and is not correct or acceptable so that students have something to aim at and some standard to judge their performance by. As they become more advanced, the variety's richness – including metaphor and idiom – should be offered for the students to absorb, provided that it is not too culture-specific. But at the same time, as Jennifer Jenkins has suggested, we need to expose our students to the reality of World English. As they become more advanced, our students should be made more and more aware of the different Englishes on offer. However, we will have to ensure that they are not swamped by diversity, but rather guided gently into an appreciation of the global phenomenon that is English.

Chapter notes and further reading

- **Native speakers**
  On the dubiousness of the term *native speaker*, see M Rampton (1990).

- **Worldwide economy**
  On the use of English in a worldwide commercial setting, see D Graddol (2006: Section 2).

- **Language death**
  On language death, see D Crystal (2000). See also R Phillipson (2003) on his view of fighting an English-only policy in Europe.

- **Languages in London**
  On the diversity of languages in London, see a report from *The Independent* at www.phon. ucl.ac.uk/home/estuary/multiling.htm. On the top 40 languages, see the CILT website at www.cilt.org.uk/faqs/langspoken.htm. See also P Baker and J Everseley (eds) (2000) and R Salverda (2002) on multilingualism in London.

- **CLIL**
  For an account of the debate on CLIL, and articles by D Marsh, G Lang and D Graddol, see www.guardian.co.uk/guardianweekly/clildebate/0,,1469879,00.html.

  A good book on teaching for CLIL is S Deller and C Price (2007).

2 | Describing the English language

A Language in use

The language we speak or write is governed by a number of rules, styles and constraints as the four examples on this page make clear. Quite apart from the meaning we wish to convey (in this case *Thank you for the invitation. I will come at eight o'clock*), we have to think about whether we are writing or speaking, texting or emailing. Whereas SMS or text messaging has developed into a sophisticated way of conveying messages in the shortest possible space (hence *thx 4 = thanks for*), more formal letters are written out in full (*Thank you very much for inviting me*). Whereas in letters we write *I will arrive ...*, in emails we will often use contracted forms (*i'll be at your place at 8*). Different email writers have their own conventions, too, such as *wbw* (= *with best wishes*), and, as our example shows, there is a greater tolerance in emails for mis-spellings and deviant punctuation (e.g. not using a capital *I* for *i'll*).

In many ways, informal emails (and Internet chatting – see Chapter 11, I2) look quite a lot like speaking in the way messages are put together. We might well send an email saying *I'll be round at 8, OK?*, but though this would approximate speech, it would be without the sounds, stress and intonation which accompany the message (and tell the listener things such as how enthusiastic the speaker is). We will look at the sounds of speech in Section F below. And informal speech is both similar to and very different from more formal written language (as we shall see in Section H).

But whether language users are texting, emailing, speaking or letter-writing, they are making choices about the language they use based on what they want to say, what medium they are operating in, how texts are typically constructed in such situations, what grammar they can use and what words and expressions they can find to express their meanings. We will examine all these in turn.

B What we want to say

The linguist Peter Grundy reports the following conversation between himself ('me' in the extract) and a student at the University of Durham where he worked some years ago:

> ME: *You're in a no-smoking zone.*
> FEMALE STUDENT: *Am I?*
> ME: *The whole building's a no-smoking zone.*
> FEMALE STUDENT: (extinguishing cigarette) *Thanks very much.*
> (Grundy 1995: 96)

We know what the words mean, of course, but why exactly did Peter Grundy give the student the information about the no-smoking zone? He clearly wasn't just offering information or passing the time. On the contrary, his purpose was to stop the student smoking. And what are we to make of the student's second utterance? Is she really thanking her lecturer for giving her information that she didn't have before? Or does her *Thanks very much* really mean *sorry*? Perhaps its purpose is to indicate to her lecturer that yes, she knows she was smoking in a no-smoking zone and since she's been 'caught', she has no option but to put out her cigarette?

Peter Grundy might have chosen different words for the purpose, especially if, instead of a student, he had found the dean, his boss, smoking in the corridor. Instead of stating, baldly, *You're in a no-smoking zone*, he might have said something like, *Umm, not sure if I should point this out or not, but this building is a no-smoking area* or maybe he would have employed a different formula of words altogether to get his point across.

The issue that faces us here is that the words we use and what they actually mean in the context we use them, are not the same thing at all. There is no one-to-one correspondence, in other words, between form and meaning.

B1 Form and meaning

Peter Grundy could have chosen a wide range of language forms to ask the student to stop smoking, e.g. *Could you put that cigarette out, please?*, *Stop smoking*, *Please extinguish your cigarette* or *If you want to smoke, you'd better go outside*. There are many different ways of saying the same thing.

This point is well exemplified by the different ways we have of expressing the future in English. Among the many alternatives on offer, we might say *I will arrive at eight o'clock* (a simple statement of fact), *I'm arriving at eight o'clock* (= that's the arrangement I have made), *I'm going to arrive at eight o'clock* (= that's my plan) or *I arrive at eight o'clock* (= that's the itinerary). Each of these constructions indicates futurity, but each means something slightly different, as we have shown.

If we take one of the grammatical constructions used to construct a future sentence, the present continuous (*I'm arriving at eight o'clock*), another startling phenomenon becomes apparent. In our example, the statement refers to the future, but if we say *Look at John! He's laughing his head off at something*, the present continuous (sometimes called progressive) is referring not to the future, but to a temporary transient present reality. A third possible meaning of the present continuous is exemplified by a sentence such as *The problem with John is that he's always laughing when he should be serious*, which describes a habitual, not a temporary action. And we can even use the present continuous to make a story about the past more dramatic, e.g. *So I'm sitting there minding my own business when suddenly this guy comes up to me ...* .

As we shall see in E2, this same-form-different-meanings situation is surprisingly unproblematic for language users since the *context* (situation) and *co-text* (lexis and grammar which surround the form, such as *eight o'clock, Look at John*, etc.) usually resolve any ambiguity. Nevertheless, it makes decisions about what forms to teach, and what meanings to teach them with, a major factor in syllabus planning.

The choice of which future form to use from the examples above will depend not only on meaning, but what purpose we wish to achieve.

B2 Purpose

Many years ago, the philosopher J L Austin identified a series of verbs which he called 'performatives', that is verbs which do what those same words mean. Thus, if a speaker says *I promise*, the word *promise* itself performs the function of promising. If a celebrity says *I name this ship 'Ocean 3'*, the use of the verb *name* performs the function of naming.

The idea that language performs certain functions is not restricted to the kind of verbs Austin mentioned, however. We saw above how *This is a no-smoking zone* had the purpose of having the student put out her cigarette, just as a sentence like *It's cold in here* might, in certain circumstances, perform the function of a request to the other person in the room to close the window.

One major result of this interest in purpose was to lead linguists to propose a category of language functions such as inviting, apologising, offering and suggesting. Thus *Would you like to come for a coffee?* performs the function of inviting, whereas *I just can't accept that* performs the function of disagreeing, with the purpose of making your own opinion quite clear. *Why don't you try yoga?* performs the function of strongly suggesting, where the purpose is to provoke action, and *I'll do it if you want*, is clearly offering help, with the purpose of being helpful.

The study of functions and how they are realised in language, has had a profound effect upon the design of language teaching materials, making language purpose a major factor in the choice of syllabus items and teaching techniques.

B3 Appropriacy and register

A feature of language functions is that they do not just have one linguistic realisation; the following phrases, for example, show only some of the possible ways of inviting someone to the cinema:

Would you like to come to the cinema?

How about coming to the cinema?

D'you fancy the cinema?

I was wondering if you might like to come to the cinema tonight?

What about the cinema?
Are you on for the cinema?
Cinema?
There's a good film on at the cinema.
etc.

Thus, when we attempt to achieve a communicative purpose (such as getting someone to agree to an invitation), we have to choose which of these language forms to use. Which form, given our situation, is the most appropriate? The same is true, of course, in our choice of language in letters, emails and text messages.

Six of the variables which govern our choice are listed below:

- **Setting:** we speak differently in libraries from the way we do in night clubs. We often use informal and spontaneous language at home, whereas we may use more formal pre-planned speech in an office or work environment.

- **Participants:** the people involved in an exchange – whether in speech or writing – clearly affect the language being chosen. However egalitarian we may want to be, we often choose words and phrases in communication with superiors which are different from the words and phrases we use when talking to, writing to or texting our friends, members of our families or colleagues of equal status to us.

- **Gender:** research clearly shows that men and women typically use language differently when addressing either members of the same or the opposite sex. This is especially true of conversation. Women frequently use more concessive language than men, for example, and crucially, often talk less than men in mixed-sex conversations.

- **Channel:** there are marked differences between spoken and written language. But spoken language is not all the same: it is affected by the situation we are in. Are we speaking face to face or on the telephone? Are we speaking through a microphone to an unseen audience or standing up in a lecture hall in front of a crowd? The examples at the beginning of this chapter have shown how the writing channel (Internet, snailmail or SMS text) will also affect how we write.

- **Topic:** the topic we are addressing affects our lexical and grammatical choices. The words and phrases that we use when talking or writing about a wedding will be different from those we employ when the conversation turns to particle physics. The vocabulary of childbirth is different from the lexical phrases associated with football. The topic-based vocabulary we use is one of the features of *register* – the choices we make about what language to employ.

- **Tone:** another feature of the register in which something is said or written is its tone. This includes variables such as formality and informality, politeness and impoliteness. For example, sophisticated women's magazines may talk of *make-up*, but teenage magazines sometimes call it *slap*. Using high pitch and exaggerated pitch movement (intonation – see F2 below) is often more polite than a flat monotone when saying things such as *Can you repeat that?*

These, then, are some of the factors that influence our choice of language. When we have our students study the way language is used in speaking or writing, we will want to draw their attention to such issues. We may ask why a speaker uses particular words or expressions in a specific situation. We may have our students prepare for a speaking activity by assembling the necessary topic words and phrases. We may discuss what sort of language is appropriate in an office situation when talking to a superior – and whether the sex of the superior makes any difference.

Language is a social construct as much as it is a mental ability. It is important for students to be just as aware of this in a foreign or second language as they are in their own.

C Language as text and discourse

We started this chapter with four examples of texts – that is collections of words, sentences and utterances (an utterance is a sentence, question, phrase, etc. in speech). Although, as we shall see, grammar and vocabulary are vital components of language (as are the sounds of English in spoken discourse), we also need to look at language at the level of text or discourse (that is texts which are longer than phrases or sentences).

C1 Discourse organisation

In order for collections of sentences or utterances to succeed effectively, the discourse needs to be organised or conducted in such a way that it will be successful. In written English this calls for both *coherence* and *cohesion*.

For a text to be coherent, it needs to be in the right order – or at least make sense. For example, if we take a paragraph from the book *Teacher Man* by Frank McCourt and put the sentences in the wrong order, the paragraph becomes incoherent:

> At the end I wondered how I lasted that long[1]. On the second day I was almost fired for mentioning the possibility of friendship with a sheep[2]. I often doubted if I should be there at all[3]. On the first day of my teaching career, I was almost fired for eating the sandwich of a high school boy[4]. Otherwise there was nothing remarkable about my thirty years in the high school classrooms of New York City[5].

But if we read the sentences in the order McCourt originally wrote them (4, 2, 5, 3, 1) the paragraph makes sense, and its internal logic – the coherent way the author sets out his thoughts – becomes clear.

However coherent a text is, however, it will not work unless it has internal cohesion. The elements in that text must cohere or stick to each other successfully to help us navigate our way around the stretch of discourse. One way of achieving this is through *lexical cohesion*, and a way of ensuring lexical cohesion is through the repetition of words and phrases (in the paragraph from *Teacher Man* above, *first day, second day/fired, fired/high school, high school*, etc.). We can also use interrelated words and meanings (or lexical set *chains*) to bind a text together (*teaching, boy, high school, classrooms* in the paragraph above).

Grammatical cohesion is achieved in a number of ways. One of the most common is the concept of *anaphoric reference*, where we use pronouns, for example, to refer back to things that have already been mentioned, as in the following example (where *his* refers back to Frank McCourt, and *it* refers back to his book *Angela's Ashes*):

> Frank McCourt first emerged on the literary scene with his book *Angela's Ashes*, a memoir of a childhood lived in poverty. It became an instant classic.

Another similar cohesive technique is that of *substitution*, using a phrase to refer to something we have already written. The last two sentences in the paragraph from *Teacher Man* above (when in the correct sequence) are *I often doubted if I should be there at all. At the end I wondered how I lasted that long.* In the first sentence, the word *there* refers back to (and substitutes for) *the high school classrooms of New York City*, mentioned in an earlier sentence, whereas *that long* refers back to *thirty years* which occurred earlier on.

Grammatical cohesion is also achieved by tense agreement since if the writer is constantly changing tense, it will make the text difficult to follow. Writers also use linkers, such as *and, also, moreover* (for addition)*, however, on the other hand, but* (for contrast) or *first, then, later* (for time).

These features are also present in spoken language, which also shows many examples of *ellipsis* (where words from a written-grammar version of an utterance are missed out without compromising the meaning of what is being said). The following two lines, for example, were spoken in a British pub:

> A: *Another round?*
> B: *Might as well.*

Another round? is probably an elliptical version of the question *Shall we have another round?* (a *round* is an order of drinks for everyone in the group), and *Might as well* is an elliptical version of the sentence *We might as well have another round.*

For conversational discourse to be successful, participants have to know how to organise the events in it. They need to know, for example, how and when to take turns – that is when to interrupt, when to show they want to continue speaking, or when they are happy to 'give the floor' to someone else. In order to do this successfully, they need to be able to use discourse markers effectively. These are the spoken equivalent of the linkers we discussed previously. Thus phrases such as *anyway, moving on* and *right* are ways of beginning a new thread of the discussion (or sometimes of closing one down); *d'you know what I mean? OK?* and *Right?* are ways of encouraging a listener's agreement and *yeah, but* and *OK* (said with doubtful intonation) are ways of indicating doubt or disagreement.

Finally, in order for conversations to proceed successfully, we need to be sure that participants are 'playing the game according to the same rules' (Thornbury 2005a: 17). Thus, for example, if speaker A asks a question, he or she expects speaker B to give an answer. This example of cooperation is at the heart of the *cooperative principle* (Grice 1975) which states that speakers should (1) make their contribution as informative as required, (2) make their contribution true, (3) make their contribution relevant, and (4) avoid obscurity and ambiguity – and be brief and orderly. Of course, these characteristics are not always present, and, as Scott Thornbury points out, we frequently excuse ourselves for disobeying these maxims with phrases such as *At the risk of simplifying things*, or *I may be wrong, but I think ...* (Thornbury 2005a: 18).

One other factor in successful spoken discourse is the way speakers use intonation. We will discuss this in F2 below.

 ## C2 Genre

One of the reasons we can communicate successfully, especially in writing, is because we have some understanding of *genre*. One way of describing this – and one much favoured by people who teach ESP (see Chapter 1B) – is to say that a genre is a type of written organisation and layout (such as an advertisement, a letter, a poem, a magazine article, etc.) which will be instantly recognised for what it is by members of a *discourse community* – that is any group of people who share the same language customs and norms.

Within the genre of advertising, however, there are many variations. The following extracts are all advertisements, but they all represent different sub-genres of advertisements.

ilavietnam

Academic Director

ILA VIETNAM
Asia & Australasia
Responsible for day to day academic management
of a new training centre.

ADVERTISEMENT 1: online job advertisement

The Life of Galileo

New version, by David Hare, of Bertold Brecht's powerful drama that looks at the conflict between faith and reason. Directed by Howard Davies.

National Theatre: Olivier, South Bank, SE1 (020-7452-3000) Sat & Mon–Wed 7.30pm, mats Sat & Wed 2pm to Oct 31, £10, £27.50. concs available

ADVERTISEMENT 2: theatre listing

Attractive and humorous, affectionate black F, 47, WLTM charming warm-hearted, open-minded M. GSOH, 42–57, any ethnic background. Ldn. Call 01730 8829741

ADVERTISEMENT 3: soulmates

However, despite their obvious differences, the advertisements all share the same basic characteristic, which is that they are written in such a way that the discourse community will know instantly exactly what they are and what they mean. Jobseekers in TEFL (the intended readership for advertisement 1) instantly recognise the meaning (and position within the advertisement) of *academic director*, and have no trouble deciphering *responsible for day to day academic management*. The British theatre-going public (a discourse community in its own right) knows that *The Life of Galileo* advertisement is a theatre listing saying when the play is on, where and how much it costs. They know that because they have seen many such listings before. This genre familiarity helps them to understand *mats* (= *matinees*) and *concs* (= *concessions*, i.e. cheaper tickets for students, the elderly, etc.). Finally, the readers of 'lonely hearts' advertisements will all understand the soulmates advertisement because that discourse community (people looking for love) know the norms and discourse patterns of such written advertisements (adjective(s) + noun → WLTM/seeks/is looking for → adjective(s) + noun + post-modification (→ for fun/companionship/long-term relationship)). And once again, it is familiarity which helps them to understand *WLTM* (*would like to meet*) and *GSOH* (*good sense of humour*), both typical abbreviations in this sub-genre.

Other experts prefer to see genre as a staged, goal-oriented social process rather than a description of text forms. A 'new rhetoric' view, on the other hand (Hyland 2002: 17), seeks to establish the connections between genre and repeated situations and to identify the way in which genres are seen as recurrent rhetorical actions. But however genre is described, the fact remains that textual success often depends on the familiarity of text forms for writers and readers of the discourse community, however small or large that community might be. And so, when we teach students how to write letters, send emails or make oral presentations, for example, we will want them to be aware of the genre norms and constraints which are involved in these events. However, we need to make sure that we are not promoting straightforward imitation, but rather making students aware of possibilities and opportunities. One way of doing this is to show them a variety of texts within a genre rather than asking for slavish imitation of just one type. We will return to this issue in Chapter 19.

Whatever text we are constructing or co-constructing (as in a conversation, for example, where speakers together make the conversation work), the sentences and utterances we use are a combination of grammar, morphology, lexis and, in the case of speaking, sounds, and it is to these elements of language that we will now turn.

D Grammar

The sentence *I will arrive at around eight o'clock* that we saw on page 25 depended for its success on the fact that the words were in the right order. We could not say, for example *I arrive will at eight o'clock around* (* denotes an incorrect utterance) because auxiliary verbs (e.g. *will*) always come before main verbs (e.g. *arrive*) in affirmative sentences. Nor can the modifying adverb *around* come after the time adverbial since its correct position is before it. There is a system of rules, in other words, which says what can come before what and which order different elements can go in. We call this system *syntax*.

Grammar is not just concerned with syntax, however. The way words are formed – and can change their form in order to express different meanings – is also at the heart of grammatical knowledge. Thus, for example, we can modify the form *arrive* by adding *-d* to make *arrived*, so that the verb now refers to the past. If we replace *e* with *-ing* to make the form *arriving*, the verb now indicates continuity. We call the study of this kind of word formation *morphology*. Speakers of a language have a good knowledge of morphology, for if they did not, they would not be able to say *I arrive*, but then change this to *he arrives*. They would not be able to use the different forms of the verb *take* (*take, took, taken*) without such knowledge, or be able to manipulate a word such as *happy* (adjective) so that it becomes an adverb (*happily*), a noun (*happiness*), or has an opposite meaning (*unhappy*).

Grammar can thus be partly seen as a knowledge of what words can go where and what form these words should take. Studying grammar means knowing how different grammatical elements can be strung together to make chains of words. The following diagram shows how the same order of elements can be followed even if we change the actual words used and alter their morphology.

I	will	arrive	at	around	eight o'clock.
They	didn't		until		last Tuesday.
She	is	arriving	in	exactly	two hours.

D1 Choosing words

In order to fill the cells in the table above (i.e. string the grammatical elements together appropriately), we need to know which words (or forms of words) can be put in those cells. For example, in the last line we couldn't put a noun in cell number 2 (*She nothing arriving*) and we couldn't put an adjective in the last cell (*in exactly happy*). They just don't fit. As a result, we choose words that are allowable. And this will often depend on the words themselves. For example, we class some nouns as *countable* (that is they can have a plural form – *chair, chairs*), but others as *uncountable* (that is they cannot be pluralised; we cannot say *furnitures*). This means that in the grammar chain *The _____ are very modern,* we can fill the blank with *chairs* but not with *furniture.* Put another way, this means that if we use the word *furniture,* we know it will be followed by a singular verb, but if we use the words *chairs,* we have to choose a plural verb form.

A similar situation occurs with verbs which are either *transitive* (they take an object), *intransitive* (they don't take an object) or both. The verb *herd* (e.g. *to herd sheep*) is a transitive verb. It always takes an object. The verb *open,* on the other hand, can be either transitive or intransitive. The dentist says *Open your mouth* (transitive), but we can also say *The dentist's surgery opens at eight o'clock* (intransitive).

Verbs are good examples, too, of the way in which words can trigger the grammatical behaviour of words around them. The verb *like* triggers the use of either the *-ing* form in verbs which follow it (*I like listening to music*) or the use of *to* + the infinitive (*I like to listen to music*), but in British English *like* cannot be followed by *that* + a sentence (we can't say *She likes that she sails*). The verb *tell* triggers the use of a direct object and, if there is a following verb, the construction *to* + infinitive (*She told me to arrive on time*), whereas *say* triggers *that* + a clause construction (*She said that I should arrive on time*).

When we construct sentences, therefore, we are constantly making choices about, for example, singular or plural, countable or uncountable, present or past, transitive or intransitive, and about exactly what words we want to use (e.g. *like, enjoy, say* or *tell*). Grammar 'is concerned with the implication of such choices' (Carter and McCarthy 2006: 4).

As far as possible, students need to understand at some level (consciously or unconsciously) what these implications are. They need to be aware of rules. The problems arise, however, when rules are complex and difficult to perceive. The fact that third person singular verbs in the present simple take an *s* in most varieties (e.g. *he plays the guitar; she sails ocean-going yachts*) is a straightforward concept which is easy to explain and easy to understand, but other rules are far less clear. Perhaps our greatest responsibility, therefore, is to help students develop their language awareness, that is their ability to spot grammatical patterns and behaviour for themselves (see Chapter 3C).

E Lexis

In this section we will look at what is known about lexis (the technical name for the vocabulary of a language) thanks, in part, to the computerised analysis of language data. Armed with that knowledge, we will discuss word meaning, how words extend through metaphor and idiom, and how they combine to form collocations and the longer lexical phrases which are a major feature of any language.

E1 Language corpora

One of the reasons we are now able to make statements about vocabulary with considerably more confidence than before is because lexicographers and other researchers are able to analyse large banks of language data stored on computers. From a *corpus* of millions of words (made up of novels, scientific articles, plays, newspapers, brochures, speeches, recorded conversations, etc. stored on computers) quick accurate information can be accessed about how often words are used and in what linguistic contexts. We can find out what other words are commonly used with the word we are interested in, and we can also state, with some confidence, how frequently words are used in the language. This is a huge advance on, say, the pioneering work of Michael West (see West 1953) who tried to get the same kind of information through manual sweat and toil and a card index. It was impossible for him and his researchers to achieve even a fraction of what computers can now tell us.

Users of computer corpora can get a *concordance* for words they are looking for. A concordance is a selection of lines from the various texts in the corpus showing the search word in use. Here for example, is a 20-line concordance for the word *asleep* in written English:

```
 1   box, would you? It would be just  like being  asleep in a box. Not that I'd like to sleep in a box
 2   hus to evade the guards who are wont to fall    asleep at that  time!"     Alianor looked uneasy. "Ca
 3   erations but those of perspective, are   fast  asleep on ground as bare and brown as an end of the
 4   ssed up like a chicken  for roasting. I fell    asleep again till the time for the evening  feed. Ye
 5   w miles further on, the eleven-year-old fell    asleep in his  saddle and Gloucester, unwilling to c
 6    Porter's room. Inside, the Porter was half     asleep behind a newspaper.      There were a great man
 7    "   His brother made no reply, seeming half    asleep in his saddle and  lagging behind. Edward dre
 8    such a  late hour, with the two guards half    asleep in the guardchamber on  the ground floor.
 9   I'd probably be quicker only I'm  still half    asleep! I wash my hair and leave it to dry naturally
10   upon her neck. He lies down. She, seeing him    asleep,  leaves him.)    GUIL: What is the dumbshow
11   en from the farm, they  found Bobbie and Jim    asleep.     The men carried Jim on a piece of flat wo
12   the cat was undisturbed by the gulls. It lay    asleep on  a piece of sacking the gardener had disca
13   thing  as small as a potato. I was probably    asleep when the robot  teacher told me the answer to
14   . I suddenly  felt very tired and I was soon    asleep.     I woke up feeling better. I wasn't hot in
15   e!" wailed the woman. "My  husband was sound    asleep with his mouth wide open when the cat ran in
16   on the rush-strewn floor. Prince Richard was    asleep  beside her, his head on his mother's lap, he
17   ter the wolf was to be cut open while she was   asleep, filled up  with heavy stones once the little
18   alaxy!    An animal is destroyed    Buff was    asleep. I told the spaceship to take us to New Earth
19   o look for them at eight o'clock, they were     asleep in the sun.    "I've found another room," Mot
20   ervant, Miles, to watch it  whilst they were    asleep, under the instruction that they should  be w
```

FIGURE 1: Twenty-line concordance for *asleep* from the British National Corpus (written), generated by the Compleat Lexical tutor (www.lextutor.ca)

Twenty lines is just a small sample of the many occurrences of *asleep* found in the written corpus. But even with such a small sample, some things are instantly clear – partly because the computer was asked to provide the lines in alphabetical order of the words immediately to the left of *asleep*. Thus we can see that in writing it seems that *fall asleep*, *half asleep* and *was/were asleep* are very common word combinations.

The Compleat Lexical Tutor (a free concordance program) allows us to look, as well, at how *asleep* is used in speaking.

```
 1   ere asleep when I went down.   She's always   asleep!   No. She don't sleep at night.     That's i
 2   p at night.    That's it! I mean, she'd been   asleep     What?    Well it were two o'clock when I
 3   is time of year really, quite he's not even    asleep up there   not pigs   you gonna watch erm J
 4   ou know he was that shattered he was falling   asleep downstairs before I put him in his cot, so i
 5   d till next morning when they were all fast    asleep you know and   mm    didn't go to bed about
 6   re doing the cars and he  had blokes    fast   asleep   fast asleep in sleeping bags   yeah    in
 7   rs and he  had blokes    fast asleep    fast   asleep in sleeping bags    yeah     in corners    yea
 8   r  and me and Russell were still in bed fast   asleep. I mean we'd  been up   Did they knock you
 9     When?    I drunk a bottle of wine and fell   asleep after the match.    Where was ?    He was sle
10   they were going up  for the cup and she fell   asleep, well you know with the wine in  you, here wa
11   before we  came out    Oh I    I'll be half    asleep all afternoon   What is it   Spanish?   Do
12    they tell their da.    Do they? That you're   asleep.    And then you know the way your he head go
13   ted the curtains out and   Mm.  once he's     asleep that's it   Yeah.   and I think it's just g
14   id eh can you turn this music down, my kid's   asleep, oh  right, oh and he went and turned it down
15   nk you're go you're tomorrow after ten ?      asleep by his side Erm how's he affording to go too?
16   u find someone else who  wants it.    I was    asleep in bed. I had to get up a    I said that's t
17   gather as soon as Paul gets in I think I was   asleep.    He's like that aren't you? He's     Yeah
18   ey we came into  the house when everyone was   asleep. That would freak me out so  much, you just w
19    that from?    Tracy. Cos she thinks she was   asleep. What, when I went down for  , so I called ba
20    her then.    Who, Kia?    Yeah.    She were   asleep when I went down.    She's always asleep!
```

FIGURE 2: Twenty-line concordance for *asleep* from the British National Corpus (spoken), generated by the Compleat Lexical tutor (www.lextutor.ca)

It becomes clear immediately that *fast asleep* is a more common word combination in speaking than in writing, but that the other combinations we noticed in writing also occur in speech.

Lexicographers work with considerably more complex concordance information than this, of course, but the principle is the same, and it allows them to provide dictionary entries which not only give definitions, but also list frequently occurring combinations (*collocations*), and say how common words are. In the dictionary entry for *asleep* (Figure 3) we see that it is one of the 2,000 most common words in speech [S2], but that it falls outside the 3,000 most common words in written English (because no frequency information is given for writing [W]).

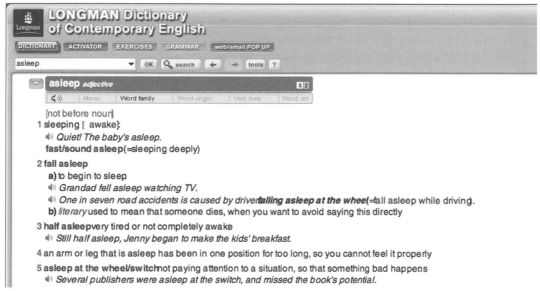

FIGURE 3: Entry for *asleep* from the *Longman Dictionary of Contemporary English* (CD-ROM version)

E2 Word meaning

The least problematic issue of vocabulary, it would seem, is meaning. We know that *table* means a thing with three or four legs which we can write on and eat off and that *book* is a collection of words between covers. But of course the situation is more complicated than this. Both words have many different meanings, quite apart from those already mentioned. We can eat off a *table*, or we can *table* a motion at a conference. We can summarise information in a *table*, too. Then again, when we have read our *book*, we can ring up a restaurant and *book* a table, but if we drive too fast on the way, we might be *booked* for speeding. Some people have been keeping a *book* on whether we will keep our job because everyone knows we've been cooking the *books* for years. The point is that the same collection of sounds and letters can have many different meanings. As with multi-meaning grammatical forms (see B1), this *polysemy* is only resolved when we see the word in context. It is understanding the meaning in context that allows us to say which meaning of the word is being used in this particular instance.

What a word means is often defined by its relationship to other words. For example, we explain the meaning of *full* by saying that it is the opposite of *empty*; we understand that *cheap* is the opposite of *expensive*. Such *antonyms* reinforce the meaning of each word in the pair, though of course because a word can be polysemous it may have more than one antonym (e.g. *a rich person – a poor person, rich food – plain food*, etc.).

Words can also have *synonyms* that mean exactly or nearly the same as each other. We say that *bad* and *evil* are synonymous, as are *good* and *decent* in certain situations, such as *She's a good/decent pianist*. Once again, much will depend on the context in which the words appear. Yet in truth it is very difficult to find real synonyms. *Costly* and *expensive* might seem on the surface to mean the same, yet they are subtly different: we tend to use the former about larger projects and larger amounts, while *expensive* has a broader range of use. We would be unlikely to say *That pen you've got there looks very costly*, but *The new building programme is proving very costly* sounds perfectly all right.

Another relationship which defines the meaning of words to each other is that of *hyponymy*, where words like *banana, apple, orange, lemon*, etc. are all hyponyms of the superordinate *fruit*. And *fruit* itself is a hyponym of other items which are members of the food family. We can express this relationship in the following diagram.

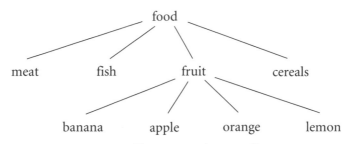

FIGURE 4: Hyponyms and superordinates

Part of a word's meaning, therefore, concerns its relations with other words, not only in terms of antonymy and synonymy, but also in terms of how it fits into the vocabulary hierarchy.

One final point should be made about word meaning, namely that what a word means is not necessarily the same as what it suggests – or rather that words have different *connotations*, often depending on the context they occur in. Thus the word *chubby* has a very positive connotation when it is combined with *baby*, but it suddenly becomes somewhat negative in tone if it is combined with *middle-aged English teacher*! And what about a sentence like *He's really smart*, where *smart* would seem to have a positive connotation of intelligence yet could be interpreted as suggesting the man is somewhat devious or self-seeking.

E3 Extending word use

Words do not just have different meanings, however. They can also be stretched and twisted to fit different contexts and different uses. We say that someone is *in a black mood* (very cross) or someone is *green* (naïve), yet we are not actually describing a colour. In such contexts *black* and *green* mean something else.

There are many examples of how the literal meaning of words can be extended. We say, for example, that *the price of mangoes went up* but *went up* here cannot mean the same as it does in *she went up the stairs*. When we say that *prices have taken a dramatic tumble*, how are we to explain the meanings of *dramatic* and *tumble*?

Such *metaphorical* use of words allows us to move beyond their purely *denotational* use (where a word only describes a thing, rather than the feelings or ideas it suggests). It helps us extend our range of expression and interpretation, allowing us the opportunity to explain our feelings about things in a way that creates readily available images. Poets use such metaphors all the time, of course. Consider, for example, these lines:

> The wind clawed through the shrunken trees
> And scratched and bit and roared with rage.

Some metaphors become fixed into phrases which competent speakers recognise at once, even though the meaning of the phrase is not decipherable from any understanding of the individual words. We all know that *She kicked the bucket* means she died and that *He has bitten off more than he can chew* means that he has attempted something that is too difficult for him. If someone says *I've got him eating out of my hand,* we understand the metaphor, but it is not original; it is a common expression, an accepted *idiom.*

The metaphorical and idiomatic use of words and phrases is not always popular, however, as the following example shows. For some years it became commonplace for people to describe someone who had suffered a disappointment as being *as sick as a parrot,* and this idiomatic expression became so widely used that it began to irritate everybody, except, perhaps, when used ironically. *As sick as a parrot* had become a *cliché,* what Crystal calls a 'lexical zombie' (Crystal 2003b: 186). *Money doesn't grow on trees, you know* qualifies as a cliché, too, so does the phrase *to add insult to injury.*

However, a cliché is not necessarily strongly metaphorical all the time as the following two lines of dialogue from a recent radio soap opera episode show:

> EX-LOVER: *I never meant to hurt you.*
> JILTED LOVER: *Oh please, Richard, not that tired old cliché.*

E4 Word combinations

Although words can appear as single items which are combined in a sentence (*She was asleep*), we have seen (E1) that they can also occur in two-or-more item groups (*She was **half asleep** all through dinner, **but fast asleep** the moment coffee was served*).

Word combinations (also known as *collocations*) have become the subject of intense interest in the recent past, in part spurred on by discoveries from language corpora (see E1 above). Collocations are words which co-occur with each other and which language users, through custom and practice, have come to see as normal and acceptable. It is immediately apparent that while some words can live together, others cannot. We can talk about a *clenched fist* and even *clenched teeth*, yet we cannot talk about **clenched eyebrows*.

The way in which words combine collocationally and in larger chunks has led people to talk about *lexical phrases*. Such phrases are often part of longer memorised strings of speech. We know, for example, what the word *ironic* means, but we can also say that it is typically used in the phrase *It is ironic that ... .*

Lexical phrases or language chunks are like pre-fabricated building units. Apart from phrasal verbs, collocations and compound words, such as *traffic lights, walking stick* and *workshop* (where two words join together to form one vocabulary item), language also chunks itself into functional phrases (*by the way, on the other hand, if you see what I mean*), idiomatic or fixed expressions (*a close shave, an only child, in love*) and verbal expressions (*can't afford to, not supposed to, don't mind*) (Baigent 1999: 51). Michael Lewis, a proponent of the Lexical approach – see Chapter 4, A7 – demonstrated how a 'lexical unit', like *I'll*, crops up time and time again in what he calls archetypal utterances, such as *I'll give you a ring, I'll drop you a line, I'll see what I can do, I'll see you later,* etc. (Lewis 1993: Chapter 5).

The chunking of language in this way suggests that talking about vocabulary exclusively in terms of words is not sufficient to account for the different kinds of meaning unit which language users have at their disposal. A *phrasal verb* (e.g. *take off, put up with*) is made up of two or more words (if we accept one definition of what a word is), yet it is only one meaning unit. We could argue that *wide awake* and *a close shave* are single meaning units, too. Some people refer to such meaning units as *lexemes* (see Crystal 2003b: 118), but whatever we call them, we need to see that words-in-combination have to be perceived as meaning units in their own right, just as single words such as *book* or *table* do.

What we are saying is that we use words either in prefabricated chunks or insert them into the templates provided by grammar. As Steven Pinker expresses it, '... the mind analyses language as some mixture of memorised chunks and rule-governed assemblies' (1999: 26).

F The sounds of the language

In writing, we represent words and grammar through orthography. When speaking, on the other hand, we construct words and phrases with individual sounds, and we also use pitch change, intonation and stress to convey different meanings.

The teaching of pronunciation will be the focus of Chapter 15, where we will also discuss how 'perfect' our students' pronunciation should be (Chapter 15, A1). In this section, however, we will look at five pronunciation issues: pitch, intonation, individual sounds, sounds and spelling, and stress.

F1 Pitch

One of the ways we recognise people is by the pitch of their voice. We say that one person has a very high voice whereas another has a deep voice. When their voice is very high, we talk about them having a 'high-pitched' voice.

While most of us have a pitch range that we normally operate at, in times of tension, for example, the pitch of our voices may change dramatically. We often speak at a higher pitch than normal if we are frightened or excited. When we are tired, bored or fed up, our pitch may be lower than is customary.

The pitch we use is, therefore, a device by which we communicate emotion and meaning. If we start speaking at a higher pitch than usual, this is noticeable. A low grunt gives some indication of mood, too!

F2 Intonation

On it's own, pitch is not very subtle, conveying, as we have seen, only the most basic information about mood and emotion. But once we start altering the pitch as we speak (e.g. changing pitch direction), we are able to convey a much subtler range of meanings. The music of speech, that is the intonation we use, is a crucial factor in speaking.

One of the uses of intonation is to show the *grammar* of what we are saying. For example, if the pitch of our voice falls when we say *clock* in the following sentence, this indicates that we are making a statement:

> I'll arrive at eight o'clock

Notice that the pitch direction changes on one syllable (*clock*). We call this the *nucleus* of the *tone unit* (*I'll arrive at eight o'clock*). A tone unit is any collection of sounds/words with one nucleus. The falling tone, therefore, indicates that this tone unit is a statement.

We could, however, use the words to mean something quite different grammatically, as in this example:

> I'll arrive at eight o'clock

The rising tone now indicates that this is a question, and the fact that *eight* is the nucleus shows that this is the information in question.

Utterances are often made up of more than one tone unit, e.g.:

> I'll arrive at eight o'clock, okay

Once again, the rising tone on *kay* indicates that this is a tag question, asking the listener to confirm the speaker's choice.

Intonation is also used to convey attitude. We have already seen how pitch tends to be higher overall when we are frightened, but the relative highs and lows of changes in pitch direction can indicate anything from surprise to excitement or even a lack of interest or dismissiveness. One of the things that characterises the way parents talk to children, for example, is the exaggerated highs and lows of pitch change. In the same way, we tend to exaggerate when we want to show particular enthusiasm or empathy, but the changes in pitch direction tend to be less extreme when we are being non-committal.

Finally, intonation plays a crucial role in spoken discourse since it signals when speakers have finished the points they wish to make, tells people when they wish to carry on with a turn (i.e. not yield the floor) and indicates agreement and disagreement. Thus a falling tone at the end of an utterance indicates that the speaker has finished their point, whereas a rising tone suggests they wish to keep going. High pitch in response to a previous speaker suggests that we wish to make a contrast with what they have said, whereas a low pitch tends to indicate that we wish to add something which is broadly in agreement with what has been said.

In this context, falling tones are sometimes called *proclaiming tones* and are used when giving new information (or adding to what has been said) whereas fall-rise tones (↘ ↗) are called *referring tones* and are used when we refer to information we presume to be shared with our listeners or when we want to check information.

Intonation is a notoriously tricky area since very many students (to say nothing of their teachers) find it difficult to hear changes in pitch direction – or rather they sometimes cannot identify which direction it is. Nevertheless, there are ways we can help them with this, as we shall see in Chapter 15.

F3 Individual sounds

Words and sentences are made up of sounds (or *phonemes*) which, on their own, may not carry meaning, but which, in combination, make words and phrases. The phonemes /k/ (like the *c* in *can*), /æ/ (like the *a* in *can*) or /t/ (like the *t* in *tooth*) are just sounds, but put them together in a certain order and we get /kæt/ (*cat*), a word that is instantly recognisable. If we change just one of these sounds (/b/ for /k/, for example) we will get a different word (*bat*); if, on the other hand, we changed /æ/ for /ɒ/ – like the *o* in *hot* – we would get another different word, /kɒt/ (*cot*).

Standard southern English has 44 phonemes as the following list shows:

iː	sheep	t	little	ə	again	z	lens	ʌ	son
ɪ	ship	d	dance	eɪ	play	ʃ	shell	ɜː	first
e	breath	k	cup	əʊ	ago	ʒ	measure	ð	then
æ	back	g	good	aɪ	climb	h	he	s	cell
ɑː	arm	tʃ	chin	aʊ	house	m	plumb	p	pen
ɒ	what	dʒ	July	ɔɪ	buoy	n	no	b	board
ɔː	law	f	fan	ɪə	cheer	ŋ	ring	j	yes
ʊ	would	v	van	eə	chair	l	let	w	when
uː	shoe	θ	think	ʊə	sure	r	wring		

The phonemes of standard southern English

Competent speakers of the language make these sounds by using various parts of the mouth (called *articulators*), such as the lips, the tongue, the teeth, the alveolar ridge (the flat little ridge behind the upper teeth), the palate, the velum (the flap of soft tissue hanging at the back of the palate, often called the soft palate) and the vocal cords (folds) (see Figure 5).

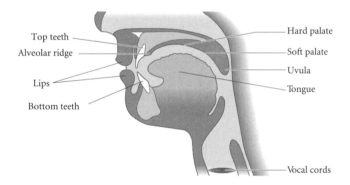

FIGURE 5: Parts of the mouth

As an example, we can see that the consonant /t/ is made when the tip of the tongue is placed on the alveolar ridge above it and when air from the lungs forces the tongue away from the ridge in an explosive burst. That is why /t/ is referred to as an alveolar plosive. Figure 6 shows which parts of the mouth are used for alveolar plosives.

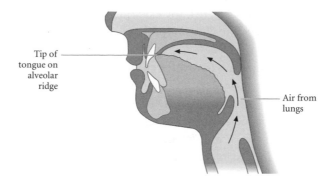

FIGURE 6: The alveolar plosive

The consonant /d/ is made in a similar way to /t/ but there are crucial differences. When we say /t/, as in /tʌn/ (*ton*), the first sound is just air expelled from the mouth (try saying *t, t, t* to yourself, holding your hand in front of your mouth). In the larynx the vocal cords (the two flaps of muscular tissue which, when pressed together, vibrate when air is forced through them) are completely open, so there is no obstruction for the air coming from the lungs. When we say /d/, as in /dʌn/ (*done*), however, the vocal cords are closed, the air from the lungs forces them to vibrate, and voiceless /t/ is now voiced to become /d/. Furthermore, there is little aspiration (air) compared to what there was with /t/ (again, if you hold your hand in front of your mouth this will become clear). Figure 7 shows the position of the vocal cords for voiceless sounds (like /p/, /t/ and /k/) and voiced consonants (like /b/, /d/ and /g/).

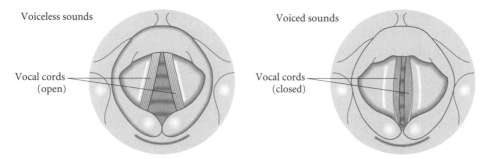

FIGURE 7: Position of the vocal cords (seen from above) for voiceless and voiced sounds

Vowels are all voiced, but there are features which differentiate them. The first is the place in the mouth where they are made. The second feature, which is easier to observe, is the position of the lips. For /ɑː/, the lips form something like a circle, whereas for /iː/, they are more stretched and spread. Figure 8 shows these two positions.

/ɑː/   /iː/

FIGURE 8: Position of the lips for /ɑː/ and /iː/

One sound which does not occur in many phonemic charts but which is nevertheless widely used, is the glottal stop, created when a closure of the vocal folds stops air completely and we say /əpɑːʔmənt/ (*apartment*), for example, instead of /əpɑːtmənt/ or /aɪsɔːʔɪt/ (*I saw it*) instead of /aɪsɔːrɪt/. The glottal stop is often used instead of other stop (or plosive) consonants.

Speakers of different languages have different sounds. Thus there is no equivalent in English for the 'click' used by Xhosa speakers, so English speakers find it difficult to produce. French people are accustomed to the awkward way in which British speakers mangle French vowels because they are not the same as English ones. Japanese speakers, on the other hand, do not have different phonemes for /l/ and /r/ and so have difficulty differentiating between them, and often find it nearly impossible to make the different sounds.

F4 Sounds and spelling

Whereas in some languages there seems to be a close correlation between sounds and spelling, in English this is often not the case. The sound /ʌ/, for example, can be realised in a number of different spellings (e.g. w*o*n, *you*ng, f*u*nny, fl*oo*d). The letters *ou*, on the other hand, can be pronounced in a number of different ways (e.g. *cloud*, /klaʊd/, *pour* /pɔː/, *enough* /ɪnʌf/, *through* /θruː/, *though* /ðəʊ/, *trough* /trɒf/, or even *journey* /dʒɜːni/. A lot depends on the sounds that come before and after them, but the fact remains that we spell some sounds in a variety of different ways, and we have a variety of different sounds for some spellings.

Words can change their sound(s), too, and this is not indicated by the way we spell them. Thus we say that *was* sounds like this: /wɒz/. However, when it occurs in a sentence like *I was robbed*, the vowel sound changes from a stressed vowel /ɒ/ to an unstressed vowel /ə/, e.g. /aɪwəzˈrɒbd/ (' before a syllable indicates that the syllable is stressed – see below). The unstressed sound in *was*, /ə/, is called the *schwa* and is one of the most frequent sounds in English, created by shortening of the vowel and the placing of stress elsewhere.

Other changes occur when sounds get close or slide into each other in connected speech: sometimes *elision* takes place where sounds 'disappear' into each other. Thus /kɑːnt/ (*can't*) finishes with the sound /t/, but when it is placed next to a word beginning with /d/, for example, the /t/ disappears (e.g. /aɪkɑːndɑːns/ – *I can't dance*). Sometimes *assimilation* takes place where the sound at the end of one word changes to be more like the sound at the beginning of the next. Thus the /d/ at the end of /bæd/ becomes a /g/ when placed next to a word starting with /g/, e.g. /bæg gaɪ/ (*bad guy*) or an /n/ becomes an /m/, e.g. /bɪm men/ (*bin men*).

F5 Stress

British and American English speakers often differ in where they place the stress in words. Thus *ballet* in British English is stressed on the first syllable (*bal*) whereas in American English, the stress usually falls on the second syllable (*let*).

Stress is the term we use to describe the point in a word or phrase where pitch changes, vowels lengthen and volume increases. In a one-syllable word like *dance*, we know which syllable is stressed since there is only one. A word with more than one syllable is more complex, however. We might stress the word *export* on the second syllable (*exPORT*) if we are using it as a verb. But if, on the contrary, we stress the first syllable (*EXport*), the verb is now a noun.

In multi-syllable words there is often more than one stressed syllable (e.g. *singularity*, *information*, *claustrophobia*). In such cases we call the strongest force the *primary stress* and the weaker force the *secondary stress*, e.g. *ˌsingulˈarity, ˌinforˈmation, ˌclaustroˈphobia*. Note that primary stress has a superscript mark whereas secondary stress is marked below the line. Secondary stress is not the same as unstressed syllables, as the presence of the schwa shows, e.g. /ˌɪnfəˈmeɪʃən/.

Words are often not pronounced as one might expect from their spelling. The word *secretary* would appear, on paper, to have four syllables, but when it is spoken, there are sometimes only three and the first one is stressed /ˈsekrətri/, or even, in rapid speech, only two, e.g. /ˈsektri/.

It is worth noticing, too, that when a word changes shape morphologically, the stressed syllable may shift as well. In English we stress *Japan* on the second syllable (*jaPAN*), but when we turn the word into an adjective the stress moves to the new syllable (*japanESE*). However, this does not always happen (e.g. *amERica, amERican*).

Stress is vitally important in conveying meaning in phrases and sentences. We have already discussed the importance of pitch and intonation, and it is on the stressed part of a tone unit (the nucleus) that intonation changes are most marked. In British English the stress often falls on the end of the phrase, to give it end weight. So a neutral way of saying *He wants to marry my daughter* might have the stress on the *dau* of *daughter*. But if the speaker changes where the stress falls (and thus where the intonation change takes place), then the meaning of the sentence changes, too, so that an affirmative statement, for example, may well become a question, e.g.

> Brad wants to MARRY my daughter? (= I can't believe the relationship is that serious.)

or

> BRAD wants to marry my daughter? (= I can't believe it! I knew Steve was keen on her, but Brad?)

G Paralinguistic features of language

A number of features of communication take place outside the formal systems of language (sounds, grammar, etc.). These *paralinguistic features* fall into two broad categories, those that involve the voice and those that involve the body.

G1 Vocal paralinguistic features

There are many ways in which we choose how we say things, depending on the situation we are in, irrespective of the sounds, stress or intonation we are using. For example, we can decide how loud or soft we wish to be (volume): whispering suggests a desire for secrecy, whereas shouting suggests either anger or determination. When we make breathiness a characteristic of our speaking, it is usually because we want to express deep emotion (or sexual desire). We can make our voices nasal (which often indicates anxiety). Whether or not these *tones of voice* (different from the tone units of intonation – see F2 above) are voluntary or involuntary, they convey intention and circumstance.

Physical paralinguistic features

We can convey a number of meanings through the way in which we use our bodies. The expressions on our faces, the gestures we make and even proximity or the way we sit, for example, may send powerful messages about how we feel or what we mean. We can look at some of these in more detail.

- **Facial expression:** facial expression is a powerful conveyor of meaning. Smiling is an almost universal signal of pleasure or welcome. Other facial expressions may not be so common, however. Raising eyebrows to suggest surprise or interest may be a part of one culture's normal currency, but may be more extreme for others. Other facial actions, such as biting your lip (indicating thought or uncertainty), compressing the lips (to show decision or obstinacy) and a visible clenching of the teeth to show anger are all powerful conveyors of meaning, too.

- **Gesture:** we use gesture to indicate a wide range of meanings, although, once again, the actual gestures we use may be specific to particular cultures. A few examples of British English behaviour show how powerful such gestures can be: shrugging shoulders may indicate indifference, an attitude of *I don't care*, or *I don't know*; crossing your arms may indicate relaxation, but it can also powerfully show boredom; waving can denote welcome and farewell, whereas scratching your head may indicate puzzlement.

   Each culture group also has its gestures for *go away*, both in its polite and ruder forms, and the use of arms, hands and fingers to make obscene gestures for insults is part and parcel of the currency of society. Other less threatening gestures may also be culture-bound.

   Some gestures, such as head-scratching, hand-clasping, 'cracking' finger joints, etc. may not be used to convey meanings. They may instead be unconscious 'ticks', or be used in some way to displace tension. Such *displacement activities* may convey a person's nervousness or distractedness, but do not send messages in the same way as a clenched fist or a beckoning finger.

- **Proximity, posture and echoing:** the physical distance between speakers can indicate a number of things and can also be used to send conscious messages about intent. Closeness, for example, indicates intimacy or threat to many speakers, while distance may denote formality or a lack of interest. Proximity is also both a matter of personal style and of culture: what may seem normal to a speaker from one culture may appear unnecessarily close or distant to a speaker from another. And standing close to someone may be quite appropriate in some situations such as an informal party, but completely out of place in others, such as a meeting with a superior.

   Posture can convey meaning, too. Hunched shoulders and a hanging head give a powerful indication of mood. A lowered head when speaking to a superior (with or without eye contact) can convey the appropriate relationship in some cultures. Direct level eye contact, on the other hand, changes the nature of the interaction, and can be seen as either open or challenging.

   A feature of posture and proximity that has been noted by several observers is that of *echoing*. An example of this sometimes occurs when two people who are keen to agree with each other find that unconsciously they have adopted the same posture, as if in imitation of each other. When it occurs naturally in this way, echoing appears to complement the verbal communication, whereas when such imitation is carried out consciously, it often indicates some form of mockery.

Paralinguistic features such as tone of voice, gesture and posture are all part of the way we communicate with each other in face-to-face encounters. When teaching, we can draw our students' attention to this, particularly when we are using video material – as we shall see in Chapter 18.

H Speaking and writing

We have already seen how ellipsis is used in speech (C1 above), and we have also alluded (in E1) to how words are used differently in speech and writing (for example *asleep* is much more common in speech than in writing). There is also evidence that we use verb tenses differently in speaking and writing. For example, in speech present verb forms outnumber past verb forms by a factor of 2:1, and simple verb forms are significantly more common in speech than in writing. In speech it appears that passive verb forms are used only rarely, whereas *will*, *would* and *can* are much more common. There are other differences, too. For example, in conversation we tend to take turns rather than speak in well-formed sentences, e.g.

> A: *Biscuit?*
> B: *Yeah.*
> A: *Here.*

In face-to-face spontaneous conversation we are likely to use small units of conversation (*biscuit, yeah, here*) rather than long sentences. Indeed, rather than using sentences, we tend to organise utterances into different tone units (see F2 above).

Another feature of this kind of conversation is that turns are not necessarily neat and tidy, e.g.

> B: *Nice (talking about the biscuit)*
>
> A: *They're my fav-*
> |
>
> B: *I like gingernuts best*
> |
>
> A: *-ourite, but I*
>   *thought ... you know when I was in town ... erm, I'm trying to cut down, you know ...*

(|) indicates two people speaking at the same time

It is also noticeable that speakers often start sentences and then abandon them (*but I thought .../you know when I was in town ...*). They use hesitators such as *erm* and *you know* to buy thinking time.

Listeners in conversations are not just passive recipients of others' words. We use interjections and other words to indicate support and to show that we are listening (e.g. *Mm, yeah, right, yeah*). We use echo questions (e.g. *San Francisco? You went to San Francisco?*) to keep the conversation going or to check that we have understood, and we employ response forms (e.g. *Yeah, OK, got you, right*) to acknowledge requests and points made.

None of these features occur in writing (unless we are providing written transcripts of spontaneous speech). Indeed, a major difference between speaking and writing is that whereas the former is often co-constructed and, as we have seen, messy, writing tends to be well-formed and pre-organised. It is precisely because conversational speech occurs in real time that it is unplanned, which accounts for many of the features we have discussed above.

However, we need to remember that speaking is not one single entity; there are major differences between the language of informal conversation and the language of a prepared lecture. The latter is likely to be more similar to written language (because it has been planned and put together in a writing-like way) than spoken language. On the other hand, Internet chat (see Chapter 11, I2) using a keyboard is more like speaking than writing, and, as we saw at the beginning of this chapter, texting is neither one nor the other. Perhaps, therefore, we should discuss different forms of speaking and writing on the basis of how speaking-like or writing-like they are. Then it will be useful to analyse different speaking and writing genres to see how they work so that we know what the conventions and constraints are for emailing, texting, giving presentations, writing postcards or letters, etc.

We have seen that face-to-face speakers have a number of features to help them indicate attitude, intimacy, etc. These include intonation, tone of voice and body movement. Writing cannot use these, of course, but it has its own range of signs and symbols, such as

 – dashes
 ! exclamations marks
 new paragraphs
 , commas
 CAPITAL letters, etc.

In this context it is interesting that emailers and text messagers frequently use emoticons as paralinguistic devices. There are many commercially produced graphics of this kind, but many people simply use keyboards to produce a range of helpful visuals to express feeling, such as smiley faces ☺, quizzical faces ☹ or unhappy faces ☹.

However, despite all the differences between writing and speaking, it is worth remembering that the vast majority of grammatical items and words are just as much at home in informal speech as they are in more formal writing. They are not different systems, but rather variations on the same system.

Chapter notes and further reading

- **Language purpose**

    The whole issue of *performatives* first came to prominence in J L Austin (1962) – a collection of his articles published by his students after his death.

    The consideration of language *notions* and *functions* was first brought to prominence by Wilkins (1976).

- **Appropriacy and register**

    In *Systemic Functional Linguistics* (M A K Halliday 1994) the three dimensions of context which account for register are *field* (the type of social action or what the text is about), *tenor* (i.e. the role relationships of the participants) and *mode* (written, spoken, etc.). Field and tenor are similar to (but not the same as) topic and tone.

- **Gender**
  See, for example, D Cameron (2006), J Sunderland (2006) and – one of the most influential (and popular) books in the field – D Tannen (1992).

- **Discourse and text**
  An excellent introduction to discourse analysis is S Thornbury (2005b). See also M Hoey (2001), M McCarthy (1991) and G Cook (1989).

- **Genre**
  See J Harmer (2004: Chapter 2), C Tribble (1996: Chapter 6) and K Hyland (2002: 10–22). The concept of genre as a goal-oriented social process is a feature of *Systemic Functional Linguistics* (M A K Halliday 1994).

- **Grammar**
  For an overview of what grammar is all about, see M Swan (2006). For clear and concise expositions of what grammar is, see the introduction to R Carter and M McCarthy (2006) and S Thornbury (1999a: Chapter 1).

  Of the many grammars on offer, serious researchers and students will want to look at D Biber *et al* (1999) and R Carter and M McCarthy (2006), both of which pay special attention to spoken as well as written grammar. M Swan (2005a) is a book which a large number of teachers and students rely on and B Cruikshank *et al* (2001) is also well worth looking at.

- **Vocabulary**
  On vocabulary in general, see N Schmitt (2002) and S Thornbury (2001a). On word meaning (and extended word meaning) see J Aitchison (1987: Chapter 4) and M Lewis (1993: Chapter 4).

  On **language corpora and language teaching**, see A Wichmann *et al* (1997). But see F Misham (2004) for discussions about problems which corpora throw up when used with learners. J Marks (2002) wants to keep corpora in perspective, too, especially in a world where ELF is more noticeable (see Chapter 1, B1 in this book). The Compleat Lexical Tutor (www.lextutor.ca) is a good place to start looking at language concordances.

  All major publishers have their own **MLDs** (Monolingual Learners' Dictionaries) and the more advanced ones are a vital resource for teachers and materials developers, too. See, for example, *The Longman Dictionary of Contemporary English, The Macmillan English Dictionary for Advanced Learners, Cambridge Advanced Learners' Dictionary, Oxford Advanced Learners' Dictionary*. Publishers generally have dictionaries for students at lower levels and some have produced thesaurus-like production dictionaries such as *The Longman Language Activator*. There are many online dictionaries and most paper dictionaries have a CD-ROM version, too.

  On **lexical phrases/chunks**, see J Nattinger and J DeCarrio (1992). On a lexical approach to language teaching see M Lewis (1993, 1997) and D Willis (1990).

  On **collocations**, see M Lewis (2000) and for material to teach collocations, see M McCarthy and F O'Dell (2005).

- **Pronunciation**

  See G Kelly (2000), A Underhill (2005), J Clark and C Yallop (1995) and C Dalton and B Seidlhofer (1994).

- **Intonation**

  See D Brazil (1997).

- **Sounds**

  J Wells (2000) provides a reliable pronunciation dictionary.

- **Speaking (and writing)**

  A full account of the grammar of speech can be found in D Biber *et al* (1999: 1066–1108). R Carter and M McCarthy (2006: 164–167) summarise speaking characteristics succinctly. See also J Harmer (2004: 6–11).

3 | Background issues in language learning

A The miracle of language

Unless there is something wrong with them mentally or physically, all children acquire a language as they develop. Indeed, many children around the world acquire more than one language and by the age of six or seven are speaking as confident bi- or trilinguals. This miraculous language 'instinct' (Pinker 1994) seems, at first glance, to happen effortlessly. The question that language teachers want answered, therefore, is whether second language acquisition – that is language learnt in the classroom – can hope to replicate the conditions in which children acquire their first language(s).

As far as we can see, children are not taught language, nor do they set out to learn it consciously. Rather they acquire it subconsciously as a result of the massive exposure to it which they get from the adults and other children around them. Their instinct – the mental capability we are all born with – acts upon the language they hear and transforms it into a knowledge of the language and an ability to speak it. It's that simple.

Or rather it isn't quite that simple. For example, if we consider the language exposure that children receive, we find that it is a special kind of language. People don't speak to two and three year olds the way they speak to adults. Instead, they (parents especially) use exaggerated intonation with higher pitch than is customary. This conveys special interest and empathy. They simplify what they say, too, using shorter sentences and fewer subordinate clauses. They choose special vocabulary which the children can understand, rather than more sophisticated lexical items which they would not. They tend to include the children in the conversation, drawing them into interactions so that the actual language used is an integral part of the interaction itself. And even before children can themselves speak, parents act as if they were taking part in the conversation, as when a mother says, for example, *Do you want some more milk?* (the baby gurgles) *You do? Yes, you do. All right, then ...* . So, in a sense, children are being taught rules of discourse even though neither they nor their parents are conscious of this. Parents – and other adults – do not choose the simplified language or exaggerated intonation consciously, either. It is usually done subconsciously, so if you asked most people exactly how they speak to children, they would not be able to say on what basis they choose words and grammar.

Finally, children have a powerful incentive to communicate effectively. Even at the pre-word phase of their development they have an instinct to let people know when they are happy, miserable, hungry or alarmed. The more language they can understand – and especially speak – the better they can function.

All of this is bound up with the age of the child and what happens to us as our brains develop and grow. Language acquisition is '... guaranteed for children up to the age of six, is steadily compromised from then until shortly after puberty, and is rare thereafter' (Pinker

1994: 293). In other words, that instinctual ability to absorb language and context and to transform them into an ability to understand and speak 'perfectly' doesn't usually last for ever. However, at around the time of puberty, children start to develop an ability for abstraction, which makes them better learners (see below), but may also make them less able to respond to language on a purely instinctive level.

Despite the fact, then, that there is something special and unique about first language(s) acquisition, a concern of many theorists and methodologists has been to try to see how, if at all, we can replicate the success of that kind of language acquisition in the language-learning classroom. We will look at a number of theories (both historical and current) that have been advanced and which methodologists have used to help them decide what methods and techniques to espouse.

A1 Acquisition and learning

Some people 'pick up' second languages without going to lessons (though true mastery is unusual via this route). Others go to language classes and study the language they wish to learn. Of the two situations, picking up a language (simply absorbing it by, for example, living in a target-language community with no formal attention to language study) is, it would appear, closer to first-language acquisition than studying a language in a classroom is. This was recognised as long ago as 1921 by the man who can be credited 'more than any other single individual' with helping English language teaching to become a 'professionhood' (Howatt 2004: 264). In his book *The Principles of Language Study*, Harold Palmer was interested in the difference between 'spontaneous' and 'studial' capabilities. The former described the ability to acquire language naturally and subconsciously, whereas the latter allowed students to organise their learning and apply their conscious knowledge to the task in hand. Palmer suggested that spontaneous capabilities are brought into play for the acquisition of the spoken language, whereas studial capabilities are required for the development of literacy.

This distinction between subconscious acquisition and conscious learning is still of concern. In the early 1980s the American linguist Stephen Krashen put forward what he called the *Input hypothesis* (summarised in Krashen 1984). He claimed that language which we acquire subconsciously (especially when it is anxiety free) is language we can easily use in spontaneous conversation because it is instantly available when we need it. Language that is learnt, on the other hand, where 'learnt' means taught and studied as grammar and vocabulary, is not available for spontaneous use in this way. Indeed, it may be that the only use for learnt language is to help us to *monitor* (check) our spontaneous communication; but then the more we monitor what we are saying, the less spontaneous we become! In Krashen's view, therefore, acquired language and learnt language are different both in character and effect.

Krashen saw the successful acquisition by students of a second language as being bound up with the nature of the language input they received. It had to be comprehensible, even if it was slightly above their productive level. He called this *comprehensible input* i + 1 (that is, information the students already have plus the next level up), and the students had to be exposed to it in a relaxed setting. This input is *roughly-tuned* (rather as parent–child language is subconsciously moderated as we saw above) and is in stark contrast to the *finely-tuned input* of much language instruction, where specific graded language has been chosen for conscious learning. Roughly-tuned input aids acquisition, Krashen argued, whereas finely-tuned input combined with conscious learning does not.

If Stephen Krashen were right, the implications would be profound. It would mean that the most useful thing we could do with students would be to expose them to large amounts of comprehensible input in a relaxed setting. Perhaps we might have students learn language consciously at some later stage for the sake of their writing, for example, but otherwise, if we wanted students to be effective at spontaneous communication, comprehensible input would be enough.

A2 The contributions of behaviourism

Anyone who has ever studied a language knows that lessons based exclusively on the acquisition view of language described above are extremely rare. From the advent of the Direct method, there has generally been more learning (in Krashen's sense) than acquisition.

The Direct method emerged at the end of the nineteenth century and it laid the foundations for classroom practices which are still around today (thanks to people like Maximilian Berlitz and, later, Harold Palmer, whom we have already mentioned). The Direct method teacher used only English in the classroom; form and meaning associations were made using real objects, pictures or demonstration. The point here is that a concentration on form (rather than subconscious acquisition) was considered to be advantageous. This is the very antithesis of a purely acquisition-based view of second-language learning. Crucially, it depends on the idea that the *input* students receive (that is the language they are exposed to) will be the same as their *intake* (that is the language they actually absorb). Yet, as we shall see below, this is shown again and again not to be the case. Students take in only some of what they are exposed to. And sometimes they take in things which are incidental to the main focus of the language input they receive.

However, the Direct method, which believed essentially in a one-to-one correspondence between input and output, really got going when it was married to the theory of behaviourism.

In an article published in the early part of the twentieth century, two psychologists, Watson and Raynor, reported the results of an experiment they had carried out with a young boy called Albert (Watson and Raynor 1920). When he was nine months old, they discovered that the easiest way to frighten him was to make a loud noise by striking a steel bar with a hammer. At various intervals over the next three months they frightened Albert in this way while he was in the presence of various animals (a rat, a rabbit and a dog). The result was that after three months Albert showed fear when confronted with these animals even when the noise was not made, and even showed unease when a fur coat was put in front of him. Pleased with their progress, the scientists then proposed to continue their experiment by turning the young baby's fear back to pleasure, but they were unable to do so because, unsurprisingly, Albert was withdrawn from the experiment by his parents.

Despite its age, Watson and Raynor's experiment is of more than academic interest because the *conditioning* it demonstrated – and the way that such research into conditioning led on to the theory of *behaviourism* – had a profound effect upon teaching of all kinds. This is especially true of language teaching where, arguably, behaviourism still exerts a powerful influence (Bruton 1998).

In behaviourist theory, conditioning is the result of a three-stage procedure: *stimulus*, *response* and *reinforcement*. For example, in a classic experiment, when a light goes on (the stimulus) a rat goes up to a bar and presses it (response) and is rewarded by the dropping of a tasty food pellet at its feet (the reinforcement). If this procedure is repeated often enough, the arrival of the food pellet as a reward reinforces the rat's actions to such an extent that it will always press the bar when the light comes on: it has learnt a new behaviour.

In a book called *Verbal Behaviour*, the psychologist Bernard Skinner suggested that much the same process happens in language learning, especially first language learning (Skinner 1957). The baby needs food (the incentive we discussed above), so it cries and food is produced. Later the infant swaps crying for one- or two-word utterances to produce the same effect, and because words are more precise than cries, it gradually learns to refine the words to get exactly what is wanted. In this *behaviourist* view of learning a similar stimulus–response–reinforcement pattern occurs with humans as with rats or any other animal that can be conditioned in the same kind of way.

In language learning, a behaviourist slant is evident when students are asked to repeat sentences correctly and are rewarded for such correctness by teacher praise or some other benefit. The more often this occurs, the more the learner is conditioned to produce the language successfully on all future occasions. As we shall see on page 64, behaviourism was directly responsible for *audiolingualism*, with its heavy emphasis on drilling (following the stimulus–response–reinforcement model). As such, the influence of behaviourism was – and is – the direct opposite of any theory of subconscious acquisition.

Behaviourism is sometimes derided and its contribution to language teaching practice heavily criticised. Yet, as Peter Castagnero suggests, the link between the audiolingual method and a simplistic view of behaviourism is 'fictitious'. 'Behaviour analysis is alive and well,' he writes, and is 'making significant contributions in applied language settings' (Castagnero 2006: 519).

A3 'Language learning will take care of itself'

In his book *Deschooling Society*, the educational theorist Ivan Illich questioned the whole purpose of formal education. As the title of his book indicates, he had a very bleak view of what happens in classrooms. We may think, he suggested, that the more input we are exposed to, the more we learn. We may even go so far as to assume that we can measure knowledge with tests and grades. But all this is a delusion.

> In fact, learning is the human activity which least needs manipulation by others. Most learning is not the result of instruction. It is rather the result of unhampered participation in a meaningful setting. (Illich 1972: 56)

At about the same time, Dick Allwright and his colleagues (who had the task of improving the English language skills of students from overseas who were soon to study on postgraduate courses at the University of Essex in England) started to question the ways they had been teaching. For example, they had asked students to study grammar; they had explained vocabulary and taught paragraph organisation. But it didn't seem to be working and it did not 'feel right'. How would it be, they wondered, if they abandoned all that and instead devoted their efforts to exposing students to English and getting them to use it, particularly given that they were highly motivated to learn. The hypothesis they were working on was, in Allwright's words, that:

> ... If the language teacher's management activities are directed exclusively at involving the learners in solving communication problems in the target language, then language learning will take care of itself ... (Allwright 1979: 170)

In the course which followed, students were given tasks to do outside the classroom (such as interviewing people and searching for library books), which involved them in speaking and reading: real tasks for which the teachers gave no language training, advice or, crucially, correction. Students also took part in communication games (see page 349) where the only objective was to complete the task using all and/or any language at their disposal. A student had to draw the same picture as their partner without looking at the partner's picture, for example, or they had to arrange objects in the same order as their partner without looking at their partner's objects – both tasks relying on verbal communication alone. The results, although not scientifically assessed, were apparently favourable. Everyone enjoyed the process far more (especially the teachers) and the students' progress appears to have been more impressive than in previous years.

Allwright and his colleagues had shifted the attention away from the *product* of learning (knowledge of grammar and lexis) to the learning *process* itself. In other words, he seemed to be suggesting, we learn to do something by doing it, and if the goal of language is communication, then communicating as we learn is the best way to go about it. Merrill Swain called this 'comprehensible output' in a clear echo of Krashen's comprehensible input (Swain 1985). Jane Willis says 'you must learn the language freely to learn to speak it, even if you make a lot of errors' (1996: 7). While not going as far as Allwright in suggesting that language learning might take care of itself, she suggests that students need chances to say what they think or feel and to experiment with using language they have heard or seen in a supportive atmosphere, without feeling threatened.

A4 Focus on form or focus on forms?

The idea that students should be involved in 'solving communication problems in the target language' – that is, performing communicative tasks in which they have to (mostly) speak their way out of trouble – has given rise to Task-based language teaching, which we will discuss in more detail in Chapter 4. Task-based learning has at its core the idea that students learn better when engaged in meaning-based tasks than if they are concentrating on language forms just for their own sake. This is not to suggest, as Allwright speculated, that language learning 'will take care of itself', but that learning should grow out of the performance of communicative tasks rather than putting the learning (of previously selected language forms) first and following it by having students perform communicative tasks.

In this context a distinction has been made between a focus on *form* and a focus on *forms*. Focus on form occurs when students direct their conscious attention to some feature of the language, such as a verb tense or the organisation of paragraphs. It can happen at any stage of a learning sequence as the result of intervention by the teacher, or because students themselves notice a language feature. It will occur naturally when students try to complete communicative tasks (and worry about how to do it – or how they did it) in Task-based learning, for example, or it might happen because the teacher gives feedback on a task the students have just been involved in. Focus on form is often incidental and opportunistic, growing out of tasks which students are involved in, rather than being pre-determined by a book or a syllabus.

Many language syllabuses and coursebooks are structured around a series of language forms, however. Teachers and students focus on them one by one because they are on the syllabus. This is often called 'focus on forms' because one of the chief organising principles behind a course is the learning of these forms.

Some commentators have argued passionately that focus on form – which grows incidentally out of communicative tasks – is significantly more effective than focusing on language forms just because they are there. Indeed Michael Long referred to the latter practices as 'neanderthal' (1988: 136). As Ron Sheen (who is largely unimpressed by the argument that focus on form in general is more effective than focus on forms) explains it, 'an underlying assumption of a focus on form approach is that all classroom activities need to be based on communicative tasks, and that any treatment of grammar should arise from difficulties in communicating any desired meaning' (Sheen 2003: 225). According to Sandra Fotos, 'Research ... suggests that task performance can significantly increase learner awareness of the target structure and improve accuracy in its use, as well as providing opportunities for meaning focused comprehension and production of the target language' (Fotos 1998: 307).

One way of focusing on form that has attracted a considerable amount of attention was described by Richard Schmidt as 'noticing'. He uses the term to describe a condition which is necessary if the language a student is exposed to is to become language 'intake', that is language that he or she takes in (Schmidt 1990). Unless the student notices the new language, he or she is unlikely to process it, and therefore the chances of learning it (and being able to use it) are slim.

According to Schmidt, and based to some extent on his own learning of Portuguese, second language learners notice a language construction if they come across it often enough or if it stands out in some way. One way of coming across it, of course, is through instruction – that is, if teachers draw their attention to it. But learners are quite capable of noticing language features for themselves (as Schmidt did) on an advertising billboard, in a TV programme or a newspaper or, for example, in what someone in a convenience store says to them every time they go to buy some milk. According to Tony Lynch, '... Noticing is certainly part of successful language learning; one can hardly imagine (adult) learners making substantial progress without it' (Lynch 2001: 25).

Noticing has one other characteristic, that of salience. Things that are salient (i.e. that stand out more) are more noticeable. Forms which call attention to themselves and are perceptually salient will have 'a greater chance of impinging on consciousness' (Skehan 1998: 49). Gerald Kelly, in his book on pronunciation, suggests that a language item needs '... to be relevant to the student at a particular time in order for there to be conscious intake and before the student can use it consistently' (Kelly 2000: 22). Salience, then, seems to apply to forms which have made themselves noticeable or prominent, and which also arrive just at the right moment because the learner is ready for them (they are relevant).

The argument might, then, go something like this: students acquire language best when they have focused on it either because they need it, or have come across it in a meaning-focused communicative task, or because in some other way they have noticed language which is relevant to them at a particular time; this kind of acquisition is intrinsically superior to asking students to focus on a series of pre-determined forms.

This, if it were true, would make the job of the syllabus or program designer extraordinarily difficult.

A5   Making sense of it all

We need to be able to make sense of the theories and hunches which have been offered to us, especially since they compete on a variety of different levels. For example, if we were to accept that noticing was a pre-condition for acquisition, then the claim that students acquire language best by subconscious exposure to comprehensible input would be untenable. If we were attracted by the notion of language conditioning, then letting language learning 'take care of itself' would make no sense. If we were convinced by arguments for a focus on form, then focusing on discrete language forms in a syllabus would not be the right thing to do.

The problem for us as teachers is that we recognise the merits of many of these arguments. For example, repetition clearly works, and we are powerfully affected by rewards (they will be called 'medals' on page 138). Hence behaviourist influences on language teaching do not seem completely absurd. It is also clear that we do acquire some language subconsciously, and that, just as Krashen suggested, an exaggerated concern for accuracy when we monitor our output can impede spontaneous speech. It is evident that trying out the language we know we are learning in meaning-focused tasks actually helps us to sort things out in our heads. Indeed, it may be that in making efforts to retrieve and then use all and any of the language, we flick a 'switch' that takes language from the learnt to the acquired store (Ellis 1982). But at the same time, the argument that this is the best or only way to do things is '... undermined by the experience of the countless people who have apparently learnt languages successfully by "traditional" methods incompatible with the hypothesis' (Swan 2005b: 379).

When examining the various claims in detail, however, certain problems crop up. A behaviourist view of language learning, for example, seems unable to cope with the fact that language learners frequently come out with language that they have never seen or used before. We make new sentences all the time, yet this creativity flies in the face of a belief which says that all language is the result of conditioning.

It seems entirely plausible to suggest that noticing specific items of language helps them to become fixed in our language store, yet the suggestion that this is in some sentences a necessary pre-condition for acquisition is somewhat problematic. Michael Swan (echoing a point made by Noam Chomsky about first-language acquisition many years before) wonders how it is possible that competent non-native speakers know that we can make sentences such as *I offered/promised/guaranteed Andrew* £100, but not **I donated/presented Andrew* £100. As he points out, this knowledge cannot come about '... by noticing exemplars, since there are no exemplars to notice; the non-use of a structure is not manifested through specific instances' (2005b: 380). Nor is the concept of salience easy to sustain at all times when it is quite clear that students seem to notice things that aren't especially salient, yet don't seem to notice other things which are prominent – or which we bring to their attention.

Finally, the suggestion that acquisition and learning are such separate processes that learnt language cannot be part of the acquired store is not verifiable unless we are able to get inside the learners' brains. Otherwise we fall back on asking people whether the language they used was learnt or acquired (in other words whether it was the result of conscious or subconscious processes), and the problem is that they usually won't be able to tell us. We are left, then, with a hypothesis which is untestable and which seems counter-intuitive, even though we cannot be confident about that either.

What we can say with confidence, however, is that learning success is closely bound up with both the method of teaching and, more crucially, the personality and age of the learner. We will examine these issues in detail in Chapter 5, but here it is worth pointing out that adults, in contrast to children, often depend upon their 'considerable intellects' (Pinker 1994: 29) to help them understand grammar; even if we wanted our students to only acquire language subconsciously (which they do some of the time), they would still think about what they were learning. Some students like to analyse what they are learning more than others.

In a wide-ranging survey article on the teaching of grammar, Rod Ellis suggests, among other things, that students need to focus not just on grammatical forms but also on their meanings, and that focus on forms is valid, provided that students are given chances to use the discrete forms they have studied in communication tasks (2006: 102). But it is also clear, he points out, that 'an incidental focus-on-form approach is of special value because it affords an opportunity for extensive treatment of grammatical problems (in contrast to the intensive treatment afforded by a focus-on-forms approach)'.

To sum up, therefore, students need considerable exposure to language for without it there is no chance of any acquisition. The best kind of language for this purpose is comprehensible input. Students also need to try to use language in meaning-focused tasks. This helps them to try out language and think through how it works. Students also need to *study* language – or focus on it – in some way or other. This may take place during or as a result of meaning-focused tasks, but it may also happen because students notice an aspect of language and think about it or because we bring that language to their attention. It is possible that some language is remembered as a result of repetitious practice – or at least that this practice leads to significant noticing – and that rewards such as success or teacher approval may help students to remember in this way.

Finally, we might agree with Guy Cook when he says that 'What is needed ... is a recognition of the complexity of language learning: that it is sometimes play and sometimes for real, sometimes form-focused and sometimes meaning-focused, sometimes fiction and sometimes fact' (1997: 231). We will discuss language play in Section F below.

B The importance of repetition

Repetition has always played a part in language learning, even if its efficiency in helping students to transfer knowledge from their short-term to their long-term memories is not firmly established. Nevertheless, we suppose that if students think about what they are repeating and try to organise it in their heads, they stand a better chance of remembering what they are learning than if they merely repeat it without thought (see Section C below).

However, one kind of repetition is of vital importance in language learning, and that is the repetition of encounters with language. It is this repetition which really helps fix things in the mind. In other words, if students see or hear some language once, they might, even when they notice it, forget it fairly quickly. But the more they come across this language – the more repeated encounters they have with it – the better chance they have of remembering (and being able to use) it.

However, repeating something a number of times, one after the other, isn't especially useful. What language students need is repeated encounters with language which are spaced out – that is, language which students come back to again and again, with time lapses in between.

Students also seem to gain from repeating tasks. Thus, if they have told a story, for example, and thought about how they did it, telling the story again allows them to re-use words and grammar, re-formulating what they said the first time in a way that helps them to think about language even as they use it. Perhaps this will provoke the structuring and re-structuring of 'noticed' language that is necessary if the learner is to adjust the hypotheses they have formed (Batstone 1994: 40–43).

C Thinking about language

Many students seem to learn better if they are asked to think about the language they are coming into contact with. For example, we could get students to repeat a sentence such as *If I hadn't overslept, I wouldn't have missed the bus* and they might well understand it. But they might forget how it was constructed unless we allowed them to think about the arrangement of sentence elements and verb tenses. Thinking about the sentence allows students to employ their 'considerable intellects' (see page 55). Of course, as we shall see in Chapter 5, different students respond differently to such analysis (and we will be less likely to use it with younger learners), but common sense tells us that if we look carefully at something, we see it better than if we just glance at it.

We can go further and say that if students have to make decisions about the words and grammar they are studying – that is if their encounter with the language has some 'cognitive depth' – they are far more likely to understand and remember that language than if they meet the new language passively. Indeed, one school of thought which is widely accepted by language teachers is that the development of our conceptual understanding and cognitive skills (in this case by thinking about and making decisions about language) is a main objective of all education, even more important than the acquisition of factual information (Williams and Burden 1997: 24). Such conceptual understanding is arrived at not through 'blind learning', but through a process of exploration which leads to genuine understanding (Lewis 1986: 165).

The practical implications of this view are quite clear: instead of explicitly teaching the present perfect tense, for example, we could expose students to examples of it and then allow them, under our guidance, to work out for themselves how it is used. Instead of telling students which words collocate with *crime*, we can get them to look at a dictionary or a computer concordance of the word (see page 34) and discover the collocations on their own. Instead of telling them about spoken grammar, we can get them to look at transcripts and come to their own conclusions about how it differs from written grammar. What we are doing, effectively, is to provoke 'noticing for the learner' (see Batstone 1994: 72 and A4 above).

One powerful reason for encouraging language students to discover things for themselves is the complex nature of language itself. While there may be an argument at lower levels for reducing its complexity into manageable pieces, students who encounter real language outside the classroom will find that it is considerably 'messier' than it may appear in a language lesson. Their response to this may well depend on how prepared they are to observe this messy language and work out, for themselves, how it is put together. Any training in language analysis we have given them will make them more able to do so.

Discovery learning may not be suitable for all students, however, especially if it conflicts with their own learning expectations or culture. One student in a piece of research by Alan Fortune which compared discovery activities with more traditionally taught grammar said, 'I feel more secure with a rule because my intuition does not tell me a lot' (Fortune 1992: 168). Nor is it clear whether such techniques work equally well with all items of grammar or lexis.

If the language that students are exposed to is over-complex, they may find it difficult to make any meaningful analysis of it on their own, even if they understand more or less what it means. But in Alan Fortune's study, quoted above, experience of such activities caused a significant number of informants to end up preferring them to more familiar activities.

Getting students to think for themselves is one aspect of what is often referred to as 'learner-centredness'. Learner-centred classrooms and lessons (where the learners are doing most of the work, often in pairs and groups) are often seen as opposite to 'teacher-centred' lessons, where the teacher is deciding what should happen and where he or she is the centre of attention. For many commentators, learner-centred teaching is preferable to teacher-fronted lessons (where the teacher is at the front, 'teaching' the class). However, as we shall see in Chapter 6, teachers are called upon to play a number of different roles, and as we shall see in Chapter 5, putting students at the heart of learning demands their willing participation and agreement to take *agency* for what they are doing.

D Arousal, affect and humanistic teaching

If, when students meet new language, they are listless and disengaged, they are far less likely to remember what they encounter than if they are engaged and emotionally open to what is going on. A very high degree of attention seems to correlate with improved recall (Thornbury 2001a: 25). In the same way, the students' feelings about a word seem to matter. Do they like what it means? Do they like how it sounds and what it looks like? Do they have good or strong associations with the word? Indeed, when we introduce students to new words, can we create a 'cuddle factor' (Harmer 1991), which will help them to have an emotional attachment to (and therefore better recall of) the word or phrase?

Students' feelings (often referred to as *affect*) go way beyond concerns about how people learn and remember language items. They relate to the whole learning experience and influence how students feel about themselves. After all, 'in the presence of overly negative feelings such as anxiety, fear, stress, anger or depression, our optimal learning potential may be compromised' (Arnold and Brown 1999: 2). The American writer Earl Stevick called these negative feelings 'alienations' and suggested that to counter these states, humanist approaches are called for (Stevick 1976). Stephen Krashen, whose ideas were discussed in A1, would probably agree. His claim for the beneficial value of comprehensible input depends upon the students being relaxed and feeling positive and unthreatened. If they are not, then their *affective filter* is raised and blocks the input from being absorbed and processed. But if, on the other hand, the affective filter is lowered – because students are relaxed – then the comprehensible input the students are exposed to will contribute far more effectively to their acquisition of new language.

How, then, can teachers ensure that their students feel positive about learning – that the affective filter is lowered? The psychologist Carl Rogers, whose impact upon this line of thinking was (and remains) profound, suggested that learners need to feel that what they are learning is personally relevant to them, that they have to experience learning (rather than just being 'taught') and that their self image needs to be enhanced as part of the process (Rogers 1969). Education should speak to the whole person, in other words, not just to a small language-learning facility. In a humanist classroom, students are emotionally involved in the learning, they are encouraged to reflect on how learning happens and their creativity is fostered. The teacher can achieve this by keeping criticism to a minimum and by encouraging them, in plain terms, to feel good about themselves. In a humanist classroom, learning a language is as much an issue of personal identity, self-knowledge, feelings and emotions as it is about language.

However, not everyone is happy with this humanistic view of the language learning experience. Some humanist activities, for example, encourage students to speak from their 'inner' selves, saying how they feel about their lives, or, perhaps, describing their closeness to different members of their families. John Morgan and Mario Rinvolucri describe such activities as allowing students to 'exteriorise their own internal text' (1988: 9). But critics question whether it is the teacher's job to ask students to reveal things of a private nature, and sometimes even to monitor and nurture the students' inner selves. There is some criticism, too, that there is a strong cultural bias to this view of teaching and learning which would be inappropriate in certain situations. Furthermore, a concentration on the inner self may limit the range of language that students can experience, with more emphasis being placed on interpersonal and informal language at the expense of other kinds. Lastly, some doubters suggest, paying too much attention to affective issues in learning may mean that teachers neglect their students' cognitive and intellectual development.

Nevertheless, it is clearly better for students to have positive rather than negative feelings about how and what they are learning. And we know that students are far more likely to learn and remember effectively if their attention is aroused and if they can 'cuddle' the lexis and grammar that they meet.

E When you're ready!

Many theorists and researchers have wondered whether a student's ability to learn new things depends on whether or not they are ready to learn it. For example, Manfred Pienemann suggests that teaching can promote acquisition if what we are teaching is close to the next form that would be acquired naturally in the learner's interlanguage. His 'teachability' hypothesis suggests that if you try to teach students language before they are ready for it, i.e. if you go directly from stage 2 to stage 4, without passing through stage 3, the student may always revert back to stage 2, because they were not ready for stage 4 (Pienemann 1998).

A similar concern with readiness informed the work of Lev Vygotsky, a psychologist working in the Soviet Union in the 1920s and 1930s. He believed that all learning, including language learning, is mediated by social interaction. Learning is 'assisted performance', and this happens when someone with more knowledge – say a parent or a teacher – helps the learner to progress. This help is called 'scaffolding', a kind of supportive framework for the construction of knowledge, and the scaffolding is only removed when the learners can appropriate the knowledge for themselves.

A key element of successful scaffolding is that the learners can only benefit from it if they are in the *Zone of Proximal Development* (ZPD) – in other words, if they are just getting to a stage (above their own current level of knowledge) where they are ready to learn the new thing with the assistance of others. Interestingly, this is not dissimilar to Krashen's idea of i + 1 (see page 50).

Patsy Lightbown and Nina Spada suggest (2006: 165) that teachability research is important primarily for helping teachers to understand why their students don't always learn what they are taught – at least not immediately. It is, perhaps, less successful in helping us to decide what to teach since individual students will often be at different levels of readiness. Nevertheless, we will try to match the language we teach (or which the students notice or are made aware of) to an individual or a group's apparent level or readiness. However, even language which is too advanced may be of use if students notice it: when they are ready for it later, there is some familiarity about it.

In recent years the concept of scaffolding – that is helping students to progress through interaction with someone with better knowledge, such as a teacher – has gained widespread credence, and helped us to focus on how teachers and students interact, especially when, for example, we reformulate what students have said (see page 145), or when we help and prompt them to try out new language. Scaffolding is thus seen as different from introducing new language in a more formal way. However, entering into such a dialogic relationship with students (Thornbury 2001b) may be more problematic with a large class.

F Language play

In recent years researchers and theorists have turned their attention to the area of language humour and language play. There are many reasons for this, chief among which is the idea that it is not just work language or the transactional language of communicative tasks which attracts people when they are free to choose, but that of 'songs, games, humour, aggression, intimate relations and religion' (Cook 2000: 159). Cook points out that language play includes mimicry and repetition, the explicit discussion of rules and the liking for 'form-driven rather than meaning-driven behaviour' (page 171).

A moment's reflection will remind us of the formulaic nature of many jokes and playful rhymes. There is often repetition of structures and lines, and the use of meaning puns to create effects. Furthermore, play (and language play) is often a collaborative affair, and according to Asta Cekaite and Karin Aronsson (who observed children with limited L2 proficiency in spontaneous peer conversations), 'Playful mislabelings and puns often generated extended repair sequences that could be seen as informal "language lessons" focused on formal aspects of language' (Cekaite and Aronsson 2005: 169). They found that student joking included artful performance, alliteration, code switching, laughter and variations in pitch among other things. In other words, there were many ingredients for successful classroom-based language learning on view when children were playing in this way.

Play is seen as something that children do, but the case being made here is that it is highly appropriate in all L2 classrooms. The right kind of laughter works powerfully on student affect. Much play and humour is co-constructed, so students have to work together. A lot of play and joke-telling is rule-bound and linguistically repetitive. And at least some people remember jokes and play routines. Finally, as Guy Cook has pointed out, humour and playful activities occupy large amounts of our real-life existence, however 'unreal' they are. For all of these reasons, the formulaic jokes and dialogues of much ELT, when properly designed, may well be extremely useful for student language development.

Chapter notes and further reading

- **Acquisition and learning**

  Probably the best (and most approachable) overview on second language acquisition research is P Lightbown and N Spada (2006).

  For more on the contribution of Harold E Palmer, see R C Smith (1999) and A Howatt (2004: Chapter 17).

  Krashen's views are effectively challenged in K Gregg (1984). See also J Harmer (1983) and a review of an earlier Krashen book in R Ellis (1983).

- **Behaviourism**

  For an easily digestible view of behaviourism, the work of Skinner (for example) and its use in audiolingualism and structuralism, see M Williams and R Burden (1997: 8–13).

- **Noticing**

  On noticing activities, leading on to structuring and re-structuring, see R Batstone (1994: Chapter 7). For a discussion about the merits of noticing, see J Harmer (2003).

- **Repetition**

  See G Cook (1994).

- **Humanistic teaching**

  Nearly ten years apart, D Atkinson (1989) and N Gadd (1998) express doubts about humanistic teaching and wonder how far it should be taken. However, humanism is defended passionately in A Underhill (1989) and J Arnold (1998). For a useful collection of articles on affect in language learning, see J Arnold (ed) (1999).

- **Readiness**

  See also M Pienemann (1999). L Vygotsky's work was not widely known for some time because of his status in post-revolutionary Russia, but see Vygotsky (1978).

- **Language play**

  See E Tarone (2000) and especially G Cook (2000). On humour in ELT, see P Medgyes (2000).

# Popular methodology

A Approaches, methods, procedures and techniques

This chapter looks at how theory has been realised in methodological practice. Within the general area of methodology, people talk about approaches, methods, techniques, procedures and models, all of which go into the practice of English teaching. These terms, though somewhat vague, are definable:

- **Approach:** people use the term *approach* to refer to theories about the nature of language and language learning which are the source of the way things are done in the classroom and which provide the reasons for doing them. An approach describes how language is used and how its constituent parts interlock – it offers a model of language competence. An approach describes how people acquire their knowledge of the language and makes statements about the conditions which will promote successful language learning.

- **Method:** a method is the practical realisation of an approach. The originators of a method have arrived at decisions about types of activities, roles of teachers and learners, the kinds of material which will be helpful and some model of syllabus organisation. Methods include various procedures and techniques (see below) as part of their standard fare.

  When methods have fixed procedures, informed by a clearly articulated approach, they are easy to describe. However, if a method takes procedures and techniques from a wide range of sources (some of which are used in other methods or are informed by other beliefs), it is more difficult to continue describing it as a 'method'. We will return to this discussion when we discuss postmethod realities in B2.

- **Procedure:** a procedure is an ordered sequence of techniques. For example, a popular dictation procedure starts when students are put in small groups. Each group then sends one representative to the front of the class to read (and remember) the first line of a poem which has been placed on a desk there. Each student then goes back to their respective group and dictates that line. Each group then sends a second student up to read the second line. The procedure continues until one group has written the whole poem (see Example 5 in Chapter 19C).

  A procedure is a sequence which can be described in terms such as *First you do this, then you do that …* . Smaller than a method, it is bigger than a technique.

- **Technique:** a common technique when using video or film material is called *silent viewing* (see Chapter 18, B1). This is where the teacher plays the video with no sound. Silent viewing is a single activity rather than a sequence, and as such is a technique rather than a whole procedure. Likewise the *finger technique* is used by some teachers; they hold up their hands and allocate a word to each of their five fingers, e.g. *He is not playing tennis* and then by bringing the *is* and the *not* fingers together, show how the verb is contracted into *isn't*. Another technique is to tell all the students in a group to murmur a new word or phrase to themselves for a few seconds just to get their tongues round it.

This use and mis-use of these terms can make discussions of comparative methodology somewhat confusing. Some methodologists, for example, have new insights and claim a new approach as a result. Others claim the status of method for a technique or procedure. Some methods start as procedures and techniques which seem to work and for which an approach is then developed. Some approaches have to go in search of procedures and techniques with which to form a method. Some methods are explicit about the approach they exemplify and the procedures they employ; others are not.

What the interested teacher needs to do when confronted with a new method, for example, is to see if and/or how it incorporates theories of language and learning. What procedures does it incorporate? Are they appropriate and effective for the classroom situation that teacher works with? In the case of techniques and activities, two questions seem worth asking: *Are they satisfying for both students and teachers?* and *Do they actually achieve what they set out to achieve?*

Popular methodology includes ideas at all the various levels we have discussed, and it is these methods, procedures and approaches which influence the current state of English language teaching.

A1 Grammar-translation, Direct method and Audiolingualism

Many of the seeds which have grown into present-day methodology were sown in debates between more and less formal attitudes to language, and crucially, the place of the students' first language in the classroom. Before the nineteenth century many formal language learners were scholars who studied rules of grammar and consulted lists of foreign words in dictionaries (though, of course, countless migrants and traders picked up new languages in other ways, too). But in the nineteenth century moves were made to bring foreign-language learning into school curriculums, and so something more was needed. This gave rise to the Grammar-translation method (or rather series of methods).

Typically, Grammar-translation methods did exactly what they said. Students were given explanations of individual points of grammar, and then they were given sentences which exemplified these points. These sentences had to be translated from the target language (L2) back to the students' first language (L1) and vice versa.

A number of features of the Grammar-translation method are worth commenting on. In the first place, language was treated at the level of the sentence only, with little study, certainly at the early stages, of longer texts. Secondly, there was little if any consideration of the spoken language. And thirdly, accuracy was considered to be a necessity.

The Direct method, which arrived at the end of the nineteenth century, was the product of a reform movement which was reacting to the restrictions of Grammar-translation. Translation was abandoned in favour of the teacher and the students speaking together, relating the grammatical forms they were studying to objects and pictures, etc. in order to establish their meaning. The sentence was still the main object of interest, and accuracy was all important. Crucially (because of the influence this has had for many years since), it was considered vitally important that only the target language should be used in the classroom. This may have been a reaction against incessant translation, but, allied to the increased numbers of monolingual native speakers who started, in the twentieth century, to travel the world teaching English, it created a powerful prejudice against the presence of the L1 in language lessons. As we shall see in Chapter 7D when we discuss monolingual, bilingual and multilingual classes, this position has shifted dramatically in the last few years, but for many decades L2-only methods were promoted all over the world.

When behaviourist accounts of language learning became popular in the 1920s and 1930s (see Chapter 3, A2), the Direct method morphed, especially in the USA, into the Audiolingual method. Using the stimulus–response–reinforcement model, it attempted, through a continuous process of such positive reinforcement, to engender good habits in language learners.

Audiolingualism relied heavily on drills to form these habits; substitution was built into these drills so that, in small steps, the student was constantly learning and, moreover, was shielded from the possibility of making mistakes by the design of the drill.

The following example shows a typical Audiolingual drill:

TEACHER: *There's a cup on the table ... repeat.*
STUDENTS: *There's a cup on the table.*
TEACHER: *Spoon.*
STUDENTS: *There's a spoon on the table.*
TEACHER: *Book.*
STUDENTS: *There's a book on the table.*
TEACHER: *On the chair.*
STUDENTS: *There's a book on the chair.*
ETC.

Much Audiolingual teaching stayed at the sentence level, and there was little placing of language in any kind of real-life context. A premium was still placed on accuracy; indeed Audiolingual methodology does its best to banish mistakes completely. The purpose was habit-formation through constant repetition of correct utterances, encouraged and supported by positive reinforcement.

A2 Presentation, practice and production

A variation on Audiolingualism is the procedure most often referred to (since the advent of Communicative Language Teaching – see below) as PPP, which stands for presentation, practice and production. This grew out of structural-situational teaching whose main departure from Audiolingualism was to place the language in clear situational contexts.

In this procedure the teacher introduces a situation which contextualises the language to be taught. The language, too, is then presented. The students now practise the language using accurate reproduction techniques such as choral repetition (where the students repeat a word, phrase or sentence all together with the teacher 'conducting'), individual repetition (where individual students repeat a word, phrase or sentence at the teacher's urging), and cue-response drills (where the teacher gives a cue such as *cinema*, nominates a student by name or by looking or pointing, and the student makes the desired response, e.g. *Would you like to come to the cinema?*). Cue–response drills have similarities with the classic kind of Audiolingual drill we saw above, but because they are contextualised by the situation that has been presented, they carry more meaning than a simple substitution drill. Later, the students, using the new language, make sentences of their own, and this is referred to as production. The following elementary level example demonstrates the PPP procedure:

- **Presentation:** the teacher shows the students the following picture and asks them whether the people in it are at work or on holiday to elicit the fact that they are on holiday.

The teacher points to the teenage boy and attempts to elicit the sentence *He's listening to music* by saying *Can anybody tell me ... Jared ...?* or asking the question *What's Jared doing ... anybody?* The teacher then models the sentence (*He's listening to music*) before isolating the grammar she wants to focus on (*he's*), distorting it (*he's ... he is ... he is*), putting it back together again (*he's ... he's*) and then giving the model in a natural way once more (*Listen ... He's listening to music ... he's listening to music*). She may accompany this demonstration of form rules by using some physical means such as bringing two hands (for *he* and *is*) together to show how the contraction works, or by using the finger technique (see above).

- **Practice:** The teacher gets the students to repeat the sentence *He's listening to music* in chorus. She may then nominate certain students to repeat the sentence individually, and she corrects any mistakes she hears. Now she goes back and models more sentences from the picture (*Usha's reading a book*, *Mrs Andrade is writing an email*, etc.), getting choral and individual repetition where she thinks this is necessary. Now she is in a position to conduct a slightly freer kind of drill than the Audiolingual one above:

TEACHER: *Can anyone tell me? ... Usha? ... Yes, Sergio.*
STUDENT: *She's reading a book.*
TEACHER: *Good.*
ETC.

In this cue–response drill the teacher gives the cue (*Usha*) before nominating a student (*Sergio*) who will give the response (*She's reading a book*). By cueing before nominating she keeps everyone alert. She will avoid nominating students in a predictable order for the same reason.

Usually the teacher puts the students in pairs to practise the sentences a bit more before listening to a few examples just to check that the learning has been effective.

- **Production:** the end point of the PPP cycle is production, what some trainers have called 'immediate creativity'. Here the students are asked to use the new language (in this case the present continuous) in sentences of their own. For example, the teacher may get the students to think about what their friends and family are doing at this moment. They must now come up with sentences such as *My mother's working at the hospital, I think, My brother's lying on the beach. I'm sure. He's on holiday*, etc.

A3   PPP and alternatives to PPP

The PPP procedure, which was offered to teacher trainees as a significant teaching procedure from the middle of the 1960s onwards (though not then referred to as PPP), came under a sustained attack in the 1990s. It was, critics argued, clearly teacher-centred (at least in the kind of procedure which we have demonstrated above), and therefore sits uneasily in a more humanistic and learner-centred framework. It also seems to assume that students learn 'in straight lines' – that is, starting from no knowledge, through highly restricted sentence-based utterances and on to immediate production. Yet human learning probably isn't like that; it's more random, more convoluted. And, by breaking language down into small pieces to learn, it may be cheating the students of a language which, in Tessa Woodward's phrase, is full of 'interlocking variables and systems' (Woodward 1993: 3). Michael Lewis suggested that PPP was inadequate because it reflected neither the nature of language nor the nature of learning (Lewis 1993: 190), and Jim Scrivener even wrote that it was 'fundamentally disabling, not enabling' (Scrivener 1994a: 15).

In response to these criticisms many people have offered variations on PPP and alternatives to it. As long ago as 1982 Keith Johnson suggested the 'deep-end strategy' as an alternative (Johnson 1982), where by encouraging the students into immediate production (throwing them in at the deep end), you turn the procedure on its head. The teacher can now see if and where students are having problems during this production phase and return to either presentation or practice as and when necessary after the production phase is over. A few years later, Donn Byrne suggested much the same thing (Byrne 1986: 3), joining the three phases in a circle (see Figure 1). Teachers and students can decide at which stage to enter the procedure.

FIGURE 1: Byrne's 'alternative approach'

A different trilogy of teaching sequence elements is ESA: Engage, Study and Activate (Harmer 2007: Chapter 4).

E stands for *engage*. As we saw on page 58, arousal and affect are important for successful learning. The point is that unless students are emotionally engaged with what is going on, their learning will be less effective.

S stands for *study* and describes any teaching and learning element where the focus is on how something is constructed, whether it is relative clauses, specific intonation patterns, the construction of a paragraph or text, the way a lexical phrase is made and used, or the collocation of a particular word. Crucially, in this model, study may be part of a 'focus on forms' syllabus, or may grow out of a communicative task where the students' attention to form is drawn to it either by the teacher or through their own noticing activities.

A stands for *activate* and this means any stage at which students are encouraged to use all and/or any of the language they know. Communicative tasks, for example, (see page 70) are designed to activate the students' language knowledge. But students also activate their language knowledge when they read for pleasure or for general interest. Indeed any meaning-focused activity where the language is not restricted provokes students into language activation.

ESA allows for three basic lesson procedures. In the first ('Straight arrows', see Figure 2) the sequence is ESA, much like PPP. The teacher engages students by presenting a picture or a situation, or by drawing them in by some other means. At the study stage of the procedure, the meaning and form of the language are explained. The teacher then models the language and the students repeat and practise it. Finally, they activate the new language by using it in sentences of their own.

A 'Boomerang' procedure, on the other hand, follows a more task-based or deep-end approach (see Figure 3). Here the order is EAS; the teacher gets the students engaged before asking them to do something like a written task, a communication game or a role-play. Based on what happens there, the students will then, after the activity has finished, study some aspect of language which they lacked or which they used incorrectly.

'Patchwork' lessons (see Figure 4), which are different from the previous two procedures, may follow a variety of sequences. For example, engaged students are encouraged to activate their knowledge before studying one and then another language element, and then returning to more activating tasks, after which the teacher re-engages them before doing some more study, etc. What the Engage/Study/Activate trilogy has tried to capture is the fact that PPP is just '... a tool used by teachers for *one* of their many possible purposes' (Swan 2005b: 380, my italics). In other words, PPP is extremely useful in a focus-on-forms lesson, especially at lower levels, but is irrelevant in a skills lesson, where focus-on-form may occur as a result of something students hear or read. It is useful, perhaps, in teaching grammar points such as the use of *can* and *can't*, but has little place when students are analysing their own language use after doing a

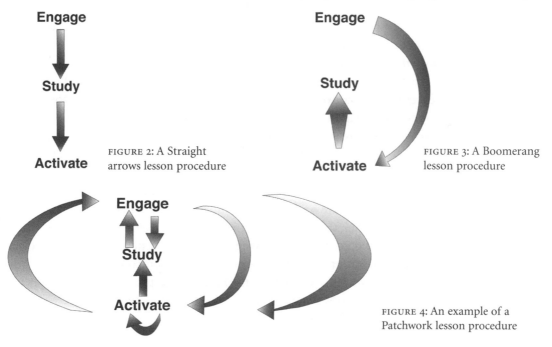

FIGURE 2: A Straight arrows lesson procedure

FIGURE 3: A Boomerang lesson procedure

FIGURE 4: An example of a Patchwork lesson procedure

communicative task. Nevertheless, a look at modern coursebooks shows that PPP is alive and well, but in a context of a wide range of other techniques and procedures. And while it is true that PPP is still used in one form or another all over the world, it is also the case that students are exposed to many other techniques and procedures. PPP is a kind of ESA, as we saw, but there are many other lesson sequences, too, such the Boomerang and Patchwork sequences mentioned above.

A4 Four methods

Four methods, developed in the 1970s and 1980s, are often considered together. While, individually, they are rarely used exclusively in 'mainstream' teaching, in different ways their influence is still felt today.

In the classic form of Community Language Learning, a 'knower' stands outside a circle of students and helps the students say what they want to say by translating, suggesting or amending the students' utterances. The students' utterances may then be recorded so that they can be analysed at a later date. Students, with the teacher's help, reflect on how they felt about the activities.

Suggestopaedia was developed by Georgi Lozanov and is concerned above all with the physical environment in which the learning takes place. Students need to be comfortable and relaxed so that their affective filter is lowered. Students take on different names and exist in a child–parent relationship with the teacher (Lozanov calls this 'infantilisation'). Traumatic topics are avoided, and at one stage of a three-part procedure, the teacher reads a previously-studied dialogue to the accompaniment of music (preferably Baroque). During this phase there are also 'several minutes of solemn silence' (Lozanov 1978: 272) and the students leave the room silently.

A typical Total Physical Response (TPR) lesson might involve the teacher telling students to 'pick up the triangle from the table and give it to me' or 'walk quickly to the door and hit it' (Asher 1977: 54–56). When the students can all respond to commands correctly, one of them can then start giving instructions to other classmates. James Asher believed that since children learn a lot of their language from commands directed at them, second-language learners can benefit from this, too. Crucially, in TPR students don't have to give instructions themselves until they are ready.

One of the most notable features of the Silent Way is the behaviour of the teacher who, rather than entering into conversation with the students, says as little as possible. This is because the founder of the method, Caleb Gattegno, believed that learning is best facilitated if the learner discovers and creates language rather than just remembering and repeating what has been taught. The learner should be in the driving seat, in other words, not the teacher.

In the Silent Way, the teacher frequently points to different sounds on a phonemic chart, modelling them before indicating that students should say the sounds. The teacher is then silent, indicating only by gesture or action when individual students should speak (they keep trying to work out whether they are saying the sound correctly) and then showing when sounds and words are said correctly by moving on to the next item. Because of the teacher's silent non-involvement, it is up to the students – under the controlling but indirect influence of the teacher – to solve problems and learn the language. Typically, the Silent Way also gets students to use Cuisenaire rods (wooden blocks of different colours and sizes, see page 180) to solve communication problems.

To some, the Silent Way has seemed somewhat inhuman, with the teacher's silence acting as a barrier rather than an incentive. But to others, the reliance students are forced to place upon themselves and upon each other is exciting and liberating. It is students who should take responsibility for their learning; it is the teacher's job to organise this.

Some of the procedures employed in these four methods may strike us as being (or having been) outside the mainstream of classroom practice, or even somewhat eccentric. Nevertheless, in their own ways, they contain truths about successful language learning. Community Language Learning, for example, reminds us that teachers are in classrooms to facilitate learning and to help students with what they want to say. Suggestopaedia's insistence on lowering the affective filter reminds us how important affect is in language learning. Nor is there any doubt about the appropriacy of getting students to move around in lessons, as in TPR. For students with a more kinaesthetic inclination (see page 89), this will be especially useful. Finally, getting students to think about what they are learning and to rely on themselves matches our concern for cognitive depth (see page 57), where close attention to language by individual students has a beneficial effect on the learning process.

A5 Communicative Language Teaching (CLT)

The real problem when attempting to define CLT (or the Communicative approach as it was originally called) is that it means different things to different people. Or perhaps it is like an extended family of different approaches, and '... as is the case with most families, not all members live harmoniously together all of the time. There are squabbles and disagreements, if not outright wars, from time to time. However, no one is willing to assert that they do not belong to the family' (Nunan 2004: 7).

One of the things that CLT embraces within its family is the concept of how language is used. Instead of concentrating solely on grammar, pioneers such as David Wilkins in the 1970s looked at what notions language expressed and what communicative functions people performed with language (Wilkins 1976). The concern was with spoken functions as much as with written grammar, and notions of when and how it was appropriate to say certain things were of primary importance. Thus communicative language teachers taught people to invite and apologise, to agree and disagree, alongside making sure they could use the past perfect or the second conditional.

A major strand of CLT centres around the essential belief that if students are involved in meaning-focused communicative tasks, then 'language learning will take care of itself' (see page 52), and that plentiful exposure to language in use and plenty of opportunities to use it are vitally important for a student's development of knowledge and skill. Activities in CLT typically involve students in real or realistic communication, where the successful achievement of the communicative task they are performing is at least as important as the accuracy of their language use. Thus role-play and simulation have become very popular in CLT. For example, students might simulate a television programme or a scene at an airport – or they might put together the simulated front page of a newspaper. In other communicative activities, students have to solve a puzzle and can only do so by sharing information. Sometimes they have to write a poem or construct a story together.

In order for these activities to be truly communicative, it was suggested from the very beginning, students should have a desire to communicate something. They should have a purpose for communicating (e.g. to make a point, to buy an airline ticket or to write a letter to a newspaper). They should be focused on the content of what they are saying or writing rather than on a particular language form. They should use a variety of language rather than just one language structure. The teacher will not intervene to stop the activity; and the materials he or she relies on will not dictate what specific language forms the students use either. In other words, such activities should attempt to replicate real communication. All this is seen as being in marked contrast to the kind of teaching and learning we saw in A1 above. They are at opposite ends of a 'communication continuum' as shown in Figure 5.

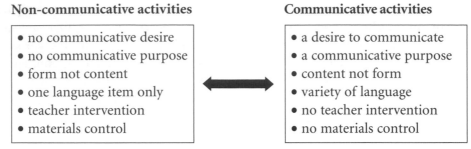

FIGURE 5: The communication continuum

Not all activities in CLT occur at either extreme of the continuum, however. Some may be further towards the communicative end, whereas some may be more non-communicative. An activity in which students have to go round the class asking questions with a communicative purpose, but using certain prescribed structures (e.g. *Have you ever done a bungee jump? Have you ever climbed a mountain? Have you ever been white-water rafting?*) may be edging towards the non-communicative end of the continuum, whereas another, where students have to interview each other about a holiday they went on, might be nearer the communicative end.

A key to the enhancement of communicative purpose and the desire to communicate is the information gap. A traditional classroom exchange in which one student asks *Where's the library?* and another student answers *It's on Green Street, opposite the bank* when they can both see it and both know the answer, is not much like real communication. If, however, the first student has a map which does not have the library shown on it, while the other student has a different map with *library* written on the correct building – but which the first student cannot see – then there is a gap between the knowledge which the two participants have. In order for the first student to locate the library on their map, that information gap needs to be closed.

CLT, therefore, with its different strands of what to teach (utterances as well as sentences, functions as well as grammar) and how to teach it (meaning-focused communicative tasks as well as more traditional study techniques), has become a generalised 'umbrella' term to describe learning sequences which aim to improve the students' ability to communicate. This is in stark contrast to teaching which is aimed more at learning bits of language just because they exist – without focusing on their use in communication.

However, CLT has come under attack for being prejudiced in favour of native-speaker teachers by demanding a relatively uncontrolled range of language use on the part of the student, and thus expecting the teacher to be able to respond to any and every language problem which may come up (Medgyes 1992). In promoting a methodology which is based around group- and pairwork, with teacher intervention kept to a minimum during, say, a role-play, CLT may also offend against educational traditions which rely on a more teacher-centred approach. CLT has sometimes been seen as having eroded the explicit teaching of grammar with a consequent loss among students of accuracy in the pursuit of fluency. Perhaps there is a danger in 'a general over-emphasis on performance at the expense of progress' (Wicksteed 1998: 3). Finally, some commentators suggest that many so-called communicative activities are no more or less real than traditional exercises. Getting people to write a letter, buy an airline ticket, find out train times (see Prabhu, quoted below), or go and look something up (see Allwright's study on page 52), is just as contrived as many more traditional exercises, and does not, in fact, arise from any genuine communicative purpose.

Despite these reservations, however, the Communicative approach has left an indelible mark on teaching and learning, resulting in the use of communicative activities in classrooms all over the world.

A6 Task-based learning (TBL)

Task-based learning (sometimes referred to as Task-based instruction, or TBI) makes the performance of meaningful tasks central to the learning process. It is informed by a belief that if students are focused on the completion of a task, they are just as likely to learn language as they are if they are focusing on language forms. Instead of a language structure or function to be learnt, students are presented with a task they have to perform or a problem they have to solve. For example, in an early example of TBL, after a class performs some pre-task activities which involve questions and vocabulary checking (e.g. *What is this? It's a timetable. What does 'arrival' mean?*), they ask and answer questions to solve a problem, such as finding train-timetable information, e.g. *When does the Brindavan express leave Madras/arrive in Bangalore?* (Prahbu 1987: 32). Although the present simple may frequently be used in such an activity, the focus of the lesson is the task, not the structure.

One way of looking at Task-based learning is to see it as a kind of 'deep-end' strategy (see Johnson 1982), or, in the words of Jane Willis, 'like a sort of PPP upside down' (Willis 1994: 19). In other words, students are given a task to perform and only when the task has been completed does the teacher discuss the language that was used, making corrections and adjustments which the students' performance of the task has shown to be desirable. This is similar to the Boomerang procedure we mentioned on page 67. However, as Willis herself makes clear, task-based methodology is, in fact, considerably more complicated than this. She suggests three basic stages: the Pre-task, the Task cycle and the Language focus (see Figure 6).

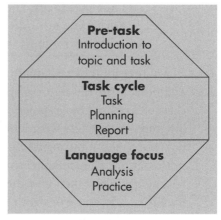

FIGURE 6: The Willis TBL framework (Willis 1996: 52)

In the Pre-task stage, the teacher explores the topic with the class and may highlight useful words and phrases, helping students to understand the task instructions. The students may hear a recording of other people doing the same task. During the Task cycle stage, the students perform the task in pairs or small groups while the teacher monitors from a distance. The students then plan how they will tell the rest of the class what they did and how it went, and they then report on the task either orally or in writing, and/or compare notes on what has happened. In the Language focus stage, the students examine and discuss specific features of any listening or reading text which they have looked at for the task and/or the teacher may conduct some form of practice of specific language features which the task has provoked.

One of the examples that Jane Willis gives of such a procedure concerns a woman's phobia about spiders (Willis 1996: 161–164). The woman lived with her husband but could never be left alone because of her fear of spiders. Part of the procedure (which I have shortened and slightly amended) goes like this:

> **Pre-task:** The teacher explains the woman's situation and asks students, in pairs, to brainstorm three consecutive steps they might take to help cure the woman of her phobia.

> **Task:** Pairs list possible ways to help the woman get over her phobia.
>
> **Planning:** Pairs rehearse how to explain the steps they recommend, and justify the order they are in.
>
> **Report and reading:** The pairs tell the class their proposals and justify them. The class listen and count how many ideas they come up with.
>
> The teacher lets the class decide and vote on which three steps might be similar to those in a newspaper report about the phobic woman's dilemma. She writes these on the board.
>
> The teacher gives out the text. She asks students to read to see whether their three steps were in the report. Finally, she asks which pair had the most steps that were similar.

> **Language focus:** The teacher helps students with any mistakes she heard during the task. She then directs students back to the article and they analyse it for topic vocabulary, time expressions, syntax elements, etc.

Another kind of task might be to ask students to give a short presentation on the life of a famous historical figure of their choice. We could start by getting them to look at some examples of brief biographies (on the Internet, for example) before discussing what is in such biographies and how we might change the sequence of the information if we were going to tell people about our figure. In pairs or groups, students now choose a figure and plan their presentation. They might consult language books or ask us to help them with grammar and vocabulary. They then give their presentations and subsequently we and they analyse what they have said and work with language items that need attention. When all that is over, we might get them to re-plan and re-deliver their presentations in order to take advantage of what they learnt from the feedback on their first attempts (see 'The importance of repetition' on page 56).

David Nunan's task sequence is somewhat different (Nunan 2004: Chapter 2). He starts with the same kind of pre-task to build the students' schema (see page 271), but he then gives students controlled language practice for the vocabulary they might need for their task. They then listen to native speakers performing a similar task and analyse the language that was used. Finally, after some free practice of language, they reach the pedagogical task where they discuss issues and make a decision. This is not at all like 'PPP upside down' since language focus activities lead towards a task rather than occurring as a result of it. This, Nunan suggests, is because 'learners should be encouraged to move from reproductive to creative language use' (2004: 37).

There is some confusion, then, about what Task-based learning means. In one view, tasks are the building blocks of a language course. Students perform the tasks and focus on language form as they do the tasks, or as a result of having done them. In another version, however, tasks are still the building blocks of the course, but we will provide students with the language to do them before they set out to perform these tasks. It is the first of these two approaches to TBL that is essentially based on the belief that 'get performance right and competence will, with some prompting, take care of itself' (Widdowson 2003: 18).

Dave and Jane Willis are quite clear that despite different approaches to TBL (see above), its advocates 'have rejected a reliance on presentation methodology' and that further 'the basis for language development is the learner's attempt to deploy language for meaning' (Willis and Willis 2003: 2).

Critics of TBL have raised a number of concerns about its overall applicability. William Littlewood, for example, has difficulty, as we have done above, in pinning down exactly what it means and so wishes to abandon the term altogether (Littlewood 2004a). Paul Seedhouse suggests that while it may be highly appropriate to base some learning on tasks, it would be 'unsound' to make tasks 'the basis for an entire pedagogical methodology' (Seedhouse 1999: 155). He points out that the kind of interaction which typical tasks promote leads to the use of specific 'task-solving' linguistic forms. These fail to include the kind of language we might expect from discussion, debate or social interactions of other kinds. As we saw on page 60, Guy Cook thinks that there is more to language learning than just 'work' language; it is one of his main arguments for the inclusion of language play. Michael Swan worries that 'while TBI may successfully develop learners' command of what is known, it is considerably less effective for the systematic teaching of new language' (2005b: 376). He also worries about how appropriate tasks are in a situation where teachers have little time, and this point is taken up by Penny Ur. Working in a state school with only three or four English lessons a week, she has to 'make sure they learn the most common and useful words and chunks as fast as possible. We don't have time to wait until such items are encountered in communicative tasks' (2006). However, as someone who wrote a book on 'task-centred discussions' (Ur 1981), she does not argue that there is no place for communicative tasks, but rather that they are a 'necessary added component of a structured, language-based syllabus and methodology' (2006: 3).

Finally, a central claim of TBL is that 'opportunities for production may force students to pay close attention to form and to the relationship between form and meaning' (Beglar and Hunt 2002: 97), although Rob Batstone wonders whether tasks which require simultaneous processing of form and meaning might 'overload the learner's system, leading to less intake rather than more' (1996: 273).

Perhaps Task-based learning, like Communicative Language Teaching before it, is really a family of slightly argumentative members who, despite their differences, really want to stay together. In its pure form (that a curriculum should be based on tasks, and that learning should emerge from the tasks rather than preceding them), it accurately reflects an approach to learning exemplified by proponents of focus-on-form, rather than those who base their curriculum on teaching a sequence of pre-selected forms. But the claims made for it, while extremely attractive, sometimes seem more like hypotheses than fact. In the end, it is indubitably the case that having students perform meaning-related tasks is good for language processing and for giving them opportunities for trying out language (and getting feedback on their language use), but whether a programme based exclusively on such tasks is appropriate (and where it might be appropriate – see Section B below) is open to question.

 ## The Lexical approach

The Lexical approach, discussed by Dave Willis (Willis 1990) and popularised by Michael Lewis (1993, 1997), is based on the assertion that 'language consists not of traditional grammar and vocabulary but often of multi-word prefabricated chunks' (Lewis 1997: 3). These are the 'lexical phrases', 'lexical chunks' and other word combinations that we discussed in Chapter 2, E4, i.e. the collocations, idioms, fixed and semi-fixed phrases which form such an important part of the language. Adult language users have literally thousands of these chunks at their disposal, such as *How are you?, See you later, You must be joking, I'll give it my best shot, changing the subject slightly ..., might as well, ... if it'll help.* Lewis proposes that fluency is the result of acquisition of a large store of these fixed and semi-fixed pre-fabricated items which are 'available as the foundation for any linguistic novelty or creativity' (1997: 15).

This highlighting of an area of language that was, perhaps, previously undervalued, has played a valuable role in provoking debate about what students should study. A Lexical approach would steer us away from an over-concentration on syntax and tense usage (with vocabulary slotted into these grammar patterns) towards the teaching of phrases which show words in combination, and which are generative in a different way from traditional grammar substitution tables. Thus, instead of teaching *will* for the future, we might instead have students focus on its use in a series of 'archetypical utterances' (Lewis 1993: 97), such as *I'll give you a ring, I'll be in touch, I'll see what I can do, I'll be back in a minute,* etc.

In the area of methodology, Lewis's account of a Lexical approach is fairly straightforward. Typical activities include asking students to add intensifiers to semi-fixed expressions, e.g. *It's obvious something's gone wrong (quite)* (Lewis 1997: 96), and getting students, once they have read a text, to underline all the nouns they can find and then to underline any verbs that collocate with those nouns (1997: 109). Word-order exercises can be adapted to focus on particular phrase components, as in this example for expressions with *get*:

Rearrange these to make fixed expressions with the verb *(get)*.

1. Things much can't worse get.
2. What we to there are supposed time get?
3. I you the very weren't happy impression got.
4. We've we as as the for can far moment got.
5. We be to don't anywhere seem getting.
6. What you I can get?

Which of these suggests:

flying   offering a drink   frustration   despair

'Sentence anagrams' from *Implementing the Lexical Approach*
by M Lewis (Language Teaching Publications)

Elsewhere, however, Lewis suggests that exposure to enough suitable input, not formal teaching, is the 'key to increasing the learner's lexicon', and that 'most vocabulary is acquired, not taught' (1997: 197).

Suggesting that language should be taught in such a Lexical approach is not without problems, however. In the first place, no one has yet explained how the learning of fixed and semi-fixed phrases can be incorporated into the understanding of a language system. Indeed, it can be argued that learning the system is a vital pre-requisite of the ability to string phrases together into a coherent whole. Otherwise we are left with the danger of having to learn an endless succession of phrase-book utterances – 'all chunks but no pineapple' (Thornbury 1998: 12).

Another problem is determining the way in which we might order such phrases for teaching and learning purposes or, if we believe that exposure to enough suitable input is the key, deciding what kind of input that should be.

Finally, we need to ask in what way a Lexical approach differs from other accounts of language teaching since there are as yet no sets of procedures to exemplify such an approach to language learning.

Despite these reservations, however, the Lexical approach has certainly drawn our attention to facts about the composition of language; what it has not yet done is to make the leap from that to a set of pedagogic principles or syllabus specifications which could be incorporated into a method. However, we will return to the issue of lexical phrases in Chapter 14.

A8 Teachers and students in dialogue together

In 1995 a group of film-makers led by the Danish director Lars Von Trier drafted the manifesto of the Dogme 95 Film-makers' Collective in which they pledged to rescue cinema from big budget, special effects-dominated Hollywood movies. They wanted to return to core values, using no artificial lighting, no special effects, etc. This prompted Scott Thornbury to write a 'short uncharacteristically provocative article' (Thornbury 2005c, describing the original article published in 2000) suggesting that ELT needed similar rescue action, notably a return to a materials- and technology-free classroom in which language emerges as teachers and students engage in a dialogic relationship. This original article provoked considerable interest and a group of teachers emerged who wanted to apply certain principles to language learning. They reasoned that language is co-constructed between teachers and students, where it emerges (as it is scaffolded by the teacher) rather than being acquired. They were hostile to materials being brought into the classroom since these interfered with the dialogic relationship between teacher and student. In this return to a 'pedagogy of bare essentials' students learn because they get to express what they want to say – rather like the consumers of Community Language Learning (see page 68) – instead of taking their cue from coursebooks and school syllabuses.

Critics of this line of reasoning point out that this kind of dialogic model favours native-speaker teachers (see page 119), that it is extremely difficult to countenance in large classes, that syllabuses are necessary organising constructs, and that materials such as coursebooks, in particular, are highly prized by both teachers and students alike for a variety of reasons (see page 181). Furthermore, in the words of Angeles Clemente, 'When I teach, I certainly do more than talk, and that is why teachers around the world still have students attending their classes' (Clemente 2001: 401). Nevertheless, the Dogme discussion provokes us into thinking carefully about our role as teachers, and about how an over-reliance on focus-on-forms, based on over-used materials, may stifle the creativity of both teacher and students.

B What methodology?

With so many different approaches and methods available, many teachers are unsure of which to choose and how to go about making that choice. In this section we will look at some of the cultural implications of the methods we use, and come to some conclusions about the bases on which we can decide on our approach to teaching.

B1 Methods and culture

The writer Adrian Holliday has come up with the term *native speakerism* to describe the way that British and American teaching methodology and practices have been exported around the world, almost without question by the exporters, though they are increasingly questioned by commentators, both native speaker and non-native speaker alike. Holliday's worry about native speakerism is that it is often premised on a view of 'us' and 'them'. Native speakerism, he worries, 'cuts into and divides World TESOL by creating a negatively reduced image of the foreign Other of non-native speaker students and educators' (2005: 16). We will discuss the specific issue of native- and non-native-speaker teachers in Chapter 6. In this section, however, it is methodology and its relationship with educational and social culture which concerns us.

Many years ago, Dilys Thorp wrote an article that identifies a problem which occurs when different educational cultures come into contact with each other. What, she wondered, are we to make of the following comment by a British lecturer about an Indonesian student: 'His work shows that he's very bright, but he's quiet in class' (Thorp 1991: 112)? If the comment was made about a British student, she suggests, it might indeed indicate that the student was of a quiet and shy disposition, and that this was a pity, whereas for the Indonesian student the judgement might not be about that student's personality at all, but rather about norms of classroom behaviour (see page 155) that the student feels are culturally appropriate. 'It is far too easy,' she writes, 'to think that our own ideas as to what constitutes "good" learning are universal, and forget their cultural specificity' (1991: 117).

The fact is that many of the approaches and teaching methods we have discussed in this chapter are based on a very western idea of what constitutes 'good' learning. For example, we have expected active participation in class, and we have encouraged adventurous students who are prepared to have a go even when they are not completely sure of the language they are trying to use. We sometimes ask students to talk about themselves and their lives in a potentially revealing way. We tell students that they should take charge of their learning, that the teacher is a helper and guide rather than the source of knowledge and authority. Yet all of these tenets may well fly in the face of educational traditions from different cultures. Thus British and American teachers working in other countries sometimes complain that their students have 'nothing to say', when in fact it is not an issue of the students' intelligence, knowledge or creativity which makes them reluctant to communicate in a British or American way, but their educational culture.

However, we are not suggesting for one minute that it is necessarily the case that ideas with an ideological origin in English-speaking TESOL are by their very nature inappropriate. On the contrary, many of them are sound and have a proven usefulness. However, what we are saying is that if teachers (native or non-native speakers) grounded in English-speaking western TESOL assume a methodological superiority (and as a result perceive other kinds of learning as inherently inferior), they will be doing their students and themselves a potential disservice.

For, as Alastair Pennycook has said, 'we need to see English language teaching as located in the domain of popular culture as much as in the domain of applied linguistics' (Pennycook 1998: 162). Our attitudes to the language, and to the way it is taught, reflect cultural biases and beliefs about how we should communicate and how we should educate each other.

When teachers from one culture (e.g. Britain, the USA, Australia) teach students from another (e.g. Cambodia, Argentina, Saudi Arabia), it is often easy to see where cultural and educational differences reside. However, as we have suggested, it is the methodological culture that matters here, not the background of the teachers themselves. In 1998 an Argentinian teacher, Pablo Toledo, posted a message on an Internet discussion list for teachers from South America which he called 'Howl' after the celebrated poem by the American Allan Ginsberg (republished in Toledo 2001). In his posting, he lamented the fact that teachers who try affective learning and humanistic teaching, who try drama and role-play and other communicative techniques, fall flat on their faces in secondary classes where the students are not interested and merely wish to get good grades. He argues passionately for a new kind of methodology to suit that kind of reality since the ideas developed in 'comfy little schools with highly motivated students' just aren't right for less 'privileged' contexts. 'Not,' he writes, 'because there is something wrong with the ideas, but they just were not made for our teaching reality, and do not deal with our problems.'

Adrian Holliday would almost certainly agree. He describes his own use of a basic Audiolingual methodology at the beginning of his career in 1970s Iran. His approach, he writes, 'was entirely methodology-centred in that students and business clients alike were expected to submit to its wisdom, as recipients of a superior treatment' (2005: 60–61). He suggests that in many situations it was entirely inappropriate and certainly 'native speakerist' (see page 119).

All we are saying here is that applying a particular methodology thoughtlessly to any and every learning context we come into contact with may not always be appropriate. What we need to ask ourselves, therefore, is how to decide what is appropriate, and how to apply the methodological beliefs that guide our teaching practice.

B2 Bargains, postmethod and context-sensitivity

One approach for context-sensitive teachers is to try to create a bridge between their methodological beliefs and the students' preferences. For example, Dilys Thorp, whose article was cited above, had what she saw as a problem with students in China when they were confronted with listening tasks. An important skill for students is listening for gist (general understanding) without getting hung up on the meaning of every single word. Yet Thorp's students were not used to this idea; they wanted to be able to listen to tapes again and again, translating word for word. It is worth quoting her response to this situation in full:

> In listening, where they needed the skill of listening for gist and not every word, and where they wanted to listen time and time again, we gradually weaned them away from this by initially allowing them to listen as often as they liked; but in return – and this was their part of the bargain – they were to concentrate on the gist and answer guided questions. These guided questions moved them away from a sentence-by-sentence analysis towards inferential interpretation of the text. Then, we gradually reduced the number of times they were allowed to listen. This seemed to work: it was a system with which they were happy, and which enabled them to see real improvements in their listening skills.
> (Thorp 1991: 115)

Thorp's solution was to make a bargain so that two essentially opposing methodological beliefs could be accommodated together as a result of negotiation between teacher and students.

A more radical suggestion is that we have reached a 'postmethod' phase. Looked at this way, taking a method into class (say Task-based learning), is actually limiting since it gets in the way of teachers and students learning how to learn together. What is needed, Kumaravadivelu suggests, is not alternative methods, but 'an alternative to method' (2006: 67). Instead of one method, he suggests ten 'macrostrategies, such as "maximise learning opportunities, facilitate negotiation, foster language awareness, promote learner autonomy" etc.' (Kumaravadivelu 2001, 2006). Of course, these aims represent a kind of methodological 'wishlist', and while not confined to a one-size-fits-all restrictive methodology, nevertheless make methodological assumptions which might, without reflection and negotiation, be as inappropriate as some of the practices Pablo Toledo 'howled' about (see page 77).

Dick Allwright is also concerned to get away from methods as the central focus of decisions about teaching. For him, the quality of life in any classroom is much more important than instructional efficiency. In what he calls *exploratory practice* (Allwright and Lenzuen 1997, Allwright 2003), teachers should determine and understand the classroom quality of life. Then they should identify a learning puzzle (find something that is puzzling in class – e.g. why certain things happen or don't happen when teaching students), reflect on it, gather data and try out different ways of solving the puzzle, reflecting at each stage on what happens in order to decide what to do next. We will discuss reflective teaching in more detail in Chapter 24.

Stephen Bax has similar concerns about the imposition of a method without taking the context where the learning is happening into account. He points out that methodology is just one factor in language learning. Other factors may be important, and other methods and approaches may be equally valid (2003: 281). His solution is for teachers to do some kind of 'context analysis' before they start teaching so that they can develop their own procedures from the range of methodological knowledge and techniques they have available to them. They then reflect on and evaluate what has happened in order to decide how to proceed (Bax 2006).

B3 Making choices

We need to be able to say, as Kumaravadivelu attempted, what is important in methodological terms, especially if we concede that a choice of one method alone may not be right in many situations. We have to be able to extract the key components of the various methods we have been describing. What is it that students need, and what should we offer them?

Six strands have emerged from our discussion in this and in the previous chapter:

- **Affect:** students learn better when they are engaged with what is happening. Their feelings and attitudes matter both in relation to their encounters with the language itself, and also in terms of the learning experience in general.

- **Input:** students need constant exposure to the language otherwise they will not learn how to use it. The input they receive may be in the form of reading or in the way the teacher talks to them. It may sometimes be roughly-tuned (see page 50) or, for more form-focused sequences, finely-tuned. Comprehensible input is not enough in itself, unless there is some language study or some opportunity for noticing or consciousness-raising to help students remember specific language. Focus on form – and especially at lower levels, on language forms – is a vital component of successful language learning.

- **Output:** students need chances to activate their language knowledge through meaning-focused tasks. This activation is achieved when they try to deploy all or any of the language they know either to produce language (spoken or written) or to read or listen for meaning.

- **Cognitive effort:** students should be encouraged to think about language as they work with it since, we are sure, this aids retention. Where appropriate, we should encourage students to do some of the work for themselves, discovering how language works rather than being given information about language construction 'on a plate'.

- **Grammar and lexis:** lexis is as important as grammar. Showing how words combine together and behave both semantically and grammatically is an important part of any language-learning programme.

- **How, why and where:** the actual way we do things depends not on the choice of a method (though it is possible that a method – or a version of a method – may be appropriate), but rather on why and where we are teaching. What do we want to achieve, with whom and in what context? We need to analyse these features and then choose from the procedures and techniques at our command those that best fit the situation we are in. At all levels and at all stages of teaching we should be able to say clearly why we are doing what we are doing – an issue we will discuss in more detail in Chapter 21.

Chapter notes and further reading

- **Approaches and methods**
  For a discussion of 'approach' versus 'method', etc., see J Richards and T Rodgers (2001: Chapter 2).

  Many teachers use metaphors to separate out these different levels of abstraction. For example, the trainer David Valente turns to the art of cooking. The approach is our belief about cooking, the method is the recipe book, the procedures are actions such as mixing, chopping, marinating, etc. and the techniques are how we mix and chop, for example.

- **Audiolingualism**
  For a concise description of Audiolingualism, see M Williams and R Burden (1997: 10–13). Chapters 2 and 3 of J Richards and T Rodgers (2001) put Audiolingual methodology into its context.

- **PPP and teaching models**
  For a classic description of PPP, see D Byrne (1986: Chapter 1). Some of the books and articles which influenced the PPP debate of the 1990s are M Lewis (1993, 1996) – whose attacks became increasingly strident – articles in Sections 1 and 2 of J Willis and D Willis (eds) (1996), T Woodward (1993) and J Harmer (1996).

  J Scrivener described lessons in terms of **A**uthentic Use, **R**estricted Use and **C**larification and focus (Scrivener 1994b). By labelling different parts of any lesson A, R or C, he was able to describe lessons as, for example, RCRA (where the teacher presents a situation, clarifies the language point, institutes restricted (controlled) practice, before getting 'authentic' use), whereas a different lesson – for example a task-based lesson – might follow a procedure such as CACACR. S Thornbury (1996) discusses Scrivener's ARC model. In a later edition of his book, Scrivener incorporates the concept of ARC into a more complex account of input, learning and use (2005: 111–117).

- **CLT**

  J Harmer (1982) described the characteristics of a communicative activity.

  The appropriacy of the Communicative approach both in and outside 'inner circle' countries (see Chapter 1, A3) has come under attack from Peter Medgyes (1986) and G Ellis (1996).

  The whole value of the Communicative approach was the subject of a bitter clash in the mid 1980s between Michael Swan (Swan 1985) and Henry Widdowson (Widdowson 1985).

- **Task-based learning**

  On TBL in general, see G Crookes and S Gass (1993a and b) and D Willis (1990). J Willis (1996) suggests a specific approach to TBL. P Skehan (1998: Chapters 5 and 6) offers a psycholinguistic perspective on TBL.

  On teacher and learner roles in TBL, see D Nunan (2004: 64–70).

  K McDonough and W Chaikitmongkol (2007) report on the positive attitudes of teachers and learners when TBL was introduced in a Thai context.

- **Four methods**

  For a concise description of the four methods mentioned here, see M Celce-Murcia (1981). J Richards and T Rogers (2001) have excellent separate chapters for each.

  On Community Language Learning, see C Curran (1976) and P La Forge (1983).

  On the Silent Way, see C Gattegno (1976) and R Rossner (1982).

  On Suggestopaedia, read G Lozanov (1978). More easily accessible examples can be found in J Cureau (1982) and M Lawlor (1986).

  On Total Physical Response, see J Asher (1977).

- **The Lexical approach**

  A major populariser of the Lexical approach has been Michael Lewis (1993, 1997). D Willis (1990) wrote about a lexical syllabus.

  An impressive critique of Lewis's work is S Thornbury (1998). An enthusiast for the Lexical approach is M Baigent (1999).

- **Methodology and culture**

  C Kramsch and P Sullivan (1996) write about appropriate pedagogy from their experiences of teaching and researching in Vietnam.

  We should avoid making assumptions about what students from different methodological cultures appreciate. J Flowerdew, for example, shows how groupwork is appropriate in a Hong Kong setting (Flowerdew 1998).

5 | Describing learners

A Age

The age of our students is a major factor in our decisions about how and what to teach. People of different ages have different needs, competences and cognitive skills; we might expect children of primary age to acquire much of a foreign language through play, for example, whereas for adults we can reasonably expect a greater use of abstract thought.

One of the most common beliefs about age and language learning is that young children learn faster and more effectively than any other age group. Most people can think of examples which appear to bear this out – as when children move to a new country and appear to pick up a new language with remarkable ease. However, as we shall see, this is not always true of children in that situation, and the story of child language facility may be something of a myth.

It is certainly true that children who learn a new language early have a facility with the pronunciation which is sometimes denied older learners. Lynne Cameron suggests that children 'reproduce the accent of their teachers with deadly accuracy' (2003: 111). Carol Read recounts how she hears a young student of hers saying *Listen. Quiet now. Attention, please!* in such a perfect imitation of the teacher that 'the thought of parody passes through my head' (2003: 7).

Apart from pronunciation ability, however, it appears that older children (that is children from about the age of 12) 'seem to be far better learners than younger ones in most aspects of acquisition, pronunciation excluded' (Yu, 2006: 53). Patsy Lightbown and Nina Spada, reviewing the literature on the subject, point to the various studies showing that older children and adolescents make more progress than younger learners (2006: 67–74).

The relative superiority of older children as language learners (especially in formal educational settings) may have something to do with their increased cognitive abilities, which allow them to benefit from more abstract approaches to language teaching. It may also have something to do with the way younger children are taught. Lynne Cameron, quoted above, suggests that teachers of young learners need to be especially alert and adaptive in their response to tasks and have to be able to adjust activities on the spot.

It is not being suggested that young children cannot acquire second languages successfully. As we have already said, many of them achieve significant competence, especially in bilingual situations. But in learning situations, teenagers are often more effective learners. Yet English is increasingly being taught at younger and younger ages. This may have great benefits in terms of citizenship, democracy, tolerance and multiculturalism, for example (Read 2003), but especially when there is ineffective transfer of skills and methodology from primary to secondary school, early learning does not always appear to offer the substantial success often claimed for it.

Nor is it true that older learners are necessarily ineffective language learners. Research has shown that they 'can reach high levels of proficiency in their second language' (Lightbown and Spada 2006: 73). They may have greater difficulty in approximating native speaker pronunciation than children do, but sometimes this is a deliberate (or even subconscious) retention of their cultural and linguistic identity.

In what follows we will consider students at different ages as if all the members of each age group are the same. Yet each student is an individual with different experiences both in and outside the classroom. Comments here about young children, teenagers and adults can only be generalisations. Much also depends upon individual learner differences and upon motivation (see Section D below).

A1 Young children

Young children, especially those up to the ages of nine or ten, learn differently from older children, adolescents and adults in the following ways:

- They respond to meaning even if they do not understand individual words.
- They often learn indirectly rather than directly – that is they take in information from all sides, learning from everything around them rather than only focusing on the precise topic they are being taught.
- Their understanding comes not just from explanation, but also from what they see and hear and, crucially, have a chance to touch and interact with.
- They find abstract concepts such as grammar rules difficult to grasp.
- They generally display an enthusiasm for learning and a curiosity about the world around them.
- They have a need for individual attention and approval from the teacher.
- They are keen to talk about themselves and respond well to learning that uses themselves and their own lives as main topics in the classroom.
- They have a limited attention span; unless activities are extremely engaging, they can get easily bored, losing interest after ten minutes or so.

It is important, when discussing young learners, to take account of changes which take place within this varied and varying age span. Gül Keskil and Pasa Tevfik Cephe, for example, note that 'while pupils who are 10 and 11 years old like games, puzzles and songs most, those who are 12 and 13 years old like activities built around dialogues, question-and-answer activities and matching exercises most' (2001: 61).

Various theorists have described the way that children develop and the various ages and stages they go through. Piaget suggested that children start at the *sensori-motor stage*, and then proceed through the *intuitive stage* and the *concrete-operational stage* before finally reaching the *formal operational stage* where abstraction becomes increasingly possible. Leo Vygotsky (see page 59) emphasised the place of social interaction in development and the role of a 'knower' providing 'scaffolding' to help a child who has entered the *Zone of Proximal Development* (ZPD) where they are ready to learn new things. Both Erik Erikson and Abraham Maslow saw development as being closely bound up in the child's confidence and self-esteem, while Reuven Feuerstein suggested that children's cognitive structures are infinitely modifiable with the help of a modifier – much like Vygotsky's knower.

But however we describe the way children develop (and though there are significant differences between, say, a four year old and a nine year old), we can make some recommendations about younger learners in general, that is children up to about ten and eleven.

In the first place, good teachers at this level need to provide a rich diet of learning experiences which encourage their students to get information from a variety of sources. They need to work with their students individually and in groups, developing good and affective relationships (see page 100). They need to plan a range of activities for a given time period, and be flexible enough to move on to the next exercise when they see their students getting bored.

Teachers of young learners need to spend time understanding how their students think and operate. They need to be able to pick up on their students' current interests so that they can use them to motivate the children. And they need good oral skills in English since speaking and listening are the skills which will be used most of all at this age. The teacher's pronunciation really matters here, too, precisely because, as we have said, children imitate it so well.

All of this reminds us that once a decision has been taken to teach English to younger learners, there is a need for highly skilled and dedicated teaching. This may well be the most difficult (but rewarding) age to teach, but when teachers do it well (and the conditions are right), there is no reason why students should not defy some of the research results we mentioned above and be highly successful learners – provided, of course, that this success is followed up as they move to a new school or grade.

We can also draw some conclusions about what a classroom for young children should look like and what might be going on in it. First of all, we will want the classroom to be bright and colourful, with windows the children can see out of, and with enough room for different activities to be taking place. We might expect the students to be working in groups in different parts of the classroom, changing their activity every ten minutes or so. 'We are obviously,' Susan Halliwell writes, 'not talking about classrooms where children spend all their time sitting still in rows or talking only to the teacher' (1992: 18). Because children love discovering things, and because they respond well to being asked to use their imagination, they may well be involved in puzzle-like activities, in making things, in drawing things, in games, in physical movement or in songs. A good primary classroom mixes play and learning in an atmosphere of cheerful and supportive harmony.

Adolescents

It is strange that, despite their relative success as language learners, adolescents are often seen as problem students. Yet with their greater ability for abstract thought and their passionate commitment to what they are doing once they are engaged, adolescents may well be the most exciting students of all. Most of them understand the need for learning and, with the right goals, can be responsible enough to do what is asked of them.

It is perfectly true that there are times when things don't seem to go very well. Adolescence is bound up, after all, with a pronounced search for identity and a need for self-esteem; adolescents need to feel good about themselves and valued. All of this is reflected in the secondary student who convincingly argued that a good teacher 'is someone who knows our names' (Harmer 2007: 26). But it's not just teachers, of course; teenage students often have an acute need for peer approval, too (or, at the very least, are extremely vulnerable to the negative judgements of their own age group).

We will discuss how teachers can ensure successful learning (preventing indiscipline, but acting effectively if it occurs) in Chapter 9, but we should not become too preoccupied with the issue of disruptive behaviour, for while we will all remember unsatisfactory classes, we will also look back with pleasure on those groups and lessons which were successful. There is almost nothing more exciting than a class of involved young people at this age pursuing a learning goal with enthusiasm. Our job, therefore, must be to provoke student engagement with material which is relevant and involving. At the same time, we need to do what we can to bolster our students' self-esteem, and be conscious, always, of their need for identity.

Herbert Puchta and Michael Schratz see problems with teenagers as resulting, in part, from '... the teacher's failure to build bridges between what they want and have to teach and their students' worlds of thought and experience' (1993: 4). They advocate linking language teaching far more closely to the students' everyday interests through, in particular, the use of 'humanistic' teaching (see Chapter 3D). Thus, as we shall see in some of the examples in Chapters 16–20, material has to be designed at the students' level, with topics which they can react to. They must be encouraged to respond to texts and situations with their own thoughts and experiences, rather than just by answering questions and doing abstract learning activities. We must give them tasks which they are able to do, rather than risk humiliating them.

We have come some way from the teaching of young children. We can ask teenagers to address learning issues directly in a way that younger learners might not appreciate. We are able to discuss abstract issues with them. Indeed, part of our job is to provoke intellectual activity by helping them to be aware of contrasting ideas and concepts which they can resolve for themselves – though still with our guidance. There are many ways of studying language (see Chapters 12–15) and practising language skills (see Chapters 16–20), and most of these are appropriate for teenagers.

A3 Adult learners

Adult language learners are notable for a number of special characteristics:

- They can engage with abstract thought. This suggests that we do not have to rely exclusively on activities such as games and songs – though these may be appropriate for some students.

- They have a whole range of life experiences to draw on.

- They have expectations about the learning process, and they already have their own set patterns of learning.

- Adults tend, on the whole, to be more disciplined than other age groups, and, crucially, they are often prepared to struggle on despite boredom.

- They come into classrooms with a rich range of experiences which allow teachers to use a wide range of activities with them.

- Unlike young children and teenagers, they often have a clear understanding of why they are learning and what they want to get out of it. As we shall see in Section D below, motivation is a critical factor in successful learning, and knowing what you want to achieve is an important part of this. Many adults are able to sustain a level of motivation (see D2) by holding on to a distant goal in a way that teenagers find more difficult.

However, adults are never entirely problem-free learners, and they have a number of characteristics which can sometimes make learning and teaching problematic.

– They can be critical of teaching methods. Their previous learning experiences may have predisposed them to one particular methodological style which makes them uncomfortable with unfamiliar teaching patterns. Conversely, they may be hostile to certain teaching and learning activities which replicate the teaching they received earlier in their educational careers.

– They may have experienced failure or criticism at school which makes them anxious and under-confident about learning a language.

– Many older adults worry that their intellectual powers may be diminishing with age. They are concerned to keep their creative powers alive, to maintain a 'sense of generativity' (Williams and Burden 1997: 32). However, as Alan Rogers points out, this generativity is directly related to how much learning has been going on in adult life before they come to a new learning experience (1996: 54).

Good teachers of adults take all of these factors into account. They are aware that their students will often be prepared to stick with an activity for longer than younger learners (though too much boredom can obviously have a disastrous effect on motivation). As well as involving their students in more indirect learning through reading, listening and communicative speaking and writing, they also allow them to use their intellects to learn consciously where this is appropriate. They encourage their students to use their own life experience in the learning process, too.

As teachers of adults we should recognise the need to minimise the bad effects of past learning experiences. We can diminish the fear of failure by offering activities which are achievable and by paying special attention to the level of challenge presented by exercises. We need to listen to students' concerns, too, and, in many cases, modify what we do to suit their learning tastes.

B Learner differences

The moment we realise that a class is composed of individuals (rather than being some kind of unified whole), we have to start thinking about how to respond to these students individually so that while we may frequently teach the group as a whole, we will also, in different ways, pay attention to the different identities we are faced with.

We will discuss differentiation in relation to mixed ability in Chapter 7C. In this section, however, we will look at the various ways researchers have tried to identify individual needs and behaviour profiles.

B1 Aptitude and intelligence

Some students are better at learning languages than others. At least that is the generally held view, and in the 1950s and 1960s it crystallised around the belief that it was possible to predict a student's future progress on the basis of linguistic aptitude tests. But it soon became clear that such tests were flawed in a number of ways. They didn't appear to measure anything other than general intellectual ability even though they ostensibly looked for linguistic talents. Furthermore, they favoured analytic-type learners over their more 'holistic' counterparts, so the tests were especially suited to people who have little trouble doing grammar-focused tasks. Those with a more 'general' view of things – whose analytical abilities are not so highly developed, and who receive and use language in a more message-oriented way – appeared to be at a disadvantage. In fact, analytic aptitude is probably not the critical factor in success. Peter Skehan, for example, believes that what distinguishes exceptional students from the rest is that they have unusual memories, particularly for the retention of things that they hear (1998: 234).

Another damning criticism of traditional aptitude tests is that while they may discriminate between the most and the least 'intelligent' students, they are less effective at distinguishing between the majority of students who fall between these two extremes. What they do accomplish is to influence the way in which both teachers and students behave. It has been suggested that students who score badly on aptitude tests will become demotivated and that this will then contribute to precisely the failure that the test predicted. Moreover, teachers who know that particular students have achieved high scores will be tempted to treat those students differently from students whose score was low. Aptitude tests end up being self-fulfilling prophecies whereas it would be much better for both teacher and students to be optimistic about all of the people in the class.

It is possible that people have different aptitudes for different kinds of study. However, if we consider aptitude and intelligence for learning language in general, our own experience of people we know who speak two or more languages can only support the view that 'learners with a wide variety of intellectual abilities can be successful language learners. This is especially true if the emphasis is on oral communication skills rather than metalinguistic knowledge' (Lightbown and Spada 2006: 185).

B2 Good learner characteristics

Another line of enquiry has been to try to tease out what a 'good learner' is. If we can narrow down a number of characteristics that all good learners share, then we can, perhaps, cultivate these characteristics in all our students.

Neil Naiman and his colleagues included a tolerance of ambiguity as a feature of good learning, together with factors such as positive task orientation (being prepared to approach tasks in a positive fashion), ego involvement (where success is important for a student's self-image), high aspirations, goal orientation and perseverance (Naiman *et al* 1978).

Joan Rubin and Irene Thompson listed no fewer than 14 good learner characteristics, among which learning to live with uncertainty (much like the tolerance of ambiguity mentioned above) is a notable factor (Rubin and Thompson 1982). But the Rubin and Thompson version of a good learner also mentions students who can find their own way (without always having to be guided by the teacher through learning tasks), who are creative, who make intelligent guesses, who make their own opportunities for practice, who make errors work for them not against them, and who use contextual clues.

Patsy Lightbown and Nina Spada summarise the main consensus about good learner characteristics (see Figure 1). As they point out, the characteristics can be classified in several categories (motivation, intellectual abilities, learning preferences), and some, such as 'willing to make mistakes', can be 'considered a personality characteristic' (Lightbown and Spada 2006: 54). In other words, this wish list cuts across a number of learner variables.

Much of what various people have said about good learners is based on cultural assumptions which underpin much current teaching practice in western-influenced methodologies.

In these cultures we appreciate self-reliant students and promote learner autonomy as a main goal (see Chapter 23). We tend to see the tolerance of ambiguity as a goal of student development, wishing to wean our students away from a need for things to be always cut and dried. We encourage students to read texts for general understanding without stopping to look up all the words they do not understand; we ask students to speak communicatively even when they have difficulty because of words they don't know or can't pronounce, and we involve students in creative writing (see Chapter 19, B3). In all these endeavours we expect our students to aspire beyond their current language level.

Rate each of the following characteristics on a scale of 1–5. Use 1 to indicate a characteristic that you think is 'very important' and 5 to indicate a characteristic that you consider 'not at all important' in predicting success in second language learning.

A good language learner:

a	is a willing and accurate guesser	1	2	3	4	5
b	tries to get a message across even if specific language knowledge is lacking	1	2	3	4	5
c	is willing to make mistakes	1	2	3	4	5
d	constantly looks for patterns in the language	1	2	3	4	5
e	practises as often as possible	1	2	3	4	5
f	analyses his or her own speech and the speech of others	1	2	3	4	5
g	attends to whether his or her performance meets the standards he or she has learned	1	2	3	4	5
h	enjoys grammar exercises	1	2	3	4	5
i	begins learning in childhood	1	2	3	4	5
j	has an above-average IQ	1	2	3	4	5
k	has good academic skills	1	2	3	4	5
l	has a good self-image and lots of confidence	1	2	3	4	5

FIGURE 1: Good learner characteristics (Lightbown and Spada 2006: 55)

Different cultures value different learning behaviours, however. Our insistence upon one kind of 'good learner' profile may encourage us to demand that students should act in class in certain ways, whatever their learning background. When we espouse some of the techniques mentioned above, we risk imposing a methodology on our students that is inimical to their culture. Yet it is precisely because this is not perhaps in the best interests of the students that we discussed context-sensitive methodology in Chapter 4B. Furthermore, some students may not enjoy grammar exercises, but this does not mean they are doomed to learning failure.

There is nothing wrong with trying to describe good language learning behaviour. Nevertheless, we need to recognise that some of our assumptions are heavily culture-bound and that students can be successful even if they do not follow these characteristics to the letter.

B3 Learner styles and strategies

A preoccupation with learner personalities and styles has been a major factor in psycholinguistic research. Are there different kinds of learner? Are there different kinds of behaviour in a group? How can we tailor our teaching to match the personalities in front of us?

The methodologist Tony Wright described four different learner styles within a group (1987: 117–118). The 'enthusiast' looks to the teacher as a point of reference and is concerned with the goals of the learning group. The 'oracular' also focuses on the teacher but is more oriented towards the satisfaction of personal goals. The 'participator' tends to concentrate on group goals and group solidarity, whereas the 'rebel', while referring to the learning group for his or her point of reference, is mainly concerned with the satisfaction of his or her own goals.

Keith Willing, working with adult students in Australia, suggested four learner categories:

> • **Convergers:** these are students who are by nature solitary, prefer to avoid groups, and who are independent and confident in their own abilities. Most importantly they are analytic and can impose their own structures on learning. They tend to be cool and pragmatic.
>
> • **Conformists:** these are students who prefer to emphasise learning 'about language' over learning to use it. They tend to be dependent on those in authority and are perfectly happy to work in non-communicative classrooms, doing what they are told. A classroom of conformists is one which prefers to see well-organised teachers.
>
> • **Concrete learners:** though they are like conformists, they also enjoy the social aspects of learning and like to learn from direct experience. They are interested in language use and language as communication rather than language as a system. They enjoy games and groupwork in class.
>
> • **Communicative learners:** these are language use oriented. They are comfortable out of class and show a degree of confidence and a willingness to take risks which their colleagues may lack. They are much more interested in social interaction with other speakers of the language than they are with analysis of how the language works. They are perfectly happy to operate without the guidance of a teacher

FIGURE 2: Learning styles based on Willing (1987)

Wright and Willing's categorisations are just two of a large number of descriptions that different researchers have come up with to try to explain different learner styles and strategies. Frank Coffield, David Moseley, Elaine Hall and Kathryn Ecclestone, in an extensive study of the literature available, identify an extremely large list of opposed styles which different theorists have advocated (see Figure 3). But while this may be of considerable interest to theorists, they 'advise against pedagogical intervention based solely on any of the learning style instruments' (Coffield *et al* 2004: 140).

convergers versus **divergers**	**initiators** versus **reasoners**
verbalisers versus **imagers**	**intuitionists** versus **analysts**
holists versus **serialists**	**extroverts** versus **introverts**
deep versus **surface learning**	**sensing** versus **intuition**
activists versus **reflectors**	**thinking** versus **feeling**
pragmatists versus **theorists**	**judging** versus **perceiving**
adaptors versus **innovators**	**left brainers** versus **right brainers**
assimilators versus **explorers**	**meaning-directed** versus **undirected**
field dependent versus **field independent**	**theorists** versus **humanitarians**
globalists versus **analysts**	**activists** versus **theorists**
assimilators versus **accommodators**	**pragmatists** versus **reflectors**
imaginative versus **analytic learners**	**organisers** versus **innovators**
non-committers versus **plungers**	**lefts/analytics/inductives/successive**
common-sense versus **dynamic learners**	**processors** versus **rights/globals/**
concrete versus **abstract learners**	**deductives/simultaneous processors**
random versus **sequential learners**	**executives/hierarchics/conservatives**
	versus **legislatives/anarchics/liberals**

FIGURE 3: Different learner descriptions (from Coffield *et al* 2004: 136)

Coffield and his colleagues have two main reasons for their scepticism. The first is that there are so many different models available (as the list in Figure 3 shows) that it is almost impossible to choose between them. This is a big worry, especially since there is no kind of consensus among researchers about what they are looking at and what they have identified. Secondly, some of the more popular methods, Coffield *et al* suggest, are driven by commercial interests which have identified themselves with particular models. This is not to suggest that there is anything intrinsically wrong with commercial interests, but rather to introduce a note of caution into our evaluation of different learner style descriptions.

It may sound as if, therefore, there is no point in reading about different learner styles at all – or trying to incorporate them into our teaching. But that is not the case. We should do as much as we can to understand the individual differences within a group. We should try to find descriptions that chime with our own perceptions, and we should endeavour to teach individuals as well as groups.

B4 ## Individual variations

If some people are better at some things than others – better at analysing, for example – this would indicate that there are differences in the ways individual brains work. It also suggests that people respond differently to the same stimuli. How might such variation determine the ways in which individual students learn most readily? How might it affect the ways in which we teach? There are two models in particular which have tried to account for such perceived individual variation, and which teachers have attempted to use for the benefit of their learners.

- **Neuro-Linguistic Programming:** according to practitioners of Neuro-Linguistic Programming (NLP), we use a number of 'primary representational systems' to experience the world. These systems are described in the acronym 'VAKOG' which stands for *Visual* (we look and see), *Auditory* (we hear and listen), *Kinaesthetic* (we feel externally, internally or through movement), *Olfactory* (we smell things) and *Gustatory* (we taste things).

Most people, while using all these systems to experience the world, nevertheless have one 'preferred primary system' (Revell and Norman 1997: 31). Some people are particularly stimulated by music when their preferred primary system is auditory, whereas others, whose primary preferred system is visual, respond most powerfully to images. An extension of this is when a visual person 'sees' music, or has a strong sense of different colours for different sounds. The VAKOG formulation, while somewhat problematic in the distinctions it attempts to make, offers a framework to analyse different student responses to stimuli and environments.

NLP gives teachers the chance to offer students activities which suit their primary preferred systems. According to Radislav Millrood, it shows how teachers can operate in the *C-Zone* – the zone of congruence, where teachers and students interact affectively – rather than in the *R-Zone* – the zone of student resistance, where students do not appreciate how the teacher tries to make them behave (Millrood 2004). NLP practitioners also use techniques such as 'three-position thinking' (Baker and Rinvolucri 2005a) to get teachers and students to see things from other people's points of view so that they can be more effective communicators and interactors.

- **MI theory:** MI stands for Multiple Intelligences, a concept introduced by the Harvard psychologist Howard Gardner. In his book *Frames of Mind*, he suggested that we do not possess a single intelligence, but a range of 'intelligences' (Gardner 1983). He listed seven of these: Musical/rhythmical, Verbal/linguistic, Visual/spatial, Bodily/kinaesthetic, Logical/mathematical, Intrapersonal and Interpersonal. All people have all of these intelligences, he said, but in each person one (or more) of them is more pronounced. This allowed him to predict that a typical occupation (or 'end state') for people with a strength in logical/mathematical intelligence is that of the scientist, whereas a typical end state for people with strengths in visual/spatial intelligence might well be that of the navigator. The athlete might be the typical end state for people who are strong in bodily/kinaesthetic intelligence, and so on. Gardner has since added an eighth intelligence which he calls Naturalistic intelligence (Gardner 1993) to account for the ability to recognise and classify patterns in nature; Daniel Goleman has added a ninth 'emotional intelligence' (Goleman 1995). This includes the ability to empathise, control impulse and self-motivate.

  If we accept that different intelligences predominate in different people, it suggests that the same learning task may not be appropriate for all of our students. While people with a strong logical/mathematical intelligence might respond well to a complex grammar explanation, a different student might need the comfort of diagrams and physical demonstration because their strength is in the visual/spatial area. Other students who have a strong interpersonal intelligence may require a more interactive climate if their learning is to be effective. Rosie Tanner (2001) has produced a chart (see Figure 4) to show what kind of activities might be suitable for people with special strengths in the different intelligences.

Armed with this information, teachers can see whether they have given their class a variety of activities to help the various types of learner described here. Although we cannot teach directly to each individual student in our class all of the time, we can ensure that we sometimes give opportunities for visualisation, for students to work on their own, for sharing and comparing and for physical movement. By keeping our eye on different individuals, we can direct them to learning activities which are best suited to their own proclivities.

Teaching Intelligently: Language Skills Activities Chart

Skill → Intelligence ↓	Listening	Reading	Writing	Speaking	Grammar	Vocabulary	Literature
Bodily-Kinaesthetic	Learners listen to three sections of a tape in three different places, then form groups to collaborate on their answers to a task.	Learners re-order a cut-up jumbled reading text.	Learners write stories in groups by writing the first sentence of a story on a piece of paper and passing it to another learner for continuation.	Learners play a game where they obtain information from various places in the classroom and report back.	Learners play a board game with counters and dice to practise tenses.	Learners label objects in the classroom with names.	Learners create a similar scene to one they have read about and act it out (eg a conflict, a time you were let down).
Interpersonal	Learners check their answers to a listening task in pairs or groups before listening a second time.	Learners discuss answers to questions on a text in groups.	Learners write a dialogue in pairs.	Learners read problem-page letters and discuss responses.	Learners do a 'find someone who ...' activity related to a grammar point (eg present perfect: find someone who has been to Spain).	Learners test each other's vocabulary.	In groups, learners discuss their preferences for characters in a book.
Intrapersonal	Learners think individually about how they might have reacted, compared with someone on a video they have seen.	Learners reflect on characters in a text and how similar or different they are to them.	Learners write learning diaries.	Learners record a speech or talk on a cassette.	Learners complete sentences about themselves, practising a grammar point (eg complete the sentence 'I am as ... as ...' five times).	Learners make their own vocabulary booklet which contains words they think are important to learn.	Learners write a diary for a few days in the life of a character in a book.
Linguistic	Learners write a letter after listening to a text.	Learners answer true/false questions about a text.	Learners write a short story.	In groups, learners discuss statements about a controversial topic.	The teacher provides a written worksheet on a grammar point.	Learners make mind maps of related words.	Learners rewrite part of a book as a film script, with instructions for the director and actors.
Logical-Mathematical	Learners listen to three pieces of text and decide what the correct sequence is.	Learners compare two characters or opinions in a text.	Learners write steps in a process, (eg a recipe).	Learners in a group each have a picture. They discuss and re-order them, without showing them, to create a story.	Learners learn grammar inductively, ie they work out how a grammar rule works by using discovery activities.	Learners discuss how many words they can think of related to another word (eg photograph, photographer).	Learners re-order a jumbled version of events in a chapter of a novel they have read.
Musical	Learners complete gaps in the lyrics of a pop song.	Learners listen to music extracts and decide how they relate to a text they have read.	Learners write the lyrics to an existing melody about a text or topic they have been dealing with in class.	Learners listen to a musical video clip (with the TV covered up) and discuss which images might accompany the music.	Learners create a mnemonic or rhyme to help them remember a grammar point.	Learners decide which new words they would like to learn from a pop song.	Learners find a piece of appropriate music to accompany a passage from a book.
Naturalist	Learners listen to sounds inside and outside the classroom and discuss what they have heard.	Learners work with a text on environmental issues.	Learners write a text describing a nature scene.	Learners discuss an environmental issue.	Learners do an activity associated with nature (eg walk by the sea) and write a story in the past tense about it.	Learners make a mind map with a word related to nature (eg bird, tree).	Learners read descriptions of nature in a novel and then write their own.
Spatial	Learners complete a chart or diagram while listening.	Learners predict the contents of a text using an accompanying picture or photo.	Learners make a collage with illustrations and text about a place in their country.	In pairs, learners discover the differences between two pictures without showing them to each other.	The teacher illustrates a grammar point with a series of pictures (eg daily activities to show present simple).	Learners cut out a picture from a magazine and label it.	Learners draw a cartoon version of a story.

FIGURE 4: Activities for different intelligences, taken from Tanner (2001)

B5 What to do about individual differences

Faced with the different descriptions of learner types and styles which have been listed here, it may seem that the teacher's task is overwhelmingly complex. We want to satisfy the many different students in front of us, teaching to their individual strengths with activities designed to produce the best results for each of them, yet we also want to address our teaching to the group as a whole.

Our task as teachers will be greatly helped if we can establish who the different students in our classes are and recognise how they are different. We can do this through observation or, as in the following two examples, through more formal devices. For example, we might ask students what their learning preferences are in questionnaires with items (perhaps in the students' first language) such as the following:

> **When answering comprehension questions about reading passages I prefer to work**
> **a** on my own.   ☐
> **b** with another student.   ☐
> **c** with a group of students. ☐

Or we might try to find out which preferred sensory system our students respond to. Revell and Norman suggest the activity shown in Figure 5.

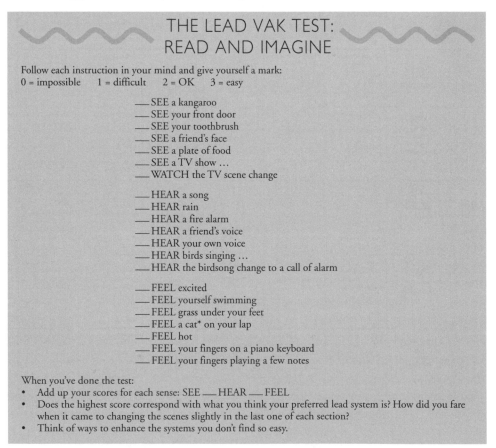

THE LEAD VAK TEST: READ AND IMAGINE

Follow each instruction in your mind and give yourself a mark:
0 = impossible   1 = difficult   2 = OK   3 = easy

___ SEE a kangaroo
___ SEE your front door
___ SEE your toothbrush
___ SEE a friend's face
___ SEE a plate of food
___ SEE a TV show …
___ WATCH the TV scene change

___ HEAR a song
___ HEAR rain
___ HEAR a fire alarm
___ HEAR a friend's voice
___ HEAR your own voice
___ HEAR birds singing …
___ HEAR the birdsong change to a call of alarm

___ FEEL excited
___ FEEL yourself swimming
___ FEEL grass under your feet
___ FEEL a cat* on your lap
___ FEEL hot
___ FEEL your fingers on a piano keyboard
___ FEEL your fingers playing a few notes

When you've done the test:
• Add up your scores for each sense: SEE ___ HEAR ___ FEEL ___
• Does the highest score correspond with what you think your preferred lead system is? How did you fare when it came to changing the scenes slightly in the last one of each section?
• Think of ways to enhance the systems you don't find so easy.

FIGURE 5: 'The Lead VAK Test' from *In Your Hands* by J Revell and S Norman (Saffire Press)

S Askey *et al* (in a webquest described in more detail on page 280), get students to do a test so that they can come up with a personal Multiple Intelligences (MI) profile which they can then share with the teacher. The students are led through a series of questions, as a result of which the software produces an MI profile for each individual student (see Figure 6).

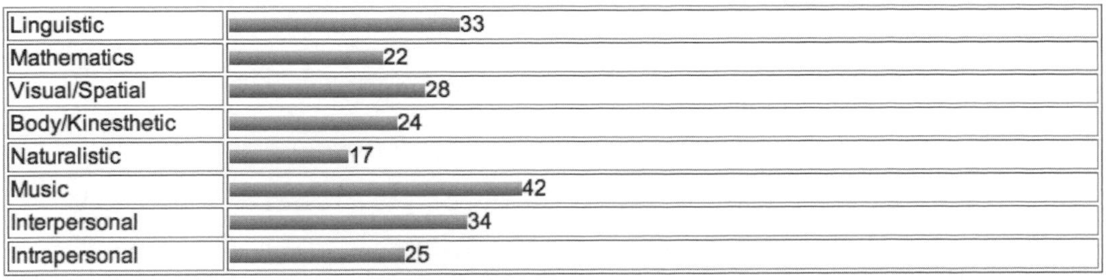

Linguistic	33
Mathematics	22
Visual/Spatial	28
Body/Kinesthetic	24
Naturalistic	17
Music	42
Interpersonal	34
Intrapersonal	25

FIGURE 6: An MI profile

As with the descriptions of learner styles above (see page 88), we might not want to view some of the results of NLP and MI tests uncritically. This is partly because of the doubts expressed by Frank Coffield and his colleagues (see above), but it is also because neither MI theory nor NLP have been subjected to any kind of rigorous scientific evaluation. However, it is clear that they both address self-evident truths – namely that different students react differently to different stimuli and that different students have different kinds of mental abilities. And so, as a result of getting information about individuals, we will be in a position to try to organise activities which provide maximal advantage to the many different people in the class, offering activities which favour, at different times, students with different learning styles. It is then up to us to keep a record of what works and what doesn't, either formally or informally. We can also ask our students (either face to face, or, more effectively, through written feedback) how they respond to these activities. The following (unedited) comments, from a multinational group of adult students in Britain, were written in response to a lesson in which they were asked to write an imaginary film scene based on a particular piece of music:

> I liked this subject because everyone could find a connection part of them. After we listened a part of music we could describe what we think by own sentences. That is why it was very attractive and that type of study was pushing us to talking a lot.

(Turkish female)

> I didn't like that kind of music. I prefer different kind of music.

(Italian male)

> I think that music is an excellent way to learn. But I think that it will be more interesting if we work with the lyrics of songs. We can learn new expressions, new words and memorize them easily because when we see the words again, we will be able to remember the song, the context the words were used in the songs and consequently your meanings.

(Brazilian female)

> I love to learn about music.

(Turkish male)

> It is difficult to express your feelings even in my mother language but finally I could written down something.

(Argentinian female)

> I was interested in this theme. Because all students can all enjoy music. But I didn't like making composition from music.

(Japanese female)

> I liked this lesson. Because it was funny. And everyone joined at this matters.

(Turkish male)

> This part was interesting as well because we had the opportunity to create something ourself (talking about music listening) using a certain language, immediate, strong and easy at the same time – what I mean is that I never thought that I could, from a piece of music, write down a scene and less of all in English! I liked it and it was not that difficult, well only because we don't have the vocabulary to write something really good.

(Italian female)

Apart from demonstrating how individuals respond differently to the same activity, these comments help us to decide whether to use a similar kind of activity again, whether to amend it or whether to abandon it.

Such feedback, coupled with questionnaires and our own observation, helps us to build a picture of the best kinds of activity for the mix of individuals in a particular class. This kind of feedback enables us, over time, to respond to our students with an appropriate blend of tasks and exercises.

This does not mean, of course, that everyone will be happy all of the time (as the feedback above shows). On the contrary, it clearly suggests that some lessons (or parts of lessons) will be more useful for some students than for others. But if we are aware of this and act accordingly, then there is a good chance that most of the class will be engaged with the learning process most of the time.

There is one last issue which should be addressed. We have already referred to the danger of pre-judging student ability through aptitude tests (see B1 above), but we might go further and worry about fixed descriptions of student differences. If students are always the same (in terms of their preferred primary system or their different intelligences), this suggests that they cannot change. Yet all learning is, in a sense, about change of one kind or another and part of our role as teachers is to help students effect change. Our job is surely to broaden students' abilities and perceptions, not merely to reinforce their natural prejudices or emphasise their limitations.

The whole area of learner difference is, as we have seen, complex and sometimes perplexing. As Frank Coffield and his colleagues write in their study of learner styles that we discussed above, teachers 'need to be knowledgeable about the strengths and limitations of the model they are using; to be aware of the dangers of labelling and discrimination; and to be prepared to respect the views of students who may well resist any attempts to change their preferred learning style' (2004: 133).

C Language levels

Students are generally described in three levels, *beginner*, *intermediate* and *advanced*, and these categories are further qualified by talking about *real beginners* and *false beginners*. Between beginner and intermediate we often class students as *elementary*. The intermediate level itself is often sub-divided into *lower intermediate* and *upper intermediate* and even *mid-intermediate*. One version of different levels, therefore, has the progression shown in Figure 7.

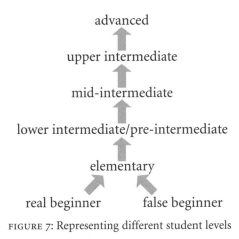

FIGURE 7: Representing different student levels

These terms are used somewhat indiscriminately, so that what one school calls intermediate is sometimes thought of as nearer elementary by others, and someone else might describe a student as advanced despite the fact that in another institution he or she would be classed as upper intermediate. Some coherence is arrived at as a result of the general consensus that exists between publishers about what levels their courses are divided into, but even here there is some variation (often depending on different views about what students at certain levels are capable of doing).

In recent years, the Council of Europe and the Association of Language Testers in Europe (ALTE) have been working to define language competency levels for learners of a number of different languages. The result of these efforts is the Common European Framework (a document setting out in detail what students 'can do' at various levels) and a series of ALTE levels ranging from A1 (roughly equivalent to elementary level) to C2 (very advanced). Figure 8 shows the different levels in sequence.

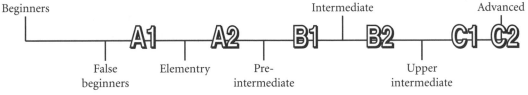

FIGURE 8: Terms for different student levels (and ALTE levels)

ALTE has produced 'can do' statements to try to show students, as well as teachers, what these levels mean, as the example in Figure 9 for the skill of writing demonstrates (A1 is at the left, C2 at the right).

Can complete basic forms and write notes including times, dates and places.	Can complete forms and write short simple letters or postcards related to personal information.	Can write letters or make notes on familiar or predicatable matters.	Can make notes while someone is talking or write a letter including non-standard questions.	Can prepare/draft professional correspondence, take reasonably accurate notes in meetings or write an essay which shows an ability to communicate.	Can write letters on any subject and full notes of meetings or seminars with good expression or accuracy.

© ALTE: Can Do statements produced by the members of the Association of Language Testers in Europe

FIGURE 9: ALTE 'Can do' statements for writing

ALTE levels and 'can do' statements (alongside the more traditional terms we have mentioned) are being used increasingly by coursebook writers and curriculum designers, not only in Europe but across much of the language-learning world (for more of the statements, see page 141). They are especially useful when translated into the students' L1 because they allow students to say what they can do, rather than having to be told by the teacher what standard they measure up against.

However, it is worth pointing out that the ALTE standards are just one way of measuring proficiency. There are also ESL standards which were developed by the TESOL organisation in the USA (see www.tesol.org/s_tesol/seccss.asp?CID=86&DID=1556), and many exam systems have their own level descriptors. We also need to remember that students' abilities within any particular level may be varied, too (e.g. they may be much better at speaking than writing).

The level students have reached often has an effect on their motivation. For example, students who have considerable trouble understanding and producing language at beginner levels often fail to progress to higher levels; this accounts for the relatively high 'drop-out' rate of some adult beginners. Sometimes students who arrive at, say, an intermediate level, tend to suffer from the so-called 'plateau effect' because for them it is not easy to see progress in their abilities from one week to the next. This can have a very demotivating effect,

Teachers need to be sensitive to the plateau effect, taking special measures to counteract it. Such efforts may include setting achievement goals (see below) so that students have a clear learning target to aim at, explaining what still needs to be done, making sure that activities are especially engaging, and sparking the students' interest in the more subtle distinctions of language use.

Other variations in level-dependent teacher behaviour are important, too, especially in terms of both methodology and the kind of language (and the topics) which we expose our students to.

C1 Methodology

Some techniques and exercises that are suitable for beginners look less appropriate for students at higher levels, and some assumptions about advanced students' abilities are less successful when transposed, without thought, to students at lower levels. This is especially true in speaking tasks. It is quite feasible to ask advanced students to get into pairs or groups to discuss a topic of some kind without structuring the activity in any way. But when asking elementary students to have a discussion in pairs or groups, we need to be far more rigorous in telling them exactly what they should do, and we will probably help them with some of the language they might want to use. The instructions we give may well be accompanied by a demonstration so that everyone is absolutely clear about the task, whereas at higher levels this may not be so necessary and might even seem strange and patronising (for an example of this, see *Speaking* on the DVD which accompanies Harmer 2007). At advanced levels it is easy to organise discussion – whether pre-planned or opportunistic (see page 201) – whereas for beginners this option will not be available.

At lower levels we may well want to have students repeat sentences and phrases chorally (see page 206), and we may organise controlled cue–response drills (pages 206–207). This is because students sometimes have difficulty getting their mouths round some of the sounds (and stress and intonation patterns) of English; choral repetition and drills can help them get over this and, furthermore, allow them to practise in an enjoyable and stress-free way. Advanced students, however, might feel rather surprised to be asked to practise like this.

In general, we will give students more support when they are at beginner or intermediate levels than we need to do when they are more advanced. This does not mean that we will not approach more advanced tasks with care or be precise about what we are asking students to do. But at higher levels we may well be entitled to expect that students will be more resourceful and, as a result, have less need for us to explain everything in such a careful and supportive way.

C2 Language, task and topic

We have said that students acquire language partly as a result of the comprehensible input they receive – especially from the teacher (see Chapter 6, D3). This means, of course, that we will have to adjust the language we use to the level of the students we are teaching. Experienced teachers are very good at rough-tuning their language to the level they are dealing with. Such rough-tuning involves, at beginner and elementary levels, using words and phrases that are as clear as possible, avoiding some of the more opaque idioms which the language contains. At lower levels we will do our best not to confuse our students by offering them too many different accents or varieties of English (see Chapter 1, B3), even though we will want to make sure they are exposed to more Englishes later on. We will also take special care at lower levels to moderate the speed we speak at and to make our instructions especially clear.

This preoccupation with suiting our language to the level of the students extends to what we ask them to read, listen to, write and speak about. As we shall see on page 273, there are things that students can do with authentic English – that is English not specially moderated for use by language students – but in general, we will want to get students to read and listen to things that they have a chance of understanding. Of course, it depends on how much we want them to get from a text, but we always need to bear in mind the demotivating effect of a text which students find depressingly impenetrable.

The same is true for what we get students to write and speak about. If we ask students to express a complex opinion and they do not have the language to do it, the result will be an unhappy one for both students and teacher. If we try to force students to write a complex letter when they are clearly unable to do such a thing, everyone will feel let down. We will discuss the concept of trying to ensure achievement below.

One problem with some beginner coursebook material in particular is the way in which quite complex topics are reduced to banalities because the language available at that level makes it impossible to treat them in any depth. The result is a kind of 'dumbing-down', which sometimes makes English language learning material appear condescending and almost childish. We must do our best to avoid this, matching topics to the level, and reserving complex issues for more advanced classes.

D Motivation

It is accepted for most fields of learning that motivation is essential to success: that we have to want to do something to succeed at it. Without such motivation we will almost certainly fail to make the necessary effort. We need, therefore, to develop our understanding of motivation – what it means, where it comes from and how it can be sustained.

D1 Defining motivation

At its most basic level, motivation is some kind of internal drive which pushes someone to do things in order to achieve something. In his discussion of motivation, Douglas Brown includes the need for ego enhancement as a prime motivator. This is the need 'for the self to be known and to be approved of by others' (Brown 2007: 169). This, presumably, is what causes people to spend hours in the gym! Such a view of motivation also accounts for our need for exploration ('the other side of the mountain').

Marion Williams and Robert Burden suggest that motivation is a 'state of cognitive arousal' which provokes a 'decision to act', as a result of which there is 'sustained intellectual and/ or physical effort' so that the person can achieve some 'previously set goal' (Williams and Burden 1997: 120). They go on to point out that the strength of that motivation will depend on how much value the individual places on the outcome he or she wishes to achieve. Adults may have clearly defined or vague goals. Children's goals, on the other hand, are often more amorphous and less easy to describe, but they can still be very powerful.

In discussions of motivation an accepted distinction is made between *extrinsic* and *intrinsic* motivation, that is motivation which comes from 'outside' and from 'inside'.

Extrinsic motivation is the result of any number of outside factors, for example the need to pass an exam, the hope of financial reward or the possibility of future travel. Intrinsic motivation, by contrast, comes from within the individual. Thus a person might be motivated by the enjoyment of the learning process itself or by a desire to make themselves feel better.

Most researchers and methodologists have come to the view that intrinsic motivation produces better results than its extrinsic counterpart (but see page 104). Even where the original reason for taking up a language course, for example, is extrinsic, the chances of success will be greatly enhanced if the students come to love the learning process.

D2 External sources of motivation

The motivation that brings students to the task of learning English can be affected and influenced by the attitude of a number of people. It is worth considering what and who these are since they form part of the environment from which the student engages with the learning process.

- **The goal:** one of the strongest outside sources of motivation is the goal which students perceive themselves to be learning for. Frequently this is provided by a forthcoming exam, and in this respect it is no surprise to note that teachers often find their exam classes more committed than other groups who do not have something definite to work towards.

However, students may have other less well-defined goals, too, such as a general desire to be able to converse in English, to be able to use English to get a better job or to understand English-language websites, etc.

Some students, of course, may not have any real English-learning goals at all. This is especially true for younger learners. In such situations they may acquire their attitude to (and motivation for) learning English from other sources.

- **The society we live in:** outside any classroom there are attitudes to language learning and the English language in particular. How important is the learning of English considered to be in the society the student lives in? In a school situation, for example, is the language learning part of the curriculum of high or low status? If school students were offered the choice of two languages to learn, which one would they choose and why? Are the cultural images associated with English positive or negative?

  All these views of language learning will affect the student's attitude to the language being studied, and the nature and strength of this attitude will, in its turn, have a profound effect on the degree of motivation the student brings to class and whether or not that motivation continues. Even where adult students have made their own decision to come to a class to study English, they will bring with them attitudes from the society they live in, developed over years, whether these attitudes are thoroughly positive or somewhat negative.

- **The people around us:** in addition to the culture of the world around them, students' attitudes to language learning will be greatly influenced by the people who are close to them. The attitude of parents and older siblings will be crucial. Do they approve of language learning, for example, or do they think that maths and reading are what count, and clearly show that they are more concerned with those subjects than with the student's success in English?

  The attitude of a student's peers is also crucial: if they are critical of the subject or activity, a student may well lose any enthusiasm they once had for learning English. If peers are enthusiastic about learning English, however, there is a much greater chance that the same student may feel more motivated to learn the subject.

- **Curiosity:** we should not underestimate a student's natural curiosity. At the beginning of a term or semester, most students have at least a mild interest in who their new teacher is and what it will be like to be in his or her lessons. When students start English for the first time, most are interested (to some extent) to see what it is like. This initial motivation is precious. Without it, getting a class off the ground and building rapport will be that much more difficult.

Even when teachers find themselves facing a class of motivated students, they cannot relax. For it is what happens next that really counts. Sustaining students' motivation is one area where we can make a real difference – and for that we need a motivation angel.

D3 The motivation angel

In the north-east of England, outside the city of Gateshead, stands a remarkable statue by Antony Gormley, the 20-metre-high *Angel of the North*. It can be seen from the motorway, from the nearby train line and for miles around. It is, by common consent, a work of uplifting beauty and inspires almost all who see it, whatever their religion or even if they have none at all.

The *Angel of the North* provides us with a satisfying metaphor to deal with the greatest difficulty teachers face in terms of motivation. For as Alan Rodgers wrote many years ago, '... we forget that initial motivation to learn may be weak and die; alternatively it can be increased and directed into new channels' (Rogers 1996: 61). In other words, we can have a powerful effect on how or even whether students remain motivated after whatever initial enthusiasm they brought to the course has dissipated. We have the ability, as well, to gradually create motivation in students where, initially, there is none. This is not to say that it is a teacher's sole responsibility to build and nurture motivation. On the contrary, students need to play their part, too. But insofar as we can have a positive effect, we need to be able to build our own 'motivation angel' to keep students engaged and involved as lesson succeeds lesson, as week succeeds week.

The angel needs to be built on the solid base of the extrinsic motivation which the students bring with them to class (see Figure 10). And on this base we will build our statue in five distinct stages.

EXTRINSIC MOTIVATION

FIGURE 10: The motivation base

- **Affect:** affect, as we said on page 58, is concerned with students' feelings, and here we as teachers can have a dramatic effect. In the words of some eleven-year-old students I interviewed, 'a good teacher is someone who asks the people who don't always put their hands up' and 'a good teacher is someone who knows our names' (Harmer 2007: 26). In other words, students are far more likely to stay motivated over a period of time if they think that the teacher cares about them. This can be done by building good teacher–student rapport (see Chapter 6C), which in turn is dependent on listening to students' views and attempts with respect, and intervening (i.e. for correction) in an appropriate and constructive way.

  When students feel that the teacher has little interest in them (or is unprepared to make the effort to treat them with consideration), they will have little incentive to remain motivated. When the teacher is caring and helpful, however, they are much more likely to retain an interest in what is going on, and as a result, their self-esteem (an important ingredient in success) is likely to be nurtured.

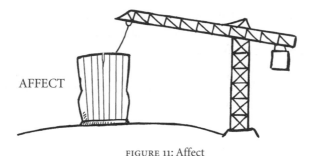

AFFECT

FIGURE 11: Affect

- **Achievement:** nothing motivates like success. Nothing demotivates like continual failure. It is part of the teacher's art, therefore, to try to ensure that students are successful, because the longer their success continues, the more likely they are to stay motivated to learn.

  However, success without effort does not seem to be that motivating. If everything is just too easy, students are likely to lose their respect for the task of learning. The same is true if success is too difficult to attain. What students need to feel is a real sense of achievement, which has cost them something to acquire but has not bankrupted them in the process.

  Part of a teacher's job, therefore, is to set an appropriate level of challenge for the students. This means setting tests that are not too difficult or too easy, and involving students in learning tasks they can succeed in. It also means being able to guide students towards success by showing them how to get things right next time.

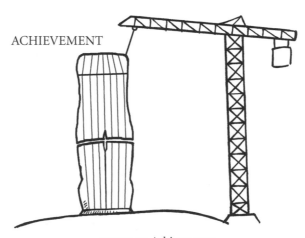

ACHIEVEMENT

FIGURE 12: Achievement

- **Attitude:** however nice teachers are, students are unlikely to follow them willingly (and do what is asked of them) unless they have confidence in their professional abilities. Students need to believe that we know what we are doing.

  This confidence in a teacher may start the moment we walk into the classroom for the first time – because of the students' perception of our attitude to the job (see Figure 13). Aspects such as the way we dress, where we stand and the way we talk to the class all have a bearing here. Students also need to feel that we know about the subject we are teaching. Consciously or unconsciously they need to feel that we are prepared to teach English in general and that we are prepared to teach this lesson in particular. As we shall see, one of the chief reasons (but not the only one, of course) why classes occasionally become undisciplined is because teachers do not have enough for the students to do – or seem not to be quite sure what to do next.

When students have confidence in the teacher, they are likely to remain engaged with what is going on. If they lose that confidence, it becomes difficult for them to sustain the motivation they might have started with.

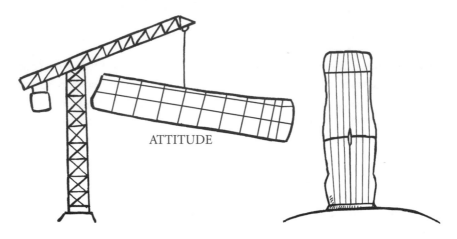

ATTITUDE

FIGURE 13: (Perceived) attitude (of the teacher)

- **Activities:** our students' motivation is far more likely to remain healthy if they are doing things they enjoy doing, and which they can see the point of. Our choice of what we ask them to do has an important role, therefore, in their continuing engagement with the learning process.

  It sometimes seems to be suggested that students only enjoy activities which involve game-like communication and other interactive tasks. However, this is not necessarily the case. Different students, as we have seen earlier in this chapter, have different styles and preferences. While some may want to sing songs and write poems, others might be much more motivated by concentrated language study and poring over reading texts.

  We need to try to match the activities (see Figure 14) we take into lessons with the students we are teaching. One way of doing this is to keep a constant eye on what they respond well to and what they feel less engaged with. Only then can we be sure that the activities we take into class have at least a chance of helping to keep students engaged with the learning process.

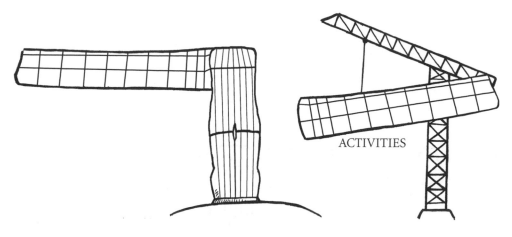

FIGURE 14: Activities

- **Agency:** *agency* is a term borrowed from social sciences (see for example Taylor 1977, Frankfurt 1988, Belz 2002). Here it is appropriated to mean something similar to the agent of a passive sentence, that is, in the words of some grammarians, the person or thing 'that does'.

  A lot of the time, in some classes, students have things done *to* them and, as a result, risk being passive recipients of whatever is being handed down. We should be equally interested, however, in things done *by* the students.

  When students have agency (see Figure 15), they get to make some of the decisions about what is going on, and, as a consequence, they take some responsibility for their learning. For example, we might allow students to tell us when and if they want to be corrected in a fluency activity (Rinvolucri 1998) rather than always deciding ourselves when correction is appropriate and when it is not. We might have students tell us what words they find difficult to pronounce rather than assuming they all have the same difficulties.

  J J Wilson suggests that wherever possible students should be allowed to make decisions. He wants to give students ownership of class materials, letting them write on the board or control the CD player, for example (Wilson 2005). For Jenny de Sonneville, while the teacher may decide on broad learning outcomes, he or she should design tasks 'in which the students are empowered to take a more active role in the course design' (2005: 11). For Lesley Painter, it was allowing students to choose what homework they wanted and needed to do that was the key to motivating her students to do the tasks that were set (Painter 1999). Real agency occurs, finally, when students take responsibility for their own learning, and we can provoke them to do this in the various ways we will discuss in Chapter 23A. A student we have trained to use dictionaries effectively has the potential for agency which a student who cannot access the wealth of information in a dictionary (especially a monolingual dictionary) is cut off from.

  No one is suggesting that students should have complete control of what happens in lessons. But the more we empower them and give them agency, the more likely they are to stay motivated over a long period.

FIGURE 15: The motivation angel

Before we leave the subject of motivation (and indeed of learner description in general), we need to remember that motivation (where it comes from and what teachers can do to sustain it) may not be the same for all students and in all cultures. Judy Chen and her colleagues (based on their study of more than 160 students in Taiwan and China) observe that an assumption that motivation for Chinese students is the same as for EFL students in the USA, is 'apt to be off the mark, as is any assumption that the components of motivation are universal' (Chen *et al* 2005: 624). What their study clearly shows is that throughout Greater China there are numerous learning strategies based entirely on memorisation (2005: 625), and that the greatest motivator is success in exams based on how much students can remember. In such situations (and until and unless the exams change so that they prioritise spoken and written communication rather than memorised vocabulary and grammar), perhaps agency may not be important in the way we have described it; nor is the need for activity variety so pronounced if all students are fixated on this kind of achievement. Indeed in Taiwan many successful ex-students, Chen and her colleagues report, promote an ever-popular 'memorize a dictionary' strategy, and some students get an idiom a day sent to their mobile phones.

We have already discussed the need for context-sensitive methodology (see Chapter 4B). The study which Judy Chen and her colleagues have undertaken reminds us again that in discussions of teaching and learning strategies we need to look carefully at who the students are, where they are learning and what their aspirations are.

Chapter notes and further reading

- **Young children**

  M Williams and R Burden (1997: Chapters 1 and 2) offer a clear account of differing theories of child development.

  On teaching children at and before primary level, see V Reilly and S Ward (1997), A Case (2007), L Cameron (2001), W Scott and L Ytreborg (1990), J Moon (2005), M Slattery and J Willis (2001) and A Pinter (2006).

  G Ellis and J Brewster (2002a) offer a storytelling handbook. M Fletcher (2005) discusses how children's emotions affect their ability to learn. M Williams (2001) discusses Reuven Feuerstein's concept of mediation and offers 12 principles for effective teaching. M Hebden and J Mason (2003) suggest different ways of organising young learner classrooms. C Linse (2004) discusses good learner behaviour. C Read (2005) writes about class management with young learners and C Bradshaw (2005) discusses giving 'great instructions'. J Bourke (2006) promotes the benefits of a topic-based syllabus for young learners.

- **Adolescents**

  On the young person's search for identity, see the work of E H Erikson reported in M Williams and R Burden (1997).

  The idea that adolescents present an ideal teaching and learning age is put forward in P Ur (1996: 286) and R Ellis (1994: 484–494). See also C Damim *et al* (2002).

  S Lindstromberg (2004) has edited a book of language activities for teenagers.

  A Leiguarda (2004) discusses the teenage brain. See also P Prowse and J Garton-Sprenger (2005) on 'teen power'. C Fowle (2002) advances the learning benefits of vocabulary notebooks for adolescents.

- **Adult learners**

  On teaching adults, see H McKay and A Tom (1999) and A Rogers (1996).

- **Individual differences in language learning**

  For a clear account of many of the issues raised in this chapter, see P Lightbown and N Spada (2006: Chapter 3) and P Skehan (1998: Chapter 10).

- **Aptitude**

  The best discussion on aptitude I know is in P Skehan (1998: Chapters 8 and 9). See also H D Brown (1994: 258–261).

  The two most widely quoted aptitude test instruments from the 1950s and 1960s were The Modern Language Aptitude Test (MLAT) designed by J Carroll and S Sapon (Carroll and Sapon 1959) and the Pimsleur Language Aptitude Battery (Pimsleur 1966).

- **Neuro-Linguistic Programming (NLP)**

  On NLP, two books well worth reading are J Revell and S Norman (1997 and 1999). However, founded/developed as it was by R Bandler and J Grinder, see also R Bandler and J Grinder (1979). J Baker and M Rinvolucri (2005a) have written a book of NLP activities, but see also articles by J Baker and M Rinvolucri (2005b), J Baker (2005) and a kind of 'for and against' account by M Rinvolucri (2005).

- **Multiple Intelligences**

  For more on Multiple Intelligences theory, read H Gardner (1983, 1993), M Zülküf Altan (2001) and R Christison's book of theory and activities (2005). H Puchta (2005, 2006a and b) discusses MI theory and H Puchta and M Rinvolucri (2005) have written a book of activities based on MI theory.

  C Green and R Tanner (2005) write interestingly about MI theory applied to online training.

- **Motivation**

  For motivation in general, see Z Dörnyei (2001) and M Williams and R Burden (1997: Chapter 6). A Littlejohn (2001) is a short helpful article on the subject and K Nicholls (2000) suggests a short questionnaire to raise students' awareness of the topic.

- **Sustaining motivation**

  L Taylor (2005) thinks the teacher's language can determine (or modify) the students' affect.

  J De Sonneville (2005) wants students to be empowered by taking some learning decisions in a 'participatory methodology'. J Harmer (2006a) discusses steps towards student agency, and J J Wilson (2005) recommends teachers 'letting go'.

6 | Describing teachers

A What is 'teaching'?

It is often helpful to use metaphors to describe what teachers do. Sometimes, for example, teachers say they are like actors because they feel as if they are always on the stage. Others talk of themselves as orchestral conductors because they direct conversation and set the pace and tone. Yet others feel like gardeners because they plant the seeds and then watch them grow. The range of images – these and others – that teachers use about themselves indicates the range of views that they have about their profession.

Many trainers are fond of quoting from *The Prophet* by Kahlil Gibran. 'If the teacher is indeed wise,' Gibran writes, 'he does not bid you enter the house of his wisdom, but rather leads you to the threshold of your own mind' (Gibran 1991: 76). Such humanist sentiments expose a dilemma in the minds of many teacher trainers and trainees. Is teaching about the 'transmission' of knowledge from teacher to student, or is it about creating conditions in which, somehow, students learn for themselves? To put it another way, if you were to walk into a classroom, where would you expect to see the teacher – standing at the front controlling affairs, or moving around the classroom quietly helping the students only when needed?

Zoltan Dörnyei and Tim Murphey see the business of teaching as the exercise of group leadership (Dörnyei and Murphey 2003: Chapter 6). It is our role as group development practitioners that really counts, they suggest. One of our principal responsibilities, in other words, is to foster good relationships with the groups in front of us so that they work together cooperatively in a spirit of friendliness and harmonious creativity. But how can this best be achieved? Dörnyei and Murphey suggest that 'a group conscious teaching style involves an increasing encouragement of and reliance on the group's own resources and the active facilitation of autonomous learning that is in accordance with the maturity level of the group' (2003: 99). When teachers and groups first meet each other, they suggest, students expect leadership and direction. This gives them a clear focus and makes them feel secure at the same time. But as groups develop their group identity, teachers will want to relax their grip and foster more democratic class practices where students are involved in the process of decision-making and direction-finding.

Two things need to be said about this view of the teacher's craft. In the first place, being democratic and letting students participate in decision-making takes more effort and organisation than controlling the class from the front. Furthermore, the promotion of learner autonomy (where students not only learn on their own, but also take responsibility for that learning), is only one view of the teaching–learning relationship, and is very culturally biased. In some situations both teachers and learners (and society in general) may feel more comfortable with a more autocratic leadership style, and while this might not suit the preferences of some, especially methodologists, it is highly attractive to others.

It is worth pointing out that being a 'democratic' teacher (where the teacher shares some of the leadership with the students) is simply one style of teaching, informed by strong beliefs, of course, but nevertheless only one way of doing things. Some teachers are effective when teaching in this way, but others may find it more difficult.

Whether or not we are more autocratic or democratic as teachers, we are called upon to play many different roles in a language learning classroom. Our ability to carry these out effectively will depend to a large extent on the rapport we establish with our students, and on our own level of knowledge and skill.

B In the classroom

'Students can pick up much from the way their teacher walks into the room at the start of that first lesson,' writes Rose Senior (Senior 2006: 93). The way we dress, the stance we adopt and our attitude to the class make an immediate impression on students. In this sense we need to make some kind of distinction between who we are, and who we are *as teachers*. This does not mean that we should somehow be dishonest about who we are when we face students. There will always be a need to be 'congruent' (Rogers 1961), that is being honest to oneself and appropriately honest with our students. But it does mean thinking about presenting a professional face to the students which they find both interesting and effective. When we walk into the classroom, we want them to see someone who looks like a teacher whatever else they look like. This does not mean conforming to some kind of teacher stereotype, but rather finding, each in our own way, a persona that we adopt when we cross the classroom threshold. The point is that we should be able to adopt a variety of roles within the classroom which facilitate learning. Some of these roles come naturally to most teachers, while others have to be thought about more carefully.

B1 The roles of a teacher

Many commentators use the term *facilitator* to describe a particular kind of teacher, one who is democratic rather than autocratic, and one who fosters learner autonomy through the use of groupwork and pairwork and by acting as more of a resource than a transmitter of knowledge. However, since we can say that the aim of all committed teachers is to facilitate learning, however they go about it, it makes more sense to describe different teacher roles in more detail and say what they are useful for, rather than make value judgements about their effectiveness in terms of their 'facilitator' credentials.

- **Controller:** when teachers act as controllers, they are in charge of the class and of the activity taking place and are often 'leading from the front'. Controllers take the register, tell students things, organise drills, read aloud and in various other ways exemplify the qualities of a teacher-fronted classroom.

  Teachers who view their job as the transmission of knowledge from themselves to their students are usually very comfortable with the image of themselves as controllers. We can all remember teachers from our past who had a gift for just such a kind of instruction and who inspired us through their knowledge and their charisma. However, not all teachers possess this ability to inspire, and in less charismatic hands, transmission teaching appears to have less obvious advantages. For a start, it denies students access to their own experiential learning by focusing everything on the teacher; in the second place, it cuts down on opportunities for students to speak because when the class is acting as a whole group, fewer individuals have a chance to say anything at all; and in the third place, over-reliance on transmission teaching can result in a lack of variety in activities and classroom atmosphere.

Of course, there are times when acting as a controller makes sense, for example when giving explanations, organising question and answer work, lecturing, making announcements or bringing a class to order. Indeed, such leadership may have a highly beneficial effect on a group, especially in the early stages. In many educational contexts it is the most common teacher role, and many teachers fail to go beyond it since controlling is the role they are used to and are most comfortable with. Yet this is a pity because by sticking to one mode of behaviour, we deny ourselves and the students many other possibilities and modes of learning which are good not only for learning itself, but also for our students' enjoyment of that learning.

- **Prompter:** sometimes, when they are involved in a role-play activity for example, students lose the thread of what is going on, or they are 'lost for words' (i.e. they may still have the thread but be unable to proceed productively for lack of vocabulary). They may not be quite sure how to proceed. What should teachers do in these circumstances? Hold back and let them work things out for themselves or, instead, 'nudge' them forward in a discreet and supportive way? If we opt for the latter, we are adopting some kind of a 'prompting' role.

  In such situations we want to help but we don't want, at that stage, to take charge. This is because we are keen to encourage the students to think creatively rather than have them hang on our every word. Thus it is that we will occasionally offer words or phrases, suggest that the students say something (e.g. *Well, ask him why he says that*) or suggest what could come next in a paragraph a student is writing, for example. Often we have to prompt students in monolingual groups to speak English rather than use their mother tongue.

  When we prompt, we need to do it sensitively and encouragingly but, above all, with discretion. If we are too adamant, we risk taking initiative away from the student. If, on the other hand, we are too retiring, we may not supply the right amount of encouragement.

- **Participant:** the traditional picture of teachers during student discussions, role-plays or group decision-making activities, is of people who 'stand back' from the activity, letting the learners get on with it and only intervening later to offer feedback and/or correct mistakes. However, there are also times when we might want to join in an activity not (only) as a teacher, but also as a participant in our own right.

  There are good reasons why we might want to take part in a discussion, for example. It means that we can liven things up from the inside instead of always having to prompt or organise from outside the group. When it goes well, students enjoy having the teacher with them, and for the teacher, participating is often more enjoyable than acting as a resource.

  The danger when teachers act as participants, of course, is that they can easily dominate the proceedings. This is hardly surprising since teachers usually have more English at their disposal than their students do. But it is also due to the fact that even in the most egalitarian classroom, the teacher is still frequently perceived of as 'the authority' and tends to be listened to with greater attention than other students. It takes great skill and sensitivity to by-pass this perception for the times when we wish to participate in the way we are suggesting here.

- **Resource:** in some activities it is inappropriate for us to take on any of the roles we have suggested so far. Suppose that the students are involved in a piece of group writing, or that they are preparing for a presentation they are to make to the class. In such situations, having the teacher take part, or try to control them, or even turn up to prompt them might be entirely unwelcome. However, the students may still have need of their teacher as a resource. They might need to ask how to say or write something or ask what a word or phrase means. They might want to know information in the middle of an activity about that activity or they might want information about where to look for something – a book or a website, for example. This is where we can be one of the most important resources they have.

  Two things need to be said about this teacher role. Firstly, no teacher knows everything about the language! Questions like What's the difference between X and Y? or Why can't I say Z? are always difficult to deal with because most of us do not carry complex information of this kind in our heads. What we should be able to offer, however, is guidance as to where students can go to look for that information. We could go further, however, and say that one of our really important jobs is to encourage students to use resource material for themselves, and to become more independent in their learning generally. Thus, instead of answering every question about what a word or phrase means, we can instead direct students to a good dictionary. Alternatively, we need to have the courage to say I don't know the answer to that right now, but I'll tell you tomorrow. This means, of course, that we will have to give them the information the next day otherwise they may begin to lose confidence in us.

  When we are acting as a resource, we will want to be helpful and available, but at the same time we have to resist the urge to spoonfeed our students so that they become over-reliant on us.

- **Tutor:** when students are working on longer projects, such as process writing (see Chapter 19, B1) or preparation for a talk or a debate, we can work with individuals or small groups, pointing them in directions they have not yet thought of taking. In such situations, we are combining the roles of prompter and resource – in other words, acting as a tutor.

  It is difficult to be a tutor in a very large group since the term implies a more intimate relationship than that of a controller or organiser. However, when students are working in small groups or in pairs, we can go round the class and, staying briefly with a particular group or individual, offer the sort of general guidance we are describing. Care needs to be taken, however, to ensure that as many individuals or groups as possible are seen, otherwise the students who have not had access to the tutor may begin to feel aggrieved.

  It is essential for us to act as tutors from time to time, however difficult this may be. In this more personal contact, the learners have a real chance to feel supported and helped, and the general class atmosphere is greatly enhanced as a result. Nevertheless, as with prompting and acting as a resource, we need to make sure that we do not intrude either too much (which will impede learner autonomy) or too little (which will be unhelpful).

The role that we take on is dependent, as we have seen, on what it is we wish the students to achieve. Where some activities are difficult to organise without the teacher acting as controller, others have no chance of success unless we take a less domineering role. There are times when we will need to act as a prompter where, on other occasions, it would be more appropriate to act as a resource. A lot will depend on the group we are teaching since our leadership style may well depend on the particular students we are working with; whereas some students might be more comfortable with using the teacher as a resource and a tutor, others may hunger for us to adopt a more controlling role.

What we can say, with certainty, is that we need to be able to switch between the various roles we have described here, judging when it is appropriate to use one or other of them. And then, when we have made that decision, however consciously or subconsciously it is done, we need to be aware of how we carry out that role, how we perform.

B2 Organising students and activities

One of the most important tasks that teachers have to perform is that of organising students to do various activities. This often involves giving the students information, telling them how they are going to do the activity, putting them into pairs or groups and finally closing things down when it is time to stop.

The first thing we need to do when organising something is to get students involved, engaged and ready. In most cases, this means making it clear that something 'new' is going to happen and that the activity will be enjoyable, interesting or beneficial. At this point teachers will often say something like *Now we're going to do this because ...* and will offer a rationale for the activity students are to be asked to perform. Thus, instead of just doing something because the teacher says so, they are prepared, hopefully with some enthusiasm, for an activity whose purpose they understand.

Once the students are ready for the activity, we will want to give any necessary instructions, saying what students should do first, what they should do next, etc. Here it is important to get the level of the language right and try to present instructions in a logical order and in as unconfusing a way as possible. It is frequently a good idea to get students to give the instructions back, in English or in their own language, as a check on whether they have understood them. An important tool in instruction is for the teacher to organise a demonstration of what is to happen. If students are going to use a chart or table to ask other students questions and record their answers, for example, getting a student up to the front to demonstrate the activity with you may be worth any number of complex instructions. Demonstration is almost always appropriate and will almost always ensure that students have a better grasp of what they are supposed to do than instructions can on their own.

Then it is time for us to start or initiate the activity. At this point students probably need to know how much time they have got and exactly when they should start.

Finally, we stop the activity when the students have finished and/or when other factors indicate that it is time to stop. This might be because the students are bored or because some pairs or groups have already finished before the others (see Chapter 10, B4). Perhaps the lesson is coming to the end and we want to give some summarising comments. At this point, it is vital to organise some kind of feedback, whether this is merely a *Did you enjoy that?* type of question (a vitally important question, of course) or whether it is a more detailed discussion of what has taken place.

Teachers should think about *content feedback* just as much as they concern themselves with the use of language forms in *form and use feedback*. The latter is concerned with our role as assessor (see below), whereas the former has more to do with the roles of participant and tutor.

When organising feedback, we need to do what we say we are going to do whether this concerns the prompt return of homework or our responses at the end of an oral activity. Students will judge us by the way we fulfil the criteria we offer them.

We can summarise the role of organiser as follows:

> Engage → instruct (demonstrate) → initiate → organise feedback

B3 The teacher as performer

In an article published at the end of the 1980s, Christopher Crouch described his experiences of observing his student teachers on teaching practice in Madrid. One of them, whom he called W, was obviously full of energy and he writes of how she 'rubbed her hands together' and 'advanced on the front row with a question, almost aggressively ...'. Later on, '... seeking students to come out to the front of the class, W strode up aisles, literally hauling individuals out of their seats' (Crouch 1989: 107). Yet amazingly, Crouch reports, the students didn't seem to mind this at all; on the contrary, they were pleased to join in and were clearly fascinated by her behaviour!

W was different from student teacher X who was 'relaxed, at ease, but his non-verbal gestures were exaggerated, larger than life'. He seemed to empathise with his students, gazing into their eyes, and generally being more 'laid back' than his colleague. But like W, he, too, was popular with students. Many of us will be able to remember teachers whose classroom behaviour was exaggerated in a way not unlike W or X – or indeed some mixture of them both.

We can be sure that neither W nor X behaved in the same way when they were walking along the street as they did in the classes that Christopher Crouch observed. On the contrary, they clearly went into 'performance' mode when they entered the classroom. When, in a piece of informal research, I asked a number of teachers *Are you a different person in the classroom than you are out of the classroom?*, the responses I got all suggested that the teachers thought of themselves as more energetic, humorous and creative in class. Frequently, too, they described themselves as 'actors' (Harmer 1995).

If, then, teachers are all performers in the classroom at some level, what does this mean for a teacher who wants to promote learner autonomy? Can we 'perform' and still act as a resource? What kind of performance should we adopt when giving feedback? Does 'performance' automatically mean that we must be standing at the front of the class putting on a show? For clearly if this was the case, teacher performance would describe only one kind of teacher role and might be criticised for the very transmissive and teacher-centred behaviour it demonstrated. But as W and X show, different teachers perform differently. Not only that, but any one teacher probably also has many different performance styles, depending on the situation. One minute we may be standing at the front commanding or entertaining, but a few minutes later we will be working quietly with a pair while the other students are working in their own pairs.

Knowing that different teachers act differently and that individual teachers vary their behaviour, depending upon what they are doing, gives us insights into classroom behaviour. It suggests that an alternative to saying *what* role teachers should be playing is to describe *how* they should be playing it. Just as stage directions give actors an insight into what lines mean, so similar descriptions in teaching may give us insights into how activities can best be managed. Thus, for an activity where the students are involved in a team game, we will want to behave energetically (because a game needs excitement and energy), encouragingly (if students need a nudge to have a go), clearly (because we don't want the game to fail through misunderstanding) and fairly (because students care about this in a competition situation). If, on the other hand, students are involved in a role-play, we should 'perform' clearly (because students need to know exactly what the parameters of the role-play are), encouragingly (because students may need prompting to get them going), but also retiringly (because, once the activity has got going, we don't want to overwhelm the students' performance) and supportively (because students may need help at various points). Figure 1 shows how we might describe these and other activities.

Activity	How the teacher should perform
1 Team game	Energetically, encouragingly, clearly, fairly
2 Role-play	Clearly, encouragingly, retiringly, supportively
3 Teacher reading aloud	Commandingly, dramatically, interestingly
4 Whole-class listening	Efficiently, clearly, supportively

FIGURE 1: Describing teacher performance styles

What seems to be clear is that while we certainly need to be aware of the roles and tasks we described in B1 above, and while we need to be able to use each of these different roles, it is also vitally important to consider how we actually behave during their performance.

C Rapport

In order to work well with the different roles we have been describing – and if we wish to develop a good learning environment in the classroom – we need to establish an appropriate relationship with our students. We need to spend time making sure that teacher–student rapport is positive and useful.

Rapport means, in essence, the relationship that the students have with the teacher and vice versa. Although it may be, in Jim Scrivener's words, 'notoriously difficult to define or quantify' (Scrivener 2005: 23), nevertheless we can recognise it when we see it: a class where there is a positive, enjoyable and respectful relationship between teacher and students, and between the students themselves.

In part, successful rapport derives from the students' perception of the teacher as a good leader and a successful professional. If, when teachers come to the class, students can see that they are well-organised and well-prepared (that is, they have thought about what they are going to do in the lesson), they are likely to have confidence in their teacher. Such confidence is an essential component in the successful relationship between students and their teachers. It extends as well to the teachers' demonstrable knowledge of the subject they are teaching and to their familiarity with classroom materials and equipment. All of these things tell the students that they are 'in good hands'.

However, rapport (and effective classroom management, as we shall see in Chapter 9) also depends on the way that we interact with students. We might be the most well-prepared and knowledgeable teachers in our school, but if that interaction isn't working well, our ability to help students to learn will be seriously compromised.

Successful interaction with students depends on four key characteristics:

- **Recognising students:** students want their teachers to know who they are. They would like their teachers to know their names, of course, but they also appreciate it when teachers have some understanding of their characters.

  It is extremely difficult for teachers to know the names of all their students, especially at the beginning of a term or semester when they have, say, nine large groups. As a result, teachers have developed a number of strategies to help them cope with this situation. One method is to ask the students (at least in the first week or two) to put name cards on the desk in front of them or stick name badges to their sweaters or jackets. We can also draw up a seating plan and ask students always to sit in the same place until we have learnt their names. However, this means we can't move students around when we want to, and students – especially younger ones – sometimes take pleasure in sitting in the wrong place just to confuse us.

  Many teachers use the register to make notes about individual students (Do they wear glasses? Are they tall? etc.) and others keep separate notes about the individuals in their classes. Some teachers study the register or class seating plan before the lesson starts or when it is finished to try to fix student names in their heads.

  There is no easy way of remembering students' names, yet it is extremely important that we do so if good rapport is to be established with individuals. We need, therefore, to find ways of doing this that suit us best.

  But knowing students' names also involves knowing about students. At any age, they will be pleased when they realise that their teacher has remembered things about them, and has some understanding of who they are. Once again, this is extremely difficult in large classes, especially when we have a number of different groups, but part of a teacher's skill is to persuade students that we recognise them and who and what they are.

- **Listening to students:** students respond very well to teachers who listen to them. Although there are many calls on our time, nevertheless we need to make ourselves as available as we can to listen to individual students' opinions and concerns, often outside the lessons themselves.

  But we need to listen properly to students in lessons, too. And we need to show that we are interested in what they have to say. Nothing demotivates a student more than when the teacher is dismissive or uninterested in what they have to say. Of course, no one can force us to be genuinely interested in absolutely everything and everyone, but it is part of a teacher's professional personality – part of our skill as teachers – that we should be able to convince students that we are listening to what they say with every sign of attention.

  As far as possible, we also need to listen to the students' comments on how they are getting on, and which activities and techniques they respond well or badly to. If we just go on teaching the same thing day after day without being aware of our students' reactions, it will become more and more difficult to maintain the rapport that is so important for successful classes.

  Finally, we should point out that listening is not just done with the ears! We need to show that we are listening and paying attention to our students, and this will mean approaching them, making eye contact and generally looking interested. As Hongshen Zhang points out, 'eyes talk' (Hongshen Zhang 2006).

- **Respecting students:** correcting students is always a delicate event. If we are too critical, we risk demotivating them, yet if we are constantly praising them, we risk turning them into 'praise junkies', who begin to need approval all the time (see page 138). The problem we face, however, is that while some students are happy to be corrected robustly, others need more support and positive reinforcement. In other words, just as students have different learning styles and intelligences, so, too, they have different preferences when it comes to being corrected. But whichever method of correction we choose, and whoever we are working with, students need to know that we are treating them with respect, and not using mockery or sarcasm – or expressing despair at their efforts!

  Respect is vital, too, when we deal with any kind of problem behaviour (see Chapter 9). We could, of course, respond to indiscipline or awkwardness by being biting in our criticism of the student who has done something we do not approve of. Yet this will be counter-productive. It is the behaviour we want to criticise, not the character of the student in question.

  Teachers who respect students do their best to see them in a positive light. They are not negative about their learners or in the way they deal with them in class. They do not react with anger or ridicule when students do unplanned things, but instead use a respectful professionalism to solve the problem.

- **Being even-handed:** most teachers have some students that they warm to more than others. For example, many teachers react well to those who take part, are cheerful and cooperative, who take responsibility for their own learning, and do what is asked of them without complaint. Sometimes teachers are less enthusiastic about those who are less forthcoming, and who find learner autonomy, for example, more of a challenge. Yet, as a teenage student once told me, 'a good teacher should try to draw out the quiet ones and control the more talkative ones', and one of her colleagues echoed this by saying that 'a good teacher is … someone who asks the people who don't always put their hands up.'

  The reasons that some students are not forthcoming may be many and varied, ranging from shyness to their cultural or family backgrounds. Sometimes students are reluctant to take part overtly because of other stronger characters in the group. And these quiet students will only be negatively affected when they see far more attention being paid to their more robust classmates. At the same time, giving some students more attention than others may make those students more difficult to deal with later since they will come to expect special treatment, and may take our interest as a licence to become over-dominant in the classroom. Moreover, it is not just teenage students who can suffer from being the 'teacher's pet'.

  Treating all students equally not only helps to establish and maintain rapport, but is also a mark of professionalism.

D The teacher as teaching aid

In a language classroom there are specific ways in which we can help our students both hear and understand language.

D1 Mime and gesture

One of the things that we are uniquely able to do on the spot is to use mime, gesture and expression to convey meaning and atmosphere. It is not difficult to pretend to be drinking or to pull a sad face. Demonstrating words like *frightened* or *old* is fairly easy for many teachers. Shrugging the shoulders can be used to indicate indifference and we can use gestures to indicate the meaning of words such as *big*, *small*, *short*, *tall*, etc., as well as to suggest concepts such as past time (a hand pointing backwards over the shoulder) or future time (a hand pointing forwards).

FIGURE 2: Mime, expression and gesture

Mime and expression probably work best when they are exaggerated since this makes their meaning explicit. However, gestures do not necessarily have universal meanings, and what might seem acceptable in one situation or place will not be appropriate in another. We need, therefore, to use them with care.

One gesture which is widely used, but which teachers should employ with care, is the act of pointing to students to ask them to participate in a drill or give some other form of response. Though it is quick and efficient, especially when we are having trouble with our students' names, it can seem aggressive and it may make it depressingly obvious to the students that, in having failed to learn their names, we are less than respectful of their identity. In many cultures it is, anyway, just plain rude. An alternative is to use the upturned palm of the hand in an inclusive gesture which is far more welcoming (see Figure 3).

FIGURE 3: Pointing and including

D2 The teacher as language model

Students get models of language from textbooks, reading materials of all sorts and from audio and video tapes. But we can also model language ourselves. This does not only mean the giving of a clear language model as in the PPP procedure described in Chapter 4, A2, but also, for example, the performance of a dialogue or the reading aloud of a text.

One way in which we can model dialogues is to draw two faces on the board and then stand in front of each of them when required to speak their lines (see Figure 4). For such activities we should make sure that we can be heard, and we should animate our performance with as much enthusiasm as is appropriate for the conversation we are modelling. We should judge the appropriate speed, too, making sure that however slowly we speak, a natural rhythm is maintained and normal intonation patterns preserved as far as possible.

FIGURE 4: Board face dialogue

Many of the same requirements apply to reading aloud, a skill which some teachers have tended to ignore. Yet the reading aloud of a particularly exciting or interesting excerpt can be extremely motivating and enjoyable for a class, especially when students have been encouraged to predict what they are going to hear. Poems, too, are very engaging for many students when teachers read them to the class.

Anyone who doubts the power of such activities only has to look at the reading circles in primary classes where children group enthusiastically around the teacher to enjoy the experience of listening to a story. Story-telling and story/poem-reading can work with adults, too, though the content and the way it is handled will be significantly different, of course.

Reading passages aloud to students can capture imagination and mood like nothing else, but in order for this to work we need to 'perform' the reading in an interesting and committed way and, as with so many other activities, we must be careful not use this activity too frequently.

D3 The teacher as provider of comprehensible input

An issue that confronts many teachers in classrooms is how much they themselves should talk, and what kind of talk this should be. Of course, there are times when teachers have to take the register, ask for quiet or suggest that students should get into pairs and groups. But there are also times when teachers simply talk to groups, engage in conversation with them, discuss the topic under consideration or ask them about their weekend, etc.

On most training courses a distinction is made between student talking time (STT) and teacher talking time (TTT). As we shall see in Chapter 10, it is the concern to maximise the former that leads many teachers to use pair- and groupwork; it has been assumed that on the whole we want to see more STT than TTT, since, as trainers frequently point out to their student teachers, 'you don't need the language practice, they do!'

It is certainly true that some teachers talk too much and that this is not necessarily advantageous for their students, especially since what those teachers say is unlikely to be always interesting. However, as we saw in Chapter 3, it is widely accepted that a vital ingredient in the learning of any language is exposure to it. The more comprehensible input the students get, the better. Yet where can they go for such language input? In the world outside the classroom, English, if they have access to it, will frequently appear incomprehensible, especially when they are at a low level. They need something or someone to provide language which has been 'roughly-tuned' to be comprehensible to them. And we are right there in the classroom to give them just that!

As teachers, we are ideally placed to provide appropriate input since we know the students in front of us and can react appropriately to them in a way that a coursebook or an audio track, for example, cannot. We know how to talk at just the right level so that even if our students don't understand every word we say, they do understand the meaning of what is being said. At such times the language gains, for the student, are significant.

As a result, it may be a good idea to consider not just how much the teacher talks, but also teacher talking quality (TTQ). It is the quality of what we say that really counts. As to when we say it, that depends on how it fits in with the need for students to get production opportunities and all the other myriad aspects of the curriculum.

Basing a lesson on using ourselves as language models and providers of input, as in the examples above, clearly has the enormous advantage of not being susceptible to technical malfunction (though that can happen!), power cuts or unavailability. However, an over-reliance on what we ourselves can offer places excessive demands upon us. It is hard to be permanently motivating and amusing, and it is taxing to have to offer a perpetually varied diet of voices, gestures and expressions. Nevertheless, the ways in which we use our voice and the ways in which we model language and employ gesture and expression are all basic and important teaching skills.

E Native-speaker teachers and non-native-speaker teachers

Jacinta Thomas, a professional with years of teaching experience and a PhD under her belt, writes of the situations where she and other non-native-speaker teachers of English have to establish their 'credibility as teachers of English' because they are not seen as 'native speakers'. She tells the following story of life in the USA:

> A 95-year-old neighbour of mine, a dear sweet old lady, recently introduced me
> to her daughter as a college teacher and quickly added 'Guess what she teaches?'
> 'What?' her daughter asked. 'English. Imagine someone coming from India to teach
> here,' replied my neighbour with a sweet chuckle.   (Thomas 1999: 2)

For many years an opposition has been created between native-speaker teachers of English and non-native-speaker teachers. And for much of that time, many non-native-speaker teachers have felt a sense of injustice and sometimes even inferiority at what they perceive as the assumed superiority of the native speaker (this is the 'enervating inferiority complex' described by Rajagopalan and quoted on page 17 of this book). Although, if and when we reach the age of 95, we might expect people to treat our opinions a little more leniently than before, nevertheless we can say that Jacinta Thomas's neighbour demonstrated a widely-held prejudice born out of ignorance about what teachers do and what effect they can be expected to have on their students. Her neighbour would have been unaware, too, of the discussions about the role of English in the modern world and the growing importance of World English (see Chapter 1, A3) which have taken place since she made her remark.

Nevertheless, what Adrian Holliday calls *native-speakerism* – which he describes as 'a pervasive ideology within ELT, characterized by the belief that "native speaker" teachers represent a "Western culture" from which springs the ideals both of the English language and English language teaching methodology' (2006: 385) – is still alive and well in some quarters, not least in the minds of some students, who seem to think that being taught by someone who has English as a mother tongue will somehow help them learn better.

But the world is changing, as we saw in Chapter 1, and English is no longer owned by anybody in particular, least of all the native speakers of the world who are in a minority which is becoming daily less significant – at least in numerical terms. It is clear, therefore, that any superiority that native speakers might once have had is rapidly becoming less sustainable. In the end, the value of a teacher depends not just on their ability to use a language, but also on their knowledge about that language and their understanding of how to facilitate both that ability and that knowledge in the minds of their students. This is not to suggest that there is anything intrinsically wrong with native-speaker teachers; on the contrary, good native-speaker teachers are worth their weight in gold. But then so are good non-native-speaker teachers, which is the whole point.

Non-native-speaker teachers have many advantages that their 'native' colleagues do not. In the first place, they have often had the same experience of learning English as their students are now having, and this gives them an instant (even if only subconscious) understanding of what their students are going through. Where they teach a group of students who speak their own native language, they are able to maximise the benefits of L1 and L2 use in the ways we will discuss in Chapter 7 (although many primary and secondary school classes around the world are becoming increasingly multilingual, especially in urban areas – see page 16). Non-native-speaker teachers are frequently considerably more familiar with local mores and learning styles than visiting native speakers are.

Native speakers, on the other hand, often have the advantage of a linguistic confidence about their language in the classroom which non-native-speaker teachers sometimes lack – indeed, it may be differences in linguistic confidence which account for some differences in teaching practices between the two groups, as Peter Medgyes suggested many years ago (Medgyes 1992).

In certain circumstances, a native-speaker teacher's inability to communicate effectively in the students' L1 (because they have only recently arrived in the country they are working in, for example) has a positive rather than a negative effect in much the same way as multilingual classes provoke inter-student communication in English. Native-speaker teachers are often – but not always – seen in a positive light by their students (which can have a good effect on motivation), and by their non-native colleagues. David Carless, for example, reporting on NET (Native English Teacher)/LET (Local English Teacher) peer teaching in Hong Kong primary schools suggests that there are 'a number of reasons why the primary school can be a positive site for NET/LET collaboration' (2006: 335).

As recently as ten years ago it would have been impossible to find a single non-native-speaker teacher working in a language school in, say, Britain or Australia. But that is no longer the case. Progress may be slow in this respect, but there are signs of such progress. In the end, provided teachers can use the language (and know about it), it is the quality of their teaching that counts, not where they come from or how they learnt or acquired English.

Chapter notes and further reading

- **Teacher's roles**
  An important book on teacher roles is T Wright (1987).

- **Teacher talking time**
  As long ago as 1985, T Lowe was discussing the value of teacher talking time as roughly-tuned input. On classroom language, see B Winn-Smith (2001). On the nature of teacher talk in more facilitative classrooms, see J Clifton (2006).

- **Native-speaker teachers and non-native-speaker teachers**
  Apart from the references in this chapter, see G Braine (ed) (1999), A and Y Tajino (2000), who talk about team teaching with native and non-native speakers in a Japanese context, A Davies (2003) and Y Park (2006), who asks whether non-natives will ever get a 'fair chance'. Icy Lee (2005a) discusses empowering non-native-speaker teachers. See also M Szwaj (1999) and J Suarez (2000).

7 | Describing learning contexts

A The place and means of instruction

We have already seen that English is studied for a number of reasons (Chapter 1, B4). People engaged in commerce – or who are hoping to work in a business environment – study business English. Students who are about go to university – or who are already there – study EAP (English for Academic Purposes), while others may study English for tourism, science and technology, medicine, etc.

- **Schools and language schools:** a huge number of students learn English in primary and secondary classrooms around the world. They have not chosen to do this themselves, but learn because English is on the curriculum. Depending on the country, area and the school itself, they may have the advantage of well-equipped rooms and the latest classroom equipment and information technology (IT), or they may, as in many parts of the world, be sitting in rows in classrooms with a blackboard and no other teaching aid.

  Private language schools, on the other hand, tend to be better equipped than some government schools (though this is not always the case). They will frequently have smaller class sizes and, crucially, the students in them may well have chosen to come and study.

- **In-school and in-company:** the vast majority of language classes in the world take place in educational institutions such as the schools and language schools we have already mentioned, and, in addition, colleges and universities. In such situations teachers have to be aware of school policy and conform to syllabus and curriculum decisions taken by whoever is responsible for the academic running of the school. There may well be learning outcomes which students are expected to achieve, and students may be preparing for specific exams.

  A number of companies also offer language classes and expect teachers to go to the company office or factory to teach. Here the 'classroom' may not be quite as appropriate as those which are specially designed for teaching and learning. But more importantly, the teacher may need to negotiate the class content, not only with the students but also with whoever is paying for the tuition.

- **Real and virtual learning environments:** language learning has traditionally involved a teacher and a student or students being in the same physical space. However, the development of high-speed Internet access has helped to bring about new virtual learning environments in which students can learn even when they are literally thousands of miles away (and in a different time zone) from a teacher or other classmates.

  Some of the issues for both real and virtual learning environments are the same. Students still need to be motivated (see pages 98–104) and we still need to offer help in that area. As a result, the best virtual learning sites have online tutors who interact with their students via email or online chat forums. It is also possible to create groups of students who are all following the same online programme, and who can, therefore, 'talk' to each other in the same way (i.e. electronically). But despite these interpersonal elements, some students find it more difficult to sustain their motivation online than they might as part of a real learning group.

Virtual learning is significantly different from face-to-face learning for a number of reasons. Firstly, for the most part, students can attend lessons when they want (though real-time chat forums have to be scheduled), rather than when lessons are timetabled (as in schools). Secondly, it no longer matters where the students are since they can log on from any location in the world.

Online learning may have these advantages, but some of the benefits of real learning environments are less easy to replicate electronically. These include the physical reality of having teachers and students around you when you are learning so that you can see their expressions and get messages from their gestures, tone of voice, etc. Many learners will prefer the presence of real people to the sight of a screen, with or without pictures and video. Of course, some communication software (such as MSN Messenger and Skype) allows users to see each other on the screen as they communicate, but this is still less attractive – and considerably more jerky – than being face to face with the teacher and fellow students. And, of course, whereas in real learning environments learning can take place with very little technical equipment, virtual learning relies on good hardware and software, and effective and reliable Internet connections.

B Class size

English language classes vary greatly in size. Some students opt for private lessons, so the teacher only has to deal with one student at a time. However, some teachers have classes of as many as 100 (and sometimes even more)! Everything depends on the particular education system that a teacher is working in. That is why, if you ask a teacher what a 'large class' is, they might answer 20, 40, 60 or 80 students.

The techniques we use will depend to some extent on how big our classes are. Whereas pairwork, for example, is extremely useful for larger groups (see Chapter 10, A4) if we want to maximise individual student talking time, it is perhaps less necessary in a group of, say, five students where everyone will have plenty of opportunities to speak during a lesson. Having students make mini-presentations is clearly less stressful for them in small groups than it is if they find themselves talking in front of 50 of their peers. Having 80 students milling around the classroom presents more extreme logistical problems than it does when there are 14 students in the room.

We will look at the two extremes of the class-size debate, one-to-one teaching and large classes.

B1 Teaching one-to-one

A special teaching context is that of an individual student working alone with a teacher over a period of hours or weeks in what are often referred to as 'private classes'. Such one-to-one teaching is extremely popular, especially for business students. But it is also ideal for students who cannot fit into normal school schedules or who are keen to have individual attention rather than being part of a group.

One-to-one lessons have considerable advantages over classes with two or more students in the group. In the first place, whereas in a group an individual student only gets a part of the teacher's attention, in a private lesson the teacher is focused exclusively on one person. In such circumstances, too, the student has opportunities to do all the student speaking, rather than only receiving a fraction of the total speaking time. Even more importantly than this, both teacher and student can tailor the course to exactly what is appropriate for that one student, rather than having to reach a compromise based on what is suitable for a group as a whole. This has enormous advantages not only for the designing of a programme of study (where the syllabus and content can be matched to a particular student's needs and interests), but also in terms of the student's learning style and what kind of stimulus (visual, audio, etc.) they respond to best (see Chapter 5, B4). One-to-one students get greatly enhanced feedback from their teachers.

It is also much easier to be flexible when teaching individual students than it is when managing a class. Changing an activity and moving on to something completely different presents less of a problem with one student than with 30. If appropriate, the teacher and the student can, on the spur of the moment, agree to leave the classroom (to do some language research, for example) and this does not cause the kind of organisational and logistical problems that moving a whole group around is likely to entail. Above all, one-to-one teaching allows teachers to enter into a genuinely dialogic relationship with their students in a way that is considerably less feasible in a large group situation.

Nevertheless, one-to-one teaching is not without its drawbacks. The intensity of the relationship makes the rapport (or lack of it) between teacher and student vitally important. Some teachers find individual students difficult to deal with – sometimes simply because they don't like them very much – and the same can be true of a student's feelings towards the teacher. Some private students are lacking in confidence or untalkative for other reasons. Some find the teacher's methodological style difficult to deal with because it is unfamiliar to them. Students and teachers can often become tired and sleepy in one-to-one sessions because the dynamic of a crowded classroom is missing. Some individual students can be very demanding and constantly expect more and more from their teacher. And some students seem to expect a private teacher to do all the work for them, forgetting that one-to-one learning demands just as much, if not more, from the student as it does from the teacher.

It is difficult to be prescriptive about one-to-one teaching, especially since so much will depend on exactly who the people involved are, but the following guidelines are almost always appropriate:

- **Make a good impression:** first impressions count with groups of any size, but are especially important when teaching one-to-one. With no group to help create an atmosphere, the way the student perceives the teacher at their first encounter is of vital importance. This is especially so since some one-to-one courses are of relatively short duration and there will be less time to change a student's misconception.

    A good impression is created by the way we present ourselves (in terms of our appearance) and how we behave during the first lesson.

- **Be well-prepared:** one of the most important ways of creating a good impression is to show the student that we are well-prepared and that we have given thought to what we are going to do in the lesson. This does not mean we are going to stick to exactly what we have planned, come what may; as with all lessons (but especially with one-to-one teaching), we must be alert to what happens and respond accordingly, perhaps moving right away from what we had intended to do. But if the student sees that we come well-prepared and with a range of possible activities which might suit them, this will greatly boost their confidence in us.

- **Be flexible:** one-to-one lessons provide enormous opportunities for flexibility for the reasons stated above. If a student is beginning to get tired, for example, it is not difficult to suggest a two-minute break involving getting up and walking around. If a planned topic is failing to arouse the student's interest (or the teacher's), it is relatively easy to switch to something else, or to ask the student whether they would like to approach the topic in another way. If language work is proving more or less difficult than anticipated, we will not find it impossible to change the pace, move forwards or go back to something we studied earlier.

- **Adapt to the student:** one of the great benefits of one-to-one lessons is that we can adapt what we do to suit a particular student's preferences and learning style. Robert E Jones, for example, had problems with a 60-year-old Japanese student who was convinced she could not learn. He was at his wits' end about how to help her make progress until, after a cycling trip with his wife, he published a little magazine with photographs of his travels around Hokkaido. Suddenly his student perked up. She was extremely interested in his trip, so interested in fact that she had read the mini-magazine, translating every single word (in defiance of orthodox wisdom), and she arrived for the next lesson happy, enthusiastic and without her usual confidence-sapping doubts. Jones (2001) referred to this as 'Machiko's breakthrough', but in a sense it was his own breakthrough because now he had found a key to open Machiko's learning door. He could adapt to her interests (she liked to hear about her teacher's life) and let her influence his methodology (however he might feel about going through texts in this way).

- **Listen and watch:** adapting to students can only take place if we are extremely observant about how individual students respond to different activities, styles and content. One-to-one teachers need to listen just as much as they talk – indeed the balance should always be in favour of listening. But we can also ask students to tell us how they are getting on, what they need more or less of, and what they would like. Our ability to be flexible means that getting such feedback (and observing our students) can help us to amend our plans to suit specific individuals.

- **Give explanations and guidelines:** when we first meet one-to-one students, it is important to explain what is going to happen, and how the student can contribute to the programme they are involved in. It is important to lay down guidelines about what they can expect the teacher to do and be, and what the teacher expects of them. It is especially important, at this stage, for students to know that they can influence what happens in the sessions by saying what they want and need more and less of.

- **Don't be afraid to say no:** one-to-one teachers should not be afraid to say no in two specific situations. Firstly, the personality match with a student is sometimes, unfortunately, completely unsuccessful. Normally we can get over this by being extremely professional, maintaining a distance between ourselves and the student, and letting the content of our lessons drive matters forward successfully. Sometimes, however, things just don't work. In such rare situations teachers should be prepared to terminate the classes (if they are working for themselves) or expect that the institution they work for will make alternative arrangements for themselves and the student.

Some one-to-one teachers feel extremely pressurised when their student appears to want more and more from them as if this will solve all their problems and teach them English effortlessly. We have to be able to tell a student when their demands are excessive and say that we cannot do everything they are asking for. Most students will understand this.

One-to-one teaching, just like teaching larger groups, has huge advantages and some disadvantages. By maximising the former, there is a good chance it can be rewarding for both teacher and student.

B2 Large classes

Many commentators talk about large classes as a problem, and it is certainly true that they present challenges that smaller classes do not. How, for example, can we give students personal attention? How can we get students interacting with each other? What can we do to make organisation smooth and effective?

However, there are also many benefits to teaching large classes. As Natalie Hess points out (Hess 2001: 2–4), in large classes there are always enough students to get interaction going, and there is a rich variety of human resources. Furthermore, there are many possible 'teachers' in the class, and, as she says, we will never get bored because the challenge is great!

There are a number of key elements in successful large-group teaching:

- **Be organised:** the bigger the group, the more we have to be organised and know what we are going to do before the lesson starts. It is much more difficult to change tack or respond to individual concerns with a large class than it is with a group of four or five students.

- **Establish routines:** the daily management of a large class will be greatly enhanced if we establish routines that we and our students recognise straight away. This will make jobs like taking the register, setting and collecting homework, getting into pairs and groups, etc. far easier. They will be done far more quickly and more efficiently if students know what is expected because they are routine operations. Part of our job at the start of a course, therefore, will be to establish good routines; this might take some time in the beginning, but will save time later on.

- **Use a different pace for different activities:** in a small class – or in one-to-one teaching – it is not difficult to vary the pace of what we do on the basis of how the students are reacting. Fairly early on in a course we will come to understand the strengths and weaknesses of individuals. However, this is far more difficult in large groups and, as a result, we will need to be more careful about how we organise different activities with them. If we ask students to say something in a large class, for example, we need to give them time to respond before charging ahead. If we are conducting drills, we may be able to work at quite a fast pace, but if we are asking students to think about something, we will want to slow the pace right down.

- **Maximise individual work:** the more we can give students individual work, even in a large class, the more we can mitigate the effects of always working with a large group 'as a whole'. Perhaps we can get students to use graded readers (see page 283) as part of their individual reading programme. We will show how this can be done in Chapter 17. When we get students to build their own portfolio of work (see page 340), we are asking them to work as individuals, too. We can get students to write individually – offering their own responses to what they read and hear. We can encourage students to make full use of a school library or self-access centre (see page 403). We can direct them to language learning websites, or we can get them to produce their own blogs (see page 193).

- **Use students:** we can give students a number of different responsibilities in the class. For example, we can appoint class monitors whose job it is to collect homework or hand out worksheets. Students can take the register (under our supervision) or organise their classmates into groups.

    We can ask some of our students to teach the others. This might mean asking individuals to be in charge of a group who are preparing arguments for a debate, for example, or who are going through a worksheet. It might mean telling individual students that it is their job to explain some language to their group.

    We need to choose our student 'leaders' with care, and we will then monitor their performance very carefully. However linguistically able a student is, we will not want to use them if they consistently offend their classmates, or if they panic when we ask them to perform a task. As far as possible, we will try to give all students some responsibility some of the time. Even where students are not doing extremely well at their language learning, there may be tasks they can do, such as handing out worksheets. This will not only be useful for us, but may give them some satisfaction, too, and this may affect their motivation very positively.

- **Use worksheets:** one solution is for teachers to hand out worksheets for many of the tasks which they would normally do with the whole class, if the class were smaller. When the feedback stage is reached, teachers can go through the worksheets with the whole group – and all the students will get the benefit.

- **Use pairwork and groupwork:** in large classes, pairwork and groupwork play an important part since they maximise student participation. Even where chairs and desks cannot be moved, there are ways of doing this: first rows turn to face second rows, third rows to face fourth rows, etc. In more technologically equipped rooms, students can work round computer screens.

    When using pairwork and groupwork with large groups, it is important to make instructions especially clear, to agree how to stop the activity (many teachers just raise their hands until students notice them and gradually quieten down) and to give good feedback.

- **Use chorus reaction:** since it becomes difficult to use a lot of individual repetition and controlled practice in a big group, it may be more appropriate to use students in chorus. The class can be divided into two halves – the front five rows and the back five rows, for example, or the left-hand and right-hand sides of the classroom. Each row/half can then speak a part in a dialogue, ask or answer a question or repeat sentences or words. This is especially useful at lower levels.

- **Take account of vision and acoustics:** big classes often (but not always) take place in big rooms. This has advantages if we want students to move around, but we also have to ensure that what we show or write can be seen and that what we say or play to the whole group (from an audio track or film clip) can be heard.

- **Use the size of the group to your advantage:** big groups have disadvantages, of course, but they also have one main advantage – they are bigger, so humour is funnier, drama is more dramatic and a good class feeling is warmer and more enveloping than it is in a small group. We should never shy away from the potential that lecturing, acting and joking offer in such a situation. We can organise activities which allow students to perform in this way, too.

No one chooses to have a large group: it makes the job of teaching even more challenging than it already is. However, some of the suggestions above will help to turn a potential disaster into some kind of a success.

C Managing mixed ability

Many teachers are extremely worried about the fact that they have students in their classes who are at different levels of proficiency. Indeed, mixed-ability classes are a major preoccupation for most of us because they appear to make planning – and the execution of plans in lessons – extremely difficult. Many teachers see mixed-ability classes as especially problematic. Yet in a real sense all classes have students with a mixture of different abilities and language levels. We know this to be true given what we said about multiple intelligences and differing primary perceived systems (what stimuli individual students respond best to – see page 90). And it is inconceivable that any two students will have exactly the same knowledge of English at any one time. Even if we were able to assemble a class of complete beginners, it would soon be clear that some were learning faster than others – or learning different things.

In private language schools and language institutes, we try to make this situation manageable by giving students placement tests (see page 379) so that they can be put into classes with people who are at roughly the same level as they are. Within other school environments, students are often streamed – that is re-grouped for language lessons according to their abilities. In other situations, however, such placement and streaming is not possible and so teachers are faced with individuals who have different language knowledge, different intelligences, different learning speeds, and different learning styles and preferences. There is particular concern for the needs not only of students who are having difficulty at the lower end of the scale, but also for 'gifted' children (Dinnocenti 1998). And even in placed and streamed groups, as we have suggested, we will still have a range of abilities in front of us.

The response to this situation is to view the teacher's role with a group in terms of *differentiation*. In a differentiated classroom there are a variety of learning options designed around students' different abilities and interests (Tomlinson 1995). We may, for example, give different students different tasks. Perhaps we could give them different things to read or listen to. We could respond to them differently, too, and group them according their different abilities. Of course, there are also times when we don't want to differentiate between individuals. For example, if we are giving students instructions or presenting new language, there are very good reasons for teaching the group as a whole (see page 161). Furthermore, in some situations (see C4 below) real differentiation is extremely difficult to achieve. Nevertheless, it is clearly desirable to respond to the needs of the individual even though they are part of a group.

C1 Working with different content

One way of working with students at different levels and with different needs is to provide them with different material, tailoring what we give them to their individual needs. Thus, for example, we might give student A a text from an English language newspaper about a certain topic. Student B might be directed to a website on the same topic but where the information is not so dense. Student C might look at a simplified reader on the topic, and we might provide Student D with a short text that we ourselves have written on the subject, written in such a way as to be comprehensible to them. In this way, all the students are working at their own individual levels.

One way of offering different content is to allow students to make choices about what material they are going to work with. For example, we can offer them a range of possible grammar or vocabulary exercises and they can choose which ones they want to do. If we wish them to read outside the class, we will encourage them to choose which books they want to read (in terms not only of topic, but also of level), since when they make their choice – rather than having books chosen for them – they are far more likely to read with enthusiasm (see Chapter 17, A1).

Giving students different content is an ideal way to differentiate between them. Nevertheless, it is extremely problematic in large classes as we shall see in C4 below. Not only does it involve considerably more teacher preparation time than non-differentiated content (because we will have to search out a range of different exercises and materials for different individuals), but giving feedback to students in class becomes a lot more complicated when we are responding to a number of different tasks than it is when we are giving feedback about one. However, content is only one area where we can differentiate between individuals.

C2 Different student actions

If we cannot (or do not want to) offer students different materials, we can, instead, get them to do different things in response to the content they are all looking at or listening to.

- **Give students different tasks:** we might ask all students to look at the same reading text, but make a difference in terms of the tasks we ask them to do in response to that text. Group A, for example, might have to interpret the information in the text by reproducing it in graphic form (say in charts and tables). Group B, on the other hand, might answer a series of open-ended questions. Group C – the group we perceive as having the greatest need of support – might be offered a series of multiple-choice questions (see page 382); their task is to pick the correct response from two or more alternatives because we think this will be easier for them than having to interpret all the information themselves.

- **Give students different roles:** within a task we can give students different roles. If students are doing a role-play, for example, in which a police officer is questioning a witness, we might give the student playing the police officer the questions they should ask, whereas the student playing the witness has to come up with their own way of expressing what they want to say. We will have done this because the student or students playing the police officer clearly need more guidance than the others. If students are preparing for a debate, we might give Group A a list of suggested arguments to prepare from whereas Group B (whom we think need less support) are told to come up with their own arguments.

- **Reward early finishers:** if all the students are doing the same tasks with the same content, some may well finish earlier than others. We need to be able to offer such students extension tasks to reward their efforts and challenge them further (see page 173). However, such tasks should be chosen with care, since asking them to do 'the regular work, plus' inevitably seems punitive to them (Tomlinson 1995: 1).

- **Encourage different student responses:** we can give students exactly the same materials and tasks, but expect (and accept) different student responses to them. Seth Lindstromberg discusses the use of *flexible tasks* (Lindstromberg 2004). These are tasks which make a virtue out of differences between students. For example, we ask students to write some true statements containing the words *in*, *tomorrow*, *my*, *hope*, *the moon* and *five*. Each sentence must contain one of these words, and the maximum number of sentences is 12. The more proficient students have a clear but high target to aim for, but everyone, including those who are not so able, have something purposeful to do. In response to a reading text, we can give students a number of tasks but know that not all of the students will complete all of them.

  Almost any time we ask students to respond creatively to a stimulus, we are allowing for differences in such a response. For example, we might ask students to complete a sentence such as *One of the things I would really like to do before I am 30 is ...*; their completions will depend to some extent on how language proficient they are. In a poetry activity we might ask them to describe someone as if they were a kind of weather. Some students might just write *You are sunshine*, whereas others might go one step further and write something like *You are sunshine after the rain*, and yet others whose language level is considerably higher might come up with *You are the gentle breeze of a dreamy summer afternoon*, which might not be great poetry, but it does suggest a degree of linguistic sophistication.

  Many activities are, by their very nature, flexible in the way that Seth Lindstromberg suggests. Such activities are extremely appropriate when considering students of mixed ability.

- **Identify student strengths (linguistic or non-linguistic):** one of the ways we can make a virtue of different student abilities is to include tasks which do not necessarily demand linguistic brilliance but instead allow students to show off other talents they have. Students who are good artists, for example, can lead the design of a poster or wall chart. A student with developed scientific intelligence may be asked to explain a scientific concept before students are asked read a science-based text. If students have special knowledge of contemporary music, we can ask them to select pieces to be played while groupwork takes place. These examples are ways of giving individual students a chance to be 'best' at something, even where they might be weaker, linguistically, than some of their colleagues.

C3 What the teacher does

Although there are many occasions when we work with the students in our lessons as one big group (see C4 below), there are others when we may want to put them in different (smaller) groups depending on their different abilities. But whether we are working with the whole class, with smaller groups or with individuals, we will treat different students differently.

- **Responding to students:** during lessons we frequently have to respond to students, giving them feedback about how they are doing (see Chapter 8), or acting as a resource or tutor (see page 110). In such circumstances we always try to tailor our response to the particular individual we are dealing with. Some students are more sensitive than others, and so we will correct them with more care than their more robust colleagues. Some students need to see things in order to be able to respond to them, whereas others respond better by having things explained to them orally.

  When students are working in pairs or groups and we are monitoring their progress (see page 172), we will react to them (or intervene) depending on how well they are getting on. Students who are experiencing difficulty may need us to help them clear up some problems; we might have to correct some language use, or help them to organise information logically, for example. If they are working on a webquest on the Internet (see page 191), we might have to show them which link to follow or what to do next. But we can also push the higher achieving groups to go further by asking them how they might say something more effectively, or suggesting an extension to what they are doing. This kind of flexible response is one of the main aspects of differentiation. However, we need to make sure that in spending time with particular groups we do not ignore or exclude others (see below).

- **Being inclusive:** a big danger for students in mixed-ability classes is that some of them may get left behind or may become disengaged with what is happening. If we spend a lot of time with the higher-level students in a class, the students who are less linguistically able may feel that they are being ignored and become demotivated as a result. If, on the other hand, we spend all our time with students who we think need our help more than others, the higher-level students may feel neglected and unchallenged. Such students can quickly lose interest in the class and develop an attitude which makes them difficult to work with.

  The skill of a mixed-ability teacher is to draw all of the students into the lesson. When setting a task with the whole group (perhaps by asking initial questions to build up a situation), teachers will want to start by working at a level that all of the students are comfortable with. She will ask questions that all the students can understand and relate to so that their interest is aroused and so that they all understand the goal they are aiming for. Once they are all involved with the topic or the task, she may allow for differentiation in any of the ways we have discussed above. But her initial task is to include and engage everyone – because students who *feel* they are excluded will soon start to behave as if they *are* excluded!

- **Flexible groupings:** we can group students flexibly for a number of tasks. Sometimes we might put them in different groups so that each group can do different tasks. We might group them so that different groups can read different texts, depending on the difficulty of the texts. At other times, however, we might put students at different levels in the same group because we believe that the weaker students will benefit from working with students at a higher linguistic level and because, at the same time, we believe the higher-level students will gain insights about the language, for example, by having to explain it to their colleagues.

In Chapter 10 we will discuss student groupings in detail since there are many issues to be taken into account when deciding when and how students should work in pairs, as a whole group or individually.

C4 Realistic mixed-ability teaching

In an ideal classroom we would have time and the opportunity to work with individuals-as-individuals all the time. However, this is extremely difficult in large classes, and especially problematic when teachers see, for example, up to nine different groups of students in any one week. Planning for significant differentiation in such a situation is a far more daunting prospect than building differentiation into lessons for a group we see all day every day (in a primary school, for example).

The degree to which we are able to differentiate between individuals depends on the physical situation in which their learning takes place. If we teach in overcrowded classrooms, it will be difficult to set up different corners in the room where different students can go to perform different tasks. On the other hand, if the school is equipped with a well-stocked self-access centre (see page 403) where students can go and work individually on a range of materials which are available there, then it will be much easier to build individual learning programmes into the curriculum. If different students can have access to different computers in a lesson, they can be doing different Internet-based tasks, but with only one computer this will be more difficult (yet even here, of course, we can have different students going to the computer at different times).

While we recognise the need for differentiation, we need to be realistic about how we can achieve it – and how much differentiation we can achieve. For example, it is much easier, logistically, to gauge our response to individuals based on their ability and who they are than it is to plan individual schemes of work for nine groups of 30 students each. Responding differently demands great sensitivity to our students, but it is physically possible, whereas handing out 25 different worksheets to different students or pairs of students presents us with greater problems. Perhaps it makes sense, therefore, to concentrate more on the kind of flexible tasks we have described above. When considering differentiation, therefore, we need to work out what is possible and what is not.

We need to remember, too, that there are times when we want to teach the class as a whole. This may be because we want to build or reinforce the group's identity or it may be because we believe that everyone in the group should learn the same thing or be offered the same information. As with so many other areas of learning and teaching, we do the best we can in the circumstances in which we find ourselves.

Finally, it is worth pointing out that learner training and the encouragement of learner autonomy (see Chapterr 23B) is the ultimate achievement of differentiation. If we can get individual students to take responsibility for their own learning, they are acting as autonomous individuals, and differentiation has thus been achieved. However, the need for such autonomy and the way that we promote it to and with our students raises many complex issues, as we shall see in Chapter 23.

D Monolingual, bilingual and multilingual

At a conference in Singapore, Peter Martin (2006) quoted an English language teacher from Brunei whom he had interviewed:

> I try not to [use Malay] but sometimes you have to. If we don't use Malay, they won't understand, especially some of the textbooks. The words are difficult. I don't like to use Malay if inspectors are here but I sometimes do. Otherwise they [the pupils] won't understand and they [the inspectors] might consider us as bad teachers.

In one short contribution this teacher encapsulates many of the issues that surround the use of the students' first language (L1) in an English-language (L2) classroom. Perhaps the most striking aspect of her contribution is the suggestion that the inspector would frown upon her use of the students' language in a lesson. Clearly, she would be doing something wrong.

The idea that the only language teachers and students can use in the foreign language classroom is the one they are learning came about because of the Direct Method (see page 63). And it came about, too, because teachers from English-speaking countries were travelling the world teaching people whose first language they themselves could not speak. Perhaps it was also the result of a methodology grounded – at least from countries such as Britain, the USA, Canada and Australia – in the problems and advantages of teaching classes where students had a mixture of first languages so that English became not only the focus of learning but also the medium of instruction. But for whatever reason, there is still a strong body of opinion which says that the classroom should be an English-only environment. However, this opinion is now seriously questioned by the majority of methodologists and, instead, a view of how and when to use the L1 in the classroom has become the main subject for debate. This is especially the case since the teacher above notes that if she doesn't 'use Malay, they won't understand'.

D1 Foreign-language students and their first language

There are some powerful arguments in favour of English-only classrooms. Chief of these is the idea that if English is the medium of communication in a classroom, then students will be provoked into more and more communication attempts, and in the process language learning may well 'take care of itself' (a view we questioned in Chapter 3, A3). Furthermore, as we have suggested, in classes where students have different first-language backgrounds, such a policy may be the only realistic option. Nevertheless some kind of a ban on the use of a person's L1 seems unfortunate for a number of reasons. In the first place, it seems highly probable that our identity is shaped to some extent by the language or languages we learn as children. This is the case when children are brought up monolingually, or more commonly bilingually, where they often have a *home* language and a *public* language. Any of these will help to shape their way of seeing and, of course, enable them to communicate in the world around them. And our natural inclination to communicate in our mother tongue is non-negotiable; it is just part of what makes us 'us', even if this is sometimes politically uncomfortable. Why else, after all, would dictators try to suppress the use of languages whose speakers they come into conflict with, as they have done countless times in history?

And so, whether we like it or not, students in our classrooms are going to be operating both in their first language and in the language they are studying. They may do this because we encourage it. They may use their L1 in the classroom to communicate with each other (whether we want them to or not – Harbord 1992), or they may be translating what they are learning in their heads. Indeed, this latter process is a natural part of any language learner's behaviour. We are bound to try to make sense of a new linguistic (and conceptual) world through a linguistic world we are already familiar with. This kind of code-switching between L1 and L2 is naturally developmental (Eldridge 1996: 310), and not some example of misguided behaviour.

Lastly, it is worth pointing out that irrespective of whether students grow up mono- or bilingually, the likelihood is that, especially in urban areas and on the Internet, they are likely to be operating in more than one language. That is the way the world is.

For all of these reasons it seems possible to make a strong case either for the careful and measured use of the students' first language or, at least, for an acknowledgement of the place of a first language in the learning of a second.

D2 The benefits of using the L1 in the L2 classroom

There are many occasions when using the students' L1 in the classroom has obvious advantages. For example, D Jabr Dajani (2002) suggests its use in planning, self-evaluation and learner training, where, if the teacher speaks the students' L1, these topics can be discussed fluently instead of in the halting English of a beginner or elementary student. Sheelagh Deller (2003) suggests that, among other things, it is useful for students to notice differences between their L1 and the target language, that when students use their L1 between themselves and with the teacher, it has a positive effect on group dynamics, and that it allows students to give ongoing feedback about the course and their experiences of learning much more fluently than they would if they were only using English. Daniel Linder (2002) suggests a number of translation activities for use in the general classroom. These include straight translation of short texts and a translation summary of a longer text. His recommendation is that these activities should be done in groups because a discussion of the issues they raise is likely to be more revealing with two or more people than when we just think about it ourselves. Boris Naimushin (2002), echoing our earlier comments about language use in the modern world, sees translation as the 'fifth skill' after reading, writing, speaking and listening.

There seem to be three strands operating here: in the first place, many commentators recognise the desirability of using the students' L1 when talking about learning. So, for example, if teachers want to discuss making a learning contract (see page 156) with their students, or to ask students what they want or need (a needs analysis), then they will get more from lower-level students if they do it in the students' L1 than if they try to struggle through with English. If we want to explain things, help students with learner training or discuss matters personally with students, then again, we will have more success at lower levels if we can use the students' L1.

Secondly, there is clearly a lot to be gained from a comparison between the L1 and the L2. Students will make these comparisons anyway, so we may as well help them do it more effectively. It will help them to understand certain classes of error (see page 137) if we are able to show them such differences. The kind of translation activities suggested above will also help in this respect, making a virtue out of the students' natural language-processing behaviour. Translation can also be a very good way of reviewing how well students have understood grammar and lexis at the end of a unit of study.

Finally, students (and their teachers) can use the L1 to keep the social atmosphere of the class in good repair. There is a case for saying that rapport is enhanced when teachers can exchange jokes with students or talk to them about aspects of their lives.

D3 The disadvantages of using the L1 in the L2 classroom

There are problems with an unquestioning use of the students' L1 in the L2 classroom, just as there were with the idea of a total ban on its appearance. The first, of course, is that as we have pointed out, the teacher may not always share the students' L1 – or at least the L1 of all the students in the classroom. This does not mean that students will no longer make comparisons between their L1 and English; as we have said, they will do this consciously or subconsciously anyway. Nor does it mean that the teacher is unable to ask students questions such as *Do you have an expression for this in your language? Is it literally the same? Can you translate it back into English?* This is extremely rich territory when discussing idioms or metaphorical usage. For example, colours have different metaphorical meanings and uses in different languages and cultures, and the variety of idiomatic ways of saying that something is obvious (*as plain as the nose on your face* in some varieties of British English) in different languages that have been reported to me (translated here into English) – *as straight as a wire* (Polish); *if it's a dog, it bites* (Cuban Spanish); *when you can see the village, you don't have to ask for directions* (Turkey); *there's an elephant in the field* (Burma-Myanmar) – is breathtaking. But we can encourage students to translate grammatical concepts and lexical items, too, and draw their attention to different writing conventions and genres (see Chapter 19). However, our interaction with the students' L1 is obviously limited when we do not, for whatever reason, share it.

A more serious objection to the use (especially the over-use) of the students' L1 is that it restricts the students' exposure to English. It is possible, for example, to make a good case for the use of their L1 when we give instructions, but this reduces their exposure to a type of English that is 'an ideal source of language for student acquisition' (Harbord 1992: 353). Indeed if, as we said in Chapter 6, D3, the teacher is a principal source of useful comprehensible input, then the more time we spend speaking English, the better.

Teachers can sometimes find themselves using the L1 more than they intended. When Linda Bawcom transcribed her lessons with two students in Spain, she found that the three of them were speaking Spanish 33 per cent of the time (2002: 50). While she speculated that this might have contributed to the good atmosphere and relaxed setting of the lessons, nevertheless she felt that there was just too much L1 being used and set out, with the students' agreement, to ration its occurrence more judiciously.

When visiting a secondary class in the Czech Republic, Simon Gill (2005) found that a particular teacher he observed only used English 5 per cent of the time, and I have encountered similar situations in classrooms in a number of countries. In such situations the students' exposure to the English language has been unnecessarily restricted; the balance has tipped too far.

There is one other situation in which the use of the L1 seems counter-productive and this is when we are encouraging students to use English in communicative speaking tasks, whose purpose, after all, is to give students chances to try out speaking in English. We may understand their natural inclination to communicate in the best way they can (i.e. in their L1), but it will not be useful for the purposes of the activity we have asked them to engage in.

D4 **Taking a stand**

In the light of the previous discussion, we need to come to some conclusions about how and when to use (or allow the use of) the students' L1 in the classroom. There are a number of points we can make:

- **Acknowledge the L1:** it makes no sense to deny the importance of the students' L1 in their L2 learning. Even where we do not share the students' language or languages, we can show our understanding of the learning process and discuss L1 and L2 issues with the class.

- **Use appropriate L1, L2 activities:** we can use sensible activities which maximise the benefits of using the students' L1. These may include translation exercises of the kind we have mentioned, or specific contrasts between the two languages in areas of grammar, vocabulary, pronunciation or discourse. We might also use the students' L1 to discuss learning matters such as the establishment of a code of conduct, or the best ways of keeping vocabulary notebooks or the giving of announcements. However, this will be done in the context of a largely English-use classroom.

- **Differentiate between levels:** while it may make sense to use the students' L1 for explanations and rapport-enhancement at lower levels, this becomes less appropriate as the students' English improves. The more they work in English, the better their English will get, and the better their English is, the less need we have of the L1 for reasons of rapport-enhancement or discussion and explanation of learning matters. However, we may still want to make comparisons between L1 and L2 and encourage the 'fifth skill' of translation.

- **Agree clear guidelines:** students need to know when mother-tongue use is productive and when it is not. While, for example, we may not worry about it when they are discussing answers to a reading comprehension in pairs, we will be less happy (as we have said) if they speak in the L1 for an oral communicative activity.

  We will discuss the issue of L1 use with our class either as the subject comes up or when establishing some kind of code of conduct (see page 156). We will ask the students for their opinions on L1 use and give our own guidelines, too, so that we can make some kind of a bargain (see page 77). Students will have then agreed about when L1 use is appropriate and when, on the contrary, it is counter-productive.

  We have seen how some teachers over-use the students' L1, often unintentionally. But if we agree clear guidelines with the class, then we should follow them ourselves if we want our students to adhere to them.

- **Use encouragement and persuasion:** teachers all over the world spend a lot of their time going round to students, especially during speaking activities, saying things like, *Please speak English!* or *Why not try to stop using Turkish/Arabic/Portuguese/Greek?* etc. and it often works, especially if students have discussed the issue of L1 use with the teacher previously.

  If such encouragement doesn't work, we can temporarily stop the activity and explain to students that since the activity is designed to give them practice in speaking English, it makes little sense if they do it in another language. This sometimes changes the atmosphere so that they go back to the activity with a new determination.

Chapter notes and further reading

- **Mixed ability**

  See C A Tomlinson (1999), J Tice (1999), B Bowler and S Parminter (2000) and S Ainslie and S Purcell (2001). J Harmer (2002) describes a dictogloss writing activity in a mixed-ability group. A Artusi (2002) shows how putting differentiated tasks up on the board can be helpful.

- **One-to-one teaching**

  See P Osborne (2005).

- **Dialogic teachers and students**

  Scott Thornbury argues for a dialogic relationship between teacher and student (Thornbury 2001b), a view discussed by Angeles Clemente (2001).

- **Using the L1/mother tongue**

  S Deller and M Rinvolucri (2002) have written a book of activities to take advantage of/ enhance the use of the mother tongue.

8 | Mistakes and feedback

In a widely-quoted study, Paul Black and Dylan Wiliam found that feedback on students' work probably has more effect on achievement than any other single factor (Black and Wiliam 1998). Such *formative assessment* (see page 379) is, they believe, 'at the heart of effective teaching' (1998: 2). They based this assumption on an extensive reading of the research evidence available to them. Richard Cullen agrees, showing how the teacher's 'follow-up moves' when a student has said something 'play a crucial part in clarifying and building on the ideas that the students express' (2002: 126). It is important, therefore, to make sure that the feedback we give is appropriate to the students concerned and to the activity they are involved in, and that we recognise feedback as a crucial part of the learning process.

A Students make mistakes

One of the things that puzzles many teachers is why students go on making the same mistakes even when those mistakes have been repeatedly pointed out to them. Yet not all mistakes are the same; sometimes they seem to be deeply ingrained, yet at other times students correct themselves with apparent ease.

In his book on mistakes and correction, Julian Edge suggested that we can divide mistakes into three broad categories: 'slips' (that is mistakes which students can correct themselves once the mistake has been pointed out to them), 'errors' (mistakes which they can't correct themselves – and which therefore need explanation) and 'attempts' (that is when a student tries to say something but does not yet know the correct way of saying it) (Edge 1989: Chapter 2). Of these, it is the category of 'error' that most concerns teachers, though the students' 'attempts' will tell us a lot about their current knowledge – and may well provide chances for opportunistic teaching.

It is widely accepted that there are two distinct sources for the errors which most, if not all, students display.

- **L1 'interference':** students who learn English as a second language already have a deep knowledge of at least one other language. Where that L1 and the variety of English they are learning come into contact with each other, there are often confusions which provoke errors in a learner's use of English. This can be at the level of sounds: Arabic, for example, does not have a phonemic distinction between /f/ and /v/, and Arabic speakers may well say *ferry* when they mean *very*. It can be at the level of grammar, where a student's first language has a subtly different system: French students often have trouble with the present perfect because there is a similar form in French but the same time concept is expressed slightly differently; Japanese students have problems with article usage because Japanese does not use the same system of reference, and so on. It may, finally, be at the level of word usage, where similar sounding words have slightly different meanings: *librería* in Spanish means *bookshop*, not *library*, *embarasada* means *pregnant*, not *embarrassed*.

- **Developmental errors:** for a long time now researchers in child language development have been aware of the phenomenon of 'over-generalisation'. This is best described as a situation where a child who starts by saying *Daddy went*, *they came*, etc. perfectly correctly suddenly starts saying *Daddy goed* and *they comed*. What seems to be happening is that the child starts to 'over-generalise' a new rule that has been (subconsciously) learnt, and, as a result, even makes mistakes with things that he or she seemed to have known before. Later, however, it all gets sorted out as the child begins to have a more sophisticated understanding, and he or she goes back to saying *went* and *came* while, at the same time, handling regular past tense endings.

  Foreign language students make the same kind of developmental errors as well. This accounts for mistakes like **She is more nicer than him* where the acquisition of *more* for comparatives is over-generalised and then mixed up with the rule that the student has learnt – that comparative adjectives are formed with an adjective + *-er*. Errors of this kind are part of a natural acquisition process.

  When second-language learners make this kind of error, therefore, they are demonstrating part of the natural process of language learning. Developmental errors are part of the students' *interlanguage*, that is the version of the language which a learner has at any one stage of development, and which is continually re-shaped as he or she aims towards full mastery. Especially when responding to errors, teachers should be seen as providing feedback and helping that re-shaping process, rather than telling students off because they are wrong.

B Assessing student performance

Assessing student performance can come from the teacher or from the students themselves.

B1 Teachers assessing students

Assessment of performance can be explicit when we say *That was really good*, or implicit when, during a language drill, for example, we pass on to the next student without making any comment or correction (there is always the danger, however, that the student may misconstrue our silence as something else).

Students are likely to receive teacher assessment in terms of praise or blame. Indeed, one of our roles is to encourage students by praising them for work that is well done. Praise is a vital component in a student's motivation and progress. George Petty sees it as an element of a two-part response to student work. He calls these two parts 'medals' and 'missions'. The medal is what we give students for doing something well, and the mission is the direction we give them to improve. We should 'try to give every student some reinforcement every lesson' (2004: 72) and avoid only rewarding conspicuous success. If, he suggests, we measure every student against what they are capable of doing – and not against the group as a whole – then we are in a position to give medals for small things, including participation in a task or evidence of thought or hard work, rather than reserving praise for big achievements only.

While it is true that students respond well to praise, over-complimenting them on their work – particularly where their own self-evaluation tells them they have not done well – may prove counter-productive. In the first place, over-praise may create 'praise junkies' (Kohn

2001), that is students who are so addicted to praise that they become attention seekers and their need for praise blinds them to what progress they are actually making. Secondly, students learn to discriminate between praise that is properly earned and medals (in Petty's formulation) that are given out carelessly. This is borne out in research by Caffyn (1984, discussed in Williams and Burden 1997: 134–136) in which secondary students demonstrated their need to understand the reasons for the teacher's approval or disapproval. Williams and Burden also point to the ineffectiveness of blame in the learning process.

What this suggests is that assessment has to be handled with subtlety. Indiscriminate praise or blame will have little positive effect – indeed it will be negatively received – but a combination of appropriate praise together with helpful suggestions about how to improve in the future will have a much greater chance of contributing to student improvement.

It is sometimes tempting to concentrate all our feedback on the language which students use, such as incorrect verb tenses, pronunciation or spelling, for example, and to ignore the content of what they are saying or writing. Yet this is a mistake, especially when we involve them in language production activities. Whenever we ask students to give opinions or write creatively, whenever we set up a role-play or involve students in putting together a school newspaper or in the writing of a report, it is important to give feedback on what the students say rather than just on how they say it.

Apart from tests and exams (which we will consider in Chapter 22), there are a number of ways in which we can assess our students' work:

- **Comments:** commenting on student performance happens at various stages both in and outside the class. Thus we may say *Good*, or nod approvingly, and these comments (or actions) are a clear sign of a positive assessment. When we wish to give a negative assessment, we might do so by indicating that something has gone wrong (see C2 below), or by saying things such as *That's not quite right*. But even here we should acknowledge the students' efforts first (the medal) before showing that something is wrong – and then suggesting future action (the mission).

  When responding to students' written work, the same praise–recommendation procedure is also appropriate, though here a lot will depend on what stage the students' writing is at. In other words, our responses to finished pieces of written work will be different from those we give to help students as they work with written drafts (see D1 below).

- **Marks and grades:** when students are graded on their work, they are always keen to know what grades they have achieved. Awarding a mark of 9/10 for a piece of writing or giving a B+ assessment for a speaking activity are clear indicators that students have done well.

  When students get good grades, their motivation is often positively affected – provided that the level of challenge for the task was appropriate (see page 101). Bad grades can be extremely disheartening. Nor is grading always easy and clear cut. If we want to give grades, therefore, we need to decide on what basis we are going to do this and we need to be able to describe this to the students (see Chapter 22, C2 on marking tests).

  When we grade a homework exercise (or a test item) which depends on multiple choice, sentence fill-ins or other controlled exercise types, it will be relatively easy for students to understand how and why they achieved the marks or grades which we have given them. But it is more difficult with more creative activities where we ask students to produce spoken or written language to perform a task. In such cases our awarding of grades will necessarily be somewhat more subjective (see Chapter 22C). It is possible that despite this our students will have enough confidence in us to accept our judgement, especially where it coincides with their own assessment of their work. But where this is not the case – or where they compare their mark or grade with other students and do not agree with what they find – it will be helpful if we can demonstrate clear criteria for the grading we have given, either offering some kind of marking scale (see page 381), or some other written or spoken explanation of the basis on which we have made our judgement.

Awarding letter grades is potentially awkward if people misunderstand what the letters mean. In some cultures success is only achieved if the grade is 'A', whereas for people in other education systems a 'B' indicates a good result. If, therefore, we wish to rely on grades like this, our students need to be absolutely clear about what such grades mean – especially if we wish to add plus and minus signs to them (e.g. C++ or A–).

Though grades are popular with students and teachers, some practitioners prefer not to award them because they find the difference between an A and a B difficult to quantify, or because they can't see the dividing line between a 'pass' and a 'distinction' clearly. Such teachers prefer to rely on comments to give feedback. They can give clear responses to the students in this way without running the risk of grading them erroneously or demotivating them unnecessarily.

If we do use marks and grades, however, we can give them after an oral activity, for a piece of homework or at the end of a period of time (a week or a semester).

- **Reports:** at the end of a term or year some teachers write reports on their students' performance, either for the student, the school or the parents of that student. Such reports should give a clear indication of how well the student has done in the recent past and a reasonable assessment of their future prospects.

  It is important when writing reports to achieve a judicious balance between positive and negative feedback, where this is possible. As with all feedback, students have a right (and a desire) to know not only what their weaknesses may be, but also what strengths they have been able to demonstrate.

  Reports of this kind may lead to future improvement and progress. The chances for this are greatly increased if they are taken together with the students' own assessment of their performance.

B2 Students assessing themselves

Although, as teachers, we are ideally placed to provide accurate assessments of student performance, students can also be extremely effective at monitoring and judging their own language production. They frequently have a very clear idea of how well they are doing or have done, and if we help them to develop this awareness, we may greatly enhance learning.

Student self-assessment is bound up with the whole matter of learner autonomy since if we can encourage them to reflect upon their own learning through learner training (Chapter 23, B1) or when on their own away from any classroom (see Chapter 23D), we are equipping them with a powerful tool for future development.

Involving students in assessment of themselves and their peers occurs when we ask a class *Do you think that's right?* after writing something we heard someone say up on the board, or asking the class the same question when one of their number gives a response. We can also ask them at the end of an activity how well they think they have got on – or tell them to add a written comment to a piece of written work they have completed, giving their own assessment of that work. We might ask them to give themselves marks or a grade and then see how this tallies with our own.

Self-assessment can be made more formal in a number of ways. For example, at the end of a coursebook unit we might ask students to check what they can now do, e.g. 'Now I know how to get my meaning across in conversation/use the past passive/interrupt politely in conversation', etc.

This kind of self evaluation is at the heart of the 'can do' statements from ALTE (Association of Language Testers in Europe) and the Common European Framework (CEF). Students – in many different languages – can measure themselves by saying what they can do in various skill areas. The ALTE statements for general overall ability (giving six levels from A1–C2), give students clear statements of ability against which to measure themselves:

LEVELS	Listening/Speaking	Reading	Writing
C2 Level 5	CAN advise on or talk about complex or sensitive issues, understanding colloquial references and dealing confidently with hostile questions.	CAN understand documents, correspondence and reports, including the finer points of complex texts.	CAN write letters on any subject and full notes of meetings or seminars with good expression and accuracy.
C1 Level 4	CAN contribute effectively to meetings and seminars within own area of work or keep up a casual conversation with a good degree of fluency, coping with abstract expressions.	CAN read quickly enough to cope with an academic course, to read the media for information or to understand non-standard correspondence.	CAN prepare/draft professional correspondence, take reasonably accurate notes in meetings or write an essay which shows an ability to communicate.
B2 Level 3	CAN follow or give a talk on a familiar topic or keep up a conversation on a fairly wide range of topics.	CAN scan texts for relevant information, and understand detailed instructions or advice.	CAN make notes while someone is talking or write a letter including non-standard requests.
B1 Level 2	CAN express opinions on abstract/cultural matters in a limited way or offer advice within a known area, and understand instructions or public announcements.	CAN understand routine information and articles, and the general meaning of non-routine information within a familiar area.	CAN write letters or make notes on familiar or predictable matters.
A2 Level 1	CAN express simple opinions or requirements in a familiar context.	CAN understand straightforward information within a known area, such as on products and signs and simple textbooks or reports on familiar matters.	CAN complete forms and write short simple letters or postcards related to personal information.
A1 ALTE break-through level	CAN understand basic instructions or take part in a basic factual conversation on a predictable topic.	CAN understand basic notices, instructions or information.	CAN complete basic forms, and write notes including times, dates and places.

FIGURE 1: Overall general ability ALTE levels at http://www.alte.org/can_do/general.php

141

A final way of formalising an assessment dialogue between teacher and student is through a record of achievement (ROA). Here, students are asked to write their own assessment of their successes and difficulties and say how they think they can proceed. The teacher then adds their own assessment of the students' progress (including grades), and replies to the points the student has made. A typical ROA form can be seen in Figure 2.

Student name: _____	Subject: _____
Student comment	
Signed: _____	Date: _____
Teacher comment	
Signed: _____	Date: _____
Grade(s)	

FIGURE 2: An ROA form

Such ROAs, unlike the more informal journal and letter writing which students and teachers can engage in, force both parties to think carefully about strengths and weaknesses and can help them decide on future courses of action. They are especially revealing for other people, such as parents, who might be interested in a student's progress.

Where students are involved in their own assessment, there is a good chance that their understanding of the feedback which their teacher gives them will be greatly enhanced as their own awareness of the learning process increases.

C Feedback during oral work

Though feedback – both assessment and correction – can be very helpful during oral work, teachers should not necessarily deal with all oral production in the same way. Decisions about how to react to performance will depend upon the stage of the lesson, the activity, the type of mistake made and the particular student who is making that mistake.

C1 Accuracy and fluency

A distinction is often made between *accuracy* and *fluency*. We need to decide whether a particular activity in the classroom is designed to expect the students' complete accuracy – as in the study of a piece of grammar, a pronunciation exercise or some vocabulary work, for example – or whether we are asking the students to use the language as fluently as possible. We need to make a clear difference between 'non-communicative' and 'communicative' activities (see page 70); whereas the former are generally intended to ensure correctness, the latter are designed to improve language fluency.

Most students want and expect us to give them feedback on their performance. For example, in one celebrated correspondence many years ago, a non-native-speaker teacher was upset when, on a teacher training course in the UK, her English trainers refused to correct any of her English because they thought it was inappropriate in a training situation. 'We find that there is practically no correcting at all,' the teacher wrote, 'and this comes to us as a big disappointment' (Lavezzo and Dunford 1993: 62). Her trainers were not guilty of neglect, however. There was a principle at stake: 'The immediate and constant correction of all errors is not necessarily an effective way of helping course participants improve their English,' the trainer replied on the same page of the journal.

This exchange of views exemplifies current attitudes to correction and some of the uncertainties around it. The received view has been that when students are involved in accuracy work, it is part of the teacher's function to point out and correct the mistakes the students are making. We might call this 'teacher intervention' – a stage where the teacher stops the activity to make the correction.

During communicative activities, however, it is generally felt that teachers should not interrupt students in mid-flow to point out a grammatical, lexical or pronunciation error, since to do so interrupts the communication and drags an activity back to the study of language form or precise meaning. Traditionally, according to one view of teaching and learning, speaking activities in the classroom, especially activities at the extreme communicative end of our continuum (see page 70), were thought to act as a 'switch' to help learners transfer 'learnt' language to the 'acquired' store (Ellis 1982) or a 'trigger', forcing students to think carefully about how best to express the meanings they wish to convey (Swain 1985: 249). This view remains at the heart of the 'focus on forms' view of language learning (see Chapter 3). Part of the value of such activities lies in the various attempts that students have to make to get their meanings across; processing language for communication is, in this view, the best way of processing language for acquisition. Teacher intervention in such circumstances can raise stress levels and stop the acquisition process in its tracks.

If that is the case, the methodologist Tony Lynch argues, then students have a lot to gain from coming up against communication problems. Provided that they have some of the words and phrases necessary to help them negotiate a way out of their communicative impasses, they will learn a lot from so doing. When teachers intervene, not only to correct but also to supply alternative modes of expression to help students, they remove that need to negotiate meaning, and thus they may deny students a learning opportunity. In such situations teacher intervention may sometimes be necessary, but it is nevertheless unfortunate – even when we are using 'gentle correction' (see page 145). In Tony Lynch's words, '... the best answer to the question of when to intervene in learner talk is: as late as possible' (Lynch 1997: 324).

Nothing in language teaching is quite that simple, of course. There are times during communicative activities when teachers may want to offer correction or suggest alternatives because the students' communication is at risk, or because this might be just the right moment to draw the students' attention to a problem. Furthermore, when students are asked for their opinions on this matter, they often have conflicting views. In a survey of all the students at a language school in south London, Philip Harmer found that whereas 38 per cent of the students liked the teacher to do correction work at the front of the class after the task had finished, 62 per cent liked being corrected at the moment of speaking (2005: 74). It is worth pointing out, too, that intensive correction can be just as inappropriately handled during accuracy work as during fluency work. It often depends on how it is done, and, just as importantly, who it is done to. Correction is a highly personal business and draws, more than many other classroom interactions, on the rapport between teacher and students. And as Philip Harmer's study suggests, different students have different preferences.

For all these reasons, we need to be extremely sensitive about the way we give feedback and the way we correct. This means, for example, not reacting to absolutely every mistake that a student makes if this will demotivate that particular student. It means judging just the right moment to correct, taking into account the preferences of the group and of individual students. In communicative or fluency activities, it means deciding if and when to intervene at all, and if we do, what is the best way to do it. Perhaps, too, if we have time, we should talk to our students about feedback and correction and explain to them what we intend to do, and when and why, and then invite their own comments so that we can make a bargain with them (see page 77) about this aspect of classroom experience.

C2 Feedback during accuracy work

As suggested above, correction is usually made up of two distinct stages. In the first, teachers show students that a mistake has been made, and in the second, if necessary, they help the students to do something about it. The first set of techniques we need to be aware of, then, is devoted to showing incorrectness. These techniques are only really beneficial for what we are assuming to be language 'slips' rather than embedded or systematic errors (due to the interlanguage stage the students has reached). When we show incorrectness, we are hoping that the students will be able to correct themselves once the problem has been pointed out. If they can't do this, however, we will need to move on to alternative techniques.

- **Showing incorrectness:** this can be done in a number of different ways:
  1 *Repeating*: here we can ask the student to repeat what they have said, perhaps by saying *Again?* which, coupled with intonation and expression, will indicate that something isn't clear.
  2 *Echoing*: this can be a precise way of pin-pointing an error. We repeat what the student has said, emphasising the part of the utterance that was wrong, e.g. *Flight 309 GO to Paris?* (said with a questioning intonation) or *She SAID me?* It is an extremely efficient way of showing incorrectness during accuracy work.
  3 *Statement and question*: we can, of course, simply say *Good try, but that's not quite right* or *Do people think that's correct?* to indicate that something hasn't quite worked.
  4 *Expression*: when we know our classes well, a simple facial expression or a gesture (for example, a wobbling hand) may be enough to indicate that something doesn't quite work. This needs to be done with care as the wrong expression or gesture can, in certain circumstances, appear to be mocking or cruel.
  5 *Hinting*: a quick way of helping students to activate rules they already know (but which they have temporarily 'mislaid') is to give a quiet hint. We might just say the word *tense* to make them think that perhaps they should have used the past simple rather than the present perfect. We could say *countable* to make them think about a concord mistake they have made, or *tell* to indicate they have chosen the wrong word. This kind of hinting depends upon the students and the teacher sharing *metalanguage* (linguistic terms) which, when whispered to students, will help them to correct themselves.

6 *Reformulation*: a correction technique which is widely used both for accuracy and fluency work is for the teacher to repeat back a corrected version of what the student has said, reformulating the sentence, but without making a big issue of it. For example:

STUDENT: *She said me I was late.*
TEACHER: *Oh, so she told you you were late, did she?*
STUDENT: *Oh yes, I mean she told me. So I was very unhappy and ...*

Such reformulation is just a quick reminder of how the language should sound. It does not put the student under pressure, but clearly points the way to future correctness. Its chief attribute – in contrast to the other techniques mentioned above – is its unobtrusiveness.

In all the procedures above, teachers hope that students are able to correct themselves once it has been indicated that something is wrong. However, where students do not know or understand what the problem is (and so cannot be expected to resolve it), the teacher will want to help the students to get it right.

• **Getting it right:** if students are unable to correct themselves or respond to reformulation, we need to focus on the correct version in more detail. We can say the correct version, emphasising the part where there is a problem (e.g. *Flight 309 GOES to Paris*) before saying the sentence normally (e.g. *Flight 309 goes to Paris*), or we can say the incorrect part correctly (e.g. *Not 'go'. Listen, 'goes'*). If necessary, we can explain the grammar (e.g. *We say I go, you go, we go, but for he, she or it, we say 'goes'. For example, 'He goes to Paris' or 'Flight 309 goes to Paris'*), or the lexical issue, (e.g. *We use 'juvenile crime' when we talk about crime committed by children; a 'childish crime' is an act that is silly because it's like the sort of thing a child would do*). We will then ask the student to repeat the utterance correctly.

We can also ask students to help or correct each other. This works well where there is a genuinely cooperative atmosphere; the idea of the group helping all of its members is a powerful concept. Nevertheless, it can go horribly wrong where the error-making individual feels belittled by the process, thinking that they are the only one who doesn't know the grammar or vocabulary. We need to be exceptionally sensitive here, only encouraging the technique where it does not undermine such students. As we have said above, it is worth asking students for their opinions about which techniques they personally feel comfortable with.

C3 Feedback during fluency work

The way in which we respond to students when they speak in a fluency activity will have a significant bearing not only on how well they perform at the time but also on how they behave in fluency activities in the future. We need to respond to the content, and not just to the language form; we need to be able to untangle problems which our students have encountered or are encountering, but we may well decide to do this after the event, not during it. Our tolerance of error in fluency sessions will be much greater than it is during more controlled sessions. Nevertheless, there are times when we may wish to intervene during fluency activities (especially in the light of students' preferences – see above), just as there are ways we can respond to our students once such activities are over.

• **Gentle correction:** if communication breaks down completely during a fluency activity, we may well have to intervene. If our students can't think of what to say, we may want to prompt them forwards. If this is just the right moment to point out a language feature, we may offer a form of correction. Provided we offer this help with tact and discretion, there is no reason why such interventions should not be helpful. But however we do it, our correction will be more 'gentle': in other words, we will not stop the whole activity and insist on everyone saying the item correctly before being allowed to continue with their discussion.

Gentle correction can be offered in a number of ways. We might simply reformulate what the student has said in the expectation that they will pick up our reformulation (see page 145), even though it hardly interrupts their speech, e.g.

STUDENT 1: *And when I go on holiday, I enjoy to ski in the winter and I like to surf in the summer. Yes, they are my favourites.*
TEACHER: *Yes, I enjoy skiing, too.*
STUDENT 1: *Ah, yes, I enjoy skiing.*
STUDENT 2: *I don't enjoy skiing. It's too cold. What I like is ...*

It is even possible that when students are making an attempt to say something they are not sure of, such reformulation or suggestion may help them to learn something new.

We can use a number of other techniques for showing incorrectness, too, such as echoing and expression, or even saying *I shouldn't say X, say Y*, etc. But because we do it gently, and because we do not move on to a 'getting it right' stage, our intervention is less disruptive than a more accuracy-based procedure would be.

However, we need to be careful of over-correction during a fluency stage. By constantly interrupting the flow of the activity, we may bring it to a standstill. What we have to judge, therefore, is whether a quick reformulation or a quick prompt may help the conversation move along without intruding too much or whether, on the contrary, it is not especially necessary and has the potential to get in the way of the conversation.

- **Recording mistakes:** we frequently act as observers, watching and listening to students so that we can give feedback afterwards. Such observation allows us to give good feedback to our students on how well they have performed, always remembering that we want to give positive as well as negative feedback.

  One of the problems of giving feedback after the event is that it is easy to forget what students have said. Most teachers, therefore, write down points they want to refer to later, and some like to use charts or other forms of categorisation to help them do this, as in Figure 3.

Grammar	Words and phrases	Pronunciation	Appropriacy

FIGURE 3: A chart for recording student mistakes

In each column we can note down things we heard, whether they were particularly good or incorrect or inappropriate. We might write down errors such as *according to my opinion in the words and phrases column, or *I haven't been yesterday* in the grammar column; we might record phoneme problems or stress issues in the pronunciation column and make a note of places where students disagreed too tentatively or bluntly in the appropriacy column.

We can also record students' language performance with audio or video recorders. In this situation the students might be asked to design their own charts like the one above so that when they listen or watch, they, too, will be writing down more and less successful language performance in categories which make remembering what they heard easier. Another alternative is to divide students into groups and have each group listen or watch for something different. For example, one group might focus on pronunciation, one group could listen for the use of appropriate or inappropriate phrases, while a third looks at the effect of the physical paralinguistic features that are used. If teachers want to involve students more – especially if they have been listening to an audiotape or watching a video – they can ask them to write up any mistakes they think they heard on the board. This can lead to a discussion in which the class votes on whether they think the mistakes really are mistakes.

Another possibility is for the teacher to transcribe parts of the recording for future study. However, this takes a lot of time!

- **After the event:** when we have recorded student performance, we will want to give feedback to the class. We can do this in a number of ways. We might want to give an assessment of an activity, saying how well we thought the students did in it, and getting the students to tell us what they found easiest or most difficult. We can put some of the mistakes we have recorded up on the board and ask students first if they can recognise the problem, and then whether they can put it right.

Alternatively, we can write both correct and incorrect words, phrases or sentences on the board and have the students decide which is which.

When we write examples of what we heard on the board, it is not generally a good idea to say who made the mistakes since this may expose students in front of their classmates. Indeed, we will probably want to concentrate most on those mistakes which were made by more than one person. These can then lead on to quick teaching and re-teaching sequences.

Another possibility is for teachers to write individual notes to students, recording mistakes they heard from those particular students with suggestions about where they might look for information about the language – in dictionaries, grammar books or on the Internet.

D Feedback on written work

The way we give feedback on writing will depend on the kind of writing task the students have undertaken, and the effect we wish to create. When students do workbook exercises based on controlled testing activities, we will mark their efforts right or wrong, possibly pencilling in the correct answer for them to study. However, when we give feedback on more creative or communicative writing (whether letters, reports, stories or poems), we will approach the task with circumspection and clearly demonstrate our interest in the content of the students' work. A lot will depend on whether we are intervening in the writing process (where students are composing various written drafts before producing a final version – see Chapter 19, B1), or whether we are marking a finished product. During the writing process we will be responding rather than correcting.

D1 Responding

When we respond, we say how the text appears to us and how successful we think it has been (we give a medal, in other words) before suggesting how it could be improved (the mission). Such responses are vital at various stages of the writing process cycle (see page 326). The comments we offer students need to appear helpful and not censorious. Sometimes they will be in the margin of the students' work or, on a computer, they can be written as viewable comments either by using an editing program or by writing in comments in a different colour. If we want to offer more extensive comments, we may need a separate piece of paper – or separate computer document. Consider this example in which the teacher is responding in the form of a letter to a student's first draft of a composition about New Year's Eve:

Dear Gabrielle,		

Dear Gabrielle,

I really enjoyed reading your draft. You have some good expressions, e.g.

... you look to the dark sky and it seems like a special party

Why don't you begin with that sentence? e.g.

I looked up at the dark sky and it seemed a special party. It was like an explosion everywhere. People were throwing fireworks into the sky, and everywhere there were lights.

Now at this point you can tell the reader what night it is:

It was New Year's Eve and everyone was celebrating.

Then you can explain what New Year's Eve means in Uruguay, how families and friends come together and how everyone has hopes for the future. You can end by coming back to the idea of fireworks.

You can organise your essay to have two times:

Past	*I looked up ...* *it seemed*	Introduction
General present	*Family celebrations in* *Uruguay are very* *important.* *People usually send* *greetings to each other...*	
Past	????	Conclusion

FIGURE 4: From *Process Writing* by R White and V Arndt (Pearson Education Ltd)

This type of feedback takes time, of course, but it can be more useful to the student than a draft covered in correction marks. It is designed specifically for situations in which the student will go back and review the draft before producing a new version.

When we respond to a final written product (an essay or a finished project), we can say what we liked, how we felt about the text and what we think the students might do next time if they are going to write something similar.

Another constructive way of responding to students' written work is to show alternative ways of writing through reformulation (see C2 above). Instead of providing the kind of comments in the example above, we might say, *I would express this paragraph slightly differently from you*, and then re-write it, keeping the original intention as far as possible, but avoiding any of the language or construction problems which the student's original contained. Such reformulation is extremely useful for students since by comparing their version with yours they discover a lot about the language. However, it has to be done sympathetically, since we might end up 'steamrollering' our own view of things, forcing the student to adopt a different voice from the one they wanted to use.

D2 Correcting

Many teachers use correction codes to indicate that students have made mistakes in their written work. These codes can be written into the body of the text itself or in the margin. This makes correction much neater and less threatening than random marks and comments. Different teachers use different symbols, but Figure 5 shows some of the more common ones.

Symbol	Meaning	Example error
S	A spelling error	*The asnwer is obvious*
WO	A mistake in word order	*I like very much it.*
G	A grammar mistake	*I am going to buy some furnitures.*
T	Wrong verb tense	*I have seen him yesterday.*
C	Concord mistake (e.g. the subject and verb agreement)	*People is angry.*
⋏	Something has been left out.	*He told ⋏ that he was sorry.*
WW	Wrong word	*I am interested on jazz music.*
{ }	Something is not necessary.	*He was not {too} strong enough.*
?M	The meaning is unclear.	*That is a very excited photograph.*
P	A punctuation mistake.	*Do you like london.*
F/I	Too formal or informal.	*Hi Mr Franklin, Thank you for your letter …*

FIGURE 5: Correction symbols

In order for students to benefit from the use of symbols such as these, they need to be trained in their use (see D3 below).

We can also correct by putting ticks against good points (or another appropriate symbol, such as, for example, a circle if the lessons are taking place in Japan) and underlining problems. We can write summarising comments at the end of a student's work saying what was appropriate and what needs correcting.

D3 Training students

If students are to benefit from our feedback on their writing, they need to know what we mean and what to do about it. This involves training them to understand the process.

We might start by writing incorrect sentences on the board, such as **I don't enjoy to watch TV*. Students come up to the board and underline the mistake in the sentence (e.g. *I don't enjoy to watch TV*). Activities like this get them used both to the idea of error-spotting and also to the convention of underlining. Later we can give them several sentences, some of which are correct and some of which are not. They have to decide which is which.

We can now introduce students to correction symbols. We can go through them one by one, showing examples of each category. Once we think students have grasped their meaning, we might get them to try using the symbols themselves. In the following example (Figure 6), the teacher has typed up some student work exactly as it was written by different members of a group. The story is on an overhead transparency. Students from a different group tried to use the correction symbols (see Figure 5) they had recently learnt about to correct the piece, with partial success:

Once upon a time, a beautif [Sp] princess lived in a castle by a river.

She was very clever.

She always read and studied.

However, she hasnt seen [T/ww] the gergous [Sp] nature around her, where she was living,

she had a stemother [Sp] that hate [T] her very much.

She had a lovely dog.

It was a very loyalty. Gr

One day, her stepmother bought a basket of red apples from the local market.

The stepmother putted [ww] poison in ⟨ apples.

Her dog saw what the [ww] stepmother do [T], so, when the stepmother gave the

apple to her, her dog jumped and ate the apple. Then, the ⟨ [P] dog died.

FIGURE 6: Students use correction symbols

The teacher then discussed the students' efforts with the class.

Once students have had a good chance to get to know how to use correction symbols, we can start to use them when looking at students' work.

D4 Involving students

So far we have discussed the teacher's feedback to students. But we can also encourage students to give feedback to each other. Such peer review has an extremely positive effect on group cohesion. It encourages students to monitor each other and, as a result, helps them to become better at self monitoring. James Muncie suggests a further advantage, namely that whereas students see teacher comment as coming from an expert, as a result of which they feel obliged to do what is suggested, even when we are only making suggestions, they are much more likely to be provoked into thinking about what they are writing if the feedback comes from one of their peers (Muncie 2000). Thus when responding to work during the drafting stage, peer feedback is potentially extremely beneficial. However, in order to make sure that the comment is focused, we might want to design a form such as the one suggested by Victoria Chan (2001) where students are given sentences to complete such as *My immediate reactions to your piece of writing are ..., I like the part ..., I'm not sure about ..., The specific language errors I have noticed are ...*, etc.

In her book on writing, Tricia Hedge suggests letting the students decide (with teacher guidance) what they think the most important things to look out for in a piece of writing are (Hedge 1988: 54). They can give their opinions about whether spelling is more important than handwriting, or whether originality of ideas should interest the feedback giver more than, say, grammatical correctness. They can be asked for their opinions on the best grading system, too. In consultation with the teacher, therefore, they can come up with their own feedback kit.

We can also encourage students to self monitor by getting them to write a checklist of things to look out for when they evaluate their own work during the drafting process (Harmer 2004: 121). The more we encourage them to be involved in giving feedback to each other, or to evaluate their own work successfully, the better they will be able to develop as successful writers.

D5 Finishing the feedback process

Except where students are taking achievement tests (see Chapter 22, A1), written feedback is designed not just to give an assessment of the students' work, but also to help and teach. We give feedback because we want to affect our students' language use in the future as well as comment upon its use in the past. This is the formative assessment we mentioned briefly at the beginning of this chapter. When we respond to first and second written drafts of a written assignment, therefore, we expect a new version to be produced which will show how the students have responded to our comments. In this way feedback is part of a learning process, and we will not have wasted our time. Our reason for using codes and symbols is the same: if students can identify the mistakes they have made, they are then in a position to correct them. The feedback process is only really finished once they have made these changes. And if students consult grammar books or dictionaries as a way of resolving some of the mistakes we have signalled for them, the feedback we have given has had a positive outcome.

If, on the contrary, when we return corrected work, the students put it straight into a file or lose it, then the time we spent responding or correcting has been completely wasted.

D6 Burning the midnight oil

'Why burn the midnight oil?' asks Icy Lee (2005b) in an article which discusses the stress of written feedback for students and teachers. For students, the sight of their work covered in corrections can cause great anxiety. For teachers, marking and correcting take up an enormous amount of time (Lee found that the 200 Hong Kong teachers she interviewed spent an average of 20–30 hours a week marking). Both teachers and students deserve a break from this drudgery.

Along with other commentators, Lee has a number of ways of varying the amount of marking and the way teachers do it. These include:

- **Selective marking:** we do not need to mark everything all the time. If we do, it takes a great deal of time and can be extremely demotivating. It is often far more effective to tell students that for their next piece of work we will be focusing specifically on spelling, or specifically on paragraph organisation, or on verb tenses, for example. We will have less to correct, the students will have fewer red marks to contend with, and while they preparing their work, students will give extra special attention to the area we have identified.

- **Different error codes:** there is no reason why students and teachers should always use the same error codes (see D2 above). At different levels and for different tasks we may want to make shorter lists of possible errors, or tailor what we are looking at for the class in question.

- **Don't mark all the papers:** teachers may decide only to mark some of the scripts they are given – as a sample of what the class has done as a whole. They can then use what they find there for post-task teaching with the whole class.

- **Involve the students:** teachers can correct some of the scripts and students can look at some of the others. As we saw in D4 above, peer correction has extremely beneficial results.

We are not, of course, suggesting abandoning teacher feedback. But we need to be able to think creatively about how it can best be done in the interests of both students and teachers.

Chapter notes and further reading

- **Analysing errors**
  On interlanguage and analysing errors, see H D Brown (2007: Chapter 9).

- **Teachers' attitudes to feedback and correction**
  In a fascinating teacher training activity, R Tanner (1992) shows how teachers do not necessarily enjoy the feedback methods which they use in class when they themselves are being corrected.

- **Using transcripts for self evaluation**
  Paul Mennim (2003) reports on a speaking 'process' approach to student presentations; students recorded their presentations, transcribed and corrected them, then gave a new transcription to the teacher who suggested changes. Only then did they give the presentation.

- **Correcting written work**
  See J Harmer (2004: Chapter 7). For alternative feedback ideas, see K Hyland (1990).

- **Written teacher feedback**
  In a small-scale study, Yoshihito Sugita (2006) found that imperative comments from teachers were far more effective on revisions than questions or statements, which suggests that students need training to understand what to do when teachers respond by asking questions and making suggestions.

- **Peer correction**
  K Hyland (2002: Chapter 6.2) reports on the beneficial results of peer-response training.

- **Online feedback**
  J Kannan and P Towndrow (2002) suggest that giving feedback online is somewhat problematical. Students make strong demands and teachers have to be careful not to spend more time than is reasonable.

9 | Managing for success

Classroom teachers do everything they can to make sure that their lessons are a success. However, sometimes things don't work as well as they had planned. There may be many reasons for this, but the one that many teachers find most difficult to deal with is when students fail to cooperate. This can disrupt the learning which should be taking place and sometimes, when individuals get significantly out of control, lessons have to stop while the teacher re-establishes order. Such moments of disruption can be unsettling, not just for teachers but also for students, especially since our aim, as classroom managers, is to promote student success, rather than to become involved in damage-limitation.

Problem behaviour from students can take many forms; Paul Wadden and Sean McGovern list disruptive talking, inaudible responses, sleeping in class, tardiness and poor attendance, failure to do homework, cheating in tests and unwillingness to speak in the target language (Wadden and McGovern 1991). Of course, their list may reflect the educational culture where they were teaching, rather than being universal. In other contexts we might add behaviours such as insolence to the teacher, insulting or bullying other students, damaging school property and refusing to accept sanctions or punishment. However, what is characterised as indiscipline '... depends on what counts as a well-ordered or disciplined classroom for the individual teacher' (Brown and McIntyre 1993: 44). Some teachers are more tolerant than others.

But whatever our own view of problem behaviour is, if we are to manage for success, we need to know why it occurs, how to prevent it and, in the last resort, what to do if it happens.

A Why problems occur

Rose Senior (2006: Chapter 5) points out that when students come to class they bring with them their own personalities and their learning expectations. Their behaviour will also be influenced by their current circumstances and by what happens in the lessons. There is always, as well, the possibility of interpersonal tensions between students and between students and their teacher.

Students' personalities are closely bound up with their levels of self-esteem – how they feel about themselves and what level of comfort and self-confidence they are experiencing. Self-esteem is influenced by a large number of factors. At the most basic level, it is very difficult to feel good about ourselves if we are not safe, or do not have food to eat or warmth or shelter. But once we have all those, we can still be both positively and negatively influenced by the people around us.

- **The family:** students' experiences in their families have a profound influence on their attitudes to learning and to authority. Sometimes indiscipline can be traced back to a difficult home situation. Sometimes home attitudes to English, to learning in general, or even to teachers themselves can pre-dispose students to behave problematically.

- **Learning expectations:** previous learning experiences of all kinds affect students' behaviour. Even at the level of 'the last teacher let me ...', students are influenced by what went before. Their expectations of the learning experience can be coloured by unpleasant memories of unhappy classroom experiences, and their behaviour can sometimes be the result of what they were previously allowed to get away with.

  Students' learning expectations are also powerfully affected by the learning culture they are operating in, where norms of thinking and behaviour may have become ingrained without anyone even questioning them. Zoltan Dörnyei and Tim Murphey discuss the 'norm of mediocrity' (2003: 36) in this context. This is the norm which says that being too good in lessons is not desirable or appropriate. And there are other norms, too, about how students should behave in lessons and about what they should think of teachers, etc. If these norms are not confronted (see page 155), problem behaviour is likely to be an ongoing reality.

- **Approval:** a student's self-esteem may result partly from the way the teacher behaves. Children seem to thrive on teacher approval (see page 82) and they are not alone. Most people who enjoy good rapport with their teacher are happy to get that teacher's approval. Where that approval is lacking, their incentive to behave well – that is to comply with the norms of the group – is often compromised.

  Students also look for approval from their peers. This is generally the case but is often most noticeable in teenagers, who may not be very impressed by learning success but are often amused or amazed by the humour or anarchic behaviour of their peers. Problem behaviour then becomes desirable rather than being a problem. Teachers will have to reverse that concept and try to find other ways that students can meet with approval.

  Despite the fact that students are often interested in their peers' antics, however, we need to remind ourselves constantly that if a class gets out of control, the people who lose out most – and who are most resentful of that loss of control – are the students.

- **What the teacher does:** a lot will depend on how we, as teachers, behave in class. In the first place, students are far more likely to be engaged with what is going on (and are therefore unlikely to be disruptive) if they have something interesting to do. If they do not – or if they see the teacher as unprepared and uncertain about what to do in their lessons – they are far more likely to lose interest. If they lose interest, their incentive to maintain their level of concentration is lessened, and if that happens, they are more likely to become disconnected with what is going on. That is when problem behaviour often manifests itself. As George Petty points out, 'Most of the discipline difficulties experienced by teachers in the classroom were created before the lesson started' (2004: 101). In other words, if teachers arrive at the classroom door without a clear idea of what they are going to do, the chances of things going wrong are greatly increased.

  The way that we react to inappropriate behaviour will have a profound influence on our students' subsequent behaviour. If they see us as decisive, effective and fair, they will be far less likely to be disruptive in the future, and the chances of their learning successfully are enhanced.

- **Success and failure:** as we saw in Chapter 5, success is a powerful agent for the sustaining of a student's motivation. If they achieve identifiable goals, our students are likely to remain engaged with what is going on. Part of a teacher's job is to make sure that students recognise their achievements, however small those achievements actually are (as we saw on page 138).

If students do not see any evidence of their own success but are presented constantly with failure (in tests, in classroom language use or in their teacher's attitude to their classroom behaviour), then their incentive to behave within the limits set by the teacher and the group is greatly reduced. Failure is a powerful engine for problem behaviour. Teachers need, therefore, to manage for student success.

- **External factors:** some external factors may affect students' behaviour, too. If they are tired, they will not be able to concentrate. If the classroom is too hot or too cold, this may result in students being too relaxed or too nervy. Discomfort then leads to disengagement. Noise from outside the classroom can impact badly upon students' concentration. Teachers at primary level, especially, notice significant behaviour changes in different weathers: a high wind, in particular, tends to make their children 'go wild'.

B Creating successful classrooms

Problem behaviour rarely occurs in successful language classrooms. When students are engaged, have a reasonable level of self-esteem and are experiencing success, there is no incentive for them to behave badly, disrupt lessons or create barriers between themselves and their teacher or their peers. We need, then, to examine how we can try to ensure that the classroom is a success-oriented environment.

B1 Behaviour norms

All groups – whether in education or anywhere else – have ways of behaving and quickly establish norms for this behaviour which delineate the ways things are done in the group. Eventually, of course, the norms of behaviour – if the group is big enough – can become full-blooded cultural norms that a whole society adheres to.

School and classroom groups have their own norms of behaviour, too. Some of these are stated explicitly by a school (e.g. the wearing of school uniforms in some countries, no running in the corridor, etc.). Some are laid down by the school and the teacher (students have to put their hands up if they want to ask a question; they must stand up when the teacher comes into the room; at the end of the lesson students must not pack their things away until the teacher tells them they may); some seem to spring up from within the group itself (or are the result of years of norms adhered to by previous groups which have been picked up by current groups – e.g. the norm of mediocrity).

If groups behave according to norms which have been laid down or picked up – or informally arrived at – then it makes sense for teachers to become personally involved in the creation of norms which the group will adhere to. One way of doing this, of course, is for the teacher to say what behaviour is or is not permissible (for example, turn off all mobile phones in class, no speaking while I am speaking, no eating or drinking in lessons). Whether or not the students agree with these rules, they are obliged to obey them. However, these rules (or norms of behaviour) will always be the teacher's rules rather than the students'. None of the members of the group (except for the teacher) have had any agency in their creation. They have no ownership of these norms, but are expected to acquiesce to them.

Schools, just like any other group-based entities, need norms of behaviour if they are to function efficiently. It is worth thinking, therefore, about how we can get the students' active agreement with such norms; for if we do so, they are far more likely to adhere to them rather than feel they have been coerced into obedience. There are three things we need to bear in mind in order to achieve this.

- **Norms need to be explicitly discussed:** it is not effective just to tell students to read a set of rules about what is considered to be normal and acceptable behaviour. We need to discuss the rules with a group, explaining what they mean and why they are there. We might give students a handout describing the kind of behaviour we expect from them. Perhaps we can have a poster or wall chart which lists the rules so that we can refer to it whenever necessary.

  If students understand what is expected of them and why it is expected of them, they are far more likely to conform to these behavioural norms than if they just seem arbitrary and capricious.

- **Norms can be jointly negotiated:** if we really want students to 'buy into' a set of rules or norms of behaviour, we will go further than just explaining them. We will actively negotiate what should go into our list with our students by creating a jointly agreed code of conduct. The code (a kind of contract between teacher and students) could include details about classroom behaviour (e.g. when someone is talking, they will be allowed to finish before they are interrupted), discuss how often homework is expected, or establish norms of learner autonomy.

  When a teacher and students have divergent views about what is acceptable and what is not, we should take the students' opinions into account and try to work with them. However, ultimately we will have to be firm about what we are prepared to accept.

  With low-level classes, teachers may need to hold the discussion in the students' first language. Where this is not possible – as in a multilingual class – we will need to show quickly and calmly, through example, what is expected and what is not acceptable.

  Some teachers adopt a formula where teacher and students produce a chart which says 'As your teacher/a learner I expect ...', 'As your teacher/a learner, I will ...'. These bind both teacher and learners to behaviours which will be mutually beneficial.

  When a code of conduct has been democratically arrived at (even when based on teacher direction) – with everyone having a say and coming to an agreement – it has considerable power. We can say to students that since they agreed to the code, they themselves have responsibility for maintaining it.

- **Norms need to be reviewed and revisited:** just because we have discussed a code of conduct at the beginning of a term or semester, it does not mean that our job is done. When students step outside the norms of behaviour, we need to be able to remind them of what we agreed on. This will be made much easier if there is a copy of the code (say on a poster or wallchart) which we can refer to.

  When the group starts behaving in ways that are not especially appropriate, we will discuss the situation with the group and get their agreement to come up with new norms to cover this new situation.

 How teachers can ensure successful behaviour

The way we work in lessons and the interaction we have with our students make a significant contribution to a group's success and, when things are going well, to successful learning.

We have already seen that the rapport we establish with our students is crucial to effective teaching and learning (see pages 113–115). Without good rapport, creating an appropriate group atmosphere and identity is extremely difficult. But there are other things, too, which we can do to ensure a positive class atmosphere.

- **Start as we mean to go on:** students will find it extremely difficult if we only begin to insist on certain behaviour when things go wrong. If, for example, we wish to start our lessons in a calm atmosphere, then we need to do that from the very first lesson by waiting for silence before we start the activities we have planned. If we have decided that we are in charge of who sits where, then we should exercise that decision-making from the very beginning rather than asking students to accept this halfway through the term.

- **Know what we are going to do:** students are far less likely to cause problems if we give them interesting things to do. They are far less likely to feel the urge to be disruptive if they understand that we have come to the lesson with clear ideas about what these things are, rather than making it up as we go along. This does not mean that we will always slavishly follow a plan (we will discuss planning in detail in Chapter 21), but it does suggest that a well-organised period of study and activity which has been thought about before the lesson has a far greater chance of success than a chaotic ill-thought-out (and ultimately frustrating) one.

- **Plan for engagement:** students who are interested and enthusiastic do not generally exhibit problem behaviour. When we plan our classes, therefore, we need to think how we can engage students in a reading or listening text before starting detailed work on it; we need to do our best to introduce topics that are relevant to our students' experience.

    Interest can be also be generated by a teacher's performance. There is no doubt that students can be engaged by the energy and enthusiasm of their teachers.

- **Prioritise success:** one of our most important tasks is to try to make our students successful. This does not mean making things easy all the time since that can provoke boredom or, at the very least, disengagement. But at the other end of the spectrum, if things are too difficult, students become demoralised. What we will try to aim for, instead, are tasks, activities and goals which challenge individual students but for which they can have a better-than-average chance of success. Getting the level of challenge right is a major factor in effective classrooms. Our use of praise (the medals and missions that we discussed on page 138) is also a way for us to show students how successful they are being.

- **Equality rules:** in any dealings with members of the group, the group has to see that we treat everyone in exactly the same way, irrespective of who they are. We should not show obvious favouritism or appear to hold a grudge against particular students. We need to treat events in the same way each time they occur, too, so that students know exactly what is likely to happen in certain circumstances. What this means is that any student who behaves in a certain way is treated exactly the same as another student who behaves similarly in the same circumstances.

- **Praise is better than blame:** a piece of research carried out four decades ago (and often cited) suggested that when students were told off for inappropriate behaviour, it had little effect. However, even 'difficult' students responded extremely positively when they were praised for appropriate behaviour (Madsen *et al* 1968). Praise works, in other words. Students are far more likely to avoid inappropriate behaviour if there is an obvious advantage (the teacher and the group's approval) in appropriate behaviour. However, as we saw on page 138, praise has to be offered in the right way and for good reasons if it is to be effective.

C Modifying problem behaviour

Despite all our best efforts to create successful learning environments, things sometimes get out of hand and students start behaving in inappropriate ways. The way we react in such situations will determine not only how serious the event becomes, but will also influence the attitude of the whole group in terms of their future adherence to the group norms which they have agreed. Punishing problem behaviour is not in itself an attractive action, but turning it into future success is.

When students behave disruptively or uncooperatively, our first task is to find out what the problem is. We can then see if we can agree a solution with the student who is exhibiting the offending behaviour so that we can set a target for them to aim at – one which will ensure the success we are striving for. There are many things to bear in mind if we wish to achieve these goals.

- **Act immediately:** it is vital to act immediately when there is a problem since the longer a type of behaviour is left unchecked, the more difficult it is to deal with. Indeed, unchecked behaviour may get steadily worse so that where it could have been deflected if it had been dealt with immediately, now it is almost impossible to deal with. Immediate action sometimes means no more than stopping talking, pausing and looking at the student in question (Brown and McIntyre 1993: 42). Sometimes, however, it may demand stronger action.

- **Keep calm:** in many students' eyes, teachers who have to shout to assert their authority appear to be losing control. Shouting by the teacher raises the overall level of noise in the classroom, too. We need to find some other way.

  The first thing to remember is that whatever we feel like, we should never appear to be flustered. Despite the fact that students sometimes appear to be attacking our personality and threatening everything we hold dear, we need to remember, in the words of a participant at a conference in Montreal Canada in 2005, that 'it's just a job'. Somehow we have to stand back from what is happening and rather than taking it personally, we need to act calmly and carefully.

  When we are trying to modify student behaviour, we need to look disruptive students in the eye, approach them, keep looking at them and speak in a measured tone. We can start by asking them questions to find out why they are behaving in the way they are. This will often be enough to defuse the situation. If more serious action is required, however, we will adopt some of the methods described below.

- **Focus on the behaviour not the student:** we should take care not to humiliate an uncooperative student. It's the behaviour that matters, not the student's character. Though it may sometimes be tempting to make aggressive or deprecatory remarks, or to compare the student adversely to other people, such reactions are almost certainly counter-productive: not only are they likely to foster hostility on the part of the student and/or damage their self-esteem, they may also be ineffective in managing the situation. Students can easily dismiss sarcasm as mere unpleasantness, but it is much more difficult to keep behaving in ways which the teacher is criticising sensibly and fairly.

- **Take things forward:** where a simple look or brief comment is not sufficient, we need to think carefully about how we respond. It is always better to be positive rather than negative. It is usually more effective for a teacher to say *Let's do this*, rather than *Don't do that*. Taking things forward is better than stopping them, in other words. Our objective will be to move on to the next stage of an activity or to get a new response rather than focusing on the old one. In extreme cases, we may decide to change the activity in order to take the steam out of the situation and allow students to re-focus. However, we should be careful not to base such decisions only on the inappropriate behaviour of one or two students.

  Other ways of going forward are to re-seat students, especially where two or more of them have encouraged one another. Once separated in an effective (but not humiliating) way, students often calm down and the problem behaviour dies away.

- **Talk in private:** it is appropriate to discuss a student's behaviour in private and talk about how to improve it. This is not always possible, of course, but disciplining a student in front of his or her classmates will not help that student's self-esteem at all. Ideally, we will try to deal with problem behaviour with the student after the class, or at least privately in a one-to-one situation, perhaps at the teacher's desk. If, however, we have to deal with the situation in front of the whole group, the more private we can keep it – by speaking quietly and approaching the student – the better.

  George Petty suggests a three-stage approach to such conversations when dealing with teenagers. He calls the stages a 'chat', a 'word' and a 'telling off' (Petty 2004: 117). In a 'chat', the teacher shows that he or she thinks the student is quite able and willing to solve the problem and that the student has the teacher's respect. When offering a 'word', the teacher is being firmer and is exerting pressure so that the students can solve their problem. But in a 'telling off', the teacher is quite clear that the behaviour is unacceptable and that it needs to change right now. And whether or not we agree with Petty's threefold division, we will all agree that we should try to deal with a problem – in the first instance – as lightly as possible before gradually becoming more serious or, finally, imposing some kind of sanction.

  One way in which we can attempt to change students' behaviour is by writing to them – a general letter to each member of the class expressing a problem and asking students to reply in confidence. In this way students have a chance to make contact with us without other people listening or having to face us directly. However, this kind of correspondence takes up a lot of time, and there are dangers of over-intimacy, too. Nevertheless, the use of letters may help to break the ice where teachers have found other ways of controlling misbehaviour to be unsuccessful.

  Dealing with indiscipline is often a matter of 'pastoral' care, helping students to recognise the problem behaviour and start to find a way towards changing it. This is far less likely to happen in class with everybody listening, than in private ongoing communication with the student outside the class.

- **Use clearly agreed sanctions:** we have already suggested that 'equality rules'. Quite apart from the need for fairness to all students, this means that students need to know what the penalties are for bad behaviour. They need to be aware that if X happens, Y will follow. There needs to be a gradual scale of action from a gentle reprimand (Petty's 'chat'– see above) to removal from a lesson and, finally, to exclusion from a school – though we will do everything we can to modify the student's behaviour so that this does not happen. Now, when X happens, the students know what to expect and they see it happening. This provides a sense of justice and a feeling of confidence in the system. What is less effective is either the teacher failing to impose a sanction that he or she has warned the group about (in which case it immediately loses its power for future occasions), or imposing a sanction far more serious than the one which the students expect (in which case they may lose respect at this arbitrary behaviour).

- **Use colleagues and the institution:** it is no shame to have disruptive students in our classroom. It happens to everyone. So when there's a problem, we should consult our colleagues, asking them for guidance. When the problem is threatening to get beyond our control (for example, a pattern of disruption which continues for a series of lessons), we would be well advised to talk to coordinators, directors of studies and/or principals. They should all have considerable experience of the kind of problems being faced and will be in a position to offer the benefit of their experience.

Whatever sector we work in (primary, secondary, tertiary, adult, state school or the private sector), we will all experience problem groups and encounter problem behaviour at some time in our teaching careers. More often than not, the problem is minor and can be easily dealt with, especially if we can refer to a previously established code of conduct, and if our responses to indiscipline are based on the principles and strategies we have outlined above. However, as we have suggested, it is far more attractive to try to avoid such problems occurring by managing for success.

Chapter notes and further reading

- **Code of conduct**
  C Kyriacou (1998: Chapter 8) calls the establishing a code of conduct 'pre-empting misbehaviour'. This pre-emption involves establishing 'clear rules and expectations regarding classroom behaviour'.

- **Self-esteem**
  Teacher approval is not just important for children. T Lowe (1987) quoted diaries from English teachers who became students of Chinese. In their Chinese classes they were very keen for approval from their teacher of Chinese.

- **Teacher authority**
  R Senior (2006: Chapter 4) discusses how teachers establish their authority through purposeful action and establishment of good teacher–student rapport (see pages 113–115 of this book).

- **Writing to students**
  On letter communication with students, see M Rinvolucri (1983, 1995). N Burbidge *et al* (1996) have a range of letter-writing activities for students, many of which involve letters to and from the teacher.

10 | Grouping students

A Different groups

There is no real limit to the way in which teachers can group students in a classroom, though certain factors, such as over-crowding, fixed furniture and entrenched student attitudes, may make things problematic. Nevertheless, teaching a class as a whole, getting students to work on their own, or having them perform tasks in pairs or groups all have their own advantages and disadvantages; each is more or less appropriate for different activities.

A1 Whole-class teaching

When people think of teaching and learning, they frequently conjure up a picture of students sitting in rows listening to a teacher who stands in front of them. For many, this is what teaching means, and it is still the most common teacher–student interaction in many cultures. Though it has many limitations, whole-class grouping like this has both practical advantages and disadvantages.

- **Advantages of whole-class grouping:**
  - It reinforces a sense of belonging among the group members, something which we as teachers need to foster (Williams and Burden 1997: 79). If everyone is involved in the same activity, then we are all 'in it together', and such experiences give us points of common reference to talk about and use as reasons to bond with each other. It is much easier for students to share an emotion such as happiness or amusement in a whole-class setting. Twenty people laughing is often more enjoyable than just two; 40 people holding their breath in anticipation create a much more engaging atmosphere than just the person sitting next to you. In other words, if language learning is a collective endeavour, then 'learning takes place most effectively when language classes pull together as unified groups' (Senior 2002: 402).
  - It is suitable for activities where the teacher is acting as a *controller* (see Chapter 6, B1). It is especially good for giving explanations and instructions, where smaller groups would mean having to do these things more than once. It is ideal for presenting material, whether in pictures, texts or on audio or video tape. It is also more cost-efficient, both in terms of material production and organisation, than other groupings can be.
  - It allows teachers to 'gauge the mood' of the class in general (rather than on an individual basis); it is a good way for us to get a general understanding of student progress.
  - It is the preferred class style in many educational settings where students and teachers feel secure when the whole class is working in lockstep and under the direct authority of the teacher.

- **Disadvantages of whole-class grouping:**

  - It favours the group rather than the individual. Everyone is forced to do the same thing at the same time and at the same pace.

  - Individual students do not have much of a chance to say anything on their own.

  - Many students are disinclined to participate in front of the whole class since to do so brings with it the risk of public failure.

  - It may not encourage students to take responsibility for their own learning (see Chapter 23). Whole-class teaching favours the transmission of knowledge from teacher to student rather than having students discover things or research things for themselves.

  - It is not the best way to organise communicative language teaching (see Chapter 4, A5) or specifically task-based sequences (see Chapter 4, A6). Communication between individuals is more difficult in a group of 20 or 30 than it is in groups of four or five. In smaller groups it is easier to share material, speak quietly and less formally, and make good eye contact. All of these contribute to successful task resolution.

A2 Seating whole-group classes

There are many different ways of seating classes when they are working as a whole group. One of the most common is to have students seated in *orderly rows* (see Figure 1).

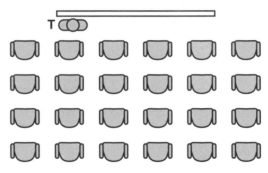

FIGURE 1: Orderly rows

There are considerable advantages to orderly row seating. The teacher has a clear view of all the students and the students can all see the teacher. Lecturing is easier with such a seating arrangement since it enables the teacher to maintain eye contact with the people he or she is talking to.

Orderly rows allow the teacher to work with the whole class. Some activities are especially suited to this kind of organisation, such as explaining a grammar point, watching a video/ DVD or a PowerPoint (or other computer-based) presentation, or using the board or an overhead projector. It is also useful when students are involved in certain kinds of language practice. If all the students are focused on a task at the same time, the whole class gets the same messages. It is often easier to create a good whole-class dynamic when students are sitting as one group – rather than many – in orderly rows.

Two other common seating arrangements are *circle* and *horseshoe* (see Figure 2). These are especially appropriate for smaller groups (i.e. fewer than 20 students). In a horseshoe, the teacher will probably be at the open end of the arrangement since that may well be where the board, overhead projector and/or computer are situated. In a circle, the teacher's position – where the board is situated – is less dominating.

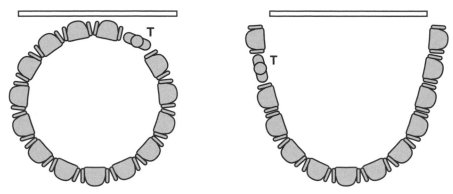

FIGURE 2: Circle and horseshoe

Classes which are arranged in a circle make quite a strong statement about what the teacher and the students believe in. With all the people in the room sitting in a circle, there is a far greater feeling of equality than when the teacher stays out at the front. This may not be quite so true of the horseshoe shape, where the teacher is often located in a commanding position, but, even here, the rigidity that comes with orderly rows, for example, is lessened.

With horseshoe and circle seating, the classroom is a more intimate place and the potential for students to share feelings and information through talking, eye contact or expressive body movements (eyebrow-raising, shoulder-shrugging, etc.) is far greater than when they are sitting in rows, one behind the other.

In some classrooms students sit in groups at *separate tables* (see Figure 3), whether they are working as a whole class, in groups or in pairs. In such classrooms, you might see the teacher walking around checking the students' work and helping out if they are having difficulties – prompting the students at this table, or explaining something to the students at that table in the corner.

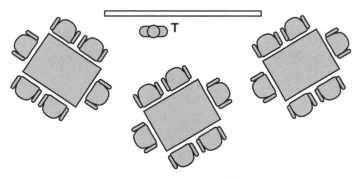

FIGURE 3: Separate tables

A huge advantage of separate tables is that groupwork is easy to arrange. Indeed, such an arrangement means that groupwork is likely to be far more common than with other kinds of seating. Separate table seating is especially useful in mixed-ability classes (see Chapter 7C), where different groups of students can benefit from concentrating on different tasks (designed for different ability levels).

Separate tables are more difficult to 'teach to' in whole-group activities, depending, of course, on the size of the room and the group. It is also important to bear in mind that students may not want to be stuck with the same three or four students for ever. Nevertheless, when students are working together, such a seating arrangement is ideal.

There are other ways of seating students, of course. Jim Scrivener, for example, suggests groupings such as 'enemy corners' (where two groups get into opposite corners of the room), opposing teams, and face-to-face (or back-to-back), where students sit in rows to make pairs (Scrivener 2005: 89).

The point of all these different sitting (and standing) arangements is that we should choose the best one for the students and, especially, the task. Insofar as we can make a general statement about it, it is worth pointing out that, where possible, varying the seating arrangements will make our lessons more dynamic and enjoyable.

A3 Students on their own

At the opposite end of the spectrum from whole-class grouping is the idea of students on their own, working in a pattern of *individualised learning*. This can range from students doing exercises on their own in class, to situations in which teachers are able to spend time working with individual students, or when students take charge of their own learning in self-access centres or other out-of-class environments (see Chapter 23C). Such individualised learning is a vital step in the development of learner autonomy.

If we wish students to work on their own in class, we can, for example, allow them to read privately and then answer questions individually; we can ask them to complete worksheets or writing tasks by themselves. We can give them worksheets with several different tasks and allow individuals to make their own decisions about which tasks to do. We can hand out different worksheets to different individuals, depending upon their tastes and abilities. We can allow students to research on their own or even choose what they want to read or listen to – especially where this concerns extensive reading (or 'learner literature' – see Chapter 17, A1).

- **Advantages of individualised learning:**
    - It allows teachers to respond to individual student differences in terms of pace of learning, learning styles and preferences (see Chapter 5B).
    - It is likely to be less stressful for students than performing in a whole-class setting or talking in pairs or groups.
    - It can develop learner autonomy and promote skills of self-reliance and investigation over teacher-dependence.
    - It can be a way of restoring peace and tranquillity to a noisy and chaotic classroom.

- **Disadvantages of individualised learning:**
    - It does not help a class develop a sense of belonging. It does not encourage cooperation in which students may be able to help and motivate each other.
    - When combined with giving individual students different tasks, it means a great deal more thought and materials preparation than whole-class teaching involves. When we work with individual students as a tutor or resource (see Chapter 6, B1), it takes much more time than interacting with the whole class.

Pairwork

In pairwork, students can practise language together, study a text, research language or take part in information-gap activities (see Example 7 in Chapter 17, B1). They can write dialogues, predict the content of reading texts or compare notes on what they have listened to or seen.

- **Advantages of pairwork:**
  - It dramatically increases the amount of speaking time any one student gets in the class.
  - It allows students to work and interact independently without the necessary guidance of the teacher, thus promoting learner independence.
  - It allows teachers time to work with one or two pairs while the other students continue working.
  - It recognises the old maxim that 'two heads are better than one', and in promoting cooperation, helps the classroom to become a more relaxed and friendly place. If we get students to make decisions in pairs (such as deciding on the correct answers to questions about a reading text), we allow them to share responsibility, rather than having to bear the whole weight themselves.
  - It is relatively quick and easy to organise.

- **Disadvantages of pairwork:**
  - Pairwork is frequently very noisy and some teachers and students dislike this. Teachers in particular worry that they will lose control of their class.
  - Students in pairs can often veer away from the point of an exercise, talking about something else completely, often in their first language (see Chapter 7D). The chances of misbehaviour are greater with pairwork than in a whole-class setting.
  - It is not always popular with students, many of whom feel they would rather relate to the teacher as individuals than interact with another learner who may be just as linguistically weak as they are.
  - the actual choice of paired partner can be problematic (see B2 below), especially if students frequently find themselves working with someone they are not keen on.

 ## Groupwork

We can put students in larger groups, too, since this will allow them to do a range of tasks for which pairwork is not sufficient or appropriate. Thus students can write a group story (see Chapter 19C, Example 7) or role-play a situation which involves five people. They can prepare a presentation or discuss an issue and come to a group decision. They can watch, write or perform a video sequence (see Chapter 20E); we can give individual students in a group different lines from a poem which the group has to reassemble (see page 297).

In general, it is possible to say that small groups of around five students provoke greater involvement and participation than larger groups. They are small enough for real interpersonal interaction, yet not so small that members are over-reliant upon each individual. Because five is an odd number it means that a majority view can usually prevail. However, there are occasions when larger groups are necessary. The activity may demand it (see the poem activity mentioned above, where the number of students in a group depends on the number of lines in the poem), or we may want to divide the class into teams for some game or preparation phase.

- **Advantages of groupwork:**

  - Like pairwork, it dramatically increases the number of talking opportunities for individual students.

  - Unlike pairwork, because there are more than two people in the group, personal relationships are usually less problematic; there is also a greater chance of different opinions and varied contributions than in pairwork.

  - It encourages broader skills of cooperation and negotiation than pairwork, and yet is more private than work in front of the whole class. Lynne Flowerdew (1998) found that it was especially appropriate in Hong Kong, where its use accorded with the Confucian principles which her Cantonese-speaking students were comfortable with. Furthermore, her students were prepared to evaluate each other's performance both positively and negatively where in a bigger group a natural tendency for self-effacement made this less likely.

  - It promotes learner autonomy by allowing students to make their own decisions in the group without being told what to do by the teacher.

  - Although we do not wish any individuals in groups to be completely passive, nevertheless some students can choose their level of participation more readily than in a whole-class or pairwork situation.

- **Disadvantages of groupwork:**

  - It is likely to be noisy (though not necessarily as loud as pairwork can be). Some teachers feel that they lose control, and the whole-class feeling which has been painstakingly built up may dissipate when the class is split into smaller entities.

  - Not all students enjoy it since they would prefer to be the focus of the teacher's attention rather than working with their peers. Sometimes students find themselves in uncongenial groups and wish they could be somewhere else.

  - Individuals may fall into group roles that become fossilised, so that some are passive whereas others may dominate.

  - Groups can take longer to organise than pairs; beginning and ending groupwork activities, especially where people move around the class, can take time and be chaotic.

A6 Ringing the changes

Deciding when to put students in groups or pairs, when to teach the whole class or when to let individuals get on with it on their own will depend upon a number of factors:

- **The task:** if we want to give students a quick chance to think about an issue which we will be focusing on later, we may put them in buzz groups where they have a chance to discuss or 'buzz' the topic among themselves before working with it in a whole-class grouping. However, small groups will be inappropriate for many explanations and demonstrations, where working with the class as one group will be more suitable.

When students have listened to a recording to complete a task or answer questions, we may let them compare their answers in quickly-organised pairs. If we want our students to practise an oral dialogue quickly, pairwork may be the best grouping, too.

If the task we wish our students to be involved in necessitates oral interaction, we will probably put students in groups, especially in a large class, so that they all have a chance to make a contribution. If we want students to write sentences which demonstrate their understanding of new vocabulary, on the other hand, we may choose to have them do it individually.

Although many tasks suggest obvious student groupings, we can usually adapt them for use with other groupings. Dialogue practice can be done in pairs, but it can also be organised with two halves of the whole class. Similarly, answering questions about a listening extract can be an individual activity or we can get students to discuss the answers in pairs. We can also have a 'jigsaw listening', where different students listen to different parts of a text so that they can then reassemble the whole text in groups.

- **Variety in a sequence:** a lot depends on how the activity fits into the lesson sequences we have been following and are likely to follow next (see Chapter 21). If much of our recent teaching has involved whole-class grouping, there may be a pressing need for pairwork or groupwork. If much of our recent work has been boisterous and active, based on interaction between various pairs and groups, we may think it sensible to allow students time to work individually to give them some breathing space. The advantage of having different student groupings is that they help to provide variety, thus sustaining motivation.

- **The mood:** crucial to our decision about what groupings to use is the mood of our students. Changing the grouping of a class can be a good way to change its mood when required. If students are becoming restless with a whole-class activity – and if they appear to have little to say or contribute in such a setting – we can put them in groups to give them a chance to re-engage with the lesson. If, on the other hand, groups appear to be losing their way or not working constructively, we can call the whole class back together and re-define the task, discuss problems that different groups have encountered or change the activity.

B Organising pairwork and groupwork

Sometimes we may have to persuade reluctant students that pairwork and groupwork are worth doing. They are more likely to believe this if pair and group activities are seen to be a success. Ensuring that pair and group activities work well will be easier if we have a clear idea about how to resolve any problems that might occur.

B1 Making it work

Because some students are unused to working in pairs and groups, or because they may have mixed feelings about working with a partner or about not having the teacher's attention at all times, it may be necessary to invest some time in discussion of learning routines. Just as we may want to create a joint code of conduct (see Chapter 9, B1), so we can come to an agreement about when and how to use different student groupings.

One way to discuss pairwork or groupwork is to do a group activity with students and then, when it is over, ask them to write or say how they felt about it (either in English or their own language). Alternatively, we can initiate a discussion about different groupings as a prelude to the use of groupwork and pairwork. This could be done by having students complete sentences such as:

> I like/don't like working on my own because ....
> ....
> I like/don't like working in pairs because..
> ....
> I like/don't like speaking in front of the whole class because ....
> ....

They can then compare their sentences with other students to see if everyone agrees. We can also ask them to list their favourite activities and compare these lists with their classmates.

When we know how our students feel about pairwork and groupwork, we can then decide, as with all action research (see Chapter 24B), what changes of method, if any, we need to make.

We might decide that we need to spend more time explaining what we are doing; we might concentrate on choosing better tasks, or we might even, in extreme cases, decide to use pairwork and groupwork less often if our students object strongly to them. However, even where students show a marked initial reluctance to working in groups, we might hope, through organising a successful demonstration activity and/or discussion, to strike the kind of bargain we discussed in Chapter 4, B2.

B2 Creating pairs and groups

Once we have decided to have students working in pairs or groups, we need to consider how we are going to put them into those pairs and groups – that is, who is going to work with whom. We can base such decisions on any one of the following principles:

- **Friendship:** a key consideration when putting students in pairs or groups is to make sure that we put friends with friends, rather than risking the possibility of people working with others whom they find difficult or unpleasant. Through observation, therefore, we can see which students get on with which of their classmates and make use of this observation later. The problem, of course, is that our observations may not always be accurate, and friendships can change over time.

  Perhaps, then, we should leave it to the students, and ask them to get into pairs or groups with whoever they want to work with. In such a situation we can be sure that members of our class will gravitate towards people they like, admire or want to be liked by. Such a procedure is likely to be just as reliable as one based on our own observation. However, letting students choose in this way can be very chaotic and may exclude less popular students altogether so that they find themselves standing on their own when the pairs or groups are formed.

  A more informed way of grouping students is to use a sociogram, but in order for this to be effective (and safe), students need to know that what they write in private will never be seen by anyone except the teacher. In this procedure, students are asked to write their name on a piece of paper and then write, in order of preference, the students they like best in the class. On the other side of the piece of paper, they list the people they do not like. It is important that they know that only the teacher will look at what they have written and that they cannot be overlooked while they do this. We can now use the information they have written to make sociograms like the imaginary one in Figure 4 (→ = likes, ------> = doesn't like):

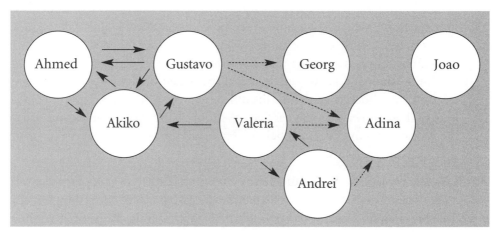

FIGURE 4: Sociogram based on *Roles of Teachers and Learners* by T Wright (Oxford University Press)

This will then allow us to make informed choices about how we should pair and group individuals. However, not everyone agrees with the idea of grouping and pairing students in this way. In the first place, sociograms are time-consuming and fail to answer the problem of what to do with unpopular students. Secondly, some people think that instead of letting the students' likes and dislikes predominate, 'the initial likes and dislikes should be replaced by acceptance among the students' (Dörnyei and Murphey 2003: 171). In other words, teachers should work to make all students accepting of each other, whoever they are paired or grouped with.

Sociograms may be useful, though, when a class doesn't seem to be cohering correctly or when pairwork and groupwork don't seem to be going well. The information they give us might help us to make decisions about grouping in order to improve matters.

- **Streaming:** much discussion centres round whether students should be streamed according to their ability. One suggestion is that pairs and groups should have a mixture of weaker and stronger students. In such groups the more able students can help their less fluent or knowledgeable colleagues. The process of helping will result in the strong students themselves being able to understand more about the language; the weaker students will benefit from the help they get.

    An alternative view is that if we are going to get students at different levels within a class to do different tasks, we should create groups in which all the students are at the same level (a level that will be different from some of the other groups). This gives us the opportunity to go to a group of weaker students and give them the special help which they need, but which stronger students might find irksome. It also allows us to give groups of stronger students more challenging tasks to perform. However, some of the value of cooperative work – all students helping each other regardless of level – may be lost.

    When we discussed *differentiation* in Chapter 7C, we saw how it was possible to help individual students with different abilities even though they were all in the same class. Streaming, therefore, seems to fit into this philosophy. However, there is the danger that students in the weaker groups might become demoralised. Furthermore, once we start grouping weaker students together, we may somehow predispose them to stay in this category rather than having the motivation to improve out of it. Successful differentiation through grouping, on the other hand, occurs when we put individual students together for individual activities and tasks, and the composition of those groups changes, depending on the tasks we have chosen. Streaming – which implies that the grouping is semi-permanent – is significantly less attractive than these rather more ad-hoc arrangements.

But in Chapter 7, C4 we said how realistic mixed-ability teaching often involves us in teaching the whole group despite the different levels. This can be replicated in groups, too, though there is always the danger that the stronger students might become frustrated while the weaker ones might get left behind. However, the benefits in terms of group cohesion may well outweigh this.

- **Chance:** we can also group students by chance, that is for no special reasons of friendship, ability or level of participation. This is by far the easiest way of doing things since it demands little pre-planning, and, by its very arbitrariness, stresses the cooperative nature of working together.

   One way of grouping people is to have students who are sitting next or near to each other work in pairs or groups. A problem can occur, though, with students who always sit in the same place since it means that they will always be in the same pairs or groups. This could give rise to boredom over a prolonged period.

   Another way of organising pairwork is the 'wheels' scenario (Scrivener 2005: 89). Here half of the class stand in a circle facing outwards, and the other half of the class stand in an outer circle facing inwards. The outer circle revolves in a clockwise direction and the inner circle revolves in an anti-clockwise direction. When they are told to stop, students work with the person facing them.

   We can organise groups by giving each student in the class (in the order they are sitting) a letter from A to E. We now ask all the As to form a group together, all the Bs to be a group, all the Cs to be a group and so on. Depending upon the size of the class, we might end up with groups of more than five, but this may not be a problem if the task is appropriate. We can also arrange random groups by asking people to get out of their chairs and stand in the order of their birthdays (with January at one end of the line and December at the other). We can then group the first five, the second five and so on. We can make groups of people wearing black or green, of people with or without glasses, or of people in different occupations (if we are in an adult class).

   It is interesting to note that modern computer language laboratories often have a random pairing and grouping program so that the teacher does not have to decide who should work with whom.

- **The task:** sometimes the task may determine who works with whom. For example, if we want students from different countries (in a multilingual group) to compare cultural practices, we will try to ensure that students from the same country do not work together (since that would defeat the object of the exercise). If the task is about people who are interested in particular leisure activities (sport, music, etc.), that might determine the make-up of the pairs or groups.

- **Changing groups:** just because we put students in groups at the beginning of an activity does not mean that they have to stay in these groups until the end. The group may change while an activity continues. For example, students may start by listing vocabulary and then discuss it first in pairs, then in groups of four, then in groups of eight – or even 16. In an interview activity, students can start working in two main groups and then break into smaller groups for a role-play. If groups are planning something or discussing, members from other groups can come and visit them to share information and take different information back to their original group. A longer sequence may start with the teacher and the whole class before moving between pairwork, individual work and groupwork until it returns back to the whole-class grouping.

- **Gender and status:** we need to remember that in some contexts it may not be appropriate to have men and women working together. Similarly, when grouping students we may want to bear in mind the status of the individuals in their lives outside the classroom. This is especially true in business English groups where different tiers of management, for example, are represented in the group. We will need, in both these scenarios, to make ourselves aware of what is the norm so that we can then make informed decisions about how to proceed.

We make our pairing and grouping decisions based on a variety of factors. If we are concerned about the atmosphere of the whole class and some of the tensions in it, we may try to make friendship groups – always bearing in mind the need to foster an acceptance for working with all students in the group eventually (see above). If our activity is based on fun (such as Example 7, *Julia's story*, on page 337), we may leave our grouping to chance. If, on the other hand, we are dealing with a non-homogeneous class (in terms of level) or if we have some students who are falling behind, we may stream groups so that we can help the weaker students while keeping the more advanced ones engaged in a different activity. We might, for example, stream pairs to do research tasks so that students with differing needs can work on different aspects of language.

One final point that needs stressing is that we should not always have students working with the same partners or group members. This creates what Sue Murray humorously refers to as ESP-PWOFP (English for the Sole Purpose of doing Pair Work with One Fixed Partner) (Murray 2000: 49). She argues persuasively that mixing and moving students around as a course progresses is good for classroom atmosphere and for individual engagement.

B3 Procedures for pairwork and groupwork

Our role in pairwork and groupwork does not end when we have decided which students should work together, of course. We have other matters to address, too, not only before the activity starts, but also during and after it.

- **Before:** when we want students to work together in pairs or groups, we will want to follow an 'engage–instruct–initiate' sequence (see page 68). This is because students need to feel enthusiastic about what they are going to do, they need to know what they are going to do, and they need to be given an idea of when they will have finished the task.

Sometimes our instructions will involve a demonstration – when, for example, students are going to use a new information-gap activity or when we want them to use cards (see Chapter 11, C3). On other occasions, where an activity is familiar, we may simply give them an instruction to practise language they are studying in pairs, or to use their dictionaries to find specific bits of information.

The success of a pairwork or groupwork task is often helped by giving students a time when the activity should finish – and then sticking to it. This helps to give them a clear framework to work within. Alternatively in lighter-hearted activities such as a poem dictation (see Example 5 on page 335), we can encourage groups to see who finishes first. Though language learning is not a contest (except, perhaps, a personal one), in game-like activities '... a slight sense of competition between groups does no harm' (Nuttall 1996: 164).

The important thing about instructions is that the students should understand and agree on what the task is. To check that they do, we may ask them to repeat the instructions, or, in monolingual classes, to translate them into their first language.

- **During:** while students are working in pairs or groups we have a number of options. We could, for instance, stand at the front or the side of the class (or at the back or anywhere else) and keep an eye on what is happening, noting who appears to be stuck, disengaged or about to finish. In this position we can tune in to a particular pair or group from some distance away. We can then decide whether to go over and help them.

  An alternative procedure is often referred to as *monitoring*. This is where we go round the class, watching and listening to specific pairs and groups either to help them with the task or to collect examples of what they are doing for later comment and work. For example, we can stay with a group for a period of time and then intervene if and when we think it is appropriate or necessary, always bearing in mind what we have said about the difference between accuracy and fluency work (see Chapter 8, C1). If students are involved in a discussion, for example, we might correct gently (see Chapter 8, C3); if we are helping students with suggestions about something they are planning, or trying to move a discussion forwards, we can act as prompter, resource or tutor (see Chapter 6, B1). In such situations we will often be responding to what they are doing rather than giving correction feedback. We will be helping them forwards with the task they are involved in. Where students fall back on their first language, we will do our best to encourage or persuade them back into English.

  When students are working in pairs or groups we have an ideal opportunity to work with individual students whom we feel would benefit from our attention. We also have a great chance to act as observer, picking up information about student progress, and seeing if we will have to 'troubleshoot' (see below). But however we monitor, intervene or take part in the work of a pair or group, it is vital that we do so in a way that is appropriate to the students involved and to the tasks they are involved in.

- **After:** when pairs and groups stop working together, we need to organise feedback (see Chapter 8). We want to let them discuss what occurred during the groupwork session and, where necessary, add our own assessments and make corrections.

  Where pairwork or groupwork has formed part of a practice session, our feedback may take the form of having a few pairs or groups quickly demonstrate the language they have been using. We can then correct it, if and when necessary, and this procedure will give both those students and the rest of the class good information for future learning and action.

Where pairs or groups have been working on a task with definite right or wrong answers, we need to ensure that they have completed it successfully. Where they have been discussing an issue or predicting the content of a reading text, we will encourage them to talk about their conclusions with us and the rest of the class. By comparing different solutions, ideas and problems, everyone gets a greater understanding of the topic.

Where students have produced a piece of work, we can give them a chance to demonstrate this to other students in the class. They can stick written material on noticeboards; they can read out dialogues they have written or play audio or video tapes they have made.

Finally, it is vital to remember that constructive feedback on the content of student work can greatly enhance students' future motivation. The feedback we give on language mistakes (see Chapter 8C and D) is only one part of that process.

B4 Troubleshooting

When we monitor pairs and groups during a groupwork activity, we are seeing how well they are doing and deciding whether or not to go over and intervene. But we are also keeping our eyes open for problems which we can resolve either on the spot or in future.

- **Finishing first:** a problem that frequently occurs when students are working in pairs or groups is that some of them finish earlier than others and/or show clearly that they have had enough of the activity and want to do something else. We need to be ready for this and have some way of dealing with the situation. Saying to them *OK, you can relax for a bit while the others finish* may be appropriate for tired students, but can make other students feel that they are being ignored.

  When we see the first pairs or groups finish the task, we might stop the activity for the whole class. That removes the problem of boredom, but it may be very demotivating for the students who haven't yet finished, especially when they are nearly there and have invested some considerable effort in the procedure.

  One way of avoiding the problems we have mentioned here is to have a series of challenging task-related extensions for early finishers so that when a group has finished early, we can give them an activity to complete while they are waiting. This will show the students that they are not just being left to do nothing. When planning groupwork it is a good idea for teachers to make a list of task-related extensions and other spare activities that first-finishing groups and pairs can be involved in (though see page 129).

  Even where we have set a time limit on pair- and groupwork, we need to keep an eye open to see how the students are progressing. We can then make the decision about when to stop the activity based on the observable (dis)engagement of the students and how near they all are to completing the task.

- **Awkward groups:** when students are working in pairs or groups we need to observe how well they interact together. Even where we have made our best judgements – based on friendship or streaming, for example – it is possible that apparently satisfactory combinations of students are not ideal. Some pairs may find it impossible to concentrate on the task in hand and instead encourage each other to talk about something else, usually in their first language. In some groups (in some educational cultures) members may defer to the oldest person there, or to the man in an otherwise female group. People with loud voices can dominate proceedings; less extrovert people may not participate fully enough. Some weak students may be lost when paired or grouped with stronger classmates.

In such situations we may need to change the pairs or groups. We can separate best friends for pairwork; we can put all the high-status figures in one group so that students in other groups do not have to defer to them. We can stream groups or reorganise them in other ways so that all group members gain the most from the activity.

One way of finding out about groups, in particular, is simply to observe, noting down how often each student speaks. If two or three observations of this kind reveal a continuing pattern, we can take the kind of action suggested above.

Chapter notes and further reading

- **Whole-class teaching**

  On the advantages of whole-class learning, see R Senior (2002). On the management of the whole class as a group, two excellent books on group dynamics are J Hadfield (1992) and Z Dörnyei and T Murphey (2003).

- **Pairwork and groupwork**

  On the advantages and disadvantages of pairwork, see S Haines (1995).

  M Courtney (1996) looks at both pairwork and groupwork for oral tasks. J Reid (1987) found that students have definite views about class grouping, and T Woodward (1995) worries about issues related to pair- and groupwork.

  M Hebden and J Mason (2003) suggest a number of different seatings and groupings for different activities with younger learners.

11 | Educational technology and other learning resources

A The technology pyramid

If you walk into some classrooms around the world, you will see fixed data projectors, interactive whiteboards (IWBs), built-in speakers for audio material that is delivered directly from a computer hard disk (rather than from a tape recorder), and computers with round-the-clock Internet access. Whenever teachers want their students to find anything out, they can get them to use a search engine like Google and the results can be shown to the whole class on the IWB.

In other classes, even in many successful private language schools around the world, there is a whiteboard in the classroom, an overhead projector (OHP) and a tape recorder. Other schools only have a whiteboard – or perhaps a blackboard – often not in very good condition. In such schools there may well not be a photocopier, though hopefully the students will have exercise books.

Finally, there are some classroom situations where neither teacher nor students have anything at all in terms of educational technology or other learning aids. Jill and Charles Hadfield represent these differing realities in a 'reversed pyramid' of resources (see Figure 1). In a world in which the pace of technological change is breathtakingly fast (so that between the writing and publishing of this book new technology will have been produced that most of us are as yet unaware of), it seems that being at the bottom of the pyramid is likely to be a bar to language learning.

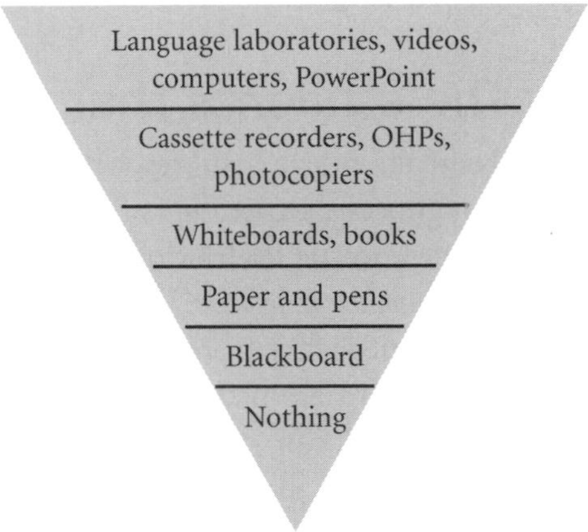

Language laboratories, videos, computers, PowerPoint

Cassette recorders, OHPs, photocopiers

Whiteboards, books

Paper and pens

Blackboard

Nothing

FIGURE 1: Reversed resources pyramid

However, Jill and Charles Hadfield argue passionately, this is not the case (Hadfield and Hadfield 2003a and b). There is a lot you can do with minimal or even no resources. For example, in one situation they taught in, there was a board and the children had exercise books, but apart from that there were no other educational aids, not even coursebooks. However, with the help of a washing line and clothes pegs they were able to hang up pictures for students to work with. Simple objects like a selection of pebbles became the focus for activities such as telling the story of the pebbles' existence; different words from sentences were written on pieces of paper or card and then put on students' backs – and the rest of the class had to make them stand in order to make a sentence from the word; paper bags with faces drawn on them became puppets; the classroom desks were rearranged to become a street plan so students could practise giving (and responding to) directions. Finally, and most importantly, the students themselves were used as source material, whether as participants in quizzes about the real world, as informants in discussions about families or as imaginers of river scenes based on teacher description. The internal world of the student is 'the richest, deepest seam of gold that you have' (Hadfield and Hadfield 2003b: 34). Indeed, (see Figure 2) Jill and Charles Hadfield propose turning the pyramid the other way up.

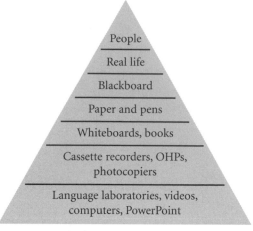

FIGURE 2: 'Other way up' resources pyramid

The resources that are currently available are truly amazing. As we shall see, they offer an amazing variety of routes for learning and discovery. Yet we should not see them as methodologies for learning, but rather as tools to help us in whatever approaches and techniques we have chosen to use. And we need to remind ourselves constantly of the fact that many classrooms both in the 'developing' and 'developed' world do not have access to very modern technology. Yet this does not prevent students – and has never prevented them – from learning English successfully. In this chapter, therefore, we will look at a range of classroom resources (both hi- and low-tech) before considering the questions we need to ask when trying to decide whether to adopt the latest technological innovation.

B The students themselves

By far the most useful resources in the classroom are the students themselves. Through their thoughts and experiences they bring the outside world into the room, and this is a powerful resource for us to draw on We can get them to write or talk about things they like or things they have experienced. We can ask them what they would do in certain situations or get them to act out scenes from their lives. In multilingual classes (see page 132), we can get them to share information about their different countries.

Students can also be very good resources for explaining and practising meaning. For example, in young learner classes we can get them to be 'living clocks'. They have to demonstrate the time with their arms (using a pointing finger for the minute hand and a fist for the hour hand) and the other students have to say what the time is. We can also get them to stand in line in the order of their birthdays (so they have to ask each other *When is your birthday?*) or in the order of the distance they live from the school. They can be made to stand in the alphabetical order of their middle names (so they have to ask), or in the order of the name of another member of their family, etc.

Students can elect one of their number to be a 'class robot'. The others tell him or her what to do. Students can mime and act out words and phrases (e.g. *Hurry up! Watch out!*) for the rest of the class to guess. They can perform dialogues taking on the personality of some of the characters the other students know (e.g. for 10- and 11-year-old beginners, Clever Carol, Horrible Harvey, etc.), and the rest of the class have to guess who they are. Most students, especially younger learners, enjoy acting out.

C Objects, pictures and things

A range of objects, pictures, cards and other things, such as Cuisenaire rods, can be used for presenting and manipulating language, and for involving students in activities of all kinds. We will look at four of them.

C1 Realia

We mentioned above how a simple pebble can be used as a stimulus for a creative activity. However, this is only one possible use for real objects: realia. With beginners, and particularly children, using realia is helpful for teaching the meanings of words or for stimulating student activity; teachers sometimes come to class with plastic fruit, cardboard clock faces, or two telephones to help simulate phone conversations.

Objects that are intrinsically interesting can provide a good starting-point for a variety of language work and communication activities. Jill and Charles Hadfield suggest bringing in a bag of 'evocative objects' that have a 'story to tell' (Hadfield and Hadfield 2003b: 32). These might be a hair ribbon, a coin, a button, a ring, a paperclip, an elastic band, an old photo frame, a key and a padlock. Students are put into groups. Each group picks an object from the bag (without looking in first). Each student in the group then writes one sentence about the object's history as if they were that object. Members of the group share their sentences to make the object's autobiography. They then read their autobiographies to the rest of the class.

We can find an object with an obscure use and ask students to speculate about what it is for (*it might/could/probably is*) and/or design various explanations to account for it (*it is used for -ing*). The class could vote on the best idea. If we bring in more than one object, especially when they are not obviously connected, students can speculate on what they have in common or they can invent stories and scenarios using the various objects. They can choose which three from a collection of objects they will put in a time capsule, or which would be most useful on a desert island, etc.

Some teachers use a soft ball to make learning more enjoyable. When they want a student to say something, ask a question or give an answer, they throw a ball to the student, who then has to respond. The student can then throw the ball to a classmate who, in turn, produces the required response before throwing the ball to someone else. Not all students find this appealing, however, and there is a limit to how often the ball can be thrown before people get fed up with it.

The only limitations on the things which we bring to class are the size and quantity of the objects themselves and the students' tolerance, especially with adults who may think they are being treated childishly. As with so many other things, this is something we will have to assess on the basis of our students' reactions.

Pictures

Teachers have always used pictures or graphics – whether drawn, taken from books, newspapers and magazines, or photographed – to facilitate learning. Pictures can be in the form of flashcards (smallish cards which we can hold up for our students to see), large wall pictures (big enough for everyone to see details), cue cards (small cards which students use in pair- or groupwork), photographs or illustrations (typically in a textbook). Some teachers also use projected slides, images from an overhead projector (see E2 below), or projected computer images (see E4 below). Teachers also draw pictures on the board to help with explanation and language work (see E1 below).

Pictures of all kinds can be used in a multiplicity of ways, as the following examples show:

- **Drills:** with lower-level students, an appropriate use for pictures – especially flashcards – is in cue–response drills (see Chapter 12, B2). We hold up a flashcard (the cue) before nominating a student and getting a response. Then we hold up another one, nominate a different student, and so on. Flashcards are particularly useful for drilling grammar items, for cueing different sentences and practising vocabulary.

  Sometimes teachers use larger wall pictures, where pointing to a detail of a picture will elicit a response, such as *There's some milk in the fridge* or *He's just been swimming*, etc. We can show large street maps to practise shop vocabulary or to get students giving and understanding directions.

- **(Communication) games:** pictures are extremely useful for a variety of communication activities, especially where these have a game-like feel, such as 'describe and draw' activities, where one student describes a picture (which we have given them) and a partner has to draw the same picture without looking at the original. We can also divide a class into four groups (A, B, C, D) and give each group a different picture that shows a separate stage in a story. Once the members of the group have studied their picture, we take it away. New groups are formed with four members each – one from group A, one from group B, one from group C and one from group D. By sharing the information they saw in their pictures, they have to work out what story the pictures together are telling.

  Teachers sometimes use pictures for creative writing. They might tell students to invent a story using at least three of the images in front of them. They can tell them to have a conversation about a specified topic, and, at various stages during the conversation, to pick a card and bring whatever that card shows into the conversation.

- **Understanding:** one of the most appropriate uses for pictures is for the presenting and checking of meaning. An easy way of explaining the meaning of the word *aeroplane*, for example, is to have a picture of one. In the same way, it is easy to check students' understanding of a piece of writing or listening by asking them to select the picture (out of, say, four) which best corresponds to the reading text or the listening passage.

- **Ornamentation:** pictures of various kinds are often used to make work more appealing. In many modern coursebooks, for example, a reading text will be adorned by a photograph which is not strictly necessary, in the same way as happens in newspaper and magazine articles. The rationale for this is clearly that pictures enhance the text, giving readers (or students) an extra visual dimension to what they are reading.

Some teachers and materials designers object to this use of illustrations because they consider it gratuitous. But it should be remembered that if the pictures are interesting, they will appeal strongly to at least some members of the class. They have the power (at least for the more visually oriented) to engage students.

- **Prediction:** pictures are useful for getting students to predict what is coming next in a lesson. Thus students might look at a picture and try to guess what it shows. (Are the people in it brother and sister, husband or wife, and what are they arguing about – or are they arguing? etc.) They then listen to an audio track or read a text to see if it matches what they predicted on the basis of the picture. This use of pictures is very powerful and has the advantage of engaging students in the task to follow.

- **Discussion:** pictures can stimulate questions such as: *What is it showing? How does it make you feel? What was the artist's/photographer's purpose in designing it in that way? Would you like to have this picture in your house? Why? Why not? How much would you pay for the picture? Is the picture a work of art?*

    One idea is to get students to become judges of a photographic competition. After being given the category of photographs they are going to judge (e.g. men in action, reportage, abstract pictures), the students decide on four or five characteristics their winning photograph should have. They then apply these characteristics to the finalists that we provide for them, before explaining why they made their choice.

    Pictures can also be used for creative language use, whether they are in a book or on cue cards, flashcards or wall pictures. We might ask students to write a description of a picture, to invent the conversation taking place between two people in a picture or, in one particular role-play activity, ask them to answer questions as if they were the characters in a famous painting.

We can make wall pictures, flashcards and cue cards in a number of ways. We can take pictures from magazines and stick them on card. We can draw them. We can buy reproductions, photographs and posters from shops or we can photocopy them from a variety of sources (though we should check copyright law before doing this). It is possible to find pictures of almost anything on the Internet and print them off.

The choice and use of pictures is very much a matter of personal taste, but we should bear in mind three qualities that pictures need to possess if they are to engage students and be linguistically useful. In the first place, they need to be appropriate not only for the purpose in hand but also for the classes they are being used for. If they are too childish, students may not like them, and if they are culturally inappropriate, they can offend people.

Ultimately, the most important thing is that pictures should be visible. They have to be big enough so that all our students – taking into account where they will be sitting – can see the necessary detail.

Lastly, we will not want to spend hours collecting pictures only to have them destroyed the first time they are used! Thought should be given to how to make them durable. Perhaps they can be stuck to cards and protected with transparent coverings.

C3 Cards

Apart from flashcards with pictures on them, cards of all shapes and sizes can be used in a variety of ways. Cards, in this sense, can range from carefully prepared pieces of thick paper which have been laminated to make them into a reusable resource to small strips of paper which the teacher brings in for one lesson only.

Of the many uses for cards, three are especially worth mentioning:

- **Matching and ordering:** cards are especially good for matching questions and answers or two halves of a sentence. Students can either match them on the desk in front of them (perhaps in pairs or groups), or they can move around the classroom looking for their pairs. This matching can be on the basis of topic, lexis or grammatical construction.

  We can also use cards to order words into sentences or to put the lines of a poem in order.

  Using cards in this way is especially good for kinaesthetic learners, of course (see page 89). But it is good for everyone else, too, especially if we can get students walking around the classroom for at least a brief period.

- **Selecting:** cards work really well if we want students to speak on the spot or use particular words or phrases in a conversation or in sentences. We can write words on separate cards and then, after shuffling them, place them in a pile face down. When a student picks up the next card in the pack, he or she has to use the word in a sentence. Alternatively, students can choose three or four cards and then have to incorporate what is on the cards into a story. Students can also pick up a card and try to describe what the word on it feels, tastes or smells like so that the other students can guess it.

- **Card games:** there are as many card game possibilities in language learning as there are in real life. We can turn the card selection into a game by introducing a competitive element – having students in pairs play against each other or against other pairs.

  A simple vocabulary game can be played in which students have cards with pictures on one side and words on the other. If they pick the picture side, they have to produce the word. If they pick the word side, they have to draw it and then compare it with the original picture. The old game of *Snap* can be adapted so that two players have a set of cards, with the same objects, etc., but whereas one player has only pictures, the other has only words. The cards are shuffled and then the players put down the cards one at a time. If a picture and word card match, the player who shouts *Snap!* first wins all the cards on the table. The object of the game is for one player to end up with all the cards.

C4 Cuisenaire rods

Originally invented by the Belgian educator Caleb Gattegno (see the Silent Way on page 68), these small blocks of wood or plastic of different lengths (see Figure 3) were originally designed for maths teaching. Each length is a different colour. The rods are featureless, and are only differentiated by their length and colour. Simple they may be, but they are useful for a wide range of activities. For example, we can say that a particular rod is a pen or a telephone, a dog or a key so that by holding them up or putting them together a story can be told. All it takes is a little imagination.

The rods can be used to demonstrate word stress, too: if one is bigger than the others (in a sequence representing syllables in a word or words in a sentence), it shows where the stress should be (see Chapter 2, F5 and Chapter 15, B2).

We can also assign a word or phrase to each of, say, five rods and the students then have to put them in the right order (e.g. *I usually get up at six o'clock*). By moving the *usually* rod around and showing where it can and cannot occur in the sentence, the students get a clear visual display of something they are attempting to fix in their minds.

Rods can be used to teach prepositions. Teachers can model with the rods sentences like *The red one is on top of/beside/under/over/behind (etc.) the green one.* They can show rods in different relative positions and ask students to describe them. Students can then position the rods for other students to describe (in ever more complex arrangements!).

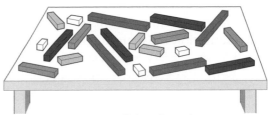

FIGURE 3: Cuisenaire rods

Cuisenaire rods are also useful for demonstrating colours (of course), comparatives, superlatives, and a whole range of other semantic and syntactic areas, particularly with people who respond well to visual or kinaesthetic activities.

D The coursebook

For years, methodologists have been arguing about the usefulness of coursebooks, questioning their role (Allwright 1981), defending their use (O'Neill 1982), worrying that they act as methodological straitjackets (Tice 1991), promoting their value as agents of methodological change (Hutchinson and Torres 1994), or arguing yet again about their relative merits (Harmer 2001, Thornbury and Meddings 2001).

D1 Coursebook or no coursebook?

The benefits and restrictions of coursebook use can be easily summarised:

- **Benefits:** good coursebooks are carefully prepared to offer a coherent syllabus, satisfactory language control, motivating texts, audio cassettes/CDs and other accessories such as video/DVD material, CD-ROMs and extra resource material. They are often attractively presented. They provide teachers under pressure with the reassurance that, even when they are forced to plan at the last moment, they will be using material which they can have confidence in. They come with detailed teacher's guides, which not only provide procedures for the lesson in the student's book, but also offer suggestions and alternatives, extra activities and resources. The adoption of a new coursebook provides a powerful stimulus for methodological development (see Hutchinson and Torres 1994).

  Students like coursebooks, too, since they foster the perception of progress as units and then books are completed. Coursebooks also provide material which students can look back at for revision and, at their best, their visual and topic appeal can have a powerfully engaging effect.

- **Restrictions:** coursebooks, used inappropriately, impose learning styles and content on classes and teachers alike, appearing to be '"fait accompli" over which they can have little control' (Littlejohn 1998: 205). Many of them rely on Presentation, Practice and Production as their main methodological procedure (see Chapter 4, A2), despite recent enthusiasm for other teaching sequences. Units and lessons often follow an unrelenting format so that students and teachers eventually become demotivated by the sameness of it all. And in their choice of topics, coursebooks can sometimes be bland or culturally inappropriate.

One solution to the perceived disadvantages of coursebooks is to do without them altogether, to use a 'do-it-yourself' approach (Block 1991, Maley 1998, Thornbury and Meddings 2001). Such an approach is extremely attractive. It can offer students a dynamic and varied programme. If they can see its relevance to their own needs, it will greatly enhance their motivation and their trust in what they are being asked to do. It allows teachers to respond on a lesson-by-lesson basis to what is happening in the class. Finally, for the teacher, it means an exciting and creative involvement with texts and tasks.

In order for the DIY approach to be successful, teachers need access to (and knowledge of) a wide range of materials, from coursebooks and videos to magazines, novels, encyclopedias, publicity brochures and the Internet. They will have to make (and make use of) a variety of home-grown materials (see below). They will also need the confidence to know when and what to choose, becoming, in effect, syllabus designers in their own right. This not only makes preparing lessons a very time-consuming business, but also runs the risk that students will end up with incoherent collections of bits and pieces of material. However, where there is time for the proper planning and organisation of DIY teaching, students may well get exceptional programmes of study, which are responsive to their needs and varied in a way that does not abandon coherence. Such an approach also ties in with a dialogic, 'Dogme'-style of teaching (see page 75).

D2 **Using coursebooks**

Around the world, however, the vast majority of teachers reject a coursebook-free approach and instead use them to help their learners and, what's more, to give structure and direction to their own teaching.

The most important aspect of coursebook use is for teachers to try to engage students with the content they are going to be dealing with. This means arousing the students' interest in a topic, and making sure that they know exactly what we want them to do before we get them to open their books and disappear, heads-down in the pages, while we are still trying to talk to them.

Many teachers want to use their coursebooks as a kind of springboard for their lessons, rather than as a manual to be slavishly followed. In other words, while they base much of their teaching on the contents of the coursebook, they reserve the right to decide when and how to use its constituent parts. There are two main ways they can do this:

- **Omit and replace:** the first decision we have to make is whether to use a particular coursebook lesson or not. If the answer is 'no', there are two possible courses of action. The first is just to omit the lesson altogether. In this case, we suppose that the students will not miss it because it does not teach anything fundamentally necessary and it is not especially interesting. When, however, we think the language or topic area in question is important, we will have to replace the coursebook lesson with our own preferred alternative.

  Although there is nothing wrong with omitting or replacing coursebook material, it becomes irksome for many students if it happens too often, especially when they have had to buy the book themselves. It may also deny them the chance to revise (a major advantage of coursebooks), and their course may lose overall coherence.

- **To change or not to change?** when we decide to use a coursebook lesson, we can, of course, do so without making any substantial changes to the way it is presented. However, we might decide to use the lesson but to change it to make it more appropriate for our students. If the material is not very substantial, we might add something to it – a role-play after a reading text, perhaps, or extra situations for language practice. We might re-write an exercise we do not especially like or replace one activity or text with something else, such as a download from the Internet or any other home-grown items. We could re-order the activities within a lesson, or even re-order lessons (within reason). Finally, we may wish to reduce a lesson by cutting out an exercise or an activity. In all our decisions, however, it is important to remember that students need to be able to see a coherent pattern to what we are doing and understand our reasons for changes.

Using coursebooks appropriately is an art which becomes clearer with experience. If the teacher approaches lesson planning in the right frame of mind (see Chapter 21), it happens almost as a matter of course. The options we have discussed for coursebook use are summarised in Figure 4.

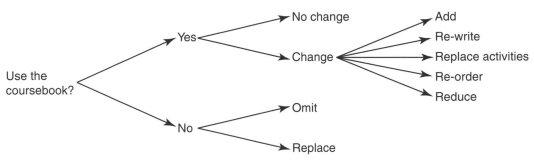

FIGURE 4: Options for coursebook use

E Ways of showing

Over the years, technology has changed the way that teachers and students are able to show each other things (one of the most important functions of classroom equipment). We will look at four major presentation aids.

E1 The board

The most versatile piece of classroom teaching equipment is the board – whether this is of the more traditional chalk-dust variety, a whiteboard written on with marker pens, or an IWB (see page 187). Boards provide a motivating focal point during whole-class grouping.

We can use boards for a variety of different purposes, including:

- **Note-pad:** teachers frequently write things up on the board as these come up during the lesson. They might be words that they want students to remember, phrases which students have not understood or seen before, or topics and phrases which they have elicited from students when trying to build up a composition plan, for example.

When we write up a word on a board, we can show how that word is stressed so that students can see and 'hear' the word at the same time (see Figure 5). We can sketch in intonation tunes or underline features of spelling, too. We can group words according to their meaning or grammatical function. Some teachers use different colours for different aspects of language.

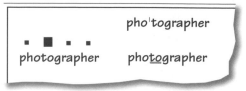

FIGURE 5: Different ways of recording word stress

- **Explanation aid:** boards can be used for explanation, too. For example, we can show the relationship between an affirmative sentence and a question by drawing connecting arrows (see Figure 6). We can show where words go in a sentence by indicating the best positions diagrammatically, or we can write up phonemic symbols (or draw diagrams of the mouth) to show how a word or sound is pronounced. The board is ideal for such uses.

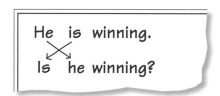

FIGURE 6: Using the board to show sentence/question relationships (elementary)

- **Picture frame:** boards can be used for drawing pictures, of course, the only limitation being our artistic ability. But even those who are not artistically gifted can usually draw a sad face and a happy face. They can produce stick men sitting down and running, or make an attempt at a bus or a car. What's more, this can be done whenever it is required because the board is always there, helping students to understand concepts and words.

- **Public workbook:** a typical procedure is to write up fill-in sentences or sentence transformation items, for example, and have individual students come up to the board and write a fill-in item, or a transformed sentence. That way the whole class becomes involved in seeing what the correct version is.

  Teachers sometimes write mistakes they have observed in a creative language activity on the board. They can ask class members who think they know how to correct them to come up and have a go.

  Such activities are very useful because they focus everyone's attention in one place.

- **Game board:** there are a number of games that can be played using the board. With noughts and crosses (also called Tic-tac-toe), for example, teachers can draw nine box frames and write different words or categories in each box (see Figure 7). Teams have to make sentences or questions with the words and if they get them right, they can put their symbol (O or X) on the square to draw their winning straight line.

  A popular spelling game involves two teams who start off with the same word. Each team has half the board. They have to fill up their side with as many words as possible, but each new word has to start with the last letter of the word before. At the end of a given period of time, the team with the largest number of correct words is the winner.

can't	won't	like
must	enjoy	want
dislike	hate	has to

FIGURE 7: Noughts and crosses (Tic-tac-toe)

- **Noticeboard:** teachers and students can display things on boards – pictures, posters, announcements, charts, etc. It is especially useful if the boards are metallic so that magnets can be used.

Handwriting on the board should be clear and easy to decipher; we should organise our material in some way, too, so that the board does not just get covered in scrawls in a random and distracting fashion. We could, for example, draw a column on one side of the board and reserve that for new words. We could then put the day's or the lesson's programme in a left-hand column and use the middle of the board for grammar explanations or games.

It is probably not a good idea to turn our back to the class while we write on the board, especially if this goes on for some time. This tends to be demotivating and may cause the class to become restless. Indeed, it is better to involve the students with boardwork as much as possible, either getting them to tell us what to write, or asking them to do the writing themselves.

E2 The overhead projector (OHP)

Despite modern computer-based presentation equipment and programs, the OHP (and the transparencies we use with it) still retains a unique versatility (see Figure 8), and, except for problems with electricity or a bulb, is much more likely to be problem-free than other more sophisticated pieces of equipment.

Just about anything can go on overhead transparencies (OHTs): we can show whole texts or grammar exercises, pictures, diagrams or students' writing. Because transparencies can be put through a photocopier or printed from any computer, they can be of very high quality. Especially where teachers have handwriting that tends to be unclear, the overhead transparency offers the possibility of attractive well-printed script.

One of the major advantages of the overhead projector is that we don't have to show everything on an OHT all at once. By covering some of the transparency with a piece of card or paper, we can blank out what we don't want the students to see. So, for example, we might show the first two lines of a story and ask students what is going to happen next, before revealing the next two lines and then the next, gradually moving the paper or card downwards. We might have questions on one side of the transparency and answers on the other. We start the teaching sequence with the answers covered, and use the same gradual revelation technique to maintain interest.

Because transparencies are, as their name suggests, transparent, they can be put on top of each other so that we gradually build up a complex picture, diagram or text. A diagram can start with one simple feature and have extra elements added to it. We can put up a gapped text and have students say what they think goes in the blanks before putting a new transparency with some or all of the filled-in items on top of the gapped one.

Sometimes we can put a text with blanks on the OHP and then lay a blank transparency on top of it so that students, using OHP pens, can come up and write in what they think should go there. Alternatively, students working in groups can list the points they want to make after they have discussed a topic (e.g. whether or not children under twelve should have a curfew from ten o'clock every evening) and show their transparency to the class while they make their presentation.

FIGURE 8: Overhead projector

Overhead projectors are extremely versatile, but they can pose some problems, too. They need electricity, of course, and bulbs do fail from time to time. Some models are quite bulky, too. They are not that powerful either, especially when they are up against natural light coming in from windows and doors. When images are projected onto shiny surfaces, such as boards, they can be uncomfortable to look at, and when they are projected onto some other surfaces, it can be very difficult to make out details.

A lot depends on how big or small the projector 'square' is on the wall or screen and whether the image is in focus. A mistake that some users make is to put too much on the transparency so that when they ask *Can people see this at the back?* the answer they get is a frustrated shaking of the head. However, if all these potential problems are taken into account and resolved, the OHP is an extremely useful resource.

E3 The flip chart

Flip charts are very useful for making notes, recording the main points in a group discussion, amending and changing points, and for the fact that individual sheets of paper can be torn off and kept for future reference. Many of these qualities (and more) are, of course, shared by computer-based technology, but flip charts are portable, relatively cheap and demand no technical expertise.

Flip charts work best in two particular situations. In the first, a teacher, group leader or group scribe stands at the flip chart and records the points that are being made. The participants – because they can see what is being written up – can then ask for changes to be made.

FIGURE 9: Flip chart

When possible, it is ideal if groups can each have flip charts of their own. When an activity is finished, students can walk round the room seeing what the different groups have written (or what points they have noted down). Flip charts can also be posted at different points in the room, each flip chart standing for a topic or a point of view. Students can walk around, adding to what is on each of the flip charts, writing up their opinions, disagreeing or merely getting an idea of what the other students are thinking, based on what is already written there.

E4 Computer-based presentation technology

Computers have changed the world of classroom presentation forever – that is for those fortunate enough to have the money and resources for both hardware and software.

The two crucial pieces of hardware are a computer and a data projector. Anything that is on our computer screen can be shown to the whole class using a data projector to put up an enlarged version of it on a screen or a white wall. This means that all the class can see a word-processed task at the same time, or we can project a picture, diagram or map, for example.

Presentation software, such as PowerPoint, increases our capacity to present visual material (words, graphics and pictures) in a dynamic and interesting way. However, the most commonly used PowerPoint template (a heading with bullet points) has suffered from overuse and may not be the most effective use of the medium. In fact, the software offers a more interesting option where we can mix text and visuals with audio/video tracks so that pictures can dissolve or fly onto and off the screen, and music, speech and film can be integrated into the presentation. Some people, of course, may find this kind of animated presentation irksome in its own way, but there is no doubt that it allows teachers to mix different kinds of display much more effectively than before such software came along.

One of the major technological developments in the last few years has been the interactive whiteboard, the IWB. This has the same properties as a computer hooked up to a data projector (i.e. you can present visual material, Internet pages, etc. in a magnified way for everyone to see), but it has three major extra advantages, too. In the first place, teachers and students can write on the board which the images are being projected onto, and they can manipulate images on the board with the use of special pens or even with nothing but their fingers. The pen or finger thus acts as a kind of computer mouse. Secondly, what appears on the board (just like the screen of a computer) can be saved or printed so that anything written up or being shown there can be looked at again.

Enthusiasts for IWBs point to this extraordinary versatility and to other tricks (such as the ability to mask parts of the board and gradually reveal information). They say that the ability to move text and graphics around the board with pen or finger is extremely attractive, especially for younger learners. They emphasise the fact that text, graphics, Internet capability, video and audio material can all be controlled from the board.

Critics of IWBs worry about the amount of money they cost. There is some concern, too, about the fact that currently most IWBs are at the front of the classroom and thus tend to promote teacher (and learner)-fronted behaviours, and are less favourable for groupwork. There are also worries about projector beams (especially in ceiling-mounted projectors) affecting the eyes of teachers who frequently find themselves looking directly at them.

 # F Ways of listening

Students get exposure to spoken language from a variety of sources. Much of it comes from the teacher, whose voice represents the single most important source of language input. Students also get language input from listening to each other and from any visiting teachers, lecturers or classroom guests.

It is still extremely common for teachers and students to listen to recorded audio material on cassette recorders. Tape recorders are versatile, cheap and convenient and, when they have efficient rewind and fast forward buttons and tape counters, they are extremely easy to use. Many teachers also use CD players, which have some of the same advantages as tape recorders, though they are often bulkier and have counter systems that are sometimes more difficult to use efficiently than those of older tape recorder models.

However, recorded material is now available (as is video material) in digital formats such as WAV and MP3. What this means in practical terms is that we can play material directly from computers and MP3 players. This has revolutionised access to listening, especially for individual listeners. The availability of podcasts (that is, downloadable files which the user can load onto their own personal MP3 players such as iPods – or, increasingly, mobile phones), means that students (and teachers) can listen to a range of material whenever they want to on devices that are so small that they are not difficult to carry around. Teachers and students can go, for example, to Podcast.net and search the site for ESL material. A search engine like Google will also enable us to find a huge variety of ESL and general podcast material.

G Ways of finding out

It has never been as easy to find things out as it is in the twenty-first century. The wide range of reference material both online and offline (in the form of CDs) is almost infinite. This is especially useful for language learners.

G1 Dictionaries

Students can access dictionaries in book form, on CD-ROMS, using small electronic handsets and on the web. We will look at these in turn.

- **Paper dictionaries:** dictionaries printed in book form have changed dramatically in the last few years. Whereas in the past, they were monochrome, with forbidding-looking entries which used various codes to denote different aspects of meaning, now they are colourful and laid out in a way that makes issues such as frequency, collocation, different meanings, pronunciation, etc. extremely clear.

  Dictionaries can be either bilingual or monolingual. In the past, teachers tended to be dismissive of the former since they frequently failed to give users sufficient information about what words meant and how they were used. Modern learners' bilingual dictionaries, however, are considerably more sophisticated, as can be seen in Figure 10.

have the day off **5 libre de impuestos** tax-free
▶ ver **aire, lucha, tiro**

librería s bookstore (AmE), bookshop (BrE)
▶ En inglés existe la palabra **library** pero significa *biblioteca*.

librero, -a *sustantivo*
■ s (persona) bookseller
■ **librero s** (mueble) bookcase: *Regresa el dicciona-*

FIGURE 10: Entry for *librería* from *Diccionario Pocket* (Pearson Education) for Latin American Spanish-speaking students of English

Here the users are given both British and American equivalents of the Spanish word *librería*, and they are also told about the fact that the English word *library* (which sounds like *librería* of course) actually translates into Spanish as *biblioteca*.

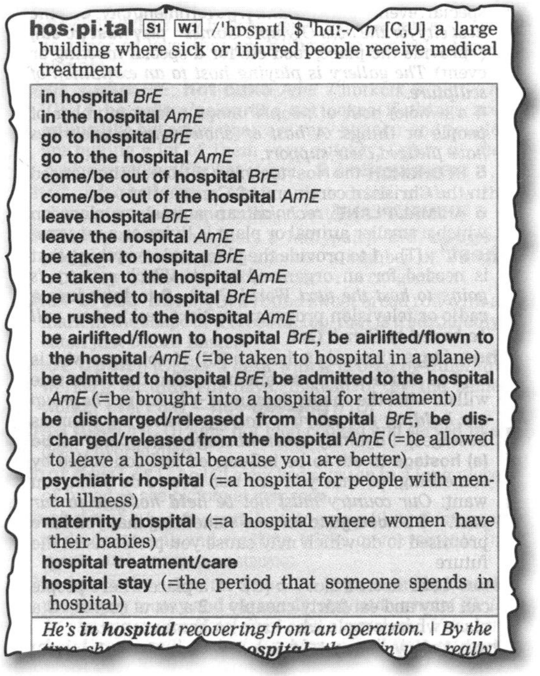

hos·pi·tal S1 W1 /ˈhɒspɪtl $ ˈhɑː-/ *n* [C,U] a large building where sick or injured people receive medical treatment

in hospital *BrE*
in the hospital *AmE*
go to hospital *BrE*
go to the hospital *AmE*
come/be out of hospital *BrE*
come/be out of the hospital *AmE*
leave hospital *BrE*
leave the hospital *AmE*
be taken to hospital *BrE*
be taken to the hospital *AmE*
be rushed to hospital *BrE*
be rushed to the hospital *AmE*
be airlifted/flown to hospital *BrE*, **be airlifted/flown to the hospital** *AmE* (=be taken to hospital in a plane)
be admitted to hospital *BrE*, **be admitted to the hospital** *AmE* (=be brought into a hospital for treatment)
be discharged/released from hospital *BrE*, **be discharged/released from the hospital** *AmE* (=be allowed to leave a hospital because you are better)
psychiatric hospital (=a hospital for people with mental illness)
maternity hospital (=a hospital where women have their babies)
hospital treatment/care
hospital stay (=the period that someone spends in hospital)

*He's **in hospital** recovering from an operation.* | *By the*

FIGURE 11: Entry for *hospital* from the *Longman Dictionary of Contemporary English* (Pearson Education Ltd)

Monolingual learners' dictionaries (MLDs), which are designed for students who can generally manage without bilingual dictionaries, use a special defining vocabulary (i.e. for the words used in the definitions) which explains meanings in clear and simple terms. They also give a wealth of information, as in the first part of the entry for *hospital* in Figure 11. *Hospital* is in red in the dictionary, which means it is one of the 3,000 most frequent words in English (S1 means it is one of 1,000 most common words in spoken English, W1 means that it is one of the 1,000 most common words in written English – therefore it is as common in writing as in speech). Users are given British and American pronunciation. There is a definition and then, most dramatically, a blue box full of the most common collocations and lexical phrases that *hospital* occurs in. As a result, students are made instantly aware of how the word *hospital* behaves in English and they understand where they are likely to meet it and how to use it.

- **CD-ROMs:** paper dictionaries are limited by the size of book that users are prepared to carry around with them. The same is not true of CD-ROMs, which can include a significantly greater amount of information (including audio material). Not only that, but CD-ROMs have one huge advantage, which is that users no longer have to search alphabetically (a skill that some people find difficult in both L1 and L2!). They can type in a word or phrase and it will appear on the screen, together with features such as collocation information, more corpus examples, a phrase-store, and even thesaurus-type word stores. Students can also hear the words being spoken and, perhaps, record themselves to compare with the spoken original. There is an example of an activity using a CD-ROM dictionary on pages 243–245.

- **Electronic pocket dictionaries:** many students like to carry around small electronic dictionaries which fit snugly into their pockets. Teachers sometimes find these problematic since students tend to refer to them frequently in lessons at times when we would prefer them not to be accessing such little machines. However, a more problematical issue has, in the past, been the size of the display screen and the information that is included in the dictionaries. Small screens mean that users are never going to get any of the incidental or insightful (and frequently unexpected) detail that we get when we look at a dictionary page or a computer screen. Furthermore, students have to scroll up and down continuously to find what they are looking for.

Recently, however, electronic dictionaries have improved somewhat. In the first place, the screens are bigger, and in the second place, more than one dictionary is often included.

Users can hear the words being spoken, too, and there are often extras such as spellcheckers, currency converters, etc.

Many teachers would still prefer students to use paper or computer-based dictionaries. But the lure of the small electronic models is powerful. We must hope that they continue to improve if students continue to buy them.

- **Online dictionaries:** finally, many dictionaries are now freely available online (although users may have to go through a complex registration process to be granted access).

  Many online dictionaries have clear definitions and useful information as in the example in Figure 12.

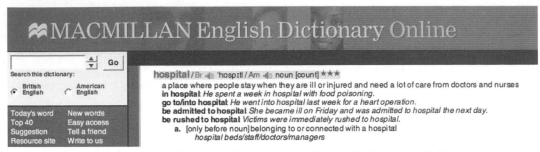

FIGURE 12: Entry for *hospital* from the *Macmillan English Dictionary Online*

Users are once again given frequency information (the entry is in red on the site), the three red stars indicating that *hospital* is one of the most frequent words in the language. By clicking on the loudspeaker symbol, users can hear the words being spoken.

G2 Concordancers

As we saw on page 34, concordancers search large corpora of language for a word or word-string that we want to know about. There are many powerful concordancing packages, but first-time users may want to try a free site at www.lextutor.ca. Users can type in a request to see 50 lines which include the search word by completing various boxes. By checking the correct boxes we can ask for the lines to be sorted alphabetically, based on the word that comes immediately before the search word. This is sometimes called left-sorting (because the words listed alphabetically are to the left of the search word). When we then click on 'get concordance' we get a concordance such as those on page 34 of this book.

Concordances are especially useful for students and teachers who want to do word research. We can also use them to design material. For example, we could print off a concordance but blank out the search word; the students have to guess what the word is. We could ask students to predict the most common words that come before and after the search word and then get them to look at the concordance lines to see if they were right.

G3 Searching the Internet

The greatest source of information not in book form is, of course, the Internet. However, its sheer size and range make it potentially awkward for users, who often find it difficult to locate the exact information they are looking for. This is partly because searching is a skill in itself which students and teachers need to acquire. For example, suppose students were doing a project on the theatre where Shakespeare's plays were first performed and they wanted to know its location, it would be unwise of them just to type the word *Shakespeare* into the popular search engine Google, because they would be offered more than 51 million sites and the vast majority of them would be irrelevant. However, if they typed in what they were really looking for in more detail (e.g. *Shakespeare Elizabethan theatre location*), they would only be offered around 420,000 sites (at the time of writing), and the first few would be of immediate relevance. Many of the others would include the words *theatre* and *location*, but would have nothing to do with Shakespeare. A way of searching precisely, however, is to type what we are looking for between inverted commas, e.g. '*Shakespeare in Love*' (the name of a fictional film about Shakespeare's life). We will then get references to that film, whereas if we type in the phrase without the inverted commas, we will get many hits about Shakespeare, and many unconnected hits on the subject of love. It is important if we want student searches to be successful, therefore, that the students know how to search effectively.

Both teachers and students can, as we have said, find almost anything they want on the Internet. They can go to online newspapers or broadcasting associations such as the BBC or CNN; they can find song lyrics or access history sites; they can find film guides and jokes sites. Two particular kinds of site are worth talking about in more detail, however.

- **Using encyclopedias:** there are a number of encyclopedia sites (and other information sites, such as biography.com) on the Internet. In their book about using technology in language teaching, Gavin Dudeney and Nicky Hockly suggest giving students charts to fill in about, say, a country, as part of a longer project (Dudeney and Hockly 2007: 46–51). They can be asked to locate the capital city, population, main languages, main cities, economy, geography, sea ports, political system, etc. Students in groups of three can look for this information on three different sites: encyclopedia.com, britannica.com and wikipedia.com (Wikipedia is an encyclopedia where any user can add to or change the information available). They can then share their information and see if the three sites agree on the information they looked for.

- **Webquests:** a particular type of information is provided by a kind of (Internet-based) extended project called a webquest. This employs Internet resources for students to use for researching, but rather than have students search on the Internet for themselves, in a webquest the teacher has prepared an introduction and then given students 'clickable' sites to visit.

  In the following webquest, designed by Philip Benz with help from Frédéric Chauthard and Michele Maurice, students have to write a report about living conditions in the tenements built for immigrants to New York in the 1820s and 1830s.

  In the *Introduction* phase, students are told about the construction of tenement houses and how people were crammed into them as tightly as possible. They are told: *You are a member of the Council of Hygiene of the Citizen's Association of New York. Your job is to investigate the living conditions in tenements and make recommendations to city officials concerning changes that need to be made.*

  In the *Task* phase, students are told that they must investigate the living conditions and write a report summarising the situation and offering solutions. They are told to use worksheets provided for them and follow the report template they are given. They are advised that they can always consult the additional resources sections on the website.

In the *Process* stage, (see Figure 13), students are given investigation stages, and, crucially, links to click on which will take them to websites that the teacher has selected so that they can complete their task.

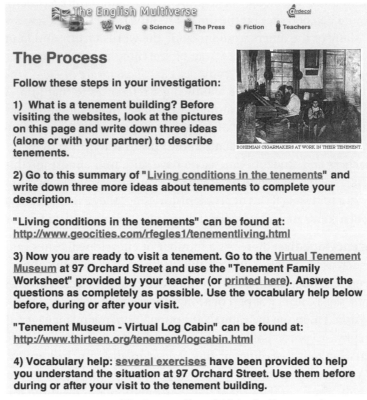

FIGURE 13: The Process (from 'Life in the Tenements' at www.ardecol.ac-grenoble.fr/english/tenement/tenementquest.htm)

Finally, in the *Evaluation* phase, students are shown how (and according to what criteria) their work will be assessed.

The point about webquests is that the Internet research is a stage towards some other goal (in this case a report). And, thanks to the wealth of material available on the Internet, students can do significant research (including text, film and audio clips) at a computer screen rather than having to go to a library (see page 280 for a fuller description of a different webquest).

H Practising language on the Internet and on CD-ROM

There are many websites on the Internet for students to practise language. Some of them are based round a school or an organisation (and need the user to register for the site), whilst others are free. Practice material is also available on CD-ROM. Some of the material is related to a particular coursebook, while other material is free-standing (i.e. it is not associated with any particular program).

1 Ways of composing

Computers and the Internet offer many opportunities for students and teachers to compose material in ways other than using pencils, pens and paper. We will examine some of the increasingly common methods of creating material both by and for students and teachers.

1.1 Word processing, word editing

In our everyday lives computers are used for writing letters, putting books together, composing reports, completing homework assignments and making lists. Of course, this can all be done by using a pen and paper. In a classroom situation when groups of writers are involved in a joint composition, we can group the students around a flip chart and have them work together with one student acting as scribe (see page 186). However, when students working in groups are using word processing software, anyone can offer and execute changes without causing unattractive crossing out, or forcing the scribe to throw a page (or sheet of paper) away and start again.

Word processed work allows teachers to give feedback in a different way, too. We can use dedicated software sub menus such as Track Changes in Microsoft Word to show where things have gone wrong or simply give comments and corrections in a different font colour from the student's original text.

1.2 Mousepals, chat and blogging

Before computers, teachers were keen for their students to correspond with penpals in different countries. This was to give students both meaningful and memorable experiences of using English, and also to help them to an appreciation of different cultures around the world.

Penpals have now morphed into mousepals and keypals; students can send each other emails instead of letters, and where such contact is well supervised and actively promoted by teachers, the benefits are soon evident. However, students will need constant attention to help them to sustain their motivation for the task.

Students can also be involved in chatting online. Indeed, many of them already do it both in their first language and in English. Teachers can organise real-time chatting events using programs such as Googletalk or MSN Messenger. It is also easy to set up groups where people exchange messages with each other, such as Yahoo Groups where people who share the same interest can post messages and reply to them.

All of this connectivity allows people to talk, whether or not they are geographically near each other. Indeed one of the great glories of the Internet is precisely this breaking down of physical barriers so that we can be in contact with each other, wherever we are and whatever the time is!

One of the most potent ways of telling people what we are thinking (and for sharing facts and events in our lives) is the weblog or blog. This is, in a sense, a public diary which anyone can read. Teachers sometimes write a blog to tell students how they are doing and what they should do next. Students or groups of students can write a diary – an instant autobiography – to tell others what they are doing and to provide feedback on how their learning is going.

Blogging is not difficult and there are many sites, such as blogger.com, which tell users how to make use of this particular resource. There is an example of a student blog on page 338.

13 **Authoring**

Of considerable interest to teachers are the many sites that allow us to download software to enable us to design our own web-based material. (This enables us to provide practice material for our students that is especially appropriate to them.) The aim of such sites is to allow teachers to key in or import their own text and then, by using the software provided, create a variety of different exercises. Perhaps the most popular of these is the Hot Potatoes site at http://hotpot.uvic.ca. We can choose whether we want students to be given multiple-choice exercises, short answer exercises, jumbled sentences, crosswords, etc. and the authoring software provides us with the type of exercise we have requested.

14 **Designing websites**

Many teachers design their own websites and even get students to make their own class websites, too. When these are put on the worldwide web (thanks to *Tripod* and *Geocities* – services of *Lycos* and *Yahoo!* respectively), anyone is allowed to visit them.

Web design is not nearly as complex as it might seem. While professional software such as Macromedia Dreamweaver and Adobe GoLive might seem a bit daunting to the beginner, Microsoft FrontPage, for example, is relatively straightforward.

Students will enjoy making their own website. Teachers can put anything they want on the web, and for private teachers (see 'Teaching one-to-one' on pages 122–125), a website is an excellent way to advertise their presence.

J Virtual learning: from emails to simulated environments

The easiest way of organising teaching, swapping material and giving feedback to students using IT is via email. Teachers can set assignments, have 'conversations' with students and give feedback on student work. However, there are Internet-based software programs designed specifically to offer teaching and training environments online.

There are a number of online courses for both students and teachers of English. These range from the downright shoddy (i.e. not worth the time that users spend on them) to serious attempts to facilitate successful learning even when groups of students are not physically present in the same space.

It is now possible to train for almost anything online, and training for English teachers is no exception. However, there is a significant difference between teacher training courses that can, apparently, be completed on websites in just a few hours, and well-designed virtual learner environments (VLEs). The idea of a VLE is that course content (including written text, audio and video lecture clips) can be stored on a website which only course participants can access. Some VLEs also contain blogs (see above) and have chat sites both in pre-arranged real time and on message boards where users can post their comments and read what others have to say. There are various platforms for VLEs (or learner management systems as they are sometimes called), including the increasingly popular *Moodle* (which is free), and *Blackboard* and *First Class* (which are not). Most VLE sites also allow for real-time tutoring so that wherever participants are situated geographically, they can participate in tutorials and even virtual classes.

A more profound learning experience takes place when we enter a new virtual world where we can move around in different buildings and different environments. *EduNation* is such a place, where people can 'go to' an island and walk around it, taking part in training activities in different buildings (see Figure 14).

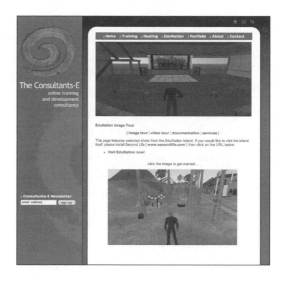

FIGURE 14: *EduNation* demonstration pictures

K Six questions

With so much technology and so many new software options available, it is sometimes difficult for teachers, directors of study and curriculum planners to know how to make choices. Almost everything sounds wonderful, and there is a temptation, sometimes, to think that all teaching and learning problems can be resolved with the purchase of a new piece of hardware or a change over to some new software-powered procedures.

The issue for decision-makers (or anyone trying to decide what to choose for their own teaching or learning) is that many of the new 'technology solutions' which are offered and updated on an almost daily basis are, indeed, very attractive. However, to adopt any one of them would require (sometimes significant) investment and, at the very least, time to learn how to make best use of it. In order, therefore, to try to think rationally and constructively about new classroom equipment of any kind, the following six questions highlight some of the considerations that should be taken into account. These questions apply not just to new technology, but also to any new methodology, procedures, coursebook or program that is offered to teachers.

Question 1: What is the pedigree?

We need to know where a new idea or piece of equipment comes from. Do its originators have a good track record in the field? A good rule of thumb is always to be suspicious, for example, of websites where you cannot find out who is responsible for them.

We are not suggesting that all new ideas have to come from tried and trusted designers or publishers. On the contrary, new people can offer new and exciting possibilities. But we still need to know who makes this thing, and what their motives are. This is partly because of question 2.

Question 2: Who gains?

If we adopt this new methodological procedure or buy this new computer or IWB, who will be the beneficiary of our purchase? If we can be sure that students will benefit, then it may be worth investing time and money in the project. The same would be true if we could say with certainty that teachers would really benefit by having their workload reduced, for example, or because their professional quality of life would somehow be enhanced.

The owner of the new technology or the proselytiser of the new method will also gain if we take on what they are offering, and there is no reason why this should not be so. However, in asking the question *Who gains?* we need to be sure that we or our students get at least as much out of what is being proposed as they do.

Question 3: Why is this the best way to do this?

FIGURE 15: Soundwave for *multicultural*

With the provision of cheap sound-editing software, it is now possible to record our voices, and, what is more, have a visual graphic of the soundwaves (Figure 15 shows the soundwave of the author saying the word *multicultural*). It certainly looks more fun than having a teacher write the word *multicultural* on the board and marking it with a board marker to show the main stress on the third syllable (see page 184 for ways of doing this). Yet most students (and teachers) are unfamiliar with soundwaves and, furthermore, do not have enough time to record and print out graphics of them. It turns out that writing words up on the board and marking them for stress actually works better (and is more cost-effective in terms of time and money) than the more high-tech option. Using soundwaves, therefore, while apparently attractive may not be the best way of showing stress. However, there are ways of using computer graphics to support pronunciation work, as we shall see on pages 261–262.

Question 4: Does it pass the TEA test?

If teachers are expected to adopt a new procedure or use a new piece of technology, it needs to pass the 'TEA' test. *T* stands for training. Unless teachers and students are helped to understand the new thing, and then given training opportunities to try it out, it will usually fail. *E* stands for the whole area of equipment. We need to be sure that the new procedure or hardware, for example, is properly supported technically. This may sound like an obvious point, but with major government-selected systems in various areas of life (health, education) sometimes failing even after huge financial investment, we should not underestimate the absolute need for teachers to be sure that the equipment is appropriate, is in place, and is properly supported by qualified professionals.

Finally, *A* stands for access. If the new technology, set of flashcards or collection of supplementary books is locked away in a cupboard for safety, it becomes inaccessible. If we have to take students down a long corridor to a computer room that has to be booked three weeks in advance, then the whole idea becomes significantly less attractive.

Question 5: What future possibilities does it open up?

When we adopt a new methodological procedure or piece of classroom equipment (or software), it is important for us to believe that it has a future. As we saw in Chapter 4, B2, many people are uneasy about one-size-fits-all methodologies, partly because they are closed to innovation and infiltration from the outside (this is especially so with procedures such as the Silent Way – see page 68). In the same way, we need to be confident that what we are investing time and money in is not a closed system – and that it has potential for expansion and future growth.

Question 6: How can I make it work?

After reading questions 1–5 above, it may seem as if we are suggesting that teachers should be extremely sceptical about new ideas and technologies, and that, in general, we should reject the new in favour of the old. However, this is far from the truth and instant rejection is just as deadening as instant acceptance can be careless.

Before rejecting any new idea or equipment, we should ask ourselves how we can make it work for us and for our students. We need to look at the 'best-case scenario' and use that to evaluate what we are being offered, not only in a cynical, but also in a positive light. That way we have a chance of judging its real worth.

Chapter notes and further reading

It is difficult to provide contemporary lists of websites that will not date. However, at the present time, readers are advised to consult the webliography at www.longman.com/methodology.

A BBC site called 'Learning English' has a wide range of ideas and activities. Dave's ESL Café (eslcafe.com) also has a lot of material for students. In the end, however, the best thing is to google areas of interest.

- **Teaching in the age of information technology**

  At the time of writing, by far the best guide to information technology and how to use it in and outside the classroom for the benefit of language teachers and students is G Dudeney and N Hockly (2007). See also D Gordon Smith and E Baber (2005).

  S Alessi and S Trollip (2001) have written a major work on multimedia for learning. R Kern (2006) has written a 'start-of-the-art' article about technology in learning and teaching.

- **'Low-tech' teaching**

  P Ahrens (1993b) designed her own rod system especially for information-gap activities which used clothes pegs and loops of string to hang pictures.

  J and C Hadfield have written a number of 'simple' activities in the Oxford Basic series (e.g. Hadfield 2001, Hadfield and Hadfield 2000).

- **Pictures**

  See K Lane (2002) on using posters, M Lewthwaite (2002) on a 'brush with art' and J Wade (2002) on 'fun with flashcards'.

- **Cuisenaire rods**

  See C Newton (2001) and J Scrivener (2005: 311–317).

- **Coursebooks**

  For more debate on the usefulness or otherwise of coursebooks, see I Freebairn (2000) and L Prodromou (2002a). J Gray (2000) looks at what teachers do with coursebooks. I McGrath (2006) investigates how teachers and students feel about coursebooks. M Rinvolucri (2002) shows how coursebooks can be 'humanised' and N McBeath (2006) advises on how to write 'really rotten materials'!

- **PowerPoint**

  A somewhat tongue-in-cheek preference for particular uses of PowerPoint as presentation software is expressed by J Harmer (2006b).

- **Interactive whiteboards (IWBs)**

  See M Hamilton (2005) and N Harris (2005). L Polkowski (2006) gives advice on 'first steps' with an IWB.

- **Dictionaries**

  See S Thornbury (2001a: 151–155). On CD-ROM dictionaries, see E Walter (2002). On electronic dictionaries, see J Stirling (2005). A Viswamohan (2005) finds that online dictionaries help her to 'keep up with the snollygosters'.

  Most major publishers have dictionaries in both book form and on CD-ROM, and many of them have online versions.

  www.dictionary.com is a website which links to many other dictionaries. There are also dictionaries of collocations and idioms, and, increasingly, highly effective bilingual dictionaries for ESL students. The best thing is to go to the individual publishers' websites and see what is on offer.

- **Concordancers**

  See G Dudeney and N Hockly (2007: Chapter 8). A Wichmann *et al* (1997) provide an important collection of applied linguistics articles about corpora in language teaching. L Dinis and K Moran (2005) and J-J Weber (2001) look at using language corpora for writing. L Gavioli and G Aston (2001) and A Frankenberg-Garcia (2005) discuss pedagogical uses of corpora. See also S Thornbury (2001a: 69–73).

- **Practising language on the Internet and on CD-ROM**

  See G Dudeney and N Hockly (2007: Chapter 9).

- **Webquests**

  The person who came up with the concept of webquests is Bernie Dodge and his website is at www.webquest.org. On webquests in general, see G Dudeney and N Hockly (2007: Chapter 4) and P Brabbs (2002).

- **Weblogs**

  J Askari Arani (2005) discusses using weblogs to teach reading and writing. See also E Catera and R Emigh (2005) who call blogs 'the ultimate soapbox'. See also G Dudeney and N Hockly (2007: Chapter 7).

- **Mousepals, chat and blogging**
  On key/mousepals see H Hennigan (1999) and D Linder (2000). G Dudeney and N Hockly (2007: Chapter 5) have a wealth of materials on how to use emailing.

- **Authoring**
  See G Dudeney and N Hockly (2007: Chapter 10) and D Gordon Smith and E Baber (2005: Chapter 9).

- **Designing websites**
  See D Gordon Smith and E Baber (2005: Chapter 8).

- **Virtual learning: from emails to simulated environments**

  See G Dudeney and N Hockly (2007: Chapter 11). See G Woodman (2005) for an account of developing online materials in a specific setting.

- **Using soundwaves**
  D Coniam (2003a) argues strongly that using soundwave software *is* useful in helping students to 'better appreciate English stress timing'.

12 | Teaching language construction

When students study the construction of a specific feature of the language, they do so either because it is new to them and they want to understand and use it or because they want to revise it in order to improve their ability to use it without making errors. The immediate goal of this kind of language study is to increase knowledge of the language system so that the longer term aim of improving productive and receptive skills can be achieved. As we shall see in the next three chapters, students do not only study language in classrooms under the direction of a teacher, but can also be involved in researching language on their own. We may also have as one of our goals the training of autonomous learners (see Chapter 23A). However, the vast majority of students of English benefit from a teacher-mediated focus on specific language forms.

A Studying structure and use

The language study which is discussed in this chapter comprises a focus on the structure and use of language forms, particularly in the following areas:

- the morphology of forms (e.g. the fact that *is* and *am* are forms of *be*, but **amn't* is not)
- the syntax of phrases, clauses and sentences (e.g. the rules of question formation or the construction of *if*-sentences)
- vocabulary, including the meanings of words, their lexical grammar (e.g. the fact that *enjoy* can be followed by an *-ing* form but not by an infinitive), and collocation rules (e.g. we say *even-handed* but not *even-footed*)
- the meanings and functions that phrases and sentences can convey
- pronunciation
- spelling

Text and paragraph construction – including the study of genre in spoken and written text – will be discussed in Chapter 19, B2.

A1 Language study in lesson sequences

The status of language study depends on why and when it occurs. It may, for example, form the main focus of a lesson: we might say, for instance, that a chief part of today's lesson will be the teaching of relative clauses, the future continuous or ways of suggesting, and design the lesson around this central purpose.

Language study may not be the main focus of a lesson sequence, however, but may be only one element in a grander design, in which case a decision will have to be taken about where the study activity should be placed in the sequence. Should the focus on any necessary language forms take place before, during or after the performance of a communicative task or a receptive skills activity? Or should students focus on language prior to using it in a task?

One approach (often taken by materials writers) is for students to study language in a variety of ways, explore a topic and then use what they have learnt to perform a task (see, for example, the *Cutting Edge* series by Sarah Cunningham and Peter Moor, published by Pearson Education, and Nunan 2004). Alternatively, the study of language forms may happen during a task-based sequence. We might focus on one or two past tense forms in the middle of an extended narrative-writing task; we might have our students study or research vocabulary to describe the weather in the middle of a sequence on holiday planning.

A third option is to study forms after the students have performed the task. This usually happens as a form of language repair when the task has shown up language problems – or when students might have found the task easier if they had been able to produce certain language forms which they did not use at all. As we saw in Chapter 4, studying language after the task has been completed is a feature of a different approach to Task-based learning from the one in the paragraph above. In other words, these three options suggest that rather than always using Straight arrows sequences, we will often find that Boomerang or Patchwork lessons are more suitable.

However, even where we have not planned when and how to include language study in a particular lesson sequence, we sometimes find opportunities presenting themselves which it is impossible to ignore. As a result, we get students to focus on language items which we had not anticipated including. Such opportunistic study may happen because a student wants to know how some element of language is constructed or why it is constructed as it is. It might take place because completely unforeseen problems present themselves; we might suddenly become aware of the chance to offer students some language which up till now they haven't been able to use but which – if they are now exposed to it – will significantly raise the level at which they are performing the task.

Opportunistic teaching – studying language which suddenly 'comes up' – exposes the tension between planning lessons in advance and responding to what actually happens (see Chapter 21). When used appropriately, the relevance and immediacy of opportunistic language study may make it the most memorable and effective kind of language study there is.

Many study activities (especially in coursebooks) have tended to follow the PPP model (see Chapter 4, A2 and A3), and there are often good reasons for this. But at other times (and with more advanced students, for example) such 'explain and practise' sequences may be entirely inappropriate. Instead, we may want to encourage students to discover or notice language before we ask them to use it. At other times, we may ask students to research language as part of an ongoing lesson sequence. We may also wish to preface a study exercise with activities which show us how much of the language in question is already known, or we may interleave the study with other elements.

A2 Choosing study activities

We will frequently decide how and when to have students study language form and use on the basis of the syllabus and/or the coursebook since it may offer an explanation and an exercise that we are happy to use almost unchanged. However, some of these sequences may not suit the particular styles and progress of our learners, and may thus need adjusting or replacing in some way. We may want to try out new activities, or may wish to avoid using the same kind of activity day after day. How then do we make such decisions?

- **Following planning principles:** when deciding how to have students study language form, we need to bear general planning principles in mind (see Chapter 21B). This means that we have to think about activities which the students do before and after this study session so that we do not simply repeat the same kind of activity again and again. We need to offer a varied diet of exercises when studying language construction both because all our students have different learning styles (see Chapter 5, B3 and B4), and also because we want help them sustain their motivation.

- **Assessing a language study activity for use in class:** when assessing an activity designed for the study of language form, we need to decide how effective it will be when we take it into class. It should justify the time we will need to spend on it both before and during the lesson. We need to believe that the activity demonstrates meaning and use clearly and that it allows opportunities for a focus on (and practice of) the construction of the language form. We have to be confident that it will engage our learners successfully.

  One way of assessing study activities is to judge their efficiency and their appropriacy. In terms of efficiency, we might want to assess the economy, ease and efficacy of the activity. Economy means that the time we spend setting up the activity is in a satisfactory ratio to the payoff the activity provides, In other words, if an activity takes three minutes to explain but only yields 45 seconds of practice, it is uneconomical. An easy activity is one that is simple for the teacher to use and organise. An efficacious activity is one that works (i.e. the students get out of it what they are supposed to get out of it). If the activity says it will teach students how the second conditional is used, it is efficacious if it does this, but it is not if it fails to explain the second conditional properly. In terms of appropriacy, we need to judge whether the activity is suitable for the time of day, the classroom conditions and for a particular group of students, taking into account their level, their educational background and their cultural sensibilities (Thornbury 1999b: 25–27).

  We often take activities and exercises into class that we have used before with other groups. We will have, therefore, a good idea of how effective they will be. Nevertheless, we need to remember that all groups are different, and that what was appropriate for one class may not work as well with other students.

- **Evaluating a study activity after use in class:** once a lesson is over, we need to evaluate the success of the activity or activities which focused on language form, whether we do this formally or informally. This is one reason why we should keep records of our classes and why we should conduct our own action research (see Chapter 24, B1).

  Evaluation of an activity answers questions such as whether or not the exercise helped students to learn the new language (efficacy), whether it was clear, whether it took more or less time than anticipated (economy), whether students were engaged by it (appropriacy) and whether or not we want to use it again. Part of this evaluation involves us in thinking about how we might modify the activity the next time we use it.

A3 Known or unknown language?

Unless we are teaching real beginners, each individual student has some degree of linguistic knowledge and ability in English. In addition to this, as we saw in Chapter 5, individual students learn at different speeds and in different ways. These two facts, taken together, explain why so many classes can rightly be described as 'mixed ability' (see page 127) – though the difference in level between students is more extreme in some cases than in others.

The fact of mixed ability throws up a problem for the study of new language forms since it will frequently be impossible to know whether such forms really are new or not for individual students in a class. And even if most of our students have come across the language before, it is not necessarily the case that they can all use it.

If – for the reasons stated above – we are not sure whether or not our students know the language we are about to ask them to study, we will need to find this information out. If we do not, we risk teaching students things they already know or assuming knowledge they do not have.

One way of avoiding teaching already-known language is to have students perform tasks and see how well they use the language forms in question before deciding whether we need to introduce those forms as if they were new. A less elaborate technique is to attempt to *elicit* the new language forms we wish them to study. If we find that students can produce them satisfactorily, we will not want to demonstrate or explain them all over again, and getting students to reproduce the new language accurately through the use of repetition and drills will be a waste of time. If elicitation is unsuccessful, however, we have good grounds for treating the language forms as new and proceeding accordingly.

B Explain and practise

Commentators have described an 'explain and practise' approach to teaching language construction as a *deductive* approach, even though this term seems somewhat unhelpful. In a deductive approach, students are given explanations or grammar rules and then, based on these explanations or rules, they make phrases and sentences using the new language. Explain and practise sequences are usually PPP-like, or what we have called 'Straight arrows' (see page 67).

In the following example for teaching the present continuous, the sequence starts when the teacher engages the students by showing them pictures of people doing various actions (painting a house, fixing the roof, cutting the grass, etc.). Following this lead-in (getting the students' interest, introducing the situation, etc.), the teacher tries to elicit the sentences he or she is thinking of teaching (in case the students know the language already, in which case explaining it all over again may not be a good idea). So the teacher might hold up a picture of someone painting a house and ask *Can anyone tell me what she's doing? Anyone? She's ...? Does anyone know?* If the students can produce the sentence, the teacher might indicate other pictures and elicit the language for them, too. If the students also perform well on this, the teacher can go straight to an activate (or 'immediate creativity') stage where the students try to make their own present continuous sentences, perhaps about what members of their family or their friends are doing right now.

If, however, as expected, the students don't manage to produce the sentences, the teacher will explain the new language. Perhaps he or she will say *OK ... look and listen ... she's fixing the roof ... listen ... fixing ... fixing ... she's fixing the roof ... everybody*, and the students repeat the sentence in chorus. The teacher will then have students make sentences about the other activities, sometimes explaining again and correcting where necessary. The students will then be involved in some repetition and cue–response drilling (see B2 below) and may do some practice in pairs. All of this stage of the lesson (repetition, drilling and controlled practice) is designed to foster accurate reproduction of what the teacher is introducing.

Finally, the teacher may ask for immediate creativity, where students use the new language (in this case the present continuous) to talk about their own lives or the actions of people they know (see above). If during this stage the students perform badly, the teacher may return either to the explanation stage or to the accurate reproduction stage to reinforce what was previously introduced.

The sequence is summarised in Figure 1.

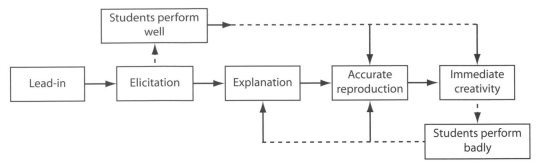

FIGURE 1: A typical explain and practise sequence

B1 Explaining things

During the explanation stage we will need to demonstrate both meaning and language construction. There are many ways to do this.

- **Explaining meaning:** one of the clearest ways of explaining the meaning of something is to show it. If we hold up a book, point to it and say *book ... book*, the meaning will be instantly clear. For actions, we can use mime: if we are teaching *He is running*, we can mime someone running. At other times we can use gesture. We can demonstrate superlative adjectives by using hand and arm movements to show *big ... bigger ... biggest*, and many teachers have standard gestures to explain such things as the past (a hand pointing backwards over the shoulder), or the future (a hand pointing forwards). We can also use facial expressions to explain the meaning of *sad, happy, frightened*, etc.

  We can use pictures to explain situations and concepts (for example, a picture of someone coming away from a swimming pool with dripping wet hair to show *She's just been swimming*). We can use diagrams, too. Many teachers use time lines to explain time, simple versus continuous verb forms and aspect (e.g. perfect tenses). For example, if we want to explain the present perfect continuous tense, we can use a time line to explain *I've been living here since* 2005.

  If we can't show something in one of the ways mentioned above, we can describe the meaning of the word. For example a *generous* person is someone who shares their time and their money/possessions with you. *Nasty* is the opposite of *nice*. A *radish* is a kind of vegetable.

  If describing meaning isn't appropriate, we can list vocabulary items to explain concepts. For example, if we want students to understand the idea of *the caring professions* (perhaps because the phrase came up in a text), we can list a number of jobs such as *doctor, nurse, social worker* and *counsellor* to explain the phrase. We can also use check questions to make sure students have understood correctly. If they are learning how to make third conditional sentences and one of the examples is *If she'd missed the train, she would have been late for the meeting*, we can ask the students questions such as *Did she miss the train?* and *Was she late for the meeting?*

A way of making meaning absolutely clear, of course, is to translate words and phrases. Sometimes this is easy; all languages have a word for *book*. Sometimes, however, it is more complex; many languages do not have an absolute equivalent for the English phrase *devil-may-care attitude* and translating idioms such as *to pull the wool over someone's eyes* means having to find an L1 equivalent, even though it may be constructed completely differently. Nevertheless, as we saw in Chapter 7, D1, translation may have an important part to play in foreign language learning.

The trick of explaining meaning effectively is to choose the best method to fit the meaning that needs to be explained. In actual fact, most teachers use a mixture of some or all of these techniques. However, check questions are especially important since they allow us to determine if our explanations have been effective.

- **Explaining language construction:** one of the most common ways of explaining language construction is through modelling sentences and phrases. For example, if we want to model *He's fixing the roof*, we may say *Listen ... he's fixing the roof ... listen ... fixing ... fixing ... he's ... he is ... he is ... he's ... he's fixing the roof*. What we have done is to say the model normally (*He's fixing the roof*) before isolating certain parts of the model (*fixing ... fixing ... he's*). We distort one of the isolated fragments (*he's*) by lengthening it (to explain its contracted form, i.e. *he is ... he is ...*) before returning to the isolated element and finally saying the whole model clearly so that students can repeat it. This procedure is represented in Figure 2:

FIGURE 2: Modelling language construction

Many teachers use fingers or hands, too, to show how *he is* turns into *he's* (see Figure 3) or how *fast* and *er* are joined together to make a comparative adjective. We can also demonstrate word and sentence stress by beating time with our arms. We can show intonation patterns by 'drawing' the tune in the air.

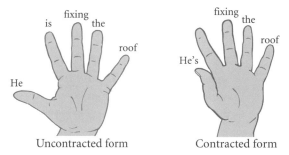

FIGURE 3: Using fingers to show how *he is* becomes *he's*

Some students will find such graphic gestures sufficient, but others like to see written explanations, diagrams on boards or overhead projectors (see page 185). For example, if we want to show how words are stressed we can use one of the markings from Figure 4.

FIGURE 4: Different ways of marking word stress

One way of demonstrating grammatical sequence is to write words on individual cards (see page 180) which can then be moved around (to show the difference between affirmative sentence order and the syntax of questions, for example). We can also manipulate a set of Cuisenaire rods (see page 180). They can be used to show parts of speech, stress patterns and sentence construction.

It is sometimes more appropriate to explain language construction with words. For example, if we want students to understand the rule about the third person singular of the present simple, we can say *Listen ... we say I play, you play, we play, they play, but with he, she and it we add an s. Listen, I play, she plays ... you play, he plays ... we play, it plays.*

However, we will need to be careful that (a) explaining the construction of the language is fairly easy to do, and (b) that we can do it in language which the students we are teaching will find easy to understand.

B2   **Practice (accurate reproduction)**

During the practice – or accurate reproduction – phase of an explain and practise sequence we will first get students repeating the new language before then moving on to practise it.

- **Repetition:** repetition can be either choral or individual. When we use choral repetition, we get all the students to say the new word or phrase together.

  For choral repetition to be effective, it is important to start the chorus clearly (so that everyone gets going at once) and to help the students with the rhythm by 'conducting' the chorus, using arms and hands to show where stress occurs, etc. Choral repetition can be invigorating, and it gives all the students a chance to speak together rather than being (possibly) shown up individually.

  Sometimes teachers divide the class in half (when working with a two-person dialogue, for example) and give each of the dialogue roles to one or other half. The conversation is then spoken in semi-chorus, with the two halves each taking their turn to speak.

  When we think students have been given sufficient repetition time in chorus (or if we don't see the need for choral repetition), we may ask for individual repetition. We do this by nominating students and asking them to give us the sentence, e.g.

TEACHER:	OK. Sam?
STUDENT 1 (SAM):	They're painting the house.
TEACHER:	Good. Kim?
STUDENT 2 (KIM):	They're painting the house.
TEACHER:	Good.
ETC.	

  It is worth remembering not to nominate students in an obvious order (e.g. by going from one end of a row to the other) since this will make the activity predictable and, as a result, will not keep students on their toes.

  A form of individual practice which some teachers and students find useful is for students to say the word or phrase quietly to themselves, murmuring it a few times as they get used to saying it. It may sound strange to hear everyone speaking the phrase quietly to themselves at the same time, but it gives them all a chance for individual repetition, a chance once again to see how it feels to say the new language.

- **Drills:** if we feel that students have done enough repetition of a phrase or phrases (or if we don't think such repetition is necessary), we may organise a quick cue–response session to encourage controlled practice of the new language. Suppose, for example, that we have taught a group of beginner students a series of phrases such as *They're painting the house, He's fixing the roof, She's mowing the grass,* etc., and that we have pictures of these actions on cards. We can use these cards as a cue, which we hope will then elicit the appropriate response, e.g.

TEACHER (HOLDS UP PICTURE OF TWO PEOPLE PAINTING THE OUTSIDE OF A HOUSE): *Sam?*
STUDENT 1 (SAM): *They're painting the house.*
TEACHER: *Good. (holds up picture of a someone fixing the roof) Kim?*
STUDENT 2 (KIM): *He's fixing the roof.*
TEACHER: *Good.*

Cues can also be verbal (e.g. *Question … film* to get the response *What time does the film start?*) or non-verbal (e.g. the teacher shrugs their shoulders to elicit *I don't know*).

Cue–response drills are an efficient way of getting the students to say the new language in a way that can be invigorating and challenging. If we think students need more controlled practice of this type, we can put them in pairs and ask them to continue saying the new words and phrases to each other. Perhaps they can take turns miming one of the actions or showing/drawing pictures of painting, fixing and mowing, etc. so that they are, in effect, conducting cue–response drills of their own.

C Discover (and practise)

In a so-called inductive approach, things are organised somewhat differently from the explain and practise sequences we have looked at above. Instead of having meaning and construction explained to them, students see examples of language and try to work out how it is put together. Thus, for example, after students have read a text, we can ask them to find examples of different past tenses and say how and why they are used. This Boomerang-type lesson (like 'PPP upside down' in Jane Willis's description – see page 71) is especially appropriate where language study arises out of skills work on reading and listening texts.

If we want students to understand how speakers in informal conversation use certain phrases as delaying tactics (or to buy 'thinking' time), we might – after letting them listen and respond to someone speaking spontaneously – get them to listen again, but this time reading a transcript of what is being said. The task we give them is to find language used for buying time – hoping that they will identify phrases like *you know, I mean, yeah, mmm,* etc.

If we want students at an intermediate or upper intermediate level to work on narrative tenses, we might show them the following text, and ask them to underline all the verbs which refer to the past:

Sarah told me an amazing story about her boyfriend, Peter. It appears that he was on holiday with a friend of his, a guy named Gordon. They had gone out for dinner in the resort they were holidaying in and had stayed out quite late. As a result they missed the last bus and had to walk home.

Peter was knocked down by a car as he crossed the road near their hotel. Perhaps he hadn't looked carefully enough before crossing the street. But a car was coming down the street, and he ended up underneath it. He was in real danger. Somehow they had to get the car off him. But there was only the female driver of the car and Gordon. That's when Gordon did this amazing thing. Despite the fact that he is not very strong (and they had, after all, just eaten a big dinner), he somehow managed to lift the car off Peter just long enough for them to get him out.

Peter stayed in hospital for some time, but he made a complete recovery. He says that he might have died if Gordon hadn't been so heroic. Gordon still can't understand how he did it, but he has quite enjoyed being a hero!

Students will underline simple past verbs (*told, was, was knocked down, ended up, had to*, etc.), past continuous verbs (*were holidaying, was coming*), past perfect verbs (*had gone out, had stayed out, hadn't looked*) and hypothetical past perfect (*would have died*). They can then discuss why each is used before going on to a practice stage and immediate creativity of their own.

As we saw on page 57, discovery activities like this suit some students very well; they enjoy working things out. Many people think that the language they understand in this way is more powerfully learnt (because they had to make some cognitive effort as they uncovered its patterns) than it would have been if they were told the grammar rules first and didn't have to make such an effort. However, not all students feel comfortable with this approach and would still prefer to be 'spoon-fed'. A lot will depend on their level. It is generally easier for more advanced students to analyse language using discovery procedures than it is for complete beginners. The Boomerang sequence is often more appropriate with students who already have a certain amount of language available to them for the first activation stage than it is with students who can say very little. Discovery activities are especially useful when students are looking at the construction of specific language for the second or third time. When we ask them to look at the use of different past tenses in a story and to work out how they are used and why, we assume that they know the individual tenses. The detective work they are doing now is intended to expand their knowledge and revise things they are already familiar with.

When students have discovered the language construction features they have been looking for, we may get them to use them either as accurate reproduction or immediate creativity. If this is a second or third visit to a particular area of language, however, accurate reproduction may be unnecessary (and inappropriate). Instead, we will encourage students to try to use the language for themselves. Of course, if they can't do this – or if they have failed to discover what they were looking for – we may have to explain things all over again, and then we will find ourselves back in the procedure we outlined in Figure 1. But this is less likely to happen in discovery activities than in explain and practise sequences.

D Research (and practise)

An alternative to explain and practise and discovery activities (but which is nevertheless a combination of the two) is to have students do language research on their own. For example, if students are working on how we use our bodies to express meaning (e.g. *waving, clenching, shrugging, wagging*), we could give them a number of collocations (e.g. *wave my arm, clench my teeth, shrug my shoulders, wag my finger*) and tell them to use them in sentences, or perhaps ask them to talk about what the actions mean. However, it might be far more memorable for them (and include the kind of agency we talked about in Chapter 5, D3) if we asked them to do the work themselves. Thus we could ask them to consult a dictionary, looking up both the verb and the various parts of the body to see if they appear to collocate. We could get them to access a concordance of various words such as *arm*, *teeth*, *shoulders*, etc. to see what collocations turn up. Or we could encourage them to use a search engine, such as Google, to see if collocations work. For example, if students want to know if *wave* and *arm* go together they can type *waved his arm* between quotation marks, and they will get something like the results in Figure 5.

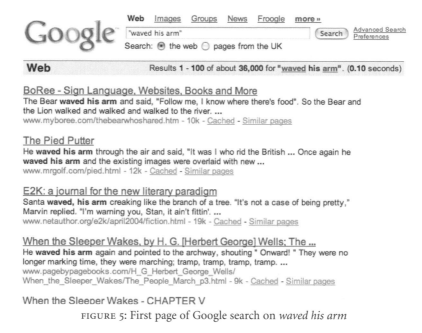

FIGURE 5: First page of Google search on *waved his arm*

When students research language, they are far more likely to remember what they find out than if they sit passively and are given words. The more we can encourage them to do this, the better – although, as we discussed in Chapter 4B, imposing such behaviour on students, whoever they are and whatever they want or need, may be inappropriate. Language research is more likely to be effective at higher levels, though much will depend on the personality of the students.

As with discovery activities, when students have researched language, we may ask them to use the language they have discovered. However, if they find this impossible to do, we may have to return to explanations and accurate reproduction. Indeed, as with everything we have discussed, the degree to which teachers use repetition and drilling depends to a large extent on their judgement of when it is appropriate and when it is not. Over-drilling, especially as students move to higher levels, can have a very demotivating effect, but as we have seen (and as all classroom learners know), in its place it can be very effective and even enjoyable. The trick is to stop it as soon as possible.

Chapter notes and further reading

On teaching language construction in general, see T Hedge (2000: Part 2).

- **Drills and drilling**

On chorus drilling, see N McIver (2000). On drills in general, see S Mumford (2003, 2006).

13 | Teaching grammar

Grammar teaching sometimes happens as a result of other work the students are doing – for example, when they study language in a text they have been reading or listening to, or when a grammar problem presents itself unexpectedly in the middle of a lesson and we feel we have to deal with it on the spot (see page 366). Grammar teaching may grow directly from the tasks students are performing or have just performed as part of a focus-on-form approach (see pages 53–54).

At other times, however, we rely on the coursebooks we are using to help us teach grammar, or we plan in advance what grammar we wish our students to be studying. Most teachers have their own favourite grammar presentation and practice activities and will often use these when they want students to study a particular piece of grammar.

Grammar can be introduced in a number of ways, or we can show students grammar evidence and ask them to work out for themselves how the language is constructed (see Chapter 3C). We will also want to provide opportunities for students to practise different grammar points, and we may want to use games to make such practice more engaging.

In Chapter 12, A2 we discussed the need for effective activities to be both efficient and appropriate. The range of activities which we will look at in this chapter all satisfy these two requirements in different ways. We will also discuss grammar books and their uses.

A Introducing grammar

The following activities represent a range of possibilities (some simple, some more elaborate) for introducing new grammar.

Example 1: The postman	Language: present simple
	Age: any
	Level: beginner/elementary

In this grammar presentation (which follows a PPP or Straight arrows sequence in terms of ESA – see page 67), students learn how to make sentences using the present simple in the third person singular. They have already learnt how to say affirmative and negative sentences in the first and second person (e.g. *I like coffee, you don't like bananas*).

The teacher holds up a number of flashcards (see Figure 1) and elicits the words *dog*s, *get up*, *doorbell*, *car*, *uniform*, *a lot of money*. The students say them chorally (see page 206) and individually before doing a quick cue–response drill using the different pictures as prompts. If the pictures are not on flashcards, they may be on OHTs or shown through a data projector – or even drawn on the board.

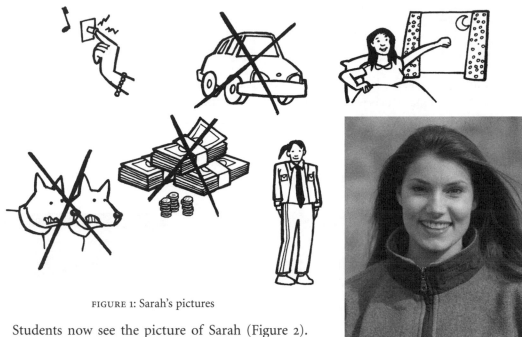

FIGURE 1: Sarah's pictures

FIGURE 2: Sarah

Students now see the picture of Sarah (Figure 2). The teacher asks the students what they think Sarah's job is, but does not confirm or deny their suggestions.

The teacher explains that she is going to tell them what Sarah does every day. She says the following sentences and the students have to choose which flashcard or picture is being talked about.

> *She doesn't like dogs.*
> *She gets up early.*
> *She doesn't drive a car.*
> *She rings doorbells.*
> *She doesn't earn a lot of money.*
> *She wears a uniform.*

When the students have guessed (confirmed their guesses) that Sarah is a postwoman, the teacher holds up the cards individually and tries to elicit the sentences about each one. She models the sentences and probably gets choral and individual repetition before moving on, in the accurate reproduction stage (see page 206), to conduct a cue–response drill by holding up, say, card C so that the students have to say *She rings doorbells.*

Once students are reasonably confident with these sentences, the teacher asks them to think of a real person (or invent their own) and what their job is. They are asked to come up with three affirmative and three negative sentences about what that person does or doesn't do every day. While they are doing this, the teacher goes round monitoring their work (offering help or correcting where necessary).

The pairs now read out their sentences and the rest of the class have to guess what profession is being described.

Example 2: Girls' night out	Language:	past simple irregular verbs
	Age:	young adult plus
	Level:	elementary

In this example, the language to be studied is presented to the students in a text.

The sequence starts when the teacher asks the students whether girls in their country often go out together and where, if they do, they go. Students can discuss this in pairs or small groups before reporting back to the class.

The students now look at two texts (see Figure 3) and try to decide if they are about a night out in Rio de Janeiro, Beijing or Moscow. When they have done this, the teacher checks they all have the same answer.

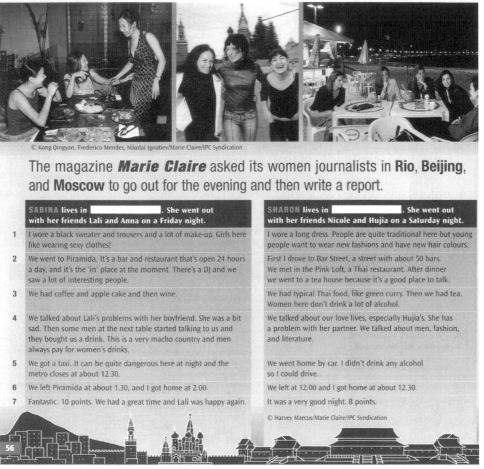

© Kong Qingyan, Frederico Mendes, Nikolai Ignatiev/Marie Claire/IPC Syndication

The magazine **Marie Claire** asked its women journalists in **Rio**, **Beijing**, and **Moscow** to go out for the evening and then write a report.

SABINA lives in [   ]. She went out with her friends Lali and Anna on a Friday night.

1. I wore a black sweater and trousers and a lot of make-up. Girls here like wearing sexy clothes!
2. We went to Piramida. It's a bar and restaurant that's open 24 hours a day, and it's the 'in' place at the moment. There's a DJ and we saw a lot of interesting people.
3. We had coffee and apple cake and then wine.
4. We talked about Lali's problems with her boyfriend. She was a bit sad. Then some men at the next table started talking to us and they bought us a drink. This is a very macho country and men always pay for women's drinks.
5. We got a taxi. It can be quite dangerous here at night and the metro closes at about 12.30.
6. We left Piramida at about 1.30, and I got home at 2.00.
7. Fantastic. 10 points. We had a great time and Lali was happy again.

SHARON lives in [   ]. She went out with her friends Nicole and Hujia on a Saturday night.

1. I wore a long dress. People are quite traditional here but young people want to wear new fashions and have new hair colours.
2. First I drove to Bar Street, a street with about 50 bars. We met in the Pink Loft, a Thai restaurant. After dinner we went to a tea house because it's a good place to talk.
3. We had typical Thai food, like green curry. Then we had tea. Women here don't drink a lot of alcohol.
4. We talked about our love lives, especially Hujia's. She has a problem with her partner. We talked about men, fashion, and literature.
5. We went home by car. I didn't drink any alcohol so I could drive.
6. We left at 12.00 and I got home at about 12.30.
7. It was a very good night. 8 points.

© Harvey Marcus/Marie Claire/IPC Syndication

56

FIGURE 3: Girls' night out from *New English File Elementary* by C Oxenden, C Latham-Koenig and P Seligson (Oxford University Press)

The students now match questions, such as *Did you have a good time? How did you go home? What did you do? What did you have to eat and drink?* and *What did you wear?* with the women's answers, marked 1–7 in the texts. Then they fill in a chart with ticks for Sabina or Sharon, depending on whether they wore a dress, went to a bar, talked about men, went home by taxi, etc.

Their attention is drawn to the irregular verbs by an exercise which asks them to find the past tense forms of certain verbs (see Figure 4).

3 GRAMMAR past simple irregular verbs

a Look at the reports again and find the past tense of these irregular verbs.

wear	_____	/wɔː/
go	_____	/went/
see	_____	/sɔː/
have	_____	/hæd/
buy	_____	/bɔːt/
get	_____	/gɒt/
leave	_____	/left/
drive	_____	/drəʊv/
meet	_____	/met/
can	_____	/kʊd/

FIGURE 4: Textsearch

The phonemic forms of these past tense verb forms are given as a back-up for those students who are comfortable reading at least some phonemic symbols.

When students have identified the past tense verb forms, the teacher gets them to say them just to check that they are pronouncing them correctly. They now look at a grammar chart (see Figure 5) before doing exercises where they fill in a short text with the correct form of the verbs *be*, *buy*, *go*, *wear*, *look*, *have*, *see*, etc.

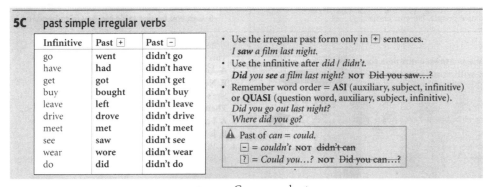

FIGURE 5: Grammar chart

Students now listen to the third girl (Silvia) talking about her night out. They can then ask and tell each other about their own experiences of going out with friends, using the verbs they have been learning.

Example 3: Disappointment	Language: Age: Level:	reported speech teenage plus intermediate

This sequence teaches students the differences between reporting speech as it happens and how this changes when we report things that were said in the past.

We show students a picture of two young men walking down the street. One of them has a mobile phone clamped to his ear and looks really happy. The other is listening to him with a look of resignation on his face. If we can't get hold of a picture, we simply draw two faces on the board (see Figure 6) and mime what follows.

FIGURE 6: Disappointment: Board drawing 1

We give the young man on the phone a name (Jack). We ask the students who Jack is talking to and we elicit the fact that he's talking to a young woman he met in the school canteen. That's why he's looking so happy. We ask the students what the young woman is saying to Jack and elicit sentences like *You're really nice, I'll see you this evening, I like your jacket, Your friend gave me your number, I've got two tickets to a concert, you can come with me.*

We now ask the students what Jack tells his friend as the conversation goes on (we point to the picture which shows him covering the mouthpiece of the phone), and we elicit and model sentences like *She says I'm really nice, She says she'll see me this evening, She says she likes my jacket*, etc. We make sure the students understand that Jack uses the present (*says*) because he's reporting the conversation as it happens. We make sure they understand how *you* changes to *I*.

We can get some students to suggest more of the girl's sentences and have their classmates pretend to be Jack and report the conversation.

We now tell the students that it is a few hours later. Jack is back at his house looking really glum (see Figure 7). We explain that he went to the concert to meet the girl but she never turned up. His mother asks him, *What did she say again?* We now elicit and model sentences such as *She said I was really nice, She said she would see me this evening, She said she liked my jacket*, etc. We ask the students why the verb *say* is in the past (because Jack is talking about a past conversation) and what effect that has (*is*

FIGURE 7: Disappointment: Board drawing 2

becomes *was, will* becomes *would, like* becomes *liked,* etc.). We can write this up on the board to help students (see Figure 8).

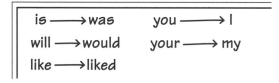

FIGURE 8: Board explanation

Students can now pretend to be having conversations with other people and report what they say in the same way, and then later they can report the conversation in the past.

Example 4: Light in space	Language: Age: Level:	*should/shouldn't have done* any intermediate/upper intermediate

In Example 2 above, the language which the students were going to study (past tense forms) was embedded in the texts which they read. This next sequence, however, uses the story of the text as a situation to provoke a number of statements using the target structure.

The sequence starts when the students are asked if they ever read science fiction, making sure that they understand what genre of fiction we are talking about. This might develop into a quick discussion of what they read and why. The point is to get them engaged and interested in what is coming. Students can be prompted to say what they would expect to find in a science fiction text.

We now ask the students to read the text in Figure 9. While they do this, they must find out information such as how many people are in the space station at the beginning and end of the text, whether they are men or women, and how long they've been there.

They had been up here for five years. Five years for five people, cut off from Earth since World War IV. True the Moonshuttle came every six months with a supply of food, but it was pilotless. They had not been able to make contact with Moonbase for two years. Cathy said it was weird.

'You say that three times a day,' Rosie answered.

'Well, it's true. It's weird and I don't think I can stand it much longer.'

'Oh for Jupiter's sake, shut up! Go and play eight-dimensional death-chess and leave me alone. You drive me crazy!'

'Thanks,' Cathy said quietly, 'I can see I'm not wanted.' She left the cabin. The door hissed behind her.

When she got to the exit chamber, she didn't look at the record book where Mitch had written 'nine – motor malfunction. Do not use'. She got into suit number nine and pressed the exit key. The outside door hissed open and she sailed out into space. She hadn't told the others where she was going (spacestation rule 345/2/Z3). It gave her a good sense of freedom.

Back in the station Rosie saw the red warning light above the exit control but she ignored it. They'd had trouble with the lights recently. Nothing serious. Captain Clarke saw it, though. She got on her personal people communicator and called Tim Hotzenfop, the station engineer.

'I think we've got a problem. You'd better come up quick.' But Tim was deep in conversation with Leila so he said 'Sure. I'll be up,' and then switched off the radio. Leila was nicer to listen to than old Clarke.

Mitch was in the repair shop next to the exit chamber when the audio-alarm went off. But he was wearing his spacewalk-man. He didn't hear a thing.

200 metres away from the station, Cathy suddenly realised that she had forgotten to close the station exit door. She must go back. She pressed the motor control on the front of her suit. There was no response. She pressed it again. Nothing. At that moment, looking back, she saw the space station she had just left roll over and she thought she heard a scream echoing out into the darkness. Her eyes widened in horror. And then she saw the light.

FIGURE 9: Light in space

When the students have read the text and shown that they have understood it by answering comprehension questions, we can then ask them to say what they think happens next. What is the light? What has happened to the space station and why? The object is to get them to be creative with language and with their response to the text.

We now ask the students to list things that people did that were 'bad' or 'not sensible' and write them on the board (see Figure 10).

a) Rosie was rude to Cathy.
b) Cathy didn't look at the record book.
c) Cathy didn't tell the others where she was going.
d) Rosie ignored the red warning light.
e) Tim switched off his radio.
f) Tim didn't do anything about the captain's call.
g) Mitch was wearing his spacewalk-man.
h) Cathy didn't close the station exit door.

FIGURE 10: Space sentences

We then ask the students if they can make a sentence about event a) using *should not* to elicit the sentence *Rosie shouldn't have been rude to Cathy*. We may write *should (not) have DONE* on the board. We then encourage students to make sentences about the other 'silly' actions, using the same construction. We may get students to come up to the board and write the sentences so that the board ends up looking like Figure 11.

a) Rosie was rude to Cathy.   She shouldn't have been rude to Cathy.
b) Cathy didn't look at the record book.   She should have looked at the record book.
c) Cathy didn't tell the others where she was going.   She should have told the others where she was going.
d) Rosie ignored the red warning light.   She shouldn't have ignored the red warning light.
e) Tim switched off his radio.   He shouldn't have switched off his radio.
f) Tim didn't do anything about the captain's call.   He should have done something about it.
g) Mitch was wearing his spacewalk-man.   He shouldn't have been wearing his spacewalk-man.
h) Cathy didn't close the station exit door.   She should have closed the exit door.

FIGURE 11: Students' responses

If students are having trouble pronouncing any of the parts of the sentences, we may model those parts and possibly have students repeat them either chorally or individually. For example we may focus on /ˈʃʊdəv/ and /ˈʃʊdntəv/, showing how the phrases are stressed and contracted.

Students are now in a position to tell stories of things in the past which they should/shouldn't have done (*I should have done my homework on time/I shouldn't have left the car unlocked*), perhaps after you have told personal stories to demonstrate what is expected.

B Discovering grammar

In the following examples, students are encouraged to work out for themselves how language forms are constructed and used. They then go on to do exercises using the language they have uncovered. It is highly possible that they have seen the language before, of course, but this may be the first time they have studied it properly.

Example 5: Comparative adjectives Language: word formation;
comparative adjectives
Age: any
Level: elementary/pre-intermediate

In this example, students have listened to a dialogue in which people have been comparing things. Before moving on to make their own sentences, the teacher wants to draw their attention to the way that we make adjectives comparative. She could have done this by giving rules, or perhaps just by ignoring such technical information and hoping that students would 'notice' the various possibilities. Instead, she chooses to put them in pairs and give them the exercise in Figure 12.

Look at this!
old → older
new → newer
light → lighter
big → bigger
thin → thinner
noisy → noisier
silly → sillier
expensive → more expensive
beautiful → more beautiful

Now work these out!
a) How do we make one-syllable adjectives into comparative adjectives?
b) Why are *big* and *thin* different?
c) What has to change when we make words like *noisy* and *silly* into comparative adjectives?
d) What is different about *expensive* and *beautiful*? Why?

FIGURE 12: Work it out

When they have finished, she checks through the answers, making sure they understand that one-syllable words which end with a vowel and a consonant double the last letter, that -*y* becomes -*i* and that longer words are preceded by *more* but otherwise stay the same.

She now moves on to a practice exercise. For example, she can put a group of words (see Figure 13) on the board. One student draws an arrow between any two of the words and the other students have to come up with sentences, such as *An elephant is bigger than a spider, A cat is cleverer than a dog.*

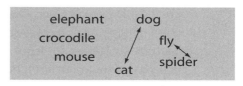

FIGURE 13: Animal comparison

There are two potential problems with the way the start of this sequence asked students to discover facts about comparative adjective forms. Firstly, it is not always easy to give a complete grammatical picture. The exercise above, for example, does not give all the necessary information about comparative forms. There are no irregular ones here (like *good – better*), nor are there examples of words that are made comparative by either taking *-er* or being preceded by *more* (e.g. *clever* in many spoken varieties of the language). Secondly, it is not necessarily the case that all students enjoy this kind of detective work. But as a way of encouraging them to think about how language works, such exercises are extremely useful, especially when, as here, the language rules they are investigating are fairly easy to discern.

Example 6: Rules and freedom	Language:	functions – expressing obligation (*can't/have to/must/allowed*)
	Age:	adult
	Level:	intermediate

In this example from an intermediate coursebook, the students are going to look at obligation language, some of which they may have already come across separately.

The teaching sequence starts when students discuss what rules they would expect to find in places such as airports, bars and pubs, beaches, hospitals, libraries, etc. They then look at a number of different signs (see Figures 14 and 15) and say where they would expect to see them and what they mean.

FIGURE 14: Signs (a) from *New Cutting Edge Intermediate* by S Cunningham and P Moor (Pearson Education Ltd)

FIGURE 15: Signs (b) from *New Cutting Edge Intermediate* by S Cunningham and P Moor (Pearson Education Ltd)

Now that students are properly warmed up and engaged with the topic, they are asked to look again at Figure 15. They have to say which signs sentences a–e (see Figure 16) apply to – and cross out those that are not true.

Finally, as a result of all the preparation work they have done, they have to put the underlined words from Exercise 3 (Figure 16) in the correct category (see Figure 17).

Once the teacher has checked that the students have been able to complete the analysis chart, she can get them to do a fill-in exercise where they have to discriminate between *have to*, *don't have to*, *should*, *shouldn't* and *are/aren't allowed*. They then make their own sentences about what the rules are in places from the first exercise (airport, bars and pubs, etc.) and read them out to their colleagues who have to guess where they are talking about.

3 Which signs on page 112 do the following relate to? Cross out the sentence(s) that are not true about each sign.

a You <u>can</u> use your credit card here.
   You <u>must</u> use your credit card here.
   You<u>'ve got to</u> use your credit card here.

b You <u>mustn't</u> smoke in the smoking area.
   You<u>'re allowed to</u> smoke in the smoking area.
   You <u>can</u> smoke in the smoking area if you want.

c You <u>mustn't</u> leave your mobile on.
   You <u>can't</u> use your mobile.
   You <u>shouldn't</u> leave your mobile on.

d Dogs <u>are allowed</u>.
   Dogs <u>are not allowed</u>.

e You <u>have to</u> be careful of the wet paint.
   You <u>don't have to</u> be careful of the wet paint.
   You <u>ought to</u> be careful of the wet paint.

FIGURE 16

Analysis

Put the underlined verbs from exercise 3 in the correct category.
1 It is necessary *have (got) to*
2 It is not necessary
3 It is OK/permitted *can*
4 It is not OK/permitted
5 It is a good idea / the correct thing
6 it is not a good idea / not the correct thing

FIGURE 17

C Practising grammar

Example 7: Where am I?	Language:	present continuous (past simple)
	Age:	younger learners
	Level:	elementary

This activity is designed to get students making sentences using the present continuous. (It can also be used to practise the past simple.) It has a slight game element because the other students have to guess what the speaker is talking about.

We tell students to think of a place they'd really like to be (e.g. a beach, a night club, on the sports field). They should keep their choice to themselves. Now we tell them to imagine they are in this place and we ask them to look around them and write down three things that they can see using the present continuous (e.g. at a football game: *A lot of people are shouting. A man is blowing a whistle. Someone is kicking a ball.*). While they are doing this, we can go round the class monitoring their progress and suggesting alternatives or prompting students who can't think what to write.

One student now comes to the front of the class, reads out his or her sentences and then says *Where am I?* The other students try to guess.

One of the advantages of the activity done in this way is that students are given time to think up their present continuous sentences rather than having to produce them spontaneously. But of course, we could do it as a quick-fire game, too, if this is appropriate.

We don't have to use the present continuous. Students could talk about a place they went to (either in reality or an imagined place) and make sentences in the past simple about what they saw there.

Example 8: Simon's adventure	Language:	past tenses
	Age:	young adults plus
	Level:	intermediate plus

The following activity is designed to get students to look again at various past tense forms, before using them for language practice.

Students are asked to read the story about Simon in Figure 18. When they have done this, they have to underline all the past tenses in the story, and then separate them into three different types (i.e. the past simple – *was, went down looked, took,* etc., the past continuous – *was rising, were breaking, were running, were just coming back,* and the past perfect – *had woken up, hadn't been able, had left, had looked for, had become*).

One day when he was on holiday with a group of friends, Simon went down to the beach at six thirty because he had woken up very early and he hadn't been able to get back to sleep.

It was a beautiful morning. The sun was rising in the sky and the waves were breaking on the shore. A few joggers were running up and down the beach and some fishermen were just coming back from a night's fishing. It looked absolutely beautiful.

Simon took a surfboard and paddled out into the bay and then he just lay on his surfboard for a bit thinking about life. He fell asleep. When he woke up and looked around, he got quite a shock because he had drifted a long way from the beach and he couldn't get back.

He decided to use his mobile phone to get help and then he realised that he had left it back in his room. And that was when he started to feel quite frightened.

They found him in the afternoon. His friends had looked for him all morning and at about lunchtime they had become very anxious. They called the air sea rescue service and a helicopter pilot saw him about two hours later.

And the moral of the story? Always tell your friends where you are going and don't fall asleep on surfboards!

FIGURE 18: Simon's surfboard story

Students check that they have underlined the same verbs (and categorised them in the right way) with their partners before the teacher goes through the answers with the class.

Students now close their books and tell each other the story of Simon and the surfboard. When they have done this, they can look at the story in the book again before, once again, telling Simon's story. Each time they do this, their fluency with the story and how to tell it increases. Repetition of this kind is extremely helpful (see page 56).

Finally, the teacher can ask the students if they know any similar stories of lucky escapes. They can talk about this in small groups and then tell the rest of the class what the most interesting story in their group was.

Example 9: Matching sentence halves	Language:	third conditional
	Age:	adult
	Level:	upper intermediate

One of the best ways of making students think of sentence construction and sentence meaning is to get them to match sentence halves. We can do this by giving them two lists that they have to match up (see Figure 19). This can be done in pairs or by students working on their own.

a	If Andrew hadn't got stuck in a traffic jam	**i**	he would have been able to answer her call.
b	If Beatrice had written down the name of his company	**ii**	they wouldn't have been late.
c	If Jed hadn't lost his mobile phone	**iii**	he wouldn't have missed his flight.
d	If Mrs Wickstead hadn't overslept	**iv**	she would have been able to call him at work.
e	If Peter and Clare hadn't missed the bus	**v**	she wouldn't have agreed to marry him.
f	If Ruth hadn't been feeling extremely happy	**vi**	she wouldn't have been there when the postman came.

FIGURE 19: Matching sentence halves

However, the activity becomes much more enjoyable and interactive if we put the sentence halves on cards. Each student then gets one card and has to walk around the room until they find their pair. They have to do this without showing their cards to other people, so they have to read them aloud and then discuss which pairings are or are not possible.

Example 10: *Find someone who ...* and other surveys	Language:	elementary
	Age:	young adult plus
	Level:	any

Find someone who ... is the name given to an ever-popular mini-survey activity. In its simplest form, students get a chart which asks them to find the names of various people by going around the class and asking questions (see Figure 20). If they ask a classmate *Do you like chocolate?* and the classmate says *no*, they do not write down a name, but if the classmate says *yes*, they write down the name and then move on to the next question.

Find someone who ...
1 likes chocolate. _____
2 often goes to the cinema. _____
3 has three brothers. _____
4 went to bed late last night. _____
5 plays the guitar. _____

FIGURE 20: A simple *Find someone who ...* chart

Find someone who ... can be adapted to suit any structure or structures. For example, we could make a chart asking students to find someone who has never been to India, has always liked music, has never eaten raw fish, has always had coffee for breakfast, etc. We can also get students to write the questions themselves to make it more interesting for them or, at the beginning of a term or semester, we can find out one interesting fact about each individual student and put these facts into the chart (e.g. *Find someone who is a keen swimmer, Find someone who plays in an orchestra,* etc.). The activity thus becomes an excellent way for them to get to know each other.

There are many mini-surveys that we can use for grammar practice in this way. For example, we can construct (or have our students construct) any number of lifestyle questions asking such things as *What time do you normally get up? What do you have for breakfast? How many cups of coffee do you drink in a day?* Or, if we want students to practise past tenses, they can design a questionnaire in order to ask *When did you last go to the cinema? Who did you go with? What was the name of the film? What did you think of the film?* etc.

Example 11: Perfect one liners	Language:	past perfect continuous
	Age:	any
	Level:	intermediate to advanced

In this activity, students practise the past perfect continuous tense by making sentences in response to prompts from the teacher. They are required to use their imaginations and/or sense of humour and the exercise is given added enjoyment by being designed as a team game.

The teacher divides the class into small teams of two to four students. She tells them that she will be reading sentences for which they have to find appropriate responses, using the past perfect continuous. She starts by giving them a sentence such as *When I got home last night, my flatmate was asleep in the car*. She asks the class, in general, what reasons they can think of to explain this, and hopes to elicit sentences like *Well, she had been listening to a programme on the radio and fallen asleep*, or *Yes, well that's because she had been talking to a hypnotist on her mobile phone*, etc.

Now that the students understand the idea of the exercise, she reads out the sentences in Figure 21. (Some of the sentences in a coursebook, such as the one about Henry VIII and, perhaps, the blood-soaked wedding clothes, may not be appropriate for all students, so we may have to come up with sentences of our own.)

a) When I came to see you yesterday, your cat was in the fridge.
b) Can you explain why you bit my dog?
c) That was my new Rolls Royce your son pushed over the cliff.
d) You had blood all over your wedding clothes after the ceremony.
e) You were the only one in the room before the theft.
f) You had different coloured socks on the other day.
g) Why did Henry VIII have his wife Anne Boleyn beheaded?

FIGURE 21: Sentences from *The Anti-grammar Grammar Book* by N Hall and J Shepheard (Pearson Education Ltd)

The teams are given a short time to come up with a good explanation for each sentence. If they are correct and/or appropriate, the teacher awards a point, but no team can offer a sentence that has been used previously.

This game-like practice forces students to make sentences using a particular verb tense. Yet by adding the element of surreal humour, it can provoke great enjoyment. And the best thing about it is that it requires no material or technology and can be slotted into lessons at many different stages.

D Grammar games

As we shall see on page 349, many games from television and radio (and games that people play at home in their everyday lives) can be adapted for classroom use. The following four examples, however, show how we can design games especially for learners. We hope they (and games like them) will engage students and encourage them to use the target structures with enthusiasm.

Example 12: Ask the right question	Language:	any
	Age:	older children plus
	Level:	elementary plus

Students sit in two teams. There is a pile of cards between them. On each card there is a word or phrase (see Figure 22). The cards are face down.

A member of team A picks up the first card and then has to ask the other team members questions until they give exactly the answer that is written on the card.

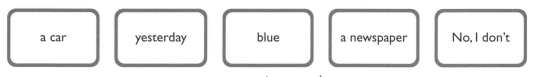

FIGURE 22: Answer cards

The game, which is suitable for all levels, forces students to think extremely carefully about the exact construction of the questions they are asking.

Example 13: Putting sentences back together again	Language:	comparatives and superlatives
	Age:	young learners
	Level:	intermediate

A common way of practising and testing syntax (see page 383) is to give students sentences with the words in the wrong order, e.g. *bananas / don't / eating / I / like* for *I don't like eating bananas.* But such word-ordering activities can be used in a more game-like way, too.

The teacher provides two sets of envelopes, each numbered 1–12 (for example). In each envelope there are the words that make up a sentence. Both envelopes marked 1 will have the same word cards (see Figure 23), and there will be two envelopes for sentence number 2 and number 3, etc.

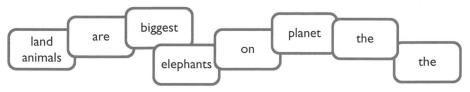

FIGURE 23: Cards for game envelope 1

The teacher then writes the numbers 1–12 on the board twice, once for each team. The two piles of envelopes are put at the front of the class. A student from each team comes up and selects an envelope (they don't have to choose them in order), and takes it back to the team. When the team have rearranged the sentence and written down on a piece of paper what they think it should be, they cross off the relevant number of the envelope on the board.

The first team to finish gets two bonus points. The teacher then looks at the sentences they have written down and each team gets a point for each correct sentence.

Example 14: One question behind	Language: Age: Level:	assorted questions teenagers plus beginner to intermediate

This game, adapted from a television programme, involves easy mental gymnastics which 'make very drill-like activities palatable' (Rinvolucri and Davis 1995: 96). It is based on the simple idea that students should answer not the question they are being asked now, but the previous question.

Students are given the questions in Figure 24. For the first question, they either don't answer at all or they just say *Mmmm*. And then for the second question (*Where do you eat?*) they give the answer they would have given to the first question (*In a bed*).

```
Where do you sleep?
Where do you eat?
Where do you go swimming?
Where do you wash your clothes?
Where do you read?
Where do you cook?
Where do you listen to music?
Where do you get angry?
Where do you do your shopping?
Where do you sometimes travel to?
```

FIGURE 24: Questions for *One question behind*, adapted from *More Grammar Games* by M Rinvolucri and P Davis (Cambridge University Press)

We could add a competitive element to this game by timing it, or seeing who can shout out the *One question behind* answer first. But the fun of it is just trying to concentrate hard enough to remember what the previous question was.

We can choose whatever grammar area we want to make the questions with (or we can get students to write their own questions to use with a partner or another team).

One question behind is very enjoyable, but remember not to let it go on for too long.

E Grammar books

Grammar books come in many shapes and sizes. They range from ones for students at lower levels (which tend to offer quick digestible explanations of grammar points and provide opportunities for practice of these specific points) to works designed for the more serious researcher, teacher or advanced student.

Many commentators make a distinction between *descriptive* and *pedagogic* grammars. The former describe everything there is, the whole of the language and its workings, whereas the latter are designed specifically to be of help to teachers and students of the language. The way in which grammar rules are offered will depend on the level the grammar is designed for, of course, and, as a result, compromises frequently have to be made about the amount of detail we may want to give about a particular grammar point. If we give too much detail, we may confuse lower level students; if we give too little, we may not be telling students things they ought to know.

Michael Swan, a noted author of pedagogical grammar material (see especially Swan 2005a – and Example 15 below), suggests that good grammar rules (for a pedagogic grammar) should exhibit *simplicity*, *truth* (because some grammar rules are more 'true' than others), *clarity* (because if a rule is unclear, it doesn't help anybody) and *relevance* (because there are some things which neither the students nor the teacher really need to know) (Swan 1994). But, of course, a lot depends on what it is we are trying to explain. For whereas the rules which govern the formation of the third person singular of the present simple (*she speaks, he drives, it watches*) may be fairly easy to state, the rules for the use of *some* and *any*, for example, are somewhat more complex. The question that grammar-focused writers have to ask themselves is how far they can simplify or complicate and still write information which will be useful and appropriate.

In their grammar practice book for elementary students, Brigit Viney, Elaine Walker and Steve Elsworth discuss the use of *a/an*, *some*, *any* and *no* with countable and uncountable nouns (see Figure 25).

5 a/an, some, any, no

We've got **some** tomatoes, **some** bread and **an** orange.
We haven't got **any** bananas or **any** cheese. We've got **no** biscuits and **no** milk.
Have we got **any** eggs? Have we got **any** juice?

- We use *a/an* with singular countable nouns (see Unit 2):
  *We haven't got **a** melon.*   *We've got **an** orange.*
- We use *some* with plural countable nouns and uncountable nouns in affirmative sentences: *We've got **some** tomatoes.   We've got **some** bread.*
- We use *any* with plural countable nouns and uncountable nouns in negative sentences and questions:
  *We haven't got **any** bananas.   We haven't got **any** cheese.*
  *Have we got **any** eggs?   Have we got **any** orange juice?*
- We use *no* with singular and plural countable nouns and uncountable nouns, to mean 'not one/not any'. We use *no* with an affirmative verb:
  *We've got **no** biscuits.   We've got **no** milk.*
- We usually use *some* (not *any*) in questions when we offer something to someone or when we ask for something:
  *Would you like **some** biscuits?   Can I have **some** juice?*

FIGURE 25: *Some* and *any* from *Grammar Practice for Elementary Students* by B Viney, E Walker and S Elsworth (Pearson Education Ltd)

The diagrammatic representations and simple explanations offered here are designed specifically for students at this level. They appear to satisfy the clarity, simplicity and relevance requirements that Michael Swan suggests, though the truth they offer is only partial.

In contrast, Ronald Carter and Michael McCarthy, in their grammar for advanced users (including teachers and language researchers), offer a significantly more complex account of how these two words are used. (See Figures 26 and 27 for the first sections of their entries on *some* and *any*.)

Some and any: strong versus weak forms   196b

Some and *any* each have strong forms, which are stressed, and weak unstressed forms. The weak form of some is pronounced /səm/.

The weak forms indicate an indefinite quantity of something:

◀ *Would you like **some cheese**?*

◀ *Are there **any messages** on the answerphone?*

The strong forms have different meanings. The strong form of *some* most typically means 'a certain' or 'a particular' when used with singular count nouns:

◀ ***Some child** was crying behind me throughout the whole flight and I never slept.*

Strong form *some* contrasts with *others*, *all* or *enough* when used with plural count nouns and with non-count nouns:

    [talking of student grants]

◀ ***Some students** get substantial amounts and others get nothing.*

    [talking of dried beans that need to be soaked before use]

◀ A: *But dry ones you have to soak them overnight and then get rid of that water and stuff.*
   B: *Right. And lentils as well?*
   A: ***Some of them**. Not all.*

◀ *We've got **some bread** but not enough for three people.*

Strong form *any* is used most typically with singular count nouns and with non-count nouns to mean 'it does not matter which':

◀ *If you have the warranty, **any authorised dealer** can get it repaired for you.*

◀ ***Any fruit juice** will make you sick if you drink enough of it.*

FIGURE 26: Screenshot 1 from the CD-ROM of the *Cambridge Grammar of English* by R Carter and M McCarthy (Cambridge University Press)

Some, any and zero determiner   196c

Although *some* and *any* indicate an indefinite quantity, they are not used for large or unlimited indefinite quantities. The zero determiner indicates an indefinite quantity without reference to size when used with non-count nouns and with plural count nouns:

◀ *There are **some extra blankets** in the wardrobe if you need them.*
   (an indefinite but limited number)

   [government spokesman after a major earthquake]

◀ *We need **help** from the international community. We need **tents** and **medicines** and **blankets**.*
   (~~We need some help from the international community. We need some tents, some medicines and some blankets.~~)

◀ *Are there **any frogs** in that pond?*
   (indefinite but probably limited expectation of quantity)

◀ *Do you have **red ants** in your garden?*
   (no expectation about quantity)

FIGURE 27: Screenshot 2 from the CD-ROM of the *Cambridge Grammar of English* by R Carter and M McCarthy (Cambridge University Press)

Carter and McCarthy's descriptions are clearly more 'truthful' than those in grammars designed for lower levels, partly because they recognise that strong and weak forms represent different grammatical behaviours for *some* and *any*, but mostly because they explain everything in far more detail than lower-level grammars do. Potential users, however, would need to apply the criteria of simplicity and clarity, too, to see whether this exemplary modern grammar matched their own needs and level.

E1 Using grammar books

Both students and teachers may consult grammar books for a number of reasons. For example, students may be drafting or re-drafting a piece of written work and may want to check that they are using some aspect of grammar correctly. Alternatively, a teacher, having noticed that a student is making a lot of mistakes in one particular area, might tell that student to look up the language in a grammar book in order to understand it better. Perhaps a student gets back a piece of written homework which has correction marks on it highlighting grammatical problems; when the student is re-writing the homework, he or she can consult a pedagogic grammar (such as the *Cambridge Grammar of English* above). But students can also work through the explanations and exercises in self-study grammars such as *Grammar Practice for Elementary Students*, either on their own or because a teacher sets exercises for homework or as classwork. Finally, teachers often use grammar books to check grammar concepts, especially where students ask difficult questions which they cannot answer on the spot, or where an area is so complex that they need to re-visit it from time to time to remind themselves of the full picture. Grammar books are also vital for the preparation of materials.

Example 15: Say and tell	Language:	verb complementation (*say* and *tell*)
	Age:	any
	Level:	intermediate and above

A student has got a corrected piece of homework back from the teacher. The teacher has underlined the sentence *He was tired of people saying him what to do*. In the margin he has written *There is a problem here with the verb 'say'. Look at 'Practical English Usage', pages 509 and 510, and re-write the sentence before the next class.*

When the student looks at *Practical English Usage*, she reads that both verbs can be used with direct and indirect speech and that *say* refers to any kind of speech whereas *tell* is only used to mean *instruct* or *inform*. Crucially, she reads that *say* is most often used without a personal object (see Figure 28).

504 say and tell

1 meaning and use

Both *say* and *tell* are used with direct and indirect speech. (*Say* is more common than *tell* with direct speech.)

> *'Turn right,' I **said**.* (OR *'Turn right,' I **told** him.*)
> *She **said** that it was my last chance.* (OR *She **told** me that it was my last chance.*)

Tell is only used to mean 'instruct' or 'inform'. So we do not use *tell* with greetings, exclamations or questions, for example.

> *He **said**, 'Good morning.'* (BUT NOT *He told them, 'Good morning.'*)
> *Mary **said**, 'What a nice idea.'* (BUT NOT *Mary told us, 'What a nice idea.'*)
> *'What's your problem?' I **said**.* (BUT NOT *'What's your problem?' I told her.*)

2 say: objects

Say is most often used without a personal object.

> *She **said** that she would be late.* (NOT *She said me ...*)

If we want to put a personal object after *say*, we use *to*.

> *And I **say** to all the people of this great country ...*

3 tell: objects

After *tell*, we usually say who is told.

> *She **told** me that she would be late.* (NOT *She told that ...*)

Tell is used without a personal object in a few expressions. Common examples: *tell the truth, tell a lie, tell a story/joke.*

> *I don't think she's **telling** the truth.* (NOT *... saying the truth.*)

Note also the use of *tell* to mean 'distinguish', 'understand', as in *tell the difference, tell the time.*

> *He's seven years old and he still can't **tell** the time.*

Tell is not used before objects like *a word, a name, a sentence, a phrase.*

> *Alice **said** a naughty word this morning.* (NOT *Alice told ...*) ▸

We do not usually use *it* after *tell* to refer to a fact.

> *What time's the meeting? ~ I'll **tell** you tomorrow.* (NOT *I'll tell you it tomorrow.*)

4 infinitives

Tell can be used before **object + infinitive**, in the sense of 'order' or 'instruct'. *Say* cannot be used like this.

> *I **told** the children to go away.* (NOT *I said the children to go away.*)

5 indirect questions

Neither *tell* nor *say* can introduce indirect questions (see 276).

> *Bill **asked** whether I wanted to see a film.* (NOT *Bill said whether I wanted to see a film.* OR *Bill told me whether ...*)

But *say* and *tell* can introduce the answers to questions.

> *Has she **said** who's coming?*
> *He only **told** one person where the money was.*

For *so* after *say* and *tell*, see 540.

FIGURE 28: From *Practical English Usage: 3rd edition* by M Swan (Oxford University Press)

Now she can re-write the homework sentence as *He was tired of people telling him what to do* and know that she has got it right. Research has offered a powerful alternative to teacher explanation.

Chapter notes and further reading

- **Grammar activities**

  See S Thornbury (1999a: Chapters 3–6) for examples of different kinds of grammar teaching and learning.

- **Grammar books**

  There are a large number of grammar books available. Two of the most impressive modern reference grammars are R Carter and M McCarthy (2006) and D Biber *et al* (1999).

  For teachers, students and researchers at a range of levels, my favourite work is M Swan (2005a), and there is also G Leech *et al* (2001), D Biber *et al* (2002) and, for language teachers especially, M Parrott (2000).

- **Grammar practice**

  For students, the most common study-and-practise grammar is the *English Grammar in Use* series by R Murphy and others (Cambridge University Press), but see also *Grammar Practice for Elementary Students* (and the other levels) by E Walker and S Elsworth (Pearson Education Ltd) and *Real English Grammar* by H Lott (Marshall Cavendish ELT).

  The *Grammar in Practice* series by R Gower (Cambridge University Press) has six levels. The *Language Practice* series (*Elementary, Pre-intermediate, First-certificate* and *Advanced*) by M Vince and others is published by Macmillan Education. *The Oxford Learner's Grammar* is written by J Eastwood (Oxford University Press).

14 | Teaching vocabulary

In Chapter 12, B1 we saw some of the many ways we can explain meaning, and when teaching vocabulary this is a major part of the teacher's art. Students need to see words in context to see how they are used. Accordingly, the best way, perhaps, of introducing new words is for students to read texts or listen to audio tracks and see or hear those words in action.

A major reason for reading texts in class (in contrast to extensive reading – see Chapter 17, A1) is to give students new language input. And whenever we ask students to read or listen, we will want them to see how words are used. That is why when students read the text on page 291 we will ask them to do exercises such as matching words from the text with their definitions. If they read the text about plastic surgery (on page 298), we may ask them to find a word in the text that means 'people whom doctors see and care for' (*patients*), etc. We may ask them to say what a word means, or ask them which word in the text is the opposite of a given word, etc. Sometimes we draw their attention specifically to chunks of language, such as *being human, Does that make sense? the whole gamut of human experience, delve deep into your own consciousness,* etc. in the audio interview on page 316.

However, at other times we set out to teach or practise a specific area of vocabulary, and the examples in this chapter show various ways in which this can be done. We will also look at activities designed to get students to research words for themselves using reference and production dictionaries.

A Introducing vocabulary

When we introduce new vocabulary, there is always a chance, of course, that it is not new to some of the students in the class. That is why elicitation is so important (see page 203). By the time students get to upper intermediate level or beyond, we can be sure that some of them will know some of the words we are asking them to focus on. Example 4 below is clearly designed to focus the students' attention on an aspect of vocabulary they certainly know quite a lot about, but they may never have studied prefixes in quite such detail before.

Example 1: Walking, running, jumping	Focus: verbs of movement Age: adult Level: beginner

The teacher starts by showing or drawing pictures, or miming the actions in Figure 1. The words are carefully modelled, and the teacher may well conduct a rapid cue–response drill where she points to a picture or mimes the action and then nominates a student to say *walk, climb,* etc.

FIGURE 1: From *Language Links* by A Doff and C Jones (Cambridge University Press)

Students are now asked to put the correct verb in the sentences in Figure 2. These can be projected or written onto the board, provided that the students can still see the pictures. This can be done with the whole class or the students can work in pairs.

If the students have worked on the exercise in pairs, the teacher now goes through the answers, making sure that the students pronounce the words correctly. They can then (depending on their age) do a quick round of *class robot*, where one student is a robot and the others give instructions, such as *run to the window*, *swim to the door*, etc. and the robot has to mime these activities.

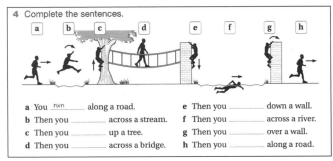

FIGURE 2: Practising *walk*, *run*, *jump*

Finally, the students can be asked to write new instructions using the new words, as in Figure 3 – or they can invent their own fitness exercise or design their own activity sequence, like the one in Figure 2. Whichever they choose, they can write (and draw) their own instructions.

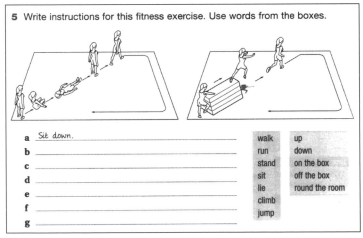

FIGURE 3: Using *walk*, *run*, *jump*, etc.

This kind of procedure, which we might call PPP, or Straight arrows if we follow the ESA form of description (see page 67), is a very effective way of teaching small numbers of individual words at beginner level.

Example 2: Inviting

Focus: functional language
Age: adult
Level: pre-intermediate

The following sequence gets students to make invitations and to accept or refuse them. Like many lessons focusing on functional language, it concentrates on lexical phrases or chunks (see page 37).

The students are shown a picture of a lake or a river where people are rowing each other around. In the foreground, a woman is talking to a young man with a broken arm. We tell the students that they should read the following dialogue and see if they can guess the word or words that are missing in each of the blanks.

> Matt: *Hi, Liz.*
> Liz: *Hi, Matt.*
> Matt: *Would you like to a _____ rowing?*
> Liz: *Rowing?*
> Matt: *Yeah. Rowing. You know. In b _____ .*
> Liz: *c _____ it's 'in a boat'. It's just that, well, you have a d _____ .*
> Matt: *You're right! e _____ I thought you could f _____ the actual rowing.*
> Liz: *Oh no.*
> Matt: *No? g _____?*
> Liz: *I'm not h _____ rowing, actually. I'm not i _____ at it.*
> Matt: *Oh … right. Well, how about a walk?*
> Liz: *I'm a bit tired.*
> Matt: *Or … a coffee?*
> Liz: *Now you're talking!*

When the students have compared their possible answers, they hear the dialogue spoken on an audio track so that they can see if they were right (the answers are *go, a boat, Of course, broken arm, That's why, do, Why not? crazy about, very good*). We can then get them to practise speaking the dialogue.

We now have the students study two elements of inviting. In the first place, we get them to make invitations by completing these phrase stems with *go rowing?* or *going rowing*?

> Invitation phrase stems
> *Do you fancy …*
> *Do you want to …*
> *How about …*
> *Would you like to …*

We can then get the students to repeat the different phrases both chorally (if appropriate) or individually.

They now look at a list of phrases and have to decide whether they mean that the speaker is saying *yes*, is not sure or is saying *no*.

Copy and complete the chart with the phrases.

I'd love to.   I'd love to but …   I'd rather not.
I'm not really sure.   No, thanks.   Perhaps.
That would be great.   What a fantastic idea!   Why not?
Yes, OK.   Yes, please.   Now you're talking!

Saying *yes*	Not sure	Saying *no*

Once again, we will have the students say the phrases correctly, paying special attention to the intonation they use. We help them to think of ways of completing the phrase *I'd love to but …* (*I'm working this evening*).

We can now get them to practise simple invitation–reply exchanges by cueing them with words like *dinner* (*How about coming to dinner? That would be great*).

In pairs they can now write longer dialogues. While they are doing this, we can go round the class monitoring their progress and helping where necessary.

Finally, the students read out (or act out) their dialogues and we give them feedback.

It is worth noticing that the level of the original dialogue is somewhat higher than the language the students are being asked to produce. That is because we think students can cope with more language when they read and listen than they can when they have to come out with it themselves.

When we teach functional language like this, we almost always end up getting students to use phrases (rather than individual words), precisely because certain common exchanges (like inviting) tend to use these pre-fabricated chunks (*I'd love to, I'd rather not, Would you like to …*) as a matter of course.

Example 3: Explaining what you mean	Focus: *type, kind, something you use …*
	Age: young adult plus
	Level: intermediate

The following sequence helps students with vocabulary that they can use when they do not know the words to describe things. The sequence starts when students talk to each other in pairs or groups and discuss situations in which they need to explain things to visitors, family and friends, etc. They then read some descriptions (see Figure 4) and have to say (guess) what is being described.

1 'It's **a type of** sport which you do in the sea. You need a board and big waves. It can be dangerous, but it's really exciting.'
2 'It's **a kind of** meal you get in Indian restaurants. It's hot and spicy and usually has meat in it. You eat it with rice.'
3 'It's **the stuff you find** under grass. It's brown. You see it when it rains.'
4 'It's **something you use for** cleaning the house. It's a machine that picks up dust and small pieces of dirt.'
5 '**They are** usually **made of** wood. They are a useful **thing** to have in the house, because you can put books on them.'

FIGURE 4: From *Total English Intermediate* by A Clare and J J Wilson (Pearson Education Ltd)

They can then check their answers with words written at the bottom of the page (*surfing, curry, mud/earth, vacuum cleaner/hoover, bookshelves*) before discussing with the teacher a) when the expressions in bold are used (when we don't know a word for something, or we want to explain the meaning of something), and b) whether *thing* and *stuff* are used for countable nouns or uncountable nouns.

Now that the words and phrases have been properly introduced, the students do a practice exercise to help them get used to them (see Figure 5).

The next stage of the lesson sequence is for students to compile lists of things so that they can use these things in subsequent exercises. In groups, they have to a) draw things which are rectangular, oval, round or square, b) name animals that are enormous/huge, tiny, etc. and c) name things that are smooth, rough, sticky, soft or hard. They then compare their choices with a speaker on an audio track.

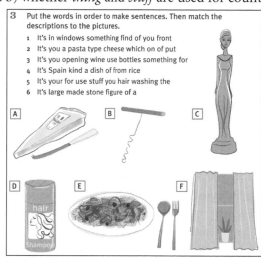

FIGURE 5: Practising 'explaining' words and phrases

Students are now in a position to describe things for each other. They do this by taking part in an information-gap activity (see page 70) where one student in each pair has the crossword for student A and the other has the crossword for student B (see Figure 6). They take turns describing the words in their crosswords by explaining what they are rather than naming them. So when, for example, student A asks student B what 1 down is, student B might reply *It is stuff you make candles with and it is sticky when it is hot.*

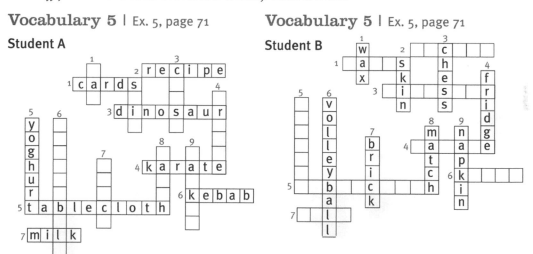

FIGURE 6: Information-gap crossword

As with the two previous examples, the sequence has followed a fairly straightforward PPP/Straight arrows type progression. As a result of what they have done, students can now start to explain themselves when and if they have trouble remembering words.

Example 4: Word formation	Focus: prefixes and suffixes
	Age: young adult plus
	Level: upper intermediate

The following sequence is from *First Certificate Gold* by Richard Acklam and Sally Burgess (Pearson Education Ltd) which, as its name suggests, is designed for people studying for the Cambridge ESOL First Certificate exam (an exam that is taken at the end of the upper intermediate – B2 – cycle of study).

Students are reminded of a sentence from a text they have just read (*And so began two hours and forty minutes of disbelief ...*), and they are then asked to say what various prefixes mean (see Figure 7). When they have discussed these with their teacher, they look at a number of words with suffixes, such as *quickly* and *backwards* (for adverbs), *employment* and *happiness* (for nouns) or *brownish* and *useless* (for adjectives).

Students are now given a kind of construction-kit exercise where they have to try to make as many words as they can by adding prefixes and suffixes (see Figure 8). This can be done in pairs or groups, or even, perhaps, as a team game where they have a set time limit.

Finally, they are asked to choose six of the words they have formed so that they can write a sentence for each. They can then share their various sentences so that other students can look at them and perhaps amend or correct them. The class can vote for the sentences they like the best, or the students can turn their own sentences into mock test-items for their classmates to try, e.g.

> **Add a prefix or suffix to the word in italics so that it has an appropriate meaning in the sentence.**
> Sienna could not hide her *appointment* when she heard that she had failed the test.

1 What do the following prefixes in **bold** mean?

EXAMPLE: *re-* means 'again'.

1 **re**play/**re**do
2 **dis**belief/**im**polite/**il**logical/**un**usual/**ir**responsible/**in**visible
3 **over**crowded/**over**charge
4 **under**estimate/**under**weight
5 **post**graduate/**post**mortem
6 **ex**-husband/**ex**-President
7 **sub**marine/**sub**way

FIGURE 7: Prefixes

3 Make as many words as you can by combining different parts of the box.

dis	**excite**	ful	ment
un	**appoint**	less	ness
im	**honest**	able	ion
in	**patient**	ly	
	success	y	
	direct	ship	
	kind		
	profit		
	help		
	friend		
	luck		
	like		

FIGURE 8: Making words

B Practising vocabulary

In the following lesson sequences the aim of the activity is either to have students use words that they more or less know, but which they need to be provoked into using, or to get them to think about word meaning, especially in context (see Example 8).

Example 5: Word circle	Focus: compound nouns Age: young adult plus Level: intermediate

In this activity, students look at a wheel of words (see Figure 9) and try to say which words combine with *book* and *TV* to make compound words.

We start by showing students the wheel and then make sure that they realise that while *book* + *case* can make *bookcase*, *TV* + *case* doesn't work in the same way.

Students are put into pairs or groups and told to come up with the combinations as quickly as possible. They should do this without using dictionaries at first, and then when we go through the answers with the class, we can put up some of them on the board and ask students to check with their dictionaries to see if they are right (some of them will not be).

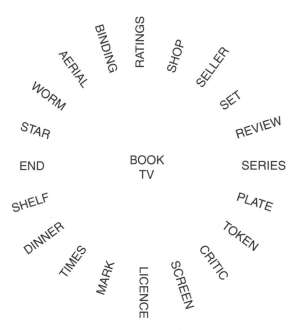

FIGURE 9: Word circle from *Have Fun with Vocabulary* by A Barnes, J Thines and J Welden (Penguin Books)

Students can now use these compound words in sentences, or some of them can be put in noughts and crosses squares (see page 256) so that students have to make sentences using them to win a square. Alternatively, students can choose any three of the words and write a questionnaire to find out about people's attitudes or habits concerning books or TV.

Example 6: Word map	Focus: houses, rooms, objects Age: any Level: any

Word maps are an extremely engaging way of building up vocabulary knowledge as well as provoking students into retrieving and using what they know.

In this sequence, the students are going to work on aspects of houses and the things in them. We start by putting the beginnings of a map on the board (see Figure 10).

Students then come to the board and add some rooms to the diagram as in Figure 11.

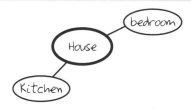

FIGURE 10: The word map begins

Students should by now have begun to get the idea (even if they haven't done a word map before this), but just to be sure, we elicit words for one of the rooms, such as the kitchen (see Figure 12).

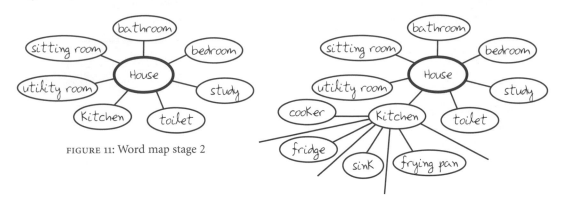

FIGURE 11: Word map stage 2

FIGURE 12: The word map takes shape

We can now put students in groups, and allocate one room per group. They are given marker pens and told to add as many words as they can to the word map for their room. It will be entirely appropriate if they think they are in competition with the other groups to see who can find the most words.

The board gradually fills up with words. Students help each other by offering words they know but which, perhaps, other members of the group have forgotten. They can look for words in dictionaries and while we walk around monitoring their progress, they can ask us for one or two words they do not know (though if there is a game element here, we will have to be fair about how much help we give).

Once the word map is complete (or as full as it is likely to be), we can make sure students can say the words correctly before going on to ask them to describe their favourite room at home or have a discussion about why people don't put televisions in the bathroom (usually) or fridges in the bedroom. We can give students a picture or plan of an empty room and ask them to decide what to put in it.

Word maps are sometimes used by teachers to show students how words group together. Getting students to build up their own maps by working in groups (as we have suggested) has the added advantage of making them try to remember some of the many words they know, while at the same time learning new words from their peers.

Example 7: In the queue	Focus: physical description
	Age: adult
	Level: beginner

In this practice activity, designed to get students using the language of description (e.g. *he's quite tall*, *she has blonde hair*, *he has a beard*), an artificial information gap is created by getting the students to look at different pictures.

The teacher starts by putting a picture of people in a queue on the board and giving the students a list of names. They can then ask questions, e.g. *What's John like?* to which the teacher replies *He's quite tall with grey hair and glasses. He has a beard.* One student then comes up and points to the correct person in the picture.

The teacher now puts the students in pairs. In each pair one student is A and the other is B. Each Student A looks at the following picture – which is in colour in the original – and is told a) to find out which of the following names apply to which of the numbered people in the cinema queue:

Alice   Cathy   Mick   Jim   Karly

and b) to answer B's questions about the other people in the picture. Thus A will ask *What's Alice like?* and B will reply *She's quite young and she has red hair. She's quite short, too.*

| 1 | Monica | 3 | 4 | Kit | Susan | 7 | 8 | Philip | Jane |

Each Student B has the same picture with different captions and is told a) to find out which of the following names apply to which of the numbered people in the queue:

Kit   Jane   Monica   Philip   Susan

and b) to answer A's questions about the people named in the picture. Thus B will ask *What's Kit like?* and A will reply *He's about 50. He's quite short and well-built. He's bald and he has glasses.*

| Jim | 2 | Cathy | Alice | 5 | 6 | Karly | Mick | 9 | 10 |

When the activity is over, the teacher has different students describe the various characters (Mick, Alice, Susan, etc.) to check that they are happy using the description language.

C **Vocabulary games**

There are many games which are appropriate for use with collections of vocabulary items. Sometimes games which are not designed especially for language students work equally well in our lessons. These include *Pictionary* (where players have to draw words which their team then have to guess), *Call my bluff* (see page 350) and *charades* (where players have to act out the title of a book, play or film).

The three game examples in this section are designed to engage students, though only one of them involves the kind of guessing which many games (such as the ones mentioned above) often include.

Example 8: Got it!	Focus: word recognition/enjoyment
	Age: any
	Level: elementary plus

This game is designed to engage students with a list of vocabulary items which will be used in the lesson sequence which follows. It does not involve any guessing or complex mental processing. But, as a result of it, students see and hear a range of words – and have a good time doing it.

Students are put into groups of four or five, all sitting round a table. The teacher gives each group a collection of 20–30 words written on individual cards or pieces of paper (e.g. words associated with cooking, such as *slice, chop, cut, frying pan, saucepan, dish*). The students have to place the cards face up on the table in front of them so that all of them can be seen.

The teacher now reads out the words one by one. The task of each individual in a group is to try to snatch the card with the word on it. When they do this (before the other members of the group), they have to hold the card up and shout *Got it!*

Each student keeps the cards they have managed to snatch, and so at the end of the game there is a winner in each group – and an overall winner who has collected the greatest number of cards.

Got it! is an entertaining way of getting a class going. The words can now be used in a lesson about cooking, they can form the basis of a word map (see above), or students can be asked to look them up in dictionaries or use them in conversations or writing.

Example 9: Backs to the board	Focus: explaining word meaning
	Age: young adult plus
	Level: intermediate plus

In the following game, students have to explain the meaning of a word or phrase to one of their team members so that he or she can guess what the word is.

Students are put into small teams. In each team one member sits with their back to the board.

The teacher now writes a word or phrase on the board. All of the group who can see this word have to explain what it means (without saying the word or phrase itself) to the team member who has their back to the board. The first student to guess the word or phrase gets a point for their team.

The game can be made more formal in structure if the students with their backs to the board have to get their information by asking *yes/no* questions only, e.g. *Is it more than one word? Can you find it in the house?*

Hidden definitions is especially effective if the teacher puts up words and phrases which the students have recently studied.

Example 10: Snap!	Focus: word meaning Age: any Level: beginner

This game is particularly useful for simple word-meaning recognition. It can be played in pairs or groups.

Two students have a pack of cards each. One pack has pictures; the other has words which relate to the pictures. The students deal their cards, putting down each card at the same time as their partner. When a picture card (e.g. a picture of a bird) matches the word card (*bird*) put down at the same time, the first person to say *Snap!* keeps the pair of cards. The object of the game is to collect as many pairs as possible.

Many games like *Snap!* have been replicated on CD-ROMs or online and, as a result, can be played by students working on their own. Figure 13 shows just this kind of activity, where the player can use the arrows under the picture or the word to find the different options so that words can be matched with their correct pictures.

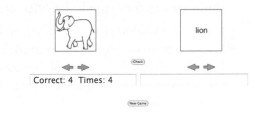

FIGURE 13: Animal matching game at www.manythings.org/lulu/d5.html

D Using dictionaries

Dictionaries, whether they are in book form, on CD-ROMs, online or bundled into the electronic machines that students like to carry around, are perhaps the greatest single resource students can have at their disposal. However, they are sometimes the least widely-used resource that learners work with. This is sad because they contain a wealth of information about words, including of course what they mean, but also how they operate (see below).

In this section we will discuss the difference between reference and production dictionaries and then look at exercises designed to train students in dictionary use or which incorporate dictionary use into lesson sequences.

D1 Reference and production dictionaries

Reference dictionaries – the kind that we most frequently use – need to be distinguished from production dictionaries, a comparatively new type of dictionary which has recently emerged.

A *reference* dictionary is one where a student looks up a word to see what meanings it has, how it is used and the way it is spelt and pronounced, as in Figure 14.

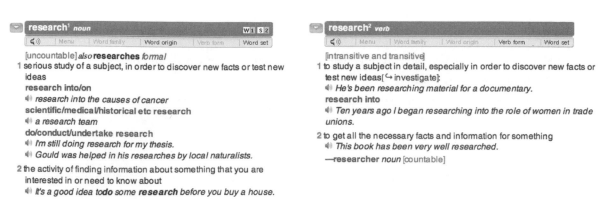

FIGURE 14: Entries for *research* in the *Longman Dictionary of Contemporary English CD-ROM* (Pearson Education Ltd)

In today's dictionaries there is a good chance that there will also be extra information telling the user about such things as:

- differences between British and American usage, for example *Monday to Friday inclusive* (British), and *Monday through Friday* (American)

- similar words, for example the difference between *gaze*, *stare* and *gape*

- frequency in different media, for example the fact that *certainly* is more common in speech than in writing (in the example in Figure 15 the noun *research* is in red, which instantly tells us that it is one of the 3,000 most common words in English; S2 = in the top 2,000 most common words in speech; W1 = in the top 1,000 most common words in written English)

- levels of formality, for example the fact that *indolent* is a formal word

- connotation, for example the fact the *vagabond* is 'especially literary' and that certain words are taboo

Dictionaries are generally used when students have already come across a word and then look it up to check that they know how to use it. Sometimes they will find a word in their bilingual dictionaries and then check with a monolingual learners' dictionary (MLD) to see if they have understood correctly.

Production dictionaries, on the other hand, are designed for students to use the other way round, starting with a meaning they wish to express and looking for the word that expresses it. Suppose, for example, that they wish to express the idea of someone secretly listening to someone else while standing near him, perhaps on the other side of a door. A native speaker would immediately choose the word *eavesdrop* to describe the situation. The

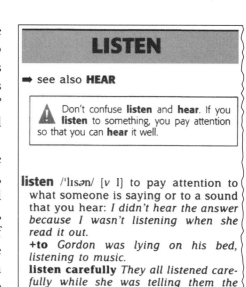

foreign student might find this in a bilingual dictionary, but would have more trouble with a reference MLD since, not knowing the word in the first place, he or she would not, of course, be able to look it up.

In a production dictionary students look for a general word that they already know, and which is a bit like the concept they wish to be able to express in English. In the case of *eavesdrop*, for example, that word might be *listen*. Opening a production dictionary (in this case the *Longman Essential Activator*), the student will find the entries in Figure 15. Going down the column, they come across a word which they can see, through its definition and the examples given, is exactly what they are looking for. They can now use it with confidence.

Reference MLDs are packed full of information which is invaluable to students checking word use. Production dictionaries, in contrast, allow students to find new words.

FIGURE 15: From the *Longman Essential Activator* (Pearson Education Ltd)

 Listen! SPOKEN (say this when you want to get someone's attention) *Listen! I've just had a brilliant idea.*

⚠ Don't say 'I listen music'. Say **I listen to music**.

pay attention /ˌpeɪ əˈtenʃən/ to listen carefully to what someone is saying: *I have some important information about travel arrangements, so please pay attention.*
+to *She went on talking, but I wasn't really paying attention to what she was saying.*

eavesdrop

eavesdrop /ˈiːvzdrɒp‖-drɑːp/ [v I] to secretly listen to someone else's conversation by standing near them, hiding behind a door etc: *"How does Jake know that?" "He must have been eavesdropping."*
+on *I used to sit in cafés and eavesdrop on the conversations around me.*

D2 Dictionary activities

The following activities are designed both to train students in how to use dictionaries and also to get them to use dictionaries as part of normal classroom work.

We need to persuade students that dictionaries can give them extraordinary power (see above). And so we will extol the virtues of dictionaries not only by talking about them, but also by using them ourselves if and when students ask us awkward questions about the meanings of words, for example.

The second stage of trying to turn our students into successful dictionary users involves training them in how to read and understand the information contained in the various entries. Finally, in stage 3, we need to make sure that we include dictionary use in our lessons.

Example 11: Training activities	Focus: understanding dictionary entries
	Age: young adult plus
	Level: pre-intermediate/intermediate

The example in Figure 16 from a coursebook for pre-intermediate learners is based on the assumption that students will be using a bilingual dictionary and points out to them some of the things they can find out from it.

☐ **How can a good dictionary help me?**

A good bilingual dictionary is very important for efficient language learning. A dictionary doesn't only tell you the meaning of a word. It also tells you the grammar, pronunciation, and stress. It sometimes gives you an example sentence too.

stress   pronunciation   meaning

listen/ˈlɪsn/ *v.*(to sth / sb) écouter   He often listens to the radio.

grammar   example sentence

1 **Dictionary abbreviations**   What do they mean?

1	sth	*something*	
2	sb	_____	
3	n.	_____	(e.g. house)
4	adj.	_____	(e.g. fat)
5	v.	_____	(e.g. go)
6	prep.	_____	(e.g. in)
7	adv.	_____	(e.g. slowly)
8	pron.	_____	(e.g. we / us)

FIGURE 16: From *English File Student's Book 2* by C Oxenden *et al* (Oxford University Press)

When students start using dictionaries – especially MLDs – for the first time, it is a good idea to include small training activities of this kind (often lasting only a few minutes each) in every lesson. For example, we could show them the entry for *swollen* (see Figure 17), and then ask them questions, such as *What parts of speech can 'swollen' be? How do you know? How many meanings of 'swollen' are given? How do you know? Are any of the uses of 'swollen' particular to any special national or regional language variety? How do you know?*

SWELL¹
swollen² *adj* **1** a part of your body that is swollen is bigger than usual, especially because you are ill or injured: *swollen glands | a badly swollen ankle | His eyes were swollen from crying.* **2** a river that is swollen has more water in it than usual **3 have a swollen head/be swollen-headed** *BrE* to be too proud and think you are very clever or important

FIGURE 17: Entry for *swollen* from the *Longman Dictionary of Contemporary English* (Pearson Education Ltd)

Example 12: Definition game Focus: working with definitions
Age: young adult plus
Level: upper intermediate

This game teaches students how to use dictionaries and, especially, gets them used to the way in which definitions are written. Modern MLDs often use a special defining vocabulary, which means that even the most complex words are explained using words that students will be able to understand. For example the word *pernickety* is described in the *Longman Dictionary of Contemporary English* as '*informal* worrying too much about small and unimportant things = **fussy**'. The game works with these same definitions. Its special feature is that the student who has to try to guess the answer is the same student who chooses (without knowing it) what the question is.

The class is divided into two teams. Each team has at least one copy of a dictionary – in this case the *Oxford Advanced Learners' Dictionary (OALD)*. One student in team A has to chose a number between 1 and 1,364 (the number of pages in the edition of the dictionary I have in front of me). They then say *left* or *right* to indicate the column on the page they have chosen (the *OALD* has two-column pages). They then give a number between 1 and 10. One member of Team B then looks for, say, the fifth word in the right-hand column on page 328 of the dictionary. They then read the definition of the word back to the Team A member who has to guess what the word is. For our example the definition is *verb: to say one does not know of, is not responsible for, or does not believe in something.* If the member of Team A guesses the word *disavow* straight away, they get three points. If they have to be given the first letter but can then guess it, they get two points. If they are given two letters, they only get one point.

Disavow is an extremely rare and difficult word, but many of the words that are chosen at random like this (because the person choosing the page number, column, etc. has no idea what the word will be) are much more common. However, if we want to make sure all the words are ones which the students should know, we can change the game slightly. The Team A student still chooses the page number, but this time they might choose the fourth red word (if red is the way that particular dictionary uses to indicate word frequency). If the word has three different meanings, the member of Team B will say that there are three different meanings and ask which one the Team A student wants. If there is no red word on the page the student has selected, the players go to the next page or the one before it.

Example 13: At home with *do*, *make* and *take* Focus: collocations
Age: teenage plus
Level: elementary

This activity is a combination of dictionary training and a language awareness exercise. It focuses on three verbs that collocate strongly with various noun phrases – but for which there are no easy rules as to why we use one verb rather than another.

Students are given the following grid and have to say which verb collocates with the noun phrases in the right-hand column. They can do this activity in pairs or small groups. If they are unsure (or if they need to check), we suggest they should look for information in their dictionaries. We will tell them to think carefully about which word to look for in each case.

do	make	take	
	✓		a lot of noise
			always _____ their homework
			always _____excuses
			breakfast
			family photographs
			friends easily
			nothing all the time
			sugar in their coffee
			supper
			the beds
			the cooking
			the dishes
			the ironing
			the laundry
			a lot of mistakes
			the housework

While the students are doing the activity, we can walk round the class monitoring their efforts and helping them to look up words either in their paper dictionaries or on a CD. This is where we can be especially useful in helping them to see what they need to find when checking an entry. For example, if they want to check which verb goes with *a lot of noise*, they can look at the word *noise* on their dictionary CD-ROM and they will find the information shown in Figure 18.

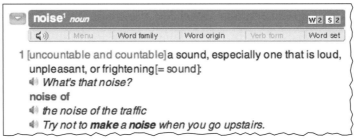

FIGURE 18: First part of the entry for *noise* from the CD-ROM for
the *Longman Dictionary of Contemporary English* (Pearson Education Ltd)

And they can investigate the collocation (in bold) further by looking at a list of phrases in which *noise* occurs, e.g.

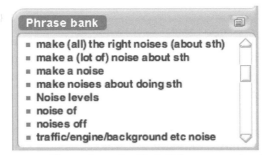

FIGURE 19: Phrases from the CD-ROM accompanying the
Longman Dictionary of Contemporary English (Pearson Education Ltd)

Once they have completed the grid, they can ask each other questions, such as *Who makes a lot of noise in your house?* or *Do you make a lot of mistakes?*

The attractive feature of this activity is that it genuinely helps students to learn more about *make*, *do* and *tell*, while at the same time ensuring that they become better dictionary users.

Example 14: Monday morning	Focus: previewing vocabulary
	Age: adult
	Level: advanced plus

When working with advanced students, the teacher Philip Harmer sometimes likes to start the week with a vocabulary worksheet. The worksheet contains various vocabulary questions which relate to words and phrases which the students are going to meet during the forthcoming week's work. These words and phrases either relate to the topics they are going to study or they come from the materials Harmer is expecting to use in the next few days.

Having prepared such a worksheet (see Figure 20 for an example) we can come to the first lesson of the week and start by getting students to work in pairs and use whatever dictionaries are available to complete the tasks.

1 Why might someone be TOLD OFF?
2 What is the difference between ...
   SYMPATHY and EMPATHY?
   CONTINUOUS and CONTINUAL?
   DISINTERESTED and UNINTERESTED?
3 How might someone be IMPOVERISHED?
4 What could be DEAFENING?
5 Which preposition?
   to put something _____ jeopardy _____ all odds
   to run the risk _____   _____ the belief that
6 What do you say when you TOSS A COIN?
7 How could someone ...
   – RISK LIFE AND LIMB?
   – TEMPT FATE?
   – TAKE PRECAUTIONS?
   – LULL someone INTO A FALSE SENSE OF SECURITY?

FIGURE 20: Monday morning worksheet

The advantage of this procedure is that the students start the week by claiming words and phrases as their own. Of course we will monitor their work, but it is they who are in charge (who have *agency* – see page 103). And by making dictionary use central to the activity, we reinforce understanding of the benefits that students can get from dictionary work.

Example 15: Films	Language: film vocabulary
	Age: teenage and above
	Level: elementary

If students are doing a project on films, they need to find appropriate words and phrases for the topic. They could rely on the teacher or the textbook, of course; both or either of these could give them everything they need. But they might be working on their own, in which case they need to consult some other source of information.

Students who consult a production dictionary will be able to research words they have, perhaps, never heard or seen before. Thus, within the topic of films, they might search for words for films and going to see them (e.g. *film, movie, cinema, go to the cinema*, etc.), types of film (*horror, comedy, war film, road movie*, etc.), people in films (*actor, actress, star*, etc.), people who make films (*director, producer, film crew*, etc.) and various other categories, including what happens in a film (see Figure 21). Provided that the dictionary designers have managed to predict the words which the students are likely to need, such production material is an ideal tool for language research. The students can now use the words for the project or task they are involved in.

7 what happens in a film

story /'stɔːri/ [n C] **a love story** *The movie is basically a love story.*

plot/storyline /'plɒt, 'stɔːrilaɪn plɑːt/ [n C] the events that happen in a film, and the way in which these events are connected: *Tom Hanks was great, but I thought the plot was really boring. | The film has a great storyline.*

scene /siːn/ [n C] one part of a film: *The first scene takes place on a beach.*
a love/war/battle scene *The battle scenes were very realistic.*

special effect /ˌspeʃəl ɪ'fekt/ [n C] an unusual image or sound that is produced artificially, in order to make something that is impossible look as if it is really happening: *The special effects were amazing – the dinosaurs looked as if they were alive.*

ending /'endɪŋ/ [n C] the way that the story in a film ends: *I don't want to give away the ending of the film.*
a happy/sad ending *I like movies with a happy ending.*

twist /twɪst/ [n C] something surprising that happens in a film, which you did not expect: *The film has a twist at the end, when we discover that the detective is the murderer.*

FIGURE 21: From the *Longman Essential Activator* (Pearson Education Ltd)

D3 When students use dictionaries

Many teachers are frustrated by their students' overuse of dictionaries, especially electronic dictionaries (see Chapter 11, G1). They find that their students want to check the meanings of words at any stage of the lesson, even when, for example, the teacher or some other student is in the middle of saying something and had hoped for the (other) students' full attention. At the same time, however, as this chapter has made clear, we want to encourage students to use their dictionaries in appropriate circumstances because we believe that they are such a valuable resource.

Students need to know when dictionary use is appropriate and acceptable and when it is less useful (as in the example in the previous paragraph). It will be useful to talk to them about how, for example, it is a good idea to try to read a text for gist (and guess the meaning of some unknown words) before later, perhaps, using dictionaries to check the meaning of words they do not know (see page 287). They need to understand that if they overuse dictionaries when they should be listening, they lose the benefit of hearing English spoken naturally – and the opportunity this gives them to practise their listening skills. However, we should also be sympathetic to the students' desire to understand every word since most people speaking a foreign language have this need.

The best way to resolve this dilemma is to come to some kind of a bargain with the students, very much like the bargain that Dilys Thorp struck with her students all those years ago (see page 77). The bargain will involve students agreeing when they will and won't use dictionaries. This, together with our use of dictionary activities like the ones mentioned in D1 above, will ensure successful and appropriate dictionary use in our lessons.

Chapter notes and further reading

- **Vocabulary activities**

  There are many different vocabulary activities in S Thornbury (2001a: Chapters 5–7). See also J Morgan and M Rinvolucri (2002), and the series *English Vocabulary in Use* by M McCarthy and F O'Dell (Cambridge University Press).

- **Games**

  Film of the first two games described in Section C is included on the DVD which accompanies J Harmer (2007). On games in language learning, see A Wright *et al* (2006). For vocabulary game activities, see F O'Dell and K Head (2003), the series *Vocabulary Games* by J and C Hadfield (Pearson Education Ltd) and the *Language Games* CD-ROM, published by Macmillan Education.

- **Dictionaries**

  See the references to dictionaries on page 198 of this book.

15 | Teaching pronunciation

A Pronunciation issues

Almost all English language teachers get students to study grammar and vocabulary, practise functional dialogues, take part in productive skill activities and try to become competent in listening and reading. Yet some of these same teachers make little attempt to teach pronunciation in any overt way and only give attention to it in passing. It is possible that they are nervous of dealing with sounds and intonation; perhaps they feel they have too much to do already and pronunciation teaching will only make things worse. They may claim that even without a formal pronunciation syllabus, and without specific pronunciation teaching, many students seem to acquire serviceable pronunciation in the course of their studies anyway.

However, the fact that some students are able to acquire reasonable pronunciation without overt pronunciation teaching should not blind us to the benefits of a focus on pronunciation in our lessons. Pronunciation teaching not only makes students aware of different sounds and sound features (and what these mean), but can also improve their speaking immeasurably. Concentrating on sounds, showing where they are made in the mouth, making students aware of where words should be stressed – all these things give them extra information about spoken English and help them achieve the goal of improved comprehension and intelligibility.

In some particular cases, pronunciation help allows students to get over serious intelligibility problems. Joan Kerr, a speech pathologist, described (in a paper at the 1998 ELICOS conference in Melbourne, Australia) how she was able to help a Cantonese speaker of English achieve considerably greater intelligibility by working on his point of articulation – changing his focus of resonance. Whereas many Cantonese vowels occur towards the back of the mouth, English ones are frequently articulated nearer the front or in the centre of the mouth. The moment you can get Cantonese speakers, she suggested, to bring their vowels further forward, increased intelligibility occurs. With other language groups it may be an issue of nasality (e.g. Vietnamese) or the degree to which speakers do or do not open their mouths. Some language groups may have particular intonation or stress patterns in phrases and sentences which sound strange when replicated in English, and there are many individual sounds which cause difficulty for speakers of various different first languages.

For all these people, being made aware of pronunciation issues will be of immense benefit not only to their own production, but also to their understanding of spoken English.

A1 Perfection versus intelligibility

A question we need to answer is how good our students' pronunciation ought to be. Should they sound exactly like speakers of a prestige variety of English (see page 24) so that just by listening to them we would assume that they were British, American, Australian or Canadian?

Or is this asking too much? Perhaps their teacher's pronunciation is the model they should aspire to. Perhaps we should be happy if they can at least make themselves understood.

The degree to which students acquire 'perfect' pronunciation seems to depend very much on their attitude to how they speak and how well they hear. In the case of attitude, there are a number of psychological issues which may well affect how 'foreign' a person sounds when they speak English. Some students, as Vicky Kuo suggests (see page 21), want to be exposed to a 'native speaker' variety, and will strive to achieve pronunciation which is indistinguishable from that of a first language English speaker. Other students, however, do not especially want to sound like 'inner circle' speakers (see page 17); frequently they wish to be speakers of English as an *international* or global language and, as we saw in Chapter 1, this does not necessarily imply trying to sound exactly like someone from Britain or Canada. It may imply sounding more like their teacher, whatever variety he or she speaks (see our discussion about native and non-native speakers in Chapter 6 E). Frequently, too, students want to retain their own accent when they speak a foreign language because that is part of their identity. Thus speaking English with, say, a Mexican accent is fine for the speaker who wishes to retain his or her 'Mexican-ness' when speaking in a foreign language. Finally, as we saw in our discussion of English as a Lingua Franca (ELF) in Chapter 1, B1, certain phonological differences (e.g. between /d/ and /ð/) may not be critical to a speaker's ability to make themselves understood.

Under the pressure of such personal, political and phonological considerations it has become customary for language teachers to consider intelligibility as the prime goal of pronunciation teaching. This implies that the students should be able to use pronunciation which is good enough for them to be always understood. If their pronunciation is not up to this standard, then clearly there is a serious danger that they will fail to communicate effectively.

If intelligibility is the goal, then it suggests that some pronunciation features are more important than others. Some sounds, for example, have to be right if the speaker is to get their message across (for example /n/ as in /sɪnɪŋ/ versus /ŋ/ as in /sɪŋɪŋ/), though others (for example /d/ and /ð/ in ELF) may not cause a lack of intelligibility if they are used interchangeably. In the case of individual sounds, a lot depends on the context of the utterance, which frequently helps the listener to hear what the speaker intends. However, stressing words and phrases correctly is vital if emphasis is to be given to the important parts of messages and if words are to be understood correctly. Intonation (see page 38) is a vital carrier of meaning; by varying the pitch of our voice we indicate whether we are asking a question or making a statement, whether we are enthusiastic or bored, or whether we want to keep talking or whether, on the contrary, we are inviting someone else to come into the conversation.

The fact that we may want our students to work towards an intelligible pronunciation rather than achieve an L1-speaker perfection may not appeal to all, however. Despite what we have said about identity and the global nature of English (and the use of ELF), some students do indeed wish to sound exactly like a native speaker. In such circumstances it would be absurd to try to deny them such an objective.

A2 Problems

Two particular problems occur in much pronunciation teaching and learning.

- **What students can hear:** some students have great difficulty hearing pronunciation features which we want them to reproduce. Frequently, speakers of different first languages have problems with different sounds, especially where, as with /b/ and /v/ for Spanish speakers, their language does not have the same two sounds. If they cannot distinguish between them, they will find it almost impossible to produce the two different English phonemes.

There are two ways of dealing with this: in the first place, we can show students how sounds are made through demonstration, diagrams and explanation. But we can also draw the sounds to their attention every time they appear on a recording or in our own conversation. In this way we gradually train the students' ears. When they can hear correctly, they are on the way to being able to speak correctly.

- **What students can say:** all babies are born with the ability to make the whole range of sounds available to human beings. But as we grow and focus in on one or two languages, we lose the habit of making some of those sounds. Learning a foreign language often presents us with the problem of physical unfamiliarity (i.e. it is actually physically difficult to make the sound using particular parts of the mouth, uvula or nasal cavity). To counter this problem, we need to be able to show and explain exactly where sounds are produced (e.g. Where is the tongue in relation to the teeth? What is the shape of the lips when making a certain vowel?).

- **The intonation problem:** for many teachers the most problematic area of pronunciation is intonation. Some of us (and many of our students) find it extremely difficult to hear 'tunes' or to identify the different patterns of rising and falling tones. In such situations it would be foolish to try to teach them.

  However, the fact that we may have difficulty recognising specific intonation tunes does not mean that we should abandon intonation teaching altogether. Most of us can hear when someone is surprised, enthusiastic or bored, or when they are really asking a question rather than just confirming something they already know. One of our tasks, then, is to give students opportunities to recognise such moods and intentions either on an audio track or through the way we ourselves model them. We can then get students to imitate the way these moods are articulated, even though we may not (be able to) discuss the technicalities of the different intonation patterns themselves.

The key to successful pronunciation teaching, however, is not so much getting students to produce correct sounds or intonation tunes, but rather to have them listen and notice how English is spoken – either on audio or video or by their teachers themselves. The more aware they are, the greater the chance that their own intelligibility levels will rise.

A3 Phonemic symbols: to use or not to use?

It is perfectly possible to work on the sounds of English without ever using any phonemic symbols. We can get students to hear the difference, say, between *sheep* and *cheap* or between *ship* and *sheep* just by saying the words enough times. There is no reason why this should not be effective. We can also describe how the sounds are made (by demonstrating, drawing pictures of the mouth and lips or explaining where the sounds are made).

However, since English is bedevilled, for many students, by an apparent lack of sound and spelling correspondence (though in fact most spelling is highly regular and the number of exceptions fairly small), it may make sense for them to be aware of the different phonemes, and the clearest way of promoting this awareness is to introduce the symbols for them.

There are other reasons for using phonemic symbols, too. Paper dictionaries usually give the pronunciation of headwords in phonemic symbols. If students can read such symbols, they can know how the word is said even without having to hear it. Online and CD-ROM dictionaries have recordings of words being said, of course.

When both teacher and students know the symbols, it is easier to explain what mistake has occurred and why it has happened; we can also use the symbols for pronunciation tasks and games.

Some teachers complain that learning symbols places an unnecessary burden on students. For certain groups this may be true, and the level of strain is greatly increased if they are asked to write in phonemic script (Newton 1999). But if they are only asked to recognise rather than produce the different symbols, then the strain is not so great, especially if they are introduced to the various symbols gradually rather than all at once.

In this chapter we assume that knowledge of phonemic script is of benefit to students.

A4 When to teach pronunciation

Just as with any aspect of language – grammar, vocabulary, etc. – teachers have to decide when to include pronunciation teaching in lesson sequences. There are a number of alternatives to choose from.

- **Whole lessons:** some teachers devote whole lesson sequences to pronunciation, and some schools timetable pronunciation lessons at various stages during the week.

   Though it would be difficult to spend a whole class period working on one or two sounds, it can make sense to work on connected speech, concentrating on stress and intonation, over some 45 minutes, provided that we follow normal planning principles (see Chapter 21B). Thus we could have students do recognition work on intonation patterns, work on the stress in certain key phrases, and then move on to the rehearsing and performing of a short play extract which exemplifies some of the issues we have worked on.

   Making pronunciation the main focus of a lesson does not mean that every minute of that lesson has to be spent on pronunciation work. Sometimes students may also listen to a longer recording, working on listening skills before moving to the pronunciation part of the sequence. Sometimes they may look at aspects of vocabulary before going on to work on word stress and sounds and spelling.

- **Discrete slots:** some teachers insert short, separate bits of pronunciation work into lesson sequences. Over a period of weeks, they work on all the individual phonemes, either separately or in contrasting pairs. At other times they spend a few minutes on a particular aspect of intonation, say, or on a contrast between two or more sounds.

   Such separate pronunciation slots can be extremely useful, and provide a welcome change of pace and activity during a lesson. Many students enjoy them, and they succeed precisely because we do not spend too long on any one issue. However, pronunciation is not a separate skill; it is part of the way we speak. Even if we want to keep our pronunciation phases separate for the reasons we have suggested, we will also need times when we integrate pronunciation work into longer lesson sequences.

- **Integrated phases:** many teachers get students to focus on pronunciation issues as an integral part of a lesson. When students listen to a recording, for example, one of the things which we can do is to draw their attention to pronunciation features on the recording, if necessary having them work on sounds that are especially prominent, or getting them to imitate intonation patterns for questions, for example.

  Pronunciation teaching forms a part of many sequences where students study language form. When we model words and phrases, we draw our students' attention to the way they are said; one of the things we want to concentrate on during an accurate reproduction stage is the students' correct pronunciation.

- **Opportunistic teaching:** just as teachers may stray from their original plan when lesson realities make this inevitable, and teach vocabulary or grammar opportunistically because it has 'come up' (see Chapter 12, A1), so there are good reasons why we may want to stop what we are doing and spend a minute or two on some pronunciation issue that has arisen in the course of an activity. A lot will depend on what kind of activity the students are involved in since we will be reluctant to interrupt fluency work inappropriately, but tackling a problem at the moment when it occurs can be a successful way of dealing with pronunciation.

Although whole pronunciation lessons may be an unaffordable luxury for classes under syllabus and timetable pressure, many teachers tackle pronunciation in a mixture of the ways suggested above.

 A5 Helping individual students

We frequently work with the whole class when we organise pronunciation teaching. We conduct drills with minimal pairs (see B1 below) or we have all of the students working on variable stress in sentences (see page 43) together. Yet, as we have seen, pronunciation is an extremely personal matter, and even in monolingual groups, different students have different problems, different needs and different attitudes to the subject. In multilingual groups, of course, students from different language backgrounds may have very different concerns and issues to deal with.

One way of responding to this situation, especially when we are working with phonemes, is to get students to identify their own individual pronunciation difficulties rather than telling them, as a group, what they need to work on. So, for example, when revising a list of words we might ask individual students which words they find easy to pronounce and which words they find difficult. We can then help them with the 'difficult' words. We can encourage students to bring difficult words to the lesson so that we can help them with them. This kind of differentiated teaching (see page 27) is especially appropriate because students may be more aware of their pronunciation problems – and be able to explain what they are – than they are with grammar or vocabulary issues.

It is vitally important when correcting students (see Chapter 8) to make sure that we offer help in a constructive and useful way. This involves us showing students which parts of the mouth they need to use (see the diagram on page 40), providing them with words in their phonological context, and offering them continual opportunities to hear the sounds being used correctly.

B Examples of pronunciation teaching

The areas of pronunciation which we need to draw our students' attention to include individual sounds they are having difficulty with, word and phrase/sentence stress and intonation. But students will also need help with connected speech for fluency and with the correspondence, or lack of it, between sounds and spelling. All of these areas are touched on in the examples below.

B1 Working with sounds

We often ask students to focus on one particular sound. This allows us to demonstrate how it is made and show how it can be spelt – a major concern with English since there is far less one-to-one correspondence between sound and spelling than there is in some other languages – especially Romance languages.

We can have students identify which words in a list (including *bird, word, worm, worth, curl, heard, first, lurch,* etc.) have the sound /ɜː/. They are then asked to identify the one consonant (*r*) which is always present in the spelling of words with this sound. We could also show or demonstrate the position of the lips when this sound is made and get students to make the sound and say words which include it.

Two more examples show specific approaches to the teaching and practising of sounds.

Example 1: *Ship* and *chip*	Sounds: /ʃ/ and /tʃ/
	Level: intermediate

Contrasting two sounds which are very similar and often confused is a popular way of getting students to concentrate on specific aspects of pronunciation.

The sequence starts with students listening to pairs of words and practising the difference between /ʃ/ and /tʃ/, e.g.:

ship	chip	washing	watching
sherry	cherry	cash	catch
shoes	choose	mash	match
sheep	cheap	wish	which, witch

From *Sounds English* by J D O'Connor and C Fletcher (Pearson Education Ltd)
The teaching sequence described here comes directly from this book.

If they have no problem with these sounds, the teacher may well move on to other sounds and/or merely do a short practice exercise as a reminder of the difference between them. But if the students have difficulty discriminating between /ʃ/ and /tʃ/, the teacher asks them to listen to a recording and, in a series of exercises, they have to work out which word they hear, e.g.:

1 Small shops/chops are often expensive.
2 The dishes/ditches need cleaning.
3 I couldn't mash/match these things up.
4 She enjoys washing/watching the children.

They now move on to exercises in which they say words or phrases with one sound or the other, e.g.

> It's very cheap.
> a grey chair
> a cheese sandwich
> You cheat!
> no chance
> a pretty child

before doing a communication task which has words with the target sounds built into it, e.g.

How much do you enjoy the things in the chart below?
1 very much   **2** not much   **3** not at all
Fill in the chart for yourself, and then ask three other people.

	You		
playing chess			
watching TV			
washing up			
going to a football match			
cooking chips			
eating chips			
lying in the sunshine			
shopping			

If, during this teaching sequence, students seem to be having trouble with either of the sounds, the teacher may well refer to a diagram of the mouth to help them see where the sounds are made, e.g.

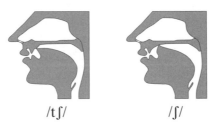

/tʃ/   /ʃ/

Contrasting sounds in this way has a lot to recommend it. It helps students concentrate on detail, especially when they are listening to hear the small difference between the sounds. It identifies sounds that are frequently confused by various nationalities. It is manageable for the teacher (rather than taking on a whole range of sounds at the same time), and it can be good fun for the students.

This kind of exercise can be done whether or not the teacher and students work with phonemic symbols.

Example 2: The phonemic chart

Sounds: all
Level: any

The writer Adrian Underhill is unambiguous about the use of phonemic symbols (see A3 above) and has produced a phonemic chart, which he recommends integrating into English lessons at various points.

This phonemic chart is laid out in relation to where in the mouth the 44 sounds of southern British English are produced. In its top right-hand corner little boxes are used to describe stress patterns, and arrows are used to describe the five basic intonation patterns (i.e. fall, rise, fall-rise, rise-fall and level).

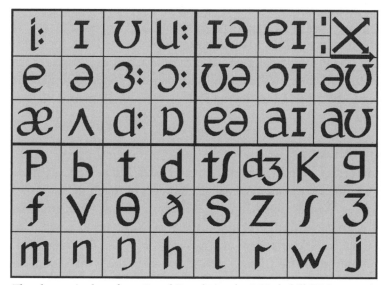

The phonemic chart from *Sound Foundations* by A Underhill (Heinemann)

What makes this chart special are the ways in which Adrian Underhill suggests that it should be used. Because each sound has a separate square, either the teacher or the students can point to that square to ask students to produce that sound and/or to show they recognise which sound is being produced. For example, the teacher might point to three sounds one after the other (/ʃ/, /ɒ/ and /p/) to get the students to say *shop*. Among other possibilities, the teacher can say a sound or a word and a student has to point to the sound(s) on the chart. When learners say something and produce an incorrect sound, the teacher can point to the sound they should have made. When the teacher first models a sound, she can point to it on the chart to identify it for the students (Underhill 2005: 101).

The phonemic chart can be carried around by the teacher or left on the classroom wall. If it is permanently there and easily accessible, the teacher can use it at any stage when it becomes appropriate. Such a usable resource is a wonderful teaching aid, as a visit to many classrooms where the chart is in evidence will demonstrate.

There are many other techniques and activities for teaching sounds apart from the ones we have shown here. Some teachers play sound bingo where the squares on the bingo card have sounds, or phonemically 'spelt' words instead of ordinary orthographic words. When the teacher says the sound or the word, the student can cross off that square of their board.

When all their squares are crossed off, they shout *Bingo!* Noughts and crosses can be played in the same way, where each square has a sound and the students have to say a word with that sound in it to win that square, e.g.

/æ/	/dʒ/	/t/
/iː/	/ə/	/d/
/ʊ/	/ɔː/	/z/

Teachers can get students to say tongue-twisters sometimes, too (e.g. *She sells sea shells by the sea shore*) or to find rhymes for poetry/limerick lines. When students are familiar with the phonemic alphabet, they can play 'odd man out' (five vocabulary items where one does not fit in with the others), but the words are written in phonemic script rather than ordinary orthography.

B2   **Working with stress**

Stress is important in individual words, in phrases and sentences. By shifting it around in a phrase or a sentence, we can also change emphasis or meaning.

As we saw in Figure 4 in Chapter 12, it is assumed that when students meet new words in class (and if the new words end up on the board), the teacher will mark the stress of those words (using a consistent system of stress marking). Another common way of drawing our students' attention to stress issues is to show where the weak vowel sounds occur in words (rather than focusing on the stressed syllables themselves). We can draw attention to the schwa /ə/ in words like /fətɒgrəfə/ (*photographer*), or /kluːləs/ (*clueless*).

However, we can also focus on stress issues in longer phrases and in sentences, as the following two examples demonstrate.

Example 3: Fishing	Sounds: phrase stress patterns
	Level: pre-intermediate upwards

The following activity (in which students are asked to recognise stress patterns in phrases) comes from a book of pronunciation games which are designed to '... engage learners in a challenge and, at the same time, highlight an aspect of pronunciation' (Hancock 1995: 1).

The sequence starts when the teacher chooses some short phrases which the students are familiar with and writes them on the board. She then reads the phrases aloud and, as she does so, she draws a large circle under each stressed syllable (which will be in the content words like *bel'ieve*, and *'later*, as opposed to grammatical words like *to*, *of* and *by*) and small circles under the unstressed syllables.

Now that students are clued in to the big and small circles, the teacher gives them a copy of the following game board:

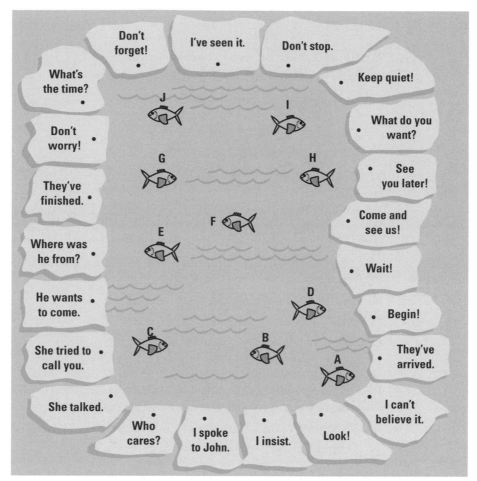

From *Pronunciation Games* by M Hancock (Cambridge University Press)

Using the 'circles' stress patterns, they have to join pairs of phrases with the same stress patterns, e.g. Look! – Wait!; Begin! – She talked; Who cares? – Don't stop etc. The object of the game is to discover which fish is caught (a fish is caught when it is completely surrounded by lines). If students get the exercise right, they will have encircled fish B.

Students can now say the phrases and the teacher can ask them to come up with their own phrases to follow the various stress patterns – or she can make her own games along similar lines.

Example 4: Special stress	Sounds: variable stress
	Level: elementary

The stress in phrases changes depending upon what we want to say. The following exercise draws students' attention to this fact and gets them to ask why it happens.

Students listen to the following conversation:

3 Special stress

1 **T.9.3.A.** Walter is a waiter in a busy snack bar.
Listen to some of his conversations with the customers.

a W So that's two coffees, a beef sandwich, and a tomato soup …
 C *No, a chicken sandwich.*
 W Sorry, sir …

b W Yes, sir?
 C A small mushroom pizza, please.
 W Okay …
 C *No, make that a large mushroom pizza.*
 W Certainly, sir …

c W Okay, so you want one coffee, six colas, four strawberry ice-creams, two chocolate ice-creams and a piece of apple pie …
 C *No, four chocolate ice-creams and two strawberry …*
 W Anything else?

From *Headway Elementary Pronunciation* by S Cunningham and P Moor (Oxford University Press)

The students are now asked to listen again and look at the lines in italics. They have to underline the words that are specially stressed and then say why they think this happens in this particular conversation (because the customer is correcting a mistake). Students can then practise saying the dialogues.

We might also give students a straightforward sentence like *I lent my sister ten pounds for a train ticket last week* and ask them what it would mean if different words took the main stress, e.g. *I LENT my sister ten pounds …* (= I didn't *give* it to her), or *I lent my sister ten pounds for a train ticket last WEEK* (= Can you believe it? She still hasn't paid me back!).

There are many other ways of teaching and demonstrating stress. Some teachers like to choose appropriate texts and have students read them aloud after they have done some work on which bits of phrases and sentences take the main stress. Some teachers like to train students in the performance of dialogues, much as a theatre director might do with actors. This will involve identifying the main stress in phrases and seeing this in relation to the intonation patterns (see below).

Cuisenaire rods (see Chapter 11, C4) are also useful in that they can provide graphic illustrations of how words and phrases are stressed. These rods of different lengths and colours can be set up to demonstrate the stress patterns of phrases and sentences as in the following example, *I'll ring you next WEEK*:

Whereas if we want to say *I'll RING you next week* (= I won't come and see you), we can organise the rods like this:

For stress in words, we can ask students to put words in correct columns depending upon their stress patterns, e.g.

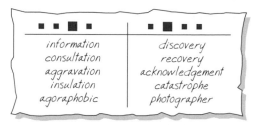

Finally, another technique that is enjoyable is to give students a list of utterances and then let them hear the phrases said with nonsense syllables (but with the right stress and intonation). The students have to match the nonsense patterns with the real thing. For example, if one of the utterances the students have is *absolutely terrible*, what they might hear is *do-di-do-di-DOO-di-di*.

B3 Working with intonation

We need to draw our students' attention to the way we use changes in pitch to convey meaning, to reflect the thematic structure of what we are saying and to convey mood.

One simple way of doing this is to show how many different meanings can be squeezed out of just one word, such as *yes*. To do this we can get students to ask us any *yes/no* question (e.g. *Are you happy?*) and answer *yes* to it in a neutral way. Now we get them to ask the question again. This time, through changing our intonation, we use *yes* to mean something different, e.g. *I'm not sure* or *How wonderful of you to ask that question* or *How dare you ask that question*? Students can be asked to identify what we mean each time by using words for emotions or matching our intonation to pictures of faces with different expressions. We can now get them to ask each other similar *yes/no* questions and, when they answer, use intonation to convey particular meanings which their classmates have to identify.

In his book on teaching pronunciation, Gerald Kelly uses the interjection *mmm* (Kelly 2000: 99). After demonstrating the different ways in which this can be said, students have to match different intonations with different meanings, e.g.

I Match the intonation tune to the meaning.

a //↘mmm//   i Reflects boredom or lack of interest.
b //↗↘mmm//   ii I agree.
c //↗mmm//   iii Strong agreement.
d //↘↗mmm//   iv I agree, but ...
e //→mmm//   v The speaker wants the listener to say more.

The point of using exercises like this is not so much to identify specific intonation patterns – especially since many languages can change the meaning of individual words in the same way – but rather to raise the students' awareness of the power of intonation and to encourage them to vary their own speech. It also trains them to listen more carefully to understand what messages are being given to them.

Example 5: Falling and rising tones	Sounds: falling and rising tones
	Level: pre-intermediate

In the following exercise, students listen to identify nuclear stress (that is the main stress where there is a change of pitch) in phrases and to hear falling and rising intonation.

1 Listen to these examples. Prominent words are in capital letters. Notice how the voice FALLS at the end.

It's MINE.   She's from ROME.   Is it YOURS?
I MET him at a DISCO.

Now listen to these examples. Notice how the voice RISES at the end.

I THINK so.   PROBABLY.   Are they HERE yet?
Is THIS the PARIS train?

From *Pronunciation Tasks* by M Hewings (Cambridge University Press)

When they have done this, the teacher may ask them to repeat the phrases with the right intonation before moving on to the next exercise where they have to listen to a recording and identify whether the voice falls or rises:

2 Listen to these sentence halves. Write (↘) in the space if the voice falls at the end and write (↗) if it goes up. Two are done for you.

1 a) I went to London ... (↘)	b) ... on Saturday. (↗)
2 a) David ... ( )	b) ... works in a bookshop. ( )
3 a) There's some cake ... ( )	b) ... in the kitchen. ( )
4 a) In Hong Kong ... ( )	b) ... last year. ( )
5 a) I'm fairly sure ... ( )	b) ... it's upstairs. ( )
6 a) Yes, ... ( )	b) ... of course. ( )
7 a) Turn left here ...	b) ... then go straight on. ( )
8 a) Oh dear, ... ( )	b) ... I *am* sorry. ( )
9 a) I like it ... ( )	b) ... very much. ( )
10 a) I don't smoke ... ( )	b) ... thank you. ( )

They then join the sentence halves together before working in pairs to answer questions with their new complete sentences, e.g. *What does your son do now? David works in a bookshop*, etc. Later they make their own conversations after noticing how a character uses a rising tone for a subject which is already being talked about and a falling tone to give new information.

This exercise not only gets students to listen carefully to intonation patterns, but by dividing sentences in two before joining them up again, it allows them to identify basic fall–rise patterns. We can also get students to listen to the way speakers react to see whether words like *OK* or *Really* indicate enthusiasm, boredom or indifference.

There are other ways to teach intonation, too: some teachers like to get their students to make dialogues without words – humming the 'tune' of what they want to say in such a way that other students can understand them. Many teachers also use a variety of devices such as arrows on the board and arm movements which 'draw' patterns in the air to demonstrate intonation. Some teachers exaggerate (and get their students to exaggerate) intonation patterns, which can be extremely amusing and which also makes patterns very clear.

Example 6: Sound waves	Sounds: intonation and stress Level: any

The following examples show how a software program (in this case the CAN-8 Virtual laboratory) can be used to help students see their intonation and stress patterns.

Students working at a computer with a headset read a sentence and hear it being said by a competent speaker of English (the first soundwave pattern at the bottom of Figure 1). They then say the sentence themselves and can instantly see how closely their version (see the second sound wave pattern in Figure 1) approximates to the first.

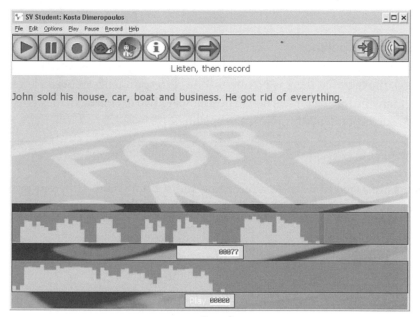

FIGURE 1: Soundwaves 1

The graphic indicates clearly that the student is speaking the sentence using different stress and intonation from the competent speaker. The student is now in a position to try to change their speed, pauses, stress and intonation. With luck, they will then produce something much more like the model (see Figure 2).

This kind of software would be especially useful with language that is more conversational than the example given here. But even with sentence-like examples, the fact that students (especially those who are more visually oriented) can 'see' what they are saying is potentially extremely useful.

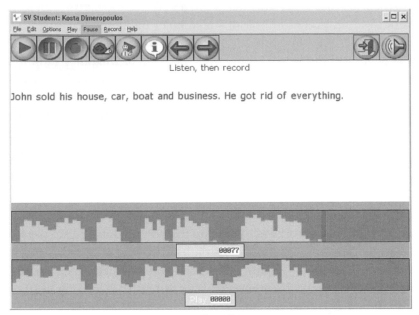

FIGURE 2: Soundwaves 2

B4 Sounds and spelling

Although there are many regularities in English spelling (such as word roots and grammatical endings), the fact that there is no one-to-one correspondence between letters and phonemes causes many problems for learners. The following two exercises are designed to teach sound–spelling correspondence for particular spellings.

Example 7: Sounds of *ou*	Level: elementary

Students are asked to listen to a recording and see how many different pronunciations they can find for the *ou* spelling in words like the following:

could	rough
country	sound
foul	thought
ground	though
house	through
out	unconscious
round	young

They can record the different sounds in their vocabulary books.

Teachers can also help students by giving them typical spellings for sounds every time they work on them. In a class on /ʃ/ and /tʃ/, for example, they can be given the following information:

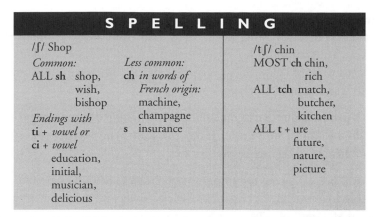

From *Sounds English* by C Fletcher and J D O'Connor (Pearson Education Ltd)

Example 8: Looking for rules   Level: intermediate and above

In this exercise, students are asked to read the following two lists of words aloud. When they have agreed that the letter *c* can be pronounced in two ways, we can ask them if they can see what the rule is which decides which pronunciation will be used. We might have to prompt them by suggesting that they look at the letter which follows the *c*.

These are the lists they see:

A		B	
centre	certain	cap	can
nice	fence	cup	coffee
city	cycle	crack	coin
policy	bicycle	call	café
decide	cinema	come	cost
		custom	could

This kind of discovery approach (see Chapter 12C) to sound and spelling rules allows students to become aware that English spelling is not quite as random as they might think.

B5 Connected speech and fluency

Good pronunciation does not just mean saying individual words or even individual sounds correctly. The sounds of words change when they come into contact with each other. This is something we need to draw students' attention to in our pronunciation teaching.

We can adopt a three-stage procedure for teaching students about features such as elision and assimilation.

- **Stage 1/comparing:** we can start by showing students sentences and phrases and having them pronounce the words correctly in isolation, e.g. *I am going to see him tomorrow* /aɪ/ /æm/ /gəʊɪŋ/ /tuː/ /siː/ /hɪm/ /təmɒrəʊ/. We then play them a recording of someone saying the sentences in normal connected speech (or we say them ourselves), e.g. /aɪmgɒnəsɪjɪmtə mɒrəʊ/. We ask students what differences they can hear.

- **Stage 2/identifying:** we have students listen to recordings of connected speech (or we say the phrases ourselves), and they have to write out a full grammatical equivalent of what they hear. Thus we could say /dʒəwɒnəkɒfi/ and expect the students to write *Do you want a coffee?* or we could play them a recording of someone saying /aɪdəvkʌmbɪfɔː/ and expect them to write *I would have come before.*

- **Stage 3/production:** in our modelling and teaching of phrases and sentences we will give students the connected version, including contractions where necessary, and get them to say the phrases and sentences in this way.

Fluency is also helped by having students say phrases and sentences (such as the ones used in stages 1–3 above) as quickly as possibly, starting slowly and then speeding up. Getting students to perform dialogues and play extracts – if we spend some time coaching them – will also make them aware of speaking customs and help them to improve their overall fluency.

Chapter notes and further reading

- **Meaning and perfection**
  For a discussion about what pronunciation norms and models we should get our students to aim for, see J Jenkins (1998). See also C Dalton and B Seidlhofer (1994: Chapter 1). R Walker (2001) discusses international intelligibility, K Keys and R Walker (2002) consider ten questions on the phonology of English as an international language, and J Field (2003) discusses the 'fuzzy' nature of intelligibility.

- **Different languages**
  For the pronunciation difficulties experienced by different first language speakers, see G Kelly (2000: Chapters 3 and 4).

- **Phonemic chart**
  G Kelly (2000: 143) has created a different pronunciation chart for students, which categorises sounds in terms of their place of articulation, and whether they are voiced or voiceless (in the case of consonants).

- **Sounds and spelling**
  See G Kelly (2000: Chapter 8). C Jannuzi (2002) suggests using phonics practice in class.

- **Intonation**
  For two brief but illuminating articles on teaching intonation, see M Hancock (2005) and G Kelly (2005). J Lewis (2001) discusses teaching focus (international prominence) in conversation.

- **Pronunciation and music**
  C Fonseca Mora (2000) suggests a connection between pronunciation (and language acquisition in general) and 'melody singing'. P Blanche (2004) suggests using dictations to teach pronunciation.

16 | Teaching language skills

Teachers tend to talk about the way we use language in terms of four skills – reading, writing, speaking and listening. These are often divided into two types. *Receptive skills* is a term used for reading and listening, skills where meaning is extracted from the discourse. *Productive skills* is the term for speaking and writing, skills where students actually have to produce language themselves.

As we shall see in Section A below, there is some concern about separating skills in this way, especially since they are seldom separated in real life. We might also want to question a once commonly-held view that receptive skills are somehow passive, whereas production skills are in some way more active.

It is certainly the case that when we speak or write we are producing language, and no one would argue with the idea that language activation (see page 67) takes place when we are doing this. But reading and listening also demand considerable language activation on the part of the reader or listener. We cannot access meaning unless our brains are fully engaged with the texts we are interacting with. In other words, we have to think to understand, using any or all of our language knowledge to get meaning from what we are seeing or hearing.

But in any case, whether we are reading or speaking we often mix what we are doing with other skills, as we shall see below.

A Skills together

It makes little sense to talk about skills in isolation since, as Eli Hinkel points out, 'in meaningful communication, people employ incremental language skills not in isolation, but in tandem' (Hinkel 2006: 113). When we are engaged in conversation, we are bound to listen as well as speak because otherwise we could not interact with the person we are speaking to (although some people, of course, are better listeners than others!). Lecturers frequently rely on notes they have written previously, and people listening to lectures often write notes of their own. Even reading, generally thought of as a private activity, often provokes conversation and comment.

Writing, too, is rarely done in isolation. Much of today's communication is electronic (via emails and text messages, for example). We read what people send to us and then reply fairly instantly. And even when we are writing on our own, we generally read through what we have written before we send it off. Sometimes, of course, this is not the case when dealing with emails and text messages, but writers and texters often regret sending their messages in haste!

Clearly, therefore, if skill use is multi-layered in this way, it would make no sense to teach each skill in isolation. We will, therefore, look at how input and output are connected in the classroom, how skills can be integrated, and how skill and language work are connected.

A1 **Input and output**

Receptive skills and productive skills feed off each other in a number of ways. What we say or write is heavily influenced by what we hear and see. Our most important information about language comes from this input. Thus the more we see and listen to comprehensible input, the more English we acquire, notice or learn. This input takes many forms: teachers provide massive language input, as does audio material in the classroom and the variety of reading texts that students are exposed to. Students may read extensively (see below) or listen to podcasts (see page 188). They may interact with other English speakers both inside and outside the classroom.

But students get other input, too, especially in relation to their own output. When a student produces a piece of language and sees how it turns out, that information is fed back into the acquisition process. Output – and the students' response to their own output – becomes input.

Such input or feedback can take various forms. Some of it comes from ourselves, whether or not we are language learners. We modify what we write or say as we go along, based on how effectively we think we are communicating. Feedback also comes from the people we are communicating with. In face-to-face spoken interaction, our listeners tell us in a number of ways whether we are managing to get our message across. On the telephone, listeners can question us and/or show through their intonation, tone of voice or lack of response that they have not understood us.

Teachers can, of course, provide feedback, too, not just when a student finishes a piece of work, but also during the writing process, for example, or when, acting as prompters or as a resource, they offer ongoing support (see Chapter 6B).

Figure 1 shows the dynamic relationship between input and output:

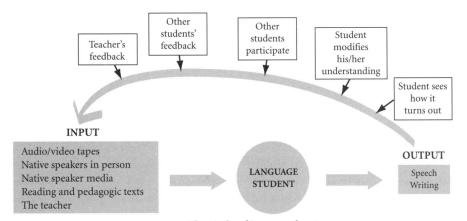

FIGURE 1: The circle of input and output

A2 **Integrating skills**

In order to replicate the natural processes of skill-mixing which we mentioned at the beginning of this chapter, and also because we want to provide maximum learning opportunities for the different students in our classes, it makes sense to integrate different skills. That is why so many learning sequences are more like the Patchwork model we discussed on page 67, rather than following the Straight arrows or Boomerang lesson types.

- **Speaking as preparation and stimulus:** we often ask students to discuss a topic as a way of activating their schemata (see below) or engaging them in a topic that they are going to read or hear about. Speaking sessions allow students to investigate their thoughts and feelings about a topic. Frequently, too, speaking is part of a longer planning sequence.

- **Texts as models:** especially where students are working with genre-focused tasks, written and spoken texts are a vital way of providing models for them to follow. One of the best ways of having students write certain kinds of report, for example, is to show them some actual reports and help them to analyse their structure and style; when getting students to give spoken directions, they will benefit from hearing other people doing it first.

  Productive work should not always be imative, of course. But students are greatly helped by being exposed to examples of writing and speaking which show certain conventions for them to draw upon. We will look at genre in detail in Chapter 19.

- **Texts as preparation and stimulus:** much language production work grows out of texts that students see or hear. A controversial reading passage may be the springboard for discussion or for a written riposte in letter form. Listening to a recording in which a speaker tells a dramatic story may provide the necessary stimulus for students to tell their own stories, or it may be the basis for a written account of the narrative. In this way, we often use written and spoken texts to stimulate our students into some other kind of work.

- **Integrated tasks:** frequently we ask students to listen to something (a recorded telephone conversation, for example) and take a message or notes. We might ask them to prepare a spoken summary of something they have read, or read information on the Internet as preparation for a role-play or some other longer piece of work.

  Almost any speaking activity is bound to involve listening, of course, but sometimes when students are involved in some kind of cooperative writing (see page 328) they will be speaking, listening, writing and reading almost simultaneously. Indeed Task-based learning (see page 71), or even just working on some single task, is almost predicated on the idea of skill integration, since it is usually impossible to complete a task successfully in one skill area without involving some other skill, too.

  Skill integration is a major factor in lesson planning, as we shall see in Chapter 21. Weaving threads of different skills and topics is a major art of teachers who plan for a sequence of lessons. Skill integration also happens when students are involved in project work, which may well involve researching (through reading or listening), speaking (e.g. in discussions or when giving a presentation) and writing (e.g. submitting a report) – as we shall see in Section D below.

A3 Language skills, language construction

Work on language skills is often a precursor to work on various aspects of language construction. As we saw in Chapter 12C, we often ask students to look at texts and discover facts about language for themselves. But whether they are trying to work out construction, or whether we are explaining things that occur in written and spoken texts, it makes considerable sense to use anything which students read as data for them to work on. For example, if we take the following text, we can see how it can be used to look at a range of different language points.

Forget satnav – it's quicker using a map, *Which?* tells motorists

Esther Addley
Friday November 10, 2006
The Guardian

Need to get from A to B? Don't bother switching on that fancy piece of kit on your dashboard. The consumer magazine *Computing Which?* has confirmed what thousands of frustrated motorists already know from bitter experience; that the best source of directions is not an expensive satellite navigation system, but a map.

In a trial that will delight Luddites and the long-suffering partners of gadget enthusiasts, the magazine tested four route-finding aids to determine the best way to reach a panlcular destination. Three hl-tech systems, including a £220 satnav box, a Microsoft software package and the government's own direction-finding website, were tested alongside the more old-fashioned method. The most effective? A copy of the AA's *Great Britain Road Atlas*, priced £8 from most petrol stations.

We could ask students to find all the adjectives in the two paragraphs, and then divide them into one-word adjectives and then compound adjectives (adjectives made from two or more words). Students could discuss how journalistic writing allows for shortened questions like *Need to get from A to B?* and *The most effective?* – forms that would be unacceptable in more formal writing. We might see if students can find descriptions of types of people (*Luddites*, *long-suffering partners*, *gadget enthusiasts*). We can discuss the reason for the use of the present perfect as against the past simple to describe the study. There is also a good example of colon usage, and a particularly revealing clause-rich sentence showing how commas can operate rather like brackets (*Three high-tech systems, including a ..., a ... and a ..., were tested ...*).

Any text or audio track can be 'mined' in this way. There is always some aspect of language that can be drawn from it. If we let the students read the whole article (from which the above is just an excerpt), it could first be the springboard for a discussion about old and new technology, and only later be used as the focus for the kind of language focus we have suggested.

A4 Integrating skill and language work

The ideal learning sequence, then, will offer both skill integration and also language study based around a topic or other thematic thread. The following example shows how it might work at the intermediate level.

Stage 1: the students complete the following questionnaire about how they respond to physical appearance. This involves them in reading and speaking.

1 When you first meet someone, what do you look at first?
  a their hair
  b their face
  c their eyes
  d their mouth
  e the front of their body
  f the back of their body
  g the clothes they are wearing
  h something else (please specify)

2 Which of the following will make you think most positively about someone (choose one only)?
  a they are well-groomed
  b they are well-dressed
  c they have a good physique
  d they look interesting

3 Think of two people that you find very attractive. What is the most physically attractive thing about them?

4 Think of two people whose appearance you find unusual or striking. What is the unusual/striking thing about them?

The class discuss their responses to the questionnaire.

Stage 2: the students read the following text from a novel about a Cantonese couple living in London, where Chen works in a Chinese restaurant.

Working in the fields Chen had once had a physique which had been lean, tanned, and sinewy; now it was almost impossible to see the outlines of his ribs for the plump flesh which clothed them. Not that he was chubby, just prosperous, as he was careful to explain to Lily.

On Lily there were two opposing views. Chen did not think she was pretty. She had a long, thin, rather horsey face, and a mouth that was too big for the rest of her features, and she smiled too frequently for a woman. She had a largish bust, and her hands and feet were a fraction too big to be wholly pleasing to her husband. It was her face, though, which really let her down (Chen had decided), being over-full of expression, particularly her bright black eyes which she had a habit of widening and narrowing when listening to something she found interesting. Probably there was too much character in her face, which perhaps explained the lack of Cantonese male interest better than any particular wrongness of an individual feature or their relationship to each other. Westerners found her attractive, though. Lily was unaware of this but Chen had noticed it with great surprise. That was if second glances and turned heads on the street were anything to go by.

From *Sour Sweet* by Timothy Mo (Abacus)

Stage 3: the students answer comprehension questions about the text before discussing Chen's views of Lily's appearance. They talk about whether or not beauty is a cultural concept.

Stage 4: students look for any language in the text which describes physical appearance. This leads on to a study section where they first discuss whether words like *thin, slim, skinny, fat, stout* or *chubby* have positive or negative connotations, and then go on to say whether words like *lean, sinewy, handsome, pretty, nubile, well-built* and *plain* can be applied to men, women or both.

Stage 5: students re-write the text from *Sour Sweet* as if Chen really approves of his wife's appearance.

Stage 6: students write physical descriptions of well-known figures. The class has to guess who they are writing about.

Stage 7: students listen to a dialogue about a police line-up before role-playing police officers taking witness statements based on descriptions of people they have supposedly seen committing a crime.

The sequence, which would, of course, be inappropriate in certain cultural contexts, provides both study and activation (see page 67). More importantly, from the point of view of this discussion, it involves the students in reading, writing, speaking and listening. As a result, students have been able to practise a wide range of language abilities.

A5 Top-down and bottom-up

A frequent distinction is made between top-down and bottom-up processing. In metaphorical terms, this is the difference between looking at a forest, or, instead, studying the individual trees within it.

It has been said that in top-down processing, the reader (or listener) gets a general view of the reading or listening passage by, in some way, absorbing the overall picture. This is greatly helped if their schemata allow them to have appropriate expectations of what they are going to come across. In bottom-up processing, on the other hand, the reader or listener focuses on such things as individual words, phrases or cohesive devices and achieves understanding by stringing these detailed elements together to build up a whole.

It is probably most useful to see acts of reading and listening (as well as speaking and writing) as interactions between top-down and bottom-up processing. Sometimes it is the individual details that help us understand (or put together) the whole; sometimes it is our overview that allows us to process the details. Without a good understanding of a reasonable proportion of the details gained or proposed through some bottom-up processing, we may find it difficult to come to a clear general picture of what a text is about, or about how to put together a coherent stretch of discourse. But without some global understanding of the topic that is written or spoken about, even an understanding of the details may not be enough.

B Receptive skills

Although there are significant differences between reading and listening, as we shall see in Chapters 17 and 18, nevertheless the basic classroom procedure we often use is the same for both.

B1 A basic methodological model for teaching receptive skills

A typical procedure for getting students to read a written text or listen to a recording involves both Type 1 and Type 2 tasks. Type 1 tasks are those where we get students to read or listen for some general understanding, rather than asking them to pick out details or get involved in a refined search of the text. Type 2 tasks, on the other hand, are those where we get students to look at the text in considerably more detail, maybe for specific information or for language points. Moving from the general to the specific by starting with Type 1 tasks and going on to Type 2 tasks works because it allows students to get a feel for what they are seeing or hearing before they have to attack the text in detail, which is the more difficult thing to do.

The procedure for teaching receptive skills generally starts with a lead in. This is where we engage students with the topic of the reading and we try to activate their *schema* (plural *schemata*), a term which was best described by Guy Cook as 'our pre-existent knowledge of the world' (Cook 1989: 69). This is the knowledge that allows many British, Australian, West Indian, Pakistani and Indian people (for example) to make sense of headlines like *England in six-wicket collapse* (a reference to the game of cricket), whereas many Canadians would instantly understand what it means to be sent to the *penalty box* and why being sent there might give another team a *power play* (both terms come from ice hockey, Canada's national sport).

All of us, at whatever age, but especially from late childhood onwards, have this pre-existent knowledge which we bring with us to all encounters with topics and events. The job of the receptive skills teacher, therefore, is to provoke students to get in touch with that knowledge or schema. They can then predict what a text is likely to be about, and what they are going to see or hear. We can provoke this kind of prediction by giving them various clues, such as pictures, headlines or book jacket descriptions. We can give them a few words or phrases from the text and ask them to predict what these might indicate about its content. We can encourage a general discussion of the topic or ask students to make their own questions for what they are going to read about. Whatever alternative we choose, the point is that prediction is vitally important if we want students to engage fully with the text.

Once students are ready to read, we set some kind of a comprehension task so that they will read or listen in a general way – trying to extract a mostly general understanding of what, superficially, the audio or written text is all about.

The students read or listen to the text and then the teacher directs feedback. Here we may suggest that students go through the answers in pairs or small groups. This is partly so that they get more opportunities to work together, and partly so that when we go through the answers with the class, individual students do not get exposed as having failed in a task.

Sometimes the teacher directs a text-related task immediately this Type 1 task has been completed. A text-related task is any kind of follow-up activity and might be either a response to the content of the text or a focus on aspects of language in the text. However, we will usually get the students to look at the text again for a Type 2 task in which they are required to examine it in more detail. The comprehension cycle is repeated and then the teacher involves the students in text-related tasks (of course, it is possible that students might be involved in more than one Type 2 task cycle).

We can summarise this procedure in Figure 2.

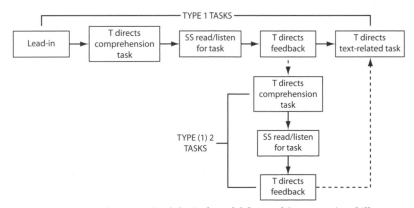

FIGURE 2: A basic methodological model for teaching receptive skills

B2 The language issue

What is it that makes a text difficult? In the case of written text, some researchers look at word and sentence length (Wallace 1992: 77) on the premise that texts with longer sentences and longer words will be more difficult to understand than those with shorter ones. Others, however, claim that the critical issue is quite simply the number of unfamiliar words which a text contains. If readers and listeners do not know half the words in a text, they will have great difficulty in understanding the text as a whole. To be successful, they have to recognise a high proportion of the vocabulary without consciously thinking about it (Paran 1996). Both sentence length and the percentage of unknown words play their part in a text's comprehensibility.

When students who are engaged in listening encounter unknown lexis, it can be '... like a dropped barrier causing them to stop and think about the meaning of a word and thus making them miss the next part of the speech' (Underwood 1989: 17). Unlike reading, there may be no opportunity to go back and listen to the lexis again. Comprehension is gradually degraded, therefore, and unless the listeners are able to latch onto a new element to help them back into the flow of what is being said, the danger is that they will lose heart and gradually disengage from the receptive task since it is just too difficult.

If, as Stephen Krashen suggested, comprehensible input aids language acquisition (see Chapter 3, A1), then it follows that 'incomprehensible' input will not. We can try to get students to read or listen to texts that are way beyond their comprehension level, but the only effect this will probably have is to demotivate them.

It is obvious, however, that the more language we expose students to, the more they will learn, so we need specific ways of addressing the problem of language difficulty. These could include pre-teaching vocabulary, using extensive reading/listening, and considering alternatives to authentic language.

- **Pre-teaching vocabulary:** one way of helping students is to pre-teach vocabulary that occurs in the reading or listening text. This removes at least some of the barriers to understanding which they are likely to encounter.

    However, if we want to give students practice in what it is like to tackle authentic reading and listening texts for general understanding, then getting past words they don't understand is one of the skills they need to develop. By giving them some or all of those words, we deny them that chance.

    We need a common sense solution to this dilemma: where students are likely to be held back unnecessarily because of three or four words, it makes sense to teach them first. Where they should be able to comprehend the text despite some unknown words, we will explain to them that they should try to understand the general meaning of the text, and that we will look at the meaning of individual words once they have done their best to read in this general way.

    One useful technique is to use some (possibly unknown) words from a reading or listening text as part of our procedure to create interest and activate the students' schemata; the words may suggest topic, genre or construction – or all three. The students can first research the meanings of words and phrases and then predict what a text with such words is likely to be about.

- **Extensive reading and listening:** most researchers like to make a difference between *extensive* and *intensive* reading and listening. Whereas the former suggests reading or listening at length, often for pleasure and in a leisurely way, intensive reading or listening tends to be more concentrated, less relaxed, and often dedicated not so much to pleasure as to the achievement of a study goal.

Extensive reading and listening frequently take place when students are on their own, whereas intensive reading or listening is often done with the help and/or intervention of the teacher.

Extensive reading – especially where students are reading material written specially at their level – has a number of benefits for the development of a student's language (see Chapter 17A). Colin Davis suggests that any classroom will be the poorer for the lack of an extensive reading programme and will be '... unable to promote its pupils' language development in all aspects as effectively as if such a programme were present' (1995: 335). He also claims that such a programme will make students more positive about reading, will improve their overall comprehension skills, and will give them a wider passive and active vocabulary. Richard Day and Julian Bamford agree, citing as two of the many goals for extensive reading 'enabling students to read without constantly stopping' and 'providing an increased word recognition' (Day and Bamford 1998).

What these commentators and others are claiming is that extensive reading is the best possible way for students to develop automaticity – that is the automatic recognition of words when they see them. It is by far the best way to improve their English reading (and writing) overall.

The benefits of extensive reading are echoed by the benefits for extensive listening: the more students listen, the more language they acquire and the better they get at listening activities in general. Whether they choose recordings of passages from textbooks, recordings of simplified readers, other listening material designed for their level or podcasts of radio programmes which they are capable of following, the effect will be the same. Provided the input is comprehensible, they will gradually acquire more words and greater schematic knowledge which will, in turn, resolve many of the language difficulties they started out with.

- **Authenticity:** because it is vital for students to get practice in dealing with written text and speech where they miss quite a few words but are still able to extract the general meaning, an argument can be made for using mainly authentic reading and listening texts in class. After all, it is when students come into contact with 'real' language that they have to work hardest to understand.

Authentic material is language where no concessions are made to foreign speakers. It is normal, natural language used by native or competent speakers of a language. This is what our students encounter (or will encounter) in real life if they come into contact with target-language speakers, and, precisely because it is authentic, it is unlikely to be simplified or spoken slowly.

Authentic material which has been carelessly chosen can be extremely demotivating for students since they will not understand it. Instead of encouraging failure, we should let students read and listen to things they can understand. For beginners this may mean roughly-tuned language from the teacher (see page 117), and specially designed reading and listening texts from materials writers. However, it is essential that such listening texts approximate to authentic language use. The language may be simplified, but it must not be unnatural. As Ronald Carter and his colleagues suggest, 'concocted, made-up language can be perfectly viable but it should be modelled on naturalistic samples' (Carter *et al* 1998: 86).

Authentic material can be used by students at fairly low levels, however, if the tasks that go with it are well-designed and help students understand it better, rather than showing them how little they know. A gently paced sequence of activities with small tasks leading to bigger ones, for example, can enable students to watch television soap operas in English and help them understand far more than they might have thought possible (Farrell 1998).

It is worth pointing out that deciding what is or is not authentic is not easy. A stage play written for native speakers is a playwright's representation of spontaneous speech rather than the real thing, so it is, in a sense, both authentic and inauthentic. A father talking to his baby daughter may be employing 'baby talk' – rough-tuning the language so that it is comprehensible – but there is nothing inauthentic about it. The language which students are exposed to has just as strong a claim to authenticity as the play or the parent, provided that it is not altered in such a way as to make it unrecognisable in style and construction from the language which competent speakers encounter in many walks of life.

B3 Comprehension tasks

A key feature in the successful teaching of receptive skills concerns the choice of comprehension tasks. Sometimes such tasks appear to be testing the students rather than helping them to understand. But although reading and listening are perfectly proper mediums for language and skill testing, nevertheless if we are trying to encourage students to improve their receptive skills, testing them will not be an appropriate way of accomplishing this. Sometimes texts and/or the tasks which accompany them are either far too easy or far too difficult.

In order to resolve these problems we need to use comprehension tasks which promote understanding and we need to match text and task appropriately.

- **Testing and teaching:** the best kind of tasks are those which raise students' expectations, help them tease out meanings and provoke an examination of the reading or listening passage. Unlike reading and listening tests, these tasks bring them to a greater understanding of language and text construction. By having students perform activities such as looking up information on the Internet, filling in forms on the basis of a recording or solving reading puzzles, we are helping them become better readers and listeners.

    Some tasks seem to fall halfway between testing and teaching, however, since, by appearing to demand a right answer (e.g. *Are these statements about the text true or false?* or questions abut the text with *what*, *when*, *how many* and *how often*), they could, in theory, be used to assess student performance. Indeed, when they are done under test conditions, their purpose is obviously to explore student strengths and weaknesses. Yet such comprehension items can also be an indispensable part of a teacher's receptive skills armoury. By the simple expedient of having students work in pairs to agree on whether a statement about part of a text is true or false, the comprehension items help each individual (through conversation and comparison) to understand something, rather than challenging them to give right answers under test-like conditions. If students are encouraged to try to predict the answers to such questions before they read or listen, expectations are created in their minds which help them focus their reading or listening (although we must be careful not to ask them to try to predict things they have no chance of being able to guess). In both cases we have turned a potential test task into a creative tool for receptive skill training.

    Whatever the reading task, a lot will depend on the conditions in which students are asked to perform that task. Even the most formal test-like items can be used to help students rather than frighten them!

- **Appropriate challenge:** when asking students to read and listen, we want to avoid texts and tasks that are either far too easy or far too difficult. As with many other language tasks, we want to get the level of challenge right, to make the tasks difficult but, nevertheless, achievable.

  Getting the level right depends on the right match between text and task. Thus, where a text is difficult, we may still be able to use it, but only if the task is appropriate. We could theoretically, for example, have beginners listen to the famous conversation between Ophelia and the prince in Shakespeare's *Hamlet* ('Get thee to a nunnery ...') and ask them how many people are speaking. We could ask students to read a few pages of *Ulysses* by James Joyce and ask them how many full stops they can find. Despite the difficulty of the texts, both of these tasks are achievable. Yet we might feel that neither is appropriate or useful. On the other hand, having students listen to a news broadcast where the language level is very challenging may be entirely appropriate if the task only asks them – at first – to try to identify the five main topics in the broadcast.

C Productive skills

Although the productive skills of writing and speaking are different in many ways, we can still provide a basic model for teaching and organising them.

C1 A basic methodological model for teaching productive skills

A key factor in the success of productive-skill tasks is the way teachers organise them and how they respond to the students' work. We will consider these in more detail in Chapters 19 and 20, but we can, here, set down a basic methodological model for the teaching of productive skills.

In the *lead-in* stage, we engage students with the topic. Perhaps we ask them what they know about a certain subject (e.g. we ask them what experience they have of tourism if we are going to have a tourism debate – see Example 7 on page 358), or we might, if we are going to role-play checking in at an airport, get them to think about the kind of conversation that usually takes place when people check in.

When we *set the task*, we explain exactly what students are going to do. At this stage we may need to demonstrate the activity in some way. For example, if we want students to work in pairs, we can show the class how the activity works by being one of a public pair ourselves so that everyone sees the procedure in action. We may get students to repeat the task instructions back to us (either in English or in their L1, depending on which is appropriate). We will also make sure that students are given all the information they need to complete the tasks (e.g. role cards, etc. for a role-play).

Once the students have started, we will *monitor the task*. This may mean going round the class, listening to students working and helping them where they are having difficulties. With writing tasks, we may become actively involved in the writing process as we respond to the students' work and point them in new directions (see Chapter 19, B7).

When the activity has finished, we give *task feedback*. This is where we may help students to see how well they have done. As we said in Chapter 8, C3 and D, we will respond to the content of the task and not just to the language the students used. We will show positive aspects of what they have achieved and not concentrate solely on their failings. Finally, we may move on from the task with a *task-related follow-up*.

In Chapter 3B we discussed the value of repetition. Frequently, then, we may re-set the task (or something very similar to it) and go through the sequence again.

We can summarise this procedure in Figure 3.

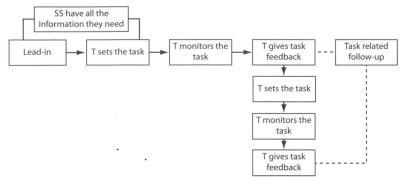

FIGURE 3: A basic model for teaching productive skills

C2 Structuring discourse

In order for communication to be successful, we have to structure our discourse in such a way that it will be understood by our listeners or readers. In writing – as we shall see in Chapter 19 – certain genres will push us to supply information in certain prescribed ways. But in order for writing to be successful, it has to be both *coherent* and *cohesive*. Coherent writing makes sense because you can follow the sequence of ideas and points. Cohesion is a more technical matter since it is here that we concentrate on the various linguistic ways of connecting ideas across phrases and sentences. These may be 'chains of reference' (Biber *et al* 1999: 42) where we use language features such as pronouns, lexical repetition and synonymy to refer to ideas that have already been expressed. We can use various linkers as well, such as for addition (*also*, *moreover*), contrast (*although*, *however*, *still*), cause and effect (*therefore*, *so*) and time (*then*, *afterwards*).

Conversational discourse, on the other hand, often appears considerably more chaotic. This is partly because it is 'jointly constructed' (Thornbury 2005a: 14) by however many people are taking part. In order for this 'construction' to be successful, participants need to know how to take turns, and what discourse markers, for example, they can use to facilitate the smooth progression from one speaker to the next. Such structuring devices include language designed to 'buy time', and quite specific organising markers, such as *firstly*, *secondly* or even *and as if that wasn't enough*.

It is worth pointing out that spoken English tends to have a higher proportion of formulaic lexical phrases than written English (Wray 1999: 227–8).

Successful communication, both in writing and in speech, depends, to some extent, on knowing the rules. Thus, as we saw in Chapter 2, C1, speakers know how and when to take turns, just as successful writers in a particular discourse community know the differences between accepted norms for writing emails and writing business letters. And there are more general sociocultural rules, too, such as how men and women address each other, whether there is any difference between talking to people of the same age or people who are considerably older, and finally, how to perform certain common speech events such as agreeing, inviting, suggesting, etc.

We are not suggesting that students need to speak or write language exactly like a British or Canadian person (for example), especially given our comments about the globalisation of

English in Chapter 1. Nevertheless, sociocultural rules of various discourse communities exist in the public consciousness (even though they change over time) so that obeying them or purposefully flouting them become acts of belonging or rejection.

C3 Interacting with an audience

Part of our speaking proficiency depends upon our ability to speak differentially, depending upon our audience and upon the way we absorb their reactions and respond to them. Part of our writing skill depends upon our ability to change our style and structure to suit the person or people we are writing for.

Where people are giving lectures, they are likely to adapt the way they are speaking and the words they are using on the basis of audience reaction. Just as good actors are expert at riding a laugh or changing their pace to suit the mood of their audience, so good presenters, salespeople and politicians keep their ears and eyes open to see how their words are going down and speak accordingly. Even when lecturers read their speeches, they will change their pace, repeat words or lines, and perhaps add in or take out some phrases on the basis of how their listeners are responding. Writers engaged in an email correspondence modify subsequent communications on the basis of the reaction of the people they are communicating with. Novelists and playwrights, at a conscious or subconscious level, identify a prototypical audience to write for. In informal spontaneous conversations, we are constantly alert for the reactions of the people we are interacting with so that we make our communication as informative as required, amending it depending on how the other participants in the interaction behave.

C4 Dealing with difficulty

When speakers or writers of their own or of a foreign language don't know a word or just can't remember it, they may employ some or all of the following strategies to resolve the difficulty:

- **Improvising:** speakers sometimes try any word or phrase that they can come up with in the hope that it is about right. Such improvisations sometimes work, but they can also obscure meaning.

- **Discarding:** when speakers simply can't find words for what they want to say, they may abandon the thought that they can't put into words.

- **Foreignising:** when operating in a foreign language, speakers (and writers) sometimes choose a word in a language they know well (such as their first language) and 'foreignise' it (in other words, pronounce it as if it was an L2 word) in the hope that it will be equivalent to the meaning they wish to express in the foreign language. This will work reasonably well if an English speaker says *content-o* because they hope that what they are saying sounds Spanish and so will be understood. Luckily for them, there is a Spanish word *contento* which means *happy*. However, if they say that they want to go to the *librario* to try to find a book, their foreignisation is less successful because there is no such word, and the closest equivalent in Spanish (*librería*) means *bookshop*, not *library* as they had hoped.

- **Paraphrasing:** speakers sometimes paraphrase, talking about *something for cleaning the teeth* if they don't know the word *toothbrush*, or saying that they *have very bad feelings about* somebody when all they want to say is that they are *cross with* that person. Such lexical substitution or circumlocution gets many speakers out of trouble, though it can make communication longer and more convoluted.

Clearly some of these difficulty strategies are more appropriate than others. As teachers we should encourage paraphrasing and improvising as more useful techniques than discarding thoughts or foreignising words blindly. However, a major reason for having students perform oral communicative tasks in class is to give them practice in just these kinds of strategy.

C5 The language issue

Learners engaged in a productive task can become very frustrated when they just do not have the words or the grammar they need to express themselves. Sometimes, of course, they can research language they would like to use (see Chapter 12D), but this can make writing a very cumbersome process, and in speaking, such an option is anyway not available, at least not in spontaneous speech.

There are a number of steps we can take which will help students achieve success:

- **Supply key language:** before we ask students to take part in a spoken or written activity, we may check their knowledge of key vocabulary and help them with phrases or questions that will be useful for the task. However, where speaking is concerned, we should remember that language which students have only just met for the first time (whether grammatical, lexical or phrasal) is often not available for instant use in spontaneous conversation; more exposure and practice is usually necessary before people can use new language fluently. We should not expect, therefore, that we can introduce new language and have students use it instantly in communicative activities. Instead, we need to plan in advance.

- **Plan activities in advance:** because of the time-lag between our students meeting new language and their ability to use it fluently, we need to plan production activities that will provoke the use of language which they have had a chance to absorb at an earlier stage.

Language production activities which fall at the communicative end of the communication continuum are not just practice activities, however. One of the strategies which speakers need to develop is the art of getting round language problems in communication; writers, too, will have to find ways of saying things even when a lack of language makes this difficult.

D Projects

Frequently, teachers ask their students to work on assignments that last for longer than say, 45 minutes or one or two lessons. Some TBL sequences (see page 71) are like this, but whatever methodology we are following, such longer-term projects have always been part of educational sequences. In schools in many education systems around the world, children may produce their own booklets or computer-based materials which combine a number of subjects they have been studying over a period of time – maths, geography, history, etc. They may produce 'books' on the life of indigenous people in their country before the arrival of settlers or conquerors from overseas, or they could write their own Aztec or ancient Egyptian cookbooks; they might do projects on animals or aspects of the natural world. Typically, their booklets will include pictures as well as writing.

In order to complete their projects, the children will look at books, consult websites, watch videos and, perhaps, conduct their own mini-experiments. The project thus becomes a perfect vehicle for skill integration and information gathering.

Project work is popular in EFL/ESOL teaching and learning, too, though its use is naturally constrained by the amount of time available for its implementation. It is far more popular, for example, on courses where students are full-time students and have access to a wide range of resources and people.

There are many possible areas for project work in an EFL/ESL setting. Many teachers, for example, encourage their students to produce a class newspaper. Other classes produce guides to their town or books on history or culture. Some projects look at people's attitudes to current issues or ask students to produce brochures for a public service or a new company.

What these examples demonstrate is that the difference between a full-blown project and some writing or speaking tasks is chiefly one of scale. When we get students to prepare for a debate (see page 358) or have them analyse reviews so that they can write their own (see page 334), we are involving them in a project of sorts. Projects are longer than the traditional essay or other written task. They demand significantly more research than a buzz group (see page 350) preparing for a quick communicative activity.

D1 ## Managing projects

Projects can be organised in a number of different ways, but they generally share the same sequence:

- **The briefing/the choice:** projects start when the teacher or the students (or the two in combination) decide on a topic. Sometimes students may bring their own ideas, sometimes the teacher may offer a list of possible topics, and sometimes the teacher may ask all the students to do the same project.

  Once the choice has been made, a briefing takes place in which teacher and students define the aims of the project and discuss how they can gather data, what the timescale of the project is, what stages it will go through and what support the students will get as the work progresses.

- **Idea/language generation:** once a briefing has taken place, what happens next will depend on how directed the project is. If students have come up with their own ideas and topics, this is where they will start on the process of idea generation. They have to decide what is going into their project. They need to make a plan about what they have to find out, and think about where they can find that information.

  If, however, teachers are directing the project very carefully, students may be told what they are looking for and where they are going to find it.

- **Data gathering:** students can gather data from a number of sources. They can consult encyclopedias or go to the Internet to find what they are looking for. They can design questionnaires so that they can interview people. They can look at texts for genre analysis or watch television programmes and listen to the radio.

- **Planning:** when students have got their ideas, generated some topic-specific language and gathered the data they require, they can start to make a plan of how the final project will be set out. In the case of a written final product, this will involve the kind of process approach we discuss in Chapter 19, B1. If students are planning to end the project with a big debate or presentation, for example, this is where they plan what they are going to say.

- **Drafting and editing:** if the project has a final written product, a first draft will be produced, consisting either of sections or the whole thing, which fellow students and/or the teacher can look at and comment on. This draft will also be self-edited by the project writers (see Chapter 8, D4).

- **The result:** finally, the goal at which the whole project has been aiming has been reached. This may take the form of a written report or a blog accompanied by photographs, for example. It may be a big role-play where people who have been gathering data about different sides of an argument get together to discuss the issue. It might be a short piece of film, a drama production or a recording. But whatever it is, this is what the whole thing has been for.

- **Consultation/tutorial:** throughout the lifetime of a project, teachers will need to be available as tutors, advising, helping and prompting students to help them progress. Such consultations and tutorials will, of course, focus on how the project is progressing. For example, we will want to be sure that students have been able to gather the data they have been looking for. We will want to be confident that they have understood the data and that they can use it effectively. A frequent problem occurs when students try to do too much in a project, so teachers may need to help them narrow down the focus of their work.

Victoria Chan, a lecturer at Hong Kong Polytechnic University, had her class do a newspaper project (Chan 2001). It is a typical example of such work. After the task briefing, students discussed newspapers and what goes into them. They analysed different aspects of newspapers (articles, reviews, comment, etc.) for both content and language, and then drafted their own stories, film reviews, etc. These were then subjected to peer review and editing before being used in the finished class newspaper. Throughout, the students were clear about the stages of the project and what they were doing and would do next. Victoria Chen reports that they were interested and motivated by what, for them, had been a highly innovative approach.

Although projects may not be appropriate in all circumstances (principally, perhaps, because of the time which teachers and students have at their disposal), still they usually involve a satisfying integration of skills. They require detailed planning and idea generation and encourage students to gather data. At the end of the whole process, students have work they can show proudly to their colleagues and friends, or they have the chance to be involved in really significant presentations both oral and/or with presentation equipment, such as overhead projectors and computer-supplied data projectors.

D2 A webquest project

As we saw on page 191, webquests allow teachers to get their students to do research from the comfort of a computer terminal. As in that example (of a webquest about city housing in New York), teachers can design the various stages of a webquest and select the sites that students can go to to gather data so that they don't waste their energies on fruitless searching.

In Chapter 5, we described a webquest which generates individual student profiles in terms of Multiple Intelligences (see page 90–91), and we can use this same webquest as an example of how such Internet-based projects are structured.

Like most webquest projects 'Teacher, have you thought about me?' (http://www.eslgo.com/classes/mi/index2.htm) starts with an *Introduction* in which the students are told that everyone learns differently and that during the webquest they are going to investigate seven or eight types of intelligence.

When students have absorbed this (the teacher can discuss the introduction with the students), they click on *Tasks* and reach the task screen. This tells them what they are going to do and, crucially, gives them clear task outcomes (e.g. 'After completing this webquest you will know about different kinds of intelligence'). It is worth pointing out that the authors of the webquest tell the students that this is more than just an assignment – it will help them learn.

Students now start to collect data using the links built into the *Process* page. In Task 1, they are offered links to short and long Multiple Intelligence questionnaires which they have to complete to find their own MI profile as in the following example:

> **Short**
> www.mitest.com/o7inte~1.htm
> http://ivc.uidaho.edu/flbrain/MIassess.html

All they have to do is to click on one of the links to go to a questionnaire. This, of course, is where the advantage of doing projects via the Internet become apparent. Task 2 gets students to click on links where they will find articles which explain the whole concept of Multiple Intelligences. Task 3 (on the same page) asks students to 'discover more about your strongest intelligence' and 'consider what medium you will use to report to your lecturer'; Task 4 asks them to 'choose another Multiple Intelligence to learn more about ... to deepen further your understanding of Multiple Intelligences'; and Task 5 tells them to 'Plan and produce your report'. There is a further page of extra resources which students can reach by clicking on the appropriate links.

When students have completed and delivered their report, they do a *Self evaluation*. Here, they rate themselves on a scale of 1–4 in different categories, such as 'General knowledge' and 'Readiness for the future'. For example, in the first of these categories, if they choose 'You learned a great deal about many types of intelligence' they would get a score of 4; in the second category, choosing 'You haven't decided how to use your knowledge yet but you're thinking about a few things that may help' would give a score of 2.

There is an evaluation grid for teachers too, and then, finally the webquest is over, and the designers end it with an upbeat message of encouragement:

> **Congratulations!** You now have the knowledge needed to take control of your own learning. You don't have to worry about your teacher's style because you are aware of your style and can learn in a variety of ways. This means you can help yourself understand difficult concepts using various kinds of intelligence at your disposal.
>
> Walk into your next class (and all future classes) with confidence, because you control what you learn. But remember you never stop learning and ideas on how we learn are always changing. You are now on an exciting road to self discovery, a road that may lead you into new areas of multiple intelligences.

This webquest is a good example of a multi-skill project. There is reading and writing, and speaking and listening (in the discussion sessions with the teacher and other students which can occur at various stages of the process). The quest promotes and supports IT literacy (see page 323), too.

Other webquests and projects may be considerably more multi-faceted than this (and take more time). Nevertheless, this example shows how technology can be harnessed to enhance successful project work.

Chapter notes and further reading

- **Authentic English**
  See S Murray (2001). A Gilmore (2004) compares textbook and authentic interactions, whereas W Guariento and J Morley (2001) compare text and task authenticity.

- **Language skills**
  See the references at the end of Chapters 17–20.

- **Projects**
  D Fried-Booth (2002) is the second edition of her ground-breaking book on the subject. See also a short article on cross-curricular projects by S Andrewes (2004) and G Beckett and T Slater (2005) who demonstrate how projects are blends of content, language and skills integration.

17 | Reading

A Extensive and intensive reading

To get maximum benefit from their reading, students need to be involved in both extensive and intensive reading. Whereas with the former, a teacher encourages students to choose for themselves what they read and to do so for pleasure and general language improvement, the latter is often (but not exclusively) teacher-chosen and directed. It is designed to enable students to develop specific receptive skills such as reading for *gist* (or general understanding – often called *skimming*), reading for *specific information* (often called *scanning*), reading for detailed comprehension or reading for inference (what is 'behind' the words) and attitude.

A1 Extensive reading

We have discussed the importance of extensive reading for the development of our students' word recognition – and for their improvement as readers overall. But it is not enough to tell students to 'read a lot'; we need to offer them a programme which includes appropriate materials, guidance, tasks and facilities, such as permanent or portable libraries of books.

- **Extensive reading materials:** one of the fundamental conditions of a successful extensive reading programme is that students should be reading material which they can understand. If they are struggling to understand every word, they can hardly be reading for pleasure – the main goal of this activity. This means that we need to provide books which either by chance, or because they have been specially written, are readily accessible to our students.

  Specially written materials for extensive reading – what Richard Day and Julian Bamford call 'language learner literature' (1998: 61) – are often referred to as *graded readers* or *simplified readers*. They can take the form of original fiction and non-fiction books as well as simplifications of established works of literature. Such books succeed because the writers or adaptors work within specific lists of allowed words and grammar. This means that students at the appropriate level can read them with ease and confidence. At their best, despite the limitations on language, such books can speak to the reader through the creation of atmosphere and/or compelling plot lines. Consider, for example, the following short extract from the second chapter of a level 1 (elementary) murder mystery for adults. In the first chapter, a man in a hospital bed appears to be suffering from amnesia. In the second chapter, that same man speaks to us directly:

> There is a man near my bed. His clothes are white. No. Some of his clothes are white. He has a white coat, but his trousers are brown. He also has brown hair. The man in the white coat says he's a doctor. He says his name is Doctor Cox. He tells me to call him Philip. He says he is going to help me.
>
> But he's not going to help me. They think I don't remember. They think I don't know anything. They know nothing, the doctors. Or the police. Nobody knows who I am. I sit in the bed and answer questions. They ask lots of questions.
>
> 'Do you know what amnesia is, John?' Doctor Cox asks me.
>
> Doctor Cox. Doctor Philip Cox. He thinks he's somebody. He's nobody. I know what amnesia is.

From *John Doe* by A Moses (Cambridge University Press)

The language is simple and controlled, but the atmosphere – in true murder-mystery style – is satisfyingly creepy. A student who enjoys this kind of story, but whose level of English is fairly low, will enjoy it enormously.

To encourage students to read this kind of learner literature – or any other texts which may be comprehensible in the same way – we need to act in the following ways:

- **Setting up a library:** in order to set up an extensive reading programme, we need to build up a library of suitable books. Although this may appear costly, it will be money well spent. If necessary, we should persuade our schools and institutions to provide such funds or raise money through other sources.

  If possible, we should organise static libraries in the classroom or in some other part of the school. If this is not possible, we need to work out some way of carrying the books around with us – in boxes or on trolleys.

  Once books have been purchased, we should code them for level and genre so that students can easily identify what kind of books they are. We should make the students aware of what the library contains and explain our classification system to them.

  We need to devise some way of keeping track of the books in the library. A simple signing-out system should ensure that our collection does not disappear over time.

  All of these setting-up procedures take time. But we can use students to help us administer the scheme. We can, if we are lucky, persuade the school administration to help us.

  If our students take part in extensive reading programmes, all the time we have spent on setting up a library will not have been wasted.

- **The role of the teacher in extensive reading programmes:** most students will not do a lot of extensive reading by themselves unless they are encouraged to do so by their teachers. Clearly, then, our role is crucial. We need to promote reading and by our own espousal of reading as a valid occupation, persuade students of its benefits. Perhaps, for example, we can occasionally read aloud from books we like and show, by our manner of reading, how exciting books can be.

  Having persuaded our students of the benefits of extensive reading, we can organise reading programmes where we indicate to them how many books we expect them to read over a given period. We can explain how they can make their choice of what to read, making it clear that the choice is theirs, but that they can consult other students' reviews and comments to help them make that choice. We can suggest that they look for books in a genre (be it crime fiction, romantic novels, science fiction, etc.) that they enjoy, and that they make appropriate level choices. We will act throughout as part organiser, part tutor (see Chapter 6, B1).

- **Extensive reading tasks:** because students should be allowed to choose their own reading texts, following their own likes and interests, they will not all be reading the same texts at once. For this reason – and because we want to prompt students to keep reading – we should encourage them to report back on their reading in a number of ways.

One approach is to set aside a time at various points in a course – say every two weeks – at which students can ask questions and/or tell their classmates about books they have found particularly enjoyable or noticeably awful. However, if this is inappropriate because not all students read at the same speed (or because they often do not have much to say about the book in front of their colleagues), we can ask them each to keep a weekly reading diary, either on its own or as part of any learning journal they may be writing (see Chapter 23, B3). Students can also write short book reviews for the class noticeboard. At the end of a month, a semester or a year, they can vote on the most popular book in the library. Other teachers have students fill in reading record charts (where they record title, publisher, level, start and end dates, comments about level and a good/fair/poor overall rating), they ask students to keep a reading notebook (where they record facts and opinions about the books they have gone through) or they engage students in oral interviews about what they are reading (Bamford and Day 2004: 77–85).

We can also put comment sheets into the books for students to write in, as the following example for a book called *The Earthquake* shows:

Rating	Your comment and your name
5	I'm afraid earthquake happens to us. Shoko
5	Great! Gabriel is nice. He is cool. TOMOKO
4	"Who is really taking care of me," I think after reading this book. YOKO
4	I had a chance to think what's the most important thing by reading this book. Hisako

From *Extensive Reading in the Second Language Classroom*
by R Day and J Bamford (Cambridge University Press)

It does not really matter which of these tasks students are asked to perform, provided that what they are asked to do helps to keep them reading as much and as often as possible.

A2 **Intensive reading: the roles of the teacher**

In order to get students to read enthusiastically in class, we need to work to create interest in the topic and tasks. However, there are further roles we need to adopt when asking students to read intensively:

- **Organiser:** we need to tell students exactly what their reading purpose is, give them clear instructions about how to achieve it and explain how long they have to do this. Once we have said *You have four minutes for this*, we should not change that time unless observation (see below) suggests that it is necessary.

- **Observer:** when we ask students to read on their own, we need to give them space to do so. This means restraining ourselves from interrupting that reading, even though the temptation may be to add more information or instructions.

  While students are reading we can observe their progress since this will give us valuable information about how well they are doing individually and collectively. It will also tell us whether to give them some extra time or, instead, move to organising feedback more quickly than we had anticipated.

- **Feedback organiser:** when our students have completed the task, we can lead a feedback session to check that they have completed it successfully. We may start by having them compare their answers in pairs and then ask for answers from the class in general or from pairs in particular. Students often appreciate giving paired answers like this since, by sharing their knowledge, they are also sharing their responsibility for the answers.

  When we ask students to give answers, we should always ask them to say where in the text they found the relevant information. This provokes a detailed study of the text which will help them the next time they come to a similar reading passage. It also tells us exactly what comprehension problems they have if and when they get answers wrong.

  It is important to be supportive when organising feedback after reading if we are to counter any negative feelings students might have about the process, and if we wish to sustain their motivation.

- **Prompter:** when students have read a text, we can prompt them to notice language features within it. We may also, as controllers, direct them to certain features of text construction, clarifying ambiguities and making them aware of issues of text structure which they had not come across previously.

A3 **Intensive reading: the vocabulary question**

A common paradox in reading lessons is that while teachers are encouraging students to read for general understanding, without worrying about the meaning of every single word, the students, on the other hand, are desperate to know what each individual word means! Given half a chance, many of them would rather tackle a reading passage with a dictionary (electronic or otherwise) in one hand and a pen in the other to write translations all over the page!

It is easy to be dismissive of such student preferences, yet as Carol Walker points out, 'It seems contradictory to insist that students "read for meaning" while simultaneously discouraging them from trying to understand the text at a deeper level than merely gist' (1998: 172). Clearly, we need to find some accommodation between our desire to have students develop particular reading skills (such as the ability to understand the general message without understanding every detail) and their natural urge to understand the meaning of every single word.

One way of reaching a compromise is to strike some kind of a bargain with a class (see Chapter 4, B2) whereby they will do more or less what we ask of them provided that we do more or less what they ask of us. Thus we may encourage students to read for general understanding without understanding every word on a first or second read-through. But then, depending on what else is going to be done, we can give them a chance to ask questions about individual words and/or give them a chance to look them up. That way both parties in the teaching–learning transaction have their needs met.

A word of caution needs to be added here. If students ask for the meaning of all the words they do not know – and given some of the problems inherent in the explaining of different word meanings – the majority of a lesson may be taken up in this way. We need, therefore, to limit the amount of time spent on vocabulary checking in the following ways:

- **Time limit:** we can give a time limit of, say, five minutes for vocabulary enquiry, whether this involves dictionary use, language corpus searches or questions to the teacher.

- **Word/phrase limit:** we can say that we will only answer questions about five or eight words or phrases.

- **Meaning consensus:** we can get students to work together to search for and find word meanings. To start the procedure, individual students write down three to five words from the text they most want to know the meaning of. When they have each done this, they share their list with another student and come up with a new joint list of only five words. This means they will probably have to discuss which words to leave out. Two pairs join to make new groups of four and once again they have to pool their lists and end up with only five words. Finally (perhaps after new groups of eight have been formed – it depends on the atmosphere in the class), students can look for meanings of their words in dictionaries and/or we can answer questions about the words which the groups have decided on.

  This process works for two reasons. In the first place, students may well be able to tell each other about some of the words which individual students did not know. More importantly, perhaps, is the fact that by the time we are asked for meanings, the students really do want to know them because the intervening process has encouraged them to invest some time in the meaning search. 'Understanding every word' has been changed into a cooperative learning task in its own right.

In responding to a natural hunger for vocabulary meaning, both teachers and students will have to compromise. It's unrealistic to expect only one-sided change, but there are ways of dealing with the problem which make a virtue out of what seems – to many teachers – a frustrating necessity.

A4 Intensive reading: letting the students in

It is often the case that the comprehension tasks we ask students to do are based on tasks in a coursebook. In other words, the students are responding to what someone else has asked them to find out. But students are far more likely to be engaged in a text if they bring their own feelings and knowledge to the task, rather than only responding to someone else's ideas of what they should find out.

One of the most important questions we can ever get students to answer is *Do you like the text*? (Kennedy 2000a and b). This question is included in the initial task in Example 2 (below). The question is important because if we only ever ask students technical questions about language, we are denying them any affective response to the content of the text. By letting them give voice (if they wish) to their feelings about what they have read, we are far more likely to provoke the 'cuddle factor' (see page 58) than if we just work through a series of exercises.

Another way of letting the students in is to allow them to create their own comprehension task. A popular way of doing this – when the text is about people, events or topics which everyone knows something about – is to discuss the subject of the text with the class before they read. We can encourage them to complete a chart (on the board) with things they know or don't know (or would like to know) about the text, e.g.

Things I/we know	Things I/we are not sure of	Things I/we would like to know

This activity provides a perfect lead-in since students will be engaged, will activate their schemata, and will, finally, end up with a good reason to read which they themselves have brought into being. Now they read the text to check off all the items they have put into the three columns. The text may not give them all the answers, of course, nor may it confirm (or even refute) what they have put in the left-hand column. Nevertheless, the chances are that they will read with considerably more interest than for some more routine task.

Another involving way of reading is to have students read different texts and then share the information they have gathered in order to piece together the whole story. This is called jigsaw reading, and we will look at an extended version of the technique in Example 7.

B   Reading lesson sequences

We use intensive reading sequences in class for a number of reasons. We may want to have students practise specific skills such as *skimming*/reading for general understanding or 'gist' (usually a Type 1 task – see page 270) or *scanning*/reading to extract specific information (also often a Type 1 task). We may, on the other hand, get students to read texts for communicative purposes (which mixes both Type 1 and Type 2 tasks), as part of other activities, as sources of information, or in order to identify specific uses of language.

Most reading sequences involve more than one reading skill. We may start by having students read for gist and then get them to read the text again for detailed comprehension; they may start by identifying the topic of a text before scanning the text quickly to recover specific information; they may read for specific information before going back to the text to identify features of text construction.

B1   Examples of reading sequences

In the following examples, the reading activity is specified, the skills which are involved are detailed and the way that the text can be used within a lesson is explained.

Example 1: AKA Diaz

Focus: reading to confirm expectations
Skills: predicting; reading for gist; reading for detailed comprehension
Age: adult
Level: intermediate

In this example, students predict the content of a text not from a picture, but from a few tantalising clues they are given (in the form of phrases from the passage they will read).

The teacher gives each student in the class a letter from A to E. She tells all the students to close their eyes. She then asks all the students with the letter A to open their eyes and shows them the word *lion*, written large so that they can see it. Then she makes them close their eyes again and this time shows the B students the phrase *racial groups*. She shows the C students the phrase *paper aeroplanes*, the D students the word *tattoos* and the E students the word *guard*.

She now puts the students in groups of five, each composed of students A–E. By discussing their words and phrases, each group has to try to predict what the text is all about. The teacher can go round the groups encouraging them and, perhaps, feeding them with new words like *cage*, *the tensest man* or *moral authority*, etc.

Finally, when the groups have made some predictions, the teacher asks them whether they would like to hear the text that all the words came from, as a prelude to reading the following text aloud, investing it with humour and drama, making the reading dramatic and enjoyable.

'This is it,' Rick said, in a cheerful voice. Through the windows of the classroom I could see the men. They were not in their seats; instead they were circling the room restlessly, like lions in a cage.

'Is there going to be a guard in the room while I teach?' I asked. I realized that this was something that should have been straightened out earlier.

Rick looked at me with deep concern. 'I'll come by a bit later, see that you're OK,' he said.

I walked through the door into the classroom. My students barely looked human. The desks were arranged in no special order, except that some of the men had got into racial groups. Many of them were smoking, and under the glare of the lights I could see their tattoos. One man with a pointed beard and a long mane of black hair circled behind me and around the other side of the desk. He was easily the tensest man I had ever seen. I thought of telling him to sit down but wondered what I would do if he refused so I kept the suggestion to myself. I placed my leather bag on the desk and faced the class. Nobody paid any attention to me. The conversation grew louder. I wanted to cut out and run. I had volunteered for this?

Every teacher has these moments of panic. We worry about rebellion: our moral authority lost, the students taking over. I had a teacher in high school, a Miss Hutchinson, who after taking roll would turn towards the board and be followed by an avalanche of paper aeroplanes and spitballs, sometimes even the bodies of students flying forward, an impromptu riot.

I unpacked my bag and began the roll. A few names down, I called out 'Diaz.'

No answer. 'Diaz,' I said again.

'Ain't my name,' a man in the front row volunteered.

'Why did you answer?' I asked.

'I'm here under another name,' he said. 'An alias. I could tell you my real name, but then I'd have to kill you.'

'We'll count that as "present",' I said. Several members of the class laughed: at least that slowed down the conversation. I finished the roll and handed out the syllabus for the class. I read it aloud and when I got to the end I looked up. 'So any questions?' I asked. The paper trembled in my hand.

'Yeah, I got a question.' AKA Diaz raised his hand. 'I want to know what the *&!* it means.'

From *Maximum Security* by R O'Connor in the literary magazine *Granta* (no. 54, 1996)

The students now read the text for themselves to answer the following detailed comprehension questions:

1 **True, false, or probably (not)?**
   a The class is in a prison.
   b There's a guard in the classroom.
   c Robert O'Connor had offered to teach the class.
   d There are white, black, Hispanic and Asian students in the class.
   e The class has both sexes.
   f Robert O'Connor was frightened.
   g The men threw paper aeroplanes at the teacher.
   h The men wanted to take the class.
   i Diaz is the man's real name.
   j AKA means 'also known as'.
   k The class was going to be a great success.

Before moving on to work with the content of the text, the teacher may well take advantage of the language in it to study some aspects that are of interest. For example, how is the meaning of *would* different in the sentences *I ... wondered what I would do if he refused* and *a teacher ... who ... would turn towards the board ...*? Can students make sentences using the same construction as *He was easily the tensest man I had ever seen* (e.g. *He/She was easily the* (superlative adjective + noun) *I had ever* (past participle)) or *I could tell you my real name, but then I'd have to kill you* (e.g. *I could ..., but then I'd have to ...*).

The discussion possibilities for this text are endless. How many differences are there between Robert O'Connor's class and the students' own class? How many similarities are there? How would they (the students) handle working in a prison? Should prisoners be given classes anyway, and if so, of what kind? What would the students themselves do if they were giving their first English class in a prison or in a more ordinary school environment?

Part of this sequence has involved the teacher reading aloud. This can be very powerful if it is not overdone. By mixing the skills of speaking, listening and reading, the students have had a rich language experience, and because they have had a chance to predict content, listen, read and then discuss the text, they are likely to be very involved with the procedure.

Example 2: Going home	Activity:	general reading
	Skills:	reading for gist; reading for detailed comprehension
	Age:	any
	Level:	upper intermediate

Over 20 years ago Michael Scott and his colleagues, working at university level with ESP students in Brazil, designed a 'standard exercise' which could be used by their students with any reading text (Scott *et al* 1984). In their version, the questions were detailed and were in Portuguese. The usefulness of the questions was assured because any students, even if they were having trouble with their spoken English, could read a text with the help of this broad-based reading 'kit'.

For general English we can use the same principle and design questions which can be given to students in English or in their own language, and which can be used for any reading text they meet. Consider the following general questions:

> **1** What is the text about?
> **2** Who was it written by?
> **3** Who was it written for?
> **4** What is the writer's intention?
> **5** Do you like the text?

In the following example, these five questions are applied to this text:

19-year-old Penny Elvey and her friend Anna are going home after six months as volunteers in a school in Nepal. But then the rain starts and the roads are flooded. This is part of their story.

At the village of Meestal there is a huge river blocking our path. We came here a few weeks ago with some students for a picnic but the innocent little stream that we sat by has now become a raging torrent.

Across the water we can see a truck. On our side a man approaches us.

'That is my friend,' he says gesturing to a man standing by the vehicle. 'You go with truck.'

Anna and I smile enthusiastically. But our guide steps forward.

'It is too dangerous. We must wait. The river will become smaller.'

Anna and I glance at each other. It is a curious philosophy since the rain is still falling steadily.

The truck driver's friend grins at me.

'We help. You give me 600 rupees.'

600 rupees is far too much but we are desperate. He knows. He knows I know he knows. Our eyes lock.

People are watching us curiously to see how we are going to react. I fold my arms and force a laugh.

'Then we will stay the night here.'

For a terrible moment I think he is going to walk away, but then he smiles nervously.

'I mean 300 for you; 300 for your friend.'

He calls two of his friends and they hold our luggage above their heads as they step into the water. Slowly and steadily they cross the river and reach the other side safely.

Suddenly a man taps my shoulder.

'For you too dangerous. You must stay here.'

My rucksack and walking boots are now sitting on a rock across the water. In the pocket of my rucksack are all my papers and money. Where my passport goes I follow. Maybe the current is not that strong.

'You can swim?'

A small crowd of people gathers on the other side. Anna goes first. Four men take hold of her and lead her safely across. Now it is my turn. I step forward gingerly but catch my ankle on a rock. The water pulls my legs away from under me. But the men drag me to the safety of the far side.

Anna and I pick up our things and climb into the old truck. The people there stare at us in amusement. We are wet through, covered in mud, our clothes in tatters. But as the truck shudders to life, we look at each other and smile. We are going to make it to Kathmandu in time for breakfast!

Adapted from *Network*, the *Gap Activity Projects* annual newsletter

When the students have discussed their answers to the general questions in the reading kit, they can go back to the text to answer more detailed questions (e.g. *Who went for a picnic? Who has to pay 600 rupees?* etc.). The teacher may want to draw their attention to certain items of vocabulary with a task such as:

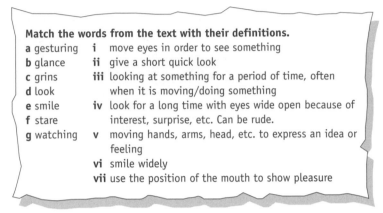

Match the words from the text with their definitions.

a gesturing	**i**	move eyes in order to see something
b glance	**ii**	give a short quick look
c grins	**iii**	looking at something for a period of time, often when it is moving/doing something
d look		
e smile	**iv**	look for a long time with eyes wide open because of interest, surprise, etc. Can be rude.
f stare		
g watching	**v**	moving hands, arms, head, etc. to express an idea or feeling
	vi	smile widely
	vii	use the position of the mouth to show pleasure

The students can now make sentences with these words using the pronouns *I* or *we*, e.g. *I like it when people smile at me.* They could discuss why Paula has written her story in the present tense, and they could then go on to talk about journeys they have made, or discuss how they feel if they spend a long time away from home. Or perhaps they could work on an exercise like the following:

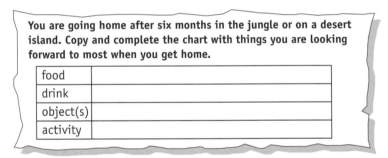

You are going home after six months in the jungle or on a desert island. Copy and complete the chart with things you are looking forward to most when you get home.

food	
drink	
object(s)	
activity	

In whatever ways the text is exploited, the use of the general questions ensures that students will approach it – for the first read anyway – in a general way. Of course, many texts can be used in this way, whether for beginners or advanced students.

Example 3: Village of snakes	Activity: modified cloze text Skills: reading for gist; reading for detailed comprehension Age: teenage Level: elementary

A popular test of comprehension is the 'modified' cloze procedure (see Chapter 22, B2) where every *n*th word is replaced by a blank. Although there may be some doubts about this as a testing technique, when used with students for fun, it can be a good way to help them arrive at a general understanding of a piece of text and a detailed understanding of the sentences in it. It may be necessary, however, for the teacher to choose some of the words that will be replaced by blanks – because some of them which happen, say, every seventh word, may cause too much trouble and should therefore be avoided.

In this example, teenage students are going to read about snakes and snake charmers in an Indian village. The teacher starts by asking students if they know any words about snakes and the people who play music to snakes. Words like *poison*, *poisonous* and *snake charmer* will then be elicited.

Students are now given the following text and asked to work with a colleague to see if they can fill in the blanks as they read.

VILLAGE OF SNAKES

by Sohan Devu

Saperagaon isn't an ordinary Indian village – (1) _____ a village of snake charmers. In (2) _____ house in the village there are (3) _____ lot of poisonous snakes; vipers, kraits (4) _____ cobras. Each one of these snakes (5) _____ poisonous enough to kill you, but (6) _____ children love playing with them.

It (7) _____ the beginning of a new day (8) _____ Saperagaon. The sun is coming up. Twelve-(9) _____-old Ravi is happy because it (10) _____ warm enough to wake the cobras. (11) _____ opens the basket and a king cobra (12) _____ its head. It hisses and then (13) _____ to bite. 'It doesn't like waking (14) _____!' says Ravi, laughing.

The villagers use (15) _____ snakes to earn money for food.'(16) _____ day we walk 15 or 20 (17) _____ to the nearest town,' says Ravi. '(18) _____ play music on the pipes and (19) _____ snakes dance. People enjoy the show,(20) _____ they don't like paying. Each day (21) _____ earn only 25 or 30 rupees.' ((22) _____ not enough for an ice cream (23) _____ the UK).

'There aren't many snake charmers (24) _____ India now,' says Sanjay Nath, (25) _____ father.

'Do many snake charmers die (26) _____ snake bites?' I ask.

'No, not (27) _____ ,' says Sanjay, 'but that isn't the (28) _____. We haven't got much money or (29) _____. It's too difficult to earn money. (30) _____ is not a good enough life (31) _____ children. They go to school now. (32) _____ learning a different way to live.

From *Go Student's Book* 2 by S Elsworth and J Rose (Pearson Education Ltd)

When the teacher and students have checked the answers to the blanks, they can read the complete text again for answers to more detailed questions such as *How many types of poisonous snakes are there?* and *Why does Ravi like the sun?* Students can then be directed to look at the text again for any language points which are interesting and/or to make sure they have understood the text as fully as is necessary. They may then say if they would like to be a snake charmer or talk about animals they like or don't like. They might listen to an interview with Ravi about his daily life and then talk about their own.

This kind of cloze procedure can be used with poems in a more interactive way, as in the following example for intermediate students.

First the students are shown, line by line, the following poem. They are told that they have to try to guess what words go in the blanks, however crazy their guesses are. We can do this by gradually revealing the lines on an overhead transparency or on a computer screen projected onto the board. Thus in the following poem ('The Confession' by Brian Patten), the students see the following lines:

> **The Confession (version 1)**
> When he showed her the (1) _____ again, she said,
> 'Yes, I remember (2) _____ it.
> I was incredibly (3) _____ then.
> You handed me the (4) _____
> And telling me over and over how to use it
> You posed, (5) _____ (6) _____ .
> You were so (7) _____ , so (8) _____ to everything.
> 'It was a July afternoon.
> The day was (9) _____and my (10) _____ hummed.
> I was (11) _____ and in search of (12) _____ (13) _____
> That seemed beyond you.
> 'Yet how can I forget that (14) _____ ?
> Look closer at the (15) _____ .
> See there (16) _____ (17) _____ (18) _____ ,
> In the (19) _____ (20) _____ you
> The other (21) _____ , (22) _____ so (23) _____ .'

The students almost certainly won't be able to come up with the original words, but they can compare their guesses to see if anyone has come up with the same idea. Throughout, they should know that this is a kind of game.

We now tell them that we will show them the lines again, but this time we will add the first letter of each word, i.e. (1) p_____ , (2) t_____ , (3) y_____ , etc.).

The next time the students see the poem, they get the first two letters of each word (i.e. (1) ph ___, (2) ta ___, (3) yo _____, etc.). By now several students will have guessed a proportion of the words.

Finally, they see the completed poem:

> **The Confession (final version)**
> When he showed her the photograph again, she said,
> 'Yes, I remember taking it.
> I was incredibly young then.
> You handed me the camera
> And telling me over and over how to use it
> You posed, smiling stiffly.
> You were so pompous, so blind to everything.
> 'It was a July afternoon.
> The day was hot and my body hummed.
> I was bored and in search of an adventure
> That seemed beyond you.
> 'Yet how can I forget that day?
> Look closer at the photograph.
> See there in the background,
> In the corner behind you
> The other boy, grinning so openly.'

This activity works extremely well because students are constantly trying to make sense of what they are seeing. They are searching for all and any of the language they know to try to complete the blanks. And because we give them a bit more information each time, they gradually get to guess almost all the words. Somewhere between reading and vocabulary practice, this activity is enjoyable and dynamic.

Example 4: The right film	Activity: researching a topic
	Skills: scanning; reading for gist
	Age: any
	Level: intermediate

The following example shows how computers and the Internet can be used in class (or in a self-access or computer centre) to get students searching for information in an entirely realistic and enjoyable way.

Students are told that they are going to the cinema in Cambridge, England. They have to find a film that is suitable for themselves and a 13 year old, and which is on in the evening. They will have to check reviews to make sure the film is a good one. Before they do this, they have the British rating system explained to them (U = anyone can go, PG = parental guidance: children can go with their parents or alone if their parents say they can, 12A = suitable for 12 year olds upwards, 15 = suitable for 15 year olds upwards, and 18 = anyone older than 17).

Students are directed to 'Guardian Unlimited', the website for one of Britain's most widely read quality newspapers at www.guardian.co.uk and then to the 'Films' pages within the website. The teacher tells them to enter a Cambridge postcode in the space provided. When they click on the 'Go' button, they will find something like the following on the screen.

They now have to click on the 'U', 'PG' and '12A' films to read summaries and short film reviews (which are also available at this site). When they have done this for all the films which suit their target audience, they have to make a choice based on the summaries and the review information. But they have to do this as quickly as possible.

> Vue
>
> Grafton Centre, East Road
>
> Barnyard (PG) Sat/Sun mat 11.10
> Borat: Cultural Learnings of America for Make Benefit Glorious Nation of Kazakhstan (15) 10.50 (Sat/Sun) 12.10 1.20 (not Sun) 2.30 3.30 5.00 6.00 (not Tue) 7.00 8.30 9.30 10.40 (Fri/Sat) 11.40 (Fri/Sat)
> Breaking and Entering (15) 11.30 (Sat/Sun) 2.20 5.30 9.00 (Sun-Thu)
> Casino Royale (12A) 9.30 (Sat/Sun) 10.00 (Sat/Sun) 11.00 (Sat/Sun) 12.30 1.00 2.00 4.00 4.30 5.30 7.30 8.00 9.00 10.30 (Fri/Sat) 11.10 (Fri/Sat) 12.07 (Fri/Sat)
> The Devil Wears Prada (PG) 1.50 4.20 (not Sat/Sun)
> Eight Below (PG) Sat/Sun mat 9.50
> Jackass Number Two (18) Thu 5.10 7.20 9.40
> Open Season (PG) Sat/Sun mat 10.10
> The Prestige (12A) 12.20 3.00 5.50 8.40 11.30 (Fri/Sat)
> Saw III (18) 6.50 9.20 11.50 (Fri/Sat)
> Tenacious D in 'The Pick of Destiny' (15) Sat/Sun 4.20

When choices have been made, the students have to explain which film they are going to see and why. They can also tell their classmates which films they would have preferred to go and see if they didn't have to worry about the 13 year old and/or they could go at different times of the day.

At this level, students will not understand all the words in the descriptions and reviews, etc. Nevertheless, they should understand enough for them to talk about what they have found.

Getting students to search for information on the web is, as we saw in Chapter 11G, immensely useful. Perhaps the best way of doing this is through webquests (see www.webquest.org). The Internet is the ideal resource tool for this kind of reading. Provided that the teacher has researched the topic (and the appropriate websites) beforehand, the reading for specific detail will be purposeful and enjoyable whether students are looking at films, weather patterns or holiday destinations. However, it is important for the teacher to have done some of the work in locating sites so that a lot of time is not spent searching uselessly.

Example 5: Look behind you	Activity:	ordering sentences
	Skill:	reading for gist; reading for detailed information
	Age:	any
	Level:	elementary

In this example, students first have to do a reading puzzle, which leads them on to complete a story. The reading is part of an integrated skills sequence which includes discussion and language work.

Students are told they are going to discuss a car journey. The teacher asks them to name the parts of a car (she can bring along a photograph or draw a car). The students end up with words like *mirror*, *tyre*, *indicator*, etc.

Students now look at the following exercise where they have to write the correct verb in the blanks to make up typical car phrases. They can do this individually or in pairs.

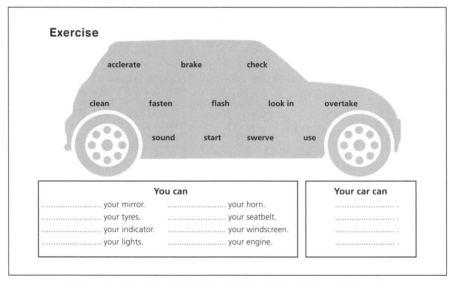

From *Reading Extra* by L Driscoll (Cambridge University Press)

The teacher goes through the answers with the class, and then gives pairs of students the set of sentences on page 297, which they have to put in order to make a story. (They are in the correct order on page 297, but the teacher will have mixed them up so that she doesn't give them out in a perfect sequence.) While they do this, the teacher goes round the class monitoring what is going on and giving help where students are stuck.

A woman was driving home along a country road late one night.

The road was completely empty except for one car behind her.

The woman thought nothing of it until the other car began to overtake.

Then it suddenly braked, swerved back behind her and flashed its lights.

The woman felt a bit nervous, particulary when the car flashed its lights again.

She accelerated, but the other car stayed right behind her.

The woman was absolutelt terrified by the time she got home.

And, what made things worse, the other car stopped behnd her.

Her only hope of escaping was to get into the house and phone the police.

She got out of her car and began to run, but so did the driver of the other car.

She screamed in terror, but he shouted, 'Quick! get inside and call the police!'

When the police arrived, the woman discovered that the man wasn't trying to kill – he had actually saved her life.

The teacher goes through the sentences with the class to make sure that everyone has the correct order. She explains that the end of the story is missing, and asks the students, once again in pairs or groups, to try to work out what the end might be. They should write a final sentence or two.

The class listen to the different endings and decide which one they like best. The teacher then shows them the following:

> **As the man was driving along behind her, he had seen someone with a knife rising from the back seat. But when he flashed his lights, the person sat back down again.**

Finally, the class discuss the fact that this story is unlikely to be true. It is one of those urban myths that everyone tells.

Re-ordering lines or paragraphs like this is a bottom-up activity (see page 270) where general meaning is only achieved by looking at how the whole thing coheres on the basis not only of the facts, but also by the use of cohesive devices (see page 29) which make the whole thing stick together.

A variation is to get students to stand up and give them each a card with a different line from a poem. They can read their lines out to each other but not show them. They have to put the poem in order (the following cards, describing an advertising photograph, are examples of this).

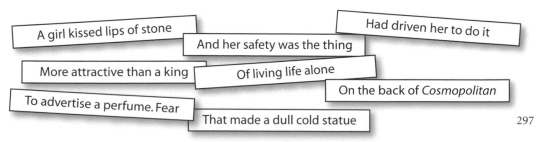

A girl kissed lips of stone

Had driven her to do it

And her safety was the thing

More attractive than a king

Of living life alone

On the back of *Cosmopolitan*

To advertise a perfume. Fear

That made a dull cold statue

Example 6: Plastic surgery	Activity:	reading for discussion
	Skills:	reading for gist; reading for more detailed comprehension.
	Age:	adult
	Level:	intermediate plus

The following example runs the risk of causing some students disquiet since it discusses an issue they may not be too comfortable with. It is an example of the kind of text which some teachers find extremely appropriate for their classes (because it engages the students' interest), whereas others would be unhappy to bring such a topic into the class.

The sequence starts when the teacher asks the students what they would say if they met someone who had just had plastic surgery (and had previously announced that they were going to do this). Would the students comment on their friend's new appearance in any way, and if so, how? Students can discuss this as a whole class or in pairs or small groups.

Students then look at the headline to the article below and speculate on its meaning. They are then asked to read the article just to say whether there is a similar trend in their country (or countries). They can discuss this in pairs before the teacher makes sure that they have got the main point of the article.

As a Type 2 task (see page 270), students answer the following questions:

1 Why are younger people turning to plastic surgery?
2 Why did the doctor refuse plastic surgery to one patient?
3 Why is plastic surgery now more popular with men?
4 Why did the man have liposuction?

YOUNGER PLASTIC SURGERY PATIENTS

Surgeons at clinics specialising in plastic surgery are reporting increasingly younger patients, according to a report released recently by the National Association of Plastic Surgery in the United States.

"They want to look like the people they see in films or the models they see in magazines. It's becoming an obsession." said one doctor in a beauty clinic in California. "Last week we had a woman in here who. at 30. said she was looking too old and wanted a facelift. I told her to come back and see me in 15 years."

The average age for patients undergoing plastic surgery over the last year was 32, down from 34 just the year before. In England recently, a 15-year-old girl was in the news for announcing that her parents were going to pay for breast enlargements as her 16th birthday present.

Her mother said, "If it makes her happy and gives her more chance of success in life, then what is the problem?" Though women still dominate the plastic surgery scene, men are growing increasingly concerned with their physical appearance and are doing something about it. According to the report, men now make up 39% of all surgeries performed — that's an increase of nearly 20% from last year.

One man, who wished to remain anonymous, said he got his liposuction – removal of excess fat – after pressure from his wife. "She's a very athletic woman and, well, I enjoy a good steak."

Liposuction tops the list of plastic surgery performed on men, followed by hair implants and breast reduction. For women the top order is still breast enlargement, followed by liposuction and facelifts.

From *Taboos and Issues* by R MacAndrew and R Martinez (Thompson Publishing)

The possibilities after a text like this are many and varied. Students could discuss different kinds of plastic surgery and what they think of them. They can take a position about whether or not plastic surgery is something they approve of or not. They could play a kind of game where they have to decide – if they had to choose – what they would have done to themselves. They might debate whether or not plastic surgery should be paid for by the state for anyone who wanted it, or they could look at a portrait from an earlier period and discuss what they could do to make the person look more like someone from the twenty-first century.

Example 7: The cellist	Activity:	jigsaw reading
	Skills:	reading for detailed comprehension
	Age:	young adult and above
	Level:	intermediate

In the following example, students are set a mystery. In order to solve it, they are put into groups of three and each student in the group is given something different to read. Without showing their texts to their colleagues, students have to share the information they have so that they can put the three pieces together, like a jigsaw, to assemble the complete story and resolve the mystery

As a lead-in, we can start the sequence by playing students an extract of music (preferably a recording of part of 'The Cellist of Sarajevo' by David Wilde). Students are asked not to say much but just to conjure up a picture in their minds based on what images this difficult and troubled music provokes. Students now read the following text:

THE CONCERT

There was only one chair on the stage of the concert hall in northern England. There was no piano, no music stand and no conductor. Just that solitary chair.

The atmosphere in the hall was tense. People were nervous and excited. Everyone in the audience of 600 people knew that they were going to hear a very special kind of music.

Finally it was time to start. Yo-Yo Ma, one of the world's most famous cellists, came on to the stage, bowed to the audience and sat down quietly on the chair. He made himself comfortable, thought for some minutes until there was complete silence, and then he started to play music that was at first empty and dangerous, but that soon became loud and painful, like the worst thing you've ever heard. It was almost unbearable but then, finally, it faded away to nothing. Yo-Yo Ma did not move. He stayed with his head bowed over his instrument.

Everyone in the hall held their breath. For what seemed like hours, nobody moved. It was as if they had all experienced something terrible and dark.

But then Yo-Yo Ma stood up. He put down his cello. He stretched out his hand to someone in the audience, asking them to come and join him. An electric shock ran through the audience when they realised what was going to happen.

A man got up from his seat and walked towards the stage. He was dressed in dirty motorcycle leathers, but Ma did not seem to mind. He rushed down from the stage, and when the two men met they flung their arms around each other in an emotional embrace.

The audience went crazy; suddenly everyone was cheering and shouting, like people do when they've just heard great music. But this was more than music.

From *Just Right Intermediate* by J Harmer (Marshall Cavendish Ltd)

We can check the students' comprehension by asking them to fill in the following chart:

Name of the concert cellist	
Number of people in the audience	
Description of the music	
Audience reaction to the music	
Description of the event after the music finished	
Audience reaction to the event	

They can check their charts in pairs and groups to see if they have understood everything.

We now tell the students that they are going to try to find out why the text says 'but this was more than music'. What, they must find out, is the connection between the music itself, the man in the audience and Yo-Yo Ma. What is the story of the music and how did it come about?

In each group of three students, one student is A, one B and the third C. Student A is directed to the following material:

STUDENT A

Read the text and make sure you understand the answers to the following questions.

a Why was there a queue of people in the street?
b What happened at four o'clock?
c How many people died?
d When exactly did they die?
e Who were they?
f Who is or was Vedran Smailovic?

In the early 1990s, there was a terrible war in Yugoslavia. Many people died, both soldiers and civilians. The city of Sarajevo was for many months one of the most dangerous places in the world. It was constantly under attack and its civilian inhabitants had to live with no electricity and little water. Only a few shops stayed open to sell food.

On May 27, 1992, one of the shops, a bakery, opened in the afternoon and a long line of men, women and children queued to buy fresh bread. But it was not to be. At four o'clock a mortar shell exploded in the street and twenty-two innocent people were killed.

A man called Vedran Smailovic lived near the scene of this terrible tragedy. He was 35 at the time, and when he heard the news he decided to do something about it.

All the A students have to be sure that they can answer the questions at the top satisfactorily so that when B and C ask them these questions, they will be able to answer them.

Student B gets a different text and question. Like the A students, all the Bs have to check their answers to the questions above the text, before asking the A and C students to answer the questions underneath the text.

STUDENT B

Read the text and make sure you understand the answers to the following questions.

a What was Vedran Smailovic's job before the war?
b What did Vedran Smailovic do when he heard the news?
c What piece of music did he play?
d Why did he play his cello?
e Was he ever hurt?

Before the war, Vedran Smailovic had been a cellist with the Sarajevo Opera. When he heard about an explosion that had killed men, women and children in a bread queue in Sarajevo, he decided to do something about it. And so he did what he did best. He played his cello.

For the next twenty-two days at exactly four o'clock in the afternoon he put on his concert clothes, took his cello and a plastic chair into the empty streets and played a piece of music by the composer Albinoni – his Adagio in G minor, one of the saddest pieces of music ever. Around him there was fighting and death. Shells fell and bullets flew while he played, but he was never hurt. With the world collapsing around him he played for compassion and peace, to ease the pain of loss and to preserve the dignity of the human race.

Find the answers to the following questions by asking Students A and C. Don't show your text to them.

a Why did Vedran Smailovic play for twenty-two days?
b Why did he play at four o'clock in the afternoon?
c Who is David Wilde and what did he do?
d What is David Wilde's connection to a concert in Manchester?

The third piece of the jigsaw is given to the C students.

STUDENT C

Read the text and make sure you understand the answers to the following questions.

a Who is David Wilde?
b What did he read about?
c What did he do then?
d Where was the first UK performance of his new music?
e Who played it?
f Who was in the audience?

David Wilde, an English composer, read a story in his newspaper which moved him deeply. It was about a man called Vedran Smailovic, who played his cello in the street in the middle of a war to honour the dead. His courage was extraordinary because he sat in the street and played while shells and bullets flew around him.

David Wilde was so inspired by the story that he wrote a special piece for solo cello which he called *The Cellist of Sarajevo*. It was performed by the cellist Yo-Yo Ma at the Manchester Cello Festival in April 1994. Incredibly, Vedran Smailovic had survived the war and was in the audience that night to hear it. When Yo-Yo Ma finished playing, the two men embraced in front of a cheering audience.

Find the answers to the following questions by asking Students A and B. Don't show your text to them.

a Exactly what happened in Sarajevo on May 27, 1992?
b What was Vedran Smailovic's job before the war?
c Why did Vedran Smailovic play his cello? What piece of music did he play?

Finally, we bring the class back together to make sure that the students have understood the whole story (that the piece 'The Cellist of Sarajevo' was written by the British composer David Wilde after he had read how cellist Vedran Smailovic played his cello in the street in Sarajevo to honour civilians killed in a bomb attack – and how Smailovic had been in the audience when Yo-Yo Ma played the piece at a concert). Once they have done that, we can ask them to decide (once again in groups) on adjectives to describe Vedran Smailovic; they can talk about how people respond to tragic events, and later they can look at some of the language chunks that occur in the texts (e.g. *He made himself comfortable, everyone held their breath*). We can then move on to ask students to study vocabulary for music and musicians.

The point of reading activities like this (quite apart from the hope that students will be engaged by the stories themselves) is that everyone is reading for a purpose and that unless they all read and do their best to pass on what they understood, the jigsaw is impossible to complete. Their participation is almost mandatory.

Chapter notes and further reading

- **Reading**
  On reading in general, see C Nuttall (1996), C Wallace (1992) and F Grellet (1981). See also articles by R Buckmaster (2005), I Cavallera and A Leiguarda (2006), P Harvey (2005, 2006) and S Pani (2004). D Dlugosz (2000) discusses the role of reading for young learners. S Urquhart and C Weir (1998) have written a substantial work on reading in the *Longman Applied Linguistics and Language Study* series.

  On encouraging students to analyse the language of texts in detail, see R Gower (1999). As a learner he found 'explicacion de texte', (i.e. describing features of a text in detail after reading/listening to it) extremely useful, however 'old-fashioned' it was; see also C Walker (1998: 172).

- **Reading and technology**
  M-L McCloskey and E Thrush (2005) talk about building a reading scaffold with web texts. M Vallance (2006) puts interactive stories on an iPod.

- **Extensive reading**
  C Nuttall (1996: 127) talks about 'vicious' and 'virtuous' reading circles. The former occur when weak readers read less and less and so read slower and less effectively, whereas a virtuous circle occurs when students read faster and therefore more effectively. R Day and J Bamford use the term 'book strapping' to describe how the effects of an action (extensive reading) are fed back into the process to achieve greater results with less effort (1998: 30).

  J Bamford and R Day (2004) have a wealth of activities for students who are reading extensively. See also P Prowse (2000), P Watkins (2001), V Brines (2001), who discusses organising a reading programme, and C Green (2005), who wants to integrate extensive reading into task-based learning.

18 | Listening

A Extensive and intensive listening

Students can improve their listening skills – and gain valuable language input – through a combination of extensive and intensive listening material and procedures. Listening of both kinds is especially important since it provides the perfect opportunity to hear voices other than the teacher's, enables students to acquire good speaking habits as a result of the spoken English they absorb and helps to improve their pronunciation.

A1 Extensive listening

Just as we can claim that extensive reading helps students to acquire vocabulary and grammar and that, furthermore, it make students better readers (see Chapter 17, A1), so extensive listening (where a teacher encourages students to choose for themselves what they listen to and to do so for pleasure and general language improvement) can also have a dramatic effect on a student's language learning.

Extensive listening will usually take place outside the classroom: in the students' home, car or on personal MP3 players as they travel from one place to another. The motivational power of such an activity increases dramatically when students make their own choices about what they are going to listen to.

Material for extensive listening can be obtained from a number of sources. Many simplified readers are now published with an audio version on cassette or CD. These provide ideal sources of listening material. Many students will enjoy reading and listening at the same time, using the reader both in book form and on an audio track. Students can also have their own copies of coursebook CDs or tapes, or recordings which accompany other books written especially at their level. They can download podcasts from a range of sources or they can listen to English language broadcasts online, either as they happen or as 'listen again' events on websites such as www.bbc.co.uk/radio.

Of course, radio broadcasts are authentic in the sense that we defined the term on page 273, and as such they may cause some learning problems for students at lower levels. However, in a short article about listening to the radio, Joseph Quinn advised students not to worry if they don't understand everything. They don't actually need to, and they're bound to take in a lot of language even if they are not aware of it. To make the most of this kind of input, students should set themselves a simple listening task, adopt a relaxed posture and 'lie down and doodle' while they listen (Quinn 2000: 14).

In order for extensive listening to work effectively with a group of students – or with groups of students – we will need to make a collection of appropriate tapes, CDs and podcasts, clearly marked for level, topic and genre – though John Field thinks that it is very difficult to judge the difficulty of a text and, therefore, difficult to grade listening (Field 2000a: 195). These can be kept, like simplified readers, in a permanent collection (such as in a self-access centre or on a hard disk so that students can either listen to them on the spot or download them onto their MP3 players). Alternatively, they can be kept in a box or some other container which can be taken into classrooms. We will then want to keep a record of which students have borrowed which items; where possible, we should involve students in the task of record-keeping.

The keenest students will want to listen to English audio material outside the classroom anyway and will need little encouragement to do so. Many others, however, will profit from having the teacher give them reasons to make use of the resources available. We need to explain the benefits of listening extensively and come to some kind of agreement about how much and what kind of listening they should do. We can recommend certain CDs or podcasts and get other students to talk about the ones which they have enjoyed the most.

In order to encourage extensive listening we can have students perform a number of tasks. They can record their responses to what they have heard in a personal journal (see Chapter 23, B3), or fill in report forms which we have prepared, asking them to list the topic, assess the level of difficulty and summarise the contents of a recording. We can have them write comments on cards which are kept in a separate comments box, add their responses to a large class listening poster or write comments on a student website. The purpose of these or any other tasks is to give students more and more reasons to listen. If they can then share their information with colleagues, they will feel they have contributed to the progress of the whole group. The motivational power of such feelings should not be underestimated.

A2   Intensive listening: using audio material

Many teachers use audio material on tape, CD or hard disk when they want their students to practise listening skills. This has a number of advantages and disadvantages.

- **Advantages:** recorded material allows students to hear a variety of different voices apart from just their own teacher's. It gives them an opportunity to 'meet' a range of different characters, especially where 'real' people are talking. But even when recordings contain written dialogues or extracts from plays, they offer a wide variety of situations and voices.

  Audio material is portable and readily available. Tapes and CDs are extremely cheap, and machines to play them are relatively inexpensive. Now that so much audio material is offered in digital form, teachers can play recorded tracks in class directly from computers (either stand-alone or on a school network).

  For all these reasons, most coursebooks include CDs and tapes, and many teachers rely on recorded material to provide a significant source of language input.

- **Disadvantages:** in big classrooms with poor acoustics, the audibility of recorded material often gives cause for concern. It is sometimes difficult to ensure that all the students in a room can hear equally well.

  Another problem with recorded material in the classroom is that everyone has to listen at the same speed, a speed dictated by the recording, not by the listeners. Although this replicates the situation of radio, it is less satisfactory when students have to take information from the recording (though see A3 below). Nor can they, themselves, interact with the speakers on the audio track in any way and they can't see the speaking taking place. For many of these reasons, students may wonder why they should get involved with such material.

Finally, having a group of people sit around listening to a tape recorder or CD player is not an entirely natural occupation.

Despite the disadvantages, however, we will still want to use recorded material at various stages in a sequence of lessons for the advantages we have already mentioned. In order to counteract some of the potential problems described above, we need to check audio and machine quality before we take them into class. Where possible, we need to change the position of the tape recorder or CD player (or the students) to offset poor acoustics or, if this is feasible, take other measures, such as using materials to deaden echoes which interfere with good sound quality.

An issue that also needs to be addressed is how often we are going to play the audio tracks we ask students to listen to. The methodologist Penny Ur points out that in real life, discourse is rarely 'replayed' and suggests, therefore, that one of our tasks is to encourage students to get as much information as is necessary or appropriate from a single hearing (Ur 1996:108).

It is certainly true that extracting general or specific information from one listening is an important skill, so the kind of task we give students for the first time they hear an audio track is absolutely critical in gradually training them to listen effectively. However, we may also want to consider the fact that in face-to-face conversation we do frequently have a chance to ask for clarification and repetition. More importantly perhaps, as Penny Ur herself acknowledges, this 'one listening' scenario conflicts with our wish to satisfy our students' desire to hear things over and over again.

If students are to get the maximum benefit from a listening, then we should replay it two or more times, since with each listening they may feel more secure, and with each listening (where we are helping appropriately) they will understand more than they did previously. As the researcher John Field suggests, students get far more benefit from a lot of listening than they do from a long pre-listening phase followed by only one or two exposures to the listening text (Field 1998a, 2000b). So even when we set prediction and gist activities for Type 1 tasks, we can return to the recording again for Type 2 tasks, such as detailed comprehension, text interpretation or language analysis. Or we might play the recording again simply because our students want us to. However, we do not want to bore the students by playing them the same recorded material again and again, nor do we want to waste time on useless repetition.

As with reading, a crucial part of listening practice is the lead-in we involve students in before they listen to recorded material, for, despite John Field's comments about long pre-listening phases, what students do before they listen will have a significant effect on how successfully they listen, especially when they listen for the first time. In a recent study Anna Ching-Shyang Chang and John Read wanted to find out what kind of listening support was most helpful for students who were doing listening tests. Overwhelmingly, whether students were 'high-' or 'low-proficiency' listeners, they found that giving students background knowledge before they listened was more successful than either letting them preview questions or teaching them some key vocabulary before they listened (Ching-Shyang Chang and Read 2006: 375–397). Of course, listening practice is not the same as testing listening; on the contrary, our job is to help students become better listeners by blending Type 1 and Type 2 tasks so that they become more and more confident and capable when they listen to English. But what this study shows is that activating students' schemata and giving them some topic help to assist them in making sense of the listening is a vital part of our role.

A3 Who controls the recorded material?

We said that a disadvantage of recorded material was that students all had to listen at the same speed – that is the speed of the recording, rather than at their own listening speed. Nevertheless, there are things we can do about this.

- **Students control stop and start:** some teachers get students to control the speed of recorded listening. They tell the teacher when they want the recording to be paused and when they are happy for it to resume. Alternatively, a student can be at the controls and ask his or her classmates to say when they want to stop or go on.

  It is possible that students may feel exposed or embarrassed when they have to ask the teacher to pause the recording. One possible way of avoiding this is to have all students listen with their eyes closed and then raise their hands if they want the recording to stop. No one can see who is asking for the pause and, as a result, no one loses face.

- **Students have access to different machines:** if we have the space or resources, it is a very good idea to have students listen to different machines in small groups. This means that they can listen at the speed of a small group rather than at the speed of the whole class.

  Having more than one machine is especially useful for any kind of jigsaw listening (see page 299 for an example of jigsaw reading).

- **Students work in a language laboratory or listening centre:** in a language laboratory all the students can listen to material (or do exercises or watch film clips) at the same time if they are in lockstep (that is all working with the same audio clip at the same time). However, a more satisfactory solution is to have students working on their own (see the pronunciation activity in Example 6 on page 261). All students can work with the same recorded material, but because they have control of their own individual machines, they can pause, rewind and fast forward in order to listen at their own speed.

The three solutions above are all designed to help students have more control even when they are members of a large group. Of course, students can go to learning/listening centres on their own and they can, as we saw above, listen on CD, tape or MP3 players (or computers) to any amount of authentic or specially recorded material in their own time.

 A4 Intensive listening: 'live' listening

A popular way of ensuring genuine communication is live listening, where the teacher and/or visitors to the class talk to the students. This has obvious advantages since it allows students to practise listening in face-to-face interactions and, especially, allows them to practise listening 'repair' strategies, such as using formulaic expressions (*Sorry? What was that? I didn't quite catch that*), repeating up to the point where communication breakdown occurred, using a rising intonation (*She didn't like the ...?*), or rephrasing and seeing if the speaker confirms the rephrasing (*You mean she said she didn't know anything?* if the speaker says something like *She denied all knowledge of the affair*) (Field 2000a: 34).

Students can also, by their expressions and demeanour, indicate if the speaker is going too slowly or too fast. Above all, they can see who they are listening to and respond not just to the sound of someone's voice, but also to all sorts of prosodic and paralinguistic clues (see Chapter 2G).

Live listening can take the following forms:

- **Reading aloud:** an enjoyable activity, when done with conviction and style, is for the teacher to read aloud to a class. This allows the students to hear a clear spoken version of a written text and can be extremely enjoyable if the teacher is prepared to read with expression and conviction.

  The teacher can also read or act out dialogues, either by playing two parts or by inviting a colleague into the classroom. This gives students a chance to hear how a speaker they know well (the teacher) would act in different conversational settings.

- **Story-telling:** teachers are ideally placed to tell stories which, in turn, provide excellent listening material. At any stage of the story, the students can be asked to predict what is coming next, to describe people in the story or pass comment on it in some other way. And as we have suggested (see page 56), re-telling stories is a powerful way of increasing language competence.

- **Interviews:** one of the most motivating listening activities is the live interview, especially where students themselves think up the questions (see Example 1 in C1 below). In such situations, students really listen for answers they themselves have asked for – rather than adopting other people's questions. Where possible, we should have strangers visit our class to be interviewed, but we can also be the subject of interviews ourselves. In such circumstances we can take on a different persona to make the interview more interesting or choose a subject we know about for the students to interview us on.

- **Conversations:** if we can persuade a colleague to come to our class, we can hold conversations with them about English or any other subject. Students then have the chance to watch the interaction as well as listen to it. We can also extend storytelling possibilities by role-playing with a colleague.

A5 Intensive listening: the roles of the teacher

As with all activities, we need to create student engagement through the way we set up listening tasks. We need to build up students' confidence by helping them listen better, rather than by testing their listening abilities (see Chapter 16, B3). We also need to acknowledge the students' difficulties and suggest ways out of them.

- **Organiser:** we need to tell students exactly what their listening purpose is and give them clear instructions about how to achieve it. One of our chief responsibilities will be to build their confidence through offering tasks that are achievable and texts that are comprehensible.

- **Machine operator:** when we use audio material, we need to be as efficient as possible in the way we use the audio player. With a tape player this means knowing where the segment we wish to use is on the tape, and knowing, through the use of the tape counter, how to get back there. On a CD or DVD player, it means finding the segment we want to use. Above all, it means testing the recording out before taking it into class so that we do not waste time trying to make the right decisions or trying to make things work when we get there. We should take decisions about where we can stop the recording for particular questions and exercises, but, once in class, we should be prepared to respond to the students' needs in the way we stop and start the machine.

  If we involve our students in live listening, we need to observe them with great care to see how easily they can understand us. We can then adjust the way we speak accordingly.

- **Feedback organiser:** when our students have completed the task, we should lead a feedback session to check that they have completed it successfully. We may start by having them compare their answers in pairs (see Chapter 10, A4) and then ask for answers from the class in general or from pairs in particular. Students often appreciate giving paired answers like this since, by sharing their knowledge, they are also sharing their responsibility for the answers. Because listening can be a tense experience, encouraging this kind of cooperation is highly desirable.

    It is important to be supportive when organising feedback after a listening if we are to counter any negative expectations students might have, and if we wish to sustain their motivation (see Chapter 5D).

- **Prompter:** when students have listened to a recording for comprehension purposes, we can prompt them listen to it again in order to notice a variety of language and spoken features. Sometimes we can offer them script dictations (where some words in a transcript are blanked out) to provoke their awareness of certain language items.

B Film and video

So far we have talked about recorded material as audio material only. But of course, we can also have students listen while they watch film clips on video, DVD or online.

There are many good reasons for encouraging students to watch while they listen. In the first place, they get to see 'language in use'. This allows them to see a whole lot of paralinguistic behaviour. For example, they can see how intonation matches facial expression and what gestures accompany certain phrases (e.g. shrugged shoulders when someone says *I don't know*), and they can pick up a range of cross-cultural clues. Film allows students entry into a whole range of other communication worlds: they see how different people stand when they talk to each other (how close they are, for example) or what sort of food people eat. Unspoken rules of behaviour in social and business situations are easier to see on film than to describe in a book or hear on an audio track.

Just like audio material, filmed extracts can be used as a main focus of a lesson sequence or as parts of other longer sequences. Sometimes we might get students to watch a whole programme, but at other times they will only watch a short two- or three-minute sequence.

Because students are used to watching film at home – and may therefore associate it with relaxation – we need to be sure that we provide them with good viewing and listening tasks so that they give their full attention to what they are hearing and seeing.

Finally, it is worth remembering that students can watch a huge range of film clips on the Internet at sites such as You Tube (www. youtube.com), where people of all ages and interests can post film clips in which they talk or show something. Everything students might want is out there in cyberspace, so they can do extensive or intensive watching and then come and tell the class about what they have seen. Just as with extensive listening, the more they do this, the better.

B1 Viewing techniques

All of the following viewing techniques are designed to awaken the students' curiosity through prediction so that when they finally watch the film sequence in its entirety, they will have some expectations about it.

- **Fast forward:** the teacher presses the play button and then fast forwards the DVD or video so that the sequence shoots past silently and at great speed, taking only a few seconds. When it is over, the teacher can ask students what the extract was all about and whether they can guess what the characters were saying.

- **Silent viewing (for language):** the teacher plays the film extract at normal speed but without the sound. Students have to guess what the characters are saying. When they have done this, the teacher plays it with sound so that they can check to see if they guessed correctly.

- **Silent viewing (for music):** the same technique can be used with music. Teachers show a sequence without sound and ask students to say what kind of music they would put behind it and why (see Section D below). When the sequence is then shown again, with sound, students can judge whether they chose music conveying the same mood as that chosen by the film director.

- **Freeze frame:** at any stage during a video sequence we can 'freeze' the picture, stopping the participants dead in their tracks. This is extremely useful for asking the students what they think will happen next or what a character will say next.

- **Partial viewing:** one way of provoking the students' curiosity is to allow them only a partial view of the pictures on the screen. We can use pieces of card to cover most of the screen, only leaving the edges on view. Alternatively, we can put little squares of paper all over the screen and remove them one by one so that what is happening is only gradually revealed.

    A variation of partial viewing occurs when the teacher uses a large 'divider', placed at right angles to the screen so that half class can only see one half of the screen, while the rest of the class can only see the other half. They then have to say what they think the people on the other side saw.

B2 Listening (and mixed) techniques

Listening routines, based on the same principles as those for viewing, are similarly designed to provoke engagement and expectations.

- **Pictureless listening (language):** the teacher covers the screen, turns the monitor away from the students or turns the brightness control right down. The students then listen to a dialogue and have to guess such things as where it is taking place and who the speakers are. Can they guess their age, for example? What do they think the speakers actually look like?

- **Pictureless listening (music):** where an excerpt has a prominent music track, students can listen to it and then say – based on the mood it appears to convey – what kind of scene they think it accompanies and where it is taking place.

- **Pictureless listening (sound effects):** in a scene without dialogue students can listen to the sound effects to guess what is happening. For example, they might hear the lighting of a gas stove, eggs being broken and fried, coffee being poured and the milk and sugar stirred in. They then tell the story they think they have just heard.

- **Picture or speech:** we can divide the class in two so that half of the class faces the screen and half faces away. The students who can see the screen have to describe what is happening to the students who cannot. This forces them into immediate fluency while the non-watching students struggle to understand what is going on, and is an effective way of mixing reception and production in spoken English (see Chapter 16, A1). Halfway through an excerpt, the students can change round.

- **Subtitles:** there are many ways we can use subtitled films. John Field (2000a: 194) suggests that one way to enable students to listen to authentic material is to allow them to have subtitles to help them. Alternatively, students can watch a film extract with subtitles but with the sound turned down. Every time a subtitle appears, we can stop the film and the students have to say what they think the characters are saying in English. With DVDs which have the option to turn off the subtitles, we can ask students to say what they would write for subtitles and then they can compare theirs with what actually appears.

    Subtitles are only really useful, of course, when students all share the same L1. But if they do, the connections they make between English and their language can be extremely useful (see Chapter 7, D2).

C Listening (and film) lesson sequences

As we saw in Chapter 16A, no skill exists in isolation (which is why skills are integrated in most learning sequences). Listening can thus occur at a number of points in a teaching sequence. Sometimes it forms the jumping-off point for the activities which follow. Sometimes it may be the first stage of a 'listening and acting out' sequence where students role-play the situation they have heard on the recording. Sometimes live listening may be a prelude to a piece of writing which is the main focus of a lesson. Other lessons, however, have listening training as their central focus.

However much we have planned a lesson, we need to be flexible in what we do. Nowhere is this more acute than in the provision of live listening, where we may, on the spur of the moment, feel the need to tell a story or act out some role. Sometimes this will be for content reasons – because a topic comes up – and sometimes it may be a way of re-focusing our students' attention.

Most listening sequences start with a Type 1 task (see page 270) before moving on to more specific Type 2 explorations of the text.

In general, we should aim to use listening material for as many purposes as possible – both for practising a variety of skills and as source material for other activities – before students finally become tired of it.

C1 Examples of listening sequences

In the following examples, the listening activity is specified, the skills which are involved are detailed and the way that the listening text can be used within a lesson is explained.

Example 1: Interviewing a stranger	Activity:	live listening
	Skills:	predicting; listening for specific information; listening for detail
	Age:	any
	Level:	beginner and above

Where possible, teachers can bring strangers into the class to talk to the students or be interviewed by them (see A4 above). Although students will be especially interested in them if they are native speakers of the language, there is no reason why they should not include any competent English speakers.

The teacher briefs the visitor about the students' language level, pointing out that they should be sensitive about the level of language they use, but not speak to the students in a very unnatural way. They should probably not go off into lengthy explanations, and they may want to consider speaking especially clearly.

The teacher takes the visitor into the classroom without telling the students who or what the visitor is. In pairs or groups, they try to guess as much as they can about the visitor. Based on their guesses, they write questions that they wish to ask.

The visitor is now interviewed with the questions the students have written. As the interview proceeds, the teacher encourages them to seek clarification where things are said that they do not understand. The teacher will also prompt the students to ask follow-up questions; if a student asks *Where are you from?* and the visitor says that he comes from Scotland, he can then be asked *Where in Scotland?* or *What's Scotland like?*

During the interview the students make notes. When the interviewee has gone, these notes form the basis of a written follow-up. The students can write a short biographical piece about the person – for example, as a profile page from a magazine. They can discuss the interview with their teacher, asking for help with any points they are still unclear about. They can also role-play similar interviews among themselves.

We can make pre-recorded interviews in coursebooks more interactive by giving students the interviewer's questions first so that they can predict what the interviewee will say.

Example 2: Sorry I'm late	Activity:	getting events in the right order
	Skills:	predicting; listening for gist
	Age:	young adult and above
	Level:	lower intermediate

A popular technique for having students understand the gist of a story – but which also incorporates prediction and the creation of expectations – involves the students in listening in order to put pictures in the sequence in which they hear them.

In this example, students look at the following four pictures:

A    B

C    D

They are given a chance, in pairs or groups, to say what they think is happening in each picture. The teacher will not confirm or deny their predictions.

Students are then told that they are going to listen to a recording and that they should put the pictures in the correct chronological order (which is not the same as the order of what they hear). This is what is on the tape:

ANNA:	*Morning Stuart. What time do you call this?*
STUART:	*Er, well, yes, I know, umm. Sorry. Sorry I'm late.*
ANNA:	*Me, too. Well?*
STUART:	*I woke up late.*
ANNA:	*You woke up late.*
STUART:	*'Fraid so. I didn't hear the alarm.*
ANNA:	*Oh, so you were out last night?*
STUART:	*Yes. Yes. 'Fraid so. No, I mean, yes, I went out last night, so what?*
ANNA:	*So what happened?*
STUART:	*Well, when I saw the time I jumped out of bed, had a quick shower, obviously, and ran out of the house. But when I got to the car ...*
ANNA:	*Yes? When you got to the car?*
STUART:	*Well, this is really stupid, but I realised I'd forgotten my keys.*
ANNA:	*Yes, that is really stupid.*
STUART:	*And the door to my house was shut.*
ANNA:	*Of course it was! So what did you do? How did you get out of that one?*
STUART:	*I ran round to the garden at the back and climbed in through the window.*
ANNA:	*Quite a morning!*
STUART:	*Yeah, and someone saw me and called the police.*
ANNA:	*This just gets worse and worse! So what happened?*
STUART:	*Well, I told them it was my house and at first they wouldn't believe me. It took a long time!*
ANNA:	*I can imagine.*
STUART:	*And you see, that's why I'm late!*

The students check their answers with each other and then, if necessary, listen again to ensure that they have the sequence correct (C, A, D, B).

The teacher can now get the students to listen again or look at the tapescript, noting phrases of interest, such as those that Stuart uses to express regret and apology (*Sorry I'm late, I woke up late, 'Fraid so*), Anna's insistent questioning (*What time do you call this? Well? So what happened? So what did you do? How did you get out of that one?*) and her use of repetition both to be judgmental and to get Stuart to keep going with an explanation she obviously finds ridiculous (*You woke up late, Yes, that is really stupid, Quite a morning! I can imagine*). The class can then go on to role-play similar scenes in which they have to come up with stories and excuses for being late for school or work.

Example 3: Telephone messages	Activity:	taking messages
	Skills:	predicting; listening for specific information
	Age:	teenage
	Level:	elementary

Although most textbooks have audio material to accompany their various lessons, there is no reason why teachers should not record their own tapes with the help of colleagues and other competent speakers of the language, provided that they take care to use a decent microphone and to record the voices as naturally as possible. This will allow them freedom to create material which is relevant to their own students' particular needs.

This sequence shows the kind of thing that teachers might have their colleagues help them with – they can get them to play the parts of the occupant of the house and the three callers.

The sequence starts when the teacher asks students the kind of short messages people might leave for members of their family if they take phone calls while they are out. The messages are often quite simple, e.g.

Students are told that they are going to hear three phone conversations in which the callers leave messages for people who are not in. They are told that Mrs Galloway has three daughters, Lyn (19), Eryn (17) and Kate (13). They are all out at the cinema, but three of their friends ring up and leave messages. All the students have to do is to write the messages which Mrs Galloway leaves for her daughters.

This is what the students hear:

MRS GALLOWAY: *Hello.*

ADAM: *Hello. Is Lyn there?*

MRS GALLOWAY: *No, she's out at the moment. Who's that?*

ADAM: *This is Adam. Any idea when she'll be back?*

MRS GALLOWAY: *About ten, I think. Can I give her a message?*

ADAM: *No ... er, yes. Can you tell her Adam rang?*

MRS GALLOWAY: *Sure, Adam.*

ADAM: *Thanks. Bye.*

MRS GALLOWAY: *Hello.*

RUTH: *Can I speak to Eryn?*

MRS GALLOWAY: *Is that Ruth?*

RUTH: *Yes. Hello, Mrs Galloway. Is Eryn in?*

MRS GALLOWAY: *No, Ruth, sorry. She's at the cinema with her sisters.*

RUTH: *Oh. Oh that's a pity, ummm ... could you ask her to bring my copy of Romeo and Juliet to college tomorrow?*

MRS GALLOWAY: *Your copy?*

RUTH:	*Yes. She borrowed it.*
MRS GALLOWAY:	*Typical! So you want her to take it in tomorrow. To college.*
RUTH:	*Yes. That's it. Thanks. Bye.*
MRS GALLOWAY:	*Oh ... bye.*
MRS GALLOWAY:	*Hello.*
JANE METCALFE:	*Can I speak to Kate?*
MRS GALLOWAY:	*I'm afraid she's not here. Can I take a message?*
JANE METCALFE:	*Yes, please. Er, my name's Jane Metcalfe. I'm the drama teacher. Can you tell Kate that the next rehearsal is at three thirty on Friday?*
MRS GALLOWAY:	*The next rehearsal?*
JANE METCALFE:	*Yes, for the school play.*
MRS GALLOWAY:	*Kate's in a play?*
JANE METCALFE:	*Yes. Didn't she tell you?*
MRS GALLOWAY:	*No ... I mean yes, of course she did.*
JANE METCALFE:	*OK, then. We'll see her on Friday afternoon.*
MRS GALLOWAY:	*Er ... yes.*

When they have written messages for the three girls, they compare their versions with each other to see if they have written the same thing. They then listen to the tape again to clear up any problems they might have had.

This sequence naturally lends itself to a progression where students 'ring' each other to leave messages. Perhaps they do this after they look at the language of the three phone calls so that they can use phrases like *I'm afraid she's not here* and *Can I take a message?*

Message taking from phone calls is a genuinely communicative act. Where feasible, students will be involved in the phone calls themselves, if possible, taking messages from someone speaking from another room or from another booth in a language laboratory (see page 306), or at least working in pairs to role-play calls.

Example 4: Breakfast	Activity:	listening to customs around the world
	Skills:	listening for general understanding; listening for detail; (re-)telling information
	Age:	young adult/adult
	Level:	elementary

In the following sequence, adapted from *New Cutting Edge Elementary* by Peter Moor and Sarah Cunningham (Pearson Education Ltd), the students have been studying words for different foods and working on the grammar of countable and uncountable nouns.

The teacher starts the sequence by getting the students to say what they had for breakfast today. They should tell other people in their pairs or groups. They then look at the pictures and information about the six people in them (see the next page). They should try to predict what these people have for breakfast.

Students now hear the audiotrack (see below) in which the six characters talk about their breakfast. They have to write down what each person says they have for breakfast – just the foods, without worrying about any extra material.

Recording 2

Kemal Well, I usually have breakfast at home before I go to work. I always have tea, black tea, maybe two or three glasses. And I have cheese and eggs and tomatoes, and in Turkey we have fantastic bread so I usually have bread with butter and jam, and sometimes I have yoghurt, too.

Mi-Kyung I always have breakfast with my family. We usually have white rice, and we have Kim-chi. We cannot live without Kim-chi! Kim-chi is a traditional dish of mixed Korean vegetables. It's very hot and spicy.

Dimitry Well, for breakfast, when I have time, I have tea, usually, black tea with lemon and lots of sugar. Never with milk. Then I have bread and cold meat and some cucumber as well. And then I sometimes have a small cake or some biscuits to finish.

Sonia In Brazil, we have very good tropical fruit, guava, mango and things like that, and we always have fruit for our breakfast – also we have coffee, of course, everybody knows in Brazil we have very good coffee, and maybe bread and jam.

José I don't usually have breakfast. I don't have time because I go to work very early about seven o'clock in the morning, so I just have a cup of coffee for breakfast, in a café with my wife Anita. But I usually stop work for a snack at about eleven, half past eleven and go to a café near my office. I have another cup of coffee and a nice big piece of tortilla – Spanish omelette made with potatoes and eggs – it's really delicious.

1 **T6.2** Listen to five people talking about their breakfast. Write down what they have.

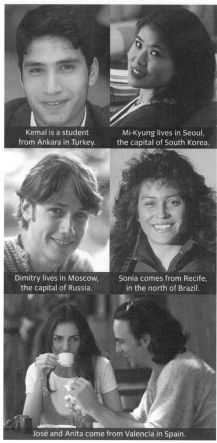

Kemal is a student from Ankara in Turkey.

Mi-Kyung lives in Seoul, the capital of South Korea.

Dimitry lives in Moscow, the capital of Russia.

Sonia comes from Recife, in the north of Brazil.

José and Anita come from Valencia in Spain.

Students now compare their answers in pairs before the teacher checks that they all agree. The teacher then asks the students to listen again to see what extra details they can find out (such as the fact that Kemal says they have fantastic bread in Turkey, that kim-chi is hot and spicy, and that José goes to work very early and then has a snack about eleven, etc.).

When students have gone through the answers with each other and with the teacher, they can choose which breakfast sounds the best. They can then think what they would say if someone interviewed them about their normal breakfast.

The class is now divided into interviewers and interviewees. The interviewers stand in a circle and the interviewees stand, facing them, in an inner circle. The interviewers now have a minute to interview the person in front of them before the inner circle moves one person to the left so that the interviewers are now facing different interviewees.

The interviewers note down what people have for breakfast.

When the activity is over, one interviewer describes what one interviewee has for breakfast and the other interviewers have to say who the interviewee is.

Example 5: Storytelling	Activity:	listening to a monologue
	Skills:	listening for gist; listening for language study; analysing language
	Age:	adult
	Level:	upper intermediate plus

In this extract, adapted from *Just Right Upper Intermediate* (Harmer and Lethaby, published by Marshall Cavendish), students are introduced to Jan Blake, and told that she is a professional story teller.

The students are given the following list of words and phrases and told to make sure they know what they mean:

a)	a mirror is held up	☐
b)	asides	☐
c)	audition	☐
d)	being human	☐
e)	decent money	☐
f)	fantastic experience	☐
g)	fascinating	☐
h)	fundamental	☐
i)	aren't we great?	☐
j)	harmony	☐
k)	hunter	☐
l)	looked back	☐
m)	judgement	☐
n)	the place was packed	☐
o)	percussionist	☐
p)	regardless of the circumstances	☐
q)	something universal	☐
r)	stupid	☐
s)	the whole gamut	☐
t)	visualising	☐
u)	word for word	☐
v)	subconscious	☐
w)	tradition	☐

Jan Blake

They can use a dictionary or the Internet (or each other) to see if they can make sense of these words and phrases.

They now listen to the following audiotrack in which Jan is speaking about the craft of story-telling. All they have to do is tick words and phrases from the first exercise which they hear.

Audioscript

What are stories for? I think, I think stories – this is my personal opinion. This isn't, er, a kind of tried and tested theory – but my personal opinion is that when someone tells a story in that arena, at the moment that the story is being told, everything about being human is accepted, yeah? The good, the bad. Every single experience of being human is in that room with everybody and it's almost, there's no judgement of what it means to be a human being at that moment. Does that make sense? So what the audience gets from it, I think, is a mirror is held up and I say to the audience this is us, aren't we great? Or aren't we stupid, or aren't we fascinating or aren't we vengeful or aren't we wonderful lovers or aren't we – this is the whole gamut of human experience can be found in a story, I think, and I think that there's something very fundamental that I can't put my finger on and say what it is. But it happens when stories are told, the visualising of the story, the sound of the story teller's voice, the contact with the audience, the, er, asides if you like, the recognition of the human condition – all of those things are in the room with you when you tell a story, when you hear a story, and I think that's what the audience gets out of it, umm, the opportunity to delve deep into your own consciousness, your own subconscious, your own imagination and experience something universal. I think that's what happens when you hear a story, that's what happens when I tell a story.

After checking through the answers, students listen to Jan again in order to see if they can summarise what she said. In pairs and groups, they see if they can come up with a one-sentence summary of Jan's main points.

We can now ask students to have a close look at what Jan says. One way is to ask them to do a cloze exercise (see page 382) on the audioscript, like the example below.

> What are stories for? I 1 _____, I think stories – this is my 2 _____ opinion. This isn't, er, a 3 _____ of tried and tested theory – 4 _____ my personal opinion is 5 _____ when someone tells a 6 _____ in that arena, at the 7 _____ that the story is being told, 8 _____ about being human is 9 _____, yeah? The good, the bad. Every 10 _____ experience of being 11 _____ is in that room with everybody and it's 12 _____, there's no judgement of 13 _____ it means to be a human 14 _____ at that moment. Does that make sense?

They try to fill in the missing words first and then listen to the track again to check their answers. This exercise makes them look at the audioscript with great care.

Another alternative is to have students look at the audioscript to see where Jan changes topic in mid-sentence (*I think stories – this is my personal opinion. This isn't, er, a kind of tried and tested theory –*), where she repeats herself (*in a story, I think, and I think*), what hesitation fillers she uses (*umm*), where she inserts new clauses into a sentence (*So what the audience gets from it, I think, is a mirror is held up*), etc. This is the kind of analysis of text we suggested on page 268 (though Jan, being a professional story teller, speaks in a far more organised way than many monologue speakers).

Example 6: Prizegiving	Activity:	word-game listening
	Skills:	listening for specific information; listening for detail; listening for acting out
	Age:	any
	Level:	intermediate plus

The technique of having students listen to see whether words (or phrases) occur in a text can be made extremely lively if we play games with it. In the following example, the teacher is going to read an extract which occurs towards the end of the book *Harry Potter and the Philosopher's Stone* by J K Rowling. The teacher wants to try to engage the students with the text in an interactive way.

The students are divided into two teams. Each team can give itself a name. The students are now shown the following words. They are told that they should choose one of the words (but make sure that no one sitting next to them has chosen the same word). They must make sure that they know exactly what their word means.

applause	curse	hugging	silent	waffle
babble	decoration	loudly	stamping	
bravery	dish	point	stars	
cheering	explosion	purple	summer	
courage	face	seat	sunburn	
cup	game	shock	tears	

Now all the students stand up. They may not sit down until they have heard their word. The teacher starts to read an extract from the story which describes Harry Potter's school's end-of-year feast, at which the headmaster, Professor Dumbledore, gives a speech and awards the 'Hogwarts Cup' to the house which has gained the most points for good behaviour, brave deeds, etc.

Any student who has chosen the word *loudly* will be able to sit down almost immediately as *loudly* occurs towards the beginning of the passage.

The teacher goes on reading until she gets to the end of the extract, which finishes with the word *decoration*.

With any luck, at least one student from each team will have chosen the word *decoration*, but even if they don't, they will listen with considerable interest for their words, and the competition between the two teams will add greatly to their engagement with the text.

The teacher can now read the text again for students to hear exactly who won what, why, and how many points the individuals were given, etc.

As a follow-up, the students can extract Professor Dumbledore's speech and study it to see exactly how it should be spoken. They can practise using the right stress and intonation as if they were going to perform the part in the film of the book.

Students can now give parts of Dumbledore's speech, one after the other. If time, space and enthusiasm permit, the whole class can act out the scene.

Of course, this particular extract will only work if students know something about Harry Potter (and how his boarding school is divided into four houses, etc.). Nevertheless, the example shows how students can have fun as they practise the skill of listening.

Example 7: Witness statement	Activity:	being observant
	Skills:	watching/listening for detail
	Age:	any
	Level:	elementary and above

In this activity, which uses a film extract, the students have to try to give as much information as they can about what they have seen – as if they were witnesses being questioned by the police. The best kind of video extract for this is a short one- or two-minute conversation in an interesting location.

After being told to remember as much as they can, they watch the sequence. In pairs, they now have to agree on everything they heard and saw: *Who said what to whom? Where did the action take place? Who was wearing what? How many people were there in the scene? What was the name of the shop? How many windows were there in the house? Was there anything in the distance? What exactly did the characters say (if anything)?*

When the pairs have finished their discussion, the teacher reads out questions and the students have to write their answers. The questions might be something like the following:

> 1 How many people did you see in total in the excerpt?
>
> 2 How many of them were women? How many were men?
>
> 3 What did the man say first?
>
> 4 Were there any vehicles in the excerpt? If so, what were they?
>
> 5 How many different buildings were there?
>
> 6 What colour was the old man's jacket?
>
> etc.

When students have written the answers, they compare them with other pairs to see whether they all agree. Now they watch the excerpt again to see how good they are as witnesses.

Example 8: Different season, different sex	Activity:	making changes
	Skills:	watching for gist; interpreting text
	Age:	young adult and above
	Level:	lower intermediate and above

In this activity, students first watch a film clip and the teacher makes sure that they understand it. They do any language work which may be appropriate.

The teacher then asks the students to watch the excerpt again. But this time they have to imagine how the scene would be different if, for example, instead of the summer which is clearly shown, the episode were taking place in an icy winter. Or, if the excerpt takes place in rain, how would it be different in bright sunshine? They can discuss the differences in pairs or groups, talking about everything from what the characters might wear to how they might speak and how they might behave.

An interesting variation on this is to ask students how the scene would be different if the participants were the opposite sex. Would the conversation between two women be different if the women were changed into men? How might the invitation dialogue they have just watched change if the sex of the participants were reversed? The responses to these questions are often revealing (and amusing). What students say will depend a lot upon their age and culture, of course, and there is always the danger of unnecessary sexism. But where teachers handle the activity with finesse and skill, the exercise can be very successful.

Having students think about filmed excerpts in this way not only helps them understand more about the language being used (and how it might change), but also directs them to insights about language and behaviour in general.

D The sound of music

Music is a powerful stimulus for student engagement precisely because it speaks directly to our emotions while still allowing us to use our brains to analyse it and its effects if we so wish. A piece of music can change the atmosphere in a classroom or prepare students for a new activity. It can amuse and entertain, and it can make a satisfactory connection between the world of leisure and the world of learning in the classroom. Some teachers, for example, like to put music on in the background when their students are working on a reading or language task or when they are involved in pairwork or groupwork. This may help to make the classroom atmosphere much warmer, and one of the methods we looked at from the 1970s (Suggestopaedia – see page 68) had background music as a central part of its design. However, it is worth remembering that not everyone is keen to have music in the background at all times, and even if they are, they may not necessarily like the teacher's choice of music. It makes sense, therefore, to let students decide if they would like music in the background rather than just imposing it on them (however well-intentioned this imposition might be). We should allow them to say what they think of the music we then play since the whole point of playing music in the first place is make students feel happy and relaxed.

Because the appreciation of music is not a complex skill, and because many different patterns of music from a variety of cultures have become popular all over the globe through satellite television and the Internet, most students have little trouble perceiving clear changes of mood and style in a wide range of world music types. In class, therefore, we can play film music and get students to say what kind of film they think it comes from. We can get them to listen to music which describes people and say what kind of people they are. They can write stories based on the mood of the music they hear, or listen to more than one piece of music and discuss with each other what mood each piece describes, what 'colour' it is, where they would like to hear it and who with.

Even those who are sceptical about their ability to respond to music often end up being convinced despite themselves. As one of David Cranmer and Clement Leroy's students wrote after hearing Honegger's 'Pacific 231' (which most people see as the composer's depiction of a steam locomotive):

> I am really puzzled by people's ability to see things in music. I can't. Take this music, for example ... if you ask me, I would visualise a train steaming through the prairie and Indians attacking it ... while some people are desperately trying to defend it. (Cranmer and Leroy 1992: 57).

One of the most useful kinds of text for students to work with is song lyrics, especially where the song in question is one which the students are very keen on. However, songs can present a problem, particularly with teenage students, because it is often difficult to know exactly which songs the students like at any particular time and which songs, very popular last week, have suddenly gone out of favour!

There are two ways of dealing with this problem: the first is to have students bring their own favourite songs to class. If they do this, however, the teacher may want to have time (a day or two) to listen to the song and try to understand the lyrics. Some of the songs may deal with issues and language which the teacher is not keen to work with. Another solution is to use older songs, and to ask students whether they think they still have merit – whether they like them, despite their antiquity. Teachers can then choose songs which they like or which are appropriate in terms of topic and subject matter, and which they themselves think pass the test of time.

According to Sylvan Payne, 'the ideal song ... repeats key phrases; attracts students' attention; and teaches some natural, interesting language without offending anyone' (2006: 42). He finds that typing in grammar points like *should have* along with the word *lyrics* into his Internet search engine often finds him exactly the kinds of songs he wants.

Chapter notes and further reading

- **Listening**

  On listening in general, see J Flowerdew and L Miller (2006), M Underwood (1989), G White (1998), A Anderson and T Lynch (1988), M Rost (1990), J Field (1998a) and P Bress (2006). In a short article B Holden (2002) offers 36 ways to integrate listening skills with learning strategies.

- **Children reflect on listening**

  C Goh and Y Taib (2006) found that young learners became better listeners after they were encouraged to think about how they listened, what made it easy and difficult, etc.

- **Live listening**

  See J Marks (2000). J McEwan (2003) discusses the benefits of bringing family and friends into the classroom for her students to listen to and interact with. See also H Keller (2003).

  There is an interesting example of conversational live listening in Lesson 13 of the Teacher Training DVD pack from International House London (for information see http://www.ihlondon.com/dvdseries/).

- **Authentic text**

  On the advantages of using authentic listening texts in class, see J Field (1998b: 13). On using transcripts of conversations in teaching, see R Carter (1998a) and G Cook (1998), who questions the use of such samples of 'authentic' speech, and a reply to his criticisms in R Carter (1998b). L Prodromou (1997a) strongly questioned the work of Carter and McCarthy, and their reply is most instructive – see M McCarthy and R Carter (1997) to which Prodromou himself replied (Prodromou 1997b).

- **Note-taking**

  On training students to take lecture notes, see H Evans Nachi and C Kinoshita (2006).

- **Podcasts**

  On using interactive stories on an iPod, see M Vallance (2006) – and for more on podcasts in general see page 188 and the reference to learning on the Internet on page 409.

  For a list of good podcast sites for students of English, see www.englishcaster.com.

- **Film and video**

  Older books on the use of video still have a lot to say about using digital film. See, for example, Stempleski and Tomalin (1990) and R Cooper *et al* (1991).

  D Coniam (2003b) writes about 'jigsaw video'. T Karpinski (2003) uses film to stimulate students' vocabulary learning. See also T Murugavel (2003) and S Ryan (2002).

- **Subtitles**

  For the use of teletext subtitles, see R Vanderplank (1988, 1996).

- **Listening sequences**

  For more listening sequences, see J Harmer (2007: Chapter 10). S Burgess and K Head look at teaching listening for exams (2005: Chapter 6). H Evans Nachi and C Kinoshita (2006) have suggestions for listeners taking notes in lectures.

- **Using music and song in the classroom**

  For more on using music in the classroom, see L Demoney and S Harris (1993) and D Cranmer and C Leroy (1992) – now sadly out of print, but a classic, nevertheless.

  On songs, see S Coffrey (2000) and C Goodger (2005). R Walker (2006) sees songs as good ways of practising pronunciation, and M Rosenberg (2006) lists some of the songs she takes into her business lessons. G P Smith (2003) writes about 'mondegreens' (where we mis-hear song lyrics) as a way of extracting meaning from song.

19 | Writing

A Literacy

In the past, people tended to view someone as literate if they could manipulate '... a set of discrete, value-free technical skills which included decoding and encoding meanings, manipulating writing tools, perceiving shape–sound correspondences, etc. which are acquired through formal education' (Hyland 2002: 53). However, as Ken Hyland points out, this view has changed radically in the last few years so that now literacy is seen as significantly more complex, located as it is in social contexts. We judge people as literate, in other words, if they can read and write in certain situations and for certain purposes, some of which are more prestigious than others. It is certainly true that to be deprived of the opportunity to write is 'to be excluded from a wide range of social roles, which the majority of people in industrialised societies associate with power and prestige' (Tribble 1996: 12). However, in different domains of life there are different literacies, and it is the exact nature of these which seems to matter. Filling in a form certainly suggests literacy at one level, but if the same person is incapable of putting together an appropriate letter of application, then they are demonstrating a lesser standard of literacy than someone who can not only write a letter of application, but also construct a short story or write a complex report. In the Christian world of the middle ages, sacred texts were only written in Latin and were only available to people with prestige and, therefore, a prestigious kind of literacy. Not that much has changed, perhaps, since in world terms we might well say that, for example, being able to use information technology successfully is a mark of a kind of literacy still denied to the majority of the world's population.

As we shall see below, the concept of genre is highly bound up with literacy of this kind, in that different written genres perform purposes for specific discourse communities. In foreign-language teaching, therefore, we need to decide what kind of writing we expect from students, and, therefore, what kind of literacies we are asking from them. This is especially important when students are studying English for academic purposes (EAP); the actual discipline and the level they are studying for will determine how 'literate' they should be.

In this chapter we will concentrate first on the 'nuts and bolts' aspects of literacy, before discussing issues to do with the writing process and genre.

A1 Handwriting

It may seem strange to worry about handwriting when so much communication takes place electronically, in emails or by using word processing software. Yet there are still many occasions, even for the most computer-literate, when we have to write by hand. Many language exams are still taken by candidates using pens and pencils, and we generally write notes, postcards, memos, journals, etc. in handwriting.

Many students whose native-language orthography is very different from English have difficulty forming English letters and may have to be taught exactly how it is done. This may involve showing them which direction the writing strokes go in. For example, the following worksheet (designed for children learning to write the letter *b*) shows writers where to start (at the star) and how the strokes go. Gradually the written *b* becomes fainter and fainter until the students are, in effect, writing it on their own.

Later on, we can get students to write words and sentences, showing them, with the help of solid and dotted lines (and little diamonds) how tall letters should be and where the round part of the *b* finishes, etc.

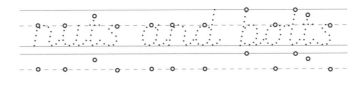

Handwriting is a personal issue. Students should not all be expected to use exactly the same style, despite copying exercises like the one above. Nevertheless, badly-formed letters may influence the reader against the writer, something which is undesirable whether the work is the product of some creative task or, more seriously, work that is going to be assessed in a test or exam. We should encourage students with problematic handwriting to improve.

A2 Spelling

Although incorrect spelling does not often prevent the understanding of a written message, it can adversely affect the reader's judgement. All too often, bad spelling is perceived as a lack of education or care. This is not necessarily the case in emails, and SMS text messages have spellings and 'words' all of their own. Nevertheless, as we saw on page 24, whereas it is perfectly acceptable in some emails to have spelling which is inexact, in other situations it is not.

One of the reasons that spelling is difficult for students of English is that the correspondence between the sound of a word and the way it is spelt is not always obvious (see Chapter 2, F4). A single sound (or more correctly, a single phoneme) may have many different spellings (*paw, poor, pore, pour, daughter, Sean*), and the same spelling may have many different sounds (*or, word, information, worry, correspond*). When students work on different phonemes, we need to draw their attention to the common spellings of those phonemes. We should also get them to look at different ways of pronouncing the same letters (or combinations of letters) or have them do exercises to discover spelling rules. When students come across new words, we can ask them what other words they know with the same kinds of spelling or sounds. When they listen to recordings, they can study transcripts and/or copy down sections of the recording.

An issue that makes spelling difficult for some students is the fact that not all varieties of English spell the same words in the same way. Which is correct: *color* or *colour*, *theater* or *theatre*? How do we decide between the use of *s* and *z* in words like *apologise* and *customize*? The former, in each case, are British spellings, and the latter are North American (though in Canada both spellings of *colour* and *theatre*, for example, are used).

To help make things clear, we should get our students to focus on a particular variety of English (British or American English, for example) as a spelling model for them to aspire to. But we should also make them aware of other spelling varieties, drawing their attention to dictionary entries which show such differences.

One of the best ways to help students improve their spelling is through reading, especially extensively (see Chapter 17, A1). We can also draw their attention to spelling problems and explain why they occur. Copying from written models is one way to do this; when students see and reflect on their copying mistakes, their spelling 'consciousness' is raised (Porte 1995).

A3 Layout and punctuation

Different writing communities (both between and within cultures) obey different punctuation and layout conventions in communications such as letters, reports and publicity materials. These are frequently non-transferable from one community or language to another. Such differences are easily seen in the different punctuation conventions for the quotation of direct speech which different languages use, or the way in which many writers use commas instead of or as much as full stops, although comma overuse is frowned on by many English-language writers and editors. Some punctuation conventions, such as the capitalisation of names, months and the pronoun *I*, are specific to only one or a few languages. Though punctuation is frequently a matter of personal style, violation of well-established customs makes a piece of writing look awkward to many readers.

Different genres of writing are laid out differently; business and personal letters are different from each other and emails have conventions all of their own. Newspaper articles are laid out in quite specific ways, and certain kinds of 'small ads' in magazines follow conventional formats. To be successful as writers in our own or another language, we need to be aware of these layouts and use or modify them when appropriate to get our message across as clearly as we can.

B Approaches to student writing

There are a number of different approaches to the practice of writing skills both in and outside the classroom. We need to choose between them, deciding whether we want students to focus more on the process of writing than its product, whether we want them to study different written genres, and whether we want to encourage creative writing – either individually or cooperatively. We will want to build the 'writing habit'.

B1 Process and product

In the teaching of writing we can either focus on the product of that writing or on the writing process itself. When concentrating on the product, we are only interested in the aim of a task and in the end product. As we shall see below, a consideration of written genre has a lot in common with a product approach to writing, i.e. an approach which values the construction of the end-product as the main thing to be focused on (rather than the process of writing itself).

Many educators, however, advocate a process approach to writing. This pays attention to the various stages that any piece of writing goes through. By spending time with learners on pre-writing phases, editing, re-drafting and finally producing a finished version of their work, a process approach aims to get to the heart of the various skills that most writers employ – and which are, therefore, worth replicating when writing in a foreign language. Indeed, it might be possible to argue that editing and re-drafting are even more important when we are writing in a foreign language than when we are writing in our first language.

In its simplest form, a process approach asks students to consider the procedure of putting together a good piece of work. We might, for example, discuss the concept of first and final drafts with our students and then ask them to say whether the activities listed here take place at first or final stages, and to put them in the best order.

In reality, the writing process is more complex than this, of course, and the various stages of drafting, reviewing, re-drafting and writing, etc. are done in a *recursive*, way: we loop backwards and move forwards between these various stages (Tribble 1996: 37–39). Thus at the editing stage we may feel the need to go back to a pre-writing phase and think again; we may edit bits of our writing as we draft it.

> **a** check language use (grammar , vocabulary, linkers)
> **b** check punctuation (and layout)
> **c** check your spelling
> **d** check your writing for unnecessary repetition of words and/or information
> **e** decide on the information for each paragraph and the order the paragraphs should go in
> **f** note down various ideas
> **g** select the best ideas for inclusion
> **h** write a clean copy of the corrected version
> **i** write out a rough version

Ron White and Valerie Arndt stress that '... writing is *re*-writing ... *re*-vision – seeing with new eyes – has a central role to play in the act of creating text' (White and Arndt 1991: 5). Perhaps, then, it is better to see writing as a kind of process 'wheel', where writers move both around the circumference of the wheel and across the spokes. And even when they have written what they think is the final version of their work, they may still, at the last moment, go back and re-plan or re-visit stages they had thought they had completed.

FIGURE 1: The process wheel

One of the disadvantages of getting students to concentrate on the process of writing is that it takes time: time to brainstorm ideas or collect them in some other way; time to draft a piece of writing and then, with the teacher's help, perhaps, review it and edit it in various ways before, perhaps, changing the focus, generating more ideas, re-drafting, re-editing, and so on. This cannot be done in 15 minutes. The various stages may well involve discussion, research, language study and a considerable amount of interaction between teacher and students and between the students themselves so that when process writing is handled appropriately, it stretches across the whole curriculum. Not all students see this as a good thing, however. Many will find it difficult to give enough time to the process and would rather finish a piece of writing straight away. And there are times when process writing is simply not appropriate, either because classroom time is limited or because we want students to write quickly as part of a communication game.

However, none of these circumstances should prevent us from explaining the process to our students and encouraging them to plan, draft, re-draft, re-plan, etc. In longer pieces of writing (or writing for portfolios – see below), the writing process is at least as important as the product, and even in exam writing tasks, the students' ability to plan (quickly) and later read back through what they have written in order to make any necessary corrections is extremely important.

B2 Genre

As we saw in Chapter 2, C2, a lot of writing within a discourse community is very genre-bound. In other words, writers frequently construct their writing so that people within that discourse community will instantly understand what kind of writing it is. We know what an advertisement is when we see it, we recognise poetry formats and we know what a formal letter should look like. Genre represents the norms of different kinds of writing.

When teachers concentrate on genre, students study texts in the genre in which they are going to be writing before they embark on their own work. Thus, if we want them to write business letters of various kinds, we let them look at typical models of such letters before starting to compose their own. If we want them to write newspaper articles, we have them study real examples to discover facts about construction and specific language use which are common to that genre. This forms part of the pre-writing phase.

Chris Tribble (1996: 148–150) suggests the following 'data collection' procedure as a prelude to the writing of letters to newspapers. Students are asked to spend some time every day for a week looking at letters to the newspapers. They are asked to make notes of particular vocabulary and/or grammar constructions used in them. For example, we might tell them to find any language which expresses approval or disapproval or to note down any *if* sentences they come across. They can use dictionaries or any other resources they need to check understanding. At the end of a week, they bring the results of their research to the class and make a list of commonly occurring lexis or grammar patterns.

The teacher now gets the students to read controversial articles in today's paper and plan letters (using language they have come across in the data collection phase) in response to those articles. Where possible, students should actually send their letters in the hope that they will be published.

A genre approach is especially appropriate for students of English for Specific Purposes. However, it is also highly useful for general English students, even at low levels, if we want them to produce written work they can be proud of.

Students who are writing within a certain genre need to consider a number of different factors. They need to have knowledge of the topic, the conventions and style of the genre, and the context in which their writing will be read, as well as by whom. Many of our students' writing tasks do not have an audience other than the teacher, of course, but that does not stop us and them working as if they did.

Asking students to imitate a given style could be seen as extremely prescriptive, encouraging them to see writing as a form of 'reproduction' rather than as a creative act. One way round this – and something that is absolutely necessary if students are to have real knowledge of a genre – is for them to see many different examples from the same genre. This means that they will be able to choose from a variety of features. However, at lower levels this may well be impractical, and so imitation may, after all, be a useful first stage, designed as much to inform as to enforce adherence to strict genre rules. Later, with exposure to different examples within a genre, it will be up to them to decide what to do with the data they have collected.

B3 Creative writing

The term *creative writing* suggests imaginative tasks, such as writing poetry, stories and plays. Such activities have a number of features to recommend them. Chief among these is that the end result is often felt to be some kind of achievement and that '... most people feel pride in their work and want it to be read' (Ur 1996: 169). This sense of achievement is significantly more marked for creative writing than for other more standard written products.

Creative writing is 'a journey of self-discovery, and self-discovery promotes effective learning' (Gaffield-Vile 1998: 31). When teachers set up imaginative writing tasks so that their students are thoroughly engaged, those students frequently strive harder than usual to produce a greater variety of correct and appropriate language than they might for more routine assignments. While students are writing a simple poem about someone they care about, or while they are trying to construct a narrative or tell stories of their childhood, for example, they are tapping into their own experiences. This, for some, provides powerful motivation to find the right words to express such experience. Creative writing also provokes the kind of input–output circle we described in Chapter 16, A1.

In order to bolster the 'product pride' that students may feel when they have written creatively, we need to provide an appropriate reader audience. In addition to ourselves as teachers, the audience can be the whole class. We can put students' writing up on a class noticeboard or copy it and include it in class magazines. We can make anthologies and distribute them to friends, parents and other teachers. We can, if we want, set up websites for our classes on the Internet, or have students write blogs (see the example on page 338) which can be read by others.

There is always a danger that students may find writing imaginatively difficult. Having 'nothing to say', they may find creative writing a painful and demotivating experience, associated in their minds with a sense of frustration and failure. A lot will depend upon how we encourage them (see B5 below). It is also important not to expect whole compositions from the very first. We need, instead, to 'build the writing habit', providing students with motivating, straightforward tasks to persuade them that writing is not only possible but can also be great fun.

B4 Writing as a cooperative activity

Although many people in their personal lives write on their own, whether at home or at work, in language classes teachers and students can take advantage of the presence of others to make writing a cooperative activity, with great benefit to all those involved. In one example of such an approach, group writing allowed the lecturer to give more detailed and constructive feedback since she was dealing with a small number of groups rather than many individual students (Boughey 1997). Individual students also found themselves saying and writing things they might not have come up with on their own, and the group's research was broader than an individual's normally was.

Cooperative writing works well whether the focus is on the writing process or, alternatively, on genre study. In the first case, reviewing and evaluation are greatly enhanced by having more than one person working on a text, and the generation of ideas is frequently more lively with two or more people involved than it is when writers work on their own. In genre-based writing, it is probably the case that two heads analyse genre-specific texts as well as, if not better, than one head would do, and often create genre-specific texts more successfully as a result.

Cooperative writing is immensely successful if students are writing on a computer. If the screen is big enough, everyone can clearly see what is being created, and everyone can make small changes both during the initial writing process and also later on. Students and teachers can also email each other, of course; and just as with Wikipedia, anyone can modify entries, so with student writing on the Internet (or on an Intranet – that is on a hard disk that everyone in the school, or from a group can access), other students can alter things that are there, and gradually co-construct a final finished product.

Writing in groups, whether as part of a long process or as part of a short game-like communicative activity, can be greatly motivating for students, including as it does, not only writing, but research, discussion, peer evaluation and group pride in a group accomplishment.

B5 Building the writing habit

Some students are extremely unconfident and unenthusiastic writers. There may be many reasons for this: perhaps they have never written much in their first language(s). Perhaps they think that they don't have anything to say and can't come up with ideas.

Whatever the reason, we need to help such students build the writing habit so that they recognise writing as being a normal part of classroom practice and they come to writing tasks with as much enthusiasm as they do other activities. One way of doing this, of course, is to give them interesting and enjoyable tasks to do. We must make sure, however, that we give them enough information to do what we have asked. We will want to make sure that they have enough of the right kind of language to do the task. We need to be able to give students ideas to complete the task, too. Sometimes we may dictate half-sentences for them to finish so that they do not have to come up with too much information of their own. Sometimes we will feed in ideas to a student or students as they do the task. Of course, we don't want to crowd the students with too many ideas if this is going to stifle creativity, but we need to be ready with enough suggestions to make sure they can never say *I can't think of anything to write*. Finally, patterns and schemes help students to write with confidence. This is the first stage of looking at different genres that we mentioned above. If students are given a model for postcard-writing, it is easy to come up with their own slightly different version. Simple poems often provide a framework in which students can say something meaningful while still being supported by a helpful structure. Giving students some kind of simple structure to write in provides the same kind of support that every writer gets when, instead of finding themselves in front of a blank screen, they are given parameters and constraints to write with. However, we are not suggesting that all writing needs to be constrained or supported in this way. The blank screen is the place where a great deal of creativity first starts.

Building the writing habit can be done with a range of activities. We can promote *instant writing* by dictating half a sentence which the students have to complete (e.g. *Before I am thirty I would like to ...*). We can get them to write three *Don't* sentences for a new school (e.g. *Don't run in the corridors*). We can get students to respond to music by writing what words or scenes a piece of music suggests, or by describing the film scene a piece of music might accompany. They can write about how a piece of music makes them feel or write stories that the music 'tells them to write' (Harmer 2004: 66).

Pictures can provide stimulation for writing-habit activities. Students can describe pictures or write descriptions of a wanted man or woman so that their colleagues have to identify that person from a group photograph. They can write postcards from a picture we give them, or create an interview with a portrait, say, from 200 years ago.

There are many writing games, too, such as story reconstruction activities where students have to build up a story from a set of pictures, each of which only one of them has seen (see below). We can get students into story circles where, in groups, they create a story together.

The whole point of all these activities is just to get students to write for the fun and practice of it, rather than have them write as a skill. Building the writing habit falls halfway between writing-for-learning and writing-for-writing (see B6 below).

B6 Writing-for-learning and writing-for-writing

We need to make a distinction between writing-for-learning and writing-for-writing if we are to promote writing as a skill.

Writing-for-learning is the kind of writing we do to help students learn language or to test them on that language. Thus, if we say *Write three sentences using the 'going to' future*, our aim is not to train students to write, but rather to help them remember the *going to* future. The same is true when we get them to write (say for a test) four sentences about what they wish about the present and the past.

When we ask students to design a good magazine advertisement, however, we are doing this so that they may become good at writing advertisements. When we get them to write a narrative, it is their ability to write a story that counts, not just their use of the past tense.

If we are to build the students' writing skills (as opposed to building their writing habits or getting them to write for language practice), we will have to use such writing-for-writing tasks as often as is appropriate.

B7 The roles of the teacher

Although the teacher needs to deploy some or all of the usual roles (see Chapter 6, B1) when students are asked to write, the ones that are especially important are as follows:

- **Motivator:** one of our principal roles in writing tasks will be to motivate the students, creating the right conditions for the generation of ideas, persuading them of the usefulness of the activity, and encouraging them to make as much effort as possible for maximum benefit. This may require special and prolonged effort on our part for longer process-writing sequences.

    Where students are involved in a creative writing activity, it is usually the case that some find it easier to generate ideas than others. During a poetry activity (see Example 6 below), for example, we may need to suggest lines to those who cannot think of anything, or at least prompt them with our own ideas.

- **Resource:** especially during more extended writing tasks, we should be ready to supply information and language where necessary. We need to tell students that we are available and be prepared to look at their work as it progresses, offering advice and suggestions in a constructive and tactful way. Because writing takes longer than conversation, for example, there is usually time for discussion with individual students or students working in pairs or groups to complete a writing task.

- **Feedback provider:** giving feedback on writing tasks demands special care (see Chapter 8D). Teachers should respond positively and encouragingly to the content of what the students have written. When offering correction, teachers will choose what and how much to focus on, based on what students need at this particular stage of their studies and on the tasks they have undertaken.

C Writing lesson sequences

In the following examples, the writing activity is specified, together with its particular focus. Some of the activities are about the nuts and bolts of writing (Examples 1, 2 and 5), some are designed to build the writing habit (Examples 5 and 6) and others are designed to give students practice in the skill of writing (Examples 3 and 4).

Example 1: Dino at the hotel	Activity: punctuating a text
	Focus: writing conventions
	Age: young adult and above
	Level: elementary

If we want students to learn about punctuation, they need to make the connection between the way we speak and the way punctuation reflects this. Commas, for example, are often placed at the points where a speaker would take a breath if they were reading the text. Full stops represent the end of a tone group, etc.

The following task – at elementary level – asks students to punctuate a prose passage using capital letters, commas, inverted commas (quotation marks) and full stops.

Students read the unpunctuated text from an elementary graded reader (see page 283) and then listen to the story on CD. This is so they can get a good idea of what it is about. In pairs, they then try to add punctuation. They can listen to the recording as many times as they like.

> 20 april was dino bracco's twenty-first birthday he worked giovanni his boss at the hotel grand brought him a cake from the hotel kitchen just twenty-one said giovanni and then he put his hand on dino's back ah dino dino … when I was twenty-one …
>
> dino ate some cake and smiled he was only twenty-one years old but he was a young man who knew what he wanted he had a plan
>
> you must know what you want dino his mother said to him when he was a child and he did he had a plan dino came from a very small town called rocella in the south of italy his mother and father were farmers rocella was beautiful but no one had any money dino was born there but now he lived and worked in venice he worked at the reception of the hotel grand

From *Hotel Casanova* by S Leather (Cambridge University Press)

We can put the unpunctuated text on the board, OHT or a projected computer screen. Students from the different pairs can punctuate it, line by line and the rest of the class can say whether or not they agree. Punctuating poems in this way is also very effective.

Example 2: The bear	Activities:	story reconstruction, story continuation
	Focus:	coherence and cohesion
	Age:	young adult and above
	Level:	upper intermediate and above

This sequence aims to make students aware of coherence – and especially cohesive devices – in writing. It is similar to Example 5 in Chapter 17 (page 296), but the objective of this whole sequence is to get students writing more coherently, using cohesive devices appropriately.

The students are told that they are going to reconstruct a text about Kitty Redcape, whose grandmother lives in the woods. Kitty frequently goes there to have tea. They are given a series of cards and told to re-order them to make a story (the first one is done for them). They need to look out for clues, such as the use of pronouns, repetition of lexical items and a coherent order of events. These are the cards they are given:

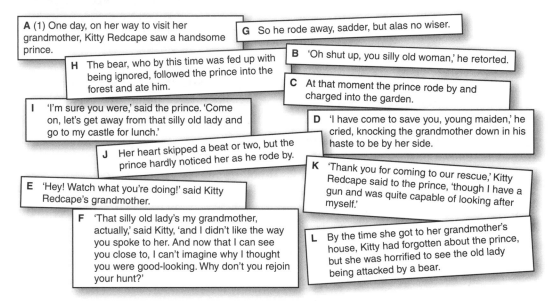

A (1) One day, on her way to visit her grandmother, Kitty Redcape saw a handsome prince.

G So he rode away, sadder, but alas no wiser.

H The bear, who by this time was fed up with being ignored, followed the prince into the forest and ate him.

B 'Oh shut up, you silly old woman,' he retorted.

C At that moment the prince rode by and charged into the garden.

I 'I'm sure you were,' said the prince. 'Come on, let's get away from that silly old lady and go to my castle for lunch.'

D 'I have come to save you, young maiden,' he cried, knocking the grandmother down in his haste to be by her side.

J Her heart skipped a beat or two, but the prince hardly noticed her as he rode by.

K 'Thank you for coming to our rescue,' Kitty Redcape said to the prince, 'though I have a gun and was quite capable of looking after myself.'

E 'Hey! Watch what you're doing!' said Kitty Redcape's grandmother.

F 'That silly old lady's my grandmother, actually,' said Kitty, 'and I didn't like the way you spoke to her. And now that I can see you close to, I can't imagine why I thought you were good-looking. Why don't you rejoin your hunt?'

L By the time she got to her grandmother's house, Kitty had forgotten about the prince, but she was horrified to see the old lady being attacked by a bear.

If students are having trouble with the sequence, we can point out, for example, that the first three cards all have *the prince* in them, and that this lexical repetition helps to tie the story together with a 'chain of reference'. We can show them how *he* is used in the same way in this two-sentence sequence:

> At that moment the prince rode by and charged into the garden. 'I have come to save you, young maiden,' he cried, knocking the grandmother down in his haste to be by her side.

After the pairs and groups have completed the task, they check to see if they have all got the same order (A, J, L, C, D, E, B, K, I, F, G, H) and discuss why and how it is arrived at.

We can now get them to develop more sentences about Kitty and her grandmother, perhaps going as far as making their own stories. For example, we might give them the following exercise:

> **Read the opening sentence and then complete the sentences which follow.**
>
> When Kitty was on her way to her grandmother's house, she stopped to talk to two woodcutters in the forest.
>
> 1. She _____.
> 2. They _____.
> 3. It _____.
> 4. The old lady _____.

Alternatively, they can be asked to re-write the following paragraphs, replacing *Kitty Redcape*, *the prince* and *the bear* by *she, her, he, him* or *it* where necessary.

> Kitty Redcape often goes to visit Kitty Redcape's grandmother in the woods. One day, on Kitty Redcape's way to Kitty Redcape's grandmother's house, Kitty Redcape sees the prince and Kitty Redcape thinks the prince is very attractive. The prince does not notice Kitty Redcape.
>
> When Kitty Redcape arrives at the cottage, Kitty Redcape sees Kitty Redcape's grandmother being attacked by a bear. Just then the prince rides into the garden to save Kitty Redcape and the prince is rude to Kitty Redcape's grandmother.
>
> The prince asks Kitty Redcape back to his castle for lunch but Kitty Redcape says no because Kitty Redcape doesn't like the prince's treatment of Kitty Redcape's grandmother and Kitty Redcape doesn't fancy the prince after all. Kitty Redcape suggests that the prince should go back to the prince's hunt and leave them alone. And that's what the prince does. The bear follows the prince into the forest and the bear eats the prince.

If students are enjoying the fairy story aspect of this sequence, we can then use a variation of 'Julia's story' (see Example 7 below) and have them write their own texts starting with a sentence we give them such as:

> *Once upon a time there was a handsome prince who lived in a castle by the river.*

They can then put their knowledge of coherence and cohesion into action.

Example 3: The genre analyser	Activity:	writing a review
	Focus:	identifying genre features
	Age:	young adult and above
	Level:	upper intermediate and above

In this sequence, we want our students to write reviews of plays, concerts or films they have seen, and to do this in a way which is appropriate for the kind of audience (either real or imaginary) that they are writing for.

Firstly, we ask our students to look at a collection of reviews of plays and films from newspapers, magazines and/or on the Internet (see Example 4 on page 295). For each one they have to use the following 'reviewers' genre-analysing kit':

REVIEWERS' GENRE-ANALYSING KIT

Answer the following questions about the review you are reading:

MEANING

What is being reviewed?

Does the reviewer like it?

What, if anything, was especially good about the thing/event being reviewed?

What, if anything, was especially bad about the thing/event being reviewed?

Who, if anybody, deserves credit for their part in it?

Who, if anybody, should be criticised for their part in it?

What, if anything, does the thing/event remind the reviewer of?

CONSTRUCTION

How is the headline/caption constructed?

What does each paragraph contain, and how are the paragraphs sequenced?

What grammar and lexis is used to show approval?

What grammar and lexis is used to show disapproval?

By studying the reviews and answering the questions above about them, students build up a picture of how they are usually written.

We can now show them a DVD or get them to go to a play or a film. While watching it, they make notes about such items as the plot, the characters, the performances, the music, the cinematography and the special effects.

Afterwards, students draft their reviews, using language – if appropriate – from the reviews they read previously. We can go round, encouraging and helping. If there is time, we can read the full drafts and give constructive feedback on each one. Students then write their final version, and later, when all the reviews have been read, the class can vote on the best one.

Writing reviews can be greatly enhanced by having students write in pairs or groups, keying their opinions directly onto a computer screen. The discussion and focus which this provides will add to the creative nature of the activity in many ways.

Studying different writing genres – whether through a genre-analysing kit, through data collection, or even by putting a variety of texts into a corpus to run with concordancing packages (see Chapter 11, G2) – is a vital first stage in having students do their own writing in specific genres.

Example 4: Unsent letters	Activity:	letter writing
	Focus:	communicative writing
	Age:	any
	Level:	intermediate and above

In this activity, students are told that they are going to write a letter to someone that they would never normally write to. For example, they could write:

> – to someone who bugs you
> – to someone you have hurt or offended
> – to an ex-boyfriend or girlfriend, or an ex-friend
> – to an unborn child
> – to an examiner
> – to a burglar who has 'done' your house
> – to a person who has helped you without knowing it
> – to the present owner of the house you used to live in
> – to a famous historical figure

From *Letters* by N Burbidge *et al* (Oxford University Press)

When students have chosen the recipient of their letter, they write it. While they are doing this, the teacher can offer help and suggestions if they want it.

When students have finished their letters, they can show them to their colleagues. Their colleagues have to be able to say who the letter is to and what points it is trying to make.

Although these letters are only pseudo-communicative – because they will not actually be sent – they nevertheless fulfil all the characteristics of a communicative activity (see Chapter 4, A5); students choose who to write to so that they compose their letters with both purpose and enthusiasm. They emphasise content rather than language for its own sake.

Example 5: A poem	Activity:	running dictation
	Focus:	writing for fun/concentrating on writing correctly
	Age:	any
	Level:	pre-intermediate and above

In the following example (adapted from Davis and Rinvolucri 1990) the basic idea of a dictation has been altered so that it is the students who dictate to each other (rather than the teacher). It has a competitive element, is very active and is often extremely enjoyable.

Students are put into groups. The teacher puts an A4 copy of the following poem on a table at the front of the classroom.

> A man bought a piano for his wife
> which she constantly tunes
> and polishes. He says her hands and fingers
> are less flexible than once they were
> which is depressing.
>
> She came home and she found it there,
> a big surprise. Its brown respectability
> dominates the room. He watches her straight back
> and fumbling fingers in the evening city, lit
> by brakes and klaxons.
>
> *Peter Hedley*

Each group sends a representative to the front of the class to read only the first line of the poem, memorise it, and then run back to their group and dictate the line. When this has happened, groups send a second (and then a third) representative to read the second (and third) line and take that back to their groups and dictate it.

The activity goes on in this way until one group has the whole poem. The teacher can then give that group a further task while the others finish, or stop the class and show everyone a complete version of the poem for them to check their own version against. They are then asked to decide on their own title for the poem (originally called 'Piano Piece').

An alternative procedure at this point is to ask all the students to write down, in complete silence, what the poem means for them – however flippant or profound their response is. They can, for example, write *nothing* if they feel like it. When they have done this, they stand up, still in silence, and go round reading what other people have written. The effect of writing and silence in this way can be dramatic and enjoyable.

There are many different ways of doing dictations, and when students have some element of control (or agency – see page 103), they are especially convincing. For example, it is possible for the teacher to read out a dictation, but have students pretend that they have a control button of the kind that you get with tape recorders, DVD players, etc. This means that they can say *pause, stop, rewind, fast forward*, etc. to control the teacher's speed and get repetition if they need it. Of course, this activity works just as well if a student is the one reading out the passage they have to write.

Example 6: Ancient monuments	Activity:	writing a poem
	Focus:	creative writing
	Age:	any
	Level:	lower intermediate plus

Simple poetry-writing activities are often extremely effective ways of getting students to write creatively, but within clearly delineated frameworks (so that they do not feel oppressed by the need to be too imaginative).

In the following example from Jane Spiro (2004: 88–90), students are going to write poems from the point of view of ancient monuments and buildings (this makes much more sense than it appears!).

The teacher brings in pictures of famous buildings, statues, landscapes and monuments, etc. which the students are likely to know. Alternatively, she can direct students to websites where they can see these things.

Students now choose one of these places. They are going to think about what the place or thing *has seen, has heard, has known,* etc. The teacher may write up the following on the board (and ask students to think of completions):

> *You have seen ...*
> *You have heard ...*
> *You have known ...*

The teacher now divides the class into small groups. She gives them a picture or name of a place. She may have a list for the students to choose from, and can move round the groups suggesting possibilities both about the monuments in question and about the kind of things the students might want to include in their poems (e.g. *the sadness of a king, camels in the desert, the sound or war, the shouts of revolution,* etc.).

The students now write their poems, but they can either write to the monument/place (*You have seen ...*) or take on its personality (and write *I have seen ...*). When they have finished their poems, they can show them (without a title) to different groups to see if they can guess what the monument or place is.

Jane Spiro quotes the following student poem, produced with the procedure we have described.

> The Pyramids
>
> I have seen camels
> And then cats
> I have seen slaves
> And then princes
> I have seen stone
> And then marble
> I have seen life
> And then death

Of course this is not a great poem, but it has the air of poetry about it, and, above all, it has given students a chance to write creatively, however restricted the poetry frame may be.

Example 7: Julia's story	Activity:	story circle
	Focus:	building the writing habit; cooperative narrative writing
	Age:	any
	Level:	elementary and above

In this activity, students join together to write a story. However, there is an element of fun built into the activity and the results are not intended to be taken too seriously.

Students are put into groups of about five, sitting in circles. The teacher then dictates a sentence such as:

That day, when Julia came back from work, she knew something was different.

Each student writes the sentence at the top of their piece of paper. They are then asked to write the next sentence in Julia's story; all they have to do is write one sentence which follows on from this introduction.

When all the students have done this, the teacher tells them to pass their pieces of paper to the person on their left. They all now have to write the next sentence of the story which has just been passed to them. When they have finished, the teacher again asks everyone to pass their papers to the person on their left. They all now have to write the next sentence of the story on the piece of paper in front of them.

The procedure continues until the pieces of paper return to their original owners. At this point the teacher tells everyone to write a sentence to finish the story off – however ridiculous!

The students are then encouraged to read out the stories they have just finished. The results are often highly amusing, and because many hands have collaborated in the process, nobody has to suffer individual responsibility for the final versions. The teacher should make sure that quite a few of the stories are heard by the class and that the rest are available for everyone else to read.

This kind of group writing is enjoyable and useful for developing writing fluency. However, it should be used sparingly otherwise it will lose its main attraction – that of spontaneity.

Example 8: Such is life	Activity:	student blogging
	Focus:	writing for communication
	Age:	adult
	Level:	any

On page 193 we discussed the value of keypals and blogging for student writing. Students can now post their own contributions onto the web so that others can comment and react in writing to what they have to say.

The following example shows a student blog in action. However, it starts with a blog by Rosa for the adult migrant English programme at St George's College of TAFE (technical, further educational and vocational classes), in Sydney, Australia.

The blog she runs (http://ourclass2006.blogspot.com at the time of writing) offers students' views on a number of topics and posts photos of student activities. It has games, descriptions and grammar activities as well as sections for teachers. But it also encourages students to write blogs and make podcasts.

In order for students to learn how to become bloggers, Rosa sends them to a tutorial site (see Figure 2). Once they have done this, they are ready to go.

One of the students, called Jessie, set up her own blog entitled 'Such is life'. One of her postings (see Figure 3) muses on how her life might change; it is accompanied by a picture Jessie has found to make her posting more interesting.

> Creating an Account   Setting up Your Blog   Blog Settings   Viewing Your Blog
>
> # Welcome to our Blogger.com Tutorial
>
> So you want to blog. We are going to walk you through all the steps you need to set up a blog. You can set up a blog very simply. You can stop when you get a confirmation that your blog is set up. Or you can customize it by changing the settings of your blog. Either way this is a simple process that can get you and your students up and running.
>
> **Create you own blog**

FIGURE 2: Rosa's blog tutorial (opening page)

FIGURE 3: Jessie's blog

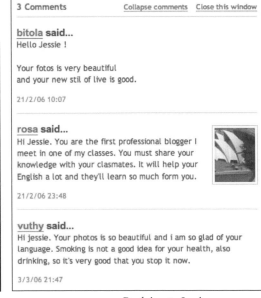

FIGURE 4: Replying to Jessie

As with all successful student blogs, she gets some replies (see Figure 4), and writing has now become real communication.

Of course the task for the teacher and the students is to keep blogs like this going. Furthermore, teachers will have to decide how much (if at all) they intervene to help students with their English. In the examples above, there are points where a writing teacher would want to intervene. In a blog (or with keypals and chatting) we have to decide how much to leave students to communicate on their own, and how much to use this as raw data for successful feedback on student work.

Example 9: College transport	Activity: report writing
	Focus: how reports are constructed; making notes
	Age: young adult +
	Level: upper intermediate

In the following sequence, students are lead through an exam-type task (for the Cambridge ESOL First Certificate exam). The clear objective is to teach report-writing skills.

The sequence (from *First Certificate Expert* by Jan Bell and Roger Gower, published by Pearson Education Ltd) starts when the teacher asks students to discuss the following questions:

1 *Which form of public transport do you prefer?*
2 *What is good and bad about public transport where you live?*

The students can discuss this in pairs or groups before the teacher talks about the questions with the class. They then look at the following task:

> It is difficult for students to get to your college. Public transport is not very good and the college car park is very small. A committee has been set up by the principal to analyse the problem and to recommend what the college should do. You are on the committee, and you have just had your last meeting.
>
> You have been asked to write a **report** for the principal.
>
> Write your **report** in **120–180** words in an appropriate style.

Students have to look at the task and decide how many parts there are to it, how informal or formal the style should be (bearing in mind who 'you' are and who you are writing to), and what will make the reader think it is a good report.

Once the teacher has discussed these questions with the class, they then start planning for the report by making notes under three headings:

Public transport	**Car park**	**Possible solutions**
buses every hour	*more students have cars*	*write to bus company*

They then match a typical four-paragraph sequence with what might be written in each of the four paragraphs.

Paragraph 1: Introducing the report	a	Focus on a minimum of two points.
Paragraph 2: Describing the first problem	b	State the purpose of the report.
Paragraph 3: Describing the second problem	c	Give a clear summary of the situation.
Paragraph 4: Summarising and recommending	d	Describe how you got the information.
	e	Only give relevant information.
	f	Give just one or two recommendations.
	g	Give the facts briefly and clearly without strong personal opinions.

They can then match their notes about public transport, car parking and possible solutions to the paragraphs.

Finally, in this phase, students are offered three titles for their report: (a) Cars, buses and trains, (b) To and from college, (c) Student transport. They are then given some language they might want to use before being asked to complete the task.

When students have written their reports, they are asked to look at them again and edit them, considering the following questions:

- Is the information relevant?

- Is the style clear and natural?

- Does the report feel balanced? (Are different viewpoints presented fairly?)

One of the reasons for this detailed writing sequence is that students are learning how to write successful exam answers (see the 'backwash effect' in Chapter 22D). But the habits being encouraged here – an analysis of the task followed by detailed planning, drafting and review – are the same habits which we have suggested for both genre and process-writing sequences.

D Portfolios, journals, letters

Many educational institutions and teachers get students to keep portfolios of examples of their written work over a period of time. These can be used for assessment, since judging different pieces of student work written over a period of time is seen by many people to be fairer than 'sudden death' final tests. However, using portfolios is a somewhat controversial alternative and not without its problems (see page 380).

Portfolios are also used as a way of encouraging students to take pride in their work; by encouraging them to keep examples of what they have written, we are encouraging them to write it well and with care.

For the Common European Framework (see page 95) portfolios are considerably more than just getting students to keep examples of their writing. *The European Language Portfolio* has three parts:

- **Language biography:** here students reflect on their language abilities using 'can do' statements (see page 96) to say things like *I can understand numbers, prices and times in English*. They can record if and why such abilities are important for them.

    The language biography asks them to say what language experiences they have had, and reveals the fact that a huge number of school students in various countries have rich and varied language backgrounds.

- **Language passport:** this is the 'public' version of the biography, and it tells, in simple tabular form, what languages the holder can speak and how well. The learners fill in this profile and can obviously amend it as their linguistic ability improves in one language or another.

    The language passport is the clearest possible statement of the advantages and benefits that accrue to people who speak more than one language, and it reinforces students' pride in their language(s) profile.

- **Dossier:** this is where students keep examples of their work – projects, reports, diplomas, PowerPoint presentations, etc. The students indicate whether this work was done individually or with other students.

The ELP is not an easy option in terms of the time needed to complete and read it by both students and teachers, and it comes with many add-ons (such as a list of 'can do' statements, see page 96) which make it somewhat cumbersome. However, it makes a powerful statement about an individual student's language identity and helps them to reflect on their learning. Indeed, portfolios may be successful mechanisms by which teachers 'can not only diagnose the learners' skills and competencies, but also become aware of their preferences, styles, dispositions and learning strategies ...' (Nunes 2004: 327). As with student journals and letter/email exchanges between teachers and students, portfolios can have a powerful effect on the development of learner autonomy, something we will discuss in more detail in Chapter 23A.

Chapter notes and further reading

- **Writing in general**
  On writing in general, see C Tribble (1996), T Hedge (2000: Chapter 9) and J Harmer (2004). T Hedge (2005) has a wealth of good writing ideas. K Hyland's important book (2002) discusses research in writing and W Grabe and R Kaplan (1996) write about the theory and practice of writing in the *Longman Applied Linguistics* series.

- **Mixed composition classes**
  N Ibrahim and S Penfield (2005) describe the benefits of mixing ESL students with first language English speakers in a freshman composition class in the USA.

- **Literacy**
  E Helmer (2005) discusses twenty-first-century literacy. P Stapleton (2005) discusses Internet literacy and its relationship to academic writing.

- **Spelling**
  R Shemesh and S Waller (2000) offer a complete book on teaching spelling. See also S Waller (2002), P Brabbs (2004), J Desmond (2006) and R Hamilton (2003), who has an 'NLP spelling strategy'.

- **Process**
  C Kelly (2003) stresses the need to focus of pre-writing rather than revision for students to understand structure. M Vince (2004) sees the educational value of a process approach. See also J Harmer (2004: Chapter 1).

  J Chau (2003) comes up with a three-step approach (ideational, sentential, relational) to help less proficient student writers. K Hill (2005) wants to link essay types and cognitive domains.

- **Genre**
  C Tribble (1996: Chapters 5 and 6) makes a strong case for a genre-based approach. H Kay and T Dudley-Evans (1998) discuss teachers' attitudes to genre. See also J Harmer (2004: Chapter 2).

- **Process and genre**

  R Badger and G White (2000) advocate a process-genre approach. J Muncie (2002) wants to find a place for grammar in composition classes. C Vickers and E Ene (2006) show how students can improve their grammatical accuracy by autonomously noticing their own writing errors.

- **Creative writing**

  C Rühlemann (2005) gives a number of ideas for students to recreate dialogue, etc. on the basis of material given to them by the teacher. S Mercer (2004) describes getting students to create different characters who can then be incorporated into play scenes. A G Elgar (2002) has students writing playscripts.

- **Penpals/keypals**

  See H Hennigan (1999) on how penpals became, in his words, 'keypals'. K Fedderholdt (2001) describes a successful keypal exchange between Japanese and Danish students.

  To set up penpal or keypal arrangements, teachers can contact the embassy of the country they are interested in, post notices at teachers' conferences or access penpal sites on the Internet such as the following three:

  www.penpalgarden.com/ – a large free penpal site where you fill in details about yourself and indicate whether you want penpals of the same or opposite gender.

  www.penpal.net – one of the largest free penpal sites on the Internet, you can select contacts by age and country.

  penpal@nationalgeographic.com – a site where children are matched to similar penpals around the world. There is a small charge per person.

- **Writing examples**

  For more writing activities, see T Hedge (2005), J Harmer (2004: Chapters 4–6, 2007: Chapter 8). On teaching writing for exams, see S Burgess and K Head (2005: Chapter 4).

- **Weblogs**

  M Vallance (2004) set up a blog project for his students with mixed results. The students were enthusiastic but Vallance himself had to intervene to (a) provide interesting topics, and (b) stop students disagreeing with each other too violently. J Askari Arani (2005) discusses teaching reading and writing in this way. S Peters (2006) gives clear tutorial information about weblogs and A P Campbell (2003) explains weblogs clearly.

- **Portfolios**

  The European Language Portfolio is clearly explained in F Heyworth and R Blakely (2005). A McDonald (2004, 2005a and b) discusses each of the three elements of the portfolio in turn.

20 | Speaking

A Elements of speaking

If students want to be able to speak fluently in English, they need to be able pronounce phonemes correctly, use appropriate stress and intonation patterns and speak in connected speech (see Chapter 15). But there is more to it than that. Speakers of English – especially where it is a second language – will have to be able to speak in a range of different genres and situations, and they will have to be able to use a range of conversational and conversational repair strategies. They will need to be able to survive in typical functional exchanges, too.

A1 Different speaking events

In his book on speaking, Scott Thornbury suggests various dimensions of different speaking events in order to describe different speaking genres (Thornbury 2005a: 13–14). For example, we can make a distinction between *transactional* and *interpersonal* functions. Transactional function has as its main purpose conveying information and facilitating the exchange of goods and services, whereas the interpersonal function is all about maintaining and sustaining good relations between people.

Whatever the purpose of the speaking event, we can characterise it as *interactive* or *non-interactive*. The conversation that takes place when we buy a newspaper at a news kiosk is interactive, whereas leaving a message on an answer phone is non-interactive.

Finally, we might make a difference between speaking that is *planned* (such as a lecture or wedding speech) and speaking that is *unplanned*, such as a conversation that takes place spontaneously when we bump into someone on the street.

These distinctions allow us to describe an event such as a job interview in terms of purpose (largely transactional), participation (interactive) and planning (partly planned).

These distinctions are not absolute, of course. Some speaking in a job interview may be for the exact purpose of maintaining and sustaining good interpersonal relations, and most interviewees do their best to plan what they are going to say (just as interviewers plan what some of their questions will be). Nevertheless, thinking of speaking in terms of purpose, participation and planning helps us to provide speaking activities in all six categories – and in different combinations of these categories.

A2 Conversational strategies

When we discussed structuring discourse in Chapter 16, C2, we said that successful face-to-face interaction depended on a knowledge (and successful execution) of turn-taking. Furthermore, speakers use various discourse markers to buy time (*ummm ... well ... you know ...*), to start a turn (*well ... I'd just like to say ...*) or to mark the beginning or the end of a segment (*right ... now ... anyway ...*).

343

- **Conversational rules and structure:** Zoltan Dörnyei and Sarah Thurrell add further categories of discourse, such as conversational openings (*How are you? That's a nice dog! At last some sunshine!*), interrupting (*Sorry to interrupt, but ...*), topic shift (*Oh, by the way, that reminds me ...*) and closings (*It's been nice talking to you ... Well, I don't want to keep you from your work ... we must get together sometime*) (Dörnyei and Thurrell 1994: 42–43).

- **Survival and repair strategies:** as we saw on page 306, students need to be able to use repair strategies when listening in interactive situations. In other words, if face-to-face conversation is to be successful, students need to be able to ask for repetition by using formulaic expressions, repeating up to the point of conversation breakdown, etc. To these repair strategies we might add such abilities as being able to paraphrase (*It's a kind of ...*), being able to use an all-purpose phrase to get round the problem of not knowing a word (*You know, it's a what-d'you-call-it*) and being able to appeal for help (*What's the word for something you play a guitar with?*).

- **Real talk:** if students are to be involved in spontaneous face-to-face conversation outside the classroom with competent English language speakers, they probably need to be exposed to more than just the kind of questions that are commonly found in coursebooks. These are sometimes well formed and take no account of ellipsis, for example. Helen Basturkmen looked at transcripts of masters-level students in conversation and found them using – among other things – questioning reformulation (i.e. repeating what someone had just said), multifunctional question forms (e.g. *Did you consider the possibility of an alliance with other organisations?* which functions as both suggestion and criticism) and the piling-up of questions one after the other (*How much technology? Who does it? Is it the suppliers?*) (Basturkmen 2001: 10).

We would not expect students to be able to use these various discourse markers or repair strategies at all levels. On the contrary, we would expect them to develop their conversational skills as their English improves. However, students need to be aware of what real conversation looks like and we should give them help in using some of the more important phrases.

To raise their awareness, we can get students to analyse transcripts of real speech, directing their attention to how speakers ask questions, respond to the questions of others, etc. We can get them to transcribe small sections of authentic speech, too, and then ask them to produce a 'clean' version, i.e. as if the original piece of conversation had been written down without all the hesitations, false starts, etc. that characterise the actual transcription.

If we want to try to get students to use typical discourse markers and phrases, we can write them on strips of paper. Each student has to pick up one of the strips and they then have to use the phrase on it in conversation. We can see who manages to use the most phrases.

We can help our students to structure planned transactional (partly interactive) discourse, such as a lecture, by giving them language like this:

> *The important thing to grasp is that ...*
> *To begin with/And finally ...*
> *What I am trying to say is that ...*
> *What I mean is ...*
> *The point I am trying to make is that ...*
> *... or, to put it another way, ...*
> etc.

If students are going to give a presentation, they can be told to include this kind of structuring/reformulating language. We can provoke its use, too, by giving those who are listening role cards like these:

> Without speaking, show that you do not understand what the speaker is saying by looking confused, scratching your head in confusion, etc. However, only do this once.

> Without speaking, show that you do not agree with something the speaker is saying by looking angry, shaking your head, etc. However, only do this once.

A3 Functional language, adjacency pairs and fixed phrases

A lot of speaking is made of up of *fixed phrases* (or *lexical chunks* – see page 38) such as *Catch you later, Back in a sec, Can I call you back in a couple of minutes?* etc.

Fixed and semi-fixed phrases crop up a lot in functional exchanges (Chapter 2, B2). Thus, for example, we can offer people things, such as a drink, a coffee, etc., by saying *D'you fancy a ...? Would you like a ...? Shall I get you a ...?*

Many functional exchanges work well because they follow a set pattern. One such pattern is the *adjacency pair* (Cook 1989: 53–57). If someone approaches you and says *Nice day isn't it?* they expect a paired response, such as *Yes, isn't it.* If we say *D'you fancy a coffee?* the adjacency pair is either *Yes, please* or *No, thank you.*

When teaching speaking, we need to make students aware of fixed phrases, functional sequences and adjacency pairs. We can do this by teaching functional exchanges. We can have students look at transcripts of typical exchanges and we can let them watch film clips (see page 308) of this kind of language use.

B Students and speaking

Getting students to speak in class can sometimes be extremely easy. In a good class atmosphere, students who get on with each other, and whose English is at an appropriate level, will often participate freely and enthusiastically if we give them a suitable topic and task. However, at other times it is not so easy to get students going. Maybe the class mix is not quite right. Perhaps we have not chosen the right kind of topic Sometimes it is the organisation of the task which is at fault. But a problem that occurs more often than any of these is the natural reluctance of some students to speak and to take part. In such situations the role(s) that teachers play will be crucial.

B1 Reluctant students

Students are often reluctant to speak because they are shy and are not predisposed to expressing themselves in front of other people, especially when they are being asked to give personal information or opinions. Frequently, too, there is a worry about speaking badly and therefore losing face in front of their classmates. In such situations there are a number of things we can do to help.

- **Preparation:** when David Wilson was trying to use German while living in Austria, he found out something that most speakers of foreign languages know. If he was to go into a restaurant and order something, it was much better if he spent some time outside the restaurant, reading the menu and then rehearsing (in his head) what he was going to say. Then, when he went in and placed his order, he did it fluently and without panic (Wilson 2005).

Wilson is describing the value of planning and rehearsal for speaking success, and students, too, will perform much better if they have the chance to think about what they are going to say and how to say it. This may involve just giving them quiet time to think in their heads about how they will speak, or it may mean letting them practise dialogues in pairs before having to do anything more public.

Marc Helgesen suggests making a feature of this thinking-in-our-heads (that is trying out a conversation in our minds). He suggests a series of ten tasks that students can do on their own (Helgesen 2003). For example, when they are on a bus, they can imagine they are in a taxi and give the imaginary taxi driver directions. They can practise telling themselves about the best thing that happened to them today or tell the person in their head about their plans for the future.

Paul Mennim describes how students record presentations they are going to make, transcribe what they have said, correct it and then hand it over to the teacher for further comment before finally making the presentation (Mennim 2003).

At other times, where students are going to take part in a discussion, we can put them in buzz groups to brainstorm ideas so that they have something to say when the real discussion happens.

Of course, there will be times when we want and expect spontaneous production from students, but at other times we will allow them to prepare themselves for the speaking they are going to do.

- **The value of repetition:** as we saw in Chapter 3B, repetition has many beneficial effects. Each new encounter with a word or phrase helps to fix it in the student's memory. Repetition has other benefits, too: it allows students to improve on what they did before. They can think about how to re-word things or just get a feel for how it sounds.

  When students repeat speaking tasks they have already done once (or twice), their first attempt is like a rehearsal for the final effort. Each rehearsal gives them more confidence as they are not attempting to get the words out for the first time when they try to speak in subsequent 'performances'.

  Repetition works even better if students get a chance to analyse what they have already done. This analysis may come from fellow students or from the teacher, but if they get a chance to evaluate what they have done – or at least get feedback about it – their performance second or third time round can only get better. Paul Howarth (2001a and b) describes this as process speaking, characterised by the pattern:

  $$\text{plan} \rightarrow \text{perform} \rightarrow \text{analyse} \longleftrightarrow \text{repeat}$$

  If we ask students to make presentations (see page 351) or tell stories, repetition obviously makes sense in the same way as getting students to draft and re-draft their writing. But letting students rehearse conversational exchanges works, too. If students have had a chance to try out the exchange, they will do it much more confidently and fluently when they do it a second time.

- **Big groups, small groups:** a major reason for the reluctance of some students to take part in speaking activities is that they find themselves having to talk in front of a big group. A way of counteracting this is by making sure that they get chances to speak and interact in smaller groups, too. As we have seen, this can be preparation for dialogue-making or discussion.

- **Mandatory participation:** in a presentation at the 2004 IATEFL conference in Liverpool, UK, William Littlewood bemoaned the presence of 'social loafers' when groups do a task – that is students who sit back and let everyone else do the work (Littlewood 2004b). How, he wondered, could he ensure that all students were equally engaged in a task. He called one of his ideas 'numbered heads': in each group of four, for example, the students are asked to assign a number from 1 to 4 to each member, without telling the teacher who has which number. At the end of an activity, the teacher indicates a group and a number (1–4) and asks that student to report on what happened. Neither the teacher nor the students knows who will be called and, as a result, all the students have to stay on-task.

  Simon Mumford (2004: 35) suggests a 'speaking grid' (see Figure 1). We start by drawing a grid and writing the names of half of the students on the vertical axis, and half on the horizontal access. We now write the numbers 1–4 in the first column of the vertical axis and then write the numbers diagonally downwards (to the right). We put the number 4 at the top of the second column and then enter it diagonally, too. We write 3 at the top of the third column and 2 at the top of the fourth column.

  Students are told that each box in the grid represents two minutes' conversation: 60 seconds of A talking to B, 60 seconds of B talking to A, so according to the example grid, for the first minute Ahmet will talk to Suzanne and then for the next minute Suzanne will talk to Ahmet. Next, Ahmet will talk to Ali and Ali will talk to Ahmet, and then he will talk (and listen) to Maria (and so on). We now give students a topic (e.g. holidays, my family, what I hope for in the future or my favourite place). Students change places after we give a signal.

	Ahmet	Lucy	Pierre	Jane
Suzanne	1	4	3	2
Ali	2	1	4	3
Maria	3	2	1	4
John	4	3	2	1

FIGURE 1: The speaking grid

Mandatory participation also lies at the heart of jigsaw reading activities (see page 299) and story-circle writing (see page 337) since both these – and other similar activities – only work when all the students take part.

B2 The roles of the teacher

As with any other type of classroom procedure, teachers need to play a number of different roles (see Chapter 6, B1) during different speaking activities. However, three have particular relevance if we are trying to get students to speak fluently:

- **Prompter:** students sometimes get lost, can't think of what to say next or in some other way lose the fluency we expect of them. We can leave them to struggle out of such situations on their own, and indeed sometimes this may be the best option. However, we may be able to help them and the activity to progress by offering discrete suggestions. If this can be done supportively, without disrupting the discussion or forcing students out of role, it will stop the sense of frustration that some students feel when they come to a dead end of language or ideas.

- **Participant:** teachers should be good animators when asking students to produce language. Sometimes this can be achieved by setting up an activity clearly and with enthusiasm. At other times, however, teachers may want to participate in discussions or role-plays themselves. That way they can prompt covertly, introduce new information to help the activity along, ensure continuing student engagement and generally maintain a creative atmosphere. However, in such circumstances they have to be careful that they do not participate too much, thus dominating the speaking and drawing all the attention to themselves.

  There is one special sense in which teachers act as participants, and that is when they are in a dialogue with the class (see Chapter 4, A8). Just as one-to-one teachers may engage in direct conversation with their students (and co-construct dialogue, thereby scaffolding their learning), so in dialogic events in larger groups, the teacher and students may talk together communicatively as near-equal participants. These are often very special moments in the lesson, although we have to be careful not to take over the classroom so that students lose opportunities for speaking (see page 118).

- **Feedback provider:** the vexed question of when and how to give feedback in speaking activities is answered by considering carefully the effect of possible different approaches.

  When students are in the middle of a speaking task, over-correction may inhibit them and take the communicativeness out of the activity. On the other hand, helpful and gentle correction may get students out of difficult misunderstandings and hesitations. Everything depends upon our tact and the appropriacy of the feedback we give in particular situations.

  When students have completed an activity, it is vital that we allow them to assess what they have done and that we tell them what, in our opinion, went well. We will respond to the content of the activity as well as the language used. Feedback for oral fluency work is described in detail in Chapter 8, C3.

A crucial part of the teacher's job when organising speaking activities is to make sure that the students understand exactly what they are supposed to do. This involves giving clear instructions and, where appropriate, demonstrating the activity with a student or students so that no one is in any doubt about what they should be doing.

C Classroom speaking activities

Many of the classroom speaking activities which are currently in use fall at or near the communicative end of the communication continuum (see page 70). There are a number of widely-used categories of speaking activity, and we will start by looking at them before going on to specific speaking examples.

C1 Acting from a script

We can ask our students to act out scenes from plays and/or their coursebooks, sometimes filming the results. Students will often act out dialogues they have written themselves.

- **Playscripts:** it is important that when students are working on plays or playscripts, they should treat it as 'real' acting. In other words, we need to help them to go through the scripts as if we were theatre directors, drawing attention to appropriate stress, intonation and speed. This means that the lines they speak will have real meaning. By giving students practice in these things before they give their final performances, we ensure that acting out is both a learning and a language producing activity.

  Laura Miccoli made drama a main feature of her work with her adult students. They started with preliminary stages which included relaxing, breathing exercises and learning how to laugh with each other. During an intermediate stage they worked on such things as emotion, action, physicalisation, gesture and how to show crying and laughing. Finally, in the presentation stage they worked on the script itself. She found that using drama (and having students write about it in their portfolios) was motivating and provided 'transformative and emancipatory learning experiences' (Miccoli 2003: 128).

  Quite apart from the benefits for pronunciation and general language use, drama also helps, according to Mark Almond (2005: 10–12), to build student confidence, contextualise language, develop students' empathy for other characters, involve students in appropriate problem-solving and engage them as 'whole' people (that is marrying emotional and intellectual characteristics of their personalities). He points out that drama practises gesture, facial expression, eye contact and movement, proxemics and prosody.

- **Acting out dialogues:** when choosing who should come out to the front of the class, we should be careful not to choose the shyest students first. We need to work to create the right kind of supportive atmosphere in the class. We need to give students time to rehearse their dialogues before they are asked to perform them. If we can give students time to work on their dialogues, they will gain much more from the whole experience.

 Communication games

There are many communication games, all of which aim to get students talking as quickly and fluently as possible. Two particular categories are worth mentioning here:

- **Information-gap games:** many games depend on an information gap: one student has to talk to a partner in order to solve a puzzle, draw a picture (describe and draw), put things in the right order (describe and arrange) or find similarities and differences between pictures. There is an example of this type of communication game on page 357.

- **Television and radio games:** when imported into the classroom, games from radio and TV often provide good fluency activities, as the following examples demonstrate. In 'Twenty questions' the chairperson thinks of an object and tells a team that the object is either animal, vegetable or mineral – or a combination of two or three of these. The team has to find out what the object is asking only *yes/no* questions, such as *Can you use it in the kitchen?* or *Is it bigger than a person?* They get points if they guess the answer in 20 questions or fewer.

  'Just a minute' is a long-running comedy contest on UK radio. Each participant has to speak for 60 seconds on a subject they are given by the chairperson without hesitation, repetition or deviation. In the radio show, as in the classroom, 'deviation' consists of language mistakes as well as wandering off the topic. If another contestant hears any of these, he or she interrupts, gets a point and carries on with the subject. The person who is speaking at the end of 60 seconds gets two points.

'Call my bluff' involves two teams. Team A is given a word that members of the other team are unlikely to know. Team A finds a correct dictionary definition of the word and then makes up two false ones. They read out their definitions and Team B has to guess which is the correct one. Now Team B is given a word and reads out three definitions of their word (one correct and two false) and Team A has to guess.

There are two more TV-inspired games in the examples below.

In other games, different tricks or devices are used to make fluent speaking amusing. In 'Fishbowl', for example, two students speak on any topic they like, but at a pre-arranged signal one of them has to reach into a fishbowl and take out one of the many pieces of paper on which students have previously written phrases, questions and sentences. They have to incorporate whatever is on the paper into the conversation straight away.

C3 Discussion

Discussions range from highly formal, whole-group staged events to informal small-group interactions.

- **Buzz groups:** these can be used for a whole range of discussions. For example, we might want students to predict the content of a reading text, or we may want them to talk about their reactions to it after they have read it. We might want them to discuss what should be included in a news broadcast or have a quick conversation about the right kind of music for a wedding or party.

- **Instant comment:** another way in which we can train students to respond fluently and immediately is to insert 'instant comment' mini-activities into lessons. This involves showing them photographs or introducing topics at any stage of a lesson and nominating students to say the first thing that comes into their head.

- **Formal debates:** in a formal debate, students prepare arguments in favour or against various propositions. When the debate starts, those who are appointed as 'panel speakers' produce well-rehearsed 'writing-like' arguments, whereas others, the audience, pitch in as the debate progresses with their own (less scripted) thoughts on the subject.

  In order for debates to be successful, students need to be given time to plan their arguments, often in groups. They can be directed to a series of points of view either for or against a proposition – or sent to websites where they will get 'ammunition' for their point of view. Webquests (see page 191) are often good ways of preparing students for debates. The teacher can divide the class into groups and then give links to different websites to the different groups.

  It is a good idea to allow students to practise their speeches in their groups first. This will allow them to get a feel for what they are going to say. There is an example of a formal debate on page 358.

  A popular debating game which has survived many decades of use is the 'balloon debate', so called because it is based on a scenario in which a number of people are travelling in the basket of a hot-air balloon. Unfortunately, however, there is a leak and the balloon cannot take their weight: unless someone leaves the balloon, they will all die. Students take on the role of a real-life person, either living or historical – from Confucius to Shakespeare, from Cleopatra to Marie Curie. They think up arguments about why they should be the survivors, either individually or in pairs or groups. After a first round of argument, everyone votes on who should be the first to jump. As more air escapes, a second round means that one more person has to go, until, some rounds later, the eventual sole survivor is chosen.

Participants in a balloon debate can represent occupations rather than specific characters; they can also take on the roles of different age-groups, hobby-enthusiasts or societies.

- **Unplanned discussion:** some discussions just happen in the middle of lessons; they are unprepared for by the teacher, but, if encouraged, can provide some of the most enjoyable and productive speaking in language classes (see Chapter 21, A2). Their success will depend upon our ability to prompt and encourage and, perhaps, to change our attitude to errors and mistakes (see Chapter 8C) from one minute to the next. Pre-planned discussions, on the other hand, depend for their success upon the way we ask students to approach the task in hand.

- **Reaching a consensus:** one of the best ways of encouraging discussion is to provide activities which force students to reach a decision or a consensus, often as a result of choosing between specific alternatives. An example of this kind of activity (with particular relevance to schools) is where students consider a scenario in which an invigilator during a public exam catches a student copying from hidden notes. The class has to decide between a range of options, such as:

> The invigilator should ignore it.
> She should give the student a sign to show that she's seen (so that the student will stop).
> She should call the family and tell them the student was cheating.
> She should inform the examining board so that the student will not be able to take that exam again.

The fact of having to make such an awkward choice gives the discussion a clear purpose and an obvious outcome to aim for.

C4 Prepared talks

One popular kind of activity is the prepared talk, where a student (or students) makes a presentation on a topic of their own choice. Such talks are not designed for informal spontaneous conversation; because they are prepared, they are more 'writing-like' than this. However, if possible, students should speak from notes rather than from a script.

For students to benefit from doing oral presentations, we need to invest some time in the procedures and processes they are involved in. In the first place, we need to give them time to prepare their talks (and help in preparing them, if necessary). Then students need a chance to rehearse their presentations. This can often be done by getting them to present to each other in pairs or small groups first. The teacher and the class can decide together on criteria for what makes a good presentation and the listener in each pair can then give feedback on what the speaker has said. The presenter will then be in a good position to make a better presentation. However, this only works if students have had a chance to discuss feedback criteria first.

When a student makes a presentation, it is important that we give other students tasks to carry out as they listen. Maybe they will be the kind of feedback tasks we have just described. Perhaps they will involve the students in asking follow-up questions. The point is that presentations have to involve active listening as well as active speaking.

Whether or not feedback comes from the teacher, the students or a combination of both, it is important that students who have made an oral presentation get a chance to analyse what they have done, and then, if possible, repeat it again in another setting so that they do it better.

C5 Questionnaires

Questionnaires are useful because, by being pre-planned, they ensure that both questioner and respondent have something to say to each other. Depending upon how tightly designed they are, they may well encourage the natural use of certain repetitive language patterns – and thus can be situated in the middle of our communication continuum.

Students can design questionnaires on any topic that is appropriate. As they do so, the teacher can act as a resource, helping them in the design process. The results obtained from questionnaires can then form the basis for written work, discussions or prepared talks. There is an example of a questionnaire on page 354.

C6 Simulation and role-play

Many students derive great benefit from simulation and role-play. Students simulate a real-life encounter (such as a business meeting, an interview or a conversation in an aeroplane cabin, a hotel foyer, a shop or a cafeteria) as if they were doing so in the real world. They can act out the simulation as themselves or take on the role of a completely different character and express thoughts and feelings they do not necessarily share. When we give students these roles, we call the simulation a role-play. Thus we might tell a student *You are a motorist who thinks that parking restrictions are unnecessary* or *You are Michelle and you want Robin to notice you, but you don't want him to know about your brother*, etc.

Simulation and role-play can be used to encourage general oral fluency or to train students for specific situations, especially where they are studying English for specific purposes (ESP).

When students are doing simulations and role-plays, they need to know exactly what the situation is, and they need to be given enough information about the background for them to function properly. Of course, we will allow them to be as creative as possible, but if they have almost no information, they may find this very difficult to do.

With more elaborate simulations, such as business meetings, mock enquiries or TV programmes, for example, we will want to spend some time creating the environment or the procedures for the simulation. Of course, the environment may be in the teacher's and the students' heads, but we want to create it, nevertheless.

Simulations and role-plays often work well when participants have to come to some kind of a decision. In one such intermediate-level activity ('Knife in the school') a boy has brought a large hunting knife into a school and the boy, his parents, the head teacher and class teacher have a meeting to decide what must be done about it. The students take the role of one of these characters based on a role card which tells them how they feel (e.g. *Jo Glassman, teacher: Two of your pupils, Sean and Cathy, told you that they had seen the knife but are afraid to confront Brian about it. You believe them absolutely but didn't actually see the knife yourself. However, you don't want Brian to know that Sean and Cathy are responsible for this meeting. You want to see Brian suspended from the school*). In groups of five, the students role-play the meeting, and at the end different groups discuss the decisions they have come to.

Clearly 'Knife in the school' might be inappropriate in some situations, but other role-plays such as planning meetings, television 'issue' shows and public protest meetings are fairly easy to replicate in the classroom.

In a different kind of role-playing activity, students write the kind of questions they might ask someone when they meet them for the first time. They are then given postcards or copies of paintings by famous artists, such as Goya, and are asked to answer those questions as if they were characters from the painting (Cranmer 1996: 68–72). The same kind of imaginative interview role-play could be based around people in dramatic photographs.

Simulation and role-play have recently gone through a period of relative unpopularity, yet this is a pity since they have three distinct advantages. In the first place, they can be good fun and are thus motivating. Secondly, they allow hesitant students to be more forthright in their opinions and behaviour without having to take responsibility for what they say in the way that they do when they are speaking for themselves. Thirdly, by broadening the world of the classroom to include the world outside, they allow students to use a much wider range of language than some more task-centred activities may do (see Chapter 4, A6). There is an example of a role-play on page 359.

D Speaking lesson sequences

In the following examples, the speaking activity is specified, together with its particular focus.

Example 1: Experts	Activity: communication game
	Focus: controlled language processing
	Age: any
	Level: elementary and above

The following game-like activity, based on a London 'Comedy Store' routine, is used by the writer Ken Wilson (Wilson 1997) for getting students to think and speak quickly.

The class chooses four or five students to be a panel of 'experts'. They come and sit in a row facing the class. The class then chooses a subject that these students are going to have to be experts on. This can be anything, from transport policy to film music, from fish to football. In pairs or groups, the class write down the questions they want to ask the experts about this particular subject. The teacher can go round the class checking the questions as they do this. Finally, once the questions have been written, they are put to the experts.

The element of this activity that makes it amusing is that each expert only says one word at a time, so the sentence is only gradually built up. Because the experts often can't think of how to continue it, it can ramble on in ever more extreme contortions until someone is lucky enough or clever enough to be in a position to finish it (with just one word). The following example shows how it might begin:

Question:	*How do fish breathe?*
Expert 1	*The*
Expert 2	*answer*
Expert 3	*to*
Expert 4	*this*
Expert 1	*question*
Expert 2	*is*
Expert 3	*an*
Expert 4	*answer*
Expert 1	*that ... etc.*

'Experts' encourages even reluctant speakers on the panel to speak, even if (or perhaps because) they only have to produce one word at a time. It keeps both experts and questioners engaged in the construction of utterances in a controlled but often surreal environment.

Example 2: Films	Activity: questionnaire
	Focus: lexis and grammar; interacting with others
	Age: young adult and above
	Level: lower intermediate and above

In this sequence, the class have recently been working on the contrasting uses of the present perfect and the past simple.

The activity starts when the teacher talks to the students about the five or six most popular films that are currently on show or which have been extremely popular in the last six months or a year. They are then told that they are going to find out which of these films is the most popular in the class.

The teacher hands out the following questionnaire form – or writes it on the board and has the students copy it. They put the names of the films they have discussed in the left-hand column.

Name of film	Tick if seen	Good (✓✓), satisfactory (✓), bad (✗) or very bad (✗✗)

The class now discuss the kinds of questions they can use, e.g. *Have you seen X? What did you think of it?* In pairs, students now interview each other and ask if they have seen any of the films and what they thought of them. They complete the charts about their partner.

The teacher now gets a student up to the board and asks them to fill in the chart based on what the other students have found out, e.g. *How many people have seen X?* and *How many people thought that X was very good?* This can then lead on to a discussion of the films in question. Students can be encouraged to say which was the best part of one of the films, who their favourite actors are, etc. The results of the questionnaires can be put on the board.

Questionnaires are often the first stage in much longer sequences, leading on to written reports and discussions. In this case, for example, students can use the questionnaire results for discussion or to write their own 'film page' for a real or imagined magazine.

Example 3: My home town	Activity:	communication game
	Focus:	lexis and grammar; language processing; information processing
	Age:	any
	Level:	elementary

In this activity, from Hadfield (1997), the whole class is involved in a matching game which involves reading and talking to others in order to solve a puzzle.

The words which students need to know in order to play this game include *north*, *south*, *east*, *west* and various places such as *university*, *cathedral*, *shopping centre*, *port* and *seaside*. The teacher makes sure that the students know them before the activity starts.

The teacher makes copies of a map of Britain in which eight towns are marked with a dot but not named. Students are also given eight town maps of which the following are the first two:

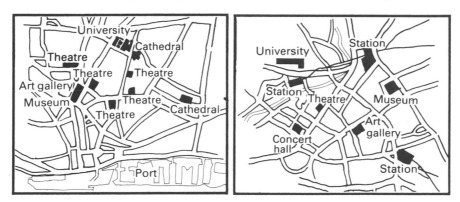

Individual students are then each given one of eight written town descriptions, such as the following:

> You come from Liverpool. Liverpool is a large port in the north-west of England. It has a university, two cathedrals, an art gallery, a museum and five theatres.

> You come from Manchester. Manchester is an industrial town in the north of England. It has a university, a concert hall, a theatre, a museum, an art gallery and three stations.

Based on the information on their card, each student now writes the name of their town in the correct place on the map, and draws a line between that place and the appropriate town plan.

The teacher then collects all the place description cards back from the students. They now have to go round the class asking each other about their towns without looking at anyone else's map. The game finishes when each student has a complete set of place names with lines linking them to the correct plans.

This game will obviously work best with students who do not have extensive knowledge of Britain and are interested in learning more. However, it can easily be adapted to make it relevant to other groups, as the author suggests, by making it about other countries. Students can even create their own imaginary countries.

'My home town' uses an information gap to create the necessary conditions for communication but shares the information around many more than two people.

Example 4: Whose line is it anyway?	Activity: improvisation game
	Focus: language processing; interacting with others
	Age: young adult and above
	Level: upper intermediate and above

'Whose line is it anyway?', taken from a British Channel 4 television game, is a challenging exercise for students.

Two students come to the front of the class. The teacher asks the rest of the class to say *who* each of the students is (e.g. police officer, nurse, teacher, president) and chooses the most interesting and communicatively generative suggestions. The pair of students might now represent a police officer and a midwife – or any other combination of occupations.

The teacher then asks the students *where* a conversation between these two is taking place; they might suggest a café, the street, a cinema or a beach. Finally, the teacher asks the students *what* they are talking about. It could be speeding, nuclear physics, childcare, a film they've both seen or football or anything else. The pair at the front might now be a police officer and a midwife on a beach talking about speeding.

The two students playing the game have to improvise a conversation straight away. They win points based on how well they manage. As an added twist, the teacher can give one of the participants a card with a word describing how they speak, e.g. *politely*, *angrily*, *ingratiatingly*, and when the conversation is over, the rest of the class have to guess what word that participant was given.

The game does not have to be quite so brutal, however. Students can practise the conversations in pairs before coming up to the front. Everything depends upon the teacher–student relationship and the relationship which the students have with each other.

A similar (but less taxing) game is called 'Royal banquet' (Mumford 2004). Here students sit along the sides of a table. The top couple are the king and queen, the others their courtiers. When the king and queen choose a topic, everyone (in their pairs across the table) must talk about the same topic. If the king and queen change the topic, all the courtiers have to change the topic, too. This can be extremely amusing (and, of course, the teacher can feed topics to the king and queen). All the couples not only have to engage in conversation, but also keep their ears open to make sure they know what the couple nearest the king and queen are talking about.

Example 5: London map	Activity: information gap
	Focus: finding the differences between two pieces of information
	Age: adult
	Level: upper intermediate

The following sequence is designed to get students talking in detail about the differences between two maps. It demands quite a lot of language from the students and significant attention to detail. It uses maps of London, but we could equally well use maps of any other city or place that the students have some familiarity with or are living in.

The activity starts when students are given two minutes to write down as many sights of London as they can. If they have access to the Internet, they can have a quick search, or they can look at a tourist guide or any other reference work. The point is for them to have to scan very quickly.

Students are put in pairs. In each pair one student is A and the other student is B. They are told that they are going to look at maps of London. But we make sure that they realise that they may not show their maps to each other. Student A is given map A and Student B is given map B. We tell them that some of the differences may be in the pictures, but others are in the writing.

Map A

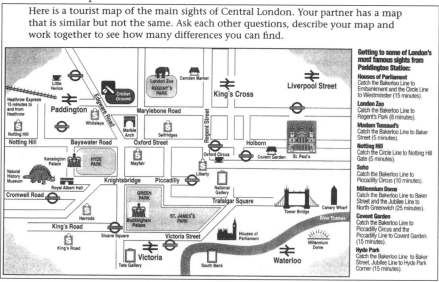

Map B

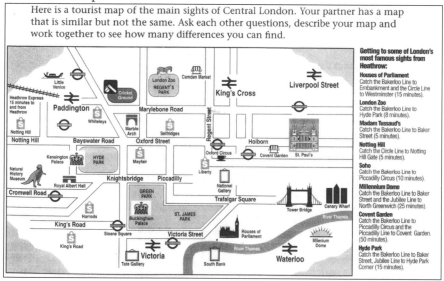

From *Pair Work Book* 3 by P Watkin Jones and D Howard-Williams (Penguin Books)

Example 6: Time capsule	Activity:	decision-making
	Focus:	information processing; interacting with others
	Age:	teenage and above
	Level:	elementary and above

A practice that is not uncommon is that of burying time capsules containing artefacts of contemporary life which, if they are found a thousand years from now, will give the finder some idea of what life was like today. In this sequence, students are told that they have a box about the size of a small suitcase. They must fill this with the largest number of things which best exemplify life today. They do not have to worry about the cost or the weight of an object, but they do have to choose things which, together, fit into the box.

The class starts with a general discussion in which the teacher and the class discuss the kinds of material which exemplify a society. Perhaps they will talk about music, books, plants, architecture, modern inventions, photography, art, teenage culture, cars, foods, etc.

When they have done this, the teacher gets students into pairs or small groups. In a short space of time (which the teacher should set and keep to) they have to make a list of everything they would like to include, however crazy. No one's suggestion is rejected at this stage.

The teacher now gets two pairs (or two small groups) to work together. They have to share their ideas, only this time they have to pare down their lists so that the items will all fit into the box. Once again, they have a short time limit for their decision-making. While they are discussing the issues that this task raises, the teacher goes round the groups, listening to what is being said and noting any points that may be worth bringing to the attention of the whole class. Where necessary, the teacher should encourage students to speak in English rather than reverting to their own language (see Chapter 7, D4).

When the groups have made their choices, the whole class listens to the suggestions and comes to a decision about the class time capsule. The teacher may want to feed in ideas or suggestions which he or she heard while going round the class. Later the teacher and class can discuss any language problems that came up during this activity.

Example 7: The debate	Activity: discussion; making speeches
	Focus: making a compelling argument
	Age: young adult plus
	Level: intermediate

In the following activity, students are going to debate a serious topic, arguing as well as they can for and against a certain point of view. The activity occurs during work on the topic of holidays.

Students are told that they are going to debate the statement 'Tourism is bad for the world'. We can start the sequence by inviting them to give any opinions on the subject so that the topic gets an airing. Perhaps we can put them into small buzz groups first just to give them time to think around the topic.

The class is now divided into two teams. In Team A students are told they should agree with the motion and in Team B they are told they should disagree with it. Point out that they will be given an opportunity to air their real views later but that debating is all about how well we argue a case.

The teams try to come up with as many arguments as they can. Perhaps they can look up facts on the Internet. If not, we can feed in arguments, e.g.

Tourism is a bad thing
- According to scientists, 15% of all greenhouse gasses will come from aeroplanes by 2050.
- Water is diverted from agricultural/poor areas to feed tourist centres.
- Tourism generates rubbish.
- Tourism destroys the countryside and pushes wildlife away.
- Tourism destroys traditional ways of life, etc.

Tourism is a good thing
- Tourism is fun.
- It's the world's largest industry.
- Tourism provides employment to many who otherwise would have no jobs.
- When tourism is restricted, only the rich can travel.
- Everyone needs a chance to relax, etc.

Students get a chance to rehearse their arguments in their teams. While they are doing this, we can go round monitoring what they are doing, offering suggestions and helping out with any language difficulties they may be having.

We can now select a proposer and a seconder, and an opposer and his or her seconder. The proposer must speak for two or three minutes, and the opposer then has the chance to state their case for the same amount of time. Now the seconders speak in their turn, probably for slightly less time (it helps if we are quite strict with the timing).

Now the subject is opened up for anyone to make their points. Once again, we may impose a time limit on their offerings.

Finally, the proposer and opposer make a short closing speech and then everyone votes on whether they agree with the motion or not. Perhaps the best way to ensure that this all works well is to have the teacher as the debate organiser and controller. But perhaps not! If a student controls the debate, it will give him or her a good role and allow the teacher to prompt students who are having trouble from the sidelines. Alternatively, we can make this into a TV-style debate, and give different students from both Team A and Team B different roles, such as an airline executive, a travel writer, an environmentalist, a holidaymaker, a hotel employee, a local fisherman, a politician and a travel agent. Each one can now use the arguments they have come up with, but from the point of view of the role they are playing.

Example 8: Travel agent	Activity: role-play
	Focus: interacting with others; information processing
	Age: any
	Level: intermediate and above

In this example, an information gap is created which gives the role-play a genuinely communicative dimension. The students have been working on the area of tourism. They are told that in pairs they are going to act out a scene in a travel agency where one student is a customer and the other is a travel agent. Student A is given the following information:

A Customer	
	• a double room
	• to go to a hotel in Miami for 7 nights. You can spend up to $1,400 on a hotel.
	• to be as near as possible to the city centre
You want	• to go to a hotel with a good discotheque
	• a children's swimming pool for your small son
	• someone to be available to look after your son at the hotel
	• the hotel to serve good food
	• a comfortable room (with a good view)

Student B gets the following hotel information. He or she can show it to the customer if necessary, but will probably have more success by explaining it.

B Travel agent

Study the following information carefully so that you can answer **A** (the customer).

	Sun Inn	Regency Park	Paradiso	Oasis
Cost (double) per night	$180	$175	$210	$130
View	☺	☺☺	☺☺☺	☺☺
Distance from centre	10 miles	12 miles	20 miles	3 miles
Disco	☺	☺☺	☺☺☺	—
Restaurant	☺☺	☺☺☺	☺☺☺	
Swimming pool				
Adults' swimming pool	☺☺☺	☺	☺☺	☺
Children's swimming pool	☺	☺☺	☺☺☺	—
Childcare facilities	—	☺☺	☺	—

Note: Various features (e.g. view, discos, restaurants, etc.) have been given different 'smile' ratings to indicate quality.

☺☺☺ = excellent, ☺☺ = very good, and ☺ = good.

As an example we can say that you get a better view if you're staying at the Paradiso than you do if you are staying at the Regency Park.

Students are given time to study their information. The teacher points out that the customer needs to select the hotel based, as far as possible, on the six qualities they want.

While students act out the scene in pairs, we can go round listening, prompting if necessary and recording examples of especially good or not very successful language use.

When the pairs have completed their role-plays, we can have them compare what happened. Did all the customers choose the Regency Park (the hotel which most closely matches the customer's needs)? What did they find difficult/easy? We can then discuss things we heard which went well – and not so well.

Example 9: The interview	Activity:	simulation
	Focus:	interacting with others; lexis and grammar; process language
	Age:	adult
	Level:	intermediate and above

In this sequence, students simulate an interview for a middle management post in a big company. We start by discussing with the class general interview issues such as the relationship between silence (on the part of interviewer and interviewee) and rising tension, and the importance of the first minutes of an interview when lasting impressions are created. We can get the students to predict some of the standard questions that usually come up, such as *Why do you want this job? Why do you want to leave the job you are in?* and *What special qualities do you have that would make you a suitable candidate for this post?* There are also the *What would you do if ...?* questions where the interviewer gives the candidate a hypothetical situation to respond to. Sometimes interviewers also ask 'best' and 'worst' questions such as *What is the best decision you have ever made and why?* We can agree with our students that good interviewees are able to tell stories of their past experience which exemplify the answers they are trying to give.

We can help our 'interviewees' by working on a variety of language phrases and chunks which will be useful to structure the discourse for this particular kind of activity (see A2 above). For example, they may want to buy time when they can't think of an immediate answer to a question. We can introduce language such as the following and, if necessary, have students try it out in a quick controlled practice activity (see Chapter 12, B2):

> That's quite a difficult question. Could you repeat it, please.
> I'm not sure if I understand your question.
> I think I'd need time to think about that.

Or we can have students look at and practise other good interview phrases such as:

> I think the best example of what I am talking about is/was ...
> Well, it's difficult to be specific, but ...
> I'm really pleased that you asked me that because ...
> One of things that attracted me to this post was ...

We now put students in two groups. In the first, the 'interviewers' group, the students write as many questions as they can think of for the particular interview in question. The 'interviewees' group try to predict what questions they will be asked.

The interviews now take place, either in groups or with the whole class watching one interview, after which we can give feedback on how well the questions were asked, how well the interviewee managed to deal with them and whether the right kind of language was used. Our simulation has provided not only an opportunity for rehearsal, but also the opportunity for the teaching of specific process language.

E Making recordings

The activities in this section suggest ways in which the camera (and/or the microphone) can become a central learning aid, as a result of which students work cooperatively together using a wide variety of language both in the process and the product of making a video or audio recording. Where sophisticated editing facilities are available and there are trained sound or film personnel on the premises, high production values can be achieved. But that is not the main point of these activities: a lot can be achieved with just a hand-held camera and a playback monitor.

Example 10: News bulletin	Activity:	presenting information clearly
	Age:	young adult and above
	Level:	elementary and above

News bulletins are especially interesting for students of English, not only because they will want to be able to understand the news in English, but also because news broadcasts have special formats and use recognisable language patterns. Recognition of such formats allows teachers to ask students to put their own bulletins together, based on the news from today's papers or on stories which they have been studying. How would television news present the deaths of Romeo and Juliet, the Spanish conquest of Mexico or the demise of Captain Ahab in his pursuit of the great whale?

Students can first watch news bulletins and analyse the language that is particular to this genre (for example, passive usage, the use of the present simple to tell stories, and the way in which speech is reported). In small groups, they then choose the stories they wish to tell and the order in which they wish to tell them. After writing the script – and editing it with the help of the teacher – they film their broadcasts; these are then watched by their classmates and by the teacher, who can lead the feedback session which ensues.

We can also have students record their own political broadcasts, advertisements or role-plays (especially where we ask them to simulate a typical TV format such as a topical debate show).

Example 11: Put it on screen	Activity:	filming a scene
	Focus:	acting from a script; interpreting text
	Age:	any
	Level:	any

When students read a story, study an extract from a novel or work with a coursebook dialogue, they form some kind of mental picture of what they are understanding. This ranges from a perception of the setting to an idea of what the characters look and sound like.

A way of really getting inside the text is to have students film the scene they have just read. If they are studying a textbook dialogue, for example, we might tell them that they should disregard the textbook illustration and focus on the words and situation only. With these in mind, they should plan and film their own versions of the text. On the other hand, we might encourage them to change aspects of the dialogue – the ending perhaps – so that even a textbook dialogue becomes their own.

Any text which involves human interaction can be exploited in this way. For example, would it be possible to film Robert O'Connor's first nerve-wracking class in the prison (Example 1, page 289)?

Filming a scene involves discussion about acting and direction and a close focus on the text in question. However, despite possible problems of logistics and time, the results can be extremely satisfying, and the activity itself highly motivating.

E1 Getting everyone involved

Because filming usually involves one camera operator and may be confined to one narrator and one overall director, there is a danger that some students may get left out of the video-making process. However, there are ways of avoiding this danger.

- **The group:** if more than one video camera is available, we can divide a class into groups. That way each member of each group has a function.

- **Process:** we can ensure participation in the decision-making process by insisting that no roles (such as actor, camera operator, director) are chosen until the last moment.

- **Assigning roles:** we can assign a number of different roles as in a real film crew. This includes such jobs as clapperboard operator, script consultant, lighting and costumes.

Chapter notes and further reading

- **Students analyse audioscripts**
  P Sayer (2005) noticed significant improvement in student speaking skills after the students had looked at transcripts and identified conversation strategies.

- **Shy students**
  See R Simunkova (2004). D Shinji Kondon and Y Ying-Ling (2004) examine strategies that students in Japan use to cope with language anxiety.

- **Teacher roles**
  On intervention during communication activities, see T Lynch (1997).

- **Discussion**
  P Ur (1981) is still a classic account of different discussion and speaking task activities. On developing discussion skills, see C Green *et al* (1997). See also B Deacon (2000) and K Harris (2002), who in a very short article writes 'in praise of whole class discussion'.

- **Drama**
  Apart from M Almond (2005), already mentioned, one of the most popular books on using drama, A Maley and A Duff (2005), is now in its third edition. See also B Bowler (2002) and A G Elgar (2002).

- **Games**
  See A Wright *et al* (2006).

- **Debate**
  On 'democratic debates' (with the students choosing the topic), see P Capone and K Hayward (1996).

- **Prepared talks**
  On student lectures see M Geldicke (1997). See also P Brown (2005), and T Edwards (2005) on poster presentations. C Mei Lin Ho (2004) argues for the viva (the oral defence of a written project).

- **Role-play and simulation**
  For an exceptional (historical) account of role-play and simulation, see K Jones (1982) (see A3 above), which includes a wonderful simulation about simulations for teachers. However, A Al-Arishi (1994) sees reasons why role-play should not be widely used.

- **Speaking sequences**
  For more speaking activity ideas, see J Harmer (2007: Chapter 9) and S Thornbury (2005a: Chapters 5 and 6). S Burgess and K Head (2005: Chapter 7) discuss teaching speaking for exams.

21 | Planning lessons

A The planning paradox

In an article some years ago, the trainer Craig Thaine described how he and his colleagues increased the emphasis on timetabling and lesson planning in their teacher training programmes. In particular, he asked participants in a methods course to design a three-day timetable sequence of five hours a day. This was because he was concerned that teacher training courses 'were often not adequately preparing candidates in the very useful skill of timetabling in daily, weekly or monthly blocks' (1996a: 7). Reactions to this extra focus on timetabling were, he reported, extremely positive both from tutors and from the trainees themselves.

In an extraordinary outburst in response this article, however, Mario Rinvolucri questioned the very assumptions on which Craig Thaine's article was based. It is worth quoting a somewhat florid paragraph from his open letter to the journal in which the article had appeared:

> The assumption behind your article seems to be that a teacher on Sunday evening should know what ... she will be doing with her class on Friday morning, five lessons on. The assumption fills me with a mixture of amazement and hilarity. How can I possibly, on a Sunday evening, know what will make sense to me and to at least some in my learning group the following Friday morning? ... Why do you consciously teach your trainees to elaborate mental structures that ignore their flesh-and-blood, here-and-now learners?
>
> (Rinvolucri 1996: 3)

Rinvolucri's concerns are echoed by David Mallows, who points out that what actually happens in a lesson is the result of an interactive system that is extremely complex. In other words, as the lesson progresses (as students interact with their teacher and with the language they are studying), things evolve and develop, depending on what has happened and what is happening minute by minute. Yet by encouraging teachers to plan lessons 'with essentially linear aims', we might be 'producing teachers who are unaware of the complex patterns that are woven in the interaction between learners and the language to which they are exposed, and which they produce' (2002: 8).

This, then, is the planning paradox. On the one hand, it makes no sense to go into any situation without having thought about what we are going to do. Yet at the same time, if we pre-determine what is going to happen before it has taken place, we may be in danger not only of missing what is right in front of us but, more importantly, we may also be closing off avenues of possible evolution and development.

In his reply to Mario Rinvolucri's letter, Craig Thaine pointed out that for inexperienced teachers, a plan – a mental structure – 'might be just the map we need initially' (Thaine 1996b: 3). New teachers, especially, need maps to help them through the landscape. And students, too, like to know what their teacher has in store for them. Evidence of teacher planning helps to ensure their confidence in the person who is teaching them. A complete failure to plan may seem irresponsible to both students and others.

The planning continuum

Whatever our reaction to the planning paradox, however, the fact remains that most teachers do think about what they are going to teach before they go into the lesson. Tessa Woodward, for example, could not think of a single teacher in all the staff rooms she had worked in who had not done 'some thinking and preparing before class' (Woodward 2002: 25).

Jim Scrivener, on the other hand, describes a situation where the teacher has no real idea what he or she is going to do before a lesson starts and where, as a result, the lesson is created moment by moment with the teacher and the learners working with whatever is happening in the room. He calls this a 'jungle path' lesson. He gives an example of the teacher walking into a classroom and asking *How was the weekend?* and, after listening to a number of answers, provoking a discussion based on what has been said. At some point the teacher may then select particular items of language that have emerged and invent instant exercises that will help students work on them (Scrivener 2005: 132). Far from being lazy or artless, he suggests, such teaching demands high skill and an ability to react appropriately minute by minute. Interestingly, this kind of lesson mirrors the Dogme proposal we discussed on page 75. But once again, it is worth pointing out that in most educational contexts, a succession of jungle path lessons will suggest to the students a degree of carelessness – or even negligence – on the part of the unprepared teacher.

At the other end of the spectrum, teachers on training courses who are about to be observed tend to produce elaborate plans of the kind we will discuss in Section B below. This is partly to give themselves confidence that they have done their best to plan for any eventuality (though of course that may be impossible – see above), but also because a detailed plan gives the observer clear evidence of the thinking that has gone into the making of the lesson.

Some teachers allow the coursebook to do the planning for them; they take in a lesson or unit and teach it exactly as it is offered in the book (though in reality, most teachers will look at the book lesson before they take it into class).

Some teachers scribble a few notes down in folders or notebooks. Perhaps these might consist of the name of an activity (e.g. different holidays – discussion), or some language (e.g. inviting). Sometimes the notes will be more elaborate than this.

Occasionally, teachers do some kind of vague 'corridor planning' in their head as they walk towards the class. Even when teachers don't make notes or write a decent plan, they generally have ideas in their head anyway.

Except in formal assessment situations, the actual form that a plan takes is less important than the thought that has gone into it; the overriding principle is that we should have an idea of what we hope our students will achieve in the class, and that this should guide our decisions about how to bring it about. At the very least, we should have what has been called 'a door into and a door out of the lesson' (Harmer 2005: 169). Where written plans act as a useful record of what we hoped to achieve, and where we amend these records (after the lesson) to say what actually happened, they become effective accounts which we can use for action research (see Chapter 24B).

Using plans in class

Planning a lesson is not the same as scripting a lesson. Lessons are not plays where students and their teacher have to remember and reproduce words in a pre-ordained sequence. Nor are they like western classical music where all the notes have to be played exactly as they are written. A better metaphor for a lesson, perhaps, would be jazz, where from an original chord sequence the players improvise their own melodies, inventing their own twists and turns so that they arrive at their own destinations by their own routes. What we take into the lesson, in other words, is a proposal for action, rather than a lesson blueprint to be followed slavishly. And once we put our proposal for action *into action,* all sorts of things might happen, quite a few of which we might not have anticipated. Classrooms are dynamic environments and, as we said on page 364, a lesson is an interactive event in which people react with each other and with the language.

Although, especially for teachers in training, it is a good idea to try to follow the plan that we have made, nevertheless in normal teaching there are a number of reasons why we may need to modify our proposal for action once a lesson is taking place:

- **Magic moments:** some of the most affecting moments in language lessons happen when a conversation develops unexpectedly or when a topic produces a level of interest in our students which we had not predicted. This is the moment when students suddenly really want to talk about the topic, or when one of them says something that, even if it falls outside the plan, is so extraordinary, challenging or amusing, that everyone, including ourselves, wants to discuss it or follow it up.

  When such magic moments come along, we have to make (often instant) decisions about what to do. We could, of course, carry on with our planned lesson as if the moment had never occurred. Yet that might not only waste a golden opportunity for real communication, but might also demonstrate to the students that we are not really respecting them and listening to them in the ways we suggested were so important for successful rapport (see Chapter 6C). A better course is to recognise the magic moment and see how it can be used, rather than denying it life because it does not fit into our plan.

- **Sensible diversion:** sometimes non-magical things happen which cause us to wonder what to do next. For example, students might start trying to use some new grammar or vocabulary which we had not planned to introduce. Yet this suddenly seems like an ideal moment to do some work on the language which has arisen, and so we take a diversion and teach something we had not intended to teach. This is the opportunistic teaching we discussed on page 201.

- **Unforeseen problems:** however well we plan, unforeseen problems often crop up. Some students may find an activity that we thought interesting incredibly boring; an activity may take more or less time than we anticipated. It is possible that something we thought would be fairly simple for our students turns out to be very difficult (or vice versa). We may have planned an activity based on the number of students we expected to turn up, only to find that some of them are absent. Occasionally we find that students have already come across material or topics we take into class, and our common sense tells us that it would be unwise to carry on. Sometimes the technology we had relied on fails to work properly.

  In any of the above scenarios it would be almost impossible to carry on with our plan as if nothing had happened. If an activity finishes quickly, we have to find something else to fill the time. If students cannot do what we are asking of them, we will have to modify what we ask them to do. If some students (but not all) have already finished an activity, we cannot just leave those students to get bored.

  It is possible to anticipate potential problems in the class (see page 373) and to plan strategies to deal with them. But however well we do this, things will still happen that surprise us.

Using a plan means having a constant dialogue between what we intended to do and what is actually happening. In other words, it is entirely right and proper to design learning outcomes which we hope our students will achieve. Indeed, many teachers will be constrained by the syllabus, exam preparation and cultural expectations (see Chapter 4B) so that the lesson outcomes will have been pre-determined. However, forcing those outcomes in the face of obvious and changing reality within the lesson itself – and continuing with a planned activity simply because it is in the plan – can be detrimental to the students' perception of us as teachers and may, if we are not careful, close off learning opportunities which our students could have benefited from. It is in the implementation and adaptation of a plan – and the interaction between the plan and ever-changing reality once a lesson has started – that the planning paradox is ultimately resolved.

B Pre-planning and planning

There is a stage that teachers go through, either consciously or subconsciously, that happens before we actually make a plan of what is going to happen in our lesson. This pre-planning stage is where we gather ideas and material and possible starting-off points. For some teachers, engaged in corridor planning, for example, this may be as far as planning goes, and jungle path teachers (see page 365) often have little more than a vague idea of how to start a lesson. For teachers who are going to produce a more formal plan, however, the pre-planning stage is the start of the whole process.

Ideas for pre-planning can come from a wide variety of sources. We could have come across a good activity that we would like to use (perhaps in a book or at a teachers' seminar). Perhaps we have seen something on the Internet or on the television which we think might be fun for a lesson. We might have made an informal decision to teach a particular item of language, or just have a vague idea about working on a unit of our coursebook.

Our pre-planning ideas are usually based on our knowledge of who we are teaching (unless we are thinking of the first few lessons with a new class). We have their personalities as individuals (and as a group) in our minds. We are conscious of their level and what we think they might be capable of. We have studied the syllabus we are following and what the students are expected to have achieved by the end of the course.

For Tessa Woodward, this pre-planning stage (considering the students and coming up with ideas from a variety of different sources) is planning itself. When she talks about planning she does 'NOT mean the writing of pages of notes with headings such as "Aims" and "Anticipated Problems" to be given in to an observer before they watch you teach' (Woodward 2001: 1). But for those teachers who are undergoing a formal observation, generalised pre-planning, with or without jotted notes, is not enough. They need to be able to show evidence of following pre-plans through into clear thinking about exactly what they intend their students to do. In the rest of this section, therefore, we will show how pre-planning ideas (based on our perception of student needs) lead on to a plan, and how this can then be translated into a formal planning document.

B1 Student needs

Lesson plans are based both on our own ideas about what will be appropriate and on what the syllabus we are working towards expects us to do. In both cases, decisions are based not only on the syllabus designer's (or lesson planner's) understanding of how language items interlock and on the kind of topics and tasks which can follow each other in effective sequences, but also on perceptions of the needs and wants of the students.

In Chapter 7, B1 we saw how teaching in a one-to-one situation has the advantage that teachers can design a programme of study based entirely on one student's needs, learning styles and learning preferences. We can do this by asking the student what he or she wants or expects from the lessons and modifying what we had intended to teach accordingly. It is more difficult to ascertain what all the different individuals in a class – or indeed a whole student population – want. However, large organisations have tried to do this, sometimes with notable success as with the 'can do' statements from the Council of Europe (see page 96).

There are all sorts of ways of conducting a *needs analysis* about what students want and need (these two may not, of course, be the same thing). We can talk to them about it, though this will not necessarily tell us anything more than the opinions of the more confident members of the class. We can give students lists of possible activities or topics and get them to rate them in order of preference. They can then compare their different lists and come to a consensus view of what the class as a whole wants and needs. We can ask students to write to us and tell us what they need, or give them a series of statements about the course for them to modify (either individually or in groups). We can administer questionnaires before, during and after the course. Alun Davies, for example, gives his questionnaires in the middle of course programmes. Students are asked to evaluate the course itself, the materials and learning activities because, he claims, 'it is impossible to overestimate the value of what learners can teach us about themselves via class-specific questionnaire surveys' (Davies 2006: 10). He does this both for *summative* assessment (that is to find out how well things have gone) and also for *formative* evaluation (that is for reasons of future course planning and professional teacher development). Other teachers have students write journals (see Chapter 23, B3) in part as a way of keeping in touch with how they feel about their lessons and modifying the programme as a result (see 'Reacting to what happens' on page 375).

Whatever means we choose to find out what our students need and want, the important thing is that our planning decisions (and the decisions of a syllabus designer) should be informed by an understanding of what is in our students' best interests.

B2 Making the plan

We will now consider a formal plan from its pre-planning phase through to the end of its formal realisation.

In the pre-planning phase we have considered a number of different parameters. In the first place, we are familiar with the syllabus and, based on its requirements, we have a number of activities and topics floating around in our heads. For example, we think it's about time we did a fluency activity with this group of students. But we quite like the idea of giving the students some reading to do, too, because that is something they have had little practice of recently. Sometime around now we should have a look at the structure *should have done,* which is in the syllabus. It would be nice to continue with the theme of transport that we have been following in the last few lessons, but we need to find something a bit different if our students aren't to get bored.

Of course, none of these thoughts occurs in a vacuum. There are things we have learnt about our students and the timetable, too. For example, we know that our class is at the intermediate level and how many people it has in it and how old they are. We know, perhaps, that they are quite prepared to have a go – that they are quite creative – but that they sometimes need waking up at the beginning of a lesson. Of course, we also know what equipment we can count on (a whiteboard or an OHP or data projector, for example, and audio equipment).

When we start to make a plan, we may want to go further than finding a door in and a door out (see page 365). We may try to aim for a 'sense of ending', to borrow the literary critic Frank Kermode's phrase, so that, once we know the end of the story (the lesson), we can give shape to the lesson as a whole. Some teachers find it useful to come up with metaphors for class sequences – a symphony, a play, a story, a TV programme, for example – to help them achieve this lesson shape. This may be extremely helpful, but what really matters, in the end, is what syllabus we are following and how we are going to realise this in terms of the activities we are going to take into class and how one activity leads into – or progresses from – another. We will discuss both of these issues in turn.

- **Syllabus type:** over the years materials designers have come up with a variety of different syllabus types. Many courses, for example, have been based around *grammatical* syllabuses (that is a list of items, such as present continuous, countable and uncountable nouns, comparative adjectives, etc.), but others have grouped their teaching items in sequences of topics (e.g. the weather, sport, the music scene, etc.). *Functional* syllabuses have listed functions, such as apologising, inviting, etc., and *situational* syllabuses have been based around situations, such as *at the bank*, *at the travel agent*, *at the supermarket*, etc. There has been talk, too, of *lexical* syllabuses (see Chapter 4, A7) and syllabuses based on lists of *tasks* (see Chapter 4, A6). There are advantages and disadvantages to any of these choices. A grammatical syllabus, for example, restricts the kind of tasks and situations which students can work with. A functional syllabus has some problems working out a grammar sequence when there are so many different ways of performing the same function (see page 27). It is difficult to sequence language if we base our syllabus on situations, and we have discussed some of the difficulties associated with task-based learning in Chapter 4, A6. What most designers and coursebook writers try to provide, therefore, is a kind of multi-syllabus syllabus, in other words, an interlocking set of parameters for any particular level or point of study which includes not only the categories discussed above, but also issues of skills and pronunciation, for example. Syllabus designers thus juggle issues of grammar, lexis, functions, topics and tasks when putting together a teaching sequence, as the coursebook example in Figure 1 makes clear. However, in reality, grammar is still often seen as the essential syllabus frame around which the other syllabuses are erected.

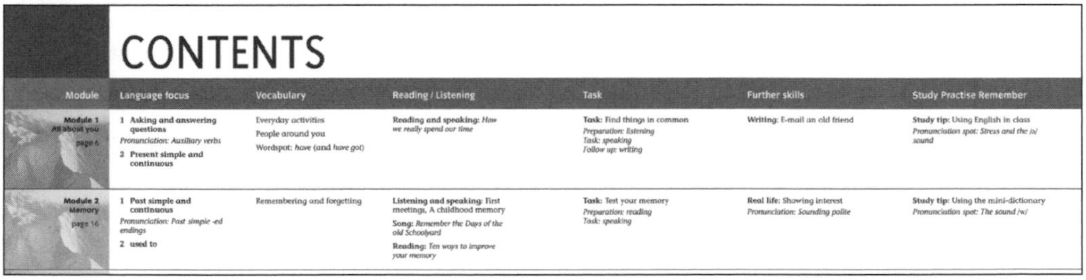

CONTENTS

Module	Language focus	Vocabulary	Reading / Listening	Task	Further skills	Study Practise Remember
Module 1 All about you page 6	1 **Asking and answering questions** *Pronunciation: Auxiliary verbs* 2 **Present simple and continuous**	Everyday activities People around you Wordspot: *have* (and *have got*)	**Reading and speaking:** *How we really spend our time*	**Task:** Find things in common *Preparation: listening* *Task: speaking* *Follow up: writing*	**Writing:** E-mail an old friend	**Study tip:** Using English in class *Pronunciation spot: Stress and the /ə/ sound*
Module 2 Memory page 16	1 **Past simple and continuous** *Pronunciation: Past simple -ed endings* 2 **used to**	Remembering and forgetting	**Listening and speaking:** First meetings, A childhood memory **Song:** *Remember the Days of the old Schoolyard* **Reading:** *Ten ways to improve your memory*	**Task:** Test your memory *Preparation: reading* *Task: speaking*	**Real life:** Showing interest *Pronunciation: Sounding polite*	**Study tip:** Using the mini-dictionary *Pronunciation spot: The sound /w/*

FIGURE 1: Part of the contents page from *New Cutting Edge* by S Cunningham and P Moor (Pearson Education Ltd)

- **Lesson stages:** the issue of how one activity leads into another is a matter of how different parts or stages of a lesson hang together. Students need to know, during a lesson, when one stage has finished and another is about to begin. This involves drawing their attention to what is going to happen next, or making it clear that something has finished by making summarising comments. Many teachers write the different stages of the lesson on the board at the beginning of each class so that students will know where they are in the lesson sequence at any given moment.

  When planning lessons, we need to think carefully, therefore, about what stages a lesson will go through and how we will get from one stage to another.

In our example – and based on our pre-planning thoughts, the syllabus we are working to, and the stages we want our students to experience – we have decided to get students to read a text about a space station (see *Light in space*, Example 4 on page 215) and use it to get students to predict before they read. We like the idea of getting students to come up with their own endings for the story. And then we think that we can organise an oral fluency activity around this topic, too. Maybe they could take part in a role-play about being in a space-station crew. There will also be a chance for language study of a current syllabus grammar point arising out of the text. These are our basic lesson blocks. Now we have to decide on the shape of the lesson – the progression from one activity to another. A possible sequence is shown in Figure 2.

Oral fluency activity
Reaching a consensus about five objects to take into space.

Students read about a space station
Predicting the content based on the title; reading to confirm predictions; reading again for detail.
↓
Students devise an ending for the story
↓
Language study
Using the space station situation to make sentences about what people should/shouldn't have done.

Immediate creativity/personalisation
Students talk about things they should/shouldn't have done.
↓
Interview role-play
Students plan and role-play interviews for jobs as members of a space station crew.

FIGURE 2: A lesson sequence

We have other ideas floating around our heads, too, and we make a note of these in case we can use them later, or instead of some element of the plan which may not be appropriate once the lesson is underway, e.g.

- Interview Cathy years later to find out what happened to her.
- Students write a 'newsflash' programme based on what happened.
- A short extract from a video on future space exploration.
- Students discuss the three things they would miss most if they were on a space station.

The same attention to detail will be necessary when we come to show the procedure for the language study part of our lesson. Here, we need to give the model sentences we are going to use and list any details (such as phonemic features) which we expect to focus on (or draw the students' attention to).

	Activity/Aids	Interaction	Procedure	Time
4	Language study	**a** T←→C	T elicits sentences based on the previous 'problem identification' session: She shouldn't have been rude to Cathy. She should have looked at the record book. She should have told the others where she was going. She shouldn't have ignored the warning light. He shouldn't have switched off his radio. He should have done something about it. He shouldn't have been wearing his spacewalk-man. She should have closed the exit door.	10"
	Textbook page 113/board	T←→S,S,S	T has SS say the sentences, and may do individual/class work on the pronunciation of the shortened form, e.g. /ʃʊdəv/ – *should've*, and /ʃʊdntəv/ – *shouldn't have*.	

Most trainers and teacher exam guidelines expect the teacher being observed to attach copies of the material which they are going to use to their plan and to say where it originates. Many trainers also like their observed teachers to submit a board plan, showing where and how they will write things up on the board. This has the advantage of making us think carefully about what the students will see so that we can use the board as effectively as possible. Where we use PowerPoint or IWB resources, most observers would expect to receive a copy of these, too.

C Planning a sequence of lessons

We have concentrated, so far, on the kind of plan we need to produce for a single observed lesson. But there are many other situations in which we may need to produce plans for a much longer sequence (e.g. a week's work, a month's work, a semester's work, etc.). Sometimes we will do this so that we ourselves have an idea of how the course will progress. Frequently, the institution teachers work for requires such long-term planning and wants to know what the learning outcomes will be for a week, month or semester. Sometimes, of course, the institution supplies teachers with the syllabus, but in this section we are concerned with situations where it does not.

When planning a sequence of lessons, there are a number of issues we need to bear in mind.

- **Reacting to what happens:** however carefully we plan, in practice, unforeseen things are likely to happen during the course of a lesson (as we saw in Section A above), and so our plans for that lesson are continually modified in the light of these. The same is true, but on a larger scale, when we plan a scheme of work for a sequence of lessons. We will have to re-visit our original series of plans continually in order to update and amend them, depending upon what has happened in previous classes. Instead of a one-off proposal for action (an individual lesson plan), we now have an over-arching map, which we may have to re-draw, sometimes quite substantially, when we find out what the country we are visiting (the lessons) is really like. We will often modify what we do based on student reactions to what has been taking place (see A2 above).

- **Short- and long-term goals:** however motivated a student may be at the beginning of a course, the level of that motivation may fall dramatically if the student is not engaged or if they cannot see where they are going – or cannot sense when they have got there.

  In order for students to stay motivated, they need goals and the potential for success in achieving them. While a satisfactory long-term goal may be 'to master the English language', it can seem only a dim and distant possibility at various stages of the learning cycle. In such circumstances (and if we are to prioritise success in the way that we suggested on page 157), students need short-term goals, too, such as the completion of some piece of work (or some part of the programme), and rewards, such as success on small staged lesson tests, or taking part in activities designed to recycle knowledge and demonstrate acquisition.

  When we plan a sequence of lessons, therefore, we need to build in goals for both students and ourselves to aim at, whether they are end-of-week tests or major revision lessons. That way we can hope to give our students a staged progression of successfully met challenges.

- **Thematic content:** one way to approach a sequence of lessons is to focus on different thematic content in each individual lesson (much as a topic syllabus – see page 369 – is organised). This will certainly provide variety, but it may not give our sequence of lessons much cohesion or coherence. It might be better, instead, for themes to carry over for more than one lesson, or at least to reappear, so that students perceive some overt topic strands as the course progresses. With such thematic threads, we and our students can refer backwards and forwards, both in terms of language – especially the vocabulary that certain topics generate – and also in terms of the topics we ask them to invest time in considering. As an example, at the upper intermediate level, we might deal with the topic of photography over a two-week period. However, if we keep on dealing with the same aspect of the topic, our students are likely to become very tired of it. And so, instead, we think of different angles. They can look at a photograph which made (or recorded) history and read about or discuss its implications. As a speaking activity, we can get them to judge a photographic competition, too. Later in the sequence of lessons, they can hear people talking about snapshots they have taken, and bring in or describe their own. They can study vocabulary for cameras and photography and role-play dialogues in which they ask people to take photographs for them. They can listen to an interview with a professional photographer about what his or her job entails, and perhaps they can read about other uses of cameras, such as speed cameras, space or scientific photography.

- **Language planning:** when we plan language input over a sequence of lessons, we want to propose a sensible progression of syllabus elements such as grammar, lexis and functions. We also want to build in sufficient opportunities for recycling or remembering language, and for using language in productive skill work. If we are following a coursebook closely, many of these decisions may already have been taken, but even in such circumstances we need to keep a constant eye on how things are going, and, with the knowledge of 'before and after', modify the programme we are working from when necessary.

Language does not exist in a vacuum, however. Our decisions about how to weave grammar and vocabulary through the lesson sequence will be heavily influenced by the need for a balance of activities.

- **Activity balance:** the balance of activities over a sequence of lessons is one of the features which will determine the overall level of student involvement in the course. If we get it right, it will also provide the widest range of experience to meet the different learning styles of the students in the class (see Chapter 5B).

  Over a period of weeks or months, we would expect students to have received a varied diet of activities; they should not have to role-play every day, nor would we expect every lesson to be devoted exclusively to language study with drilling and repetition. While some of the oral activities they are involved in can be discussions, others, by contrast, might involve them in making presentations. Sometimes we will encourage students to work in pairs or groups for consensus-reaching activities, but at other times, we will work with the whole class for lecture-type teaching or divide them into two teams for a game.

- **Skills:** the balance of skills depends to a large extent on the kind of course we are teaching. Some students may be studying principally to improve their speaking and listening. Others may need to concentrate on reading and writing. But many general English courses are designed to involve students in all four skills.

  Different skills need to be threaded through a sequence of lessons so that writing, for example, does not get forgotten, and reading does not predominate. We need to have special tasks devoted exclusively to speaking before, then, integrating that speaking task into other skill-area activities.

  Although we don't want to inflict anarchy on our classes, we do want to make sure that with skills, as with other areas, such as activities, etc., we are not too predictable. If every Friday is the reading class, every Monday is the presentation class and every Wednesday is where we do speaking and writing, there is a danger that students might become bored.

C1 Projects and threads

Some lesson sequences may, of course, be devoted to longer project work of the kind we discussed in Chapter 16. In such a case, we will try to ensure that a good balance of skills, language, activities and thematic strands is achieved throughout the time in which the students are working on the project. A good project of this kind will involve students in reading, discussion, writing (with language input) and, possibly, oral presentation.

However, where students are not involved in a long-term project, we can still build threads and strands into a sequence. These are the varied connections of themes, language, activities and skills which weave through the sequence like pieces of different coloured thread. They should have sufficient variety built into them so that they are not numbingly predictable, but, at the same time, students and their teachers should be able to trace the threaded elements so that some kind of a loose pattern emerges. Planning a sequence of lessons is somewhat like creating a tapestry, in other words, but a tapestry full of light, variety and colour rather than some of the darker heavier works which can be found in old houses and museums.

Figure 3 shows an example of five lessons planned around three different threads (vocabulary, tenses and reading), but we could, of course, add other threads, such as activity threads, theme threads and skill threads.

LESSON NOTES					
Threads	MONDAY	TUESDAY	WEDNESDAY	THURSDAY	FRIDAY
Animals vocabulary thread (10 mins each time)	Parts of cat's body	Review + cat verbs	Review + cat metaphors	Review and start fish vocab	Review and start fish verbs
Tenses thread (30 mins each time)	Regular past simple first person	Review + all persons	Review + negatives	Review + some irregulars	Review and start 'Did you …?' questions
Reading thread (20 mins each time)	Introduction of graded reader	First two pages + comp. questions	Review and Chap. 1	Study of past forms in Chap. 1	Oral summary of Chap. 1 + vocab in notebook

FIGURE 3: Lesson threads from Woodward (2001: 195)

Chapter notes and further reading

- **Lesson shapes and metaphors**

  S Thornbury (1999b) quotes Frank Kermode's 'sense of ending' and both he and P Ur (1996: 213) suggest seeing lessons as, for example, a show, a menu, a story and a film.

  M Cattlin (2003) calls his approach to lesson planning Reactive-Proactive. D Kent (2001) suggests a topic-driven strategy for lesson planning within a TBL framework. H A Smith (2003) shows how you can enter a planning cycle through grammatical structure, skills, functions or vocabulary.

  T Woodward (2003) is a short article which says how plans can be successful.

- **Student needs**

  A Walters and M L Vilches (2001) propose a needs analysis framework when implementing ELT innovations. See also A Boon (2005) and A Almagro Esteban (2005).

- **Aims and objectives**

  See G Petty (2004: Chapter 27).

- **Unforeseen problems**

  See R Gower *et al* (1995: 178).

22 | Testing and evaluation

A Testing and assessment

Teachers and other education professionals spend a lot of time testing, evaluating and assessing students. Sometimes this is to measure the students' abilities to see if they can enter a course or institution. Sometimes it is to see how well they getting on. Sometimes it is because the students themselves want a qualification. Sometimes this assessment is formal and public, and sometimes it is informal and takes place in day-to-day lessons.

We can make a difference between *summative* and *formative* assessment. Summative assessment, as the name suggests, is the kind of measurement that takes place to round things off or make a one-off measurement. Such tests include the end-of-year tests that students take or the big public exams which many students enter for (see the list at the end of this chapter).

Formative assessment, on the other hand, relates to the kind of feedback teachers give students as a course is progressing and which, as a result, may help them to improve their performance. This is done at a micro-level every time we indicate that something is wrong and help students to get it right (see Chapter 8), but can also take place when teachers go through the results of progress and achievement tests. The results of such formative assessment could well, in certain circumstances, suggest that the teacher change the focus of the curriculum or the emphasis he or she is giving to certain lesson elements. Formative assessment, in other words, means that teachers as well as students may have to change and develop. It is perhaps because of this that many teachers are not keen on adopting a rigorous approach to formative testing (Leung and Lewkowicz 2006: 227), quite apart from the fact that in many institutions such ongoing modification is not encouraged.

However, it is worth remembering that handing back any piece of assessed homework or progress test presents teachers and students with ideal learning opportunities – opportunities which will be wasted if the work is immediately put away, rather than being used as a vehicle for development.

A1 Different types of testing

There are four main reasons for testing, which give rise to four categories of test:

- **Placement tests:** placing new students in the right class in a school is facilitated by the use of placement tests. Usually based on syllabuses and materials the students will follow and use once their level has been decided on, these test grammar and vocabulary knowledge and assess students' productive and receptive skills.

  Some schools ask students to assess themselves as part of the placement process, adding this self-analysis into the final placing decision.

379

- **Diagnostic tests:** while placement tests are designed to show how good a student's English is in relation to a previously agreed system of levels, diagnostic tests can be used to expose learner difficulties, gaps in their knowledge and skill deficiencies during a course. Thus, when we know what the problems are, we can do something about them.

- **Progress or achievement tests:** these tests are designed to measure learners' language and skill progress in relation to the syllabus they have been following.

  Progress tests are often written by teachers and given to students every few weeks to see how well they are doing. In this way they can form part of a programme of formative assessment (see above).

  Achievement tests only work if they contain item types which the students are familiar with. This does not mean that in a reading test, for example, we give them texts they have seen before, but it does mean providing them with similar texts and familiar task types. If students are faced with completely new material, the test will not measure the learning that has been taking place, even though it can still measure general language proficiency.

  Achievement tests at the end of a term (like progress tests at the end of a unit, a fortnight, etc.) should reflect progress, not failure. They should reinforce the learning that has taken place, not go out of their way to expose weaknesses. They can also help us to decide on changes to future teaching programmes where students do significantly worse in (parts of) the test than we might have expected.

- **Proficiency tests:** proficiency tests give a general picture of a student's knowledge and ability (rather than measure progress). They are frequently used as stages people have to reach if they want to be admitted to a foreign university, get a job or obtain some kind of certificate. Most public examinations are proficiency tests of this type.

  Proficiency tests have a profound backwash effect (see Section D below) since, where they are external exams, students obviously want to pass them, and teachers' reputations sometimes depend (probably unfairly) upon how many of them succeed.

- **Portfolio assessment:** achievement tests and proficiency tests are both concerned with measuring a student's ability at a certain time. Students only get 'one shot' at showing how much they know. For some people, who say they are 'not good at exams', this seems like an unfair situation, and many educators claim that 'sudden death' testing like this does not give a true picture of how well some students could do in certain situations. As a result, many educational institutions allow students to assemble a portfolio of their work over a period of time (a term or semester), and the student can then be assessed by looking at three or four of the best pieces of work over this period.

  Portfolio assessment of this kind has clear benefits. It provides evidence of student effort. It helps students become more autonomous, and it can 'foster student reflection (and) help them to self monitor their own learning' (Nunes 2004: 334). It has clear validity since, especially with written work, students will have had a chance to edit before submitting their work, and this approach to assessment has an extremely positive washback effect.

  However, portfolio assessment is not without its pitfalls. In the first place, it is time-consuming, and in the second place, teachers will need clear training in how to select items from the portfolio and how to give them grades. Some students may be tempted to leave their portfolios until the end of the course when, they expect, their work will be at its best (though there are ways to counter this tendency). But above all, when students work on their own away from the classroom, it is not always clear that the work reflects their own efforts or whether, in fact, they have been helped by others. It is largely for this reason that the British Qualifications and Curriculum Agency, for example, has recommended phasing out coursework in many disciplines in secondary education in Britain and replacing it with external exams, the equivalent of proficiency tests (Qualifications and Curriculum Agency 2006). However, this view is not shared by all; the argument about whether continuous assessment (represented by portfolio assessment) or 'sudden death' (represented by external proficiency tests) is the most appropriate method of assessment is set to continue for some time to come.

A2 Characteristics of a good test

In order to judge the effectiveness of any test, it is sensible to lay down criteria against which the test can be measured, as follows:

- **Validity:** a test is valid if it tests what it is supposed to test. Thus it is not valid, for example, to test writing ability with an essay question that requires specialist knowledge of history or biology – unless it is known that all students share this knowledge before they do the test.

    A test is valid if it produces similar results to some other measure – that is if we can show that Test A gives us the same kind of results as Test B (or some other test).

    A test is only valid is there is validity in the way it is marked; if we score short written answers to a listening test for spelling and grammar, then it is not necessarily a valid test of listening. We are scoring the wrong thing.

    A particular kind of validity that concerns most test designers is face validity. This means that the test should look, on the face of it, as if it is valid. A test which consisted of only three multiple-choice items would not convince students of its face validity, however reliable or practical teachers thought it to be.

- **Reliability:** a good test should give consistent results. For example, if the same group of students took the same test twice within two days – without reflecting on the first test before they sat it again – they should get the same results on each occasion. If they took another similar test, the results should be consistent. If two groups who were demonstrably alike took the test, the marking range would be the same.

    In practice, reliability is enhanced by making the test instructions absolutely clear, restricting the scope for variety in the answers and making sure that test conditions remain constant.

    Reliability also depends on the people who mark the tests – the scorers. Clearly a test is unreliable if the result depends to any large extent on who is marking it. Much thought has gone into making the scoring of tests as reliable as possible (see C2 below).

B Types of test item

Whatever purpose a test or exam has, a major factor in its success or failure as a good measuring instrument will be determined by the item types that it contains.

B1 Direct and indirect test items

A test item is *direct* if it asks candidates to perform the communicative skill which is being tested. *Indirect* test items, on the other hand, try to measure a student's knowledge and ability by getting at what lies beneath their receptive and productive skills. Whereas direct test items try to be as much like real-life language use as possible, indirect items try to find out about a student's language knowledge through more controlled items, such as multiple-choice questions or grammar transformation items. These are often quicker to design and, crucially, easier to mark, and produce greater scorer reliability.

Another distinction needs to be made between *discrete-point* testing and *integrative* testing. Whereas discrete-point testing only tests one thing at a time (such as asking students to choose the correct tense of a verb), integrative test items expect students to use a variety of language at any one given time – as they will have to do when writing a composition or doing a conversational oral test.

In many proficiency tests where students sit a number of different papers, there is a mixture of direct and indirect, discrete-point and integrative testing. Test designers find that this combination gives a good overall picture of student ability. Placement tests often use discrete-point testing to measure students against an existing language syllabus, but may then compare this with more direct and integrative tasks to get a fuller picture.

B2 Indirect test item types

Although there is a wide range of indirect test possibilities, certain types are in common use.

- **Multiple-choice questions:** a traditional vocabulary multiple-choice question (MCQ) looks like this:

The journalist was _____ by enemy fire as he tried to send a story by satellite phone.			
a wronged	**b** wounded	**c** injured	**d** damaged

  For many years, MCQs were considered to be ideal test instruments for measuring students' knowledge of grammar and vocabulary. Above all, this was because they were easy to mark. Moreover, since the advent of computers, the answer sheets for these tests can be read by machines, thereby cutting out the possibility of scorer error.

  However, there are a number of problems with MCQs. In the first place, they are extremely difficult to write well, especially in terms of the design of the incorrect choices. These 'distractors' may actually put ideas into students' heads that they did not have before they read them. Secondly, while it is possible to train students so that their MCQ abilities are enhanced, this may not actually improve their English. The difference between two student scores may be between the person who has been trained in the technique and a person who has not, rather than being a difference of language knowledge and ability.

  MCQs are still widely used, but though they score highly in terms of practicality and scorer reliability, their validity and overall reliability are suspect.

- **Cloze procedures:** cloze procedures seem to offer us the ideal indirect but integrative testing item. They can be prepared quickly and, if the claims made for them are true, they are an extremely cost-effective way of finding out about a testee's overall knowledge.

  Cloze, in its purest form, is the deletion of every *n*th word in a text (somewhere between every fifth or tenth word). Because the procedure is random, it avoids test designer failings. It produces test items like this:

> They sat on a bench attached 1 _____ a picnic table. Below them they 2 _____ see the river gurgling between overgrown 3 _____. The sky was diamond blue, with 4 _____ white clouds dancing in the freshening 5 _____. They could hear the call of 6 _____ and the buzzing of countless insects. 8 _____ were completely alone. etc.

Cloze testing seems, on the face of it, like a perfect test instrument, since, because of the randomness of the deleted words, anything may be tested (e.g. grammar, collocation, fixed phrases, reading comprehension), and therefore it becomes more integrative in its reach. However, it turns out that the actual score a student gets depends on the particular words that are deleted, rather than on any general English knowledge. Some are more difficult to supply than others, and in some cases there are several possible answers. Even in the short sample text above, it is clear that while there is no doubt about items such as 1 and 8, for example, item 4 is less predictable. Different passages produce different results.

Despite such problems of reliability, cloze is too useful a technique to abandon altogether because it is clear that supplying the correct word for a blank does imply an understanding of context and a knowledge of that word and how it operates. Perhaps it would be better, therefore, to use 'rational' or 'modified' cloze procedures (Alderson 1996: 222) where the test designer can be sure that the deleted words are recoverable from the context. This means abandoning the completely random nature of traditional cloze procedure. Instead, every eighth or tenth word is deleted, but the teacher has the option to delete a word to the left or right if the context makes this more sensible.

Modified cloze is useful for placement tests since students can be given texts that they would be expected to cope with at certain levels – thus allowing us to judge their suitability for those levels. They are useful, too, as part of a test battery in either achievement or proficiency tests.

- **Transformation and paraphrase:** a common test item asks candidates to re-write sentences in a slightly different form, retaining the exact meaning of the original. For example, the following item tests the candidates' knowledge of verb and clause patterns that are triggered by the use of *I wish*.

> I'm sorry that I didn't get her an anniversary present.
>
> I wish _____

In order to complete the item successfully, the student has to understand the first sentence, and then know how to construct an equivalent which is grammatically possible. As such, they do tell us something about the candidates' knowledge of the language system.

- **Sentence re-ordering:** getting students to put words in the right order to make appropriate sentences tells us quite a lot about their underlying knowledge of syntax and lexico-grammatical elements. The following example is typical:

> **Put the words in order to make correct sentences.**
>
> called / I / I'm / in / sorry / wasn't / when / you
>
> _____

Re-ordering exercises are fairly easy to write, though it is not always possible to ensure only one correct order.

There are many other indirect techniques, too, including sentence fill-ins (*Jan _____ to the gym every Tuesday morning*), choosing the correct tense of verbs in sentences and passages (*I have arrived/arrived yesterday*), finding errors in sentences (*She noticed about his new jacket*), and choosing the correct form of a word (*He didn't enjoy being on the (lose) _____ side*). All of these offer items which are quick and efficient to score and which aim to tell us something about a student's underlying knowledge.

B3 Direct test item types

For direct test items to achieve validity and to be reliable, test designers need to do the following:

- **Create a 'level playing field':** in the case of a written test, teachers and candidates would almost certainly complain about the following essay question:

> *Why was the discovery of DNA so important for the science of the twentieth century?*

since it unfairly favours candidates who have sound scientific knowledge and presupposes a knowledge of twentieth-century scientific history.

However, the following topic comes close to ensuring that all candidates have the same chance of success:

> Present a written argument or case to an educated non-specialist audience on the following topic:
> **Higher mammals, especially monkeys, have rights and should not be used in laboratory experiments.**
> You should write at least 250 words.
> You should use your own ideas, knowledge and experience to support your arguments with examples and relevant evidence.

General writing question from the *IELTS* exam (see notes at the end of this chapter)

Receptive skill testing also needs to avoid making excessive demands on the student's general or specialist knowledge. Receptive ability testing can also be undermined if the means of testing requires students to perform well in writing or speaking (when it is a test of reading or listening). In such a situation we can no longer be sure that it is the receptive skill we are measuring.

- **Replicate real-life interaction:** in real life when people speak or write, they generally do so with some real purpose. Yet traditional writing tests have often been based exclusively on general essay questions, and speaking tests have often included hypothetical questions about what candidates might say if they happened to be in a certain situation. More modern test writers now include tasks which attempt to replicate features of real life (Weir 1993: 167). They will often look similar to the kind of speaking activities described in Chapter 20.

    Tests of reading and listening should also, as far as possible, reflect real life. This means that texts should be as realistic as possible, even where they are not authentic (see Chapter 16, B2). Although there are ways of assessing student understanding (using matching tasks or multiple-choice questions) which do not necessarily satisfy these criteria, test items should be as much like real reading and listening as possible.

The following direct test item types are a few of the many which attempt to meet the criteria we have mentioned above:

SPEAKING
- An interviewer questions a candidate about themselves.
- Information-gap activities where a candidate has to find out information either from an interlocutor or a fellow candidate. (The role-play on page 359 would not need too much modification to serve as a suitable test item.)
- Decision-making activities, such as showing paired candidates ten photos of people and asking them to put them in order of the best and worst dressed.
- Using pictures for candidates to compare and contrast, whether they can both see them or whether (as in many communication games) they have find similarities and differences without being able to look at each other's material.
- Role-play activities where candidates perform tasks such as introducing themselves or ringing a theatre to book tickets.

WRITING
- Writing compositions and stories.
- 'Transactional letters' where candidates reply to a job advertisement or write a complaint to a hotel based on information given in the exam paper.
- Information leaflets about their school or a place in their town.
- A set of instructions for some common task.
- Newspaper articles about a recent event.

READING
- Multiple-choice questions to test comprehension of a text.
- Matching written descriptions with pictures of the items or procedure they describe.
- Transferring written information to charts, graphs, maps, etc. (though special care has to be taken not to disadvantage non-mathematically-minded candidates).
- Choosing the best summary of a paragraph or a whole text.
- Matching jumbled headings with paragraphs.
- Inserting sentences provided by the examiner in the correct place in the text.

LISTENING
- Completing charts with facts and figures from the listening text.
- Identifying which of a number of objects (pictured on the test paper) is being described.
- Identifying who (out of two or three speakers) says what.
- Identifying whether speakers are enthusiastic, encouraging, in disagreement or amused.
- Following directions on a map and identifying the correct house or place.

In the interests of reliability, listening tests are most often supplied on tape or CD to ensure that all candidates have the same opportunities, irrespective of the speakers' voices, speed or expressions. Sometimes, as in the computerised TOEFL test (see the notes at the end of this chapter), candidates work with headphones from an individual computer. Where a group of students listen to the same recording, however, we need to be sure that it is clearly and easily audible.

C Writing and marking tests

At various times during our teaching careers we may have to write tests for the students we are teaching, and mark the tests they have completed for us. These may range from a lesson test at the end of the week to an achievement test at the end of a term or a year.

C1 Writing tests

Before designing a test and then giving it to a group of students, there are a number of things we need to do:

- **Assess the test situation:** before we start to write the test we need to remind ourselves of the context in which the test takes place. We have to decide how much time should be given to the test-taking, when and where it will take place, and how much time there is for marking.

- **Decide what to test:** we have to list what we want to include in our test. This means taking a conscious decision to include or exclude skills such as reading comprehension or speaking (if speaking tests are impractical). It means knowing what syllabus items can be legitimately included (in an achievement test), and what kinds of topics and situations are appropriate for our students.

  Just because we have a list of all the vocabulary items or grammar points the students have studied over the term, this does not mean we have to test every single item. If we include a representative sample from across the whole list, the students' success or failure with those items will be a good indicator of how well they have learnt all of the language they have studied.

- **Balance the elements:** if we are to include direct and indirect test items, we have to make a decision about how many of each we should put in our test. A 200-item multiple-choice test with a short real-life writing task tacked onto the end suggests that we think that MCQs are a better way of finding out about students than more integrative writing tasks would be.

  Balancing elements involves estimating how long we want each section of the test to take and then writing test items within those time constraints. The amount of space and time we give to the various elements should also reflect their importance in our teaching.

- **Weight the scores:** however well we have balanced the elements in our test, our perception of our students' success or failure will depend upon how many marks are given to each section of the test. If we give two marks for each of our ten MCQs but only one mark for each of our ten transformation items, it means that it is more important for students to do well in the former than in the latter.

- **Make the test work:** it is absolutely vital that we try out individual items and/or whole tests on colleagues and other students before administering them to real candidates.

  When we write test items, the first thing to do is to get fellow teachers to try them out. Frequently they spot problems which we are not aware of and/or come up with possible answers and alternatives that we had not anticipated.

  Later, having made changes based on our colleagues' reactions, we will want to try out the test on students. We will not do this with the students who are going to take the test, of course, but if we can find a class that is roughly similar – or a class one level above the proposed test – then we will soon find out what items cause unnecessary problems. We can also discover how long the test takes.

Such trialling is designed to avoid disaster and to yield a whole range of possible answers/responses to the various test items. This means that when other people finally mark the test, we can give them a list of possible alternatives and thus ensure reliable scoring.

C2 Marking tests

When Cyril Weir gave copies of the same eight exam scripts to his postgraduate students (who were doing an MA in TESOL) some years ago, they marked them first on the basis of 'impressionistic' marking out of a possible total of 20 marks. The results were alarming. Some scorers gave higher marks overall than others. But for some of the scripts, the range of marks was excessive. For one, the lowest mark awarded was 5, whereas another scorer gave it 20. For another, the range was between 1 and 15. As Cyril Weir writes, 'the worst scripts ... if they had been marked by certain markers, might have been given higher marks than the best scripts' (1993: 157)!

There are a number of solutions to this kind of scorer subjectivity.

- **Training:** if scorers have seen examples of scripts at various different levels and discussed what marks they should be given, then their marking is likely to be less erratic than if they come to the task fresh. If scorers are allowed to watch and discuss videoed oral tests, they can be trained to 'rate the samples of spoken English accurately and consistently in terms of the pre-defined descriptions of performance' (Saville and Hargreaves 1999).

- **More than one scorer:** reliability can be greatly enhanced by having more than one scorer. The more people who look at a script, the greater the chance that its true worth will be located somewhere between the various scores it is given. Two examiners watching an oral test are likely to agree on a more reliable score than one.

  Many public examination boards use *moderators* whose job it is to check samples of individual scorer's work to see that it conforms with the general standards laid down for the exam.

- **Global assessment scales:** a way of specifying scores that can be given to productive skill work is to create 'pre-defined descriptions of performance'. Such descriptions say what students need to be capable of in order to gain the required marks, as in the following assessment (or rating) scale for oral ability:

Score	Description
0	The candidate is almost unintelligible, uses words wrongly and shows no sign of any grammatical understanding.
1	The candidate is able to transmit only very basic ideas, using individual words rather than phrases or fuller patterns of discourse. Speech is very hesitant and the pronunciation makes intelligibility difficult.
2	The candidate transmits basic ideas in a fairly stilted way. Pronunciation is sometimes problematic and there are examples of grammatical and lexical misuse and gaps which impede communication on occasions.

Score	Description
3	The candidate transmits ideas moderately clearly. Speech is somewhat hesitant and there are frequent lapses in grammar and vocabulary use. Nevertheless, the candidate makes him/herself understood.
4	The candidate speaks fairly fluently, showing an ability to communicate ideas with not too much trouble. There are some problems of grammatical accuracy and some words are inappropriately used.
5	The candidate speaks fluently with few obvious mistakes and a wide variety of lexis and expression. Pronunciation is almost always intelligible, and there is little difficulty in communicating ideas.

Global assessment scales are not without problems, however: perhaps the description does not exactly match the student who is speaking, as would be the case (for the scale above) where he or she had very poor pronunciation but was nevertheless grammatically accurate. There is also the danger that different teachers 'will not agree on the meaning of scale descriptors' (Upshur and Turner 1995: 5). Global assessment, on its own, still falls short of the kind of reliability we wish to achieve.

- **Analytic profiles:** marking gets more reliable when a student's performance is analysed in much greater detail. Instead of just a general assessment, marks are awarded for different elements.

  For oral assessment we can judge a student's speaking in a number of different ways, such as pronunciation, fluency, use of lexis and grammar and intelligibility. We may want to rate their ability to get themselves out of trouble (repair skills) and how successfully they completed the task which we set them.

  The resulting analytic profile might end up looking like this:

Criteria	Score (see analytic scales)
Pronunciation	
Fluency	
Use of vocabulary	
Use of grammar	
Intelligibility	
Repair skills	
Task completion	

For each separate criterion, we can now provide a separate 'analytic scale', as in the following example for fluency:

Score	Description
0	The candidate cannot get words or phrases out at all.
1	The candidate speaks hesitatingly in short, interrupted bursts.
2	The candidate speaks slowly with frequent pauses.
3	The candidate speaks at a comfortable speed with quite a lot of pauses and hesitations.
4	The candidate speaks at a comfortable speed with only an occasional pause or upset.
5	The candidate speaks quickly with few hesitations.

A combination of global and analytic scoring gives us the best chance of reliable marking. However, a profusion of criteria may make the marking of a test extremely lengthy and cumbersome; test designers and administrators will have to decide how to accommodate the competing claims of reliability and practicality.

- **Scoring and interacting during oral tests:** scorer reliability in oral tests is helped not only by global assessment scores and analytic profiles but also by separating the role of scorer (or examiner) from the role of *interlocutor* (the examiner who guides and provokes conversation). This may cause practical problems, but it will allow the scorer to observe and assess, free from the responsibility of keeping the interaction with the candidate or candidates going.

  In many tests of speaking, students are now put in pairs or groups for certain tasks since it is felt that this will ensure genuine interaction and will help to relax students in a way that interlocutor–candidate interaction might not. However, at least one commentator worries that pairing students in this way leads candidates to perform below their level of proficiency, and that when students with the same mother tongue are paired together, their intelligibility to the examiner may suffer (Foot 1999: 52).

D Teaching for tests

One of the things that preoccupies test designers and teachers alike is what has been called the *washback* or *backwash* effect. This refers to the fact that since teachers quite reasonably want their students to pass the tests and exams they are going to take, their teaching becomes dominated by the test and, especially, by the items that are in it. Where non-exam teachers might use a range of different activities, exam teachers suffering from the washback effect might stick rigidly to exam-format activities. In such a situation, the format of the exam is determining the format of the lessons.

Two points need to be taken into account when discussing the washback effect, however. In the first place, modern tests – especially the direct items included in them – are grounded far more in mainstream classroom activities and methodologies than some earlier examples of the genre. In other words, there are many direct test questions which would not look out of place in a modern lesson anyway. But secondly, even if preparing students for a particular test format is a necessity, 'it is as important to build variety and fun into an exam course as it is to drive students towards the goal of passing their exam' (Burgess and Head 2005: 1).

And we can go further: many teachers find teaching exam classes to be extremely satisfying in that where students perceive a clear sense of purpose – and are highly motivated to do as well as possible – they are in some senses 'easier' to teach than students whose focus is less clear. When a whole class has something to aim at, they may work with greater diligence than when they do not. Furthermore, in training students to develop good exam skills (including working on their own, reviewing what they have done, learning to use reference tools – e.g. dictionaries, grammar books, the Internet – keeping an independent learning record or diary, etc.), we are encouraging exactly those attributes that contribute towards autonomous learning (see Chapter 23, A and B).

Good exam-preparation teachers need to familiarise themselves with the tests their students are taking, and they need to be able to answer their students' concerns and worries. Above all, they need to be able to walk a fine line between good exam preparation on the one hand,

and not being swept away by the washback effect on the other. Within this context there are a number of things we can do in an exam class:

- **Train for test types:** we can show the various test types and ask the students what each item is testing so that they are clear about what is required. We can help them to understand what the test or exam designer is aiming for. By showing them the kind of marking scales that are used, we can make them aware of what constitutes success. Getting 'inside the heads' of the test designers will help students to focus on what they are being asked to do and why. After students have completed a test item type, we can tell them what score an examiner might give and why.

  We can then give students training to help them approach test items more effectively. As an example, for speaking tasks, we will equip students with appropriate negotiating language to help them get over awkward moments in such tasks. When training students to handle reading test items, we will discuss with them the best way to approach a first reading of the text, and how that can be modified on second reading to allow them to answer the questions asked.

  If the test or exam is likely to contain multiple-choice questions, we can help students to appreciate the advantages of finding the obvious distractor(s) first. They can then work out what similarities and differences the other distractors have so that they can identify the area of meaning or grammar that is being targeted.

  In all this work our task is to make students thoroughly familiar with the test items they will have to face so that they give of their best, and so that, in the end, the test discovers their level of English, rather than having it obscured by their unfamiliarity with the test items.

- **Discuss general exam skills:** most students benefit from being reminded about general test and exam skills, without which much of the work they do will be wasted. For example, they need to read through questions carefully so that they know exactly what is expected. They need to pace themselves so that they do not spend a disproportionate amount of time on only part of an exam. In writing, for example, they need to be able to apply process skills (see Chapter 19, B1) to the task. As they build up to an exam, they need to be able to organise their work so that they can revise effectively.

- **Do practice tests:** students need a chance to practise taking the test or exam so that they get a feel for the experience, especially with regard to issues such as pacing. At various points in a course, therefore, students can sit practice papers or whole practice tests, but this should not be done too often since not only will it give teachers horrific marking schedules, but it will also be less productive than other test and exam preparation procedures.

- **Have fun:** as we said above, just because students need to practise certain test types does not mean this has to be done in a boring or tense way. There are a number of ways of having fun with tests and exams.

  If a typical test item asks candidates to put words in order to make sentences (see B2 above), the teacher might prepare the class for this kind of item by giving students a number of words on cards which they have to physically assemble into sentences. They can hold them above their heads (so that they cannot see the words on them) and their classmates have to tell them where to stand to make a 'human sentence'. Students can play 'transformation tennis', where one student 'serves' a sentence, e.g. *India is the country I would like to visit more than any other* and the receiving student has to reply with a transformation starting with *The country*, e.g. *The country I would most like to visit is India* (Prodromou 1995: 22–23). They can change the sex of all the people in direct and indirect test items to see if the items still work and if not, why not.

Students can be encouraged to write their own test items, based on language they have been working on and the examples they have seen so far. The new test items can now be given to other students to see how well they have been written and how difficult they are. This helps students to get into the minds of their test and exam writers.

- **Ignore the test:** if students who are studying for an exam only ever look at test types, discuss exam technique and take practice tests, lessons may become monotonous. There is also the possibility that general English improvement will be compromised at the expense of exam preparation.

  When we are preparing students for an exam, we need to ignore the exam from time to time so that we have opportunities to work on general language issues, and so that students can take part in the kind of motivating activities that are appropriate for all English lessons.

Chapter notes and further reading

- **Public exams**
  There are many international exams which students can take.

  - Cambridge exams are offered by the University of Cambridge ESOL Cambridge, UK (www.cambridgeesol.org). These include exams in general English, e.g.

    Key English Test (KET) for elementary candidates (A2)

    Preliminary English Test (PET) for lower intermediate candidates (B1)

    First Certificate in English (FCE) for upper intermediate candidates (B2)

    Certificate of Advanced English (CAE) for upper intermediate/advanced candidates (C1)

    Certificate of Proficiency in English (CPE) for very advanced candidates (C2)

    BEC (Business English Certificate) offered at three levels

    Cambridge ESOL also offers three exams for young learners (YLE tests): Starters (below A1), Movers (A1) and Flyers (A2).

  - City and Guilds Pitman qualifications are offered by City and Guilds, London (www.city-and-guilds.co.uk). Exams are offered in:

    International ESOL (6 levels)

    International Spoken ESOL (6 levels)

    ESOL for Young Learners

    Spoken ESOL for Young Learners

English for Business Communications (3 levels)

Spoken English Test for Business (6 levels)

English for Office Skills (2 levels)

- IELTS (International English Language Testing System) exams are administered jointly by Cambridge ESOL (see above), the British Council and IDP Education, Australia (www.ielts.org).

  IELTS scores (on a 0–9 band) are used especially by British and Australian universities to gauge the level of would-be students or trainers/teachers.

  There are papers in listening and speaking. Candidates then choose general or academic writing, and general or academic reading.

- GESE (Graded Exams in Spoken English) and ISE (Integrated Skills in English) exams are offered by Trinity College, London (www.trinitycollege.co.uk). The spoken English exams are one-to-one interviews with an examiner at a level to suit the candidate.

- TOEFL (Test of English as a Foreign Language) is offered by Educational Testing Services, New Jersey, USA (www.toefl.org).

  TOEFL scores are used by colleges and universities in North America and elsewhere to measure English proficiency for would-be students. The tests are now computer-administered in parts of the world where this is possible.

- TOEIC (Test of English for International Communication) is offered by TOEIC Service International, Princeton, New Jersey (www.toeic.com).

  TOEIC scores are used by a number of companies in the USA and elsewhere to judge the level of English of potential employees.

- Exams for business are offered by Cambridge ESOL (see above), City and Guilds (see above) and by the London Chamber of Commerce and Industry (LCCI) (www.lccieb.com).

- **Testing in general**
  On testing in general, see McNamara, T (2000), A Hughes (2003) and C Weir (1993). See also C Alderson *et al* (1995). On the history of language testing, see C Weir (2005: Chapter 1).

- **Validity and reliability**
  For an investigation into issues of test validity and 'establishing the validity of the interpretation of scores', see C Weir (2005). For a polemical view of 'learner validity' (e.g. how tests can benefit learners), see B Tomlinson (2005) and a reply to it (Figueras 2005).

- **Portfolio assessment**
  For a positive view of portfolio assessment, see K Smith (2002). W Trotman (2004) summarises advantages and disadvantages and P Whitaker (2005) worries about some of the problems associated with this kind of assessment.

- **Cloze procedures**
  A Hughes (2003: 191–193) gives an example of a cloze test based on informal spoken English and suggests this is an effective way of measuring oral ability.

- **Oral testing**
  B Knight (1992) describes a workshop in which teachers investigate how to measure students' speaking skills.

- **Using rating scales**
  J Upshur and C Turner (1995) suggest replacing descriptive rating scales with scales where test markers have to answer a series of binary (*yes/no*) questions about student performance.

- **Washback/backwash**
  See A Hughes (2003: Chapter 6), T Green and R Hawkey (2004) and L Prodromou (1995).

- **Teaching for exams**
  The best book on the subject – with many examples for different exams tasks – is S Burgess and K Head (2005).

- **Testing in the age of EIL**
  In an interesting exchange of views, J Jenkins (2006b) and L Taylor (2006) discuss how testing may have to change in the light of discussions about English as an International language (EIL) – another term for Global English (see Chapter 1B), i.e. the English that is intended for international communication, also referred to as ELF (see page 20).

23 | Learner autonomy: learning to learn

However good a teacher may be, students will find it difficult to learn a language unless they aim to learn outside as well as during class time. This is because language is too complex and varied for there to be enough time for students to learn all they need to in a classroom. Even if students have three English lessons a week, it will take a great number of weeks before they have had the kind of exposure and opportunities for use which are necessary for real progress. The problem for teachers is the knowledge that not everything can be taught in class, but even if it could, a teacher will not always be around if and when students wish to use the language in real life (Cotterall 1995: 220).

To compensate for the limits of classroom time and to boost the chances for successful language learning and acquisition, students need to be encouraged to develop their own learning strategies so that as far as possible, they become autonomous learners. As we suggested in Chapter 5, D3, giving students *agency* (enabling them to be the doers rather than the recipients of learning action) is one way of helping to sustain their motivation. However, students are sometimes reluctant to adopt this kind of agency. Attitudes to self-directed learning are frequently conditioned by the educational culture in which students have studied or are studying (see Chapter 4, B1) and this may not always prioritise learner autonomy. And whereas some students see the need to learn for themselves, others, for whatever reason, are less enthusiastic about taking responsibility for their learning, even when we give them every encouragement and opportunity to develop as autonomous learners. This was borne out in a study by Icy Lee (in Hong Kong). She reports that some of her students responded well to learner training work after they had signed a 'learner contract' with their teacher, but that others were not nearly so successful (Lee 1998). The more enthusiastic of her learners spent more time learning on their own and felt more positive about themselves and about learning both during and after a term in which self-directed learning had been actively promoted by their teacher. They were confident that they would continue learning on their own after the course. The less enthusiastic learners, however, suffered from low self-esteem, had an ambivalent attitude to learner autonomy and spent less time in self-study than their peers. They were unlikely to continue studying on their own after the course had finished.

Nevertheless, and despite the danger that some students will find assuming agency a nearly impossible challenge, various commentators see autonomy and associated learner behaviour as crucial. Mark James suggests that a basic goal of English language teaching is that 'students will apply outside the classroom what they have learnt inside the classroom' (2006: 151). For Sarah Cotterall, learner autonomy is not just a goal for highly committed students completing optional courses, but should be seen as 'an essential goal of all learning' (2000: 109).

Learner autonomy is important, in other words, yet it is easier for some than for others. In the face of such a reality, what can teachers do to try to promote autonomous learning, and how far can and should they go? These are the questions which this chapter will attempt to answer.

A Promoting autonomy

Most teachers are keen to talk to students about the importance of becoming autonomous learners. But just telling students that autonomy is in some way a good thing will have little effect unless it is part of a wider course design – and unless we find ways of helping students to become more independent.

Sarah Cotterell suggests that language courses which aim to promote learner autonomy should have a number of defining characteristics. In the first place, the course should reflect the learners' goals in its language, tasks and strategies. This means raising the students' awareness of ways of identifying goals, specifying objectives and identifying resources which will help them to realise these goals. Next, the course tasks should be explicitly linked to a simplified model of the language learning process. In other words, Sarah Cotterell suggests, students are unlikely to be able to manage their own learning if they have no idea of how learning works; it is by developing an awareness of language-learning theory that they are able to adopt learning strategies for themselves. Course tasks should replicate real-world communicative tasks (or provide rehearsal for such tasks) and, finally, the course should promote reflection on learning (Cotterall 2000: 111–112).

Joanne McClure shares some of the same goals. Working at Nanyang Technological University in Singapore, she wanted her students to develop an awareness of themselves as learners. Among other things, she wanted them to develop a systematic approach to their reading, writing and research and to become increasingly aware of the way in which successful writers structure their research (McClure 2001: 143).

What both writers are talking about is how to get students thinking about how they learn so that the more they think in this way, the more they will be able to take charge of their own learning.

A1 Students and teachers

The problem, for some teachers, with getting students to think about learning is that students do not necessarily see the world in the same way as their teachers do. In a memorable article, Kumaravadivelu found that the learners' perceptions of what was going on frequently failed to match the teacher's intentions. For example, when a teacher wanted students to practise scanning by reading advertisements, the students (in post-lesson discussion) veered between thinking they had been studying how to buy through newspaper advertisements to supposing the lesson had something to do with capital letters and commas, even though the teacher had not mentioned this at all, though they had looked at the issue a week previously (Kumaravadivelu 1991: 103).

Ten years later, Carol Griffiths and Judy Parr were interested to see if the learning strategies which students relied on matched their teachers' perceptions of the strategies they were using. The strategies they looked at included using review and flashcards to remember words (memory strategies), trying to find patterns in English or deliberately reading for pleasure (cognitive strategies), making guesses and skipping words they did not know (compensation strategies), noticing mistakes for future correction (metacognitive strategies), trying to relax when they felt afraid of using English or giving themselves a 'prize' if they did well (affective strategies), and asking English speakers to correct them when they talked and trying to learn about the culture of English speakers (social strategies).

The teachers reckoned that of the six strategies under investigation the priority ratings for the students would be as follows:

6 (most frequent)	Memory strategies
5	Cognitive strategies
4	Social strategies
3	Metacognitive strategies
2	Compensation strategies
1 (least frequent)	Affective strategies

However, the students came up with a very different frequency list:

6 (most frequent)	Social strategies
5	Metacognitive strategies
4	Compensation strategies
3	Cognitive strategies
2	Affective strategies
1 (least frequent)	Memory strategies

(Griffiths and Parr 2001: 252)

Roger Hawkey found the same kind of perception mismatch when he asked his students to rate the prominence of 13 activity categories, such as *listening to the teacher talking to the whole class* and *pair discussions*. Students saw things very differently so that whereas, for example, the teacher thought that pair discussions were the second most common activity type, for students they came in at number eight (Hawkey 2006).

When we train or encourage students to be autonomous, therefore, we need to try to ensure that both we and they are hearing the same things. Furthermore, we will need to offer them choices in learning strategies. What may feel appropriate from the teacher's point of view may not seem so appropriate for students. And as we saw in Chapter 5B, what is appropriate for one student may not be appropriate for all.

B Learner training, learner autonomy

It is possible that some students will be keen to take responsibility for their own learning from the very beginning of a course. However, most teachers know that this is unlikely unless they are given help in thinking about how they learn and how this learning can be made more effective (as we saw in Section A above). Learner training, in other words, is a first step on the road to self-directed learning. Together with activities where students are encouraged, or even (sometimes) forced, to take responsibility for what they are doing, learner training gives those who are prepared to take it the possibility of real autonomy.

B1 **Thinking about learning**

In the following learner training examples, students are encouraged to think about what (and how) they have been learning, are made to think about different ways of listening and are offered different strategies for them to choose from.

Example 1: Finishing a unit	Focus: reflecting on learning

Under the influence of the Common European Framework (see page 95), many teachers and materials writers have students go through a checklist of 'can do' statements at the end of each unit. For example, they have to tick statements such as *I can use the present continuous to talk about the future* or *I can construct a business letter using appropriate language and layout*. If they don't feel they can tick a statement, they have a clear indication that they should go back and study the language or the language skill they still seem to have trouble with.

A more elaborate way of getting students to reflect on what they have done recently is to ask them to complete sentences about, say, last week's work, e.g.

- The thing(s) that I enjoyed most in last week's lessons was/were ...
- The thing(s) I learnt last week that I did not know before was/were ...
- The thing(s) I am going to do to help me remember what I learnt last week is/are ...
- The thing(s) I found most difficult in last week's work was/were ...
- The question(s) I would like to ask about what we have done is/are ...

'Can do' statements and sentences like this prompt the students to think about what they have learnt and start to get them reflecting on their learning.

Example 2: Listening to different things	Focus: listening strategies

In the following activity, students are reminded that one way of making listening easier is to use their knowledge of the world. In other words, if the moment they hear something, they can recognise what kind of a 'something' it is (e.g. a radio commercial, an airport or station announcement, etc.), they will be ready to predict what is coming next and so it will be easier for them to understand what they are listening to.

Students listen to audio clips, such as the beginning of a radio news bulletin (*It is six o'clock. Here is the news ...*), a recorded message (*Welcome to the Clifton Cinemas automated booking service ...*), or the introduction to a lecture (*So I'd like you to give a special welcome to Professor Martha Ellis who is going to address us on the subject of ...*). They have to identify what the listening genres are in each case.

They now have to say how they will listen to each of the listening genres they have just identified. They complete the following chart:

Listening for gist	**Listening for specific detail**	**Listening for all details**
(Getting a general understanding on first listening)	(Trying to hear one or two specific pieces of information only)	(Listening for any relevant information in order to know what to do next)

When they have done this, they compare their answers in pairs or small groups before discussing it with the whole class.

Just as Joanne McClure wanted her students to develop a systematic approach to their writing and studying (see page 395), so here we are asking students to think carefully about different ways of listening and how each one suits different listening genres. Although there are no completely right answers, still this kind of activity gets students to start thinking about how they can approach the task of listening so they do it more efficiently when they are on their own without the guidance of a teacher.

| **Example 3:** Note-taking | Focus: choosing strategies |

One of the skills that our students need, especially (but not only) at tertiary level is that of note-taking. Many students of English are studying the language precisely because they wish to attend academic courses delivered in English. They need to know, therefore, what the best way of taking notes is.

However, here we have a problem since note-taking is a highly personal matter and there is no right way of doing it. And if we looked at the notes of all the students as they left a lecture, we would find a whole range of possibilities. Some would have taken copious notes, while others would only have noted down a few points. Some notes would be highly organised, while others would look chaotic. Yet even notes that seem chaotic to us may be effective (that is, they help students to remember and understand what they have experienced) for some students whose minds and visual memories work in that way.

What this suggests is that rather than telling students how to take notes, we should offer them various possibilities for them to choose from (see Figure 1).

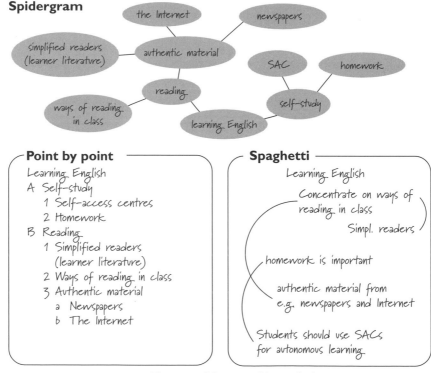

FIGURE 1: Three possible note-taking techniques

However, even these three examples may act only as springboards to a discussion about the best way to make notes for each individual student. The purpose of the activity is, after all, to get students to select a strategy so that they can take responsibility for their own note-taking method, not merely to imitate what we ourselves might think or do.

We can do the same when we encourage students to keep their own vocabulary/lexical notebooks. We can offer them various possibilities starting with (a) a simple alphabetical listing of words (*ankle, elbow, goalkeeper, manager*), (b) words plus translation (*ankle – tornozelo, elbow – cotovelo, goalkeeper – goleiro, manager – técnico*), (c) words in alphabetical order with example sentences (*ankle – I sprained my ankle when I slipped on a banana skin, goalkeeper – The goalkeeper couldn't stop the ball going into the back of the net*) – with or without translation, or (d) words grouped together in lexical fields (*people in football – goalkeeper, manager, referee; parts of the body – ankle, elbow, knee*). We can advise students which of these are the most effective, but in the end, *they* must be the ones to choose the best way of recording words and phrases so that they will remember them.

B2 Taking over

The ideal situation is for the students to take over their own learning – in other words, to do it without having to be shown how by the teacher. There are various ways of trying to bring this about.

In the first place, what we have called the 'immediate creativity' phase (see Chapter 12B) is the moment when we get students to take the language for themselves. They are no longer just repeating what we have told them to; instead, they are trying to use the new language to say things they want to. When we get students to make their own dialogues with new language, the same thing is true; the moment they invent their very own conversations, they are, to some extent, taking the language into their own hands. However, this kind of teacher-provoked creativity is some way from the agency we discussed in Chapter 5, D3.

Magdalena Kubanyiova wants us to leave the students alone (Kubanyiova 2004) and let them decide, for example, how to write questionnaires if they have been asked to do a survey. For her, students do fine if we let them get on with it.

In Chapter 14, D2 we looked at a number of dictionary activities in which students both learnt how dictionaries worked and then learnt how to use them. Once students are capable of using dictionaries in this way, they have, in effect, taken over since they can get word information with or without our help.

When students get to make (or help to make) decisions about what happens in and out of class, they can be seen to have at least partly taken over in the same way. Thus, for example, when a teacher says *You can decide what we do next. We can either listen to someone talking about different kinds of education, we can read a text about a special education experiment or we can have a discussion about different kinds of discipline ...* and the students choose which of these they are going to do, they have a degree of agency. In the same way, Lesley Painter's decision to let students decide what homework they wanted to do (Painter 1999 and see page 103 of this book) is entirely consistent with Jenny De Sonneville's suggestion that students should take a more active role in course design (De Sonneville 2005: 11).

Except in exceptional circumstances, we are not suggesting that students should take over the whole design and running of a course. That, surely, is our job and we bring our professional skills to bear when we decide on the programme we are going to ask students to follow. But within that programme, the more we can get students to rely on their own decision-making, the better. We can get them to tell us what they want and need to do next via discussion, needs analyses or other forms of action research (see Chapter 24B). We can ensure that some of their time is spent in a self-access centre (see Section C below), and we can do our best to ensure that they learn outside the classroom and after the course.

B3 Learning journals

One way in which teachers try to encourage students to become autonomous is by encouraging them to write journals. But journal writing has other benefits, too. In the first place, writing journals provides good writing practice and helps to improve the students' general writing skills. In the second place, journals allow students to express feelings more freely than they might do in public, in class. If they know that their journals are not going to be read by everyone (unless they want people to read them), they will write more openly. And because the act of writing is less immediate than spontaneous conversation, they have more time to access those feelings. Journals can also provide a kind of teacher–student dialogue that is often impossible in a whole-class environment. We can often learn things about our students which we were previously unaware of when we read what they write in these journals. For example, when Lakshmy Krishnan and Lee Hwee Hoon asked students to keep diaries at the Nanyang Technological University in Singapore, they found themselves 'listening to voices' which gave them strong messages about individual concerns and needs. As a result of reading these journals, the course leaders found themselves thinking up new ways of helping students from outside Singapore who had shown, through their journal entries, that they were homesick and disoriented (Krishnan and Hoon 2002).

From the point of view of learner autonomy, journals provide an opportunity for students to think both about *how* they are learning (i.e. what is easier or more difficult, and why and how they achieve success), and also about *what* they are learning (i.e. aspects of the language and how it all fits together). This kind of introspection may well lead them to insights which will greatly enhance their progress. Just as teacher journals provoke their writers into reflecting on how and why things have happened so that they can decide what to do next (see Chapter 24, A1), so student journals may well provoke creative introspection in their writers. A marked benefit of such introspection when it occurs is its effect on memory. There are good reasons for supposing that when we have a chance to reflect carefully on what we have done, we are far more likely to remember it than if we simply discard an experience the moment it is over.

Although some students may have kept diaries in the past (and some may still do so), the majority may be either unfamiliar with or unenthusiastic about journal writing. Because of this we need to consider carefully why we want students to take part in the activity so that we can communicate this purpose to them. For example, we might want to set up a teacher–student channel where we can offer help and support on a one-to-one basis. Alternatively, we might want them to write down their reactions to individual lessons or keep a record of what is going through their heads during and after classes. We can then respond to what they write. Perhaps, on the other hand, we may just want them to write about anything that comes into their heads (probably as a result of the lessons they have been taking with us).

Having decided what kind of journal we want students to keep, we will then explain why we want them to write and what kind of thing we want them to say when they are writing. We will tell them what kind of an exercise book or notebook they might want to use or we can, if we think this will help, provide the notebooks ourselves. We are now ready to get the process under way.

- **Starting out and keeping going:** it may help, when we first introduce the idea of journal writing, to give students some examples of possible journal entries. When and if we have done this, we might give them an opportunity or opportunities to write practice journal entries which we can then comment on.

  We now have to decide when and how often we expect students to write their journal entries. If we really want to give them agency, this will be up to them, of course, but if we are worried that, despite initial enthusiasm, they might get bored with the idea, we can institute regular journal-writing sessions of about, say, ten minutes a week. At the very least, this gives students good writing practice.

  If we are going to respond to student journals in any way (see below), we can institute a regime so that they know when the journals will be collected each week (or fortnight). Together with a regular journal-writing slot, this will ensure that students bring journals with them and continue to focus on making journal entries.

  To keep students' interest in their journals going, we should emphasise that it is up to them to decide what they want to put in them (though of course we will make it clear that we do not accept material that is inappropriate or insulting). They can personalise their journals with pictures or drawings, too.

  The continuing success of journal writing may well depend upon whether or not we offer written responses to their entries (see below) and, if we do, what kind of response this is.

- **Public or private:** when we encourage students to write journals, they have to know who, if anyone, will be reading them. It is quite feasible to suggest, for example, that students should be allowed to keep what they write completely private. If this is the case, our role would mainly be to provide writing time and to encourage students repeatedly to keep writing. We might also lead discussions in which students talk about the experience of journal writing.

  Many students will welcome their teacher's response to their journals. This will give them the motivation of writing for someone apart from themselves (though this is not without its problems – see below). There are good reasons for us to read our students' journals, partly since this give us insights into what they are thinking and worrying about, but also because it informs us about their progress and their reactions to their learning experiences.

  A more public version of the journal is to get students to write a blog (see page 338). This has the advantage of providing some excitement about 'going live' online, but will probably have a negative impact if the blog is never replied to by anyone else. There is no point in going public if the public are not interested once you get there!

  The best way to resolve the public/private dichotomy is to discuss the most appropriate kind of journal with the students so that they can decide whether they want to stay private, write for the teacher only or go totally public. It will be our job to make sure that they understand the advantages and disadvantages of each alternative.

- **Responding to journals:** there are many different ways of responding to students' journals, and the one we choose may well determine the success or failure of the whole journal-writing enterprise. We could, for example, write a comment at the end of a journal entry which only showed that we had read what the student had written (e.g. *I enjoyed reading your journal this week. Well done*), or we could refer to a particular part of the entry (e.g. *I think your description of the difficulty of understanding English on the phone is very interesting*). Both comments (especially the second) show that we have at least read the journal. However, we might go further and offer advice (e.g. *The next time you are talking to an English speaker on the phone, you can use phrases such as 'Could your repeat what you just said?' or 'Would you mind speaking a bit more slowly?'*). We could also offer language comments such as *Be careful about 'since' and 'for'. We use 'for' with a period of time (three weeks, two hours, etc.) and 'since' with an actual time (1999, six o'clock, etc.).* Of course, we can go further than this and underline the mistakes in the students' writing in the same way as we correct some of their written homework.

  One of the best ways of deciding how to respond to student journal entries is to discuss what kind of responses they would feel most comfortable with. That's what Richard Watson Todd and his colleagues in Thailand did with their students. What was clear to them was that the students wanted feedback from the teachers who read their journals, provided that trust was established between them and the teacher. It was in this way that appropriate dialogue was established and maintained. But when asked, students made it clear that for them a general comment at the end of a journal entry was not enough. These journal writers wanted comments at the place in the text where the teacher had concerns or other reactions (the same could be achieved, of course, with footnotes). The comments that the students most valued were suggestions, positive evaluation or supportive back-up (Watson Todd *et al* 2001). However, it is worth remembering that individual students may have different views from the group as a whole. We should be sensitive to this and, where possible, ask individual students if they are comfortable with the level and type of feedback that they are receiving.

  Responding to learner journals can dramatically increase a teacher's workload, especially if more than one class is involved in doing this. No teacher can reply adequately to 150 journal entries a week on top of lesson preparation, classroom teaching and homework marking. But there are ways round this. We can, for example, make 'appointments' to read an individual's journal. Instead of reading it every week, we might say we will read it twice a term, and say when that will be. We could read one group's journals one week and another group's the next. We can ask students to restrict themselves to writing no more than one or two pages.

Journal-writing provokes students into reflecting on their own learning while also giving them good English writing practice. If we organise it properly, it can have enormous benefits for both students and teachers.

B4 **Forcing agency?**

Before we leave the subject of getting students to assume agency (to take responsibility for their learning), we need to discuss limits to our attempts to make this happen. If, as we have suggested, learning is conditioned both by the student's educational culture and also by his or her individual learning styles and preferences, then the idea that all students should be forced to become autonomous seems unnecessarily prescriptive. Why should students who are, for whatever reason, reluctant to become autonomous, have autonomy thrust upon them?

The fact is that in the words of an old English proverb, you can lead a horse to water but you can't make it drink. And if it doesn't want or need to drink, you shouldn't make it do so anyway. Some students, like horses at the water's edge, just don't get it; for them the teacher is the one who is responsible for their learning, and they expect the teacher to do their job.

Faced with the reluctance of at least some of the students in a group to assume agency, we have to consider what we can do both for those students and for others in the group who are keener on the idea of taking learner responsibility.

The first thing we will offer our students is the kind of learner training we discussed in B1. It will never be wasted, even if some students respond to it less enthusiastically than others. The second thing we will do is give students the chance to take over as often as possible, whether this is in the form of getting them to tell us if they want to be corrected during a fluency activity (see Chapter 8, C3), allowing them to make decisions about homework tasks or simply leaving them alone to construct their own questionnaires, for example.

But however much students do or do not take up our offer of training for autonomy, there is a group of activities which at the very least make their participation mandatory. These are activities where students have to take part in order for the activity to be a success. For example, the story-circle writing on page 337 only works because every member of the group is obliged to write a new sentence every time they are given a new piece of paper. Opting out is not an option (unless, of course an individual student has a serious behaviour problem, but that is another issue – see Chapter 9A). The jigsaw reading activity on page 299 also encourages mandatory participation since the story of why a concert was so special (which the students are introduced to at the beginning of the sequence) can only be fully understood – the jigsaw can only be successfully completed – if every student shares the knowledge they have read in their own short texts. William Littlewood's numbered heads technique (see page 347) also ensures that all individual students are more or less obliged to participate.

C The self-access centre (SAC)

A useful adjunct to classroom learning – or indeed alternative to it – is the self-access or (open) learning centre. In SACs students can work on their own (or in pairs and groups) with a range of material, from grammar reference and workbook-type tasks to audio and video excerpts. They can work with books, worksheets, CDs and DVDs, or they can access material from computers, whether hooked up to an Intranet – that is all programs working from a main server run by the institution where the SAC is located – or whether they have access to the Internet.

Some modern SACs consist of little but banks of computers. Others, which rely on books and paper, will almost certainly have large collections of learner literature (see Chapter 17,

A1), dictionaries (see Chapter 11, G1), reading texts and listening materials. Where possible, SACs either have separate rooms or have one large room divided into sections for different kinds of material, though it is also possible to put large amounts of self-access material on a trolley that can be wheeled from class to class. As Lum Yoke Lin and Ray Brown make clear, each self-access centre is unique. Working in Malaysia, they showed that each of the 28 centres they were involved in which incorporated SACs had 'their own unique local problems and preferences, and this gives them their individual characters' (Lum and Brown 1994: 155).

In well-regulated SACs, students drop in either as a regular part of the timetable or in their own spare time. Some students may have signed up to be allowed to use the SAC even though they are not in any English class; they are, therefore, not actually following a regular course. Once inside the room (or hooked up to a computer), they will decide what work to do, find the right kind of material and activities, and settle down to complete the learning task.

C1 Characteristics of a good self-access centre

One way of setting up a SAC is just to put piles of material in a room or have computers that students can hook themselves up to. However, this is unlikely to be advantageous for students who may not know what to do or where to go to do it. In order for a SAC or a computer website to work successfully, various issues have to be resolved.

- **Classification systems:** nothing will demotivate a student more than trying to work on something that is too easy or way outside their reach. Yet this is a distinct possibility unless there is a clear system of classification which details the type of material and the level it is designed for. Thus when students access the main screen of the SAC computer, they should find it easy to get to the listening menu (if listening is what they want to do), there should be a clear description of what listening material there is, and the levels should be clearly signposted. In general, the website should be easy to navigate around.

  Where SACs have a preponderance of book and paper materials on bookshelves, in files or in boxes, these should be clearly classified by skill, activity and level. Such classification information should be visually prominent, using colour coding and/or clear labelling. Students should also be able to consult a card index or database.

- **Pathways:** once students have completed an exercise, they can be given suggestions about where to go next. The material they have been using can list other items on the same topic; on the computer screen, students can return to the main menu when they have completed an exercise, and that menu can offer a range of further possibilities. With paper worksheets, suggestions can be incorporated for related material, e.g. *Now you have done this scanning exercise, you might want to try R/6/32 which asks you to skim a text – another important reading skill.* In both cases, the activity becomes a jumping off point for students to follow pathways suggested by software and SAC.

  SAC assistants and teachers have a major role to play in helping students to use the centres successfully and follow appropriate pathways. Students can be shown where things are, can be helped with hardware and software problems and directed down new pathways. In order to help students in this way, assistants and teachers need to be fully aware of a centre's contents and benefits, and trained – through induction materials, specially designed SAC lessons, and staff seminars – to help students appropriately (O'Dell 1992).

- **Training students:** most students, left to their own devices in a SAC or on a computer website, will not know how to use the facility to its best advantage, however good the menu or classification system is. Websites and SACs are likely to look either boring or intimidating. To prevent this situation, students need to be trained to use programs and centres appropriately.

  Some teachers provide training in class, giving students clear tasks and then taking them directly to the SAC to have them complete these. This can happen on a regular basis over a period of weeks, at the end of which time the students are thoroughly familiar with what is in the centre and how best to use it. Many teachers design quizzes to get students hunting around the website or the centre itself. Alternatively, we could tell students to explore the website or SAC on their own so that they can produce leaflets or computer-based manuals showing other students what is on offer and how to use them. With highly motivated and potentially autonomous learners, the need to make things clear for their colleagues will force them to get to grips with what is on offer.

  Even when students have been trained to use a SAC, they will still benefit from the help that assistants and teachers can give them in the centre itself.

- **Making self-access centres appropriate for students:** one view of a SAC has a group of individual students sitting apart from each other in silence (often at a computer screen), working profitably and autonomously. Yet as Jeremy Jones points out, 'To make autonomy an undiluted educational objective in a culture where it has no traditional place is to be guilty at least of cultural insensitivity' (Jones 1995: 229). Working at Phnom Penh University in Cambodia, he was concerned to make SAC use appropriate to the styles of learning which his students found most comfortable. Clear evidence suggested that students enjoyed working collaboratively and so, instead of the usual individual seating spaces in many SACs, students could choose more 'coffee-table' places, designed specifically to have groups working together. There was a higher tolerance of noise than might be expected in some other places, and tasks were designed which specifically encouraged pair and group interaction.

  Anyone setting up a SAC or designing material and tasks for use in it should think carefully about who is likely to use it and what patterns of use will be most culturally appropriate. One way of doing this is to set up a student advisory panel to take part in planning and evaluating the centre. Apart from guaranteeing the involvement of those particular students, this has the potential for a SAC design which really meets the needs of its users.

- **Keeping interest going:** SACs really come into their own when students take the decision to go and study there by themselves – and continue to do so over a period of time. For this reason, administrators and teachers have to devise methods to keep users involved and interested.

  One way of doing this is to give students a feedback sheet to fill in after every activity. Though such forms are ostensibly for the centre's use, the process of reflecting on an activity helps to maintain the user's engagement and prepares them for the next task.

  Another means of maintaining student involvement is through a SAC-users' committee which students can apply to become members of. With monthly meetings which bring about change and improvement, they have a genuine part to play in directing the centre's present and future course.

  An ideal way of keeping users on board is for the centre to provide a monthly or quarterly newsletter and/or website in which students and centre administrators list new material and new ways of using things. Different pathways can be explored and different users can be profiled. The newsletter/website can run competitions and include the kind of news and gossip that newsletters in other fields use to keep their members involved.

Many computer programs can track an individual student's use and progress through the various activities available. Students can also be asked to sign in every time they visit a SAC, and attendance can be rewarded in some way (or made part of a course requirement).

C2 Evaluating self-access resources

In order to make sure that SACs or computer sites are fulfilling their functions of allowing students to work and study on their own, we need some process of evaluation, some way of measuring whether or not the centres or sites are effective.

Hayo Reinders and Marilyn Lewis have designed a checklist for self-access materials which is 'an attempt to strike a balance between the ideal, lengthy survey which would leave no question unasked and a shorter one which had more chance of being used' (Reinders and Lewis 2006: 277). In their case, their concern has been with self-access material in book form (see Figure 2). It is clear that for them selection, ease of access, clear learning goals and procedures and learner training are key characteristics for book-based self-access materials.

Features	Yes/No/Unsure	Comments
Selecting the resource		
Claims to be suitable for self-access		
Clearly describes the student level		
Needs to be used sequentially		
Accessing parts of the resource		
An index		
A table of contents		
A detailed 'map'		
A glossary		
Chapter previews or summaries		
The learning process		
Information summarised		
Examples provided for tasks		
Objectives provided for tasks		
Keys/answers/criteria for tasks		
Learning to learn		
Notes on the learning process		
Shows how to set goals		
Other features		

FIGURE 2: An evaluative checklist for self-access material (Reinders and Lewis 2006: 277)

The authors have included a comment column so that users can say how useful the checklist is and what they might want added to it (or amended).

A checklist for computer-based self-access materials would look somewhat different from this, of course. We would be unlikely to talk about chapters and indexes or tables of contents.

Instead, we would be concerned with issues such as menus, ease of navigation, interactivity and whether or not (and in what form) answers or hints were provided on the screen. But whatever kind of checklist we make, we will want to design a questionnaire, list or table which allows us to measure whether the material we are asking students to access matches the criteria we discussed in C1 above.

D After (and outside) the course

As Susan McLean Orlando suggests, the kind of learning that occurs in formal settings 'may represent only a fraction of the learning experienced by participants' (McLean Orlando 2006: 45). If they are studying in a target-language community such as Australia, Britain, Canada, New Zealand or the USA, for example, they are likely to hear and see English all around them in shopping malls, on advertising billboards or on TV or the radio. Increasingly, even when they are studying in what were once considered EFL situations (see page 19), they may have access to the Internet for a wide variety of genres from newspaper reports to blogs, from poetry to pop songs. As English becomes more and more of a lingua franca (see Chapter 1, B1), there is more and more chance that students will be exposed to English in the real world outside the classroom, too. In most situations, teachers and students can have access to competent English speakers who, for example, work for international companies or who take part in English-language theatre productions or other recreational activities.

When students are attending our lessons, we can do our best to make them aware of all these resources. We need to remind them of all the ways they can access English on their own. We can set them tasks, such as bringing in English they have found on their own every Monday morning, or having them report on what they have done to enhance their English outside the class. We will promote extensive reading and listening, of course, and we can also ask them to use their learning journals (see B3 above) as records of the English they have investigated on their own.

However, sooner or later students will stop attending our lessons (or may not want to or be able to attend lessons of any kind). Now they really are on their own, and unless they can find some way of continuing to learn autonomously, their English is unlikely to improve and might even begin to deteriorate. There is a lot we can do to help our students plan for the teacher-free future.

D1 Training students to continue learning

Much of the advice that students are given about continued learning is not taken up (Braymen 1995). It is too general and though students know it is all sound counsel, they cannot follow the advice because the whole idea is too 'big', too amorphous. We need, therefore, to offer specific guidance which will allow them to focus on exactly what suits them best.

The first thing we need to do is to include 'continuing learning' as a topic in the syllabus. We can involve students in awareness-raising activities; together we can list all available sources of English before discussing which are most appropriate for their individual needs and how and where to get hold of them. We can consider the various skills that the students might want to work on, and re-visit various styles of language study and language research which they can usefully carry out on their own.

To train students in ways of using resources at their disposal, we can organise 'self-study' projects in class, which they can later replicate when they are on their own. For example, we might direct them to watch an English language news channel on TV and note down the main story headlines before following up those stories in newspapers or on the Internet. We can start, perhaps, by providing the material on CD, tape or DVD. Later, students can start accessing news material on their own, using the techniques we have practised earlier. By the time the course is over, they may have acquired the habit of accessing this kind of material on their own.

We can get students to use classroom techniques on their own, encouraging them to predict the content of texts before they read in detail, and then decide on a maximum of ten unknown words to look up in their dictionaries after they have read. We can train them to be their own language researchers by looking for new words and patterns that they have come across in subsequent texts. In this sense, all the learner training we do in class (see B1 above) has enormous potential for students working on their own, since, once having considered the best ways to learn, they can use these ways to improve without the necessity of teacher supervision.

One way of helping students to continue learning once a course is over is to negotiate *personal plans* which they can use for the weeks after lessons finish. The following example is the personal plan of an intermediate level student who works in an office where the British magazine *The Economist* is available, who has their own MLD (see Chapter 11, G1), and who has a copy of the vocabulary book *English Vocabulary in Use* by Michael McCarthy and Felicity O'Dell (published by Cambridge University Press):

Aim: to improve my vocabulary

Tasks:

1. Read at least three magazine articles from *The Economist* every week. For each article note down three words I want to know the meaning of. Look the words up in my dictionary. Find the words again in next week's articles and check (with the dictionary) that they mean the same in the new articles.

2. Do one unit from *English Vocabulary in Use* every week and check with the answer key and my dictionary.

Of course, we may not have time for personal plans if we have a large number of students. Instead, we can offer general work plans for anybody and everybody in which we list, for example, three good techniques for maintaining listening ability (and where to find listening material), or give details of Internet sites for language learners.

A powerful way of getting students to continue with their language use, especially where a successful group is coming to an end, is to encourage them to stay in touch with each other. They can do this by email or by setting up a users' group on the Internet (e.g. with Yahoo groups – see http://groups.yahoo.com – where it is extremely easy to set up a discussion group so that people can talk to a whole group at the same time).

Finally, students can access the many sites for language learners which are available online. Some of these are attached to schools the students have studied at, but there are many other sites, too, which provide free language exercises and other material for people who want to continue studying on their own.

Chapter notes and further reading

- **Learner autonomy**

  For theoretical studies of learner autonomy, see P Benson and P Voller (eds) (1997) and P Benson (2001). B Sinclair *et al* (2000) edit a collection of articles about the future – from a 2000 perspective – of learner autonomy and A Scharle and A Szabó (2000) have written a book about the practical side of learner autonomy. See also a short article by J Taylor (2002).

- **Learner training**

  G Ellis and B Sinclair (1989) expound a theory of learner training and then provide a range of activities for preparation and skills training. M Geldicke (2000) describes how she gives learners 'action plans' to guide their learning.

- **Student journal writing**

  See J Harmer (2004: Chapter 8) and K Richards (1992). A Kwamlah Johnson (2002) discusses the kind of notebooks that students can use for journal writing.

- **Self-access centres (SACs)**

  See D Gardner and L Lambert (1999). P Vettori's short article (2005) discusses setting up a SAC. C Gierse (1993) and L Barnett and G Jordan (1991) discuss SAC pathways.

  G Aston (1993) describes getting students to write leaflets, etc. for their colleagues.

- **Learning outside the classroom**

  Two articles which are well worth reading are D Braymen (1995) and N Pickard (1996).

- **Learner sites on the Internet**

  It is impossible to list all the sites that are available for students of English, but a few which are worth recommending are:

  - *Learning English* (bbc.co.uk/worldservice/learningenglish), a site run by the World Service arm of the BBC, has a good range of activities.

  - *Dave's ESL Café* (elscafé.com) has a large number of activities for students and a great links page which will take users to many other different websites.

  - *The Internet Tesol Journal* has lots of activities for students (including quizzes) at http://a4esl.org/. But their links page (at http://iteslj.org/links/) is a great place for students to start looking around. For example, they have a large list of podcast sites as well as grammar exercises, webquests and quiz links.

  - *The University of Illinois, Chicago*, has a good links page for students at www.uic.edu/depts/tie/coolsites.htm.

  In reality, however, students are best served by either getting sites from their school or tutors, or by using Google or another search engine to track down good English material.

24 | What teachers do next

In her course for language teachers, Penny Ur discussed the difference between teachers 'with 20 years' experience and those with one year's experience repeated 20 times' (Ur 1996: 317). Naturally we admire the first teacher and disapprove of (or sympathise with) the second. Nothing could be more deadening for a teacher than 20 years of repetition, especially in the interactive and dynamic world of the classroom. Our students, too, deserve teachers who are alive to the possibility of change and who keep up-to-date with what is going on, not only in the world of English language teaching, but also in the world at large.

The truth, however, is that no matter how much we enjoy meeting new students at the beginning of a new course, it is sometimes difficult to maintain a sense of excitement and engagement when using the same old lesson routines or reading texts time after time. The increasing predictability of student reactions and behaviour can – if we do not take steps to prevent it – dent even the most ardent initial enthusiasm. Teaching should be different from this, though. It can and should be a permanent process of change and growth.

At the beginning of our careers we go on teacher training courses where we are taught what to do. It is as our careers develop, however, that instead of being trained (or in addition to be trained), we should seek to develop ourselves and our teaching.

Teacher development means many different things to different people. Brian Tomlinson suggests that in a teacher development approach teachers are given new experiences to reflect and learn from (Tomlinson 2003). For him, the best of these tools is to involve teachers in writing teaching materials since when they do this they have to think carefully about what they want to do, why they want to do it and how to make it happen. Bill Templer, on the other hand, thinks that 'we need to hold up mirrors to our own practice, making more conscious what is beneath the surface' (Templer 2004). Paul Davis says that 'as development becomes more powerful, the role of the trainer will become less important' (Davis 1999). Sandra Piai was extremely impressed to hear a participant in a teacher development workshop say 'You can train me, and you can educate me, but you can't develop me – I develop' (Piai 2005: 21).

In this chapter we will look at a variety of ways in which people can either hold up mirrors to their practice, investigate what is going on in their classes, develop in cooperation with others, look outside the immediate world of the classroom for stimulation or continue studying.

A Reflection paths

Holding up mirrors to our practice (in Templer's words – see above) means being a reflective teacher. In other words, we need to think about (to reflect on) what we are doing and why. Some reflection is simply a matter of thinking about what is happening in our lessons (and our lives) as we take the metro home from work, but there are a number of more organised ways of doing this.

A1 Keeping journals

One way of provoking self-analysis and reflection on our teaching is by keeping our own journals in which we record our thoughts about our teaching and our students. Journals are powerful reflective devices which allow us to use introspection to make sense of what is going on around us. Bill Templer calls the classroom journal, kept on a regular basis, 'the best single interactive mirror' (Templer 2004).

Naoko Aoki came to realise that proper action research (see Section B below) was too much for the teachers she was working with. This, coupled with her belief that teachers' knowledge is narrative-based, led her to try something that was less time-consuming. Accordingly, she got her trainees to write stories about their teaching (of Japanese as a foreign language). The results were stories of emotional conflict with – and pressure from – senior colleagues and difficulty in classroom management. But they also referred 'to dilemmas between the ideals the students hold and the reality they face. I saw tears in the eyes of story tellers' (2004: 4).

Although the journals that Naoki Aoki is describing were produced as part of a training exercise, they nevertheless tell us something of the power of journals that we might keep by ourselves and for ourselves – in other words, as part of our own development. Lindsay Millar suggests six stages in journal-keeping (Miller 2004b). These include deciding what kind of journal we want to keep, preparing a format for the journal, deciding which class we want to write our journal about, and setting aside a time when we are going to write up our journal. This last stage is of crucial importance since unless we build routine into our journal-writing, it will often be difficult to sustain the momentum necessary to write it.

As we shall see in D1 below, journal-keeping is also a valuable tool for teachers who engage in self-development by learning another language. The journals that people have kept in such situations have often led to powerful insights into the nature not only of their own learning but also of the way they teach.

Journal-writing is powerful for two main reasons. In the first place, the act of writing the journal forces us to try to put into words thoughts which, up till then, are inchoate, offering, in this condition, little chance for real introspection. Secondly, the act of reading our own journals makes us engage again with what we experienced, felt or worried about. As a result of this re-engagement, we might quite possibly come to conclusions about what to do next.

A2 Negative and positive

If real development can only come from within, then it is by looking inside ourselves and seeking to understand or change what we find there that is likely to be the most effective way of moving forward and making things better.

Linda Bawcom, in an article devoted to preventing stress and countering teacher burnout, suggests making lists and seeing what they tell us. For example, we might draw up a list of professional priorities, such as the one in Figure 1. In the left-hand column we say what actually happens by numbering the items 1–12. Then, in the right-hand column, we re-prioritise the items as we would like them to be. The difference between the reality and what we wish for gives us the beginnings of a development plan.

_____ Attending conferences		_____
_____ Getting a certificate/diploma/degree		_____
_____ Peer observations		_____
_____ Peer counselling (time spent talking to colleagues)		_____
_____ Lesson planning/creating materials		_____
_____ Reading professional journals/books		_____
_____ Time with students (outside the classroom)		_____
_____ Time getting to and from place of work		_____
_____ Writing articles		_____
_____ Syllabus design/writing a (text)book		_____
_____ Doing (classroom) research		_____
_____ Doing administrative duties		_____

FIGURE 1: Professional priorities (from Bawcom 2005: 50)

We can do the same, Linda Bawcom suggests, with personal priorities, too (such as spending time with partners, children, friends or attending to our spiritual growth, having holidays, etc.).

Bill Templer suggests questioning other teachers as a lead-in to examining our own beliefs and practices. In an activity called 'Ghostwriter' (Templer 2004), he offers various questions for us to put to colleagues, such as _What are your two greatest strengths/weaknesses as a teacher? Or Reflect on a recent class. What worked well and why? OR What didn't work and why?_ Once we have discussed this with another teacher, he suggests we should write a brief sketch as if we were the person we have just interviewed.

What both Bawcom and Templer are suggesting is that we can think for ourselves, about ourselves. What we need to do, perhaps, is to set time aside to do this so that by making lists (in Bawcom's case) or trying to see ourselves from the outside (Templer's suggestion) we can come to conclusions about where we are with a view to deciding where we want to be.

A3 Recording ourselves

Another way of reflecting upon our own teaching practice is to record ourselves. Bill Templer (see above) suggests using a cheap tape recorder which we can leave running during the lesson. When the lesson is over, we can listen to the tape to remind us of what went on. Frequently, this will lead us to reflect on what happened and perhaps cause us to think of how we might do things differently in the future.

Many teachers have derived benefit (and some surprise) from having their lessons filmed. Watching ourselves at work is often slightly uncomfortable, but it can also show us things which we were not aware of. Here, for example, is a teacher (Louise) who has just seen a film of herself teaching:

> Um, it was quite a shock the first time, um, because I think you tend to focus in on all the negative things rather than any of the, any of the positives. Um, but it was, it was interesting to sort of see how the students would, would see you, um, and see it from a, from a different perspective.

Louise's colleague Philip found it interesting to watch film of himself because of 'the way I'm acting, the way I'm – my body language, things, gestures that I don't know, for example, that I have or things that I don't know I do in class'. Both gained significant insights from what they saw. Louise, for example, noticed

> ... this sort of perspective of the timing when you ask students things; often when you're waiting for a reaction it seems like it takes forever, um, and I saw that I had a tendency to sort of put words into their mouths or answer their questions for them and sort of push them along a bit. So I think what I might change is giving them a bit more time, because actually from their perspective, having seen the video clips, they might need that extra thinking time.

Rolf Tynan, a teacher whose lesson is included on the DVD which accompanies this book, found watching himself 'frightening and slightly disturbing', but

> ... after watching it a few times, it's definitely made me much more aware of what I do and what I think I do. And that is definitely one of the most valuable things I've had in a long time.

Watching film of other people teaching can also be extremely insightful. A colleague of Louise and Philip's (mentioned above), having watched film clips of other teachers in his school said:

> I think it's really good to put oneself in the context of other teachers as well because I think if – if one only watched oneself, um, it might – you might run the risk of being quite solipsistic, but watching other people puts you in the context and you see your own strengths and weaknesses and particularly you see other teachers', other teachers' strengths which you can, um, you can perhaps learn from.

A4 Professional literature

There is much to be learnt from the various methodology books, journals and magazines produced for teachers of English. Books and articles written by teachers and theorists will often open our eyes to new possibilities. They may also form part of action research or 'search' and 'research' cycles (see Section B below), either by raising an issue which we want to focus on or by helping us to formulate the kinds of questions we wish to ask.

There are a number of different journals which cater for different tastes (see the list at the end of this chapter); whereas some report on academic research, others prefer to describe classroom activities in detail, often with personal comment from the writer. Some journals impose a formal style on their contributors, whereas others allow for a variety of approaches, including letters and short reports. Some journals are now published exclusively on the Internet, while others have Internet archives of past articles.

When teachers join professional teacher organisations (see C4 below), they often receive that organisation's journal or newsletter. Members of special interest groups (such as the Teacher Development Special Interest Group – TD SIG – of IATEFL) will also get publications for that SIG. These newsletters and journals are a valuable way of keeping in touch with what is going on in the world of English language teaching. Not only do they inform us about new developments and ideas, but they also keep us in touch with colleagues whose concerns, it soon becomes apparent, are similar to ours.

B   Action research

Action research is the name given to a series of procedures teachers can engage in, perhaps because they wish to improve aspects of their teaching, or, alternatively, because they wish to evaluate the success and/or appropriacy of certain activities and procedures. Teachers sometimes embark on action research because there is a problem that is worrying them and they want to try to decide what to do about it. In all of these cases they gather data to enable them to make decisions about what they or their students do in class.

Alan Maley sees a significant difference between research and what he calls *inquiry*. The former is often done by outsiders and concerns itself with either building or testing out some kind of hypothesis. The principal aim is to abstract a theory from classroom practice. The main reason for pursuing inquiry, on the other hand, is 'to solve immediate problems, or answer urgent personally-relevant questions' (Maley 2003). We want to find out why certain things happen, what would happen if we did something differently or whether we can find a different way of doing something. This kind of inquiry is a continuing process of development leading us to both small and sometimes more significant insights.

Although the difference between theoretical research and inquiry may not be as great as Alan Maley has suggested, nevertheless action research (i.e. teachers investigating their own and their students' behaviour) is far more like inquiry than scientific research conducted by outsiders.

B1   Action research cycles

Julian Edge describes a process where a teacher, feeling unhappy about what she is doing, sets out on her own course of action to see how she might change things for the better (Edge 1999 – see also Edge 2003). The teacher is worried about the kind of feedback she gives in distance-learning courses. She feels her criticisms often seem very negative. How, then, can she (a) find out if what she fears is true and (b) do something about it if this proves to be the case.

The teacher starts by doing some reading on the subject of feedback and then sends out her conclusions about the best way to give feedback (based on this reading) to students and colleagues for their opinions. Once she has synthesised all these opinions, she issues her new criteria for giving feedback. Her students are then asked to grade her feedback according to these criteria. Now she tries giving recorded spoken feedback on tape and finds that student response is very favourable (though one student points out that written notes were much easier to refer back to later). The teacher then talks to her colleagues about what has happened so far. Some of them decide to try taped oral feedback; some decide to remain with written feedback. The teacher then writes up the whole process as an article for a teachers' magazine.

Edge's teacher has conducted the kind of action research inquiry we discussed above. Michael Wallace suggests using case studies as a form of action research. Such case studies should have special significance for the teacher concerned, and the boundaries of the case study should be clearly set (in other words, we should know exactly what we are looking at and for). We must make sure that we will end up having sufficient evidence to draw conclusions from, and that what we are investigating has at least the potential for having an impact on our practice. And finally, any case study (any piece of research we do) should allow for alternative perspectives (i.e. the opinions of others) (Wallace 2000: 16).

What we have described are versions of a classic action research cycle (see Figure 2). This starts when we identify an issue we wish to investigate. We may want to know more about our learners and what they find motivating and challenging. We might want to learn more about ourselves as teachers – how effective we are, how we look to our students, how we would look to ourselves if we were observing our own teaching. We might want to gauge the interest generated by certain topics or judge the effectiveness of certain activity types. We might want to see if an activity would work better done in groups rather than pairs, or investigate whether reading is more effective with or without pre-teaching vocabulary. We might want to find out why something isn't working.

Whichever of these issues we choose, we will want to formulate questions we want answered so that we can decide how we are going to gather data. Having collected the data, we analyse the results, and it is on the basis of these results that we decide what to do next. We may then subject this new decision to the same examination that the original issue generated (this possibility is reflected by the broken line in Figure 2). Alternatively, having resolved one issue, we may focus on a different problem and start the process afresh for that issue.

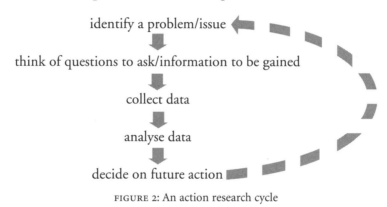

identify a problem/issue

think of questions to ask/information to be gained

collect data

analyse data

decide on future action

FIGURE 2: An action research cycle

B2 Gathering data

In order for our inquiry or case study to be effective, we have to gather data. There are many ways of doing this, but two of them have already been mentioned in Section A above. For example, we might decide to keep a journal about one specific aspect of teaching (e.g. what happens when students work in groups) and write entries about this at the end of every day's teaching. After, say, 14 days of this, we will have a lot of evidence. Alternatively, we might record ourselves (or have ourselves filmed) doing particular tasks so that we can assess their effectiveness. But there are other data-gathering methods, too.

- **Observation tasks:** we can design data-gathering worksheets which are easy to use, but which will give us valuable information. For example, we could have a list of student names in a column. Each time a student says something, we can put a tick against his or her name. After a few lessons we will have a much clearer and more accurate idea of individual participation. We might restrict our ticks to times when students ask us for help. Perhaps we will keep a written record of who chooses to sit with whom in freely-chosen pairs. We could design a form where we could record how many times specific words are used in the three weeks following their introduction during a PPP sequence (see page 65). We could keep

415

a record of what we wear to class and in columns next to this record examples of student indiscipline (to see if there is any correlation between the two). And, of course, quite apart from having ourselves filmed or audio-recorded (see above), we can film just the students at certain stages of lessons and watch (or listen) to these incidents again and again in order to gain some insight into students' reactions and behaviour.

- **Interviews:** we can interview students and colleagues about activities, materials, techniques and procedures. However, a lot will depend upon the manner and content of such interviews. When we discuss something with the whole class, for example, the results we get will be unreliable since not all students are prepared to offer an opinion, especially if it runs counter to a perceived majority opinion. Even with one-to-one interviews (if there is enough time for this), a lot will depend upon the questions we ask and how well we listen to the answers we are given.

  If we are going to interview students, it makes sense to plan our questions very carefully. This involves being clear about what we want to find out and perhaps brainstorming a set of questions with colleagues before trying them out with the students. When we get to the interview itself, we should tell the students what we are doing and why.

  All this preparation is designed to make the interview effective and successful. If possible, it helps to record the interview, too, so that we can listen to it again and, perhaps, transcribe it.

- **Written questionnaires:** questionnaires, which are sometimes more effective than the interviews we described above, can get respondents to answer open questions such as *How did you feel about activity X?*, *yes/no* questions such as *Did you find activity X easy?* or questions which ask for some kind of rating response, e.g.

> **Activity X was:**
> extremely easy ☐　easy ☐　quite easy ☐
> difficult ☐　very difficult ☐　impossible ☐

We can also ask students to rate the qualities of an activity in order of importance or write a short paragraph about an activity, some material or a unit.

When Philip Harmer wanted to know if and how his correction techniques were effective, he conducted research by sending a questionnaire to all 150 students in the language school where he worked. Among the questions that students had to answer were:

> **Speaking**
> **A.** Which of the following correction techniques do you prefer?
> - I like being corrected at the moment of speaking.
> - I like the teacher to do correction work at the front of the class after the task has finished.
> - I don't like being corrected at all.
>
> **Writing**
> **B.** Which of the following correction techniques do you prefer?
> - Underlining.
> - The teacher writes the correct answer.
> - The teacher highlights the type of mistake (e.g. SP for spelling).
> - The teacher only corrects a certain type of mistake (e.g. *This time I'm only going to correct tenses*).

As a result of his research, he writes that he is not sure that he now corrects differently, but what has changed is 'that I now incorporate the questionnaire into long-term courses ... for the learner it provides an opportunity for actively contributing to the way the class works' (Harmer, P 2005: 75).

We can also ask students to fill in charts or priority lists to see how they perceive what is happening in lessons (though we should bear in mind the potential for teacher–student mismatch that we discussed in Chapter 23, A1).

- **Breaking rules and changing environments:** in a groundbreaking work, John Fanselow (1987) suggested that one way of developing is to break our own rules and see what happens. If we normally teach one way, in other words, we should try teaching in the opposite way and see what effect it has. If we normally move around the class all the time, perhaps we should see what happens if we spend the whole lesson sitting in the same place. The results may be surprising and will never be less than interesting.

  Luke Prodromou decided after some years of teaching adults and young adults that he needed to reassess what he was doing, and one way was to be 'Luke in Lilliput' (Prodromou 2002b: 57) – in other words, to involve himself in teaching a completely different age group (in this case eight year olds).

  Breaking rules and changing environments are not for the faint-hearted. We need to have the confidence and enthusiasm for investigation and discovery. Sandra Piai and Kate Threadgold got their trainees to try something new and different as a piece of supervised action research because this 'gave them a *real* reason for trying out, reflecting on, ideas and activities' (2001: 12). Teacher schemes such as the DELTA (see page 428) do the same kind of thing.

  One way to help us think about doing things differently is a technique called 'Cataloguing nightmares' (see Figure 3). In this we complete the left-hand column with a list of the things that go wrong – or that we are frightened might go wrong – in our lessons. In the next column, we say what happens which makes these things go wrong. Finally, in the right-hand column, we write down an opposite procedure from the one described in the middle column. We now have a plan of action for breaking rules – or at least completely upending the routines we use. Our new 'opposite procedure' may not work, but at least it will allow us to view the problem differently and maybe gain some insights into how to change things (again) in the future.

Nightmares	Procedure	Opposite procedure
When I put students in pairs and give them instructions, they never listen and the pairwork is always chaotic.	I put students in pairs, give out material and then give instructions.	Give instructions, hand out material, put students in pairs.

FIGURE 3: Cataloguing nightmares

C Developing with others

Not all reflection, reading or action research needs to be done by teachers working alone. There are many ways teachers can confer with each other and develop together, either face-to-face or, increasingly, online.

C1 Cooperative/collaborative development

Teachers, like anyone else, need chances to discuss what they are doing and what happens to them in class so that they can examine their beliefs and feelings. However much we have reflected on our own experiences and practice, most of us find discussing our situation with others helps us to sort things out in our own mind. The question, however, is how 'the others' – that is the people we are talking to – should behave. Do we want them merely to listen to our stories and thoughts, or are we expecting them to give us suggestions and advice? We are all familiar with occasions when we think we want people to advise us and then resent them when they do.

Julian Edge coined the term *cooperative development* (Edge 1992a and b) to describe a specific kind of relationship between speakers and the people listening to them – whose role is crucial since 'the queen of facilitative skills is listening in a non-judgmental, respectful and empathetic way' (Underhill 1992: 79).

In cooperative development 'a relationship of trust is necessary' (Edge 2003: 58) between *speakers* who interact with *understanders*; a teacher, in this case, talks to an empathetic colleague. The empathetic colleague (the understander) makes every effort to understand the speaker but crucially, in Edge's realisation, does not interpret, explain or judge what he or she is hearing. All that is necessary is for the understander to say 'This is what I'm hearing. This is what I've understood. Have I got it right?' (Edge 1992a: 65). The understander's side of the bargain is that 'she will put aside her own thoughts, ideas and evaluations in order to concentrate on understanding what the speaker has to say' (Edge 2003: 58).

This style of empathising is similar to 'co-counselling', where two people agree to meet and divide the allotted time in half so that each is a speaker and listener for an equal time period (Head and Taylor 1997: 143–144).

Charles Lansley, while sympathetic to the idea of empathetic colleagues, suggested that just listening does not change anything (Lansley 1994) and that 'phatic communion' may even reinforce the opinions that the speaker started with. He cites conversations where unconfrontational listening can reinforce negative stereotyping, as when people on train journeys wish to avoid argument and so end up agreeing with propositions they really disagree with, e.g.

> A: *I don't think much of the government.*
> B: *Oh, they're not so bad.*
> A: *I don't say they're bad.*
> B: *They're all right.*
> A: *Yes.*
> (Lansley 1994: 53)

Something similar seems to happen when speakers use tag questions, with the implicit assumption that what they are saying is so obvious that listeners couldn't possibly disagree, e.g. *Adults find learning a new language difficult, don't they?* or *It's difficult to get Japanese students to speak in class, isn't it?* According to Charles Lansley, 'The danger of being in the teaching profession for too long (especially without much or any INSETT [in-service teacher training]) is that one's teaching can end up being based on one's own uncritical subjective principles' (1994: 54). He proposes, instead, a form of *collaborative development* where the listener engages in active debate with the speaker, provoking them to question their assumptions and justify their opinions.

Steve Mann wants the understander to go further, too, and suggests other moves that can be made. For example, the understander can ask *focusing* questions, such as *From what you've talked about so far, is there one thing that you think is the most important?*, thematising questions, such as *Earlier you were talking about classes being better if they are unplanned, and then you were talking about giving students more responsibility for choosing materials. Are they connected for you?* or challenging questions, such as *A while back you said that correcting learners in class seems like a waste of time and now you're saying that Keiko and Junko have really responded to correction. Do these two statements hang together for you?* (Mann 2001: 59).

Perhaps the best way to reconcile these differing views of similar processes is to suggest that co-development is a three-stage process. At first, it is the job of the understander to help establish trust by listening empathetically. Once the trust is there, stage 2 allows understanders to challenge what they are hearing, so that in stage 3 there can be some kind of resolution of the situation the speaker is talking about. But if at any time the relationship of trust is broken and the speaker loses confidence, the understander can go back to stage 1 until that relationship is re-established.

Talking with colleagues is one of the best ways of resolving our doubts and uncertainties and it can help us understand what it is we think. As listeners (understanders), too, we can have a powerful effect on our colleagues' development.

C2 Peer teaching, peer observation

In our teaching lives we are frequently observed by others. It starts on teacher training courses and goes on when academic coordinators or directors of study come into our lessons as part of some quality control exercise. In all these situations the observed teacher is at a disadvantage since the observers – however sympathetically they carry out their function – have power over the teacher's future career. There are very few teachers who welcome this kind of visitation.

However, many of us would welcome the opportunity to talk to someone about a lesson we have just taught, hoping that they would help us to understand what happened at certain moments or suggest ways of making things more effective. This was the case with a teacher called Poh in Hong Kong who invited her colleague Thomas Farrell into her lessons as part of her own self-development. She wanted an outsider's view of her teaching practices, a view which was not totally dependent on her own or her students' reactions. Thomas Farrell thus became her 'critical friend' and soon noted, with interest, that even before Poh had seen his observation notes, she 'addressed most of the issues I had raised'. Perhaps Farrell had taken on a 'proactive role of promoting reflection within our friendship by acting as a catalyst for Poh to look at her teaching' (Farrell 2001: 372).

It sounds like the ideal arrangement – equal colleagues observing each other so that they (or at least one of them) can develop. And there are various ways of doing this. In the first, two teachers hold a dialogue in front of the class about a language point, a text or an aspect of culture. Students gain from hearing different views on the same topic, and the participating teachers learn through their public interaction with each other. Sometimes two teachers can take different parts of the same lesson so that at one stage one might be acting as organiser and then observer, while the other plays the roles of prompter and resource (see Chapter 6, B1). At other points in the lesson, one teacher could explain a grammar point before the other takes over to run a short controlled practice session. All of these techniques mean that both teachers can discuss what went on after the lesson and understand the lesson better since, in the old cliché, 'two heads are better than one'.

A more formal way of organising peer teaching and observation is for two teachers to plan a lesson which one of them then teaches and the other observes. After the lesson, they both describe what happened to their joint plan and detail their experiences of the lesson. They can then discuss how it could be improved. For the next class, the position is reversed. As a result, both teachers get the benefit of each other's advice and insights.

However, peer teaching of this sort is not without its problems. Thomas Farrell, whose 'critical friendship' we discussed above, suggested that his observation worked because his colleague was comfortable with her teaching and so was 'in a strong psychological state to allow someone to observe her classes' (2001: 373). But even in such a situation he sometimes felt reluctant to give his opinions, partly because neither he nor the teacher had established any ground rules. Aliye Kasapoglu and Bill Snyder, in an admittedly small-scale study, found that while the participating teachers enjoyed being observed, they all wanted to be observed by someone more experienced than themselves. The younger teachers, especially, seemed to have wanted training rather than development. And like Thomas Farrell's colleague, observation seemed a one-way street where the observer helps the person being observed.

But this is to underuse the enormous development potential of peer observation. Being observed is never an entirely comfortable experience, of course, and where peer observation is part of an institutional scheme in which colleagues are obliged to watch each other, teachers often view it with some trepidation. Jill Cosh, in the ELT department of Anglia Ruskin University in Cambridge found that 'teachers will still feel nervous about being observed and implicit judgements being made about their teaching' (Cosh 1999: 25).

The scheme that Jill Cosh worked on tackled this situation in two ways. In the first, she and colleagues recognised that the great development potential of peer observation is for the observer, not the person being observed. The observer doesn't judge whoever he or she is observing based on their own assumptions, but rather assesses those same assumptions on the basis of what he or she sees the observed teacher doing. And the only way to make this happen is to make sure that the observer has some kind of feedback form which guides his or her observation. Jill Cosh feels strongly that we should not be making judgements about the teaching of others because 'notions of good teaching are very subjective; they are to a large extent intangible and unable to be addressed through a list of criteria, and giving constructive feedback is a difficult skill where the observer risks giving offence' (Cosh and Woodward 2003: 20). But questioning one's own assumptions while observing can be a genuinely intrapersonal development event.

Teachers' groups

One of the most supportive environments for teachers, where real teacher development can take place, is in small teacher groups. In this situation colleagues, usually working in the same school, meet together to discuss any issues and problems which may arise in the course of their teaching.

Some teacher development meetings of this kind are organised by principals and directors of study. Outside speakers and animators are occasionally brought in to facilitate discussions. The director of studies may select a topic – in conjunction with the teachers – and then asks a member of staff to lead a session. What emerges is something halfway between bottom-up teacher development and top-down in-service teacher training (INSETT). At their best, such regular meetings are extremely stimulating and insightful. In many schools an INSETT coordinator is appointed to arrange a teacher development programme. Where this is done effectively, he or she will consult widely with colleagues to see what they would most like to work on and with.

Paul Davis suggested that this kind of organisation, while helpful, is not teacher development in the sense that he wants to see it. For him, a teacher development group will 'normally be comprised of people who work together or work in the same geographical area. Although they may have different levels of experience and/or status, because their participation in the group is voluntary or because they come from different workplaces, they should be able to act as a peer group' (Davis 1999). What he is proposing is a situation where a group of teachers makes the decision to meet once a week and runs what is, in effect, its own support group (Plumb 1994). Any member of the group can suggest topics for future meetings; topics can range far and wide, from new ideas for pronunciation teaching to how to react when students make complaints, from the most appropriate kind of clothes to wear for teaching to five new uses for the camera. Teachers themselves are in charge of the group and, indeed, as Paul Davis suggests, certain people such as academic and administrative managers may be deliberately excluded so that the group can maintain its peer status.

Teachers' associations

There are many teachers' associations around the world. Some of them are international, such as IATEFL, based in Britain and TESOL, based in the USA; some are country-based, such as JALT (in Japan), FAAPI (in Argentina), ELICOS (in Australia) or ATECR (in the Czech Republic); still others are smaller and regional, such as APIGA (in Galicia, Spain) or CELTA (in Cambridge, England).

Teachers' associations provide two possible development opportunities:

- **Conferences and seminars:** conferences, meetings and workshops allow us to hear about the latest developments in the field, take part in investigative workshops and enter into debates about current issues in theory and practice. We can 'network' with other members of the ELT community and, best of all, we learn that other people from different places, different countries and systems even, share similar problems and are themselves searching for solutions.

  Perhaps the best moments in conferences are the conversations that participants have with each other after they've been to talks and workshops. As we walk out of other people's sessions, we compare notes with fellow attenders, and as we do so, we find ourselves having to justify why we have reacted as we have to what we have heard. These exchanges are often

421

significantly more important than the sessions themselves since they offer very real (even if short) self-development opportunities as we grapple with our feelings and thoughts about what we have experienced.

- **Presenting:** submitting a paper or a workshop for a teachers' association meeting, whether regional, national or international, is one of the most powerful catalysts for reflecting upon our practice. When we try to work out exactly what we want to say and the best way of doing it, we are forcing ourselves to assess what we do. The challenge of a future audience sharpens our perceptions.

  Some teachers get very nervous about presenting, and it is true that standing up in front of colleagues can be extremely daunting, especially when there are a lot of them wanting to listen to you. Yet most presenters find that audiences of their peers are on the whole overwhelmingly supportive and friendly. As a result, teachers who present to them, work with them or lead discussions usually find their self-esteem enhanced, their beliefs challenged and expanded, and their possibilities for the future enlarged.

  Giving (and preparing) presentations has many of the better advantages of other development opportunities since not only do we have to think about our topic in a more 'inquiring' manner than we normally do, but also because we are actually undertaking real professional development by learning a new skill and by perhaps making ourselves visible to future employers or collaborators.

C5 The virtual community

When Paul Davis suggested that teachers' groups were normally made up of people from the same geographical area, he was writing in 1999 when the virtual world was considerably less developed than it is today and when broadband access was less ubiquitous than it has become.

There is no real substitute for people meeting together in the same physical space to share experiences, ideas, hopes and fears. But there are alternatives, and the plethora of different sites and user groups on the Internet offers teachers considerable scope in talking to colleagues all over the world at all hours of the day or night. There are many different groups of this kind. There are also people who meet when taking part in real-time chat forums (quite apart from conference calls using audio or videoware). In the future it will be increasingly common and unsensational for people to contact each other online like this.

We have said that real face-to-face communication is always better than online discussion whether or not it takes place in real time or whether it is the result of emails posted on a group noticeboard at different times. Yet the huge advantage of online communication is the fact that someone from Ankara, say, can talk to someone from Vermont very easily – and that all the other members of the group, whether or not they are participating or lurking (i.e. reading all the postings without replying), can be members of the group wherever they are located.

D Moving outwards and sideways

In order to enhance professional and personal growth, teachers sometimes need to step outside the world of the classroom where the concentration, all too frequently, is on knowledge and skill alone. There are other issues and practices which can be of immense help in making their professional understanding more profound and their working reality more rewarding.

D1 Learning by learning

One of the best ways of reflecting upon our teaching practice is to become learners ourselves again, so that our view of the learning–teaching process is not always influenced from one side of that relationship. By voluntarily submitting ourselves to a new learning experience, especially (but not only) if this involves us in learning a new language, our view of our students' experience can be changed. As Luke Prodromou found when he decided to learn Spanish, 'Going back to school, and being on the receiving end of the foreign language learning process, confronted me with challenge after challenge to my assumptions about good language teaching' (2002b: 58).

Language teachers who have started to learn a new language are often surprised by what they discover about themselves – and about language learning in general. Some have become aware, as if for the first time, how frightening it can be to speak in class (Lowe 1987). Patricia Ahrens, on the other hand, discovered that many 'communicative' activities she was asked to take part in were mundane and uninvolving. She found it extremely difficult to talk in a foreign language in class when she had nothing to say (Ahrens 1993a). Roger Gower, meanwhile, realised, among other things, how much he wanted to understand every single word in the reading texts he worked with (Gower 1999).

It can be eye-opening to find out how important our teacher's approval is to us, how susceptible we are to teacher criticism, or to realise how important it is for the teacher to set us clear goals and guide us in other ways.

Those who teach a language which they themselves learnt as a foreign or second language – such as the vast majority of EFL/ESOL teachers in the world – will, of course, have highly relevant memories of the experience of learning that language. Teachers who teach their first language will not have the same history and for them going back into the language classroom as students will be extremely challenging but, as Luke Prodromou points out, 'learning a foreign language has the advantage of offering personal and professional development at the same time for the same price' (2002b: 58).

Even if we cannot or do not want to learn a foreign language, however, the experience of learning almost anything will be of benefit, not only for our own development, but also for our understanding of the process of learning. Taking up a musical instrument, enrolling in an art class or trying to master any other new skill will help us to see what the world looks like from our students' point of view, and this can only help us and, we hope, them.

D2 Supplementing teaching

One way of countering the potential sameness of a teacher's life is to increase our range of occupations and interests so that teaching becomes the fixed centre in a more varied and interesting professional life.

There are many tasks that make a valuable contribution to the teaching and learning of English. First among these is writing materials – whether these are one-off activities, longer units or whole books. Materials writing can be challenging and stimulating, and when done in tandem with teaching can provide us with powerful insights, so that both the writing and the teaching become significantly more involving and enjoyable.

Teachers often find it difficult to break into the world of publishing, but in fact publishers are always looking for people with new and exciting ideas, and for people who would be prepared to trial new materials or write reports. The first thing that teachers need to do if they want to become involved with writing, therefore, is to get in touch with publishing houses and say that they are eager to pilot material or write reports. They can find out how to get in touch with publishers by visiting their representatives at the book exhibitions which are a feature of teachers' conferences, or they can find the addresses of the publishers of their favourite books by searching on the Internet.

Some of the best materials have been written by teachers who have found themselves producing teaching ideas because they were not satisfied with what was on offer. This is certainly a powerful motivation for writing, but it is what happens next that may make the difference between being published and being ignored. Publishers are sent large numbers of unsolicited manuscripts, and many of these works are fairly swiftly rejected. Authors are more likely to be successful, however, if they start by first finding out the name of the individual in the publishing house who deals with the area they work in and then writing a short letter to that person, explaining who they are and what they are working on. It may be helpful to include a brief one- or two-page synopsis of their proposal at this stage, but that is all. Publishers are far more likely to be interested in this approach than in a large pile of paper that they are too busy to wade through.

The publishers of magazines and journals (see the chapter notes on page 427) are also extremely interested in hearing from potential contributors. Editors are always looking for people to write articles, send in teaching ideas or review books. However, before submitting articles for possible publication (or offering book reviews or teaching ideas), teachers should read the notes for contributors very carefully since material that is sent in but which does not match the editor's requirements is unlikely to get accepted.

Teachers can become involved in far more than just materials (or article) writing, however. The various exam boards such as Cambridge ESOL, Trinity Exams, TOEFL and TOEIC are always on the lookout for markers, examiners and item writers. As with publishing, teachers who are interested in this area should find out the name of the relevant subject officer and write to them, expressing their interest and saying who they are and where they work.

Many people now set up their own websites where they provide material either by subscription or free of charge. It is no longer difficult or expensive to record material which can be made available as MP3 files (and so be downloaded as podcasts). Other teachers help to organise entertainments for their students or run drama groups, sports teams or conversation get-togethers.

Many teachers see a change of teaching sector as a developmental move, both as a way of researching teaching (see B2 above), and also as a way of making life more challenging and more interesting. Perhaps the most interesting move, in this sense, is to become involved in training teachers since this is not only extremely rewarding but also forces us to examine what we do and how we do it in a way that has huge developmental benefits. But any move to a different kind of teaching (such as one-to-one, exam teaching or business English, if these are things we have not done before) will force us to look at our teaching afresh and, by providing us with new challenges, has the power to revitalise our professional lives.

Finally, some teachers become involved in the running and organising of teachers' associations (see page 426). Most associations allow any member to stand for election and there is no doubt that those who become committee members, treasurers and presidents of, say, IATEFL or TESOL get a huge amount of personal satisfaction from being involved in running organisations like this. When things go well, they also have the satisfaction of knowing that they are doing something incredibly important and valuable for their fellow teachers. Equally, we can become involved in running small teachers' groups such as those mentioned in C3 above.

D3 More training?

One way of developing as a teacher is to undertake more training. Those who have an initial teaching certificate such as the TKT (Teaching Knowledge Test), CELTA (Certificate in Language Teaching for Adults), offered by Cambridge ESOL, or the Trinity Certificate may want to think of going further in the future. They might, for example, enhance their basic course by doing a special supplement on the teaching of young learners or business English, for example. They might want to study for a more advanced qualification such as the Cambridge ESOL DELTA (Diploma in English Language Teaching for Adults).

Many organisations offer their own specialised courses for different teaching sectors, and if and when teachers have exhausted these, they can think of going forward to study at Master's or Doctoral level.

What we choose to study depends entirely on our own interests and what we hope to achieve as a result of the course of study we undertake. However, it is worth remembering that we should be especially careful to make sure that the institution we choose to study with has the appropriate accreditation and that its reputation among colleagues and the world at large is a satisfactory one. As with many other professions and specialities, English language teaching has its fair share of unscrupulous and untrustworthy operators. Further training usually costs money and so, as with any other expenditure, we should try to ensure that our money will be well and wisely spent.

E Being well

In his article 'Finding the centre', Alan Maley suggested that because teachers have stressful jobs they need to pay attention to their physical well-being, not only so that they can teach better, but also so that they can survive, learn and grow as people (1993: 14).

Teachers need to care for their bodies to counteract stress and fatigue. Katie Head and Pauline Taylor (1997: Chapter 6) suggest techniques for breathing and progressive relaxation. They advocate the use of disciplines such as tai chi, yoga and the Alexander technique to achieve greater physical ease and counteract possible burnout.

One of a teacher's chief physical attributes is the voice. Roz Comins observes that at least one in ten long-serving teachers need clinical help at some time in their career to counteract vocal damage (1999: 8). Yet voice is part of the whole person, both physically and emotionally. When we misuse it, it will let us down. But when we care for it, it will help to keep us healthy and build our confidence. We can do this by breathing correctly and resting our voice and ourselves when necessary. We can drink water or herbal tea rather than ordinary tea, coffee or cola if and when we suffer from laryngitis; we can adjust our pitch and volume and avoid shouting and whispering.

Many teachers work long hours in stressful and challenging situations. At the primary level they seem to be vulnerable to many of the minor illnesses that their students bring with them to school. Keeping healthy by taking exercise and getting between six and a half and eight hours' sleep a night are ways of counteracting this.

Chapter notes and further reading

- **The developing teacher**
  On teacher development, see especially the excellent K Head and P Taylor (1997), S Bax (1995), D Nunan (1989) and J Edge (ed) (2002).

- **Reflective teaching**
  The concept of the reflective teacher was first (and best) articulated in D Schön (1983) and further developed in Schön (1987). J Richards and C Lockhart (1996) have a book devoted to reflective teaching in second language classrooms.

- **Keeping journals**
  The most impressive published teacher journal is J Appel (1995) – a whole book of reflections on his teaching experiences. On journals as training tools, see J McDonough (1994).

- **Action research**
  See the excellent M Wallace (1997). On teachers as researchers, see L Miller (2004a).

- **Observation tasks**
  D Kurtoglu Eken (1999) suggests having students themselves perform observation tasks as a way of collecting lesson data.

- **Teachers interview students**
  See L Miller (2005).

- **Teacher development groups**
  K Head and P Taylor (1997: Chapter 5) describe different experiences with teacher development groups.

- **Teachers as learners**
  See J McDonough (2002) and B Hyde (2000).

- **Voice**
  A Maley (2000) has written a book on the teacher's voice. See also R Comins (1999) and R Whitehead, quoted in K Head and P Taylor (1997: 137–139).

- **Teachers' associations**
  Two of the major international teachers' associations are:

  - (IATEFL) The International Association of Teachers of English as a Foreign Language, 3 Kingsdown Chambers, Kingsdown Park, Tankerton, Whitstable, Kent CT5 2DJ, UK (www.iatefl.org).

- (TESOL) Teachers of English to Speakers of Other Languages, 1600 Cameron Street, Suite 300, Alexandria, Virginia 22314, USA (www.tesol.edu).

Most countries have teachers' organisations. Some of these are affiliated to either TESOL (e.g. Mextesol in Mexico, TESOL Greece) or IATEFL (i.e. IATEFL Poland, IATEFL Chile). A list of 12,871 links to teachers' associations (at the time of writing) can be found at http://iteslj.org/links/TESL/Associations/.

- **Journals for teachers**
  Some of the more useful journals for teachers are:

  - *English Language Teaching Journal* (*ELTJ*), published by Oxford University Press (www.oup.co.uk/eltj/). Articles are both practical and research-based and cover the full range of topics to do with language, methodology, class management and theory.

  - *TESOL Quarterly*, published by TESOL (see www.tesol.org/s_tesol/seccss.asp?CID=209&DID=1679). This contains largely research-based articles and covers a full range of topics to do with language, culture, bilingualism and methodology.

  - *Modern English Teacher* (*MET*), published by Keyways Publishing, has a variety of practical articles with classroom ideas, current issues, 'about language' sections, and tips and hints for individual activities (www.onlinemet.com).

  - *English Teaching Professional* (*ETP*) published by Keyways Publishing is a practical magazine with (usually) short articles on background theory, classroom activities, teacher development, etc. (www.etprofessional.com).

  - *Essential Teacher*, published by the TESOL organisation (see www.tesol.org/s_tesol/secet.asp?CID=1391&DID=7400) has short articles offering guidance for teachers working in varied ESL and EFL workplaces.

  - *Humanising Language Teaching* (www.hltmag.co.uk) is a free online journal published by Pilgrims that offers an eclectic mix of articles, comments, jokes and book reviews. It has an extremely useful search by author and topic facility.

  - *The Internet TESL Journal* (see http://iteslj.org). This site from Japan (which has been going since 1995) offers articles, lessons, techniques, questions, games, jokes and a fantastic series of links to other websites.

- **Teacher examination schemes**
  Among the international exams which teachers can take are the following:

  - Cambridge exams are offered by the University of Cambridge ESOL Cambridge, UK (www.cambridgeesol.org).
    – TKT (Teaching Knowledge Test): this is a PET-level (see page 391) multiple-choice exam which tests basic knowledge of some teaching theory.
    – CELTA (Certificate in English Language Teaching to Adults): this is a (mostly) pre-service practical course which prepares candidates to teach English to adults.

– CELTYL (Certificate in English Language Teaching to Young Learners): as its names suggests, this is an exam for people who want to specialise in teaching English to children. It includes a large practical element.

– DELTA (Diploma in English Language Teaching to Adults): this is for candidates who have substantial experience before they start studying for the DELTA. It examines both theoretical knowledge and practical skills.

There are other qualifications too, such as ICELT (In-service Certificate in English Language Teaching) which helps to develop teacher knowledge and competence within the context where they are working and IDLTM (International Diploma in Language Teaching Management).

- Trinity College (www.trinitycollege.co.uk) offers a range of teacher certification schemes. These include:
  – CertTESOL: this is designed for those with little or no knowledge of teaching English. It equips candidates with basic teaching skills.
  – LTCL Diploma TESOL: this is designed for experienced teachers and has four distinct units.
  – CertTEYL (Certificate in Teaching English to Young Learners): this is designed for people whose first language is not English and who have little or no knowledge of teaching English, but who wish to teach children between 6 and 12 years of age.
  – ICT in the Classroom: designed in collaboration with The Consultants-E (www.theconsultants-e.com), this course is for teachers who want to become better users of information technology.

Individual institutions offer their own qualifications. For example, the International House World Organisation (www.ihworld.com) offers qualifications in teaching English, teaching other languages, teaching younger learners and business teaching. In the USA many teachers enter the profession via an MA in TESOL such as that offered online by the New School (a university in New York – www.newschool.edu/matesol). Many universities in the USA, the UK and many other countries – e.g. Australia, Canada, New Zealand, etc. – offer similar face-to-face or online undergraduate or postgraduate courses of study.

Bibliography

Ahrens, P 1993a Diary of a language learner/teacher. *Modern English Teacher* 2/2.

Ahrens, P 1993b Displaying visuals. *Modern English Teacher* 2/4.

Ainslie, S and Purcell, S 2001 Mixed Ability Teaching in Language Learning Resource Pack. CILT Publications.

Aitchison, J 1987 *Words in The Mind* Blackwell.

Al-Arishi, A 1994 Role-play, real-play, and surreal play in the ESOL classroom. *ELT Journal* 48/4.

Alderson, J C 1996 The testing of reading. In Nuttall, C.

Alderson, J C, Clapham, C and Wall, D 1995 *Language Test Construction and Evaluation* Cambridge University Press.

Alessi, S and Trollip, S 2001 *Multimedia for Learning* 3rd edn Allyn and Bacon.

Allwright, A 2003 Exploratory practice: Rethinking practitioner research in language teaching. *Language Teaching Research* 7.

Allwright, A and Lenzuen, R 1997 Exploratory practice: Work at the Cultura Inglesa, Rio de Janeiro. *Language Teaching Research* 1.

Allwright, R 1979 Language learning through communication practice. In Brumfit, C and Johnson, K (eds) *The Communicative Approach to Language Teaching* Oxford University Press.

Allwright, R 1981 What do we want teaching materials for? *ELT Journal* 36/1 and in Rossner and Bolitho (eds).

Almagro Esteban, A 2005 Developing needs. *English Teaching Professional* 36.

Almond, M 2005 *Teaching English with Drama* Modern English Publishing.

Anderson, A and Lynch, T 1998 *Listening* Oxford University Press.

Andrewes, S 2004 Cross-curricular projects. *English Teaching Professional* 33.

Aoki, N 2004 Teachers' conversations with partial autobiographies. *The Teacher Trainer* 18/3.

Appel, J 1995 *Diary of a Language Teacher* Macmillan Heinemann.

Arnold, J 1998 Towards more humanistic English teaching. *ELT Journal* 52/3.

Arnold, J (ed) 1999 *Affect in Language Learning* Cambridge University Press.

Arnold, J and Brown, H D 1999 A map of the terrain. In Arnold, J 1999.

Artusi A 2002 Mixed level: the board, an invaluable tool. *IATEFL Issues* 166.

Asher, J 1977 *Learning Another Language Through Actions: The Complete Teacher's Guidebook* Sky Oaks Productions.

Askari Arani, J 2005 Weblogs: teaching writing and reading English through a web-based communicative medium. *Modern English Teacher* 14/4.

Askey, S, Trotta, J and Fleming, T 2003 Teacher, have you thought about me? A multiple intelligences webquest for adult learners of English http://www.eslgo.com/classes/mi/index2.htm.

Aston, G 1993 The learner's contribution to the self-access centre. *ELT Journal* 47/3.

Atkinson, D 1989 'Humanistic' approaches in the language classroom: an affective reaction. *ELT Journal* 43/4.

Austin, J, L 1962 *How to do Things with Words* Clarendon Press.

Badger, R and White, G 2000 A process genre approach to teaching writing. *ELT Journal* 54/2.

Baigent, M 1999 Teaching in chunks: integrating a lexical approach. *Modern English Teacher* 8/2.

Baker, J 2005 Neuro-Linguistic Programming 2. *English Teaching Professional* 38.

Baker, J and Rinvolucri, M 2005a Neuro-Linguistic Programming. *English Teaching Professional* 37.

Baker, J and Rinvolucri, M 2005b *Unlocking Self-expression through NLP* DELTA Publishing.

Baker, P and Eversley, J 2000 *Multilingual Capital, London* Battlebridge.

Bamford, J and Day, R 2004 *Extensive Reading Activities for Teaching Language* Cambridge University Press.

Bandler, R and Grinder, J 1979 *Frogs into Princes* Real People Press.

Barnett, L and Jordan, G 1991 Self-access facilities: what are they for? *ELT Journal* 45/4.

Basturkmen, H 2001 Descriptions of spoken language for higher level learners: the example of questioning. *ELT Journal* 55/1.

Batstone, R 1994 *Grammar* Oxford University Press.

Batstone, R 1996 Key concepts in ELT: Task-Based learning. *ELT Journal* 50/3.

Bawcom, L 2002 Over-using L1 in the classroom? *Modern English Teacher* 11/1.

Bawcom, L 2005 Preventing stress and burn-out. *Modern English Teacher* 14/2.

Bax, S 1995 Principles for evaluating teacher development activities. *ELT Journal* 49/3.

Bax, S 2003 The end of CLT: a context approach to language teaching. *ELT Journal* 57/3.

Bax, S 2006 Rethinking methodology? The role of context. Paper delivered at the English Australia Conference, Perth, Australia.

Beckett, G and Slater, T 2005 The project framework: a tool for language, content, and skills integration. *ELT Journal* 59/2.

Beglar, D and Hunt, A 2002 Implementing task-based language teaching. In Richards, J and Renandya, W (eds) *Methodology in Language Teaching: an anthology of current practice* Cambridge University Press.

Belz, J 2002 Social dimensions of telecollaborative foreign language study. *Language Learning and Technology* 6/1.

Benson, P 2001 *Teaching and Researching Autonomy in Language Learning* (Applied Linguistics in Action) Longman.

Benson, P and Voller, P (eds) 1997 *Autonomy and Independence in Language Learning* (Applied Linguistics and Language Study) Longman.

Biber, D, Johansson, S, Leech, G, Conrad, S and Finegan, E 1999 *Longman Grammar of Spoken and Written English* Pearson Education Ltd.

Biber, D, Johansson, S and Leech, C 2002 *Longman Students' Grammar of Spoken and Written English* Pearson Education Ltd.

Bisong, J 1995 Language choice and cultural imperialism: a Nigerian perspective. *ELT Journal* 49/2.

Black, P and Wiliam, D 1998 Inside the black box: raising standards through classroom assessment. *Phi Delta Kappan* 80 and at https://www.pdkintl.org/kappan/kbla9810.htm.

Blanche, P 2004 Using dictations to teach pronunciation. *Modern English Teacher* 13/1.

Block, D 1991 Some thoughts on DIY materials design. *ELT Journal* 45/3.

Boon, A 2005 Tell me what you want, what you really, really want! *Modern English Teacher* 14/4.

Boughey, C 1997 Learning to write by writing to learn: a group-work approach. *ELT Journal* 51/2.

Bourke, J 2006 Designing a topic-based syllabus for young learners. *ELT Journal* 60/3.

Bowler, B 2002 The play's the thing. *English Teaching Professional* 22.

Bowler, B and Parminter, S 2000 Mixed-level tasks. *English Teaching Professional* 15.

Brabbs, P 2002 WebQuests. *English Teaching Professional* 24.

Brabbs, P 2004 A magic spell. *English Teaching Professional* 35.

Bradshaw, C 2005 Giving great instructions. *English Teaching Professional* 38.

Braine, G (ed) 1999 *Non-native Educators in English Language Teaching* Lawrence Eribaum Associates.

Braymen, D 1995 Training students for continued learning. *Modern English Teacher* 4/2.

Brazil, D 1997 *The Communicative Value of Intonation in English* Cambridge University Press.

Bress, P 2006 Listening skills. *Modern English Teacher* 15/1.

Brines, V 2001 Read on: the organisation of an extensive reading programme. *Modern English Teacher* 10/3.

Brown, H D 1994 *Principles of Language Learning and Teaching* 3rd edn Pearson Education Ltd.

Brown, H D 2007 *Principles of Language Learning and Teaching* 5th edn Pearson Education Ltd.

Brown, P 2005 Student presentations. *Modern English Teacher* 14/2.

Brown, S and McIntyre, D 1993 *Making Sense of Teaching* Open University Press.

Bruton, A 1998 PPP, CLT, NA, TBI, ARC, ESA. CFPU: for what? *IATEFL Teacher Training SIG* 21.

Buckmaster, R 2005 Reading and reading skills: exploiting reading texts to the full. *Modern English Teacher* 14/2.

Burbidge, N, Gray, P, Levy, S and Rinvolucri, M 1996 *Letters* Oxford University Press.

Burgess, S and Head, K 2005 *How to Teach for Exams* Pearson Education Ltd.

Byrne, D 1986 *Teaching Oral Skills* Pearson Education Ltd.

Caffyn, R 1984 Rewards and punishments in schools. A study of their effectiveness as perceived by secondary school pupils and their teacher. MEd dissertation unpublished. University of Exeter.

Cameron, D 2006 *On Language and Sexual Politics* Routledge.

Cameron, L 2001 *Teaching Languages to Young Learners* Cambridge University Press.

Cameron, L 2003 Challenges for ELT from the expansion in teaching children. *ELT Journal* 57/2.

Campbell, A P 2003 Weblogs for use with ESL classes. *Internet TESOL Journal* 9/2 at http://iteslj.org/Techniques/Campbell-Weblogs.html.

Canagarajah, A S 2005 Globalisation of English and changing pedagogical priorities: the postmodern turn. In Beaven, B (ed) *IATEFL 2005 Cardiff Conference Selections* IATEFL Publications.

Capone, P and Hayward, K 1996 Democratic debates. *Modern English Teacher* 5/4.

Carless, D 2006 Collaborative EFL teaching in primary schools. *ELT Journal* 60/4.

Carroll, J and Sapon, S 1959 *The Modern Language Aptitude Test* The Psychological Corporation.

Carter, R 1998a Orders of reality: CANCODE, communication, and culture. *ELT Journal* 52/1.

Carter, R 1998b Reply to Guy Cook. *ELT Journal* 52/1.

Carter, R, Hughes, R and McCarthy, M 1998 Telling tails: grammar, the spoken language and materials development. In Tomlinson, B (ed).

Carter, R and McCarthy, M 2006 *Cambridge Grammar of English* Cambridge University Press.

Case, A 2007 Should my English teaching school be a pre-school school? *Modern English Teacher* 16/1.

Castagnero, P 2006 Audiolingual method and behaviourism: from misunderstanding to myth. *Applied Linguistics* 27/3.

Catera, E and Emigh, R 2005 Blogs, the virtual sopabox. *Essential Teacher* 2/3

Cattlin, M 2003 The RP reactive-proactive approach to lesson planning. *Modern English Teacher* 12/2.

Cavallera, I and Leiguarda, A 2006 Developing the reading brain. *Modern English Teacher* 15/1.

Cekaite, A and Aronsson, K 2005 Language play, a collaborative resource in children's learning. *Applied Linguistics* 26/2.

Chan, V 2001 The newspaper project: working together to make a class newspaper. *Modern English Teacher* 10/1.

Chau, J 2003 A three-step approach. Helping less proficient students in writing. *Modern English Teacher* 12/1.

Chen, J, Warden, C and Chang, H-T 2005 Motivators that do not motivate: the case of Chinese EFL learners and the influence of culture on motivation. *TESOL Quarterly* 39/4.

Ching-Shyang Chang, A and Read, J 2006 The effects of listening support on the listening performance of EFL learners. *TESOL Quarterly* 40/2.

Clark, J and Yallop C 1995 *An Introduction to Phonetics and Phonology* Blackwell.

Clemente, A 2001 On Thornbury's 'Unbearable lightness'. *ELT Journal* 55/4.

Clifton, J 2006 Facilitator talk. *ELT Journal* 60/2.

Coffield, F, Moseley, D, Hall, E and Ecclestone, K 2004 Learning styles and pedagogy in post-16 learning: a systematic and critical overview. Learning Skills and Research Centre of the Learning and Skills Development Agency. www.lsda.org.uk/files/PDF/Unplearnstylespost16.pdf.

Coffrey, S 2000 'Turn, turn, turn.' Alternative ways of presenting songs. *Modern English Teacher* 9/1.

Comins, R 1999 Voice, the neglected imperative. *Modern English Teacher* 8/2.

Coniam, D 2003a Using speech-digitising software to better appreciate English stress timing. *The Teacher Trainer* 17/1.

Coniam, D 2003b Jigsaw video. *Modern English Teacher* 12/2.

Cook, G 1989 *Discourse* Oxford University Press.

Cook, G 1994 Repetition and learning by heart: an aspect of intimate discourse, and its implications. *ELT Journal* 48/2.

Cook, G 1997 Language play, language learning. *ELT Journal* 51/3.

Cook, G 1998 The uses of reality: a reply to Ronald Carter. *ELT Journal* 52/1.

Cook, G 2000 *Language Play, Language Learning* Oxford University Press.

Cook, G 2001 *Discourse* Oxford University Press.

Cooper, R, Lavery, M and Rinvolucri, M 1991 *Video* Oxford University Press.

Cosh, J 1999 Peer observation: a reflective model. *ELT Journal* 53/1.

Cosh, J and Woodward, T 2003 A new focus for peer observation: an interview with Jill Cosh. *The Teacher Trainer* 17/3.

Cotterall, S 2000 Promoting learner autonomy through the curriculum: principles for designing language courses. *ELT Journal* 54/2.

Courtney, M 1996 Talking to learn: selecting and using peer group oral tasks. *ELT Journal* 50/4.

Cranmer, D 1996 *Motivating High-Level Learners* Pearson Education Ltd.

Cranmer, D and Leroy, C 1992 *Musical Openings* Pearson Education Ltd.

Crookes, G and Gass, S 1993a *Tasks in a Pedagogical Context* Multilingual Matters.

Crookes, G and Gass, S 1993b *Tasks and Language Learning* Multilingual Matters.

Crouch, C 1989 Performance teaching in ELT. *ELT Journal* 43/2.

Cruikshank, B, Conrad, S and Ivanovic, R 2001 *An A–Z of English Grammar and Usage* Pearson Education Ltd.

Crystal, D 2000 *Language Death* Cambridge University Press.

Crystal, D 2003a *English as a Global Language* 2nd edn Cambridge University Press.

Crystal, D 2003b *The Cambridge Encyclopaedia of the English Language* 2nd edn Cambridge University Press.

Cullen, R 2002 Supportive teacher talk: the importance of the F-move. *ELT Journal* 56/2.

Cureau, J 1982 Harnessing the power of suggestion. *Practical English Teaching* 2/3.

Curran, C 1976 *Counseling-Learning in Second Languages* Apple River Press.

Dalton, C and Seidlhofer, B 1994 *Pronunciation* Oxford University Press.

Damim, C, Peixoto, M and Wasenkeski, W 2002 Teaching teenagers. *English Teaching Professional* 23.

Davies, A 2003 *The Native Speaker: Myth and Reality* Multilingual Matters.

Davies, A 2006 What do learners really want from their EFL course? *ELT Journal* 60/1.

Davis, C 1995 Extensive reading: an expensive extravagance. *ELT Journal* 49/4.

Davis, P 1999 What is teacher development? *Humanising Language Teaching* 1/1.

Davis, P and Rinvolucri, M1990 *Dictation* Cambridge University Press.

Day, R and Bamford, J 1998 *Extensive Reading in the Second Language Classroom* Cambridge University Press.

De Sonneville, J 2005 Empowerment in action: using a participatory methodology in course design. *IATEFL Global Issues SIG 2005 Brighton Event Papers*.

Deacon, B 2000 Timed conversation: an activity for engaging large groups. *Modern English Teacher* 9/4.

Deller, S 2003 The language of the learner. *English Teaching Professional* 26.

Deller, S and Price, C 2007 *Teaching other Subjects through English CLIL* Oxford University Press.

Deller, S and Rinvolucri, M 2002 *Using the Mother Tongue* DELTA Publishing.

Desmond, J 2006 English spelling. *Modern English Teacher* 15/2.

Dinis, L and Moran, K 2005 Corpus-based tools for efficient writing instruction. *Essential Teacher* 2/3.

Dinnocenti, S 1998 Differentiation: definition and description for the gifted and talented. NRC/GT 1998 Spring Newsletter at http://www.sp.uconn.edu/~nrcgt/news/spring98/sprng985.html.

Dlugosz, D 2000 Rethinking the role of reading in teaching a foreign language to young learners. *ELT Journal* 54/3.

Domoney, L and Harris, S 1993 Justified and ancient: pop music in EFL classrooms. *ELT Journal* 47/3.

Dörnyei, Z 2001 *Teaching and Researching Motivation* Pearson Education Ltd.

Dörnyei, Z and Murphey, T 2003 *Group Dynamics in the Language Classroom* Cambridge University Press.

Dörnyei, Z and Thurrell, S 1994 Teaching conversational skills intensively: course content and rationale. *ELT Journal* 48/1.

Dudeney, G and Hockly, N 2007 *How to Teach English with Technology* Pearson Education Ltd.

Edge, J 1989 *Mistakes and Correction* Longman.

Edge, J 1992a Co-operative development. *ELT Journal* 46/1.

Edge, J 1992b *Co-operative Development: Professional Self-development through Co-operation with Colleagues* Pearson Education Ltd.

Edge, J 1999 In place of strife. Paper given at the International House Teacher Training Conference.

Edge, J (ed) 2002 *Continuing Professional Development* IATEFL Publications.

Edge, J 2003 Collegial self-development. *English Teaching Professional* 27.

Edwards, T 2005 Poster presentations. *English Teaching Professional* 38.

Eldridge, J 1996 Code-switching in a Turkish secondary school. *ELT Journal* 50/4.

Elgar, A G 2002 Student playwriting for language development. *ELT Journal* 56/1.

Ellis, G 1996 How culturally appropriate is the communicative approach? *ELT Journal* 50/3.

Ellis, G and Brewster J 2002a *Tell It Again! The New Storytelling Handbook for Primary Teachers* Pearson Education Ltd.

Ellis, G and Brewster, J 2002b *The Primary English Teacher's Guide* Penguin English Guides.

Ellis, G and Sinclair, B 1989 *Learning to Learn English* Cambridge University Press.

Ellis, R 1982 Informal and formal approaches to communicative language teaching. *ELT Journal* 36/2.

Ellis, R 1983 Review of Krashen, S 'Principles and practice in second language acquisition'. *ELT Journal* 37/3.

Ellis, R 1994 *The Study of Second Language Acquisition* Oxford University Press.

Ellis, R 2006 Current issues in the teaching of grammar: an SLA perspective. *TESOL Quarterly* 40/1.

Evans Nachi, H and Kinoshita, C 2006 Lecturing in miniature. *English Teaching Professional* 43.

Fanselow, J 1987 *Breaking Rules* Pearson Education Ltd.

Farrell, T 1998 Using TV 'soaps' for listening comprehension. *Modern English Teacher* 7/2.

Farrell, T 2001 Critical friendships: colleagues helping each other develop. *ELT Journal* 55/4.

Fedderholdt, K 2001 An email exchange project between non-native speakers of English. *ELT Journal* 55/3.

Field, J 1998a Skills and strategies: towards a new methodology for listening. *ELT Journal* 52/2.

Field, J 1998b The changing face of listening. *English Teaching Professional* 6.

Field, J 2000a 'Not waving but drowning': a reply to T Ridgeway. *ELT Journal* 54/2.

Field, J 2000b Finding one's way in the fog: listening strategies and second-language learners. *Modern English Teacher* 9/1.

Field, J 2003 The fuzzy notion of 'intelligibility': a headache for pronunciation teachers and oral testers. Special IATEFL All-SIGS newsletter.

Figueras, N 2005 Testing, testing, everywhere, and not a while to think. *ELT Journal* 59/1.

Fletcher, M 2005 Focus on feelings. *English Teaching Professional* 39.

Flowerdew, J and Miller, L 2006 *Second Language Listening: Theory and Practice* Cambridge University Press.

Flowerdew, L 1998 A cultural perspective on groupwork. *ELT Journal* 52/4.

Fonseca Mora, C 2000 Foreign language acquisition and melody singing. *ELT Journal* 54/2.

Foot, M 1999 Relaxing in pairs. *ELT Journal* 53/1.

Fortune, A 1992 Self-study grammar practice: learners' views and preferences. *ELT Journal* 46/2.

Fotos, S 1998 Shifting the focus from forms to form in the EFL classroom. *ELT Journal* 52/4.

Fowle, C 2002 Vocabulary notebooks: implementation and outcomes. *ELT Journal* 56/4.

Frankenberg-Garcia, A 2005 Pedagogical uses of monolingual and parallel concordances. *ELT Journal* 59/3.

Frankfurt, H 1988 Freedom of the will and the concept of a person. In *The Importance of What We Care About – Philosophical Essays* Cambridge University Press.

Freebairn, I 2000 The coursebook – future continuous or past? *English Teaching Professional* 15.

Fried-Booth, D 2002 *Project Work* 2nd edn Oxford University Press.

Gadd, N 1998 Towards less humanistic English teaching. *ELT Journal* 52/3.

Gaffield-Vile, N 1998 Creative writing in the ELT classroom. *Modern English Teacher* 7/3.

Gardner, D and Lambert, L 1999 *Establishing Self-access: From Theory to Practice* Cambridge University Press.

Gardner, H 1983 *Frames of Mind: The Theory of Multiple Intelligences* Basic Books.

Gardner, H 1993 *Multiple Intelligences: The Theory of Practice* Basic Books.

Gattegno, C 1976 *The Common Sense of Teaching Foreign Languages* Educational Solutions.

Gavioli, L and Aston, G 2001 Enriching reality: language corpora in language pedagogy. *ELT Journal* 55/3.

Geldicke, M 1997 Lectures in the classroom. *English Teaching Professional* 4.

Geldicke, M 2000 Action plans. *English Teaching Professional* 14.

Gibran, K 1991 *The Prophet* Pan Books.

Gierse, C 1993 Ideas on how to motivate learner independence. *Modern English Teacher* 2/4.

Gill, S 2005 The L1 in the L2 classroom. *Humanising Language Teaching* 7/5.

Gilmore, A 2004 A comparison of textbook and authentic interactions. *ELT Journal* 58/4.

Goh, C and Taib, Y 2006 Metacognitive instruction in listening for young learners. *ELT Journal* 60/3.

Goleman, D 1995 *Emotional Intelligence. Why Can it Matter More than IQ?* Bloomsbury.

Goodger, C 2005 Songs in action. *English Teaching Professional* 40.

Gordon Smith, D and Baber, E 2005 *Teaching English with Information Technology* Modern English Publishing.

Gower, R 1999 Doing as we would be done by. *Modern English Teacher* 8/4.

Gower, R, Phillips, D and Walters, S 1995 *Teaching Practice Handbook* Heinemann.

Grabe,W and Kaplan, R 1996 *Theory and Practice of Writing* Longman.

Graddol, D 2006 *English Next* The British Council.

Gray, J 2000 The ELT coursebook as cultural artefact: how teachers censor and adapt. *ELT Journal* 54/3.

Green, C 2005 Integrating extensive reading in the task-based curriculum. *ELT Journal* 59/4.

Green, C and Tanner, R 2005 Multiple intelligences and online teacher education. *ELT Journal* 59/4.

Green, C, Christopher, E and Lam, J 1997 Developing discussion skills in the ESL classroom. *ELT Journal* 51/2.

Green, T and Hawkey, R 2004 Test washback and impact. *Modern English Teacher* 13/4.

Gregg, K 1984 Krashen's monitor and Occam's razor. *Applied Linguistics* 5/2.

Grellet, F 1981 *Developing Reading Skills* Cambridge University Press.

Grice, H P 1975 Logic and conversation. In Cole, P and Morgan, J (eds) *Syntax and Semantics*, vol. 3 speech acts Academic Press.

Griffiths, C and Parr, J 2001 Language-learning strategies: theory and perception. *ELT Journal* 55/3.

Grundy, P 1995 *Doing Pragmatics* Edward Arnold.

Guariento, W and Morley, J 2001 Text and task authenticity in the EFL classroom. *ELT Journal* 55/4.

Hadfield, J 1992 *Group Dynamics* Oxford University Press.

Hadfield, J 1997 *Elementary Communication Games* Pearson Education Ltd.

Hadfield, J 2001 *Simple Writing Activities* Oxford University Press.

Hadfield, J and Hadfield C 2000 *Simple Listening Activities* Oxford University Press.

Hadfield, J and Hadfield C 2003a Hidden resources in the language classroom 1. *Modern English Teacher* 12/1.

Hadfield, J and Hadfield C 2003b Hidden resources in the language classroom 2. *Modern English Teacher* 12/2.

Haines, S 1995 For and against: pairwork. *Modern English Teacher* 4/1.

Halliday, M A K 1994 *An Introduction to Functional Grammar* 2nd edn Edward Arnold.

Halliwell, S 1992 *Teaching English in the Primary Classroom* Pearson Education Ltd.

Hamilton, M 2005 Straight from the chalkface: test driving the interactive whiteboard. *Modern English Teacher* 14/3.

Hamilton, R 2003 The NLP spelling strategy. *Modern English Teacher* 12/1.

Hancock, M 1995 *Pronunciation Games* Cambridge University Press.

Hancock, M 2005 Three takes on intonation. *English Teaching Professional* 40.

Harbord, J 1992 The use of the mother tongue in the classroom. *ELT Journal* 46/4.

Harmer, J 1982 What is communicative? *ELT Journal* 36/3.

Harmer, J 1983 Krashen's input hypothesis and the teaching of EFL. *World Language English* 3/1.

Harmer, J 1991 The cuddle factor. *Practical English Teaching* 11/2.

Harmer, J 1995 Taming the big 'I': teacher performance and student satisfaction. *ELT Journal* 49/4.

Harmer, J 1996 Is PPP dead? *Modern English Teacher* 5/2.

Harmer, J 2001 Coursebooks: a human, cultural and linguistic disaster? *Modern English Teacher* 10/3.

Harmer, J 2002 Ways of coping: random grouping and mixed ability dictogloss. *ELT Forum* www.eltforum.com/.

Harmer, J 2003 Do your students notice anything? *Modern English Teacher* 12/3.

Harmer, J 2004 *How to Teach Writing* Pearson Education Ltd.

Harmer, J 2005 And in the end the love you take ... In Pulverness, A (ed) *IATEFL 2004 Liverpool Conference Selections* IATEFL.

Harmer, J 2006a Engaging students as learners. *English Teaching Professional* 42.

Harmer, J 2006b 10 things I hate about PowerPoint. *The Teacher Trainer* 20/3 and *Humanising Language Teaching* 8/3.

Harmer, J 2007 *How to Teach English* 2nd edn Pearson Education Ltd.

Harmer, P 2005 How and when should teachers correct? In Pulverness, A (ed) *IATEFL 2004 Liverpool Conference Selections* IATEFL.

Harris, K 2002 In praise of whole-class discussion. *IATEFL Issues* 167.

Harris, N 2005 Interactive whiteboards: ELT's next best thing? *Modern English Teacher* 14/2.

Harvey, P 2005 What makes reading in a second language difficult? The reader. *Modern English Teacher* 14/4.

Harvey, P 2006 What makes reading in a second language difficult? *Modern English Teacher* 15/1.

Hawkey, R 2006 Teacher and learner perceptions of language learning activity. *ELT Journal* 60/3.

Head, K and Taylor, P 1997 *Readings in Teacher Development* Heinemann.

Hebden, M and Mason, J 2003 Classroom organisation. *English Teaching Professional* 28.

Hedge, T 2000 *Teaching and Learning in the Language Classroom* Oxford University Press.

Hedge, T 2005 *Writing* 2nd edn Oxford University Press.

Helgesen, M 2003 Talk to yourself. *English Teaching Professional* 29.

Helmer, E 2005 21st-century literacy. *English Teaching Professional* 36.

Hennigan, H 1999 Penpals to keypals. *Modern English Teacher* 8/2.

Hess, N 2001 *Teaching Large Multilevel Classes* Cambridge University Press.

Heyworth, F and Blakely, R 2005 Language for everyone: the European Language Portfolio. *Modern English Teacher* 14/3.

Hill, K 2005 Linking essay types and cognitive domains *Essential Teacher* 2/4 TESOL.

Hinkel, E 2006 Current perspectives in teaching the four skills. *TESOL Quaterly* 40/1.

Hoey, M 2001 *Textual Interaction: An Introduction to Written Discourse Analysis* Routledge.

Holden, B 2002 Listen and learn. *English Teaching Professional* 23.

Holliday, A 2005 *The Struggle to Teach English as an International Language* Oxford University Press.

Holliday, A 2006 Native-speakerism. *ELT Journal* 60/4.

Hongshen Zhang 2006 Eyes talk. *TTEd SIG* 2006/1.

House, J 2001 A 'stateless' language that Europe should embrace. *The Guardian Weekly* 19–25 April.

Howarth, P 2001a Process speaking 1: preparing to repeat yourself. *Modern English Teacher* 10/1.

Howarth, P 2001b Process speaking 2: preparing to repeat yourself. *Modern English Teacher* 10/2.

Howatt, A with Widdowson, H G 2004 *A History of Language Teaching* Oxford University Press.

Hughes, A 2003 *Testing for Language Teachers* 2nd edn Cambridge University Press.

Hutchinson, T and Torres, E 1994 The textbook as agent of change. *ELT Journal* 48/4.

Hyde, B 2000 Teachers as learners: beyond language learning. *ELT Journal* 54/3.

Hyland, K 1990 Providing productive feedback. *ELT Journal* 44/4.

Hyland, K 2002 *Teaching and Researching Writing* Pearson Education Ltd.

Ibrahim, N and Penfield, S 2005 Dynamic diversity: new dimensions in mixed composition classes. *ELT Journal* 59/3.

Illich, I 1972 *De-schooling Society* Harrow Books.

Jabr Dajani, D 2002 Using mother tongue to become a better learner. *Modern English Teacher* 11/2.

James, M 2006 Teaching for transfer in ELT. *ELT Journal* 60/2.

Jannuzi, C 2002 Phonics triptych. *Modern English Teacher* 11/1.

Jenkins, J 1998 Which pronunciation norms and models for English as an International Language? *ELT Journal* 52/2.

Jenkins, J 2004 ELF at the gate: the position of English as a lingua franca. In Pulverness, A (ed) *Liverpool Conference Selections* IATEFL Publications.

Jenkins, J 2006a Current perspectives on teaching World Englishes and English as a lingua franca. *TESOL Quarterly* 40/1.

Jenkins, J 2006b The spread of EIL: a testing time for testers. *ELT Journal* 60/1.

Johnson, K 1982 The deep-end strategy in communicative language teaching. In *Communicative Syllabus Design and Methodology* Pergamon Institute of English.

Jones, J 1995 Self-access and culture: retreating from autonomy. *ELT Journal* 49/3.

Jones, K 1982 *Simulation and Role-play* Cambridge University Press.

Jones, R 2001 Machiko's breakthrough: a magic classroom moment. *Humanising Language Teaching* 3/1.

Kachru, B 1983 Introduction: the other side of English. In Kachru, B (ed) *The Other Tongue – English Across Cultures* Pergamon.

Kachru, B 1985 Standards, codification and sociolinguistic realism: the English language in the outer circle. In Quirk, R and Widdowson, H (eds) *English in the World. Teaching and Learning the Language and Literature* Cambridge University Press in association with the British Council.

Kachru, B 2004 *Asian Englishes: Beyond the Canon* Hong Kong University Press.

Kannan, J and Towndrow, P 2002 On-line feedback. *Modern English Teacher* 11/1.

Karpinski, T 2003 The use of films as a stimulus to learn vocabulary. *Modern English Teacher* 12/1.

Kay, H and Dudley-Evans, T 1998 Genre: what teachers think. *ELT Journal* 52/4.

Kay, R 2006 Arguments against teaching English as an international language in Brazil. *Humanising Language Teaching* 8/1.

Keller, H 2003 Guests – the friendly human resource for intercultural awareness. *IATEFL Issues* 171.

Kelly, C 2003 From process to structure. *English Teaching Professional* 26.

Kelly, G 2000 *How to Teach Pronunciation* Pearson Education Ltd.

Kelly, G 2005 Can intonation be taught? *English Teaching Professional* 39.

Kennedy, A 2000a 'Did you *like* the text?' Reading without language-focused questions. *Modern English Teacher* 9/2.

Kennedy, A 2000b 'Did you *like* the text?' Engaging with the coursebook. *Modern English Teacher* 9/3.

Kent, D 2001 A topic-driven strategy for language lesson design: reconciling reactive TBL principles within a proactive, syllabus-oriented ELT world. *IATEFL TT SIG Newsletter* 2/2001.

Kern, R 2006 Perspectives on technology in learning and teaching languages. *TESOL Quarterly* 40/1.

Keskil, G and Tevfik Cephe, P 2001 Learner variables in learning English: is a 10-year-old the same as a 12-year-old? *Modern English Teacher* 10/1.

Keys, K and Walker, R 2002 Ten questions on the phonology of English as an international language. *ELT Journal* 56/3.

Knight, B 1992 Assessing speaking skills: a workshop for teacher development. *ELT Journal* 46/3.

Kohn, A 2001 Five reasons to stop saying 'Good job'! *Young Children* September 2001.

Kramsch, C and Sullivan, P 1996 Appropriate pedagogy. *ELT Journal* 50/3.

Krashen, S 1984 *The Input Hypothesis* Longman.

Krishnan, L and Hoon, L H 2002 Diaries: listening to 'voices' from the multicultural classroom. *ELT Journal* 56/3.

Kubanyiova, M 2004 Leave them alone! *English Teaching Professional* 33.

Kumaravadivelu, B 1991 Language-learning tasks: teacher intention and learner interpretation. *ELT Journal* 45/2.

Kumaravadivelu, B 2001 Toward a postmethod pedagogy. *TESOL Quarterly* 35.

Kumaravadivelu, B 2006 TESOL methods: changing tracks, challenging trends. *TESOL Quarterly* 40/1.

Kuo, I-C V 2006 Addressing the issue of teaching English as a lingua franca. *ELT Journal* 60/3.

Kurtoglu Eken, D 1999 Through the eyes of the learner: learner observations of teaching and learning. *ELT Journal* 53/4.

Kwamlah Johnson, A 2002 Journal writing for an audience. *Modern English Teacher* 11/2.

Kyriacou, C 1998 *Effective Teaching in Schools* 2nd edn Simon and Shuster Education.

La Forge, P 1983 *Counseling and Culture in Second Language Acquisition* Pergamon.

Lane, K 2002 Why posters? And How? *IATEFL Issues* 167.

Lansley, C 1994 'Collaborative development': an alternative to phatic discourse and the art of co-operative development. *ELT Journal* 48/1.

Lavezzo, M and Dunford, H 1993 To correct or not to correct? *Modern English Teacher* 2/3.

Lawlor, M 1986 The inner track method as successful teaching. *Practical English Teaching* 6/3.

Lee, I 1998 Supporting greater autonomy in language learning. *ELT Journal* 52/4.

Lee, I 2005a Empowering non-native speakers for English language teaching: the case of Hong Kong. *The Teacher Trainer* 19/1.

Lee, I 2005b Why burn the midnight oil? Marking student essays. *Modern English Teacher* 14/1.

Leech, G, Cruickshank, B and Ivanic, R 2001 *An A–Z of English Grammar and Usage* Pearson Education Ltd.

Leiguarda, A 2004 Teenagers! Motivating the teenage brain. *Modern English Teacher* 13/4.

Leung, C and Lewkowicz, J 2006 Expanding horizons and unresolved conundrums: language testing and assessment. *TESOL Quarterly* 40/1.

Lewis, J 2001 Teaching focus for conversational use. *ELT Journal* 55/1.

Lewis, M 1986 *The English Verb* Language Teaching Publications.

Lewis, M 1993 *The Lexical Approach* Language Teaching Publications.

Lewis, M 1997 *Implementing the Lexical Approach* Language Teaching Publications.

Lewis, M (ed) 2000 *Teaching Collocation* Language Teaching Publications.

Lewthwaite, M 2002 A brush with art. *English Teaching Professional* 23.

Lightbown, P and Spada, N 2006 *How Languages are Learned* 3rd edn Oxford University Press.

Linder, D 2000 Making e-mail exchanges really work. *Modern English Teacher* 9/3.

Linder, D 2002 Translation. *English Teaching Professional* 23.

Lindstromberg, S 2004a Towards better results with mixed-proficiency classes: use of flexible tasks. *Humanising Language Teaching* 6/3.

Lindstromberg, S (ed) 2004b *Language Activities for Teenagers* Cambridge University Press.

Linse, C 2004 On their best behaviour. *English Teaching Professional* 32.

Littlejohn, A 1998 The analysis of language teaching materials: inside the Trojan horse. In Tomlinson, B (ed).

Littlejohn, A 2001 Motivation: where does it come from? Where does it go? *English Teaching Professional* 19.

Littlewood, W 2004a The task-based approach: some questions and suggestions. *ELT Journal* 58/4.

Littlewood, W 2004b Structuring classroom interaction for task-based learning. Paper presented at the 38th annual IATEFL conference, Liverpool, UK.

Long, M H 1988 Instructed interlanguage development. In Beebe, L (ed) *Issues in Second Language Acquisition: Multiple Perspectives* Newbury House.

Lowe, T 1987 An experiment in role reversal: teachers as language learners. *ELT Journal* 41/2.

Lozanov, G 1978 *Suggestology and the Outlines of Suggestopody* Gordon and Breach.

Lum, Y L and Brown, R 1994 Guidelines for production of in-house self-access materials. *ELT Journal* 48/2.

Lynch, T 1997 Nudge, nudge: teacher interventions in task-based learner talk. *ELT Journal* 51/4.

Lynch, T 2001 Seeing what they meant: transcribing as a route to noticing. *ELT Journal* 55/2.

Madsen, C H, Becker, W C and Thomas, D R 1968 Rules, praise, and ignoring. *Journal of Behavioural Analaysis* 1.

Maley, A 1993 Finding the centre. *The Teacher Trainer* 7/3.

Maley, A 1998 Squaring the circle – reconciling materials as constraint with materials as empowerment. In Tomlinson, B (ed).

Maley, A 2000 *The Language Teacher's Voice* Macmillan ELT.

Maley, A 2003 A modest proposal: from research to inquiry. *Humanising Language Teaching* 5/6.

Maley, A and Duff, A 2005 *Drama Techniques* 3rd edn Cambridge University Press.

Mallows, D 2002 Non-linearity and the observed lesson. *ELT Journal* 56/1.

Mann, S 2001 From argument to articulation. *English Teaching Professional* 20.

Marks, J 2000 Listening in. *English Teaching Professional* 16.

Marks, J 2002 All change or small change? The corpus revolution: what's in it for me? *Modern English Teacher* 11/2.

Martin, P 2006 Language teacher training: sociolinguistic and multilingual realities. Paper delivered at the XX RELC conference in Singapore.

McBeath, N 2006 How to write really rotten materials. *Modern English Teacher* 15/1.

McCarthy, M 1991 *Discourse Analysis for Language Teachers* Cambridge University Press.

McCarthy, M and Carter, R 1997 Octopus or hydra? *IATEFL Newsletter* 137.

McCarthy, M and O'Dell, F 2005 *English Collocations in Use* Cambridge University Press.

McCloskey, M-L and Thrush, E 2005 Building a reading scaffold with web texts. *Essential Teacher* 2/4.

McClure, J 2001 Developing language skills and learner autonomy in international postgraduates. *ELT Journal* 55/2.

McCourt, F 2005 *Teacher Man* Fourth Estate.

McDonald, A 2004 A frame for learning 1. *English Teaching Professional* 35.

McDonald, A 2005a A frame for learning 2. *English Teaching Professional* 36.

McDonald, A 2005b A frame for learning 3. *English Teaching Professional* 35.

McDonough, J 1994 A teacher looks at teachers' diaries. *ELT Journal* 48/1.

McDonough, J 2002 The teacher as language learner: worlds of difference. *ELT Journal* 56/4.

McDonough, K and Chaikitmongkol, W 2007 Teachers' and learners' reactions to a task-based EFL course in Thailand. *TESOL Quarterly* 41/1.

McEwan, J 2003 Be my guest. *English Teaching Professional* 26.

McGrath, I 2006 Teachers' and learner's images for coursebooks. *ELT Journal* 60/2.

McIver, N 2000 How do I organise a chorus drill? *English Teaching Professional* 15.

McKay, H and Tom, A 1999 *Teaching Adult Second Language Learners* Cambridge University Press.

McLean Orlando, S 2006 The importance of informal learning in EFL. *Modern English Teacher* 15/1.

McNamara, T 2000 *Language Testing* Oxford University Press.

Medgyes, P 1986 Queries from a communicative teacher. *ELT Journal* 40/2 and in Rossner and Bolitho (eds).

Medgyes, P 1992 Native or non-native: who's worth more? *ELT Journal* 46/4.

Medgyes, P 2000 *Laughing Matters* Cambridge University Press.

Mei Lin Ho, C 2004 Viva la viva. *Modern English Teacher* 13/4.

Mennim, P 2003 Rehearsed oral output and reactive focus on form. *ELT Journal* 57/2.

Mercer, S 2004 Getting into character. *English Teaching Professional* 32.

Miccoli, L 2003 English through drama for oral skills development. *ELT Journal* 57/2.

Miller, L 2004a Teachers as researchers: adapting research methods to the classroom. *Modern English Teacher* 13/2.

Miller, L 2004b Teachers as researchers: teacher journals. *Modern English Teacher* 13/4.

Miller, L 2005 Teachers as researchers: interviews. *Modern English Teacher* 13/4.

Millrood, R 2004 The role of NLP in teachers' classroom discourse. *ELT Journal* 58/1.

Misham, F 2004 Authenticating corpora for language learning: a problem and its resolution. *ELT Journal* 58/3.

Moon, J 2005 *Children Learning English* Macmillan ELT.

Morgan, J and Rinvolucri, M 1988 *Vocabulary* Oxford University Press.

Morgan, J and Rinvolucri, M 2002 *Vocabulary* 2nd edn Oxford University Press.

Mumford, S 2003 Drilling can be fun: getting the most out of your drills. *Modern English Teacher* 12/4.

Mumford, S 2004 Organising free speaking. *Modern English Teacher* 13/4.

Mumford, S 2006 Another look at drills. *Modern English Teacher* 15/4.

Muncie, J 2000 Using written teacher feedback in EFL composition classes. *ELT Journal* 54/1.

Muncie, J 2002 Finding a place for grammar in EFL composition classes. *ELT Journal* 56/2.

Murray, S 2000 Don't just sit there … Getting students to change places in class. *Modern English Teacher* 9/4.

Murray, S 2001 Authentic interest: using authentic text with low-level learners. *Modern English Teacher* 10/1.

Murugavel, T 2003 Using video. *English Teaching Professional* 29.

Naiman, N, Froelich, M, Stern, H and Todesco, A 1978 The good language learner. *Research in Education* series, no. 7, Ontario Institute for Studies in Education.

Naimushin, B 2002 Translation in foreign language teaching. *Modern English Teacher* 11/4.

Nattinger, J and DeCarrio, J 1992 *Lexical Phrases and Language Teaching* Oxford University Press.

Newton, C 1999 Phonemic script – the pros and cons. *English Teaching Professional* 12.

Newton, C 2001 A box of tricks. *English Teaching Professional* 19.

Nicholls, K 2000 Motivation – can we do anything about it? *Modern English Teacher* 9/2.

Nunan, D 1989 A client-centred approach to teacher development. *ELT Journal* 43/2.

Nunan, D 2004 *Task-Based Learning and Teaching* Cambridge University Press.

Nunes, A 2004 Portfolios in the EFL classroom: disclosing an informed practice. *ELT Journal* 58/4.

Nuttall, C 1996 *Teaching Reading Skills in a Foreign Language* Heinemann.

O'Dell, F 1992 Helping teachers to use a self-access centre to its full potential. *ELT Journal* 46/2.

O'Dell, F and Head, K 2003 *Games for Vocabulary Practice: Interactive Vocabulary Activities for all Levels* Cambridge University Press.

O'Neill, R 1982 Why use textbooks? *ELT Journal* 36/2 and in Rossner and Bolitho (eds).

Osborne, P 2005 *Teaching One to One* Modern English Publishing.

Painter, L 1999 Homework. *English Teaching Professional* 10.

Palmer, H 1921 *The Principles of Language Study* Harrap. Republished by Oxford University Press 1964.

Pani, S 2004 Reading strategy instruction through mental modelling. *ELT Journal* 58/4.

Paran, A 1996 Reading in EFL: facts and fictions. *ELT Journal* 50/1.

Park, Y 2006 Will nonnative-English-speaking teachers ever get a fair chance? *Essential Teacher* 3/1.

Parrott, M 2000 *Grammar for Language Teachers* Cambridge University Press.

Payne, S 2006 A song-based grammar lesson in record time. *Essential Teacher* 3/1.

Pennycook, A 1994 *The Cultural Politics of English as an International Language* Longman.

Pennycook, A 1998 *English and the Discourse of Colonialism* Routledge.

Peters, S 2006 Create your own ESL/EFL Weblog. *TOPICS Online Magazine* at http://www.topics-mag.com/call/blogs/ESL_EFL.htm.

Petty, G 2004 *Teaching Today* 3rd edn Nelson Thornes.

Phillipson, R 1992 *Linguistic Imperialism* Oxford University Press.

Phillipson, R 1996 Linguistic imperialism: African perspectives. *ELT Journal* 50/2.

Phillipson, R 2003 *English-only Europe? Challenging Language Policy* Routledge.

Piai, S 2005 You can train me, and you can educate me, but you can't develop me – I develop. *Essential Teacher* 2/4.

Piai, S and Threadgold, K 2001 Using action research as a means of evaluation on a teacher training course. *The Teacher Trainer* 15/3.

Pickard, N 1996 Out-of-class language learning strategies. *ELT Journal* 50/2.

Pienemann, M 1998 Determining the influence of instruction on L2 speech processing. *AILA Review* 5/1.

Pienemann, M 1999 *Language Processing and Second Language Deveopment: Probability Theory* John Benjamin

Pilger, J 1998 *Hidden Agendas* Vintage.

Pimsleur, P 1966 *Pimsleur Aptitude Test Battery* Harcourt, Brace and World.

Pinker, S 1994 *The Language Instinct* Penguin.

Pinker, S 1999 *Words and Rules* Weidenfeld and Nicolson.

Pinter, A 2006 *Teaching Young Language Learners* Oxford University Press.

Plumb, K 1994 Teacher development: the experience of developing within a peer-group. *IATEFL Teacher Development SIG Newsletter* 25.

Polkowski, L 2006 First steps with the interactive whiteboard in ESOL. *Modern English Teacher* 15/1.

Porte, G 1995 Writing wrongs: copying as a strategy for underachieving EFL writers. *ELT Journal* 49/2.

Prabhu, N 1987 *Second Language Pedagogy* Oxford University Press.

Prodromou, L 1995 The backwash effect: from testing to teaching. *ELT Journal* 49/1.

Prodromou, L 1997a Global English and the octopus. *IATEFL Newsletter* 135.

Prodromou, L 1997b From corpus to octopus. *IATEFL Newsletter* 137.

Prodromou, L 2002a The great ELT textbook debate. *Modern English Teacher* 11/4.

Prodromou, L 2002b Crossing frontiers. *English Teaching Professional* 23.

Prowse, P 2000 Open your books. *English Teaching Professional* 14.

Prowse, P and Garton-Sprenger, J 2005 Teen power. *English Teaching Professional* 39.

Puchta, H 2005 Making the most of Multiple Intelligences. *English Teaching Professional* 41.

Puchta, H 2006a Multiple intelligences in action 1. *English Teaching Professional* 42.

Puchta, H 2006b Multiple intelligences in action 2. *English Teaching Professional* 43.

Puchta, H and Rinvolucri, M 2005 *Multiple Intelligences in EFL: Exercises for Secondary and Adult Students* Helbling Languages.

Puchta, H and Schratz, M 1993 *Teaching Teenagers* Addison Wesley Longman.

Qualiifications and Curriculum Agency 2006 A review of GCSE coursework. http://www.qca.org.uk/downloads/QCA-06-2736_GCSE_coursework_report-June-2006.pdf.

Quinn, J 2000 Wavelengths. *English Teaching Professional* 14.

Radosh, D 2005 One billion. *The New Yorker* 02/28 – and at www.newyorker.com/talk/content/?050228ta_talk_radosh.

Rajagopalan, K 1999 Of EFL teachers, conscience, and cowardice. *ELT Journal* 53/3.

Rajagopalan, K 2004 The concept of 'World English' and its implications for ELT. *ELT Journal* 58/2.

Rampton, M 1990 Displacing the 'native speaker': expertise, affiliation and inheritance. *ELT Journal* 44/2.

Read, C 2003 Is younger better? *English Teaching Professional* 28.

Read, C 2005 Managing children positively. *English Teaching Professional* 38.

Reid, J 1987 The learning style preferences of ESL students. *TESOL Quarterly* 21/1.

Reilly, V and Ward, S 1997 *Very Young Learners* Oxford University Press.

Reinders, H and Lewis, M 2006 An evaluative checklist for self-access materials. *ELT Journal* 60/3.

Revell, J and Norman, S 1997 *In Your Hands* Saffire Press.

Revell, J and Norman, S 1999 *Handing Over: NLP-based Activities for Language Learning* Saffire Press.

Richards, J and Lockhart, C 1996 *Reflective Teaching in Second Language Classrooms* Cambridge University Press.

Richards, J and Rodgers, T 2001 *Approaches and Methods in Language Teaching* 2nd edn Cambridge University Press.

Richards, K 1992 Pepys into a TEFL course. *ELT Journal* 46/2.

Ridgeway, T 2000 Listening strategies – I beg your pardon. *ELT Journal* 54/2.

Rinvolucri, M 1983 Writing to your students. *ELT Journal* 37/1.

Rinvolucri, M 1998 Mistakes. *Modern English Teacher* 7/3.

Rinvolucri, M 1995 Language students as letter writers. *ELT Journal* 49/2.

Rinvolucri, M 1996 Letter to Craig Thaine. *The Teacher Trainer* 10/2.

Rinvolucri, M 2002 *Humanising Your Coursebook* DELTA Publishing.

Rinvolucri, M 2005 NLP suits some people extremely well. *Modern English Teacher* 14/4.

Rinvolucri, M and Davis, P 1995 *More Grammar Games* Cambridge University Press.

Rogers, A 1996 *Teaching Adults* 2nd edn Open University Press.

Rogers, C 1969 *Freedom to Learn* Charles Merrill.

Rogers, C R 1961 *On Becomng a Person* Houghton Mifflin.

Rosenberg, M 2006 In the music business. *English Teaching Professional* 43.

Rossner, R and Bolitho, R (eds) 1990 *Currents of Change in English Language Teaching* Oxford University Press.

Rossner, R 1982 Talking shop: a conversation with Caleb Gattegno. *ELT Journal* 36/4.

Rost, M 1990 *Listening in Language Learning* Pearson Education Ltd.

Rubin, J and Thompson, I 1982 *How to be a More Successful Language Learner* Heinle and Heinle.

Rühlemann, C 2005 Creative re-writing. *English Teaching Professional* 41.

Ryan, S 2002 Digital video: using technology to improve learner motivation. *Modern English Teacher* 11/2.

Salverda, R 2002 Multilingualism in metropolitan London. *English Today* 18.

Saville, N and Hargreaves, P 1999 Assessing speaking in the revised FCE. *ELT Journal* 53/1.

Sayer, P 2005 An intensive approach to building conversation skills. *ELT Journal* 59/1.

Scharle, A and Szabó, A 2000 *Learner Autonomy* Cambridge University Press.

Schmidt, R 1990 The role of consciousness in second language learning. *Applied Linguistics* 11/2.

Schmitt, N 2002 *Vocabulary in Language Teaching* Cambridge University Press.

Schön, D 1983 *The Reflective Practitioner: How Professionals Think in Action* Basic Books.

Schön, D 1987 *Educating the Reflective Practitioner* Jossey-Bass.

Scott, W and Ytreborg, L 1990 *Teaching English to Children* Pearson Education Ltd.

Scott, M, Carioni, I, Zanatta, M, Bayer, E and Quintilhana, T 1984 Using a 'standard' exercise in teaching reading comprehension. *ELT Journal* 38/2.

Scrivener, J 1994a PPP and after. *The Teacher Trainer* 8/1.

Scrivener, J 1994b *Learning Teaching* Heinemann.

Scrivener, J 2005 *Learning Teaching* 2nd edn Heinemann.

Seedhouse, P 1999 Task-based interaction. *ELT Journal* 53/3.

Seidlhofer, B 2004 Research perspectives on teaching English as a lingua franca. *Annual Review of Applied Linguistics* 24.

Senior, R 2006 *The Experience of Language Teaching* Cambridge University Press.

Senior, R M 2002 A class-centred approach to language teaching. *ELT Journal* 56/4.

Sheen, R 2003 Focus on form – a myth in the making? *ELT Journal* 57/3.

Shemesh, R and Waller, S 2000 *Teaching English Spelling* Cambridge University Press.

Shinji Kondon, D and Ying-Ling, Y 2004 Strategies for coping with language anxiety: the case of students of English in Japan. *ELT Journal* 58/3.

Simunkova, R 2004 The shy speaker. *English Teaching Professional* 35.

Sinclair, B, McGrath, I and Lamb, T (eds) 2000 *Learner Autonomy, Teacher Autonomy: Future Directions* Pearson Education Ltd in association with the British Council.

Skehan, P 1998 *A Cognitive Approach to Language Learning* Oxford University Press.

Skinner, B 1957 *Verbal Behaviour* Appleton.

Slattery, M and Willis, J 2001 *English for Primary Teachers* Oxford University Press.

Smith, G P 2003 Music and mondegreens: extracting meaning from noise. *ELT Journal* 57/2.

Smith, H A 2003 Getting to the language point: lesson planning for real world teaching practice. *The Teacher Trainer* 17/2.

Smith, K 2002 Learner portfolios. *English Teaching Professional* 22.

Smith, R C 1999 *The Writings of Harold E Palmer* Hon-no-Tomosha.

Spiro, J 2004 *Creative Poetry Writing* Oxford University Press.

Stapleton, P 2005 Evaluating web-sources: internet literacy and L2 academic writing. *ELT Journal* 59/2.

Stempleski, S and Tomalin, B 1990 *Video in Action* Prentice Hall.

Stevick, E 1976 *Memory, Meaning and Method: Some Psychological Perspectives on Language Learning* Newbury House.

Stirling, J 2005 The portable electronic dictionary. *Modern English Teacher* 14/3.

Suarez, J 2000 'NATIVE' and 'NON-NATIVE': not only a question of terminology. *Humanising Language Teaching* 2/6.

Sugita, Y 2006 The impact of teachers' comment types on students' revision. *ELT Journal* 60/1.

Sunderland, J 2006 *Language and Gender: An Advanced Resource Book* Routledge.

Swain, M 1985 Communicative competence: some rules of comprehensible input and comprehensible output in its development. In Gass, S and Madden, C (eds) *Input in Second Language Acquisition* Newbury House.

Swan, M 1985 A critical look at the Communication Approach. *ELT Journal* 39/1 and 2.

Swan, M 1994 Design criteria for pedagogic language rules. In Bygate, M, Tonkyn, A and Williams, E (eds).

Swan, M 2005a *Practical English Usage* 3rd edn Oxford University Press.

Swan, M 2005b Legislation by hypothesis: the case of task-based instruction. *Applied Linguistics* 26/3.

Swan, M 2006 *Grammar* Oxford University Press.

Szwaj, M 1999 The paradox of a non-native EFL teacher. *Humanising Language Teaching* 1/8.

Tajino, A and Tajino, Y 2000 Native and non-native: what can they offer? Lessons from team teaching in Japan. *ELT Journal* 54/1.

Tannen, D 1992 *You Just Don't Understand: Women and Men in Conversation* Virago.

Tanner, R 1992 Erroroleplay. *The Teacher Trainer* 6/2.

Tanner, R 2001 Teaching intelligently. *English Teaching Professional* 20.

Tarone, E 2000 Getting serious about language play: language play, interlanguage variation and second-language acquisition. In Swierbin, B, Morris, F, Anderson, M, Klee, C and Tarone, E *Social and Cognitive Factors in Second Language Acquisition: Selected Proceedings of the 1999 Second Language Research Forum* Cascadilla Press.

Taylor, C 1977 What is Human Agency? In Mischel, T (ed) *The Self: Psychological and Philosophical Issues* Oxford University Press.

Taylor, J 2002 The road to autonomy. *English Teaching Professional* 24.

Taylor, L 2005 Investigating affect through analysis of teacher-generated language. *IATEFL TTEd SIG Newsletter* 2005/3.

Taylor, L 2006 The changing landscape of English: implications for language assessment. *ELT Journal* 60/1.

Templer, B 2004 Reflective teaching in the low-resource classroom: reinventing ourselves as teachers through self-scrutiny. *Humanising Language Teaching* 6/3.

Thaine, C 1996a Dealing with timetabling on second language teacher training courses. *The Teacher Trainer* 10/1.

Thaine, C 1996b Letter to Mario Rinvolucri. *The Teacher Trainer* 10/3.

Thomas, J 1999 Voices from the periphery: Non-native teachers and issues of credibility. In Braine, G (ed).

Thornbury, S 1996 'ARC': does it have restricted use? *The Teacher Trainer* 10/3.

Thornbury, S 1998 The lexical approach: a journey without maps? *Modern English Teacher* 7/4.

Thornbury, S 1999a *How to Teach Grammar* Pearson Education Ltd.

Thornbury, S 1999b Lesson art and design. *ELT Journal* 53/1.

Thornbury, S 2000 A Dogma for EFL. *IATEFL Issues* 153.

Thornbury, S 2001a *How to Teach Vocabulary* Pearson Education Ltd.

Thornbury, S 2001b The unbearable lightness of EFL. *ELT Journal* 55/4.

Thornbury, S 2005a *How to Teach Speaking* Pearson Education Ltd.

Thornbury, S 2005b *Beyond the Sentence* Macmillan Education.

Thornbury, S 2005c Dogme: dancing in the dark? *Humanising Language Teaching* 7/2.

Thornbury, S and Meddings, L 2001 Coursebooks: the roaring in the chimney. *Modern English Teacher* 10/3.

Thorp, D 1991 Confused encounters: differing expectations in the EAP classroom. *ELT Journal* 45/2.

Tice, J 1991 The textbook straightjacket. *Practical English Teaching* 11/3.

Tice, J 1999 *The Mixed-ability Classroom* Richmond Publishing.

Timmis, I 2002 Native-speaker norms and International English: a classroom view. *ELT Journal* 56/3.

Toledo, P 2001 'Howl'. A modest proposal revisited. *IATEFL Issues* 159.

Tomlinson, B 2003 Developing materials to develop yourself. *Humanising Language Teaching* 5/4.

Tomlinson, B 2005 Testing to learn: a personal view of language testing. *ELT Journal* 59/1.

Tomlinson, C A 1995 Differentiating instruction for advanced learners in the mixed-ability middle school classroom ERIC EC Digest E536 at http://www.kidsource.com/kidsource/content/diff_instruction.html.

Tomlinson, C A 1999 The differentiated classroom: responding to the needs of all learners. Association for Supervision and Curriculum Development, USA.

Tribble, C 1996 *Writing* Oxford University Press.

Trotman, W 2004 Portfolio assessment: advantages,drawbacks and implementation. *Modern English Teacher* 13/4.

Underhill, A 1989 Process in humanistic education. *ELT Journal* 43/4.

Underhill, A 1992 The role of groups in developing teacher self-awareness. *ELT Journal* 46/1.

Underhill, A 2005 *Sound Foundations* 2nd edn Macmillan Education.

Underwood, M 1989 *Teaching Listening* Pearson Education Limited.

Upshur, J and Turner, C 1995 Constructing rating scales for second language tests. *ELT Journal* 49/1.

Ur, P 1981 *Discussions that Work* Cambridge University Press.

Ur, P 1996 *A Course in Language Teaching* Cambridge University Press.

Ur, P 2006 A different ball game: contrasting contexts and methodologies. Unpublished article based on a talk given at the IATEFL Conference in Harrogate, April 2006.

Urquhart, S and Weir, C 1998 *Reading in a Second Language: Process, Product and Practice* (Applied Linguistics and Language Study) Longman.

Vallance, M 2004 Using weblogs to encourage English language learners to write. *Modern English Teacher* 13/2.

Vallance, M 2006 Interactive stories on an iPod. *Modern English Teacher* 15/1.

Vanderplank, R 1988 The value of teletext sub-titles in language learning. *ELT Journal* 42/4.

Vanderplank, R 1996 Really active viewing with teletext subtitles and closed captions. *Modern English Teacher* 5/2.

Vettori, P 2005 Accessorise! *English Teaching Professional* 39.

Vickers, C and Ene, E 2006 Grammatical accuracy and learner autonomy in advanced writing. *ELT Journal* 60/2.

Vince, M 2004 Writing revalued. *English Teaching Professional* 35.

Viswamohan, A 2005 Keeping up with the snollygosters. *English Teaching Professional* 37.

Vygotsky, L 1978 *Mind in Society* MIT Press.

Wadden, P and McGovern, S 1991 The quandary of negative class participation: coming to terms with misbehaviour in the language classroom. *ELT Journal* 45/2.

Wade, J 2002 Fun with flashcards. *English Teaching Professional* 23.

Walker, C 1998 Books on reading. *ELT Journal* 52/2.

Walker, R 2001 International intelligibility. *English Teaching Professional* 21.

Walker, R 2006 Going for a song. *English Teaching Professional* 43.

Wallace, C 1992 *Reading* Oxford University Press.

Wallace, M 1997 *Action Research for Language Teachers* Cambridge University Press.

Wallace, M 2000 The case for case studies. *IATEFL Research SIG and Teacher Development SIG Special Joint Issue*.

Waller, S 2002 The spelling dilemma. *English Teaching Professional* 24.

Walter, E 2002 CD-ROM dictionaries. *Modern English Teacher* 11/1.

Waters, A and Vilches, M L 2001 Implementing ELT innovations: a needs analysis framework. *ELT Journal* 55/2.

Watkins, P 2001 Getting the most from your graded reader. *English Teaching Professional* 21.

Watson Todd, R 2003 How to be a creative teacher. *English Teaching Professional* 29.

Watson Todd, R, Mills, N, Palard, C and Khamcharoen, P 2001 Giving feedback on journals. *ELT Journal* 55/4.

Watson, J R and Raynor, R 1920 Conditioned emotional reactions. *Journal of Experimental Psychology* 3/1.

Weber, J-J 2001 A concordance-and genre-informed approach to ESP essay writing. *ELT Journal* 55/1.

Weir, C 1993 *Understanding and Developing Language Tests* Prentice Hall.

Weir, C 2005 *Language Testing and Validation* Palgrave Macmillan.

Wells, J 2000 *Longman Pronunciation Dictionary* Pearson Education Ltd.

West 1953 *A General Service List of English Words* Longman.

Whitaker, P 2005 More to portfolio assessment. *Modern English Teacher* 14/4.

White, G 1998 *Listening* Oxford University Press.

White, R and Arndt, V 1991 *Process Writing* Pearson Education Ltd.

Wichmann, A, Fligelstone, S McEnery, T and Knowles, G 1997 *Teaching and Language Corpora* (Applied Linguistics and Language Study) Longman.

Wicksteed, K 1998 Where next for the National Curriculum? *The Linguist.*

Widdowson, H 1985 Against dogma: a reply to Michael Swan. *ELT Journal* 39/3 and in Rossner and Bolitho (eds).

Widdowson, H 2003 *Defining Issues in English Language Teaching* Oxford University Press.

Wilkins, D 1976 *Notional Syllabuses* Oxford University Press.

Williams, M and Burden, R 1997 *Psychology for Language Teachers* Cambridge University Press.

Williams, M 2001 Learn to mediate: mediate to learn. *English Teaching Professional* 21.

Willing, K 1987 *Learning Styles in Adult Migrant Education* Adult Migrant Education Programme, Adelaide.

Willis, D 1990 *The Lexical Syllabus* Collins ELT.

Willis, D and Wills, J 2003 The principles of TBL: a reply to Anthony Bruton. *IATEFL Issues* 175.

Willis, J 1994 Task-based language learning as an alternative to PPP. *The Teacher Trainer* 8/1.

Willis, J 1996 *A Framework for Task-based Learning* Longman.

Willis, J and Willis, D (eds) 1996 *Challenge and Change in Language Teaching* Heinemann.

Wilson, D 2005 Be prepared! *English Teaching Professional* 36.

Wilson, J J 2005 Letting go! *English Teaching Professional* 39.

Wilson, K 1997 *Fastlane Teacher's Book 1* Pearson Education Ltd.

Winn-Smith, B 2001 Classroom language. *English Teaching Professional* 18.

Woodman, G 2005 Designing online training materials for German–British intercultural encounters. *Folio* 9/2.

Woodward, T 1993 Changing the basis of pre-service TEFL training in the UK. *IATEFL Teacher Training SIG Newsletter* 13.

Woodward, T 1995 Pair and groupwork – confessions of ignorance. *The Teacher Trainer* 9/1.

Woodward, T 2001 *Planning Lessons and Courses* Cambridge University Press.

Woodward, T 2002 Perspectives on planning. *English Teaching Professional* 24.

Woodward, T 2003 The secret of success. *English Teaching Professional* 26.

Wray, A 1999 Formulaic language in learners and native speakers. *Language Teaching* 32/4.

Wright, A, Betteridge, D and Buckby, M 2006 *Games for Language Learning* 3rd edn Cambridge University Press.

Wright, T 1987 *Roles of Teachers and Learners* Oxford University Press.

Yu, M-C 2006 The effect of age on starting to learn English. *Modern English Teacher* 15/2.

Zülküf Altan, M 2001 The theory of multiple intelligences: what does it offer EFL teachers? *Modern English Teacher* 10/1.

The Practice of English Language Teaching DVD

Lesson stories and teachers talking

There are three types of film clip on the DVD:

    A *Meet the teachers*: The teachers whose lessons are included on the DVD introduce themselves.

    B *Lesson stories*: Nine complete lesson sequences have been carefully edited down to provide short but clear 'stories' of the lessons.

    C *Teachers talking*: In interviews, the nine teachers discuss issues arising out of their filmed lessons.

Contents (B and C)

The *Lesson stories* and *Teachers talking* sections are listed alphabetically by teacher. Where a topic is written in SMALL CAPITALS, you can follow up references to it in this book by using the Contents list on pages 2–9 or the Index.

Lesson stories	Teachers talking
Allan [Intermediate] Allan uses LIVE LISTENING to train students in LISTENING SKILLS.	**Allan** talks about LIVE and PRE-RECORDED LISTENING and about how students reconstruct what they hear.
Barbara [Intermediate] Barbara uses an INTERACTIVE WHITEBOARD to teach an INTEGRATED listening-and-speaking SKILLS lesson on the topic of annoying rules.	**Barbara** talks about the advantages of using INTERACTIVE WHITEBOARDS, and about the importance of giving good INSTRUCTIONS.
Bill [Elementary] Bill elicits words to help him gradually build up a dialogue which the students can then use freely to make their own conversation. He focuses on teaching stress and intonation in phrases.	**Bill** talks about SCAFFOLDING and dialogue frameworks and discusses the place of PRONUNCIATION TEACHING, especially the importance of STRESS and INTONATION.
Elli [Beginner] Elli is teaching the STRUCTURE *going to* to a class of BEGINNERS.	**Elli** talks about the importance of giving good MODELS, about what is especially important in TEACHING BEGINNERS, and about the teacher as provider of COMPREHENSIBLE INPUT.
Kit [Pre-intermediate] Kit teaches students to ask for and give directions.	**Kit** talks about signposting and summarising lesson content for students. He discusses reasons for his choice of lesson TOPIC and his attitude to COURSEBOOK USE.
Laura [Upper-intermediate] Laura uses a READING TEXT to create the conditions for a SPEAKING ACTIVITY.	**Laura** talks about ROLE-PLAY, CORRECTION when using FLUENCY ACTIVITIES, OPPORTUNISTIC TEACHING, and the importance of getting students to move around.
Rolf [Upper-intermediate] Rolf tells a story about a British Christmas to teach GRAMMAR INDUCTIVELY. [Note: in many British homes, presents for children are left under a Christmas tree. Young children often believe that the presents are put there by Santa Claus on Christmas Eve (December 24th).]	**Rolf** talks about DICTOGLOSS and other GRAMMAR-TEACHING TECHNIQUES, and explains his choice of story.
Silvana [Pre-intermediate] Silvana uses an INTERACTIVE WHITEBOARD to teach a number of phrases about feeling unwell.	**Silvana** talks about the impact of interactive whiteboards in classrooms and about the relative status and advantages of NATIVE- and NON-NATIVE-SPEAKER TEACHERS.
Tony [Upper-intermediate] Tony teaches LEXICAL PHRASES to describe feeling happy and sad.	**Tony** talks about the importance of RAPPORT and what the students did next in the LESSON SEQUENCE.

Lesson story observation sheet

When watching the *Lesson stories*, copy and complete the following observation sheet in note form.

Teacher's name	
Level	
What the teacher was trying to achieve (check the opening screen caption)	
What teaching equipment (paper, books, technology) the teacher used – and your reactions to this	
Techniques the teacher used (e.g. grammar explanation, pronunciation teaching, speaking organisation)	
Things you noticed about the teacher's behaviour/manner in the lesson	
Things you noticed about the students' behaviour/manner in the lesson	
Your favourite part of the lesson	
Your overall impression of the lesson	

If possible compare your observation sheet with a colleague.

Reflection questions

Consider the following questions after watching the *Lesson stories* and the relevant *Teachers talking* sections.

Allan	• What is special about live listening? Assess its advantages and disadvantages in comparison to pre-recorded listening extracts. • How can teachers choose successful topics for lessons?
Barbara	• What are the advantages and disadvantages of using an interactive whiteboard? • How important is it to give instructions clearly? What are the best ways of doing this?
Bill	• How important is the teaching of pronunciation? • When teaching pronunciation, what should teachers concentrate on?
Elli	• Why is teaching beginners different from teaching other levels? • How should teachers speak to beginners?
Kit	• What are the advantages and disadvantages of having a clear shape for a lesson? • What is the place of coursebooks in language teaching?
Laura	• What are the advantages and disadvantages of role-play? • When should teachers correct during a fluency activity?
Rolf	• If you were learning a foreign language, would you prefer to be taught grammar overtly or deductively? Why? • How useful is a dictogloss procedure for students studying grammar?
Silvana	• If you were learning a foreign language, would you prefer a native-speaker or a non-native-speaker teacher? Why? • How teacher-centred are presentation techniques such as the interactive whiteboard?
Tony	• How important is it for students to learn the metaphorical use of language? • What is the importance of good teacher–students and student–student rapport?

Subject index

Note: References in *italic* are to Chapter notes; those to figures are indicated as, for example, 41*f*.

Author index

Pearson Education Limited
Edinburgh Gate
Harlow
Essex CM20 2JE
England
And Associated Companies throughout the World.

www.longman.com

© Pearson Education Limited 2007

Second impression 2007
Printed in China CTPSC/02
Book for pack ISBN – 978 1 4058 4772 8
Book/DVD Pack ISBN – 978 1 4058 5311 8

Acknowledgements

We are grateful to the following for permission to reproduce copyright material:

Text: Adult Migrant Education programme: Adelaide for an extract from Learning Styles in Adult Migrant Education by K Willing © 1987; Association of Language Testers in Europe EEIG for 'ALTE: Can Do statements' produced by the members of the Association of Language Testers in Europe; Cambridge University Press for the following: A figure from Extensive Reading in the Second Language Classroom by Richard Day and James Bamford © 1998, 3 illustrations from Language Links by Adrian Doff and Christopher Jones © 2005, an extract from More Grammar Games by Mario Davis Rinvolucri © 1995, a figure from Planning Lessons and Courses by Tessa Woodward © 2001, an illustration from Pronunciation Games by Mark Hancock © 1995, 2 figures from Pronunciation Tasks by Martin Hewings © 1993 and a figure from Reading Extra by Liz Driscoll © 2004; Cambridge ESOL for a general writing question from IELTS exam administered jointly with the British Council and IDP Education, Australia; Cambridge University Press in association with the British Council for 2 figures by Kachru adapted from English in the World edited by Randolph Quirk and H.G. Widdowson © 1985; Frank Coffield, David Moseley, Elaine Hall and Kathryn Ecclestone for an extract from "Learning Styles for Post 16 Learners – What Do We Know?" by Coffield, Hall, Moseley & Ecclestone published on www.isda.org. uk; GAP Activity Projects (GAP) for an extract adapted from GAP Annual Newsletter 1996 by Penny Elvy; Guardian News & Media Ltd for an extract from "Forget Satnav it's quicker using a map" by Esther Addley published in The Guardian 10th November 2006 © Guardian 2006; Jill Hadfield, Charlie Hadfield and Modern English Publishing for 2 diagrams by Jill and Charlie Hadfield published in Modern English Teacher 12/1 and 12/2; Jill Hadfield for "My Home Town Game" from Elementary Communication Games published by Nelson 1997 © Jill Hadfield; Hong Kong University Press for a figure adapted from Asian Englishes: Beyond the Canon by Braj B. Kachru © 2004; IATEFL for an extract from "How and when should teachers correct?" by Philip Harmer edited by Alan Pulverness © IATEFL 2004 Liverpool Conference Selections; ICM Talent for an extract from Maximum Security by Robert O'Connor published by Granta Publications 1996 © Robert O'Connor; Macmillan Publishers Ltd for the "Phonemic Chart" published in Sound Foundations by Adrian Underhill © Macmillan 1994; Marshall Cavendish Limited for extracts from "Just Right Intermediate Students Book" by Jeremy Harmer from Just Right Course (c) 2004 and "Just listening and Speaking Upper Intermediate" by Jeremy Harmer and Carol Lethaby from Just Skills series (c) 2005 both published by Marshall Cavendish Limited www.mcelt.co.uk/justright; Harvey Marcus for the article "TFI Friday" published in Marie Claire October 2002 © Harvey Marcus; Modern English Publishing for 'Teaching English Intelligently' by Rosie Tanner published in English Teaching Professional 20; 'Organising free speaking' by Simon Mumford published in Modern English Teacher 13/4 and 'Preventing Stress and Burn-out' by Linda Bawcom published in Modern English Teacher 14/2; The National Theatre for their advertisement

for The Life of Galileo; Oxford University Press for extracts from "Confused Encounters: Differing Expectations in the EAP Classroom" by Dilys Throp published in ELT Journal 45 Volume 2: 108-118, 1991, "An Evaluative Checklist for Self-Access Materials" by Hayo Reinders and Marilyn Lewis published in ELT Journal 60 Volume 3: 272-278, 2006, "Language-learning strategies: theory and perception" by C Griffiths and J Parr published in ELT Journal 55 Volume 3: 247-254, 2001, Headway Elementary Pronunciation by Sarah Cunningham and Peter Moor © 2002, New English File Elementary by Clive Oxenden, Christine Latham-Koenig and Paul Seligson © 2004, and an extract from Practical English Usage by Michael Swan © 2005; an illustration from English File Students' Book 2 by Clive Oxenden, Christina Latham-Koenig, Paul Seligson © 2004; a figure from How Languages are Learned by Patsy Lightbown and Nina Spada © 2006; The poem 'The Pyramids' and an illustration from Creative poetry writing by Jane Spiro © 2004; Pearson Education Ltd for extracts from the following titles: The Anti-Grammar Grammar book by Nick Hall and John Shepheard, First Certificate Expert by Roger Gower and Jan Bell, GO Students Book 2 by Steve Elsworth and Jim Rose, Grammar Practice for Elementary Students by Walker & Elsworth, How to Teach Pronunciation by Gerald Kelly, New Cutting Edge Elementary by Sarah Cunningham & Peter Moor, Process Writing by Ron White and Valerie Arndt, Longman Essential Activato; Sounds English by JD O'Connor & Clare Fletcher, for figures from the following titles: First Certificate Gold by Aclam & Burgess, A Framework for Task-based Learning by Jane Willis, How To Teach Writing by Jeremy Harmer, Teaching Oral English by Donn Byrne, Total English Intermediate by Antonia Clare and JJ Wilson, for a table from New Cutting Edge Intermediate by Sarah Cunningham & Peter Moor, for 2 map illustrations from Pairwork 3 Upper Intermediate Advanced by Watcyn Jones & Howard Williams, for a definition from Diccionario Pocket ©2003 and 3 definitions from Longman Dictionary of Contemporary English © 2005; Penguin Group (UK) for an extract and figure 'Word circle' figure from Have Fun with Vocabulary by Annette Barnes, Jean Thines and Jennie Welden (Penguin English 1996) © Annette Barnes, Jean Thines and Jennie Welden 1996; Rogers, Coleridge & White Ltd and Brian Patten for the poem "Confession" by Brian Patten from Collected Love Poems (HarperCollins 2007) © Brian Patten; Saffire Press for 'The Lead VAK Test' from In Your Hands by Jane Revell and Susan Norman © Saffire Press 1997; Thomson Learning Global Rights Group for the extract "Sentence anagrams" published in "Implementing the Lexical Approach: Putting Theory into Practice 1st edition" by Lewis © 1997, Heinle, a division of Thomson Learning www. thomsonrights.com; and Sabiha Tunc, Baskent University Turkey and Elka Tobeva for their online exchange concerning the 2006 IATEFL conference, Harrogate published on www.yahoogroups.com 23rd March 2006.

Photos (Key: b-bottom; c-centre; l-left; r-right; t-top)
25 PunchStock: PhotoAlto; 100 Alamy Images: Mike Kipling Photography; 186 Photolibrary.com: Index Stock Imagery; 211 PunchStock: RubberBall.; 218 Corbis: Dennis Wilson (no diving); Matthias Kulka (no mobile phones); Nik Wheeler (dress code; Imagestate: Age fotostock / Glamour International (smoking area); Age fotostock / Claver Carroll (flag); Age fotostock / Ken Welsh (no parking); Impact Photos: Ray Roberts (no dogs); Jeff Moore (jeff@jmal.co.uk): (credit cards, cyclists and pedestrians only, staff only); page 299: Redferns; page 300: Panos (Paul Lowe); page 301: (t) Panos (Paul Lowe), (b) David Wilde ©2002 Delphian Records Ltd
316 © Jan Blake used with kind permission

Picture Research by: Sarah Purtill

Screenshots 93: Learning Disabilities Resource Community; 190: Macmillan Publishers Ltd; 192: www.ardecol.ac-grenoble.fr; 195: The Consultants-E, online training and development consultancy (www.theconsultants-e.com) (Nicky Hockley, Director of Pedagogy); 209: Google™ Google is a trademark of Google Inc; 239: www.mannythings.org (Charles Kelly); 261 & 262: Kosta Dimeropoulos; 295: Guardian Unlimited; 324: www.handwritinghelpforkids. com; 324: www.tampareads.com; 338: ©Joel Bloch, ESL Composition Programme, The Ohio State University; 338: BlogSpot. All other images © Pearson Education.

Every effort has been made to trace the copyright holders and we apologise in advance for any unintentional omissions. We regret that we have been unable to make contact with the copyright owners of the material shown on pages: 93, 190, 192, 295, 324 & 338. We would be pleased to insert the appropriate acknowledgement in any subsequent edition of this publication.